THE JOURNEY

Cecilia Sternberg

THE JOURNEY

The Dial Press/James Wade
New York 1977

Originally published in Great Britain
by William Collins Sons & Co., Ltd.

Manufactured in the United States of America

Second Printing—1978

Library of Congress Catalog Card Number 77-014-691

ISBN 0-8037-4270-3

In memory of my cousin Eddie Bismarck
who asked me to write about our family

ILLUSTRATIONS

CONTENTS

PART ONE

EUROPE

I

Dawn had come at last and with it the first day in our lives as emigrants.

The train was speeding through France. The child Diana, eleven years old when we left Czechoslovakia, slept next to me. The door to my husband's compartment in the *wagon-lit* was closed; I hoped he too was asleep.

We had crossed three frontiers without mishap. Our passports and travel documents had been inspected and returned to us without comment. Fears that we would be stopped at the Czech border had proved groundless; yet several of our friends who had tried to leave the country before us with seemingly valid exit permits had had their passports taken from them. 'New regulations' they had been told; all they could do was to return to Prague and try again. Later anyone who wanted to leave would have to cross the frontier illegally and on foot, taking with them only what they could carry, shot at by the Czech guards if they were seen and imprisoned for years if caught.

I had not dared to undress or lie down. I went out into the corridor of the train, sat on the hard little window seat, and looked out. We were passing through a forest – old and splendid trees, oaks and beeches of such height that the rising sun slanted bright rays on to green ferns and moss beneath them. I looked at my watch, a gift from Steinhardt. It was one of those expensive and complicated Swiss mechanisms that give year, month, day and time. It said 5 a.m. 30 July 1948.

Where were we? I wondered. We were not due in Paris for several hours. A map hung in the corridor; I saw we were passing through the Ardennes and I remembered that one of the last and most desperate battles of the war had been fought there. Yet all seemed untouched, peaceful and beautiful again. How soon and how generously nature covers all traces of destruction and death! Something like happiness touched me for the first time since we had left home, but it was tinged with guilt: how dared I find comfort in the beauty of an alien landscape so soon? I hoped my husband slept; the forests he had owned and loved had been just as splendid as these, rich in valuable timber, filled with game and birds. Was he watching these trees pass by, reminded of all he had lost, with more pain than I could feel?

Leopold had been kept too busy on the Czech frontier for regrets, and his personal success in keeping our three large trunks and numerous suitcases practically unopened and quite unexamined by the frontier-guards had pleased him. This luggage contained all the good clothes we still possessed, much of our household linen, and quite a lot else that no permit for a month's cure in Vichy for my husband's leg (the pretext for our journey) could have justified. In the last moments before we left I had secreted in the trunks whatever valuables I could still find in our town flat – the silver tea and coffee sets in use on the last day, some gilded forks and spoons I found in a drawer, cigarette-boxes and my furs. 'Personal belongings only, no valuables or currency', our instructions read. Though I might have got away with travelling with my teapot and coffee-jug, and the cutlery to use in Vichy, a mink coat and a white fox fur could hardly have seemed necessary in August.

I had been too nervous to go with my husband to unlock the luggage that had been carried to the guard-house. Besides, I could not leave the child; she was very quiet and good but clutched her small bag, just as fearful for her belongings as I was for mine. I need not have worried; my husband returned smelling strongly of Slivovice, our local plum brandy. 'They never even looked,' he laughed. 'We could have taken anything. They drank my health and wished us good fortune. Odd – ' he added, 'they all recognized me.'

There was certainly nothing odd about that, I thought. Who throughout the country did not recognize him? His great height, and breadth, his limp, his stick – not an elegant cane but a thick stem of gnarled oak, for nothing less robust would have taken his weight – and the broad-brimmed felt hat he always wore out of doors to control his unruly mass of grey curls, all made his appearance memorable. Anyone who had ever been on a race-course knew him and his racing colours, blue and gold; anyone who had frequented nightclubs knew him. In the streets of Prague and Vienna they knew him, and in every restaurant, hotel and bar. He was the favourite of all head-waiters because of his large but discriminating appetite and his generous tips. He was a most willing victim of all scroungers, hangers-on, destitute tarts, alcoholics and down and outs. I think he never refused a request for help in his life, and the more disreputable and undeserving the applicant the more readily he gave.

I suppose he was exceedingly wealthy after inheriting from his father, but just how rich I never really knew. It was not customary at that time to discuss finance with one's wife, nor in polite society as a whole. I never saw a household account or knew how much the servants were paid, or what our journeys cost, nor even the price of my dresses and shoes. I ordered them and had them fitted and never saw the bills; it was the same with furniture, carpeting, upholstery and curtaining materials that I chose.

However, my husband, though obviously well off, a generous spender and fond of the good things of life, worked remarkably hard for his estates, paying back what he took from them by widespread improvements. His time was spent in reforesting, cultivating and draining the soil, and keeping the two castles and various farms he owned in good order; also in rebuilding tenant cottages and restoring the churches – he was patron of nine – at his own expense.

But his success went beyond the boundaries of his lands for his unique character allowed him to prosper even under the new regime of the time. The young republic of Czechoslovakia had brought in land reform, abolition of aristocratic titles, and a variety of new laws and measures with which to curb the powers of the great landowners. Naturally most of the aristocracy resented this. Deprived of part of their lands, their incomes reduced, they withdrew with pique on to what was left of their estates, or went to Vienna or abroad for their pleasures, and would have nothing to do with a government they felt was bent on ruining them and a people who did not seem to want them any more.

My husband's reactions were different. He couldn't have cared less what he was called – Sternberg was good enough on its own. His coat of arms was the star of Bethlehem: legend said his ancestor Caspar had been one of the three kings who came to worship the Christchild. In any case the Knights of Sternberg were first mentioned in Czech history in the year eleven hundred, and Sternbergs had prospered and survived in the kingdom of Bohemia for nearly a thousand years since, in spite of changing rulers, adversities and defeats. Why, he thought, should not he? If the country was to be called Czechoslovakia now what did he care? This was his land and these were his people, for better or worse.

He was not an intellectual. Like many of his class he lacked education; he rarely read a book and spelt incorrectly all his life. It was as if he sensed that too much thought or knowledge might somehow impair his primitive unfailing instinct for survival. He was as canny as a fox and as strong as a bear, but blessed with an irrepressible sense of humour that was not only very human but also humane; if often extremely coarse it was never wounding.

He was a true democrat; not by conviction – he had no convictions –
but by nature. He quite simply liked people, all people of whatever
kind or class. Nothing could have profited him more in a country that,
after the euphoria of its newly acquired freedom and independence
had somewhat abated, had to learn to connect the past with the
future by way of the uncertain present.

Leopold Sternberg had always been popular on the land. Now he
became so in Prague. He made friends wherever he went, both among
the new élite and in government circles, his natural geniality and warmth
disarming those still rather unsure of themselves and wary of aristocratic superiority. His Rabelaisian jokes went from office to office
where he bargained for tax relief or compensation for confiscated
lands – jokes to be taken home and told to laughing wives in bed. He
invited all and anyone who had never stayed in a castle before to spend
the night, wining and dining them and never seeming to notice if
some of his guests' manners at table and otherwise were rather strange.
Soon he was able to achieve almost anything he wanted as to concessions
and loans, which benefited not only himself but other members of his
class. He pioneered reconciliation between those in power and those
that feared theirs lost. Soon many of the younger, more forward-
looking members of the aristocracy began to follow his example.
Even the abolished titles were restored; not officially of course, but
quite simply by ninety out of a hundred Czechs respectfully using them
again.

But to return to our journey.

'Go to sleep,' my husband said to the child, seeing how tense and
exhausted she looked. She shook her head.

He was very fond of children, especially naughty children whose
misdeeds probably reminded him of his own unruly youth. Diana was
never naughty – at worst she sulked or looked at us with stern disapproval. She was a very solemn little girl. He was as gentle and kind
to her as he was towards anything young and helpless, but I doubt
if he felt much more for her than he would have for any other child in
his care. Traditionally he should have wanted a son and heir; my
disappointment at not having produced one was very great at the time,
and the ensuing knowledge that I would never bear another child
saddened me. Yet he did not seem to care.

'We can always adopt one of the cousins' boys – Hugili or Peter;
or perhaps Franzi or Adam [his brothers] will have sons.'

16

'But that's not the same,' I protested.

'Just so. I wouldn't want it to be the same.'

'Because of your father?'

'Yes, I wouldn't like that situation repeated.'

My father-in-law had been one of the most courteous, gentle and charming of men, very cultured and much interested in the arts, which was unusual at a time when the diversions of gentlemen were mainly shooting, eating, drinking, riding and womanizing. But he was formal and strict as to manners, very proud of his ancestry and the royal connections that had occasionally blossomed on his family tree, and he lived still according to the stern conventions of the Austrian Imperial court.

He was a kind and loving husband, and a good and tolerant father to all of his children except for his eldest son and heir; of him he expected too much too early. There was no doubt about the young giant's physical health and strength, his ingenuity in evading discipline and the inventiveness of his crude practical jokes. But Leopold was the despair of every tutor. He refused to, or simply could not, learn to read as a boy, and there was not much improvement in his readiness to acquire knowledge later. Instead he was always involved in some scrape or other, always laughing, joking, playing the fool; incapable, it seemed, of serious thought, indisciplinable and unable to concentrate on anything but his pleasure. Was this a suitable heir, my father-in-law sadly asked himself, to a great name, estates and responsibilities? That his mother adored and spoilt him, that the younger children worshipped him and tried to imitate him only made things worse. Sending him to the Theresianum, the Viennese academy for young noblemen, brought no improvement; he had many admirers among the pupils but none among the teachers. In despair his father tried a Czech university, in Brno, soon to discover that though his son had made many friends in the town he rarely attended a lecture.

Then the First World War started. Eldest sons of prominent noble families were, by tacit agreement with military and court authorities, spared the dangers of the battle-front; yet, true to his irresponsible character, Leopold joined the regiment of the 9th Dragoons and after very brief training was fighting on the Russian front. Except for infrequent periods of leave he remained there all through the war; posted here and there with his regiment, travelling always with his tent, his bathtub, cases of champagne, his valet and often a mistress.

'If nothing else the boy has courage, and is as great a soldier as his forebears,' his father reassured himself, sharing his wife's pride in the decorations awarded to his son: first the silver and then the gold medal for bravery.

Apart from a glancing Cossack sword-thrust that only superficially grazed his chest, he had not been wounded. 'My prayers keep him safe,' my mother-in-law said. But on one of the last days of that war, knowing that the end was in sight, she may have forgotten to pray for her son. A shrapnel burst shattered his leg. He was found unconscious, so weak from loss of blood that no amputation could be risked, and he was transported to a hospital in Vienna.

'Death isn't unpleasant,' he once told me. 'I died several times in that hospital. One gets very cold and sleepy and the only thing one wants is not to be woken up. But Mumsy always did; she shook me and scolded till I had to come back. And she forced the whole family, even Father, to kneel down and pray for me round the bed.'

There were no antibiotics at that time, and the doctors declared there was no hope at all of saving his life without amputation. 'You wouldn't believe,' he said to me many years later, 'how that leg stank. It was full of fat white maggots for months – the doctors used them to clean up the pus. It was Mumsy who saved my leg; she refused to let them cut it off. "So then let him die," she told the doctors quite calmly. "Here or in heaven my son shall keep his two legs." '

He survived, for he was very strong and so was his mother, but he spent three years in and out of hospitals. He was given morphia, not only to ease the pain but also to calm his impatience and keep him quiet. Soon he became an addict and needed five injections daily. Then his mother, collaborating with the doctors, arranged that salt water should replace the morphine in the syringes and he was given huge quantities of alcohol as a stimulant.

When at last he had completely recovered, except for a limp (one leg was now much shorter than the other), he did his best, gloriously drunk most of the time, to make up for all he had missed in the years in hospital. His excesses shocked and delighted scandal-loving Viennese society. Not only did he use his absent parents' Palais for parties to which all the ladies of the *demi-monde* were invited and give dinners in the famous marble-panelled *separée* in the Hotel Sacher, when the entire ballet of the Opera were made to drink so much champagne that they had to be practically swept out by the waiters next morning, but he also won and lost vast sums of money gambling in the Jockey Club. Since he only played with friends he could never bring himself to ask for payment of the IOUs which they gave him instead of money, and so of course in the end he lost a fortune.

During this time he acquired a permanent mistress; I once saw her in Monte Carlo after my marriage, and never have I seen a more exquisitely beautiful creature – but she was expensive too, and so were his race-horses. Soon his debts could not be ignored by his parents; his mother paid them again and again out of her own considerable fortune, trying to persuade her husband that their son was just sowing his wild oats and would soon settle down and not become, as he by then firmly believed, a disgrace to the family.

'It's nothing I can explain,' my husband answered rather irritably years later, when I ventured to question him about his strained relationship with his father. 'I was fond of him, I admired him. I wouldn't have minded in the least if he had been angry with me or reproached me – it would have been natural if he had. But he never did; he was always as gentle and polite as if we were strangers, not father and son. I know he secretly disliked me, I could sense it.'

He was right of course; my husband's instinctive insights were often surer than any reasoning.

In any case a day came when his father was forced to act. No fortune, however great, could withstand the constant drain of his son's extravagances. The ultimatum was that his debts would be paid off once and for all on condition that he left Vienna and established himself permanently in the country. He was to retire to Zasmuky, the second property owned by the Sternbergs near Prague, and try to manage it for his father. If he did not agree to this his allowance would be stopped and his father never wished to see or hear of him again, implying disinheritance. All this by letter – my father-in-law disliked violent confrontations.

His son knew he had to accept; all in all it was not an ungenerous offer. He moved to Zasmuky; not into the castle – that had not been modernized and was cold and bleak – but into a charming old lodge where his mother established him, finding him a good cook; while his valet Jenicek, without whom he never moved anywhere, saw to his comforts. Furniture, pictures, household linen and other necessities were sent from Castolovice. There was room enough for guests and it became a most attractive small house in which I was later to spend the first years of my married life very happily.

My future husband certainly did not reform immediately. Prague was only an hour's journey by car, and he frequently went there for a night's revelry; nor did he lack the sort of light female company that he had become accustomed to. Only gradually did he change. More and more he became interested in the management of the estate till after a year or so he was working from dawn to dusk, superintending the planting and harvesting, choosing trees to be felled in the forests, replanting orchards, doubling the output of beer from the brewery by growing hops. Though he had no agricultural training, his instinctive understanding of the land and its needs surprised even his sceptical labourers; accustomed to an indifferent superintendent, interested only in his own cut of profit, they soon realized that they were now working for someone who cared. It had been many years since any member of the family had come to Zasmuky except for brief visits in the summer. True, the day of the aristocrats was over now that they had a republic, but their Pan Hrabe (Mr Count) was different. He talked to them as if he and they were equals. They liked him and they helped him discreetly, realizing his lack of experience, but also declaring with pride that he might have been born a farmer, so few were the mistakes he made.

My father-in-law should have been well content with his son, and to all appearances he was; but secretly he never forgave him for having succeeded where he had expected failure.

The train had started to move again.

'I'll put you to bed now, darling,' I said to the child. 'Oh, please not while we are in Germany,' she begged. Then anxiously: 'They won't come and take you away with them, will they, Papi?'

'No, the Germans won't bother us any more,' he reassured her. He offered me the hip-flask he always carried in his pocket; I drank and he finished the rest. His days of heavy drinking were long past, but he liked a few stiff drinks before lunch and in the evening, and by that time so did I.

Diana wrinkled her nose in disgust at the rank smell of Slivovice that pervaded the compartment. 'Anyway I have this,' she declared. She opened her bag and produced a penknife, flicking it open expertly to contemplate the sharp blade. 'In case they do come in and are from the Gestapo!' Poor child, I thought; years had passed since their terrifying visits to our flat in Prague, yet she still remembered.

The train had stopped again. Germans in long coats walked up and down, their faces gaunt and sinister in the swaying light of their lanterns. Only one entered our compartment; he checked our papers marked 'transit' and left, without a word or a smile. I wondered if he didn't think it served us right that we too had to leave our country now, cast out as so many Germans living in Czechoslovakia had been when the war had ended.

'A pity we can't see what's been bombed,' my daughter said, staring out into the darkness as the train started moving again. I put her to bed and went into my husband's compartment.

'Well, it's all over now,' I sighed with relief; 'thank God!' 'Or thank Steinhardt?' questioned my husband. I looked at him closely but there was no resentment visible in his face. Not in twenty years of marriage had I been able to tell from his expression what he was feeling, if he wished to conceal it – only his acts gave a clue. In spite of his outgoing nature and his outspokenness, in everything that concerned his inmost feelings he could be very reticent.

I kissed him goodnight and went back to the compartment I shared with Diana, who blessedly slept. I sat down and began to think of Laurence Steinhardt, US Ambassador to Prague, to whom we owed our freedom.

2

After the war ended the properties confiscated from us by the Germans were returned to us, and for two and a half years before the communist government came into power we lived and entertained in Castolovice much as we had before the war. We had shooting parties and house-parties for old friends and neighbours, and our newly acquired friends among the Western diplomats.

Of these latter our most frequent guests were the Steinhardts, the Nicholses and the Rotters. Laurence Steinhardt had been US Ambassador in Moscow in the war and now had the embassy in Prague; Phil Nichols, British Ambassador to the Czech government in exile, continued in office on President Benes's return to the country. Adi Rotter had been a staunch friend of ours all through the war; he had resigned from the diplomatic service after Austria lost its independence, but was now reinstated pending his appointment as ambassador.

Castolovice was not the most beautiful of castles. It had suffered too many alterations; gothicized in the last century and partially rebuilt in the Renaissance style by my parents-in-law. But it was large and impressive, and had a certain rather barbaric splendour with its tower and great courtyard, and frescoed walls on which some unknown artist of the seventeenth century had colourfully depicted Jaroslaw Sternberg's legendary victory over the Tartars in the twelfth century.

I don't know how many rooms there were; in the vast servants' quarters at ground level the only room I knew was my maid's, and I had only been in the kitchen once, when my husband was away and the cook had chopped off a finger by accident. It was Leopold who ran the house, with the help of a competent housekeeper, two butlers, three footmen, his valet, a chef, and the various house- and kitchen-maids considered necessary for such a large establishment. It was my duty to see that the guest-rooms were in good order; there were over thirty, and I had to arrange the flowers, select the china and silver for big dinner parties, and suffer the chef's visit every morning at nine, while breakfasting in bed, so that I could check the menu for the day – obviously he knew more about cooking than I did, so I seldom altered his plans. These chores, however, were my only ones, and it would have been resented by the entire household and by my husband had I tried to do more. Only in the gardens was I given a free hand.

Our living-rooms were: the hall, five drawing-rooms of various sizes, two dining-rooms – one for winter, one for summer – a library, and a chapel where mass was still said daily when my parents-in-law were alive, and in which I had been rebaptized before my marriage. I had always yearned to be a Roman Catholic when a child: those pretty pictures, rosaries, medals, the splendid vestments and the incense, the mass with its Latin incantations – all had seemed to me wonderful and full of mystery. So I had no scruples about changing my religion when my parents-in-law asked me to do so. However, I had been quite properly christened at my birth in London by an Anglican bishop, and had the document to prove it. Therefore, at seventeen, I resented having to stand in that unheated chapel, my head and neck being deluged with icy water from a jug, while the Czech archbishop and two village priests saved me once more from the devil. My kind mother-in-law, who acted as my godmother, sensing my disquiet explained that the ceremony was 'just in case' – and presented me with a pretty diamond and garnet brooch.

The chapel adjoined what was called the Grand Salon; this was thirty feet wide and almost a hundred feet long, with a great carved stone fireplace at each end. All the wall space between the tall windows was filled with family portraits – hundreds of Sternbergs in the armour or dress of their day. The floor was of parquet, inlaid with stars set in squares of the same size as the pictures on the unique ceiling, which had been brought by cart from Italy in the sixteenth century when the castle was built. These pictures, in ornately framed panels, told the whole of the Old and the New Testament stories. This was our main room for entertaining.

We had been fortunate. When we returned to Castolovice we found that neither Germans nor Russians had stolen or destroyed anything, although the castle of Zasmuky, in which German soldiers and then Russian troops had been stationed, was irreparably damaged. Only the gardens in which I had worked so hard, planning and planting, had been neglected and looked sad and overgrown. We had to find a new gardener, for the last had left years ago. We engaged a Frenchman who had been in a German labour camp; he had Czech relations and wanted to stay in our country. He seemed suitable, but what we did not know at first was that he was a rabid communist and agitator. Warned by the villagers who feared him, we treated him with care, but he was a good gardener and there seemed no reason to dismiss him till, without my husband's consent, he hired German prisoners from the nearest town jail to work in the gardens. I would not have minded so much had they been men but these were frail, elderly women. What crimes could they possibly have committed? I could not bear to see them kneeling as they weeded nettles and brambles in the borders under my window. Should I go out and speak to them? I did not dare; anti-German feelings still ran so high among our people that any sign of pity or sympathy for the enemy, even though defeated, was suspect.

After the war ended, since victory parades could not go on for ever, there was much political propaganda for voluntary agricultural work to restore the ravished lands. Even I and several friends had joined groups that were transported by bus to the hills above Prague, where we planted sugar-beet seedlings in the blazing summer sun.

In the villages too there was a call for all good patriots to give at least one extra hour daily to field or garden work. Armed with a trowel I confronted our gardener, who was superintending the German women's labours; communist or not, we were on quite friendly terms because I spoke French.

'I want to work,' I said. 'I want to give an hour a day to help our country, too.'

He looked at me with total incomprehension. 'But Madame would soil her hands!' he exclaimed.

I knelt down and started to weed – I had gardened all my life and knew what I was doing. After that, day after day I did my hour's work among the old women; we never spoke and they ignored me. Probably they thought me mad or, worse, that I was mocking them. Then once one passed me a trowel with a half-smile and another helped me lift a particularly heavy load of weeds, and I felt better. Perhaps, after all, they had understood.

Then they were gone. 'What happened to those Germans?' I asked the gardener casually. '*Ces sales boches*,' he exclaimed. 'I didn't like to see Madame working among them. I sent them back to the prison where they would have stayed for life if it had been my decision. Unfortunately our present weak government has allowed them to be returned to Germany.'

Soon we found other help in the garden. All our old and well-trained servants, loyal throughout the war and having anxiously awaited our homecoming, came back to us: among them was our aged but still excellent chef. Food which had been scarce for years was plentiful again: there was butter and cream in abundance from the farms, fish from our lakes, crayfish and trout from our streams, partridges and pheasants from the fields, deer and wild boar from the forests, and vegetables from the garden.

Once again we had duck shoots and pheasant shoots and gay picnics in the woods, fishing expeditions and mushroom hunts, and at night much drinking, dancing and flirting under the great biblical ceiling of the Grand Salon. Little did we realize the danger that hung over our heads in that room; the great expanse of painted panelling was suspended by chains from the roof beams, and, unknown to us, woodworms were gradually reducing the rafters to dust. However it was only after we had left that it finally collapsed. I was glad to learn that the communists have since repaired it. The Grand Salon is now a tourist attraction and the star, our coat of arms with its motto 'It will not set', is sold – cast in tin and even silver as tiepins, brooches or other souvenirs.

There is no doubt that we lived in a fools' paradise in those post-war years; but neither we nor our friends the Western diplomats believed or, more accurately, wanted to believe that a country that had suffered so much under German occupation would choose communism and so lose its freedom and sovereignty once more. If there were warning voices: 'Sell some land, take out what you can. Buy something in a safer country. Insure your future in case things go wrong,' we ignored them. My husband was too patriotic to listen to such advice, nor was I able to contemplate any action that would prove lack of confidence in the future of our country.

Because of my mixed ancestry, I might have claimed almost any European nation as my own – France or Denmark, Spain, Austria, Hungary or even Germany. But I was born in England, my two grandmothers were English, it was my first language; and I was taught to believe, and still do, that it is the only really decent country in the world. The only people to whom I was in no way related except through my husband were the Czechs; and yet, through the comradeship of shared suffering and persecution in the war, I came to feel I was Czech.

3

In February 1948 the coalition government fell and our country became communist.

Masaryk's terrible death followed. We had dined with him at the Chinese Embassy, joking over birds' nest soup and experimenting with chopsticks, only two weeks earlier. But I could see his gaiety was forced and he looked pale and ill.

After dinner we walked out on to the snow-covered terrace that overlooked the domes and spires of Prague. It was a beautiful clear night, strangely warm for the time of year; I even remember the dress I wore – it was pale grey and pink chiffon, and floated round me like a soft cloud in the wind.

'You will catch cold,' he said.

'But Mr Masaryk, it's spring,' I laughed. 'It's blowing from the west.'

'A false spring, little Countess,' he said, 'and the wind is from the east.'

We mourned him as did the whole nation; but was everything really lost? Even if communist rule had begun in earnest, we still hoped to be allowed some form of survival, albeit under much reduced material circumstances. Surely some special arrangements would be made for those twelve families who had risked property and even life by having at the onset of the war declared themselves loyal to President Benes, anti-German, and willing to fight for their country?

My husband had been one of the twelve; and, as a class, we had our
martyrs too. My husband's old uncle Count Kinsky, who had been the
leader of the group that went to Benes, was mercilessly interrogated
by the Gestapo and then sent to a concentration camp, where he nearly
died. He was our closest neighbour in the country, frail of health in
spite of imposing height and magnificent appearance; a man of great
courage and keen intellect, whom both my husband and I loved and
admired. He was only saved, on grounds of ill-health, by the intervention of my cousin Gottfried Bismarck, then a prominent member of the
Nazi party. Handsome young Humprecht Czernin was killed in a
concentration camp; Charlie Rohan was locked up for a long time, and
so was Franzi Schoenborn.

It was to avail us nothing.

It was Steinhardt, only just returned from Washington where he
had seen President Truman, who finally made us face the truth;
it was as disappointing to him as it was painful for us, for he had worked
so hard to keep our country for the West. He came to our flat in Prague
to tell us it was just a question of time till Russia took over completely.

Steinhardt knew our flat well; it was within walking distance from
his embassy. We had lived in the apartment, which was in the Palace of
the Knights of Malta, all through the war, and had kept it on afterwards. There were many reasons by then why we were more often in
Prague than in the country; Steinhardt would drop in almost daily to
ask Leopold about people who had come to him with demands or
requests, or to gossip with me. His wife Dulcie was a semi-invalid and
rarely left the Peczek Palais, but she liked to know what was going on.

The house and its gardens had been bought by the US government
from the Peczeks, who had wisely left for America before the war, and
who did not want to return to Prague. The lovely old embassy in the
Schoenborn Palace, though sufficient for official use, had, or so at least
the Steinhardts thought, inadequate living quarters and was much too
small for entertaining. The Peczek Palais was built in the eighteenth-
century French style, and furnished likewise. Everything was gilt –
over-ornate mirrors everywhere, gilded panelling, heavy satins and
brocades. But since it was all almost new with not a genuine piece of
period furniture in it, only over-elaborate copies, its opulence and
extreme gaudiness were rather overwhelming. 'Just like an expensive
brothel,' Leopold told Dulcie, who was shocked and offended. Both
Steinhardts liked the house; it was modern, well-heated and extremely
comfortable.

His Excellency (it amused me to so address Steinhardt, however intimate we had become; nor did he dislike being reminded of his official status) was a very attractive man. A lawyer by profession, he was a younger member of a New York Jewish family, whose affluence and success went back three generations; a democrat, he had been a protégé of Roosevelt, whom he greatly admired. He had been given Lima as his first post, when still very young to be an ambassador, then Teheran, Moscow and Prague. He was still in the prime of life when we met – a handsome, vivacious man, radiating energy and optimism. Forceful and dynamic, he worked hard; but he was not by nature a diplomat, being too frank and outspoken. If he had a fault it was vanity, and a weakness for pretty women.

Though Steinhardt was ambitious, he was not half as ambitious or shrewd as his wife was for him. In fact she saw no reason why, with her help, he should not become President of the United States. She came from a half-Jewish family, was an only child and an heiress. Steinhardt, though successful as a young lawyer, had to earn his living and could never have afforded ambassadorial posts without her money; nor, perhaps, would he have wanted them. Dulcie had been educated in Europe and spoke five languages fluently, had travelled much, was well-read and cultured. She queened it on all social occasions: people were brought to or came to her – she never went to them. She was very much Madame l'Ambassadrice, and apart from her health was eminently equipped for the job.

I never exactly knew from what it was she suffered; Steinhardt did not like to talk about it. When I first met her she was not noticeably ill, though she sometimes walked awkwardly, supporting herself with a gold-headed cane. She seemed to feel cold all the time. She would go visiting here and there and, however warm the room, would sit tightly wrapped in a voluminous Russian sable coat, with a fur hood over her head and nothing but her small, pretty face visible. It was quite unlined though I knew she was fifty-five; bare of any cosmetics and as pale as wax.

Later I was to know that, though weeks might go by in which she seemed quite well, there were days when Dulcie could not walk and appeared semi-paralysed. Yet on the next evening she might go to a nightclub with us, and even dance. She had strange moods: on some days she seemed perfectly normal, gracious and dignified, yet on others she would constantly burst into tears or laugh uncontrollably, losing all composure.

My husband soon became a favourite with the ambassadress; he acted on her like a tonic. Distrustful of people who made up to her because of her position and wealth, she shrewdly realized that my husband could not have cared less if she had been the Empress of China. She knew that he quite simply liked her. As for him, he was sorry for her; she was small and pretty and often in obvious distress. He treated her like a sick child, wiped her tears with his large coronet-embroidered handkerchiefs, lifted her out of cars and even into bed, when she came to stay with us. He teased her out of moods and tempers, laughed at her airs and graces, shocked her with ribald jokes, and hugged and kissed her most disrespectfully whenever they met.

Dulcie loved it all. There was nothing erotic about their friendship – she did not approve of sex. Any lapse of that kind in her embassy staff was severely reprimanded; any woman who wore too low or revealing a dress soon learned to cover up. 'D'you think there's anything nasty going on between X and Z?' she would ask me sometimes.

Nasty or not, the Steinhardts had a daughter, not found like Moses in the bulrushes, but very much their own. She was seventeen when she came to Prague, an attractive quiet girl, with her mother's oval face and white skin, and her father's large almond-shaped eyes. Unfortunately she had also inherited her father's nose, and her face was too small for it; with less of it she could have been a great beauty. She was at that time somewhat overshadowed by her parents, but devoted to both of them, and astonishingly loyal and discreet for so young a person about anything that concerned them.

I liked her very much. I was fond of Dulcie too, but in the same protective, amused, indulgent way as my husband. Of course she could not accept that from me; what she wanted from me, if anything, was heart-to-heart woman's talk of which I was incapable, and gossip which I had learned to dread. All through the war our flat in Prague had been a centre of intrigue and resistance, where men had come to talk freely of their fears, hopes and plans, because of their trust in my husband. I had learned to be careful of what I said, and not give anything away – above all not myself.

Sometimes there would be embarrassing questions like: 'Do tell me, was there a little romance between you and Laurence before I came to Prague? I wouldn't blame you in the least. After all you didn't know me then – and he is very attractive to women.'

'Romance? What do you mean, Dulcie? Do you mean sex?'

She retreated, as I knew she would.

'I didn't mean anything as crude as that. But tell me, where did you first meet?'

'At a cheap little tart's apartment – Bibicka's. She was then sleeping as readily with the young members of your staff as she was formerly with German officers.'

She looked at me aghast. Both Leopold and I loved shocking Dulcie. 'Of course Laurence couldn't have known. He'd only just arrived, I suppose?'

'It was his first evening in Prague.'

'But how could you and Leopold have gone there, knowing what the woman was?'

'Because we had been sent an invitation, on embassy paper, to meet the Ambassador of the United States.'

'Impossible! I'll have to look into that.'

'Dulcie, don't. It's all so long ago.'

Indeed it was; so much had happened since. And yet how vividly I remembered that evening when I met Steinhardt for the first time.

I opened the window of our compartment, which had become stifling. Smoke and ashes blew into my face. I closed the window again and lay down against cushions that looked clean but smelled of long use. I sprayed some Chanel No. 5 on them, and the scent brought back the whole scene.

We had arrived late at Bibicka's flat. A young American in uniform seemed to be acting as host. The apartment was dense with smoke, crammed with people, and the noise they made was deafening. Then I saw Steinhardt across the crowded room. Someone introduced us, garbling our names. He looked at my tall husband; he couldn't have mistaken him for anything but what he was, but, as he told me later, he could not place me at all. Because I was so oddly dressed, he thought I might be some actress Leopold had brought. (Since all clothes were dressmaker-made in those days I often designed my own; I had copied my high-necked tight-fitting black velvet suit from the picture of a Florentine youth, and added a vivid crimson pillbox cap.) Steinhardt was much too experienced not to have noticed that many of the ladies present were anything but 'ladies' – most of them girls or women whose profession was obvious from their behaviour and dress.

Our hostess Bibicka disentangled herself from the variously uniformed men that surrounded her. I had never met her socially, but had seen her frequently in nightclubs, often with people I knew. She was small, dark, almost Oriental in lushness, and very pretty.

'The Russian military attaché very much wants to meet you,' she said; 'I'm sure the Ambassador will excuse you for a moment.' She drew me away and, reluctantly, I went with her.

'I can't speak Russian,' I protested. 'Doesn't matter, he speaks German,' was the reply.

I had rarely seen a more repulsive-looking man. Though he was tall and slim, his neat uniform resplendent with decorations, his domed head was covered with strange tufts of bright red hair. His face was egg-shaped, and neither eyes, nose or mouth were prominent enough to disrupt its smooth pale surface. It was as self-contained as an egg, except that the shell would have been impossible to crack; only his eyes, green, bright, inquisitive and alert, looked outward through narrow slits.

'*Sie sind Aristocratin?*' he asked in halting German. I was startled; Bibicka had obviously informed him about us.

'Czechoslovakia is a republic,' I reminded him; 'but by birth, yes.'

He peered at me as if I was some curious species which he had never seen before, and which he might like to collect – alive or dead, I thought with a shudder.

'I think my husband wants to leave,' I said. He looked across to where Steinhardt and Leopold were still talking.

'*Kleiner Jud,*' he shrugged.

'Well, he's not so little! The American Ambassador must be over six feet,' I said indignantly.

'Your husband is bigger, too big. Czechoslovakia is a very small country.' He made an odd gesture as if measuring something between finger and thumb and then casting it away. When I think of it now I know it was a warning; then I was only shocked at his rudeness.

By the time I had pushed my way through the crowd and reached Leopold, Steinhardt had left. 'What did you talk about?' I asked on our way home.

'Well, obviously he had no idea who we were, and was being careful. And your going off with that Russian must have made him suspicious, too; I saw him watching you. Anyway, I asked him if he liked shooting and fishing, and when he said yes, I said I hoped he would come and stay with us in the country.'

'And will he?'

'I don't know. He said he was very busy, having only just arrived, but that if it was at all possible later, he would try.'

We met him again, of course. He was guest of honour at many official receptions to which we were also asked; but he was always surrounded by members of our government or visiting American generals, senators or journalists. Not that he had forgotten us; reassured, no doubt, as to our respectability by then, he would greet us and exchange a few friendly words, and I would often catch his eye as he looked at me thoughtfully across some room.

There was a lot going on in Prague in those after-war months. The town was occupied by Russian troops; they were no great threat to the populace as they had strict orders not to rape or steal, and if there were occasional lapses of discipline the transgressors were immediately shot. Nevertheless they were everywhere, with their short guns that looked like flutes, their squat women in uniform directing the traffic. The whole town was in a constant state of movement, with welcoming or victory parades every day. Montgomery came, Eisenhower came, but Churchill, though expected, did not – to everyone's disappointment. There were endless festivities in honour of British, Russian and American generals, and all the diplomats were kept very busy – Steinhardt most of all, since he was senior ambassador of the diplomatic corps.

At last the town returned to normal. The Russian troops were withdrawn, prominent visitors became less frequent and the people, exhausted by both war and the joys of liberation, went back to work.

4

We sent Steinhardt an invitation to our autumn duck shoot. I wrote the letter myself, and rather to our surprise he accepted, saying, however, he could not come the night before as I had suggested since he had a party to attend, but would arrive in the morning at ten, in time for the shoot.

He arrived two hours late.

It was an unheard-of offence, but then what could he know of our shooting customs? The head forester, the gamekeepers, loaders, and a hundred beaters had all been kept waiting, and so had the chef, with the carefully prepared picnic lunch. Our impatient guests, the men all crack shots, as were even some of the women, had all grown up in a tradition in which the ritual of the shoot had to be as precisely timed and as strictly followed as that of the mass in church.

Leopold did not shoot, because of his leg injury. His balance was too uncertain for him to handle a gun safely, but we had been to hundreds of shooting parties together, and always walked with the guns. Both of us knew all the rules – I had known them even in childhood, as my father was an excellent shot and a stern teacher. I had grown accustomed, like everyone else, to ignoring all that was cruel and ugly about shooting: the scream of the wounded hare, the sad thud of a dead or dying pheasant. Instead I had learned to enjoy the beauty of a perfect autumn day, the soaring flight of the birds, and the clean shot that picked them out of the sky.

I liked being with the well-groomed, handsome men, as clean, well-tended and as potent as their guns; I liked to share their restrained excitement and to acclaim their prowess. I knew they were not consciously cruel; in fact I never walked with a man who did not spare a second shot for a wounded animal if it had not already been picked up and clubbed to death by the following beaters or gamekeepers.

Yet the slaughter of so many harmless creatures – once at a world-famous shoot in Hungary I saw eleven thousand pheasants shot in one day – demanded certain ritualistic practices to absolve those taking part. These came in the final ceremony at the end of the shoot when everyone assembled.

Birds or game were laid out in neat squares or circles like those of a formal garden, sorted according to colour and kind, the pheasants, hare, rabbits or ducks lying on a bed of ferns. At a stag or wild boar shoot, the dead beasts would have been wiped clean of all blood, their limbs decently composed and fresh pine branches laid on their gutted stomachs. Then the head forester would step forward and read out the list of the animals shot, and by whom. Every man bared his head and stood silent, in homage to the dead animals. The Halali was blown on a single horn, the lament mournfully echoing through the forest. The shoot was over; everyone saluted the head forester and proclaimed '*lovuzdar*', meaning 'successful hunting'.

Steinhardt must have left his car outside because he entered the courtyard on foot. We were all assembled there waiting, men and women from the different shoots, wearing the same uniform as their gamekeepers – dark green or brown costumes of heavy water-repellent wool, with felt hats, decorated with silver medallions. These last were engraved with coats of arms or emblems, and had been awarded on previous shoots for successful performance.

Steinhardt looked much smaller than I had remembered him,

perhaps because I was surrounded by Kinskys, our closest neighbours – four tall young men all over six feet, and their father Uncle Franzi even taller. Besides, the size of the courtyard through which he had to walk would have dwarfed anyone. It struck me that we must seem rather formidable to him, viewed as a group all in semi-uniform, and the loaders standing by with their guns. But he seemed quite unperturbed, walking jauntily towards us, rather oddly attired, with a broad, shiny, very new-looking cartridge belt strapped tightly round his waist, and a largish felt hat on his head.

'Here comes the wild west,' Alphy whispered, making me giggle. He was the second eldest of the Kinsky boys who were all close friends, but he was by far the most handsome, and my favourite. My husband hastily introduced everyone to Steinhardt, then I showed him his room to which his luggage had meanwhile been brought.

'Have I time for a bath?' he asked.

'We've been waiting for two hours, your Excellency.'

'I'm sorry, I had a late night and overslept.' He opened his bag and took out a small parcel. 'This is for you,' he smiled. I unwrapped it: a dozen nylons and a bottle of Chanel No. 5. I nearly laughed out loud – the typical GI gift to his girl! I thanked him, told him his bathroom was next door, and begged him for God's sake to hurry; I then rejoined my guests in the courtyard.

'Diplomatic customs seem to have changed,' Aunt Paula Kinsky said sharply. 'In my day ambassadors were always punctual.'

'Incredible to hold up a shoot for so long,' Charlie Parish grumbled.

'How can he know our routine?' I asked. 'Or even how to shoot,' someone said.

'He's very handsome,' my sister-in-law Toti remarked; 'Spanish-looking.'

'Spanish! Jewish, you mean,' said Princess Marika.

'Sephardic,' Uncle Franzi declared.

At last he came hurrying down the steps to join us. Everyone piled into cars; they were all chauffeur-driven, since very few of our friends knew how to drive. 'I'll take my car – it's outside. Can I give anyone a lift?' Steinhardt asked.

'I'll come,' my husband said; 'the deer-park is miles from here and I'll have to show you the way.'

They went off together; Steinhardt's car was long, low and bright, obviously more powerful than our slower vehicles, soon left behind.

The deer-park was enclosed by fences, but was large enough – about four hundred acres of forest – for red deer and wild boar to roam freely. The duckponds were small lakes in which rushes and water-lilies grew, surrounded by tall oaks. There were always stationary ducks on the ponds, fed by the gamekeepers throughout the winter. In the spring their call would bring hundreds of migratory birds to settle and breed, and in the autumn, before they were due to leave, they were shot. Places had been marked out on one side of the lake, about ten feet apart. It was customary for the ladies of the party to stand behind whatever man they chose; they themselves rarely shot in our country. I stood as usual with Uncle Franzi Kinsky; he shot so superbly that I could be certain every bird would drop stone dead. Steinhardt's stand was next to ours, and Leopold was with him.

'We may be in great danger from the ambassador,' Uncle Franzi whispered. 'I've been peppered before, but you don't want to get it full in your pretty face. Stand close behind me.'

The call of the beaters and the splash of their boots among the reeds drew near. The head forester blew a single note on his horn, then came the great soaring of ducks rising from the water and volley after volley of shots. To my amazement I saw Steinhardt raise his gun and accurately and neatly bring down one bird after another.

'Well, I'll be damned,' exclaimed Uncle Franzi. 'Not that some of them weren't mine,' he added.

The surviving ducks had vanished among the trees; they would settle on the next lake which we would take later, when the beaters had reached it. Hunting dogs splashed in the water, retrieving dead birds or flushing those wounded out of the bushes.

'Good shooting!' Uncle Franzi called over to Steinhardt. 'I didn't know there was much duck-shooting in America.'

'But all the north of New York State has lakes. My uncle had a place near Lake George; I spent all my holidays there, and learned to shoot as a boy,' was the answer.

I breathed a sigh of relief, and catching my husband's eye I saw that he too was pleased. Neither of us could ignore how useful the ambassador's friendship might be for us all in the uncertain future. Yet we knew the stupid arrogance of our own class only too well; Steinhardt, having proved himself their equal at a gentleman's sport, would impress them far more by this than by the fact that he was the representative of the most powerful nation in the world. I gave him a warm and grateful look, and he smiled back.

I walked with Uncle Franzi to the second lake. I was very fond of him; all through the war, except for the time when he was in a concentration camp, his sane advice and his certainty of eventual allied victory had sustained us. He was a self-taught historian, and had studied military strategy as a hobby.

'The ambassador didn't do too badly, did he?' I asked happily.

'Remarkably well for a little Jew.'

Again with a shudder, I remembered the Russian's words: '*kleiner Jud*'. 'Why,' I asked crossly, 'shouldn't a Jew shoot as well as a Christian?'

'Because of their ancestry. They were never killers – we are.'

'Anyway, I wish no one ever used the word Jew again.'

'But it's no worse, surely, than saying Italian, English, or Greek, or whatever?' He smiled down at me rather maliciously, I thought, from his great height. 'Why do you mind? Is it because of what happened to them in the war?'

'Because of what happened even before – ' I hesitated. 'Sometimes I think it was people like us that killed them . . .'

He did not look at all surprised. I continued: 'The way people of our class talked –

"What a brilliant man, but then of course he's a Jew."

"The best surgeon I know, but he's of the chosen people," or

"Very intelligent, but then he's Jewish."'

'Quite complimentary if you see it that way,' Uncle Franzi smiled.

'I can't,' I said. 'We were always somehow disparaging, setting them apart as if they were a different species.'

'But they are – '

'That's exactly what the Germans said, exploiting the prejudices of our class and the upper classes. It's easy enough to rouse the rabble once guidance comes from their leaders. I know we are guilty.' Then I told him what I had never told anyone else before, except my husband: that in the war when the persecution began I had gone again and again to what used to be the old ghetto, surrounding one of the most ancient synagogues in Europe, where the Jews awaiting transportation were gathered together like cattle, branded with the yellow star.

'There were young pretty girls,' I told him; 'they had sewn themselves Halinkas, high yellow boots out of the same felt to match their star, as if in defiance. But oh! the sad frightened faces of the old people . . . What could I do but press a little money stealthily into their hands? There were German guards everywhere; I'm such a coward!'

'You might well have been shot for pro-Jewish activities, if you had been caught.' He was looking at me very kindly; encouraged, I continued:

'Then from one day to the next they were all gone – to their death,

I had no doubt about it, even then. I went to the old Jewish cemetery – it was still open, though later the Germans put a barbed wire fence around it; I found Rabbi Loew's grave . . .'

'The miracle Rabbi that created the Golem?'

'Yes. Jews who needed help would place a small stone or pebble on his grave, but now there were no Jews left in Prague to do it. So I did it for them.'

'You are an absurd and fanciful child,' Uncle Franzi said. For a while we walked together in silence through the autumn-tinted forest.

'You are of course in some ways right,' he said at last. 'Certainly we as a class can also be blamed for proclaiming them different from us. But, you see, they were. Not even Hitler or Goebbels can have believed in their own propaganda that the Jews were an inferior race. It was because they were intellectually superior that they were feared, envied and distrusted. Inferior? A people who had been worshipping the single God we believe in for thousands of years, while we were crawling around half-naked in the forests of Europe, lawless beasts, preying on each other, and at best revering some stone idol? The people of whom Christ was born? But envy and the wish to destroy what is superior is one of the most natural of human instincts; all Hitler needed to do was to exploit it. Read your history: the Romans envied the Greeks because of their superior culture so they destroyed Greece; the barbarians envied Roman power and civilization, so they conquered Rome; the crusaders envied the great empire of Byzantium so they brought about its downfall. But the Jews had no country to conquer or wreck; they carried their civilization and religion with them wherever they went, and their power was within themselves. Only by physically exterminating them could they be conquered.'

'Six million innocent people?'

'It is the most monstrous crime in history, but had they died in a war defending their beliefs you would not find it so awful. In a way, they did; we must think of them as martyrs who died for their faith and trust that their homeland, which those who are left are now regaining, will provide them with a secure future. Cheer up, child, it's not your fault!'

'But I have one German great-grandmother,' I protested.

'Well, so have I, but I doubt if either of them indulged in pogroms.'

I sighed. 'I think I'll go and sit with the ambassador now,' I said.

His wise old eyes, as clear blue as the sky, crinkled with amusement. 'To absolve your guilt or because he's handsome?'

'Both,' I laughed, and left him.

I found Steinhardt balancing backward and forward on his shooting stick, his loader was with him. He looked, I thought, rather tired and bored – but there was instant recovery as I sat down beside him. The meadow was bright with pink autumn crocus, which grew wild in the deer-park, and the noon-day sun was warm and pleasant.

'What a beautiful place this is,' he said, looking round appreciatively.

'Yes, we missed it very much during the war.' I told him a little of our experiences in those years, and of Uncle Franzi's time in concentration camp.

The horn blew; a duck rose, then two or three more. The loader who had been consigned to Steinhardt handed him his gun. He took it and laid it across his knee.

'But why don't you shoot?' I asked.

'Because I'd much rather talk to you. Besides, I don't much like killing animals for sport.'

More ducks rose, flying directly above. 'Please shoot,' I said; 'the others won't understand if you don't.'

Obediently he stood up, raised his gun and brought down first two, then five more birds. 'Satisfied?' he asked.

The horn blew, proclaiming the end of the shoot. I walked with Steinhardt to where our lunch had been laid out on long trestle tables. There were surrounding benches but the formality of my parents-in-law's time, when all the male household servants were assembled to serve, and when every guest was seated according to rank, had been abolished by us. It would not have looked very democratic in front of loaders and gamekeepers, in a country on the brink of communism.

'Sit where you like,' Leopold said, 'and help yourselves.'

However, I asked Steinhardt to sit at my right and Prince Lobkowitz, who was no relation and so had second highest rank, on my left. The latter had been one of my most cherished friends for years. No one could have called him handsome; tall, like nearly all the members of his class, Prince Jenda had a pronounced stoop and seemed to find it difficult to manage his awkward, heavy body. He had the high and bumpy forehead of a musician and the dreamy eyes of a poet, but though gifted with rare sensitivity and insight, and appreciative of all the arts, he excelled in none. Nor was he good at managing his financial affairs: he had five children and only a small estate, so that he and his wife Meggy found it difficult to make ends meet. She had been a great beauty in her youth, the daughter of Count Czernin, Austrian minister of foreign affairs and a rather controversial figure in the First World War. She had been very spoilt as a girl in Vienna, yet she had loyally stood by her husband, suffering the consequences of his anti-German and pro-Czech attitude: poverty, hardship and danger for herself and her children. They were a couple much loved by all of us.

Leopold had placed Meggy on his right and Princess Marika, who was a distant relation, on his left. I will call her Marika although it was not her name. There had been no reason at all to invite her to the shoot except that she had so much wanted to come, and Leopold, always good-natured and hospitable, could not refuse her request. She was then about fifty; she too, like Meggy, had been a beauty and her husband the senior member of a great Czech family. Both he and her twelve-year-old son, her only child, had died together in a motor accident. She was left with a magnificent castle, vast estates, great wealth – and very little else. Her face and body had coarsened with age and self-indulgence; she was not very intelligent and did not know how to fill her leisure or use her riches. She had no real friends, only sycophants who flattered her, making her believe she was as important and attractive as she had been in the past. She had become rather aggressive, pride of rank and intolerance being all she had left to make herself noticeable. We all knew this and, feeling sorry, paid her as much attention as possible.

I had asked Aunt Paula Kinsky to sit on Steinhardt's other side; she spoke perfect English and would, I knew, interest him. She was a big handsome woman, immensely capable, the despair of any other female in the country; her gardens more beautiful than those of anyone else, her house better kept than any other, her children and the dogs she bred both superb examples of health, good looks, and behaviour. She was a devoted wife and Uncle Franzi adored her. Soon she and Steinhardt were deep in conversation about his experiences in Russia during the war.

I glanced along the table. We were five women and nine men, and everyone seemed to be having a good time. The various platters of pâté, roast venison, ham, salad, cold pheasant, and cakes were passed around, and so were the carafes of red and white wine, and plum brandy. Leopold was facing me across the narrow table, joking with Meggy Lobkowitz, but no one was paying any attention to Marika. She was staring at Steinhardt's plate, on which he had heaped a lot of ham. Suddenly she pushed a dish of cold pheasant towards him across the table:

'Would your Excellency not prefer this?' she asked.

'Thank you, later perhaps. This ham is delicious, as good as our Virginia ham.'

'But it's pork; I thought perhaps because of your religion . . .' Marika had at last got all the attention she craved. The whole table was reduced to silence. '. . . like we Catholics don't eat meat on Friday,' she explained, seeing Steinhardt's amazement.

He laughed: 'Oh that! I'm not very Orthodox, I'm afraid. Our biblical ancestors had very good reason to forbid the eating of pork, because of the danger of trichanosis, but by now it's tested in every country and quite safe.'

His voice was not loud but it carried. 'Neatly countered,' Jenda whispered appreciatively into my ear; 'what a bitch!' Conversation was resumed.

After lunch the head forester came to tell us he was ready, and the game had been laid out. 'Count Kinsky, a hundred and twenty ducks,' he proclaimed; 'Baron Parish, eighty-five; the Ambassador of the United States, fifty-seven,' and so on in diminishing numbers. In all three hundred and fifty-seven ducks were shot. The Halali was blown, and Steinhardt stood bareheaded to attention, like all the others.

'Aren't such apparently absurd ceremonies rather difficult for an American to understand, in this day and age?' I asked him. 'Not at all – our Indians and those of South America have much the same customs. The spirits of the animals killed have to be appeased lest they never return to the hunting ground. Come, I'll drive you home. It's a brand new car they've sent me – let's see how fast she can go.'

I climbed in beside him. How lightly and almost casually his hands rested on the wheel, yet how certain his control of the powerful car.

'I think you and I are going to be great friends,' he said.

'Not at a hundred miles an hour,' I complained, watching the speedometer. He slowed down immediately. 'I didn't want to frighten you,' he said. 'It's just that I'm rather impatient by nature. Once I know my way and where I want to go, I like to get there fast. Do you understand?'

'Yes,' I replied.

He returned to Prague that afternoon, and Leopold and I followed two days later. Next time he came to Castolovice, a couple of weeks afterwards, it was with his wife and daughter. Meanwhile the friendship which he had foreseen had been firmly established between us, and lasted throughout his term as ambassador to Prague.

5

When the day came that was to decide our future, it was towards evening, I remember, that Steinhardt came to our flat. He had only just returned from Washington. He seemed to have aged since I had last seen him; his face, always golden brown as if tanned by some ancestral sun, looked grey and worn, and his dark eyes lacked their usual sparkle.

'Please don't tell anyone yet, but I wanted you to be the first to know,' he began. 'We will be leaving quite soon. It will take me a month or two to wind things up at the embassy, and for Dulcie to pack, but then we're off.'

He must have sensed my anguish and fear. The Nicholses gone, and now the Steinhardts; were we to be left entirely without protection from the West?

'I must advise you to leave too,' he then said. 'There's not a hope left for people of your kind in this country.'

My husband made a movement of protest. He knew his popularity, and still felt he had friends and protectors even among those who had turned communist almost overnight.

'You'd be crazy to stay,' Steinhardt told him brutally. 'Save your lives at least. Everything else is lost. I fear for your safety.' He added more gently; 'I can't be responsible for letting you stay – your pro-Western sympathies are too well known. Once the Russians take over, as of course they eventually will – ' he gestured expressively, hand against throat.

'But where should we go?' I pleaded.

'To America, of course, where else?' He saw the amazed gratitude in my eyes. 'Though perhaps you might wish to settle in England instead,' he said rather acidly. 'Phil, I'm sure, would look after you there.' He had always been rather jealous of my affection for the Nicholses. 'I talked it over with them both before they left; they were as anxious for your and Leopold's safety as I was.'

'So you always knew,' my husband said angrily. 'Why didn't you tell us?'

'I couldn't – too dangerous. There was still hope. Why rock a boat before it sinks? Anyway,' he continued, turning to me, 'Phil said there would be difficulties in getting even you into England. Though you were born there, you are Czech by marriage, wife of a friendly, not an enemy alien. Had you been married to a German you would have had your British nationality back immediately; it doesn't seem fair, but that's how it is. Then there's the child, a Czech child; you know how fussy the British are about laws and regulations. As for Leopold,' he shrugged: 'I doubt if they'd even grant him entry. Come to America,' he then said warmly. 'It's a great country and anyone with any sense can still make a living in it. It may not be easy to get you your entry permits, but I think I can manage it and I'll look after you once you are there.

'The main problem now is to get you out of here. You need a cure,' he told my husband. 'I've been informed they only allow travel by now in cases of bad health. Vichy in France would do wonders for your leg. Send in your passports immediately, and whatever other documents they ask for. Say you desperately need a cure and that you are too ill to travel without your wife; naturally she cannot leave her child. It may just work.'

He stood up laughing, made us a little bow like a conjuror who has successfully pulled a rabbit out of his hat, then, reassuring us once more that he would see to everything, he left.

He kept his word. Meanwhile the sad truth that there was nothing left but to try and emigrate had dawned too upon our friends and relations. Steinhardt helped where he could, so did de Jean, the French Ambassador and many other diplomats, above all our great friend Adi Rotter, the Austrian Ambassador. All the right-wing members of our government had fled or were in prison; we heard President Benes had resigned and shortly afterwards he died, following a stroke.

Phyllis Nichols returned from The Hague to visit and bring whatever comfort she could to poor Mrs Benes, her many friends, and us. She flew in and out several times, taking with her on her own children's passport the children of Czechs who had flown for Britain during the war and had married English women. She took much else – small fortunes in jewellery and valuables, to be returned to their grateful owners after they had managed to escape. In the general confusion of the communist takeover it was incredible what could be and was done to help and save, with diplomatic immunity still not questioned; though there were cases in which desperate Czechs confidently handed over their valuables to some diplomat or other, never to set eyes on them again!

Meanwhile we had sent in our passports and other documents applying for exit permits, to hear a month later on further anxious enquiry that unfortunately all our papers had been mislaid. Would we send in duplicates? Of course we had none.

'Bastards,' Steinhardt said when we told him about it. 'I feared something like this might happen; I know their tricks. Don't worry, I'll have your papers back and your exit permits too by next week. I'll make some deal – I've traded with communists before.'

Next evening he came back to say everything would be all right but would give us no details. He questioned us closely as to what possessions of value we had that were easily transportable; there were only the china and silver, and the pictures which were still in our flat. We did not dare to ransack Castolovice, because of the servants. Someone was bound to talk and our permission to leave might be cancelled. Jewels? I told him they were in Venice, that I had been there when war seemed inevitable and had left them with Italian friends.

'I doubt if you'll ever see them again,' he said.

Then he enquired what friends or relations we had outside the country, on whom we could rely for help. I knew that some of my husband's Austrian relations would do anything for him but many were by then deprived of their Bohemian estates and as poor as we. Neither he nor I mentioned any names; there had to be something he could depend on for himself, beyond Steinhardt's assistance.

American friends? We knew America only from a Cook's tour we had made when young, but we had seen little of the real America, nor had we made any friends. Later we were to know many Americans in Vienna and abroad, and some had come to stay with us in Castolovice. Rather hesitantly I mentioned a few names. Friends? We had had much to offer in the past – but now? Yet Steinhardt seemed pleased with what he had noted down in an address book.

Then night after night he came to our flat after dark. Undoubtedly he was watched – every diplomat of any importance expected to be shadowed at that time, and he most of all. But there was nothing unusual in his visiting me, or in carrying a briefcase on his way home from the embassy. If it was somewhat augmented in weight and size when he left, who was to notice in the dark? Nor was anyone to know that under his fine vicuna coat, which he wore unbelted, several pictures, old masters that had been in my husband's family for centuries, also left the flat.

Steinhardt asked Leopold to withdraw whatever he could from the bank, without arousing suspicion. It was not by then permissible to take out currency, except for the small amount needed for a month's cure in Vichy, so Steinhardt pocketed the rest and returned it to us later in US dollars. He even bought or sold our car for us. It was a big Tatra coupé, specially built for my husband, dark blue, and upholstered in red leather. Leopold had practically given it to his chauffeur, who had driven him for twenty-five years. Steinhardt felt this to be wasteful and Czerni, although a member of the communist party (perhaps because he had seen too much of our way of life) much to our amazement loyally brought the car back to my husband.

Perhaps the most painful part of our departure was saying goodbye to our old servants. We dared not tell them we would not return, but of course they knew. They had depended on us as much as we had on them; what would become of them now?

At the end of the week, as Steinhardt had assured us, we had our passports back and our exit permits signed. By then I was glad to leave – Leopold still very reluctant. He did not like to leave friends less fortunate than he at finding a means of escape, and though his closest relations – his two younger sisters and two brothers – were all abroad, there was still Annicka.

He had acquired her more by accident than intention towards the end of the war. In one of his spells of circulatory trouble, and when gangrene had been feared in his leg, he had been given a new medicine by his doctor to stimulate his circulation. It cured his leg but it had the most amazing side effects: for weeks no woman was safe from his attentions. The Novaks were a nice little couple of the Czech bourgeoisie; he was well off, a small insignificant man; she was red-haired, not particularly attractive as to face, but with a beautiful figure. They lived in a smart modern flat where we went occasionally to cocktail parties because other friends of ours went. There was nothing interesting about either of them except that they seemed rather touchingly devoted to each other.

Poor woman! My husband's sudden amorous advances so amazed, overawed and flattered her, while impressing her little husband, that there was no defence. Soon all Prague was talking of the affair.

At first I was only amused. My husband and I had been reasonably faithful to each other through the years, though there had been brief lapses from which each of us had rapidly recovered. Certainly nothing as permanent as this became had ever happened before.

Once an old princess, an aunt of Leopold's, whose past had been far from blameless, advised: 'If you are ever jealous, dear child, of some lady who is pursuing your husband or your lover, there are only three ways by which to defeat her – cut her dead, make her your best friend or seduce her yourself. Of course,' she added hastily, 'this doesn't apply if the woman is a *cocotte* or of the lower class; anyway, they don't count.'

Her advice was useless in this case. I could not cut Annicka dead, though I would have liked to, just because she was not of my class. My Czech, though I had worked hard at learning it in wartime, was not good enough for persuasive friendships, and she spoke no other language. Besides, what would I have had in common with her, except my husband? Even he said she was feather-brained and had the mentality of a child of eight. As for seducing her – !

But she was certainly no tart. She had been a perfectly respectable, happily married young woman before Leopold took that medicine, and though its effects wore off in time, he was definitely stuck with her. He swore he didn't love her, but I knew that in some ways he did. Her simplicity made him laugh, her humble adoration touched and flattered him; she made him feel even taller and more handsome and important than he was.

By then her husband had left her. She had no money of her own and when she heard we were leaving she threatened suicide if Leopold did not get her out of the country too. He had not liked to ask Steinhardt to help; it had embarrassed him less to go to de Jean, the then French Ambassador who, he felt, would understand better, being French. De Jean did, and promised to do his best. Annicka had a married sister in France, and if this sister would write and say she was seriously ill and needed help, de Jean thought he could get Annicka out. Though I did not relish the idea of her joining us in emigration, I was too much in love with Steinhardt by then to think it fair to object.

The Steinhardts were to return to America a week or two after our departure, to discuss his new post. Dulcie wanted Paris, he said he preferred Ottawa. He had been away from his own country too long, he said, and this would be near New York: 'I will fly over every week to visit you, once you are there,' he reassured me. Amongst other things, he would see to our entry permits when in Washington, and contact some of our former friends in New York. After that both he and Dulcie would return to Paris, she for her clothes, he, I hoped, to be with me. There was of course no question of any of us going to Vichy; he had ordered rooms for us at the Cambon, a little hotel just behind the Ritz, he said, and very convenient and cheap.

*

I looked at my watch once more. It was seven thirty and we were nearing the end of our journey. From somewhere came the delicious smell of fresh coffee; I rang for the sleeping-car attendant and ordered our breakfasts.

My child was still asleep, clutching her knife. What weapon had I with which to face the uncertain future? I asked myself. My husband's briefcase was crammed with 'to whom it may concern' letters from diplomats and former members of the Czech government, who had since also fled, recommending him to the Czech refugee commission already established in Paris and linked to one in New York. Would he find the work he hoped for there? Could he still serve his country abroad and make a living of it? I doubted it even then. An old tree, uprooted from its native soil, rarely thrives after being transplanted. How would I be able to support and protect him?

I peered into the small mirror above the washbasin; my hair was in a mess, my face grey and pinched-looking. Hastily I applied paint:

'"Where are you going to, my pretty maid?"

'"I'm going a-milking, Sir," she said.

'"And what is your fortune, my pretty maid?"

'"My face is my fortune, kind Sir," she said.'

As I hummed it, I wondered if the old nursery rhyme was applicable to myself. I had never been a beauty, and though I still had a good figure, I was nearing forty.

But in a way my face was my fortune, and it hadn't changed much through the years. My head was so small that it looked as if it could not contain any brains whatsoever, and my face was that of a child – mischievous perhaps, but disarmingly innocent, frank and gay. It was totally unrevealing of my real nature. Had I chosen a mask in which to get away with murder, I would have chosen my face. Soon, I thought, it will sag and crumple, or harden into ugly lines, and the childish charm would be gone, just as my figure would go. What then would I be able to depend on? Steinhardt?

Never in my life had I dared to cheat myself. I had few illusions and only one left: that I was going to make a fortune in America, entirely on my own.

I had always been quite good at drawing and painting and modelling in clay. In the war I had made small figurines, copies of the baroque saints that graced every church, town square and bridge in Prague. I had them cast in plaster, painted them up and sometimes even sold them. We had no income then, of course, as our estates were confiscated, and though my husband somehow managed to keep our household going thanks to loans from his friends, I was always short of pocket money. St Wenceslas, our country's patron, sold best, and another saint whose name I have forgotten – I think it was Thaddeus, or the one to pray to if imprisoned – sold equally well. But my greatest success came with a small copy of the miraculous Infant Jesus of Prague, moulded in wax as was the original in the church of the Carmelites, and dressed like it in gold-threaded brocade. Czechs, religious or not, bought the figure as a charm against danger and death; German soldiers leaving for the front bought it for the same reasons. But moulding the Infant was laborious and sewing its clothes took endless time. Why not cast it in ceramic? Surely, if mass-produced, it would sell in America too?

Steinhardt, though he admired my artistry, seemed somewhat dubious – also of the buttons I was later to show him hopefully. In the months before we left, knowing I must quickly learn some trade, I had secretly visited, three times weekly, an old White Russian gentleman who had found refuge in Czechoslovakia after the Revolution. He earned his meagre living by making ceramic buttons. I knew nothing of ceramics but he taught me how to make moulds, fire a kiln, glaze and gild. Poor man, after the communist coup, in fear of being deported back to Russia, he had killed himself.

I learned to make as pretty buttons as he did. I had my samples with me, rainbow-coloured and gilt, of every size and shape, and they filled me with hope.

'Paris in an hour,' announced the sleeping-car attendant, bringing our breakfast trays. I woke my family.

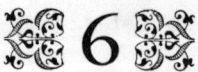

We arrived at our hotel in the Rue Cambon only after a fierce encounter at the railway station with porters incensed by the amount of our luggage, and reluctant to move it except at exorbitant cost. It had finally been loaded into two taxis; my husband went in one with most of our trunks, while I followed, with Diana and the suitcases. On the way to the hotel our driver stopped, and, without any word of apology, got out to relieve himself behind one of those corrugated iron screens that were still abundant in Paris. Manners seem to have deteriorated in France since before the war, I thought.

'He is telephoning, darling,' I explained to the enquiring child.

'Rather wet,' she decided, seeing the man's boots and the stream of water descending into the gutter.

On reaching the hotel I found Leopold standing in front of it, surrounded by trunks. He was listening with unconcealed amusement to the way in which a very plump, but tightly corseted, woman in black satin dealt with first his, and then my taxi-driver's demands for payment. Insults and imprecations echoed through the Rue Cambon, bringing out even the uniformed doorman of the Ritz, whose back entrance was almost opposite the front of our hotel.

At last, having dealt with the drivers to her satisfaction, the lady gestured to my husband to pay the sum she had settled for, shrugged off further muttered insults from the drivers, and turned to me smiling, and in no way embarrassed or perturbed.

'Welcome to my hotel,' she said in awkward English. 'The apartments are awaiting you.' Then, catching sight of my daughter who had cautiously retreated behind me, she leapt forward. '*Oh, la pauvre petite!*' She swept the reluctant child into her arms and held her tight. 'She has lost her country. Oh, those *sales boches* – ' She was obviously not very accurately informed as to why we had left Czechoslovakia.

This formidable woman was Madame Poisson, the owner of our hotel; we were to get to know her very well. Her husband, a shadowy figure to be found behind the desk when not busy in the kitchen, was a person of less importance.

Madame led us through the dark, narrow foyer, past an equally dark dining-room smelling strongly of garlic, and preceded us up several flights of stairs, puffing and blowing and apologizing that *le lift* was temporarily out of order. Seeing it, a small shaky-looking birdcage, stuck half-way between ceiling and ground floor, I thanked God it was. She flung open a door. '*Voilà,*' she said.

The apartment consisted of two largish bedrooms and a bathroom but, being under the mansard roof, very low-ceilinged and stiflingly hot. '*Mais comment, on a oublié les fleurs!*' she exclaimed, indignantly looking round. We had not expected flowers, but somewhat more comfortable accommodation; the rooms were very sparsely furnished. She was too shrewd not to sense our disappointment. '*En tout cas,*' she said, 'it's not expensive. One must help the refugees as best one can, as Monsieur Steinhardt wrote.'

Soon our luggage, carried by a very old man and a boy who couldn't be more than twelve, filled the entire floorspace of our rooms. My husband sat disconsolately on one bed, my daughter perched on the other. 'We won't be here for long,' I said comfortingly and started to unpack. Since none of us could remember what was in any of the suitcases, I had to undo them all. The room grew more and more untidy and seemed to get warmer every minute. Its small windows opened on to a courtyard below, where one could see tables and chairs shaded by dusty parasols. Under them some people were having breakfast or lunch; their voices were clearly audible and so was the clatter of knives and forks. A rank smell of food rose in the hot air.

'I'm hungry,' the child complained.

'Go into the bathroom and wash. Here's your dressing gown.' I had found it at last. 'When we are clean we will go down and eat.'

'Let's go to the Ritz,' Leopold said.

'But mustn't we economize?' I asked, rather shocked at his suggestion.

'Certainly not,' he grinned, pulling a wad of crumpled bank notes out of his pocket. He always carried his money this way. It was, I suppose, all that had been allowed us in French currency for the cure in Vichy; yet it seemed quite a lot, and soon, I hoped, Steinhardt would bring the rest.

There was a scream from the bathroom. I rushed in fearing the child had scalded herself, though I need not have worried – the water in the Hotel Cambon was never more than lukewarm. I found her still in her dressing gown, but drenched from head to foot, a fountain rising from the bidet, towards the ceiling, spraying the entire bathroom.

'Mummy, I only turned the handle,' she explained, her face wet with water or tears, or both.

Though it was just the sort of joke that Leopold would usually have enjoyed, he seemed more irritated than amused. He was tired and emotionally exhausted, I knew; he too had wanted to bath and change. He looked at the flooded bathroom with distaste and, leaving me to mop up, walked out as he was in his rumpled old suit, saying he needed a drink and would wait for us in the Ritz bar. I couldn't blame him, but I rather wondered how we were going to manage with all three of us living in such close proximity. Diana's nursery had been a long way from our rooms in Castolovice, and also in Prague; even when her nanny left she had always had someone to look after her. My husband and I had had separate bedrooms and bathrooms for many years.

Still, it was good to be in Paris again, I thought as, washed and changed into clean summer dresses, the child and I crossed the hot sunlit street and entered the cool Ritz. Except for a few American tourists the bar was quite empty but then of course August was the time of year when everyone left town.

'What do you want to drink?' Leopold asked as we sat down beside him on the red plush bench. 'I've been having several Martinis.' I could see he had. 'The same for me,' I said, 'Lemonade for the child.'

He ordered our drinks. 'Do you know,' he said indignantly, 'the barman didn't recognize me? Yet I'm sure it's the same man who was here before the war.'

'Darling, all barmen look the same. It must be ten years since we were last here.'

We started remembering people, famous and infamous, that had frequented the Ritz bar in the past. Then it had been a meeting and market place of international society. All the elegant, rich and distinguished – or those who aspired to be so – from all over the world could be seen there. Whoever was in Paris for business or politics, to shop or just to enjoy themselves met in the Ritz bar before lunch. How sadly deserted it seemed now.

'May I go?' the child asked, obviously bored. Where? I remembered the long corridor full of shops that used to lead from the back entrance of the Ritz to that on the Place Vendôme. Although I doubted there would be much left to see in those shops after the war I took her there. To my amazed delight I saw that everything was quite unchanged; the most expensive luxuries were as beautifully and tastefully displayed as before – jewels and dresses, furs and feathers, negligées, leatherware and hats, perfumes and a profusion of equally heady-smelling flowers gardenias, carnations and tuberoses. No woman could have resisted, certainly not I. I told Diana to walk around and went back to my husband in the bar.

'You know, it's extraordinary,' I told him, 'how quickly everything has recovered here since the war and what's for sale again.' 'Paris always was a whore,' he muttered.

'I saw a dress, well, perhaps two,' I said hesitantly, 'and several things we need desperately. Do I dare buy them?' 'But of course. Here,' he said, pulling the bundle of notes out of his pocket and putting it on the table. 'Take what you want.'

I took too much and I spent it all. What a way to start our future, I thought, buying luxuries in the most expensive shopping arcade in Paris, on the first day of emigration. But it had done me good – I felt gay and reckless. After all, thanks to Steinhardt, there was more than enough left to safeguard our future for years to come. I had everything sent to the Hotel Cambon – a silk dressing gown, ties and socks for Leopold, two dresses and some pretty underwear for myself, and the toys the child had chosen.

When we returned to the bar I saw to my amazement that Leopold was not alone: Gloria Fürstenberg was sitting beside him. I hadn't seen her for years; she was looking smarter and more lovely than ever in a white silk suit, her abundant black hair tied back with a white chiffon scarf. She got up to embrace us. 'Poor darlings,' she said. 'Leopold has told me everything.' Her funny accent had not changed – she was half-Mexican by birth, her father a well-known writer and journalist. When very young she had married a German, a Count Fürstenberg, and had been counted with Mathilde Mumm, Biene Goldschmidt, and one or two others whose names I have forgotten as one of Berlin society's most celebrated beauties.

I first met Gloria at one of Prince Ulrich Kinsky's shooting parties in Czechoslovakia. There were then a lot of amusing English people and some German couples there, but only very few Czechs or Austrians, and those bachelors. Ulrich had recently divorced his first wife and remarried, without a Church annulment, a woman who was also divorced. Mathilde was half-German, half-Argentinian; she was indeed a great beauty with a face of classical perfection, accustomed to move in the best society in Germany to which her birth, her good looks and behaviour fully entitled her. She was a sweet-natured, gentle and rather simple woman, extremely virtuous and conventional, who neither understood nor deserved the way her husband's relations and most of Austrian society treated her because she had not been married in church. They refused to meet her. Had she been Ulrich's mistress and not his legal wife everything would have been all right; as it was she was practically ostracized and she suffered. I was very sorry for her and fond of her; Leopold had always been a great friend of Ulrich's, so to the horror of our parents-in-law we frequently stayed with this couple 'living in sin', as they said. We enjoyed the foreign guests they invited to their parties much more than the staid relations and often very dull members of his own class that Ulrich used to have at his houseparties before.

Gloria and Mathilde had been friends in Berlin; rivals too perhaps, because of their equal beauty, but both women in their different ways were devoid of feminine envy or meanness. Everyone liked Gloria. In our country, her Christian name was unfamiliar except for the very familiar 'Gloria in Excelsis Deo' heard at mass. With the flippancy only devout Roman Catholics can afford when speaking of their religion, we called her Gloria in Excelsis.

Even women liked her. She was no threat to husbands or lovers and no easy prey for any man; only at poker, bridge or backgammon, all of which were played at those house-parties for high stakes, was she a menace.

She must have liked me I think because after my challenging her to backgammon in Mestec, Ulrich's castle, she refused to play with me. 'I'd sooner pluck a chicken,' she said. She was very intelligent and witty, with a keen sense of humour which was only cruel when with her dark almond-shaped eyes sparkling with fun, her black hair in disarray from the restless movements of her hands, she mimicked and mocked anyone she thought pompous, stupid or pretentious.

We met several times later: in Berlin and in Baden-Baden where we went for the races, and in Frankfurt where we stayed with Carlo Weinberg for the polo week. After the war had begun I heard no more of her. Ulrich had died of a heart attack, Mathilde had managed to get their children, twin girls and a baby son, safely to Argentina, rejoining her relations there.

It must have been towards the end of the war, that Gloria called me up from the Ambassador Hotel in Prague, a by then rather shabby hotel frequented mainly by Czechs since the Germans preferred the more modern and more luxurious Bristol or Alcron. 'I'm so ill,' she gasped, coughing and sneezing into the phone, 'and so tired, and sick of Germany and all the bombing. I am here for a little rest. Please come and visit me.'

I found her in the most luxurious suite the hotel afforded, lying in bed draped in pink chiffon, looking too lovely for words, and sneezing into a small handkerchief. There were red roses everywhere, six dozen at least.

'I've caught such a cold,' she said. 'I left just like that.' She snapped her fingers. 'I put my nightdress and my toothbrush into my handbag and left in only my mink coat and very little underneath. I didn't know how cold it was here.'

We talked for a while, of her problems and ours; she was hoping to get to Spain with her children. Then suddenly she drew some type-written pages from under her pillow and handed them to me. 'I want to know if you think them very good.'

I started reading. They were love poems written in German by a man to a woman. Not too bad if one wasn't as much of an admirer of the poet Rilke as I was. Whole sentences and images all too familiar.

'Quite good,' I said, 'but not very original.'

'Second-rate would you say?'

'Second-hand rather, I'm afraid.'

'It is what I had feared. Anyway, how can one write good poems in a language where the moon is masculine and the sun feminine? It's all wrong.'

Next day she telephoned to say she felt much better and was leaving and sending me all her roses. Who the poet was I never found out. After the war had ended I heard she was living in Spain and was separated from her husband. And now here she was, really not very surprisingly since she was the sort of woman who would not stay away from Paris for long if she could help it.

She got up. 'Come,' she said, 'you must be my guests for lunch on this your first day of freedom. I'm broke, that's why I'm staying here at the Ritz where I have credit. I had a run of bad luck at the tables in Deauville. Who cares? Let's have all the caviar we can eat and let's drink champagne.'

At the mention of food, whatever food, my poor child's tired little face brightened. We had the most delicious lunch with the *maître d'hôtel* paying us every attention, Leopold quite sure he had been recognized at last. We talked of mutual friends, saddened by the fate of some, rejoicing for those that had survived and were safe.

'Biene and Erich Goldschmidt? They got to Switzerland in time,' Gloria told us. 'They are in New York now, Marion Goldschmidt too escaped to Switzerland. Poor Horstman, well I suppose you know?'

We didn't. We had heard very little about our German friends and acquaintances during and since the war.

'The Russians got him. Do you remember how he cherished his fabulous collection of Dresden china? Because of the bombing of Berlin he had stored it in his country place in Silesia. After the war had ended he went back to try and save it from the Russians. He was too late – they were already there. He has never been heard of since.'

'But Lalli?'

'She's all right. She's living in Rome.'

Much as I had liked Lalli Horstman, I had never been able to grow fond of her husband. He had been one of the great hosts of pre-war Berlin, his house in the Tiergartenstrasse almost a museum of all that was most exquisite and rare of eighteenth-century furniture, china and bibelots. He had wonderful taste in collecting antiques as well as in acquiring beautiful women. But though he handled the former with great care and reverence, his coarse treatment of the latter was proverbial. He was fat, physically very unattractive and had, I thought, very parvenu manners.

'I wonder he survived the war,' Leopold said. 'Wasn't he half-Jewish? Lalli certainly was.'

'Of course. But he kept his position under the Nazis all through the war, living much as he did in our day. Goering was a friend of his, they had many tastes in common. I think it was about him that Goering said *"Wer Jude ist bestimme ich"*!' Gloria laughed.

'And the Weinbergs? Old Carlo survived, I hear.'

'Only just. He lives in Rome now in a little flat. His brother, the head of the IG Farben, was killed in a concentration camp. Carlo is a very old and broken man by now.'

'I'm sorry. He was a good friend,' Leopold said.

'And madly generous,' Gloria added.

He certainly was to me, I remembered. I still have a necklace he had given me when he took us to shop in Frankfurt. I had admired it at the jewellers, a little wreath of jade flowers set with rubies and diamonds. Of course I never expected him to give it to me. Next morning at Waldfried it was on my breakfast table.

We remembered Waldfried, that absurd group of rustic chalets supposed to look like shooting boxes in the forest near Frankfurt in which Carlo entertained his guests. The interiors were even more bizarre – suite after suite of rooms, Renaissance or rococo, medieval or empire with furniture, pictures, statuary and tapestries all of the appropriate period. We would dine at long refectory tables covered with gold-fringed crimson velvet, up to a hundred guests, served on gold plate. Carlo's own polo ground adjoined the forest. Though seventy then he still played, and teams from everywhere came with their ponies and were his guests for the famous polo week to which we were always invited. He was the best and most considerate of hosts, a kind, generous, sweet-tempered old man, beloved by everyone.

'It's been a bad time for so many, for all of us,' Gloria sighed. 'One must find the courage to start all over again.'

When the bill came, Leopold took it automatically. 'But you're my guests,' Gloria protested.

'But I really can't,' Leopold said, hopelessly embarrassed. I understood why. Never in his life I think had he not paid the bill when lunching with a lady.

No doubt Gloria understood too. 'No,' she said, waving the waiter away, 'times have changed.'

'You make me feel like a gigolo,' Leopold laughed. She looked at him very kindly. His face was flushed with the many drinks he had had and the rich food he had eaten; his curly grey hair was disordered and stood up on end, his suit was rumpled and shabby. 'Darling Leopold, no one in the world would mistake you for one.'

She kissed us goodbye saying she had to leave for St Tropez next day to join some friends on a yacht bound for Greece.

Years later I was to meet her again in America. She was then Mrs Lowell Guinness. Her house in Palm Beach was beautiful and as luxurious as only great wealth and great taste could have made it. She was better-looking than ever, and surrounded by adoring friends. 'I'm so very happy,' she told me. 'Lowell has so much!' Obviously I thought, scanning the beautifully furnished rooms and the great windows overlooking garden and blue sea. 'As a man, you understand!'

7

Meanwhile, cheered by our lunch, we returned to the hotel. I praised the child for her behaviour, for not having interrupted our conversation, and having eaten with restraint in spite of having been ravenously hungry. 'Such good food,' she said dreamily as I put her to bed for her afternoon rest.

I went into my husband's room; he seemed to feel the same. 'I wish we could have stayed in the Ritz,' he complained, 'being there reminded me so much of the past.'

'Do you remember our honeymoon?' 'Also that,' he laughed, 'and when you tried to rape me.' It was an old joke between us but it still made me blush. 'You've had too much to drink,' I said severely. He yawned. 'Yes, I think I'll sleep. Later we must call up a lot of people.'

I went back into the other room and lay down too, thinking with some amusement of what he had said. It was almost true. After our wedding in Vienna, now twenty years ago, we had left by train for Paris accompanied by Leopold's valet Jenicek, without whom he never travelled anywhere. I detested him; he was a cheeky, sneaky little man, his manners far too familiar, I thought. But he amused Leopold and they would joke together in Czech, which I did not then understand, or they would study the racing papers, ignoring me.

It was customary even for a young girl of good family to travel with

a maid in those days; much more so a married woman. Aunt Diana
had sent me a maid from Emkendorf thinking I should have someone
to remind me of my home in a strange country; but I didn't need a fat,
untrained, Holstein peasant girl to remind me of Emkendorf and except
for someone to look after my clothes I didn't need a maid at all. I
always dressed and undressed myself, much to the surprise of my sister-
in-law, who even had her stockings put on by her maid. My hair needed
only the attention of a comb, being cropped as short as a boy's, and
since I intensely disliked being touched by strangers I washed and cut
it myself. I refused to take Wilhelmine to Paris and she was sent instead
to Zasmuky to await our arrival.

To have to travel with Jenicek was, I knew, going to be bad enough.
I was right: all night long I had to suffer his constant invasion of our
privacy. He was in and out of our sleeping compartment where I lay
looking lovely, I hoped, in my best trousseau nightgown, between
pink *crêpe de chine* sheets – one always travelled with one's own sheets
on trains in those days – enquiring almost all through the night what
he could bring and do for our comfort. Except for a few furtively
exchanged kisses nothing further took place on that journey, thanks
to Jenicek's attentiveness.

But once settled in our apartment in the Ritz, everything unpacked,
Leopold and I were left alone at last. I felt rather frightened. All
through my life when afraid I have been more liable to attack than to
retreat. I did then. I was seventeen, I had no mother to tell me anything
about sex, my Aunt Diana was a spinster and my grandmother too
Victorian to have been capable of enlightening me.

I knew everything animals did of course; horses, dogs, cows, pigs
and poultry – no one had objected to my seeing them mating on the
farms and in the paddocks of Emkendorf. But that I felt was very
different from what human lovemaking must be, and I wanted to
please my husband. He was an experienced man of the world, known
to have had many mistresses, and I did not want to prove inadequate.
So I had resorted to literature. A girl-friend of mine warmly recommended the *Kama Sutra*. The man in the shop had looked at me with
some surprise when I asked for it; its name meant nothing to me and
the picture on the cover of Indian gods embracing seemed quite innocent. I read and re-read the book, growing ever more confused at the
gymnastics necessary for perfection in the art of love. Nevertheless
I thought at last I knew something positive. 'Let's get it over with,'
I felt, and tearing off my clothes in front of my amazed husband I
advanced towards him with the peculiar sort of dance the *Kama* recom-

mended with which to arouse the beloved.

I think I have never seen, nor I hope ever will see anyone as shocked as Leopold looked then. He had believed me an innocent child; nevertheless he accepted my challenge, soon to realize that I knew nothing and had to be taught the facts of life kindly and gently. After the first shock I learnt quickly and I think made him as happy as I became myself.

Was it really twenty years ago? We had been married in Vienna in 1928 with all the pomp and circumstance still considered essential then. It was in January; the bridesmaids would have frozen to death in St Stephen's Cathedral, but the small well-heated Kapuziner Kirche was considered just as elegant, since its vaults contained all the tombs of the Imperial family.

For some reason I have never fathomed, except that perhaps my grandmother thought it smart, we were married by the French Papal Nuncio. He looked very splendid in his violet-coloured robes but he spoke no German and of course no Czech. Leopold spoke no French. He had the night before attended not only the *Brautsoirée* which was given in my honour and ended at twelve, but also the bachelor party given for him by his male friends. All the *demi-monde* of Vienna had been present, with the many lovely ladies that had adored him, laughed at his jokes, profited from his generosity, and now had reluctantly come to bid him goodbye.

The party in the Sacher *separée* had lasted till five in the morning. Leopold was tired and soon gave up repeating the vows of the wedding service in an unknown language and certainly no one heard him say '*Oui*' in French or 'Yes' in any other language because he quite simply didn't.

'The child can get annulled from that libertine any day,' Uncle Alec Hoyos, who was one of the wedding witnesses, told my grandmother, 'I can swear to it that Sternberg never said yes.'

'Of course,' my father-in-law told his wife, 'if this marriage that you have so much encouraged proves disastrous, Leopold can easily get out of it and remarry someone more suitable. The marriage sacrament cannot be considered valid by the Church since he never agreed to bind himself.'

Worse followed. Of the rings we had exchanged in church, Leopold immediately lost his, on purpose I'm sure, because he disliked wearing a ring; offended, I refused to wear mine. This was noted by everyone at the wedding breakfast. Bets were made in the Jockey Club as to how long the marriage would last – one year, two years at best; after that the odds were exorbitant.

It was to last nearly thirty years.

My grandmother, English by birth, Countess Hoyos by marriage, had made all the wedding arrangements. She had chosen my trousseau at Spitzers, Vienna's best dressmaker at the time. A dozen each of nightdresses, day dresses, evening dresses, coats, hats, and shoes to match, and the household linen embroidered with crowns and with interlaced C S. Aunt Diana, my father's only sister, who had looked after me and my two younger brothers when our mother died, paid for it all, though she could ill afford to do so. She did not come to the wedding; she had done her best for me. I was a girl without a fortune; my father had left nothing but debts, and my home in Schleswig-Holstein – beautiful, neoclassical Emkendorf, built in the late eighteenth century, decorated by Italian artisans, who had spent eleven years there painting and stuccoing walls and ceilings – was heavily mortgaged and would have to be sold.

It was Aunt Diana too, who, reluctantly because in her own strange way she loved me as much as I loved her, had persuaded me to accept my grandmother's invitation to be given a season in Vienna and a winter in Rome. This was still before my father's death. Both he and she knew that the company he kept, mainly living abroad after my mother had died, was not suitable for a young girl.

'Countess Hoyos may not be quite . . .' Aunt Diana sniffed; (she refused to call my grandmother Alice) 'but she has made herself a considerable position in Vienna and married off all her daughters well.' The 'not quite . . .' and the sniff were because my grandmother had been born plain Miss Whitehead whereas Aunt Diana's mother had been related to half the nobility of Scotland and England.

Omama, as all her grandchildren called her, was well over sixty when I joined her in Vienna. Tiny, still rather pretty with short-cropped yellow-white curls and china blue eyes, she was always very smartly dressed. She looked very like a doll, which was deceptive, because she was unbreakable. Small as Omama was, she was the most forceful of matriarchs and dominated her entire family. She was strictly Victorian as to morals, Edwardian in her respect for titles and wealth, and very social and worldly.

When I first arrived at her house in Vienna, she gave me a peck on the cheek then told me to take off my jacket. She had seen me last at my mother's funeral when I was still a child. 'Stand up straight,' she said, 'I'll never find you a husband if you slouch like that. There, that's better. Quite a good figure. We must get you some decent clothes.

You're a bit young to be taken out. Still, I was married at sixteen and had seven children before I was thirty. We'll start slowly, it wouldn't do at all for you to become cheap by being seen everywhere at first.'

Some days later she invited Prince Festetitz, a distant relation on her husband's side, to tea. He was, she knew, as good a judge of women as of horses. I served the buttered toast trying to look graceful, but I tried too hard, tripped and fell over a rug. There was nothing to do but laugh and Prince Festetitz laughed with me, gallantly raising me from the floor and holding me longer than was necessary. I went to my room to clean off the buttered toast from my dress. When I returned Prince Festetitz had left.

'How could you be so clumsy?' Omama asked, but she looked more amused than angry.

'Sorry if I made a bad impression,' I said, but I knew I hadn't. I wasn't so naïve as not to know when a man liked me, even then.

'What did he say?' I asked.

'Well, it wasn't very nice, I don't know why men these days use such horsy language.'

'Oh, do tell me.'

'It was a warning really. He said, "You have a fast filly there – she may make it, but don't let her have her head." '

'In case I stumble,' I laughed.

She took his advice. She did indeed fear very much that because of my unconventional upbringing and high spirits I might be labelled as fast, which would have been disastrous to my marriage chances. She was very strict with me; never was I allowed to go anywhere unchaperoned, never allowed to talk to any man she considered unsuitable. But I had grown up in almost complete freedom, and reverting to the language of Prince Festetitz, I could be led, but not ridden on too tight a rein. The more Omama tried to curb me, the faster I went. She could not object to my dancing at balls. It was the time of the Charleston, and I was certainly the highest kicker among the young girls of Vienna – not because I was morally lighter as some thought, but physically, compared to the heavily built Austrians. I flirted outrageously, I even let young men kiss me. There was always a conservatory or a garden adjoining the ballroom and they were very innocent kisses – no improper advantages were taken of young girls in those days. Also I didn't even like being kissed very much then. What I really enjoyed was shocking my grandmother. Definitely I was fast.

I was so fast that to her amazement I came first in the marriage race, beating all the other *Contesserln*, as the young girls of Austria were called, to the post by becoming engaged to Leopold Sternberg, an eldest son of one of the wealthiest families of the Austro-Hungarian Empire. Never will I forget my grandmother's face when I told her of my engagement. She had never met Leopold. She knew his parents of course; she and they moved in the same social circles revolving at different levels round the imaginary axis of the court. Austria was by then a republic.

But there was still the *Erste Gesellschaft*, the élite, all *Hoffähig* (entitled to be received at court) nobles of impeccable ancestry and flawless family trees, owners of vast estates often in Czechoslovakia or Hungary, magnificent castles and palaces in Vienna and Prague. The *Zweite Gesellschaft*, or second-class society was made up of some aristocrats whose grandmothers, mothers or wives had been commoners and so not acceptable at court; also the highly cultured Viennese bourgeoisie and the intelligentsia – artists, writers and musicians.

Then there was the *demi-monde*, the glamorous half-world, its existence supposedly veiled from young girls, and respectable women, its mysteries only penetrable by men. The world of *separées*, houses of assignation and of the famous Viennese *cocottes*. Of course, through the indiscretion of sons, brothers and even husbands and the gossip of hairdressers and dressmakers one was always fully informed. One knew their names – Stephie, Mitzi, Lilie and so on – and discussed their jewels, their clothes and their habits and price. On Sundays it was even possible to see them. All of Vienna attended the twelve o'clock mass at St Stephen's Cathedral, and then sauntered along the Kärtnerstrasse towards the Sacher Hotel where many had lunch or a drink in the bar. These ladies always walked in pairs, either with a female friend or maid, and would pass one holding themselves very straight, looking neither to left nor right, beautiful, arrogant and self-assured – only their scent lingering on after them, a reminder and an invitation.

If a man, walking with a woman of society, showed the slightest start of recognition on meeting these ladies, or worst of all *faux pas*, bowed and doffed his hat, he would be frozen by a glance of such cold and haughty disdain as some great queen might have cast on a subject that had transgressed. The *demi-monde* had conventions stricter perhaps than any of the other societies. But then most of the Viennese still lived according to the conventions established by the Imperial court.

The only set that broke all rules were *Die Gloriosen* – the glorious ones, as they had been named – all of the *Erste Gesellschaft*, so called perhaps because of the glorious beauty of their women or their glorious disregard of all social conventions. Their prodigality, high spirits and recklessness scandalized and delighted all of Vienna. They gambled and drank, they danced till dawn to the new jazz music in nightclubs in which it had been unheard of for a lady to be seen before, rubbing shoulders with pimps and prostitutes, or sat through many hours of the night listening to the haunting melodies of Hungarian gipsy bands, or drove out to the Heurigen where the young wine was drunk by rich and poor alike and everyone sang Viennese folk-songs together. It was to this set that my husband had belonged. Last but not least there was *Schmud'l*. It was the most condemning word in the Viennese dialect. It was applicable to the most sovereign of families, it might be said of an archduke or a prince, or it might mark a beautiful woman of impeccable ancestry as it would deprive a *cocotte* of her values in the *demi-monde*. It was a word used by the aristocracy and the middle class alike. What did *Schmud'l* mean? Difficult to explain because one simply knew who was *Schmud'l* or not. Unsmart, inelegant, dull and unsuccessful? Unwashed, shabby or mean? Even my grandmother, who because of her English birth had remained free of Austrian intolerance, would not have invited anyone who was *Schmud'l* to her house.

There was another more subtle and even crueller form of discrimination which my grandmother was by nature too democratic not to dislike. Although her German was fluent, she never spoke it if she didn't have to. When I first came to Vienna, unable to comprehend the importance of *Du* and *Sie*, she advised me not to bother. 'Speak English,' she said, 'everyone here can understand it. It's safer.'

All male members of the aristocracy called each other by Christian names and said '*Du*' or 'thou' to each other, related or not. All females of the same class called each other '*Du*' or 'thou' except in the case of an older lady whom one addressed somewhat like this – 'Hast thou slept well, Princess Norah?' To a man not related, but of her own class, a girl or woman would say 'Count Kari, will you bring me an ice?' never the '*Du*' or 'thou'. It was a custom used in French and Italian society too, but never to the cruel extent in which it stressed aristocratic superiority in Austria.

Because anyone not of noble birth, however distinguished, intelligent or charming, was discriminated against by being called '*Sie*', or 'you', it needed great diplomacy and much genealogical knowledge not to offend superiors or inferiors. For instance, those of royal blood had to be addressed by '*Sie*' and the full title, Imperial Highness. As if all this were not enough, in terms of intimacy among husband and wife, parents and children, and often in addressing the servants too, the 'he' and 'she' were used. 'Will she come and kiss me goodnight?' a child would ask its mother. 'I hear he has been good at his lessons,' from father to son, 'Will he bring me my coat?' to a servant.

Having discovered the value of '*Du*', I gave it too freely for my grandmother's satisfaction. I had quite simply called everyone '*Du*' whom I thought nice. Omama's social position in Vienna was by then so assured that for the sake of variety she received members of the second society in her house as well, knowing that many of them were more intelligent and interesting than those of the first. But of course it was not proper for me to call Doctor Kassner '*Du*', nor Frau Kuhn, however great a philosopher the one and an artist the other.

Soon I took my grandmother's advice and spoke nothing but English in Austria. Probably she in her youth had also met and resented the knife-thrust of the '*Sie*' when she had first learned to speak German. She had been born plain Alice Whitehead, the daughter of an engineer born in Bolton, Lancashire. After briefly serving in the merchant navy and having somehow acquired engineering training, he designed the first workable torpedo. In the beginning his genius remained unrecognized in England and his plans were not accepted by the navy. Austria, however, showed interest and first in Pola on the Adriatic and later in Fiume he was given every facility for developing his invention, the Whitehead torpedo. The Fiume factory was the largest – a smaller one in Weymouth followed. He became rich and prosperous and acquired several country estates in England; he sent his sons to Eton and his daughters to be educated in Florence.

In his portrait he had a red-gold beard and eyes as blue as the sea – so straight and powerful in their glance that, I imagine, they must have intimidated the impecunious Austrian naval officer who had nothing to offer but his title in exchange for the hand of Robert Whitehead's treasured little daughter Alice.

George Hoyos wasn't even young, nearing forty, and my grandmother just sixteen. Worse, he was a Roman Catholic. Robert Whitehead had all the Englishman's contempt for foreign titles and dislike of the papacy. But however small she was, my grandmother must even then have had a formidable will of her own. She was still almost a school-girl, had never been courted before, and was impressed by the handsome naval officer in his smart uniform. She persuaded her father to accept him as a son-in-law, provided George changed his faith. Whether for love's sake or that of partnership in the torpedo works, George Hoyos became a Protestant and promised the same for whatever children he might have.

My grandfather was a younger son with no property of his own and so had no objection to his family being brought up in England or to living there himself on his father-in-law's estate. Winters were always spent in Fiume in the big villa with its lovely gardens overlooking the Adriatic that Robert Whitehead had built for his family and where most of his Hoyos grandchildren were born.

My grandmother hardly knew Vienna or her husband's relations before her daughters reached marriageable age. Since her children had Austrian titles and were after all Austrians, she persuaded her reluctant husband that the girls must be given a season or two in Vienna. Both her sons were still at Oxford. George Hoyos had every reason for objecting, knowing that his Hungarian relations (his was a minor line of a great family, originally Spanish, that became Austrian under Charles V) would be of very little help socially to his children in Vienna. His brothers and sisters had at best married into the Hungarian gentry and were poor and quite unimportant; he feared his rich and socially prominent Austrian cousins might not receive his wife at all, since she was a commoner, a Protestant, and unacceptable at court.

My grandmother ignored his warnings. Her three eldest daughters, befeathered and betrained, had been presented at Buckingham Palace. One of her brothers was in the diplomatic service and had married a lord's daughter, and was soon to become an ambassador. Her other brothers, though they continued to superintend the highly profitable manufacture of torpedoes, lived on their estates as country gentlemen. Her family in England was by then extremely wealthy, respected, and definitely upper class. She would not take her husband's pessimism as to her social prospects in Vienna seriously. Wisely he retired to Fiume to await events.

My grandmother rented the largest palace she could find in Vienna. It is now the Hotel Bristol. There she started to entertain, and invited all her husband's Austrian relations. They came, but many of their wives and daughters did not. She gave dinner parties and receptions and balls which many diplomats attended, and all the young Austrian bachelors, but remarkably few young girls. '*Die Alice Hoyos hängt wirklich den Schinken aus,*' all of society laughed. Which, translated from the dialect, meant that if one supplies the ham, everyone will come to one's house. They did; they came to eat and drink and enjoy themselves and flirt with the three pretty girls, but that was all. There were no marriage proposals. Invitations to the palaces of the great Austrian families were rare and of acceptance at court there was no hope at all. My grandmother was not a stupid woman, but she was wilful and would not acknowledge defeat. It was her daughters who rather cruelly enlightened her at last.

'Mama, you try too hard,' Marguerite, called Maggie, said. 'People laugh at us, they think us parvenu and ridiculous.'

'You'll never marry us off here, if that's what you want,' my mother, Lilly, the most rebellious and independent-thinking of the three declared. 'And we will never be invited to the *Hofball*,' beautiful Polly complained, 'only at best to the *Ball bei Hof* where all the common people go.'

'Why can't we go back home?' Lilly asked. 'Do you know what they call us here? "The Whitehead Torpedoes." '

My grandmother knew herself beaten, though not for long. The family returned to England and by an odd chance she later married off all three daughters to what she considered eminently suitable husbands. The girls' nursery governess who had taught them German, I think she was called Fraulein Orpen, was still teaching the youngest of Omama's children, Camilla. She had been formerly employed by a Count Plessen in Schleswig-Holstein, and she had always kept in touch with them. The Hoyos girls knew all about the Plessens and had admired their photographs, especially that of the eldest, Ludwig, who sat his horse so well. Pictures of the Hoyos family were annually sent to the Plessens by Fraulein Orpen too. One day she came to my grandmother in great excitement. Young Count Plessen was now in the German diplomatic service, stationed in London. Would he be permitted to call on the family of which he had heard so much? Of course my grandmother agreed. She had grown very fond of the faithful and loyal Fraulein.

He came to stay in the country at Becket in Wiltshire where my grandparents then lived. He proved himself a good rider, he spoke perfect English and was a handsome man, even if the girls thought him rather old. His glance went from one pretty face to another, to rest longest on my Aunt Polly's perfect features. She was by far the most beautiful of my grandmother's daughters, as fair as an angel but also as reserved and remote as one would expect angels to be. He chose her. A few days later he formally proposed, was accepted by Polly and, more important, by my grandparents.

Count Plessen's most intimate friend in Germany was Prince Herbert Bismarck, the son of the Iron Chancellor. He often came to England to visit the Roseberys. He had been advised to have a look at the remaining Hoyos girls, after meeting Polly and finding her admirable. There were still four left, but poor Ella was mentally retarded and unmarriageable and Camilla was still in the nursery. Only Maggie and Lilly, my mother, were available. She was, I'm told, by far the most physically attractive of the sisters; her temperament, vitality and humour flashed from blue eyes. She had more character than the others and had been the most difficult to control of all the children, as my grandmother knew to her sorrow. Maggie, more intelligent, with a thoughtful, delicate, serious face, was tall and slim and moved with a dignity and grace all her own. Prince Bismarck, who was an even older and more experienced bachelor than his friend Ludwig, gave my mother a regretful look and chose gentle Maggie.

My father was a friend and neighbour of the Plessens in Holstein. He met my mother when she came to stay with her sister, fell in love with her, proposed and was accepted. A widower in his forties but by all accounts a most charming and good-looking man of whom it was said that no woman could refuse him anything. My mother didn't even try.

All in all, my grandmother had every reason to be satisfied with her sons-in-law. Two counts and a prince, and many grandchildren soon on their way. She was not worried that her three daughters might not be very happily married to men much older than themselves and forced to live among the stiff German nobility, accustomed as they had been to the freedom of the English way of life and the gaiety of Vienna.

Meanwhile her sons too had found highly satisfactory wives. Eddie Hoyos, the eldest's, marriage was a social triumph though he had to convert to the Roman Catholic faith. 'Paris vaut bien une Messe,' as Henri IV had said. My grandmother might have quoted the same about Vienna, since her daughter-in-law Ilona was of the most illustrious family Kinsky of Chlumec. Her second son Alec married an exquisite Frenchwoman, Edmée de Lois-Chandieu, of impeccable Huguenot ancestry. Finally Camilla, who had grown almost as beautiful as Polly and who had several English suitors whom she alienated by too great a religious fervour, married an American of an old Virginian family. Not rich, but that didn't matter; all the daughters had their own fortune.

9

Omama had often been called a snob and a social climber, and perhaps she was; but when I came to stay with her she had certainly arrived. All through the war she had remained in Vienna, as loyal an Austrian as an Englishwoman could be. She worked for the Red Cross in which she proved a most competent organizer as well as generous with donations, and had gained much respect. But it was after the war, when the monarchy collapsed, that she really came into her own. For soon afterwards the krone, the Austrian currency, lost its value while the English pound remained stable.

Omama spent most of her large income on entertaining. 'Let's go and have lunch with little Alice Hoyos,' even archdukes and archduchesses would suggest, grateful for a free meal, since it took a million kronen at that time to buy even a cup of coffee. And my grandmother would welcome the royal personages with a deep curtsy and, needless to say, with some secret satisfaction that those by whom she had formerly not been received now came to her.

The post-war years in Vienna were hard on everyone. There was acute poverty and unemployment and much disruption of law and order. All classes suffered. The aristocrats, though still in possession of their estates, feared a Russian-type revolution, the thrifty middle class saw their savings vanish, and the workers, out of work, saw their only hope in socialism. The once great Austrian Empire had fallen apart. The Emperor Charles had abdicated and gone into exile with his family. An Austrian republic was finally established under the socialist chancellor Carl Renner. By then any form of monetary stability and any return to order under no matter what government was welcomed by all classes. Soon Viennese humour revived.

My husband's uncle, Count Adalbert Sternberg, better known as Monschi, who was a member of what was somewhat approximate to the Austrian House of Lords, would rock the house with his wit and humour; he died of too much drink, but not before he had distributed his visiting cards all over Vienna. The republic had of course abolished aristocratic titles. 'Adalbert Sternberg,' his card read, 'ennobled by

Charles the Great, disennobled by Charles Renner.'

I had met my future husband not in Vienna, but much earlier, when I was only fifteen, at my Aunt Maggie Bismarck's home Friedrichsruh in Germany. I had just been expelled from boarding school in Lausanne for having escaped from it to go dancing with my cousin Eddie Bismarck in one of the hotels. Eddie was then studying in Geneva. We were great friends even then and Aunt Maggie, who adored her youngest son, had asked me to Friedrichsruh to please him. It was at this annual house-party given by my cousin Otto Bismarck for the Hamburg Derby that I first met Leopold. Since I was still a schoolgirl Aunt Maggie did not approve of my mixing too much with the much older hard-drinking Swedes and Austrians who were her eldest son's guests, but of course I did. I loved their crude practical jokes, their free manners and total lack of convention or morals, and had been delighted and flattered when what was obviously the joker of the pack, the limping, red-faced Austrian giant whom they all seemed to love, pursued me all over the house. I had of course not realized that he was very drunk as I had never seen anyone drunk before. He made me laugh so much as he fell over chairs and tables. 'He was wonderful,' I told my aunt, who reproached me for having spent a whole evening with him. 'He didn't try to kiss you?' she asked anxiously. 'Often,' I said, 'but I was much too quick for him.'

Some of her disapproval must have reached Prince Kinsky, with whom Leopold had come, because they suddenly moved to Hamburg. There Leopold had a horse running in the Derby, and Ulrich's polo team was playing. Also the town, with its varied nightlife, probably offered more interesting diversions than those permissible at Friedrichsruh. I was disappointed, I had liked the funny giant.

Two years later I met him again in Carlsbad in Czechoslovakia where I was staying with my father who was very ill in a sanatorium there. Leopold had come to visit his mother who was taking the cure. She was very kind to me; she knew my grandmother, and many of my Austrian relations, but even if I had been a complete stranger I think she would have tried to help and comfort me in my distress.

She was a small, plumpish woman, neither very distinguished-looking nor elegant, but with a face radiating kindness and good humour. They took me to see a play in Carlsbad's charming little theatre and to dine in good restaurants. The health food in the sanatorium had made me very hungry. They even took me to dance in the Hotel Imperial because I told them it was the thing I most longed to do.

There Leopold called one of the sleek-haired scented young males employed by the hotel to exercise ladies anxious to lose weight in the least unpleasant way possible by dancing off their fat. My pro was an excellent dancer, and Leopold and his mother watched as I performed the most intricate steps. They watched, I think, with some admiration. Perhaps my looks had also somewhat improved since Leopold had seen me in Friedrichsruh. Anyway, the season in Vienna and Rome had given me some poise and self-confidence and I had pretty clothes. After I had danced with each of the six pros I returned to our table breathless and happy. 'That was wonderful,' I said gratefully. 'You like dancing so much?' Leopold asked. 'Oh, more than anything in the world.' Something in his mother's expression told me that I had been tactless because, with his lame leg, her son could not dance. Next day, his mother told me that he had gone back to his country place.

Soon I forgot all about him. After an emergency operation my father grew progressively worse and died. I had only begun to really know my father since he became ill; he had taken little interest in us as children, and after my mother's death left us in the care of his sister. He had loved my mother deeply; if we saw him rarely after her death I believe it was not so much from lack of affection but because our very existence reminded him too painfully of his wife and of his duties as a father in which he feared he was failing. He knew he had forfeited our inheritance (through foolish speculations and reckless extravagance) and that Emkendorf would probably be lost to him and to us. Soon nothing seemed to matter to him any more. If all that he loved was gone or doomed to go, why bother? He was still a very handsome man of immense charm; women were only too ready to comfort him, and in them and drink he found a sort of oblivion. But when he became ill he needed me, much more than I had ever needed him. Children rarely resent neglect as much as they do parental restraint, which he had spared me. In the months before he died we became friends. I learnt to admire him, and the courage, dignity and gaiety with which he faced certain death. I learnt too late what I was losing.

Except for the doctors at the sanatorium there was no one to help me in Carlsbad. I could have called on my grandmother to come to my assistance, but I didn't. Somehow the idea seemed distasteful. My brothers were too young to be asked to deal with death, and my Aunt Diana too busy with the preparations for the funeral in Emkendorf. Somehow I managed and returned home with my father's coffin.

Aunt Diana greeted me with her usual calm. She had lost the only person she had been devoted to throughout her life and to whom she had sacrificed much of her independence and most of her fortune. She didn't shed a tear. 'Ladies don't cry,' she had taught me when I was still a child. Only later, when I told her how fearlessly her brother had faced his end and how handsome he had looked in death did her still-beautiful old face become momentarily contorted as if by some acute physical pain.

My father's coffin had been placed in the hall, surrounded by the four life-sized marble Venuses that always graced it. There were wreaths and flowers everywhere. I can't remember much about the funeral except that numerous friends and relations came. He was buried in the crypt of our village church in Westensee; the church itself embellished by my father's far from Protestant taste by Caravaggios and Guido Renis, of which there had been a surplus in Emkendorf.

For a few weeks after the funeral I, with my two brothers, one a schoolboy and the other still in the nursery, was allowed to relive all the joys of childhood, to roam through gardens, parks and forests all so familiar and fraught with memories and to marvel at the decorative Italianate phantasies of the house itself. It was the last time I was to see Emkendorf. Aunt Diana persuaded me to return to Vienna. 'Certain sacrifices have to be made by women, for their family,' she told me. 'I never married because I felt it my duty to look after mine. You will have to marry for your brothers' sake. There may be just enough left to give them a start in life if you are provided for. Try and find a rich husband.'

Thank God I didn't have to try very hard. As I was in mourning I couldn't go to dances or parties in Vienna, but it was quite proper for me to accept an invitation to a shooting party in Czechoslovakia given by Ulrich Kinsky. His first wife (he was later to remarry) was a relation of mine, Katalin Szecheny, a Hungarian by birth. It was at Mestec that I met Leopold again. I think I first fell in love with him when, inadequately dressed for a shoot being ignorant of the rigours of the Czech climate, I stood cold, miserable and wet in sleet and snow with no one paying me any attention. He came limping up to me, took off his great fur-lined coat, and put it round my shoulders and without a word walked away coatless into the falling snow.

There must have been about thirty guests at dinner that night, everyone in evening dress. I, being the youngest, was placed at the end of the table between Ulrich's secretary and a pimply-faced nephew of his. Since both my neighbours were even shyer than I was, I turned my attention to the rest of the table. Not all of the women were beautiful; some were obviously aunts or relations of Ulrich's, rather dowdy in dress but covered with magnificent jewels. The men's faces were flushed from the many hours of shooting in the cold, most of them with swollen cheeks from the kick of their guns; over two thousand pheasant had been shot that day. It had certainly given them a healthy appetite and made them thirsty. Of all the six courses, very little was left when it reached my end of the table, at which my two neighbours grumbled, making up for their lack of food by emptying their glasses as rapidly as they were refilled. A different wine was served with each course. Conversation with them became progressively more difficult.

Beyond the candelabras, the silver centre piece with the vases all filled with hothouse flowers and maidenhair ferns, I could just see Leopold sitting between two very pretty young women in extremely *décolleté* dresses, both leaning against him and laughing at whatever he said. I was too far away to hear what the joke was. If he looked in my direction, at all, it was so absent-mindedly that I thought he had forgotten he had ever met me.

After dinner, however, when I was sitting feeling rather forlorn between three elderly ladies who enquired as to my parentage and then turned to each other to discuss their own relations with greater interest, he broke away from the group of laughing men and women sipping their brandy out of huge balloon-shaped glasses in the adjoining room and came up to me. 'Come along, we need a fourth for bridge,' he said. Before I had time to say I couldn't play very well he had taken me into another room. There were indeed bridge tables and packs of cards prepared, but no players. He drew me down on to a sofa. 'You weren't very happy with Ulrich's old aunts, were you? Or at dinner with his idiotic nephew?' So he had noticed; and suddenly I felt as comforted and protected as I had when he had wrapped me in his coat.

We talked a while. He knew of my father's death. I told him how kindly his mother had written to me. 'Mumsy' (he always called her that) 'likes you. She thinks the only way for me to settle down is by marrying me off; she thought you'd suit me. Though God knows my father wouldn't be too pleased. You have no royal blood tucked away anywhere, have you?' I didn't know what to say or what I really felt. Was this supposed to be a proposal? Or just one of his jokes? 'You hardly know me,' he said, 'I thought I'd ask Ulrich to invite you.' So that was why my distant relationship with Katalin had been remembered. But was he serious?

I temporized. 'I've seen how you make everyone laugh. Is it my turn now? Surely you are only joking? But please continue, it's all most amusing.' 'Not really,' he said. He took my hand and pressed it against his thigh; indignantly, I tried to withdraw it. I knew enough of male anatomy to be shocked and affronted. 'Silly child,' he said, 'for once this is no joke. I can't take off my trousers here to show you, someone might come in. But feel my leg, it wouldn't be fair for you not to know. It's decently covered with skin and doesn't pain or impede me much, but it's ugly. Feel it.' He pressed my hand against the upper part of his leg above the knee. It seemed to me just a bone without flesh. I didn't flinch, I felt neither disgust nor horror, only pity and tenderness, so that it was I who kissed first.

A couple in search of the bridge partners came in and left hurriedly. 'Now your reputation is ruined you'll have to become engaged to me,' Leopold laughed. Agreeing to meet in Vienna after he had talked to his father we parted.

'Were there any suitable young men?' my grandmother enquired on my return. It was always her first question. 'None,' I said, 'except for Leopold Sternberg, and he's not very young and I'm sure you wouldn't think him suitable.'

'Oh, poor Fanny's dreadful son. I hope you didn't talk to him, he has a terrible reputation.' 'And what if he had asked me to marry him?' Her hard bright blue eyes widened with surprise. 'Do you mean he seriously proposed?' she gasped. 'Well, yes, do you think I should accept?' 'Oh my dear child . . .' She was so tiny that I had to bend down to be embraced and kissed. 'Of course you must. This is indeed most wonderful news.' 'Don't spread it around yet,' I warned, 'he has to ask his father's permission first.' By evening all of Vienna knew and next day there was an announcement of my engagement in the paper.

I later heard how much my father-in-law had resented this, and my poor mother-in-law, overwhelmed by his anger, had her first of many strokes. She was seriously ill for a time, and Leopold, who adored his mother, remained with her, but he wrote; short notes on any sort of paper, always in pencil, telling me not to worry and that everything would be all right, and many kisses. But only after she had recovered and I had been formally invited to Castolovice to meet the entire family was my engagement approved of – after all, there was nothing really wrong with me, they thought, but my religion and my grandmother's being born a commoner. It was decided to change the former and forget the latter. Two months later Leopold and I were married, my grandmother hurrying the preparations as much as she decently could lest the prey escape.

When Omama died many years later leaving sixty-seven descendants she was eighty-seven. In her last years she had become gentle, frail and rather pathetic and I had grown much fonder of her than I had been in my youth.

All of Vienna tried to crowd into the English church in which she had attended the Anglican service every Sunday of her life in Vienna to pay her their last respects. I know she was sincerely mourned by many. Her two most intimate friends, Princess Norah Fugger and Princess Ida Schwarzenberg, because of their rank and venerable age, sat in front pews with Omama's close relations. Both ladies were very deaf and rather blind though they still had the sharpest tongues in town. Neither of them had ever seen an English coffin before, its flat narrow shape quite unlike the ornamental domed ones used on the continent.

'Look,' cried Princess Norah to Princess Ida, for all the congregation to hear. 'They are going to bury poor little Alice in a torpedo!' 'How suitable,' Princess Ida boomed back.

10

Even in the first years of our marriage Leopold and I travelled frequently. Zasmuky's estate, then in perfect working order, did not need his constant attention. I would have been happy to remain with him in the little house, decorating it, planting and tending its garden, but he was accustomed to leading a very social life and bored without it. So we went to Vienna for what was called the *Jubelwoche* ('the Week of Rejoicing'), which consisted of a month of tennis tournaments, polo games, and the Vienna Derby. After that came the Berlin Derby, polo in Frankfurt, races in Baden-Baden and journeys in winter to Monte Carlo or Cannes, these last always unfortunate. Leopold still enjoyed gambling and was as lucky as it is possible to be with every chance against one. As for me, I only needed to place the counter anywhere on the roulette board and it would be certain to be raked in after the turn of the wheel.

Then there were family events which had to be attended, funerals and weddings. The most splendid of the latter was my cousin Otto Bismarck's nuptials in Berlin. Many hundreds of people had been invited to it from all over Europe. Otto had finally chosen a lovely bride, a young Swedish girl, Ann-Mari Tengbom. Her father was a famous architect who had built the city hall in Stockholm.

The religious ceremony, impressive and imposing, took place in Berlin's cathedral (bombed into ruins in the last war), with President Hindenburg assisting. In the evening there was a dinner party given by the Bismarcks for five hundred guests in the Hotel Adlon. I had been placed at one of the separate tables of which there must have been over a hundred dispersed through the immense ballroom. Leopold was sitting with a party of Swedes, with Countess Ebba Bunde beside him. They were old friends and drinking companions, both able to consume greater amounts of alcohol than others without ill effects. Only once, the story goes, had Countess Ebba suffered from a hangover. Walking with the King of Sweden on the race-course at Stockholm she had, with a polite 'Excuse me', removed his top hat from his head, been sick in it, and had handed it back to him. The sight of the hatless king had after that encouraged more casual fashions on the race-course.

At my table there was no one I had ever seen before. I studied my two neighbours' cards surreptitiously. Herr Herborus von Bismarck, Herr Hermann von Bismarck. I knew relations of a different line to that of my cousin's family existed, but I had never met any of them in Friedrichsruh. I was not prepared for their appearance. Both Bismarcks had bright red hair, red bristling beards and faces rather like the rooting snouts of the wild boar that still survived in the East German forest. There were two other more normal-looking men seated at the table and three dowdy women. 'Brothers?' I asked, trying to start a conversation, looking from Hermann to Herborus. 'Cousins,' they said, after they had pondered the question. I realized my accent puzzled them as much as theirs did me. It was more like Polish than German. 'And where do you come from?' I asked. 'Hinterpommern,' they said in unison, then started to eat their soup.

This, I thought, is not going to be much fun. I looked longingly at the many tables of handsome Swedes. Why, I wondered, had I been seated where I was? I had on my best evening dress, a sheath of crystal sequins, my shoulders bare except for jewels, and though I knew I couldn't outshine the lovely bride, I looked my best. All wasted on my uncouth neighbours. Resentfully I gulped my champagne, then waved to the waiter to pour me some more; the two Prussian ladies stared disapprovingly.

All right, I thought, let's be gay. I dropped my soup spoon on the floor; Herborus's red beard and my head collided under the table, trying to pick it up. He won, and to my surprise put it back on my plate. When the fish came, I dropped my fork; I made no effort to retrieve it, nor did anyone else, and I started to eat with the fish knife instead, spooning sole suprême into my mouth.

'Aren't you afraid of cutting yourself?' asked a more-or-less civilized-looking man who was seated facing me.

'Oh no, it's quite blunt.' A sudden thought came to me. I smiled apologetically, looking from face to face. 'You see, I'm not really accustomed to such smart society, I've not always been a countess, you know,' I said, fingering my place card. 'It takes a while to learn party manners. I was very young when my husband took me off the streets in Vienna.' That's done it, I thought happily, gulping more champagne. One woman half-rose from her chair, but sat down again realizing, I suppose, that she couldn't make her indignant way out all alone past the many tables. My two neighbours flushed redder than their beards, while the man facing me turned away in horror, I hoped, but then I saw he was only trying to conceal his laughter. This should have made me suspicious; I was later to find out that he was a great friend of my cousin Hannah's, knew all about me, and told her all of my very silly behaviour the next day.

I was stopped from further elaborating on my past because President Hindenburg, who was seated next to the bride, got up to speak. The main table was too far away for much to be audible, but there was great dignity about the tall old general, the ribbons of his many decorations spread across his heart. I suddenly remembered having hammered nails into him as a child.

We had been travelling through Berlin with our parents, and Nanny had taken us for a walk in the park. At the end of some avenue there was a gigantic statue of Hindenburg carved in wood; its purpose was to collect money for the widows and orphans of the First World War. Each brass nail hammered into him cost a German mark. Millions of brass nails had transformed his statue into a towering golden idol.

'God bless the bride and groom.' He finalized his speech loud enough for five hundred people to hear and raised his glass. 'Hoch soll'n sie leben, Dreimal Hoch,' everyone sang. It is untranslatable into English without sounding very odd, though it was the usual Austrian and German toast, 'High may they live, three times high.'

Much later I was to remember President Hindenburg's simple 'God bless'. Powerless to stem the rise of Nazism, the old man was forced to accept what he hadn't the strength left to oppose, yet he had to be present at the political rallies at which Hitler spoke. After having patiently listened to several of these rabble-rousing speeches in which one of the Führer's favourite turns of expression were 'Thanks to Providence', 'According to Providence', and 'Providence will decide', Hindenburg could bear it no longer. 'Say God for a change,' the old general had thundered.

After dinner and the serving of coffee and liqueurs, we were all photographed, Hindenburg standing between bride and groom.

Leopold was with Biene, the wife of one of Otto's first cousins. Though they were Bismarcks from Pomerania too, their style of living was very different from that of their more distant relations of the other line of the family. They had a magnificent country house at which we had stayed, and large estates.

I saw Leopold was laughing, and no wonder. Biene was a beautiful woman, highly educated, speaking foreign languages fluently, her family of unquestionable ancestry, but when she spoke German one would have believed her father to have been a Prussian sergeant-major and her mother a Berlin whore. Where she had ever learnt to speak the way she did remained a mystery, but there's no doubt she had a wonderful ear for accents, a strong inclination to shock and surprise and a curious sense of humour.

I went up to them. As dark as a gipsy, and marvellously dressed, Biene was commenting caustically on the wedding ceremony. Soon I was in fits of laughter too. Someone came up to us and said the President would like Leopold to be introduced to him. 'For God's sake, why?' Leopold asked.

'The eagle eye must have spotted that,' Biene said, touching the war medals Leopold had pinned in discreet miniature on his coat, the wedding invitation having said 'Decorations worn'. 'You will have to go.'

We went of course, Leopold limping even more than usual, not so much because his leg impeded him but because he was slightly drunk and had lost his stick somewhere. Otto, who stood beside the President, introduced us. 'I see you have the golden medal for courage,' Hindenburg said. 'Well done! Wounded too? Russia?' Leopold nodded, acutely embarrassed. Otto, who hadn't listened properly, perhaps preoccupied with the next introduction, said, 'Count Sternberg is from Czechoslovakia, Herr President.' 'Bohemia,' the general corrected. 'What was it, Bismarck, that your grandfather said about that country?' Since it was one of the Iron Chancellor's most famed comments, Otto had no difficulty in remembering. 'Who rules Bohemia, rules Europe.' 'Still true! It was a pleasure to meet you, Count Sternberg.'

Soon after that we made up a party with some Swedes and went to explore the more curious and notorious Berlin nightclubs together. The inspection lasted till dawn.

The next day I met my cousin Hannah von Bredow at a family lunch. She was a tall woman, very slim and elegant, in spite of having had seven children. Her good looks were marred by a purple birthmark that disfigured part of her face, her neck, breast and arm. Aunt Maggie, her mother, always remained convinced that it had been caused by the shock of seeing a beggar expose his sores in the streets of Naples when she was pregnant, though no doctor would seriously confirm that this would have marked the unborn child. Hannah concealed her blemishes as best she could, to reveal instead a remarkable mind and such scintillating wit that her disfigurement was ignored by everyone. It was said of her that had she not been a woman, she would have become another Iron Chancellor.

After lunch, she drew me aside. 'You've been very naughty,' she remarked sternly. She was old enough to have been my mother and I respected and liked her. I had no idea to what she was referring; I'd forgotten the dinner party, and was not certain what scandals Leopold, the Swedes and I might not have caused in the nightclubs later. 'I've been told that you shocked and horrified our very worthy if slightly backward and provincial East Prussian relations by your behaviour last night.'

Relieved, I began to laugh. 'Why the hell did you have to seat me like that?' I knew she had been responsible for most of the wedding arrangements as Aunt Maggie had been suffering from a bad cold. 'You must have known it would end in disaster.'

'I grant it was a mistake, but just try and seat five hundred people according to their rank and satisfaction.'

'Were the wild boars very angry?'

'The women were furious. They are extremely *Adelslstolz* and virtuous, and naturally felt insulted at having had to sit at table with a little tart, which is what you made yourself out to be. Very convincingly too,' Hannah started to laugh, 'I hear both Hermann and Herborus have made discreet enquiries as to where you can be found.'

❧ II ❧

Leopold recalled me from my memories. 'Time to telephone people,' he said, coming from his room draped in his new dressing gown and wiping the sweat from his brow with its satin cuffs. Our parcels from the Ritz had meanwhile come and the child was unpacking her toys. I looked longingly at the cool dresses I had unwrapped. 'First you must telegraph Toti to tell her we have arrived,' he ordered. Toti Radetzky was my sister-in-law who was now safely in Vienna; I had always been very fond of her. She was about my age and when I first came to Castolovice as a rather frightened young girl she had tried to make me feel at home. Later she made a most unfortunate marriage which didn't last and was with us all through the war in Prague, incredibly brave and resourceful in the time of the worst German persecutions.

'Then call up Kira,' Leopold demanded, 'and Loisl Vollgruber, of course. And the Charles Roux. And Ripka, that's very important. Find out when he can see me. And Madame Millesrois. Ask her if she has written to Annicka or de Jean.' 'Have you any of the numbers?' 'Only Ripka's. Here.'

There were no telephones in our rooms at the Hotel Cambon. As I went downstairs I realized with some consternation how much Leopold would need my help, at least in France, since he spoke no French. Would he not come to resent having to depend on me after the many years in which I had depended on him for everything?

In the hot little booth I struggled with the heavy chained telephone books. I called the Austrian Embassy first. No, His Excellency was not in town, but staying in the country until September. I found Kira Troubetzkois's number. He had been a great friend of my husband's in his bachelor days, and his beautiful sister Sonia had married a Czech neighbour of ours, Count Kolovrat. Kira now lived in Paris and had, we knew, recently married a Frenchwoman. No, once again, the Prince and Princess were in the South of France, to return early in October. I called Madame Millesrois; she was holidaying in Venice on the Lido, the servant didn't know when she would be back.

I got Ripka's office, gave my name and was told in Czech that the minister was busy, would I leave a message. I said my husband would like to see the minister as soon as possible. I was asked to wait a minute – it was more like twenty – to be told that the minister would see him on Tuesday at ten. Well, even if the appointment was only in three days' time, that was something accomplished. I called the Charles Roux. I didn't know them too well, they had been at the French Embassy in Prague long before the war when we had not bothered much with diplomatic society, but they had been very popular there. All our friends had liked them and they had often returned to our country as visitors. We had been advised to call on them the moment we arrived and told they were still very pro-Czech and helpful to everyone who came to them from Prague. Surely they would be out of town too, I thought.

'C'est Edmonde,' said a rather charming voice; whoever it was, she must have been expecting some other call. 'Madame Charles Roux?' I enquired. 'That's my mother,' came the answer in English, obviously having noticed my accent. 'Who is it?' I gave my name. Madame Charles Roux came to the telephone. She seemed pleased that I had called and anxious to hear the latest news from Prague. She invited us to lunch the next day. I wrote out Toti's telegram at the desk and returned to our hot room and lay down. My head ached.

'Papi's gone for a walk,' the child told me. She was playing contentedly with one of her new toys. 'I hope he won't get lost.' 'Oh, he knows Paris quite well,' I assured her, thinking that all we both knew of the town in which we had frequently stayed was no more than any visiting tourist did. Like them we had come to shop and have a good time with friends equally in search of pleasure, which meant eating in the best restaurants, viewing fashion shows, dining at Maxim's and going on to nightclubs in Montmartre or to the then very resplendent *Folies Bergères*. It had been the time of the young Maurice Chevalier who sang, danced and joked in his straw boater; of Mistinguette with her songs. Crowned with a head-dress of ostrich feathers and trailing even more of them, she would regally descend from spectacular heights on to the stage, down stairs or simulated waterfalls, flanked by chorus and dancers, all partially nude, to reveal at every step the most famous legs in France. There was golden-brown Josephine Baker too, dancing naked except for a bunch of bananas. It was all very entertaining; it was Paris; it was not France.

We knew very few French people, a few aristocrats, no one in the government or in the world of business; none of the intelligentsia or of the bourgeoisie. Of the real France itself we knew practically nothing.

77

I was only familiar with its people through its classical literature, with its countryside and landscapes only through the vision of artists who had painted them. Yet my ancestry was partially French. My great-great-grandfather, the Marquis de Criminil, had fled his country at the time of the Revolution and emigrated to Denmark. There he married the wealthy daughter of the minister of finance, Count Schlmmelman; they had one son. His sister-in-law Julie was the wife of Count Carl Reventlow who owned several estates in Holstein – then still Danish – including Emkendorf. This couple was childless. They adopted their half-French nephew and made him their heir. He and his descendants then bore the joint name of Counts of Reventlow Criminil, which had been my father's and my name before I married.

In our childhood my brothers and I, informed of our French ancestry by Aunt Diana, always called the old Marquis the coachman, however much she tried to explain that being master of the stable at the court of Versailles to Louis XVI's brother, the Comte de Provence, was a post of honour and didn't mean that he drove carriages. But she couldn't deny that he had proved himself as a coachman on one important occasion. When he first left France, he did not leave alone. In a covered cart, and with horses from his farm, dressed in peasant clothes and taking the reins himself, he drove Madame, the Comte de Provence's wife, and her lady-in-waiting out of France and to safety in Coblenz in Germany, where her husband awaited her. After the restoration of the Bourbons the Marquis returned to his country to receive the order of St Louis from his grateful sovereign, but that seems to have been the only reward given him for saving Madame, by then the Queen of France, from the guillotine.

Nevertheless, he came back to Denmark with several more cartloads, not driven by himself in this case. They were filled with very fine pieces of French eighteenth-century furniture. These, and the statues and paintings bought by Carl and Julie Reventlow on their travels in Italy, added much to the beauties of Emkendorf. Where the old Marquis got the furniture will always remain a mystery; it seems extremely doubtful that the small Château de Criminil, part manse, part farm, which had been his family's home, had contained furniture worthy of Versailles. Or so at least my father thought when he visited the château before the First World War. It was a small castle with three towers still standing intact as they must have been for a long time since they were on our coat of arms; the rest of the place was in a sad state of crumbling deterioration. Two sisters, the Desmoiselles de Criminil, both very ancient spinsters, lived there in genteel poverty; they were the last of that line of the family. The château near Amiens was destroyed in the war.

There was the sound of footsteps racing up the stairs. *Le garçon* rushed into the room. '*Prague vous appelle, Madame. L'Ambassade d'Amerique,*' he cried. I went downstairs. It was Steinhardt enquiring how we were. How had we travelled? Was Leopold's leg better? Was the hotel comfortable, and how soon were we going on to Vichy? For a moment I was confused, then I realized that he was being careful. Calls from the American Embassy would be listened in to now in Prague. I gave the expected answers. 'We will be flying home next week,' he then said. 'They are sending us a special plane. I have a lot to do in Washington, but we hope to be in Paris in a month or two. They've given me Ottawa, but Dulcie will need to come to Paris for some winter clothes. Write to me,' he added, and he gave me his office address in the city. 'If there's anything you need, let me know. Take care of yourself.' That was all. Did I need anything? I needed him. Still, it was good to hear his warm laughing voice. But two months? Had his voice really been so warm?

Leopold's call from Prague came an hour later after he had returned from his walk, which I'm certain had included a visit to the Ritz bar. It was as unsatisfactory as mine had been, but with a difference. Where I thought I had sensed waning affection, Annicka, calling from the French Embassy in Prague had left him in no doubt as to the warmth of hers. 'Poor little fool,' he said. 'She's desperate. Her sister hasn't answered any of her letters. She says she'll die rather than not join me.' 'Let her,' I thought. I still resented Annicka's existence, unfairly, as I knew. Leopold and I had not been lovers for years, though I think we had come to trust each other more than in the times of jealous passion. 'I feel so responsible,' he said sadly. I sighed. 'Look here,' I said, 'I'll have to go to Venice anyway to see about the jewels. I could talk to Madame Millesrois. I'm certain I could persuade her to do something about Annicka.' He looked at me gratefully. 'And I'll write to Eddie and ask him to meet me there. Even if Mona's in Capri he could come to Venice for a day or two,' I added.

Eddie Bismarck was my favourite cousin, who would have come to see me in Czechoslovakia immediately the war had ended had not his name Bismarck, stamping him so obviously as a German, made it impossible. Nor could he for the same reason join us in post-war Paris, where anti-German feeling was running higher than in the war. 'He'd be a great help about America too,' Leopold remarked. 'After all, he knows it well.' 'But if I leave, what about the child?' 'Oh, I can look after her, she's no trouble,' Leopold declared.

Probably she wouldn't be, I thought, taken to the Ritz bar every morning, lunching there later, or at Pruniers, taken shopping in the afternoon, and, for all I knew,,to Montmartre at night. The French find it perfectly natural for a child to sit in bistros, bars, and even night-clubs drinking wine if accompanied by its parent, and so might Leopold. 'Impossible,' I said. 'Anyway, I'll have to find someone to keep her occupied, teach her French perhaps. I'll ask Madame Poisson if she knows of a temporary governess.'

We dined in the little courtyard of the hotel. Only a few tables were occupied by French-speaking families, some with children whom my daughter watched with interest. It was quite pleasant sitting there in the cool of the evening, and the food was not too bad. Madame Poisson hovered around us, recommending this or that dish, all atten-tion. Obviously the telephone calls from the two embassies in Prague had impressed her. She had smartened herself up for the night. Though still in black, part of her voluminous bosom was now bare, her golden hair piled in an impressive coiffure on top of her head, her wrinkled face masked with powder and rouge – she was certainly over sixty.

I had told Leopold that Ripka could only see him in a couple of days and that nearly all our friends were out of town. He was not in the best of tempers, and was rather bored. Because of it I knew he could not be trusted not to seek some diversion and the only possible one at present was Madame Poisson herself. She was standing over him enquiring if the *garçon* should bring another carafe of wine, of which we had already drunk two, when to my horror I saw one of his hands disappear under the table and a very startled look distort Madame's face. She leapt from his side as if stung, and muttering something unintelligible left the courtyard. The child, who was very observant, stared at Leopold and frowned. 'Papi, you pinched her behind,' she said, 'I saw it.' 'Certainly not,' he answered, grinning happily. 'I just wanted to know where that corset ended.'

I knew it would have been futile to reproach him, but the child had been taught to respect her father whom she had previously only known at a distance. All I could hope for was that in the future she would learn to accept his occasional lapses into very unconventional behaviour without embarrassment, as I had. He had too much person-ality not to have become a law unto himself – if he enjoyed shocking people and playing the *enfant terrible*, I certainly could not stop him. Nor did I want to, because it often made me laugh.

To my relief Madame Poisson returned looking quite unruffled and smiling. Had she mistaken Leopold's pinch for a compliment? I asked her if she could spare us a moment, saying I had a problem I wished to discuss with her. She sat down at our table. 'Go to bed now, darling,' I told the child. 'We'll be down here if you need me, you can call out of the window. I'll be up soon anyway.' 'Will you share a bottle of wine?' Leopold asked Madame politely when the child had left. 'This one at my expense then,' she said, equally forthcoming. She sipped delicately, her expression rather wary, perhaps she was thinking that I was going to ask for the price of the apartments to be reduced.

'Madame, I was wondering,' I said, 'if you would know of a respectable woman who would be willing to take my daughter for walks in the parks and teach her a little French. A sort of temporary governess.' She pondered, but not for long. 'I think I know exactly the right person,' she exclaimed. 'She's a highly-educated lady who has seen better days, a spinster and very proper; a relation of mine [it later proved to be her sister], she shall come tomorrow.'

She came. She was old, dressed in shabby black, had a narrow, sallow face and a sharp beak-like nose. She looked exactly like a crow. She spoke no English, but was extremely voluble in French about the beauties of the parks of Paris where *la petite Diane* would meet the right children; that of course was understood, since she knew well who was who, even if she had been forced to retire from the *monde* to which she had once belonged. I engaged her. The weekly payments she demanded seemed rather high, but then it would only be for a short while and I was really by then at my wits' end as what to do with the child all day long. She was bored, she was homesick, she missed her friends, she resented being constantly asked to be quiet and play with her toys or read in the hot hotel room while we wrote letters or discussed our uncertain future.

I had taken her out window-shopping, but she quite sensibly refused to look at things that I had to tell her we couldn't afford to buy. The Louvre had always been a great source of pleasure to me, so I took her there. On ascending the stairs to the picture galleries, I saw with joy that the Nike of Samothrace, surely one of the most beautiful examples of Greek sculpture in the world, had returned to France and was back in her place. Having her stolen had not brought Hitler the winged victory she represented. 'Look how wonderfully the wind of her flight stirs her gown. Isn't she lovely?' I asked my daughter. 'She'd be better if she hadn't lost her head,' was Diana's comment.

In the galleries I showed her many of my favourite pictures. She was not a stupid or insensitive child; surely, I thought, she would appreciate the great works of art of the past as I did. She listened dutifully while I tried to explain composition, subtlety of colour, significance of light and shade. She looked at the pictures and looked away with an expression more fearful than enthusiastic on her face. Then I realized that to a child only the subject matters, and that the crucifixion of Christ and his death and the torture of blood-spattered martyrs, however beautifully painted, could not be contemplated with pleasure by her. Neither did she like the many Madonnas pensively brooding over the infant Jesus. 'Of course they all look sad,' she said, 'she knows what will happen to her baby when he grows up.'

Landscapes bored her, except when she recognized in them some animal she knew, a deer or a rabbit, a squirrel or a bird. What she thought of the pictures of mythological subjects I didn't dare ask, knowing how strange the posturing Venuses or embracing gods and goddesses and frolicking nymphs and satyrs, most of them nude, must seem to her. As far as I knew, she had never seen anyone naked, certainly neither of her parents. It was not customary at the time to familiarize children with nudity at an early age, as young couples seem to do now. Even husbands and wives only saw each other naked when they made love.

When I first married, having soon lost all shyness, I started to walk about our bedroom without clothes. I had a perfect figure, and nothing to be ashamed of, I thought. But Leopold knew very much more about the erotic than I did then. 'Put your dressing gown on,' he said firmly. 'No woman should ever allow her husband or her lover to grow accustomed to her nakedness.'

The only thing that seemed to give my daughter real pleasure was food. Perhaps it was because she had not had enough sweets in the war and the insecurity she now felt after having lost her home reminded her of that time; in any case, we could never pass a *patisserie*, a cake or sweet shop without her imploring to be allowed to buy and eat. If I constantly let her over-indulge, it was because it seemed to do her no harm and because it was the least expensive way of making her happy.

Keeping Leopold content throughout our stay in Paris was going to prove much more difficult and costly. He had to use taxis wherever he went since his stiff leg made it impossible to step into buses or use the moving stairs of the metro. Also he discovered that with Madame or Monsieur Poisson's obliging help he could call up friends in Vienna and even in Prague, which he frequently did, ignoring the expense.

❦ 12 ❦

After our first day and night in Paris all of us slept, utterly exhausted, only to wake just in time to go to the Charles Roux for lunch. Theirs was one of those architecturally perfect town-houses of which there are still many left in Paris. *Entre court et jardin*. There is no blatant splendour about them like that of the Roman palaces, they do not overwhelm and crush with heavy baroque opulence like those of Vienna or Prague, and they are quite unlike the tall narrow London houses. They are unique in their unostentatious perfection and there is a country air about them. Two little stone lodges and a tall wrought-iron gate to give privacy and protection to those living in a big city, a paved courtyard, then the house, plain rather than ornate, built of silvery stone. Inside, the hall and dining-room are usually small, whereas the salon with its french windows leading into the garden is almost as long and wide as the house. Most of the rooms still have the original eighteenth-century panelling, usually there are four or five bedrooms under the mansard roof, and servants' quarters and the kitchen in the basement. They are the sort of house that make one feel that no more or less could ever have been wanted for pleasant living in the past or present by people of discriminating taste.

Madame Charles Roux, a small, neat, elegantly dressed woman, embraced us affectionately. She remarked that the child, whom she had not seen before, was *gentille* and very like her father. Not even in miniature, neither in looks, mentality nor behaviour did Diana then or later ever resemble her father. She introduced her daughter Edmonde, an attractive girl in her twenties, and apologized for her husband's absence; for business reasons he was not in Paris. 'We are just among ourselves,' she said smiling warmly, 'so you can tell us everything.'

We told her about our journey and the escapes of some of her and our friends from Czechoslovakia. Also about those still there, as fearful to leave as they were afraid to stay. 'But are they in any real danger?' Edmonde asked. Leopold shrugged his shoulders. 'Under a system where even having been born into the upper classes is considered a crime?' 'But how could it happen?' Madame Charles Roux asked.

'Even if the Yalta agreement re-zoned the spheres of interest in Europe, why didn't Czechoslovakia put up a better fight for its sovereignty? Surely by going communist, Russian rule is inevitable?' 'I'm afraid so,' Leopold agreed, 'perhaps the country had too little time to have become truly unified and for the spirit of independence to mature. After all, it was only for thirty years that Czechoslovakia was really free. German oppression followed too soon after centuries of Austrian suppression for national self-confidence to have grown. All the Czechs had learnt was to fear their Germanic neighbours more than ever. Munich had taught them that their friends in the West were not to be trusted, having betrayed and forsaken them in their hour of need. Their only hope seemed to be in a close alliance with Russia, the great Slav brother who promised friendship and protection.'

'But surely it was not necessary for the whole nation to vote for communism?' Edmonde asked. 'The Russians are realists, they accept any sort of regime, provided that it is friendly or of use to them.' Leopold laughed. 'The election was a farce. There were enough quite ruthless communists in the government by then to see to it that votes for the right-wing parties were miscounted or discarded.' 'So you don't think the Czechs really wanted communism?' 'Certainly not, but fear and greed influenced many.'

We had meanwhile gone in to lunch. Edmonde sat next to me. 'What your husband says is very interesting,' she said, looking at him thoughtfully; her eyes, I saw, were not only rather beautiful, but shrewdly observant. 'But why greed?' Madame Charles Roux, who was sitting next to him, asked. 'Surely everyone knows that not much personal fortune can be acquired under communism?' 'I'll give you an example,' Leopold said. He then told her how in the last months before we left, dozens of his labourers and peasants had come to him for advice. They had been told that his property would be divided up between them, everyone receiving up to five or ten acres if they voted for the communist party. Quite unembarrassed, and with the confidence they had learnt to have in him, they asked him which acres were the most profitable and which would be the best for each of them to claim. 'Poor devils,' Leopold added. 'Of course now the land will be communized, they'll get nothing and will even lose their own small plots.

'And then,' he continued, 'there were many that voted for communism out of fear. Quite a few had collaborated with the Germans and so hoped to escape punishment, and many others who had suffered under the occupation, influenced by communist propaganda, believed that the Western allies would soon be on friendly terms with the

Germans again and Czechoslovakia would be left unprotected once more. Only communist Russia could now be trusted to defend the nation.'

I had listened to Leopold with some pride. He rarely took the trouble to voice the thoughts in his mind at such great length, and I felt he had spoken convincingly and well. Perhaps being able to do so in German, which both mother and daughter spoke fluently, helped. He and I usually spoke English together, but Czech and German were his native languages. 'It s all so sad,' Madame Charles Roux sighed. 'Such a wonderful country now lost to us all.'

Edmonde turned to me and asked what our plans for the future were. I told her we were hoping to go to America. 'Oh,' she said, 'I know it well. I worked there for over a year as a reporter for *Vogue*.' 'And did you like America?' I inevitably asked. 'I might have, but my job meant doing the social rounds day and night since I was fashion correspondent. It rather bored me, I'm a solitary sort of person really, I'd rather sit at home and write.' 'Novels?' I asked. 'Perhaps.' 'We too will have to find work in New York,' I said, 'I hope the Czech Refugee Committee will have something for Leopold.'

'And you?' 'I've learnt a little about ceramics. I make figurines. They sold rather well in Prague. Do you think there would be a market for that sort of thing in New York?' I asked her anxiously. She looked at me rather doubtfully, I thought. 'If they were very original perhaps, but the competition in America is terrific, and you must consider that everything sold there is chosen from what the best artists and designers from all over the world produce.'

'Mummy makes lovely ceramic buttons,' remarked the child, who had been politely silent all through lunch. 'Oh, those,' Edmonde laughed. 'They were used by dressmakers here too during the war when metal was scarce. Imagine, they even made ceramic jewellery. It's quite out of fashion now of course.' I hoped my face didn't show my disappointment. 'But seriously,' she continued, 'the difficulties an artist has in New York, however good he or she may be, are very great. The reason is that Americans need to be reassured by advertising and their press as to the artistic quality of what they buy. They don't trust their own taste and their minds have to be made up for them by experts. Then they will pay any price for what is recommended. Because of this, any artist who is not world-famous needs an agent in America to "put it across" as they say to the public, and these agents are very expensive. Believe me, I know this from experience. There is of course an easier way to success if you have the right social connections. The Americans look up to their aristocracy of wealth and fashion with much more respect than we ever have for our people of title. If you can get anyone socially prominent in that set to buy whatever it is you make, it's the best advertisement you can get.'

'I don't know many Americans,' I told her, 'but Ambassador Steinhardt and his wife became great friends of ours when they were in Prague. I'm sure they would help. Then there's Mrs Harrison Williams, she's always been very kind to me.' Edmonde's eyebrows rose. 'Mona Williams? Why, if she takes you up, you can even sell buttons.' 'Of course, I'm still rather inexperienced,' I confessed. 'I don't know much about kilns and firing. I'll have to learn a lot more before I can start selling anything.' 'A friend of mine here in Paris is a very successful artist in ceramics,' Edmonde said. 'It might interest you to see her studio. I could drive you there tomorrow morning if you think it might be of use to you.' 'I'd be ever so grateful,' I said truthfully.

Meanwhile Madame Charles Roux had started to argue with Leopold about the wisdom of our emigrating to America. 'Surely it would make much more sense to go and live in Austria where you have so many relations and friends who would welcome and help you,' she said to him. 'After all, you were as much at home in Vienna as you were in Prague.' 'That's a long time ago,' Leopold said. 'After the Germans took over in Austria I never went back.' 'But that's all over now. Do consider it, Count Leopold. You'd be so much happier there among your own people than among strangers in a strange country.' 'No I wouldn't,' Leopold said firmly. 'But why?' 'I'm afraid it's too complex to explain.'

We had left the dining-room by then and had finished our coffee. Leopold got up rather abruptly, looked at the tiny gold watch that had belonged to his mother and from which he was never parted, and said that it was time to go as he had an appointment at four. We thanked Madame Charles Roux with the usual polite phrases but also with real gratitude for her kindness, and left.

'What is this appointment you have at four?' I asked Leopold as we drove back to our hotel. 'Just an excuse to get away.' 'I thought so. Yet Madame Charles Roux was right about Austria.' 'Now don't you start bothering me about it too,' he said angrily. 'You know I won't go there.' Secretly of course I was relieved and glad since I very much wanted us to emigrate to America. For his own good I would have had to accept it even if he had decided to settle in Vienna, knowing that it was the most natural and sensible thing for him to do, and that it was only his stubborn pride that deterred him.

Not that he would have been too proud to accept charity or have minded being financially supported by some of his still very wealthy relatives there. He was much too generous himself not to feel that he could take what under reversed circumstances he would have gladly given. It was a different sort of pride that forbade him to return to the Vienna of his youth. 'They would laugh at me there,' he once told me, 'and I know what they'd say. *"Hast's notwendig gehabt so ein Oberczeche zu sein? Was hast Du am ende davon gehabt? Rausgeschmissen habn sie Dich genau so wie uns."'* Roughly translated from the Viennese it meant What necessity was there for you to be so pro-Czech? They chucked you out exactly as they did us. But its real meaning and connotation is more complex to translate and explain since it has its roots in the past.

In the days of the Austrian Empire the Czechs and the Slovaks were looked down on as inferior people. A race of good servants at best, disloyal and subversive at worst. Their language to which they clung so tenaciously was ridiculed, the history of their past in which they took such pride ignored as unimportant and their aspirations to great independence within the framework of the monarchy denied. The Imperial court was, of course, all-powerful at the time, and its influence on opinions and fashions absolute. To be pro-Czech, to sympathize with its people, to prefer living in provincial Prague to Imperial Vienna, as some resentful Bohemian nobles did, was considered unsmart, unadvantageous, and politically suspect.

Although the Austrian Emperor had honoured the Hungarians by being crowned King of Hungary with the crown of St Stephen, he had offended the Czech nobles as well as the Czech people by disdaining the crown of St Wenceslas. Had he given the Czechs the same rights of independence as the Hungarians had been granted, he would have gained loyal friends in Bohemia and there might never have been a Czechoslovak republic.

After the end of the First World War, the Austrian monarchy collapsed. All efforts of the Emperor Charles to preserve his empire intact had failed; he died in exile. Many Austrians felt that the Czechs were to blame for the disaster. Not only had Czech troops deserted by the thousands and joined the Russians towards the end of the war but the swift establishment of a Czechoslovak republic under President Masaryk, thanks to American aid, encouraged Serbs, Croats and Poles to seek equal independence. The once great Austrian Empire disintegrated and fell apart.

Then came further cause for Austrian resentment against the Czechs. The koruna soon became a stable currency, while the Austrian krone inflated into worthless paper millions and billions. Affluent Czechs took full advantage of the rate of exchange. Vienna was still a city where pleasure could be bought by those who were able to pay. Meanwhile many of its formerly prosperous population had been reduced to begging in the street. Then, when, after years of insecure and impotent governments in Austria, shifting from right to left and vice versa, Hitler annexed the country without much opposition and soon afterwards occupied Czechoslovakia, the Austrians who had properties there frankly rejoiced.

Thanks to Hitler, it was they that were in power again, and the Czech traitors were getting the treatment they deserved. But what they could not understand was why their cousins ignored the benefits Hitler was ready to bestow on all members of the aristocracy loyal to the Reich. After all, Germany was winning on all fronts by then. How could their relations so foolishly and stubbornly insist on sharing the fate of the Czechs? Whatever the final outcome, Leopold did not want to live among people who would mock his patriotism and point out that all he had gained from it in the end was loss of property and exile from the country he had loyally served.

13

The next morning Leopold set out hopefully for the Czech Refugee Committee. The reluctant child was taken for her walk; she did not seem to like the swarthy Mademoiselle. Edmonde Charles Roux came to fetch me in her little car as the studio was on the outskirts of Paris.

We drove through many shop-lined streets. Even outside the town centre the goods displayed in the windows seemed of a quality I hadn't seen since before the war and the people looked well-fed, well-dressed and happy. It was all very unlike the Prague I had left. 'It's wonderful how Paris has recovered from what it must have suffered during the war,' I remarked. 'We didn't suffer all that much,' Edmonde remarked dryly. 'Business went on as usual here.' 'In spite of the occupation?' 'Because of the occupation. Paris has always sold to foreigners. In the war it was to Germans.'

'But wasn't that,' I hesitated, 'rather unpatriotic?' 'On the contrary, it was the only way a shopkeeper, who after all has to earn his living, could harry the enemy.' 'But how?' I asked. Edmonde laughed. 'By overcharging, cheating, selling inferior goods and not delivering. There was really very little the Germans could do about it. Our Parisians are tough, resourceful and resilient. If one remembers how much French blood was shed in these streets in the name of liberty, equality and brotherhood! There has been more civil strife here than in any other city in the world. What Frenchmen have done to Frenchmen in the past was infinitely worse than what the Germans could do to France. As a matter of fact, the ordinary German soldiers here in Paris behaved very correctly. The Gestapo of course was *autre chose*.' She shuddered and fell silent.

After a while she stopped the car in front of a long, low wooden building. It stretched the full expanse of one side of a narrow street. We entered an enormous room blazing with colour. Its walls were covered with mosaics and vividly painted tiles that combined and formed large pictures. There were jars, pots and vases as tall as the men who were turning them on wheels or spraying them; at least ten men in overalls were at work. Everywhere were the most astoundingly bizarre life-sized animals. Cats and dogs, camels and elephants, unicorns and dragons glazed vivid emerald green, lapis lazuli blue or turquoise.

A small youth in overalls came to meet us; or so I thought till he pulled off his cap, revealing a lot of brown hair and the very smudged face of a young woman. 'It's the clay dust,' she apologized, trying to clean her face with hands equally dirty before she kissed Edmonde. It was obvious they were great friends. They laughed and gossiped together when not kindly and politely showing me everything there was to see. Too much unfortunately not to undermine my confidence in ever becoming an expert in ceramics.

'First you must look at my new kiln,' the young woman had said. 'It's my pride and joy. I had it specially built.' She led us to the end of the studio. The kiln was the size of a small house. She pressed some buttons and the iron door swung open. 'Enter if you please. Have no fear,' she added, 'I won't bake you in my oven. It's quite cool, we only fire once a week, it's more economical.' The interior, in spite of its thick walls of firebrick through which the electric wires were threaded, was the size of a little room.

'Perhaps,' she laughed, 'because I am so small myself, I like making big things. With this kiln I can. Do you know a Count Coudenhove?'

she asked me. 'I think he was Czechoslovak.' 'I know several,' I said. 'Well, one of them ordered me to make a stove which was to be an exact portrait of himself dressed in a fur coat and with a hat on his head. He sat for me several times; he was rather fat, and his tummy made an excellent stove. It was sent to Czechoslovakia and he wrote that he was very satisfied, and making fires in it.

'You wouldn't believe the strange requests I get, and from all over the world. A ceramic palm-tree with monkeys and nuts suspended from it, and a man who wanted his entire room tiled with a map of Texas. I have an order now for a mermaid, to sit at the edge of someone's bath. It's all a challenge, often an amusement, and occasionally very profitable. Then of course I do murals for banks, hotels and night-clubs. But most of all I like making my strange beasts. They don't sell too badly, even here in Paris. Look, isn't the iridescent blue and gold of that dragon's scales superb?'

'It's lovely,' I said truthfully. 'It's been fired four times, each time with a different glaze superimposed to give that lustre. A very expensive process, not to speak of the danger of the block cracking as it cools. But of course you know all our difficulties,' she smiled. 'Edmonde said you'd like my advice on kilns and glazes. I wouldn't recommend anything quite as large as mine in the beginning, it would cost you a fortune to ship it to America. They don't make them there, the best medium-sized ones come from England and so really do all the best clays and glazes. Let me give you some of the catalogues. You'll find everything you could possibly want in them, and most of these firms have representatives in America.

'The best of luck in the USA,' she said to me as we left. 'I wish you every success.'

'Any help to you?' asked Edmonde as she drove me back. 'Of course,' I said, hoping that she hadn't noticed how impressed I had been. 'She's very talented.' 'Not only that. She's also a very good business-woman. From quite small beginnings she's built up a most prosperous industry; she's worked hard for years, she's not as young as she looks, you know.

'I was wondering,' Edmonde added, 'if I could give you any addresses in New York that might be of use to you, but most of my friends who worked with me on the magazine were not of much social importance, although they were nice girls. They had to struggle hard to make a living, and had little time for amusements. New York is terribly expensive, and all you might learn from them is how to live very frugally and uncomfortably. I hope you won't need that sort of advice.'

'I'm sure I will,' I said sadly. My hopes of making a fortune in ceramics had sunk very low after what I had seen. 'Anyway, I'll send you some addresses. My mother and I are leaving for Italy in a few days, but I do hope we meet again.'

We never did. Years later I bought a novel made famous by having won the *Prix Goncourt*, the French literary prize. I saw to my amazement that it was written by Edmonde Charles Roux.

I returned to the hotel room . . . It was hotter and more untidy than ever, but at least I was alone. Leopold and the child had not yet returned. I glanced through the catalogues, not understanding their terminology at all. I lay down on my unmade bed and cried as I had not since we left home. One of the few advantages of our rooms under the roof was that whoever came up the last flight of stairs could only be coming to us. Besides, Leopold's limping step was unmistakable, and I had time to wash my face and compose myself before he entered the room. He detested tears and I only indulged in them rarely; self-pity and failing courage were things he couldn't understand.

When I saw his face I knew that he was in more need of comfort than I was. He confessed that his interview with ex-minister Ripka, from which he had expected so much, had not even been worth the taxi fare. 'He simply didn't want me,' Leopold said bitterly. 'Oh, he was quite polite about it, but he said that there were no vacancies in the Committee except perhaps for a clerk. I had to confess that I couldn't read, write or speak French, and that I didn't know how to type.' 'I'm sorry, darling,' I said, trying to comfort him. 'But work here wouldn't have been permanent anyway.'

'Ripka was a bit more encouraging about New York. He said that with our connections I would probably find something. He knew all about Steinhardt of course. He suggested that I might try to speak on the Czech American broadcast and that since I'd been so popular at home there was a chance that people might even listen.' 'But isn't that a rather good idea?' I asked. 'How could I?' Leopold said. 'I'd endanger the lives of any relations we still have there, and of many of our close friends if I broadcast anti-communist propaganda, which is what it would amount to. Even Ripka had to concede that there was that risk.

'He was quite without hope for the future of our country, and I had the impression that by now all he cares about is his own survival and that of his family and friends. I'm certain he didn't count me among the latter,' Leopold remarked, 'a certain envy and resentment was obvious. "You aristocrats have so many rich and influential relations in every country that you'll always find help somewhere," he told me.'

When the child returned, she was not enthusiastic about her morning's walk. 'That woman wouldn't allow me to play on the swings with the other children,' she said indignantly. 'She said they were *sales*. What does that mean?' 'Dirty,' I explained.

'And her table manners,' continued the child, her eyes wide with feigned horror, knowing how strict we were about hers. 'She eats her cheese with her knife, and mops the gravy from her plate with a piece of bread.' Leopold laughed. 'Most French people do,' he told her. 'It's not very nice, is it?' 'No,' I conceded, 'but we will have to try and get accustomed to manners different from our own when we travel.'

She was not listening, I could see that she was thinking of something else. 'Mummy, there's this pond in the park where all the children sail their boats. If we could buy the tiniest little sailing boat with a lot of string . . .?' she pleaded. Next day I bought her the largest toy boat I could find; I think the model of a yacht – all its rigging and sails looked authentic, and it was very expensive. She was pleased with it, and went on her walks with Mademoiselle with greater enthusiasm until the day the boat sank. After that I had to buy a doll's perambulator which she could push in the park, in which she bedded the three dolls she had been allowed to take with her. The hundreds she had left behind in Castolovice were later to form the nucleus of a Czech dolls museum.

Leopold grew more cheerful in the week that followed; his visit to Ripka had consequences. Many Czechs, working in the Refugee Committee, had recognized him. They came to call, bringing relations and friends. Leopold received them each evening under the dusty striped umbrella in the courtyard of the hotel. They were mainly ex-diplomats and former government employees who had fled, and businessmen and shopkeepers who hoped to make a living elsewhere. There were endless political discussions and arguments about the past. Doubts and fears for the future were discussed too. I don't know which was more appreciated, Leopold's advice or the wine which they drank at our expense. As long as these night sessions with compatriots reassured him that he was still a person of importance, what, I thought, did the expense matter, except that something would have to be done about money, and soon.

I had written to Steinhardt expressing all the gratitude and affection I felt for him as best I could, without being indiscreet. I told him how comfortable and happy we were in Paris and how we had found many old friends.

What I didn't dare confess in my letter was that we were in need of money. After all, he was carefully and kindly planning our future in America, and had saved enough of our belongings at some risk to his diplomatic status, to ensure us a reasonable start in the New World. He was a generous man, but certainly not wasteful, and it had been well known in embassy circles that Dulcie kept a tight purse. If I had told him that in a week we had managed to spend what was supposed to last for months, he might well have been shocked. However fond of me he was, Dulcie might certainly encourage doubts as to the wisdom of importing us to the USA.

'There must be some other way of getting money,' I thought. Everything would be all right if I still found my jewels intact in Venice, but how was I going to pay for the journey? I must sell something. I went through our trunks. My furs? Even in the stifling August heat I knew I would need them later, although they seemed unnecessary then. The silver? It wasn't worth much to anyone except me; I had poured tea or coffee, offered sugar and milk out of the various pots and bowls and the rare cigarettes out of the boxes to friends all through the war. I found the gold fruit-knives and forks, a dozen of each in a pretty tooled leather case. Their handles were hand-painted porcelain. Surely they were eighteenth century, and would be worth quite a lot? Yet simply to walk into any shop and try to sell them without knowing their value seemed foolish, and besides I might be mistaken for a thief. I decided to consult Madame Poisson.

I found her sitting at a desk doing accounts in her small, dark office behind the hall, and asked her if she could spare me a moment. 'Certainly,' she said, pulling out a chair for me to sit on. 'I'm sure you will understand, Madame, that sometimes a woman wants to sell something without letting her husband know,' I said.

'*Naturellement.*'

I knew by then that there was very little she didn't understand. 'So I thought I'd try and sell this,' I explained. 'I just chanced to throw it into my trunk at the last moment. It is totally useless to me, and my husband doesn't even know it exists.' I opened the box and put it on her desk.

'But they are pretty!' she exclaimed, taking out a fork and examining it carefully. 'Not gold of course, silver gilt, *vermeille*, and here in Paris we prefer Sèvres to Saxe.'

'I don't know where to go to sell it, or what its value is.' 'You are right to have confidence in me,' she declared. 'I will take you to Duroque. He's a man of great honesty and a friend of mine. He will give you the best possible price, I'll take you to him tomorrow afternoon when I have an hour free. Is that agreeable?' 'You're very kind, Madame,' I said, and I meant it.

No doubt she was a shrewd businesswoman, and as mercenary as only a Parisian can be, but she was too clever to be dishonest and too kind-hearted to take undue advantage of people she liked. She seemed to have grown fond of us. I had rather rashly told Leopold that the maiden name of Madame de Pompadour had been Poisson, and as Pompadour was easier for him to remember than the latter, he called her Pompadour on the frequent occasions on which they met. It did not offend her at all. *'Comme le Comte est rigolo,'* she would laugh.

Next day she in her usual black but with an elegant feather hat and gloves and I carrying the box in a paper bag, walked together the length of the Rue Cambon. It was a street scented like so many around the Place Vendôme with the perfumes wafted from open shop doors and worn by most of the men and women who walked those streets.

It wasn't a shop that Madame Poisson took me to, but a rather dingy office on a third floor. *Le lift* was in this case in order. She and the old man behind the desk greeted each other effusively, and when that was over I displayed my wares. Monsieur Duroque applied his magnifying glass to his eye and inspected knives and forks closely.

'Nice,' he said. 'If they had been eighteenth- instead of nineteenth-century, they would have been of some value.'

'But I was so sure they were,' I protested.

'If Madame does not believe me, see the mark.' He handed me his glass. I looked, but since I didn't know one silver mark from another I didn't dare contradict.

'Do you nevertheless wish to sell?'

'Well, now that we are here,' I said, looking at Madame Poisson for help. Instantly she sprang into action.

'How much?'

He quoted a sum in francs. 'How much would that be in dollars?' I asked. We had used up nearly all the French francs we had been allowed for the cure in Vichy, and I was unsure of the French rate of exchange in any other currency.

'I can't offer more than three hundred dollars,' he said. Of course I had hoped for more, but would have accepted almost anything.

'But this is absurd!' Madame Poisson exclaimed. 'Why, I would buy that cassette for a much greater sum myself if I did not already have one like it. Five hundred dollars is what I would have been ready to pay.'

'Unfortunately I can't,' Monsieur Duroque said firmly.

'You don't know the circumstances of this poor and unfortunate lady, cast out from her country by the Germans with a small child to support, selling the last of her possessions,' she pleaded. He glanced at me briefly, recognizing of course as every Parisian would that my newly bought dress didn't indicate poverty, but one of the city's best fashion houses. 'Four hundred and fifty dollars then,' Madame Poisson conceded, 'or we go elsewhere.'

He sighed. 'I would not want to take advantage of this lady's misfortunes. But where would my profit be if I paid such an exorbitant price?' he added pathetically.

'*Mon Dieu!*' cried Madame Poisson. 'Haven't you profited enough by the customers I send you? It's four hundred and fifty, or I will come to you no more.'

He was defeated. He went to his safe, took out a sheaf of notes, counted them carefully, and handed them over to me. To my amazement, Madame Poisson's parting from him was just as friendly and effusive as their greeting had been. He bowed low over her hand and watched her with unconcealed admiration as she sailed out of his office. Once on the street, she apologized to me for what she had said about my poverty, hoping it hadn't embarrassed me too much. 'Duroque has a kind heart,' she explained. 'It was worth at least fifty dollars more, that sad story.'

'But the rest was all thanks to you, Madame. I'm ever so grateful to you,' I said.

'*De quoi?* I wouldn't be owner of all that,' she said, looking at her hotel which we were approaching with as much pride as if it were the Ritz that faced it, 'if I didn't know how to drive a bargain.'

I brought Leopold the money. 'It will have to last till Steinhardt comes,' I warned.

'But this is quite a lot,' he said, counting the notes before bundling them into his pocket. 'Wherever did you get it?'

'I've been walking the streets.' I laughed.

'Really? I didn't think you were worth so much.' I told him the whole story. 'Good old Pompadour,' he said. As I had thought, he hadn't even known that the dessert-set existed.

That evening he must have been at his best, surrounded by the devoted Czechs who applauded his jokes. I could hear the roars of their laughter in my room above the courtyard till late at night. I wondered rather sadly if his form of witticisms at which all of Vienna and Prague had laughed for so many years, and on which much of his popularity had depended, would ever be understood in any other language. They were mainly jokes based on a play of words in the vernacular, and their humour was untranslatable and incomprehensible to anyone who hadn't grown up in the Austro-Hungarian Empire. It was the tragic-comic humour of the soldier Schwejk, of the Frau Pollack jokes, and the Graf Feri stories, or of Jewish self-deprecating wit, all told in Austrian jargon which incorporated words taken from the vocabularies of all its subject peoples.

It was a sort of *lingua franca* and it gave a unique richness of expression to the language. Poets and writers benefited from its variety, as did the theatre. Vienna's famous comic actors took full advantage of the *double entendres*, puns, and extremely funny misunderstandings which this jargon made possible. It was no wonder that only very few Austrian writers or actors were ever successful abroad. Viennese subtlety of expression and humour was untranslatable.

When Leopold at last came to bed that night, it was past one, yet he insisted we must go to mass next morning at eight thirty. 'But why,' I asked, 'when there's a mass at the Madeleine at twelve?' He drew a piece of paper from his pocket. 'They wrote this down for me. It's a church where there are services for exiles, Poles, Hungarians and Czechs. The Czech mass is at nine, and I'd like to go.'

At home we went to mass every Sunday, and also when travelling if there was a Roman Catholic church available. I was as zealous about my newly acquired faith at first as are all converts, much to Leopold's distaste. 'What,' he had asked, 'is there to be so damn serious about?' when I remonstrated about his behaviour in church. I had been accustomed to the austere solemnity of Protestant services and the attention paid to the sermon and prayers. I was not prepared to understand the seeming lack of respect for the service that Leopold and most of his friends and relations had.

Only at certain moments in the mass, at the consecration and the elevation of the host, when the little acolytes rang their bells, did they kneel and bow their heads, making the sign of the cross, in silent devotion. All through the sermon there was a complete lack of attention. People yawned, coughed loudly, looked round and smiled at each other; Leopold always seemed to behave worst of all because he was so conspicuous. He could not kneel because of his stiff leg, and, towering above everyone else, he would repeat the prayers in a very loud voice accompanied by gestures that caused stifled laughter.

'But why,' I asked, 'are you all so casual about your religion? I can't understand why you go to church at all if you behave no differently there than at home.'

'It's our Father's house, isn't it?' I understood after that, and also why Leopold would never discuss religious subjects. Once a very stupid woman who thought she was being clever asked Leopold how, in this day and age, he found it possible to believe. 'You might as well ask me why I breathe,' had been his abrupt answer.

Next morning the three of us, all sleepy and in a bad temper because of having had to use the bathroom at the same time, were taxied through half of Paris until we reached an ugly modern church. It was crowded. How could there be so many Czechs in town? I wondered. There seemed to be no place for us to sit, but, as usual, Leopold was recognized, and without ceremony some people were cleared from the front benches and we took their places.

One of our neighbours whispered that the officiating priest was a Dominican from the convent of Strahov in Prague. How well I remembered the beautiful baroque convent. Its great library, surely one of the finest in the world, was occasionally open to the public, though its walled garden was secret except to those who knew certain paths that overlooked it, from which one could see the white-cassocked monks digging, weeding, or reading their breviaries. I wondered if they had all been expelled by now.

The priest read the gospel, and the sermon followed. Among this congregation there was no lack of attention, every face, upturned towards the pulpit, seemed to ask for hope and comfort. The priest gave what he could in the Christian sense, speaking of the rewards of martyrdom in heaven and asking us to pray for those that had suffered and died for their faith and country, and those who would in the future.

The mass followed. Many took communion, not only old men, women and children, as I had grown accustomed to in Prague of late, but also young and middle-aged people, who were probably quite unaccustomed to receiving the host. They knelt humbly at the altar because it was also the altar of their lost country. Then the organ intoned the first bars of our national anthem, sacred to all Czechs, and doubly so then because singing it in the war during the German occupation had been punishable by death. It has a lovely haunting melody; its words do not speak of power and glory, only of the beauty of the Czech lands. 'Kdé Domov Muj?' 'Where is my home?' The child beside us sang clearly and distinctly; all the many voices rose in unison asking the same question. Then came the answering verses. They sing of sparkling

97

streams and rushing rivers, of mountains and forests, of fertile fields and flowering meadows. 'Země české domov muj,' it ends. 'It's on Czech soil I have my home.'

After that we left the church. We spoke to no one and no one talked to us. 'Never again,' Leopold said as we drove back to the hotel. 'I thought it was lovely,' said the child. 'Did I sing all right?' 'Beautifully, darling,' I said, kissing the top of her head since I did not want my tears to wet her face.

From then on we went to mass at twelve in the church of the Madeleine where all the smart Catholic Parisians met to admire or envy each other's clothes, and gossip on the marble steps afterwards.

14

Leopold had become impatient for me to leave for Venice. I had no doubts that Annicka, who managed to telephone him from the French Embassy in Prague almost every day, was imploring him to do something about her sister. I had written to my cousin Eddie and, as I had expected, he was as pleased as I was at the thought of our being able to meet again after our long separation. He wrote that all that was needed was for me to telegraph the hour of my arrival.

I cannot remember a time when we were not close friends, in childhood, in youth and in later years. Only the war parted us for a while. Eddie Bismarck was a grandson of the Iron Chancellor. He was christened Albrecht Edward, but his first name soon changed to Eddie as no one could pronounce Albrecht in the countries in which he preferred to live. He was the youngest of my Aunt Maggie's five children. Of them all, her eldest daughter Hannah, later Frau von Bredow, was probably the most intelligent and certainly the wittiest. Goedella, who was very pretty, became the wife of Count Herman Keyserling. He was of Baltic origin and a philosopher whose books had brought him some fame in Germany as well as abroad.

Aunt Maggie's eldest son, Otto, was the cleverest, Gottfried the most complex, and Eddie the most charming and gifted. But from his family's point of view Eddie had one serious fault; since his earliest youth he showed a marked dislike for everything German. Some blamed Miss

Rosser, his English nanny, others thought that Aunt Maggie's secret distaste for the Germanic, though she concealed it heroically, must have influenced him.

Eddie was sent to a school in Plöhn which was considered smart because the Hohenzollern princes went there. He ran away three times and he was finally tutored at home. He loathed his staid German teachers and laughed at them and mocked them until they despaired and left. Finally, after years of frustration on all sides, in which he had nevertheless managed to learn very much more than could have been expected, he was allowed to study in Switzerland.

I know how happy he was there, for I was at school in Lausanne then and he often came to visit me. I met many of his young friends, none of them German!

Aunt Maggie had been a widow for many years. Although she was guardian of her children according to her husband's will, two co-guardians had been appointed to advise her. They insisted that her youngest son might become estranged from his country if he stayed abroad too long, and suggested that after his studies in Geneva had been completed he should spend a term or two at the University of Bonn to harden him into a true Prussian.

Bonn had the most famous, or rather infamous, student corps in Germany, the *Bonner Borussen*, whose members were all Prussian *Junkers* of the nobility, their barbaric customs hallowed by tradition. Neither attendance at lectures nor study were expected or demanded in Bonn, but proficiency at fencing and drinking was. Those who were challenged to compete in the drinking bouts drank beer until they had to leave the room to be sick, and returned to drink more. Whoever survived and was semi-sober by morning was acclaimed victor.

As for the fencing, after some preliminary training with masks and foils came the final confrontation in which two opponents, with no protection save a band about the throat, slashed each others' faces with swords. The horrible gashes inflicted were not even properly sewn up lest these marks of honour should fade into insignificant scars in later years. Eddie was a good fencer; he was lithe, agile and quite fearless, but he had too much common-sense to wish to be disfigured for life, and he loathed drinking beer.

Very soon the friends that he had inevitably made felt as he did about Bonn. Peter Yorck, Toffy Doenhoff, Goetz von Berlichengen all fled the university with him. He brought them to Emkendorf, then took them to the Plessens in Nehmten and Sierhagen where they met enough of his pretty young cousins to be grateful that they had escaped disfigurement. Count Peter Yorck was the only one of the young Prussians I liked. His hair curled, even though it was shortly cropped, and he had the face of a shy faun. He wrote me long, carefully penned letters during the time I was at school in Lausanne. Letters were only distributed among the pupils on Saturdays as was the ration of chocolate one was permitted to buy.

I looked forward to both all through the week, but if forced to choose between the Toblerone which I preferred to all other chocolate and Peter's letters, I would have chosen the Toblerone. Even now I cannot see any of those three-cornered pieces without remembering him. We never met again. I married, he married, and we lived in different countries. After the unsuccessful attempt to assassinate Hitler in which my cousin Gottfried Bismarck had also been involved, Peter Yorck was executed.

After leaving Bonn, Eddie went to England to stay with relations and friends, and then joined my grandmother and me in Rome. Except for brief visits to his mother, he remained in Italy from then on. It was the country he most loved all of his life, and where he felt most at home.

Eddie's appearance was rather deceptive. He was a slim, graceful, golden-haired youth who charmed his way wherever life was pleasantest, gay, frivolous, making friends wherever he went. The fact that he spoke every language like a native, was well-read and artistic in his tastes, didn't detract from the impression he made of being a rich and idle young aristocrat, and what is now called a playboy.

However, those who saw his flat in Rome, which he had decorated and furnished himself, realized that he was either very rich indeed or that he knew a lot about antiques. Only the latter was true.

Eddie had no fortune of his own, but depended on his brother Otto's monthly *appanage*, to which he was legally entitled.

Since Eddie's brother felt that he should live and work in Germany like a good Bismarck and Eddie refused to do this, there were often quarrels, and his allowance became conditional upon his returning to the fatherland. Sometimes Eddie was very short of money, so he began to earn by decorating flats and houses for his more affluent friends. He had an expert's knowledge of antiques and was as shrewd as any dealer in bargaining and acquiring them for his customers at very reasonable prices.

He did not earn very much at first, but he loved his work. It allowed him to gratify his awareness of beauty, for he could now discover and buy rare and precious objects for others and encourage their acquiring derelict palaces and villas which he then restored. Sometimes, and this gave him the greatest satisfaction, he was even commissioned to build. Although he had no architectural training, he showed great originality in his designs and plans, and also saw to it that the work was properly completed at not too great a cost.

There was rarely a month in which he didn't write to tell me of some new project in Rome, Naples or Capri. Then suddenly he wrote to confess that he had fallen in love. He had indulged in plenty of casual affairs in the past, but this time he wrote that it was serious, and I was rather jealous. Not that we had ever been in love with each other, we were far too alike for that, even physically. We were always taken to be brother and sister when we travelled together. We knew that we were closer to each other than to any other members of our families; we had the same strengths and weaknesses, we had many interests and tastes in common, and we laughed at the same things. Above all, we liked being together, enjoying each other's company above all others. Leopold understood this and never resented our friendship. He too was fond of Eddie.

'Her name is Mona Williams,' Eddie wrote. 'She's an American and a married woman. I am taking her to Friedrichsruh to meet my mother and then we will motor to Vienna to see Omama and come on to you, if that's all right. You're not sick all the time, are you?' He knew that I was at last expecting a child.

I read the letter to Leopold. 'Don't you think it sounds as if he was introducing a fiancée?' I asked him anxiously.

'Don't worry. A man doesn't necessarily have to marry every woman he travels around with, especially if she is already married.' 'But Americans come unstuck so easily.'

We were then living in Zasmuky, our home before Leopold inherited Castolovice. It had been the former lodge of the adjoining castle, that had never been modernized. We had made the little house quite comfortable, but it was in no way luxurious, and, because it had very small windows, it was rather dark and gloomy on the autumn afternoon when Eddie and Mona finally arrived.

I had of course expected her to be attractive, but not that her beauty would be such that it illuminated the dark little house as if a hundred candles had been lit. There was a radiance about her that I've never seen in another woman. Her hair was bright silver, though she cannot have been more than thirty. It curled upwards in shining waves which crowned a perfect face. Her large eyes, slanting at the outer corners, were the brightest of turquoise blue. Her complexion was dazzling. Her skin glowed as if transfused by an inner light.

She was so incredibly beautiful that she seemed to me like some marvellous being from another world that had come to grace our humble dwelling. Even her clothes, her scent, her jewels, the gem-studded boxes and cigarette lighters she used, seemed too exquisitely rare and precious to have been made by mortals. Far from being jealous, all I could do was worship. As for Leopold, he just stared in speechless admiration.

After she had gone to her room to dress, Eddie and I were left alone together. 'Well?' he asked, grinning delightedly at my awed expression.

'It simply doesn't seem possible,' I said. 'It's what I imagine an angel looks like; that unearthly radiance.'

'I know it's strange,' he said, 'but I assure you that she's very human.'

'You should have prepared me.'

'You might have heard. Did her name mean nothing to you? Mona Williams? She is known as the most beautiful woman in America.'

'Boy, are you lucky,' I said, falling into slang.

'Not really,' he said rather sadly. 'She is very fond of her husband.'

'But wherever did you meet her?' I asked.

'It was an absurd meeting,' he laughed. 'It was in Venice, I was on Spoleto's yacht with Eileen, and the Harrison Williams' yacht was anchored near it. Suddenly I saw someone dive from it into the sea. I didn't know if it was a man or a woman, but I heard a cry for help. I jumped in and swam towards whoever it was who was struggling in the water. I saw then that it was a woman; far from drowning, her distress was only due to her having lost the upper part of her bathing suit which she couldn't retie. I helped, she invited me to her yacht, introduced me to her husband, and we became friends.'

'So she came to you out of the sea like Venus?'

'Exactly,' he laughed.

'But doesn't her beauty frighten you?'

'It did at first, but now, for her sake, I try to ignore it as much as possible.'

'But why?'

'Because such beauty is more of a curse than a blessing,' Eddie said. 'It sets her apart. Men dread her, for obvious reasons; a kind word or two, a look from those turquoise eyes, and they are lost, enchanted. Women envy her and fear for their men. She has hundreds of acquaintances and very few real friends. Except for her husband who adores her she is a very lonely woman. Yet she's a perfectly normal, nice, warm-hearted human being – a bit capricious and spoilt of course because of the amount of admiration she gets and her husband's incredible wealth, which allows her to satisfy every whim. But in spite of that, she is simply the most lovable creature I ever met.'

'And the husband, I suppose he's awful?'

'No, not at all. He's old and he's as shrewd as they come, but he's a gentleman and has charm.'

'But do you want to marry her, Eddie?'

'Of course I do. But she will never leave Harrison as long as he lives. She's a loyal sort of person.'

Mona came to sit with me by the fire before dinner, wearing a rose-coloured satin tea-gown. I had also changed for the evening, but I knew how unattractive I must look, for, whatever I wore, there was no concealing my condition by then. I would have liked to have made a better impression; after all, she had come a long way to meet Eddie's favourite cousin. She spoke with a very low voice and I sensed that she was shy and not quite at her ease.

It was only much later when I saw her own luxurious houses in New York, Palm Beach and on Long Island, her apartment in the Palazzo Borghese in Rome, the villa Eddie was to build for her in Capri, and finally the two wonderful houses in Paris, that I realized how strange she must have felt in such unfamiliar surroundings. How she must have marvelled that civilized people could live in a little house like ours, with only one bathroom. Although we took her to see Castolovice the next day, driving there through the bleak, already wintry countryside, I can't imagine that the great gaunt pile of the castle, whose interior was still furnished in my parents-in-law's Edwardian taste, can have appealed much to her either.

We talked a little about Eddie's mother and his brother Otto's beautiful Swedish wife Ann-Mari whom she had met at Friedrichsruh, and we regretted my grandmother's failing health. It was all very formal until she told me that she had bought a piece of land in Capri on which she wanted to build. 'That will amuse Eddie, don't you think?' Suddenly there was a lilt in her voice that offered friendship and asked for understanding.

'Building has always been his greatest passion,' I said.

'And now perhaps we can share it,' she smiled.

Women have rarely attracted me physically, but I had to turn in confusion from the seductive enchantment of that smile. 'I so long to build something new with him . . .'

'She really loves him,' I thought, and felt ashamed at feeling surprised. Because I could so easily identify myself with Eddie and knew our exact worth, her extraordinary beauty seemed somehow too great a gift to have been bestowed on him.

'Couldn't you come and help?' she then asked. 'The place I've bought is just a heap of rubble now, but you could stay with us at the hotel. Eddie has told me how talented you are, I'd so love to have your advice too. You and he are so alike.'

Next day she and Eddie left for Capri.

'Wasn't she marvellous?' I asked Leopold.

'Yes,' he conceded, 'but a man prefers a woman he can take on his knee to one he has to kneel to. I'd sooner make advances to a statue of the holy Virgin in church than I would to her.'

<h1 style="text-align:center">15</h1>

A few weeks later I went to stay with them in Capri. Eddie and I had frequently escaped there when we had been in Rome together. My father had lived there for a while before he became seriously ill and we had joined him. We both knew the island well; we had explored it together, venturing into caves and grottoes and bathing in the sun-warmed pools among the rocks. We had climbed the highest peaks, ascending through lemon, orange and olive groves and sweet-scented freesias blooming under the trees, up to where there was just rock, sparsely covered with thyme and rosemary, aromatic in the hot sun. From there we would look down on the expanse of blue sea below.

We had made friends too in Capri. Axel Munthe was still busy building his fantastic San Michele; Eddie and I agreed that we thought it quite hideous, despite its superb position – *Rumba di Tiberio*. We always deplored the incorporation of what was really no more than Roman rubble – pieces of mosaic, broken pots and dismembered statuary – into buildings. Possibly they were of historical interest, but depressing and sad, as are all remnants of past glory.

Norman Douglas was still living there though he had become a recluse. His books had done too much to publicize the charms of the island, much to his own disadvantage. He disliked Capri being overrun by tourists. Compton MacKenzie came and went. My father's old cousin, Hugo Wemyss, never left the island. He was always dressed in white tweed, with a barefooted little Capri boy walking beside him holding a scarlet sunshade over his white but not very venerable head.

There had been many others, whose names I have since forgotten, in that strangely assorted coterie of writers, painters, musicians and artists from all over the world. They came to Capri free to indulge in tastes accepted by the Caprese since the time of the Emperor Tiberius, at very little cost, and with no danger to themselves. But now there was none of the old group left except for old Dr Munthe; he was almost totally blind and no longer lived at San Michele, the house made famous by his book, but in a tower by the sea.

Capri had become a fashionable and expensive tourist resort, and the Hotel Quisisana, where Mona had a large apartment, now equalled in comfort any other international first-class hotel. Although I deplored finding Capri so changed, Eddie was much too busy to care. Day after day, sometimes asking me to join them, more often forgetting to do so, Mona and he would take one of the *carozzas* and drive down to the Fortino. These horse-drawn carriages were then the only form of transport on the island, except for the funicular.

I rather dreaded these drives because of my pregnant condition. The horses were smartly attired with feather head-dresses and sometimes even straw hats, their manes and tails tasselled with scarlet fringe, and they had brass bells attached to their harness. They were driven at a terrific pace up and down the steep inclines of the narrow roads, one carriage often racing another, with a great cracking of whips, jingling of bells, and fierce-sounding cries from the drivers. Quite often the *carozzas* upset, spilling their passengers on to the road.

I much preferred taking the funicular down to the harbour and walking up the short distance from there to the Fortino. The remains of the old fortress and the surrounding land formed a large plateau backed by olive-clad hills. It overlooked the *Marina Grande* from which small steamers shuttled between Capri and Naples, and the fishing boats with their orange sails went out at sunrise to return at sunset. Beyond the sparkling stretch of sea Vesuvius was clearly outlined against the eternal blue of the Mediterranean sky. The Fortino itself was just a ruin, a mass of rubble overgrown with weeds. Steep terraces, considerably eroded by rainfall and spray, descended to a small beach.

Eddie and Mona tirelessly explored, visualizing what they would build. They climbed rocks, stumbled over boulders, balanced on the edge of precipices, and sometimes were even lost to each other among the tall scrub. The site of the fort was planned to be that of the main house, with a wide terrace overlooking harbour and sea. Towards the hills would stand the guest-house and cottages for servants and labourers. The rest would be gardens, terrace upon terrace descending towards the beach.

These gardens, when they were later landscaped and planted, were to become Mona's pride and joy; creating and tending them was one of her greatest personal achievements. Eddie knew all about building, furnishing and decorating, but very little about plants. Mona's love for flowers must have seemed almost abnormal to anyone who didn't know her well. I have never seen her in a house or room of her own that was not full of fresh flowers which she would arrange and re-arrange with the greatest care, her touch so gentle that no leaf was bruised and no petal fell. I wondered if she didn't know that flowers were more closely related to herself than human beings, their fragile beauty so like her own.

Her husband Harrison Williams arrived while I was in Capri. He was not in the least like my expectations of a self-made American millionaire. He was neither brash nor self-assertive; he was a tall, spare, rather elegant old man who chose his words carefully, if he spoke at all, obviously reserved but with a keen and sharp sense of humour when he relaxed. He would sometimes join Eddie and Mona at the Fortino and sit on a rock enjoying the sun, gazing out to sea; he had been a great yachtsman in his youth. He would watch them at their planning and exploring with as much tolerant amusement as he might have watched children at play.

He was, I think, fonder of Eddie than Eddie was of him. There was no doubt about who was in power and to whom Mona belonged, which Eddie knew and resented. Harrison was a very shrewd old man. His vast enterprises still left him with very little time for leisure, and he accepted that Mona needed occasional younger company. He could only accompany her rarely on her trips to Europe, and Eddie seemed an eminently suitable protector. Eddie knew his world, and no doubt Harrison thought that he would certainly keep Mona from becoming the victim of fortune hunters and predators. Her kind-heartedness and generosity were only too easy to exploit. If she insisted on travelling around 'meeting God knows what sort of titled crook' (Harrison's opinion of central-European aristocracy was not very high) he knew that Eddie was the best bodyguard she could have. After agreeing that Eddie should be in charge of building the rose-coloured palace by the sea that Mona had visualized, Harrison left for New York.

In half a year the main house was completed and the other buildings were in various stages of construction. Eddie employed local workmen wherever possible, fearing that more sophisticated builders might have ideas which conflicted with his own. The Caprese were good artisans. They had built villas since the time of Tiberius, and all they needed was authoritative guidance. Eddie was better suited to give this than anyone else not born in southern Italy. Latins of the working class are as quick to exploit weakness as they are to respect strength; with sure instinct they assess a man's true qualities behind his appearance and manner, and act accordingly. Very soon the Caprese knew that the elegant, handsome young Signor Conte was no fool and could not be fooled by them; they also discovered that he was rather like themselves.

He was hard-working and never spared himself; he could drive as hard a bargain as the peasants and fishermen, and was as quick to recognize fraud and deceit as any of them. Above all, he spoke their language fluently. If necessary, he could match insult with insult in the dialect, and was adept at the lusty vociferations and the lightning-quick give-and-take of Neapolitan humour. Those that worked for him on the island addressed him with an amused sort of respect as *Altezza*, 'Highness', though they knew quite well that he was no royal prince. It was a friendly hint that his arrogance was noted but not resented. If Eddie was imperious with those he commanded it was not from a feeling of superiority, and they all knew this. If he was their head, they were his hands and feet – all had to work together as one body; failure was mutual, and so was the pride of achievement.

16

I returned home after my fortnight in Capri glad to leave although Mona and Eddie had both begged me to stay longer. She had been very kind, and had given me many presents, lovely flowing silken garments to conceal my pregnancy, but there was no question of either of them really needing me there, involved as they were with each other and their plans for the future. I feared I had lost Eddie for ever. I was mistaken. He wrote as often as before to tell me how the work was progressing and to enquire about my health. Mona returned to New York for Christmas and Eddie joined her there. Later they toured Mexico with a party of friends.

My daughter was born on 22 February in Vienna. A few days later I got a letter dated 22 February from Mexico City. Eddie wrote that he had suddenly felt worried about me and had gone to pray for me and the child I was expecting in the church of the miraculous holy Virgin of Guadeloupe. Eddie was not then a Roman Catholic, but was soon to become one.

He enclosed a picture of the Madonna who had converted the Mexican Indians to Christianity after appearing to a peasant near a shrine sacred to the Mexican pagan earth-goddess. The Church had disbelieved the humble Indian's story, and had asked him for proof. The Madonna gave it. To the bishop's amazement, the peon's arms were suddenly filled with flowers such as had never bloomed before in winter on the high plateau where Mexico City now stands. The miracle was accepted, and the church sacred to the Virgin of Guadeloupe was built.

Eddie knew of course approximately when I was expecting my child, but of the exact day he was as ignorant as I was. Naturally I had been rather frightened when the pains started, and I was taken to the hospital. I checked with Eddie later, and discovered that, allowing for the difference in time, the hour he had spent in church was the same as that in which Diana was born. A coincidence? I don't think so. All our lives we were able to read each other's thoughts, why not at a distance?

I suffered very little pain, and the baby was healthy and normal. She was christened Francisca Diana after her two godmothers, my sister-in-law and my Aunt Diana, Alice in memory of my grandmother, and Maria Guadeloupe in gratitude for my safe delivery thanks to Eddie's prayers. Later he brought me a gold medal of the Virgin which I pinned to the child's cot until she was old enough to wear it round her neck.

Eddie returned to Capri to complete the Fortino and by autumn the house was partially ready for Mona to live in, not that she could go there very often at that time, or even in the first years after its completion. Harrison's wealth and social position and her beauty brought sovereign duties to them both that they could not ignore. Prominent American politicians, visiting foreign statesmen, and writers and artists of importance had to be invited and entertained, as well as the cream of New York's society.

Mona, acclaimed as the best-dressed woman in America, had to live up to her reputation by travelling at least twice a year to Paris, where her dresses were specially designed for her; she could hardly spare the time even for that. The many houses that Harrison owned were continually being redecorated according to her whims and tastes, and the gardens she loved, whether in Palm Beach or on Long Island, needed her personal attention, no matter how many gardeners she employed.

It was an entirely public life, with very little privacy or leisure, and in later years the Fortino became a sort of retreat and escape for Harrison too from a world of which he had wearied. He had built up his financial empire until it towered above him like his own monument. There was little left to do but enjoy the fruits of his labours, and he had grown too old for that. Towards the end he counted the figs that ripened in the Fortino's gardens with much more interest than he did his dividends.

As for Mona, she was happier living on the island than she had ever been anywhere else. There she did not have to entertain anyone but real friends, she did not have to dress up any more but could give herself to the sea, diving into it from the rocks as she did every morning, relishing its cool embrace. She could spend all day in her gardens, weeding and planting; above all, in the beauties of her surroundings, she could forget her own.

17

It was two years after my first stay with them that I returned to Capri; because of my father-in-law's death and our subsequent move to Castolovice I had not travelled. Although Leopold didn't suffer as acutely at his father's dying as he had at his mother's three years earlier, it was nevertheless a time of mourning for both of us.

My father-in-law died surrounded by his entire family, to whom of course I then belonged. I had been alone with my father in his last hour in the sanatorium at Carlsbad; it had been a gentle, private death, a going to sleep, his hand in mine. I was not prepared for the almost public event that dying still was at that time among the Austrian aristocracy. Not only the immediate family attended, but also distant relations and friends, a doctor, a priest of course, a lawyer, and the servants. It had been so too at my mother-in-law's death.

To have to listen to each rasping breath of the death struggle in case some last word was said or wish expressed, to watch the administering of the last sacrament and to see a familiar face contort and grow un-recognizable had shocked me deeply. Had they been my parents who were dying I would in my sorrow have perhaps forgotten the indecency of those who stood by dry-eyed and stared so avidly at physical dis-solution. As it was, I felt deeply ashamed even of my own presence.

Soon after we had moved from Zasmuky to Castolovice I began to completely redecorate the castle. It was, I knew, a tactless thing to do, and I would have been surprised had my sisters- and brothers-in-law not resented it, since most people love and admire their childhood surroundings. My parents-in-law had had the fashionable taste of their day; everything had to be made to look very English. Vast amounts of chintz decorated with large cabbage roses covered most of the furniture, and curtained the windows. All the beds were Edwardian cages of brightly polished brass and every drawing-room was crowded with little tables on which stood photographs in silver frames, bronze knick-knacks, or even plaster statues – and all this in a house that was to a large extent still pure Renaissance!

I couldn't have lived there without getting rid of a lot of what it so incongruously contained, and trying to give back to the place its former dignity and splendour. There were some good tapestries, some fine carpets, a certain amount of furniture of the right epoch, and quite a few pictures of high quality. If my in-laws missed the familiar clutter they had known, they had to grant that the large and beautifully proportioned rooms with their painted ceilings and just a few pieces of the right furniture and tapestries were an improvement.

I had the village smith saw off all the brass head- and foot-boards from the beds and turned them into four-posters, covering the posts with the material I curtained the beds with. I hadn't needed to buy any new stuffs. One large room was entirely covered with a very ugly bright brick-red velvet; I had it torn down and sent to the wash-house as it was dirty. What the washerwomen did to it, I don't know, but it came back as hundreds of yards of the most beautiful pale peach-coloured material with a silvery sheen. After that I experimented with some dark green brocade curtains, sending them to the wash-house as well as some repellent bright blue satin ones. They were returned the softest lime, and the blue a pearly grey.

Of course, their colours were uneven, but just because of that I thought them more beautiful, as if centuries had mellowed and faded them. I was grateful to the washerwomen for such miracles of transformation, achieved probably by using a strong bleach, and I presented them with all the flowered chintz in the house. I'm sure that even now it still curtains many cottage windows in the village of Castolovice. I had enough pleasing material by then for bed-hangings and curtains throughout the castle, and what I needed to cover old chairs, stools and benches, I had collected years earlier in Zasmuky.

The Franciscan monastery there had been founded many centuries ago by Sternbergs. Its church was a resting place for their remains, and the friars were obliged to pray for their souls day and night. Leopold, as head of his family, was the monastery's patron, and I, as his wife, was the only woman allowed to enter the friars' quarters. If the idea had certain fascinations, what I was privileged to see was mostly disappointing.

There were by then very few friars left, and they were old and far from clean, like their cells. Only the monastery's library was interesting. It contained many illuminated missals of great beauty, which I greatly desired to possess. I'm quite sure the friars would have given them to me had I asked them to do so, for I saw that they had no idea of the treasures in their keeping; but I resisted the temptation. However, I had no scruples at all in accepting the prior's offer to exchange old vestments for new.

It seems there are changing fashions even in ecclesiastical clothes; they can be cut too high or too low, too wide or too short, as the prior explained. I begged him to buy whatever he thought suitable, and I was given in exchange great seventeenth- and eighteenth-century copes of flowered brocade threaded with gold, and equally rare and beautiful vestments. With these I covered the best of the furniture in Castolovice.

Leopold's father and mother, his famous Uncle Monschi and one of his brothers were buried in the garden of the monastery. My father-in-law had chosen the small plot for himself and his family in preference to the crypt under the church. In a year of flood all the coffins of the former Sternbergs had disintegrated, and their bones had become so inextricably mixed that all that could be done was to close the vault with cement. In the well-tended garden overlooking my in-laws' graves stood a stone crucifix with St John and the sorrowing mother looking up to the dying Christ. It had been designed and commissioned by my father-in-law and carved by a very gifted Czech artist.

I wonder what has happened to it? Soon after the communists

took over I heard that the monastery had been abolished, the friars dispersed. My parents-in-law's remains had been unearthed, they had not even been permitted the small piece of ground in which they had hoped for eternal rest. The village commissar had declared the land was needed for agricultural use. But that was still all in the unforeseeable future.

Meanwhile I had redecorated Castolovice and was quite proud of what I had achieved. I thought that even Eddie would approve. He wrote that he was too busy to leave, but asked if I would come for a month or two with the child to see how the Fortino had progressed. He said he would find us somewhere to live in Capri.

He had rented a villa on the Punta Tragara, the only level road on the island where a nanny could push a child in a pram. It was a small white-washed house with the domed roof and ceilings typical of Capri's Moorish-influenced architecture. Purple bougainvillaea rambled all over it, olive groves surrounded it, and beyond, hazed by their grey foliage, was a glimpse of the sparkling sea.

There was a friendly peasant woman who cooked and looked after us, and there was the white rabbit which Eddie proudly presented to my daughter on our arrival. It had pink eyes and a pink ribbon round its neck. He couldn't know that Diana was not quite old enough to appreciate his gift. She and the rabbit did play occasional games together on the terrace but the rabbit, who was more nimble on its four feet than the child, got the best of every contest by butting Diana into retreat with its head. Miss Dunkley, charmed by Eddie, did not protest at first, but when the animal, instead of sleeping in the hutch provided for it on the terrace, jumped into the child's cot, she became adamant. 'Either the rabbit goes or I do.' I told her it would hurt my cousin's feelings if we gave it away, and we compromised. From then the rabbit slept in my bed; it was very clean and house-trained like a dog.

Eddie lived in the Fortino then; he had arranged two rooms for himself with his own furniture in a small pavilion separate from the main house. It had a balcony from which one looked down on to the sea hundreds of feet below; the light and graceful furniture was all Empire, with shapes reminiscent of the chairs and couches and tables depicted on the walls of rooms in Pompeii and Herculaneum. There were a few fine Etruscan vases, many books, a beautiful, albeit fragmentary, head of a Roman youth and photographs and drawings portraying Mona. Otherwise, everything was white.

'Colour is for the north,' Eddie said, 'here nothing should compare with the views from the windows; sun, sky, sea and landscape are bright enough.'

Although the outside was washed a pale terracotta, the interior of the house was mainly white or off-white and cream, the floors amber marble, the high ceilings domed and white-washed. Many rooms, such as the library and the big dining-room, would be added later; then there was only a very large drawing-room, a small dining-room and two bedrooms with adjoining bathrooms and dressing-rooms upstairs.

Mona had sent a lot of furniture from New York. Eddie told me it had come from a house of Harrison's on Long Island which he had pulled down to make room for a small golf course and to enlarge Mona's garden there. The furniture was English eighteenth-century, more plain than ornate, and of a very fine quality. The sheen and warm glow of the polished wood were a pleasing contrast to the cool white of the upholstered sofas, chairs and curtains. 'Mona wanted this room to be as plain a background for her flowers, and perhaps for herself, as possible,' Eddie explained. 'It looks like nothing now, but you ought to see it when she's here,' he added.

'I think it's lovely,' I said, 'but why is it that everything is white and yet it isn't? There's a sort of sheen like mother-of-pearl everywhere.'

'It's a trick. All the white materials are interlined with pink, grey or yellow, and the walls were painted with coats of different colours before they were white-washed, which accounts for the iridescent lustre. Come, you must see Mona's bedroom.'

We walked up the short flight of marble steps that led from the hall and separated on a half-landing, leading from there to the two different apartments. Mona's bedroom was white too; one wall was all window, and framed what some consider the most beautiful view in the world, the Bay of Naples crowned by Vesuvius. Her bed was a curving, convoluted seashell carved in wood, resting on dolphin feet; an eighteenth-century phantasia of great charm. Whoever had designed it must have had in mind Venus sleeping in her ocean bed before she rose from the sea.

'How perfect,' I said appreciatively.

'It's very uncomfortable,' Eddie remarked. 'That chaise longue is amusing, don't you think? We found it in Venice.'

Indeed it was. It was intricately carved and painted with faint traces of gold, with a monkey sitting on its high back, holding a small parasol on a gilded bamboo cane over its head. The floors of the room were covered with white fur, and all the upholstery materials were of the coarse handwoven raw cream silk that was then still made in southern Italy. Mona's large dressing-room was all mirrored cupboards, and her bath was a sunken pool of pale pink marble.

Harrison's rooms looked north and windowed the olive-clad hills. They were more conventional, but very perfect, except for his black marble bath that rather reminded me of a tomb.

Beyond the large terrace and above the sea there was a separate building like a pavilion with a domed roof. It contained only one large room and all its walls were mirrored panels on which, among gold and silver trees and flowers, birds flew and monkeys played. It had been painted for Mona by Driand.

'It's a bit too rich for here, but Mona wanted to use the panels,' Eddie explained. 'So we built this separate room for them. It's nice to come into after the bright sunlight for drinks before lunch and in the evenings with the fire burning it's a sort of world in itself.'

The guest-house with its six bedrooms and bathrooms was only completed later, as were several of the other buildings. All were to be painted the same pale terracotta which brought a sort of unity to the different groups of buildings which all stood on different levels. Seen from the harbour the Fortino, with its domes and high stone walls, looked like a Moorish citadel.

The terraced gardens were being planted, promising something of their future beauty by the rarity and variety of plants and trees. Because of the hot, dry summers, few people living in Italy tried to grow much more than orange and lemon trees, bright geraniums and the native marguerites that did not mind the heat frothing in great white clouds from the rocks, pink bougainvillaea and oleander.

But Mona wanted every flower she had once known and thought beautiful in her gardens. Camellias, gardenias and magnolias to remind her of the American South where she had been born, blue jacarandas which she knew from Florida, scarlet flame trees she had seen in the tropics and the sweet-scented jasmines. All these grew well and rapidly in the mild Capri climate; wonderful orchids and ferns too in the shaded greenhouses she had built.

'It's that damn English lawn which she insists on having in front of the house,' Eddie complained. 'I have to keep a sprinkler going on it all through the year, and all the water has to come from the mainland by boat at incredible expense. Who ever heard of wanting to grow cowslips and primroses and daffodils and all our spring flowers in this climate? Not to speak of the large rose-garden. Yet somehow we manage. It's hard work, but who cares, as long as it makes her happy.'

I didn't see Mona that time. She only came a month later; meanwhile I had Eddie all to myself for the length of my stay, which I thoroughly enjoyed.

18

Confident that Madame Poisson would look after Leopold and the child, I had started off on my journey to Venice with much of the anticipatory excitement with which I had travelled towards it in former years. Not only was I looking forward to meeting Eddie, but to seeing Venice again, and the family Arrivabene who had added so much to the city's enchantment for me in the past. Even if Granny and her daughter Countess Arrivabene, both of whom I had been very fond, had since died, Loni, who had been believed shot towards the end of the war, had survived, I knew, and so had his sisters Niki and Madina.

I had written to Niki while I was still in Czechoslovakia asking for news. She had answered immediately that Loni had married at last, and that she was very happy about his choice, a young Venetian girl of great beauty, faultless ancestry, and considerable fortune. Madina had separated from her husband (both sisters had married Visconti brothers) and was in Venice with her children. 'When,' Niki asked, 'will I see you again?' She added that though she knew I would miss her mother, those of the family who were left were longing to welcome me to the Palazzo Papadopoli just as before. There was no mention of the jewels I had given to her mother to keep for me.

I had telegraphed from Paris that I was coming to Venice for a few days and would stay at the Grand Hotel with Eddie. Niki wired back saying we were expected with great pleasure. 'I'm rather doubtful I'll find the jewels,' I had told Leopold before I left. 'Anything can happen in wartime. If the Arrivabenes' survival depended on selling them, I couldn't blame them much.' Leopold shrugged. 'What's one loss more or less? At least this may have benefited friends, not enemies.'

I had not taken a sleeping compartment; it was cheaper to travel first class, however large the tip one had to give the conductor to ensure privacy and the right to open any window one pleased. Besides, this was a journey on which I had never been able to sleep more than the first few hours, too impatient for dawn and seeing the Swiss mountains unveil snow-covered peaks mirrored in the dark waters of the great lakes. As the train crept higher and higher there would be Alpine meadows still deep in snow, or vivid green or starred with flowers, and waterfalls cascading down from the high glaciers.

Then the sudden fearful plunge into darkness as the train entered the Simplon tunnel, and what seemed a lifetime, though it was barely an hour, of claustrophobic fears. The great weight of the mountains pressing down, the black walls of the tunnel closing in, now and then a lantern hung in some rock crevice revealing how near they were, the compartment growing ever more stifling and oppressive since all the windows had to be shut against the engine's fumes. Hands had to be tightly clasped to one's ears to avoid the pressure of changing altitudes or to shut out the thundering roar the train made in the confined spaces of the pass, before it emerged blessedly out into the bright sunlight and Italy.

Smiling faces. Even from the frontier guards the warm, all-enveloping glance that is like an embrace with which all Latins greet a half-way pretty woman. I would comb my hair and go to wash as best I could in the smelly lavatory. Lago Maggiore, its great expanse of shining water surrounded by mountains, villages, castles and villas clinging to its shore among orange and lemon groves, then soon Milan. Time to get out and have an espresso and to buy buns and oranges and salami. Return to the train; much shunting and bumping as it separated into two parts which different engines would take to Florence and Rome. And then the swift descent of the train rushing like a river towards the sea, past the sun-dappled lake of Garda down into the plains of the Emilia and the Veneto.

Verona and Vicenza, Mantova and Este, Bologna and Padova; evocative names, their mere sound recalling so much of art and history. Small towns, almost unchanged except for their loss of power since the past centuries in which they had grown and ruled, owing their wealth to the bounty of the sea. Then at last Venice, sovereign city of them all.

I had first met Niki and her father in Rome. My involvement with the entire Arrivabene family and Venice came only ten years later. When I was seventeen and still unmarried, my grandmother had taken me with her to Rome for the winter months and the social season of receptions and balls given in the great palaces of the Roman aristocracy or at the various embassies. Grateful as I was to be allowed the benefits of a Roman début, I knew that taking me there was a mere pretext for my grandmother's making the journey.

Though over sixty-five, she was very much in love. Signor Bordonaro, Principe di . . . (he had a string of Sicilian titles too long to list), had been first secretary at the Italian Embassy in Vienna for some years then became ambassador and had been recalled to the foreign office in Rome. It had been a long friendship, based primarily, I think, on Bordonaro's side, on the fact that only very few women in Viennese society spoke such perfect Italian as my grandmother did. He had never become very expert at speaking German or English. But she was also extremely useful to him. Thanks to her large international circle of relations, acquaintances and friends he could, at one of her small, select luncheon parties, or by having tea with her in the afternoon, gather more interesting political and social information in much greater physical comfort and with less tiresome effort than he could anywhere else.

He showed his appreciation and gratitude by courting her much as Disraeli must have courted Queen Victoria. Huge bunches of violets instead of primroses arrived twice a week, filling my grandmother's drawing-rooms with their scent. Parcels of books were constantly being delivered, or little notes marked 'By hand'. He took her to the opera where he had a permanent box – often I was allowed to go with them. It was always Verdi or Puccini, I must have seen *Tosca* at least six times.

Since my grandmother knew herself safe from any crude physical involvement, she felt free to indulge in romantic fancies. I wonder if she would not even have married Bordonaro if he had asked her to do so. He was only a few years younger than she was, and Omama knew that for her age she still looked remarkably trim and attractive. Her face was almost unlined, her china blue eyes undimmed, her hair, though growing rather sparse and dyed a reddish-gold, was smartly fluffed into curls by Vienna's best hairdresser, her clothes expensive and in the latest fashion. Naturally it came as a great shock to her when one day Bordonaro asked if he could come and introduce his fiancée, assuring my grandmother that she would approve of his choice. There was certainly nothing Omama could object to in Donna Diana. A handsome, healthy, intelligent and well-bred young woman, who treated my grandmother with almost daughterly respect and consideration. Nevertheless, after Bordonaro's marriage, Omama gradually lapsed into old age. She allowed her hair to turn white, which it had been anyway for years, and only recovered some of her former energy when

Bordonaro died suddenly from a heart attack. 'I warned him,' she declared with evident satisfaction, 'a young wife can be a terrible strain on the heart.'

But in those months Omama and I spent in Rome, Bordonaro was still a bachelor, coming to the Hotel Elysée twice a week with flowers, and if it was a warm and sunny day he had a carriage or his car waiting to take her for a drive through the gardens of the Villa Borghese or along the Via Appia. He even arranged for her to meet Mussolini since she very much wanted to see the great man.

She returned from her interview with the Duce in a state of triumphant elation, carrying a large photograph inscribed 'To my dear Alice Hoyos, Friend of Italy', signed Benito Mussolini. She had it set in an ornate silver frame and she would frequently gaze at it. 'What supreme power in those eyes!' she would exclaim.

Power of a different sort attracted her just as much. Through my grandfather Hoyos we were distantly related to the Orsinis. Prince Domenico Orsini was *Assistente al Solio* to the Pope, and at many ceremonies in St Peter's had to stand on the altar steps beside the Holy Father, draped in a long mantle of black lace. When it was not his turn to assist, Prince Colonna had to do so. It was a hereditary office held by the two families for many centuries. Domenico's younger brother Lelio Orsini was in the papal guards. Thanks to the help of these relations, my grandmother and I were received in private audience by the Pope.

We had to wait in the antechamber, veiled and dressed all in black. Uncle Lelio Orsini, who was escorting us, led me to the window on the pretext of showing me the view over St Peter's Square. Behind the crimson damask curtains, half-drawn against the bright sunlight, he pinched my bottom hard. Though this is considered a rough compliment if it happens to one in the streets of Rome, I had not expected it in the Vatican.

Pope Pius XI received us most graciously. We knelt of course, but he raised my grandmother, who was trying to kiss his toe, from her knees and gave her his hand so she could kiss his ring instead. He talked to her in German about Vienna and about the family Hoyos, and said he knew of their devotion to the Church. Obviously no one had told him that we were Protestants, and it certainly was not the right moment to enlighten him. Then he blessed us, and the audience was over. After that a photograph of the Holy Father joined that of Mussolini on my grandmother's desk.

A few weeks later there was to be one of the most splendid of papal

ceremonies in St Peter's Church, the beatification of a saint. People
came to take part from all over the world, believers and unbelievers.
My grandmother hadn't realized until it was too late that one needed
tickets to be suitably seated on one of the tiered stands that had
been erected on each side of the high altar. Diplomats, important guests
and the Roman aristocracy had their reserved seats there, and no more
were by then available, nor could they be bought. Yet she insisted on
going.

Even in St Peter's Square the crowd was dense. We pressed our way
through the entrance doors with some difficulty, to find that the greatest
church in the world was also filled with the largest number of people
I have ever seen or hope to see again gathered in one place. All that was
visible to us above the tens of thousands of heads were the pillars of
the central altar and the raised benches on which the cardinals sat in
rows of crimson and ermine, the archbishops in violet robes, and the
stands where the nobility of Rome, dressed in sombre black, had their
seats.

'That's where we have to go,' my grandmother pointed.

'It's impossible,' I protested.

'Nonsense,' she said. Small as she was, she shoved and pushed her
way through the crowd, calling at intervals in a loud, shrill voice
'Orsini, Orsini!' like a battle cry. I followed in her wake, acutely
embarrassed.

The Italian crowd, appreciative of eccentricity and madness, let us
pass. On and on she pressed, until finally we reached the pews in which
our startled relations, who had watched some of our spectacular
progress through St Peter's, made room for us on their benches. Princess
Orsini handed Omama, who was quite out of breath, a glass of wine.
Everyone came with picnic baskets to these long ceremonies.

Laura was Domenico's second wife, and an American by birth. She
looked very regal and beautiful with a diamond tiara holding her long
black lace veil, more diamonds at the wrists and neck, but I saw that
she was shaking with silent laughter. My grandmother's Anglo-Saxon
tenacity of purpose and brazen audacity had obviously delighted her;
the rest of our Italian relations looked less amused.

We had reached our, or rather their, seats, just in time. Christ's
representative on earth was approaching the high altar, announced
by a flourish of trumpets, carried high above the crowd in a golden
chair, wearing the triple crown and encased in gem-studded robes.
Great fans of peacock feathers waved, and there was a deafening roar
of applause. '*Viva il Papa.*' I thought of the gentle old man in his simple

white robes who had talked to us so kindly a few weeks ago, now so exalted and dehumanized a symbol of the power of the Church. The impassive face might have been that of a waxen image, only the gloved hands moved in ritual gestures of benediction. The splendid ceremony that followed lasted for three hours and even my grandmother was totally exhausted when we returned to our hotel.

Not that she tired easily. She could sightsee all day, and go to two or three evening receptions afterwards. She had incredible stamina as long as she was interested or found someone interested in her. Fortunately for me she didn't like going to balls. They started very late in Rome, after eleven, and continued till dawn. Sitting with all the elderly ladies on uncomfortable little gold chairs lined up against the wall through the night did not appeal to her.

My cousin Eddie Bismarck, who loved dancing as much as I did, was always willing to escort me and to bring me home. She thought him a suitable chaperon, little knowing that once in the ballroom we only met again when it was time to leave.

It was a good year for dances, there was one almost every night in one of the palaces. Tulle or net was the fashion in evening dresses then. Women and girls looked like many-petalled flowers in the layers of net, and it was a most pleasing sight when hundreds of couples revolved in those immense marble-floored ballrooms, enveloped in rainbow-coloured floating clouds of tulle.

In Rome, as in Vienna, the young unmarried and the married belonged to different sets, mingling only at dances, receptions, the race-course or in church. Only two of the Italian girls, most of whom were attractive, were considered beauties that year, Bona Aliotti and Niki Arrivabene. Competition was fierce among the young females of Rome. Somewhere a rumour started that 'Alas, poor Bona had the *castatore*, the evil eye. She had looked at a horse, and it had fallen dead at her feet.' This was in no way surprising since Roman cab horses were overworked and underfed and frequently died in harness. There followed other examples of the spells she cast, all equally nonsensical. Yet these did the poor girl's reputation more harm than if she had indulged in the utmost depravity.

After that, Niki ruled supreme. Almost as lovely as Bona, popular with the young of both sexes, distinguished as to birth, manners and reputation, she could well afford to be kind and generous to less fortunate girls, and she was always nice to me. Of course, I was no threat in the marriage market. If the Romans ever married foreigners, it was rich Americans. However, I never lacked dancing partners, and even had two dependable admirers, neither of whom I was the least bit in love with.

Prince Giuseppe Giovanelli was of rather unattractive appearance, his large nose his only outstanding feature, but he had other assets. His family was very wealthy and owned a palace in Venice, large country estates in the Veneto and the *Tempesta*, one of the most mysterious and beautiful of Giorgione's pictures. He was an eldest son, and there was not a girl in Rome who didn't hope to marry him. He had grown wary of pursuit and attached himself to me, assured that I couldn't possibly presume to have matrimonial intentions since I wasn't Italian.

And there was Pupo, Marchese di Bagno. His parents owned a perfect Palladian villa near Bologna. He was not much older than I was, and as vital and full of energy as the racing cars he drove. Everyone liked Pupo, and no one took him seriously. He was good-natured, frank, unaffected, always in love, but too young to be considered marriageable. Even my grandmother thought Pupo too much of a child to endanger my virtue, at least in broad daylight, and in an open racing car in which there wasn't even room for my legs since the exhaust pipes went right through it; I had to crouch above them like a monkey.

Generously she allowed me many morning drives with Pupo provided I was punctually back for lunch – after all it was spring, and Bordonaro was being very attentive. But I had discovered that in ninety minutes Pupo could drive to Ostia and back with enough time to spare for a quick exhilarating swim in the sea, provided he forced his Bugatti to the utmost speed it was capable of; we would arrive back at the hotel with engines smoking, and the pipes so hot that Pupo had to lift me out of the car. My legs would have been badly burnt had I slipped against the red-hot metal.

I don't think Omama knew that I was in much greater danger of losing my life than my virtue on these expeditions which forced Pupo to drive at such a reckless pace. But I was much more afraid of her disapproval should we not return in time than I was of speed, which I rather enjoyed. In any case, she was still of a generation to whom physical courage and daring were natural. Runaway horses, upsetting carriages, accidents when out hunting, these were risks any lady had to take. A fast racing car seemed to her no more dangerous than a mettlesome horse. A reputation for courage in her days had never stopped any girl from making a good marriage, quite the contrary. A reputation for being fast in other ways inevitably did.

In Rome, much as it had been in Vienna, young girls accepted the restrictions imposed on them without protest. Though competitive

within the narrow means permitted, and mildly jealous of each others'
successes, what they really envied were the glamorous young married
women, their freedom and independence, their lovers and their clothes.
To walk into a room with the imperial grace of Princess Paula Cajetani,
more beautiful even than the jewels she wore! Or to be able, as Princess
Paula Medici of the exquisite sad, pale face, to clown a whole dinner
party into uproars of laughter!

To resemble Princess Isabella Colonna, so slim, sleek and elegant,
and as quick to strike with her witty tongue as a viper! Even Countess
Dorothy Frasso, American by birth, plump and rather blowsy, was
envied for her uninhibited freedom of speech and behaviour, as well as
for her house, the Villa Madama, with its frescoes painted by Raphael.
There were many others, legendary even in their lifetime, whose names
I've since forgotten. They never spoke to us, they were not interested
in callow youth. But their glamour haunted us and our fantasies
endowed them with amorous adventures beyond any possible truth.

The men that accompanied them, husbands, friends or lovers, didn't
pay us any attention either, nor would we have liked it if they had.
What would have been the good? Divorce was impossible in Italy then.
On that one subject Mussolini and the Pope were in complete agreement.
And because of that, 'liaisons' became almost as binding and permanent
as marriages.

However attractive some of the bachelors of the older set, one knew
that none of them were free to marry, and no young girl would have
dared get involved with anyone's husband or established lover. Not
that there was much danger. No married man or bachelor would,
except in case of extreme provocation, have compromised a young
girl of his own class and nationality. However, as I had seen in Vienna
and was to learn in Rome, any girl of foreign origin was considered
fair game.

I had met Count Arrivabene at various receptions and balls. If I
had noticed him at all, it was because he was Niki's father. Though
probably no more than fifty then, he seemed an old gentleman to me.
But there was something puzzling about his face; I was drawn to look
at him frequently in an effort to recognize why it was so familiar. Then
suddenly I knew. Those curving nostrils and slanting eyes, the curling
hair, pointed ears and beard. That face had laughed and leered at me on
numerous sightseeing tours in museums and gardens and from
fountains carved in stone or marble.

'Look, just like Count Arrivabene!' I pointed out to my grandmother,
contemplating the smiling features of a small bronze figure on one of

our walks through an art gallery. My grandmother adjusted her *lorgnon* (she only wore glasses in private) and peered at the little figure with its goat legs and at what left no doubt as to its sex. 'No likeness at all,' she said indignantly, 'Count Arrivabene is one of Rome's most distinguished gentlemen, and this . . . Well, it's not in very good taste, is it?' She hurried on, drawing my attention to less realistic works of art.

At a reception at the Palazzo Colonna, Count Arrivabene singled me out, not much to my surprise, since he must have noticed my frequent glances at him on former occasions. My grandmother was sitting next to me, but she showed no disapproval when he led me away. He walked me through the various salons, pointing out the beauties of the frescoed ceilings, pictures and statuary. I knew somewhat more about art than most girls of my age. My comments seemed to surprise and please him, and my vanity was flattered. Then he asked me if I would come and have tea with him the next day in his house. Since I was so appreciative and knowledgeable, he would like me to view his own small collection.

'I'd love to,' I said delighted, 'I haven't seen Niki for weeks.' 'I'm afraid the children are with their mother in Venice, my wife hasn't been very well.' He drew a small flat gold notebook from his pocket and with a golden pencil wrote an address on a slip of paper. He tore it out and gave it to me. 'Tomorrow at half past four?'

'But would we be alone?' I asked anxiously.

He laughed. 'I wouldn't want anyone to disturb us.'

'Then I'm afraid I can't come,' I said firmly.

'But dear child, there's nothing to fear, I'll certainly respect your virginity, if that's what's worrying you. Tomorrow then.'

He walked away leaving me blushing and angry. Old goat. Did he think I didn't know what kind of legs were concealed under his smart striped trousers? But I was even more furious with myself than I was with him. Vain, silly fool for having even for a moment believed that it was my knowledge of art that he had admired.

I returned to the Elysée, a small, very respectable, family hotel which overlooked the Borghese gardens, in which my grandmother had an apartment, and I a small room adjoining hers. In one of the corridors competing for the bathroom I had met a young American girl called Sally. She was touring Europe with an aunt. Since my grandmother doubted that she was a fit friend for me to have, as she was always rather extravagantly dressed and had a loud laugh, I used to meet her when my grandmother rested in the afternoons, in a remote dark writing-room downstairs. Sally was, I thought, very attractive, and I knew she was much worldlier than I was.

'Would you like to see a beautiful palace tomorrow afternoon?' I asked her. 'And have tea with a genuine Italian nobleman?'

'Oh, do let's go!' she said enthusiastically.

'The trouble is, I can't, I've got to go to the British Embassy for tea with my grandmother,' I explained. 'Lady Sybil Graham is somehow related.' I didn't mention her niece, my friend Joan Marchbankes, whom I was longing to see again since every moment with her meant laughter. She had the most bizarre sense of humour I think I've encountered in my life; I didn't want Sally to be jealous. 'Count Arrivabene will be just as pleased to see you, as he would have been to see me. All he wants is to show his picture collection.' But after all, she was a friend, perhaps I should warn her. 'You know what Italians are – even if he's an old gentleman, be careful, Sally.'

'Sure,' she laughed. 'What can I lose?'

Sally went. On her return she said that the old Count, though very polite, had been rather stiff and distant, and had listened without comment to her explanation of why she had come alone. He had shown her a few dark pictures and given her tea, a miserable tea she said, not even a biscuit, and then excused himself for having to leave for his club. And nothing else? Nothing. Sally left the week afterwards for Vienna with her aunt. I gave her some addresses and letters of recommendation to various young men that I knew would appreciate her uninhibited and courageous attitude towards life.

Count Arrivabene bowed to me stiffly whenever we met after that, but never spoke to me again. Niki returned from Venice and was as friendly as before. In late spring my grandmother went back to Vienna and I joined my father, who was very ill in Carlsbad.

19

Years later my husband and I, accompanied by my daughter and her nanny Miss Dunkley, travelled to Venice. I had not been well after a minor operation, and sea-bathing had been recommended, so we stayed at the Lido. While we were there, Henlein, the Sudeten German leader, demanded independence for his people, nominally within the framework of the Czechoslovak republic. This would, if accepted, mean handing over the frontier fortifications to the Germans. President Benes refused. It seemed possible that Hitler would intervene on behalf of his compatriots. Leopold, advised by letter that there might be partial mobilization, thought he should return home, but he saw no reason why we shouldn't stay. 'I'd rather have you here than there if anything does happen,' he said, 'though I'm sure Hitler won't risk war because of the Sudeten. It will probably all blow over in a week or two.'

In the end he was right, though it took over a month until he wrote that he felt it was safe for us to come home. He had advised me before he left to contact the Weiningers in Switzerland should I be in need of money. I soon was. The Excelsior was expensive, and also, since I became bored and lonely after he had left, I found much comfort in shopping in Venice.

The Weiningers were Jewish friends of ours who had fled from Germany and had rented our former home the lodge in Zasmuky for a summer, hoping to find peace and safety there, but had then moved on to Switzerland. We had asked them to keep what they owed us in rent in case we ever needed money abroad – there were currency restrictions in Czechoslovakia even then.

Leopold and I had rarely been separated from each other, and I missed him. As the season on the Lido drew to its close the weather changed, as it always does there in mid-September. The sea became too cold for swimming, the beach deserted, and the hotel grew emptier every day. Service became poor, the food inadequate, and Nanny started to complain. Mice in the child's bedroom, scorpions in the bath, the milk no longer fresh, and the butter rancid. But what was I to do? Leopold wrote that there had been certain incidents that might still bring a crisis, and that I was to wait.

More and more often I fled to Venice, escaping into its timeless dream-like unreality, roaming its narrow streets, wandering into churches and palaces to marvel at the riches they contained. Frequently too I would take the child and Miss Dunkley to walk around St Mark's Square and to sit at one of the tables at Florians for lunch or tea. 'The greatest and most splendid drawing-room in the world,' Piazza San Marco is rightly called. 'If you sit in it long enough, anyone you have ever known will eventually walk by,' so at least I had read.

Sailors of every nation came and went, some belated tourists, but no one I knew. And then one day when I was laboriously reading the Italian papers, trying to find news of Czechoslovakia, and Diana was feeding the pigeons with Miss Dunkley, there suddenly was Niki Arrivabene laughing down at me, quite unchanged since I had seen her last in Rome ten years ago. She held a small boy by the hand, who was about my daughter's age. She sat down. How gladly, and with what relief I answered all her questions and read the sympathy in her charming face.

'Look here,' she finally said, 'half our house is rented and we fill what's left. There's Granny and my mother, Loni, Madina and I and our children. Otherwise of course I would ask you to stay with us. But in any case,' Niki decided, 'you can't go on living on the Lido. You'll die of melancholia there at this time of year. Have you any money?'

'More than enough,' I said. I had since I contacted the Weiningers who had sent the amount they owed us to a bank in Venice, opening an account in my name.

'Then go to the Grand Hotel. And come to our house tonight after six. You never met my mother, I think? She was rarely in Rome that winter. Daddy died, did you know?' I said I was sorry, though secretly much relieved.

'Loni's the only male Arrivabene left now. He's been rather ill, he works too hard, poor sweet. Well, you'll see them all tonight. Look, our children have made friends already.' They were indeed feeding the pigeons together, eyeing each other solemnly, Miss Dunkley hovering over them.

We moved to the Grand Hotel that afternoon, then, that evening and every following evening throughout the next weeks I stepped into my gondola and with a thrill of anticipation pronounced the magic words, 'Palazzo Papadopoli.'

To approach it along the Grand Canal was in itself enchantment. Palaces to right and left mirrored their crumbling splendour in the darkening waters. The gentle rocking of the gondola, the rhythmic thrust of the oar, the hiss and lisp of small waves breaking against stone and marble are sounds so typically Venetian that they have become part of the sibilant dialect still spoken by its people. Then the great marble arch of the Rialto and, just before reaching the bridge, the tall, square block of severely classical Renaissance architecture looming immense, the Palazzo Papadopoli.

'I really don't know what you think is so special about those Arrivabenes,' a cousin of Leopold's who had often stayed in Venice said, when she came to visit us in Czechoslovakia. 'Granted they are all very good-looking, and somewhat better educated than most Italians of their class. But they're so eccentric and precious, and really almost incestuously in love with each other. And so arrogant and proud. I really can't see what there is to be so proud of. They have no money. Well, perhaps the two married girls will be better off once old Visconti dies, but Loni has nothing but his palace and a mother and grandmother to support. His only income is from renting the Papadopoli in the season to rich Americans. Did you know that the family actually had to move into the attics to save money?'

In a superficial sense it was all true. But it was also rather obvious that our cousin neither knew the Arrivabenes well, nor had she seen those attics under the vast roof of the palace, in which my friends lived among clouds like the beautiful gods, goddesses and nymphs on a ceiling painted by Tiepolo. Literally among clouds, huge billowing white and gold clouds and swirling draperies all made of plaster, flowing out from walls and ceiling, suspended from arches and pillars in nearly all the many rooms which I was to get to know so well.

Each member of the family had a self-contained apartment, and I was taken from one to the other by Niki on the evening when a rickety lift had carried me up to those Olympian heights for the first time. Countess Arrivabene received me in the big drawing-room. She had been famed for her beauty in her youth; tall and dignified, she moved rather stiffly – I only knew later how much she suffered from arthritis. Her features were still very perfect, age had only mellowed them, as it does antique marble. She was gracious but reserved and it was only much later that she showed me her rooms.

They were like a museum. Unlike other women of her time and class she had seriously studied archaeology, travelled much, and brought back from various sites and excavations objects of too early a date for me to be able to appreciate them. Pottery shards, bits of glass, strangely shaped stone objects and pins and bracelets of copper or brass, with notes attached, littered the shelves in her rooms and there were books everywhere.

Niki's rooms were all white and gold, golden stars shone from the ceiling between the clouds, and the walls of her bathroom and the bath itself were entirely encrusted with seashells.

I had only met Niki's sister Madina once or twice in Rome. She was several years younger than Niki, and still in the schoolroom then. A quiet, dreamy, very beautiful child, as fair as Niki was dark. But when I saw her again in Venice her loveliness had become quite extra-ordinary. I have never seen greater distinction and grace of movement and gesture. There was something ethereal, almost unreal about her beauty, and she seemed to move and have her being in some remote world of her own. She reminded me of an Ondine in search of a human soul.

Her rooms were entirely appropriate. She slept in a bed hung with sea-green silk, surrounded by water. A small river, contained in a sort of canal lined with turquoise-coloured tiles, seashells and bits of glass that gleamed like jewels, flowed perpetually round her room. 'It keeps me cool,' she explained. I quite understood. 'Chaste nymph of the shaded secret pools and streams,' how could she sleep otherwise than surrounded by water?

It was late when we finally came to Loni's apartment that evening. Niki had excused his not having been able to receive me in the drawing-room because he still had to spend a lot of time in bed after a severe attack of bronchitis. I had never met him before. He had been at a naval academy when I was in Rome. I wondered if he would resemble his father, but there was nothing of the satyr about Loni's looks.

He welcomed us wearing a dressing gown of coarse white silk rather like a monk's robe, and I was struck by his likeness to the saints and knights painted by El Greco. Those narrow pale faces with their haunting dark eyes, the expressive hands, those elongated forms posed in dramatic attitudes, the exaggerated gestures of pathos or ecstasy were all his. How much his sisters cherished him was obvious to me even then. They fussed over him, enquired about his comforts, ran to help him as he mixed a cocktail for me. I also realized that I had been brought to him on approval, in the hope that I might distract and amuse him. Next day a great bunch of headily scented tuberoses arrived at my hotel with a note begging me to call again in the evening from Loni. So I had been a success.

After that I went to the palace every night. In the big drawing-room, presumably built for entertaining, I only found guests rarely. The Arrivabenes really only enjoyed entertaining each other. Often I would find Granny sitting there laying a patience game or playing cards, chess or backgammon with her daughter. I had soon learnt to call her Granny as they all did. Princess Papadopoli was over eighty, and Austrian by birth, the daughter of a famous general. She liked to talk German to me. She was tiny and rather wizened, but bright and alert and had a much keener sense of humour than the rest of her family.

Except for Loni's valet Celura, I never saw any servants in those apartments. I suppose there must have been a cook and a kitchen somewhere, but I never saw either, nor, as far as I could ascertain, was there a dining-room. Like the celestials, the Arrivabenes didn't seem to need food. Only once did I have a meal, in Loni's room where I had stayed much later than usual to hear one of Hitler's most aggressive speeches concerning Czechoslovakia.

Loni always had a bottle of brandy in his room which I ruthlessly depleted. None of the family drank anything but an occasional glass of wine. That night I was also very hungry. 'Don't you ever eat?' I asked Loni.

'But of course,' Loni said, 'what would you like?'

'Anything. Spaghetti?'

He went out, to tell Celura I suppose, who appeared an hour later with two golden plates engraved with the Arrivabene coat of arms and their motto, 'Arrived in time'. It seems some great battle had been won by the fortuitous appearance of one of Loni's ancestors with his troops, hence the name. However, the spaghetti had not arrived in time. It was cold, dry and quite unpalatable and when Loni went to fetch some wine I fed it to one of the many cats that freely roamed the Papadopolis.

Loni's apartments were rather austerely masculine, and devoid of the stucco decorations that embellished the others. There was instead a definitely nautical touch. The round windows were reminiscent of portholes, there was much white linen and dark blue upholstery edged with rope. After all, he was a captain in the Italian navy.

One evening he led me through a door so cleverly fitted into the mahogany panelling that I could never have discovered it myself and down a narrow winding staircase. 'This is the most valuable thing I still own,' he said, opening another door. 'I couldn't let the Americans have it. Yet the rooms could easily be dismantled; I could get a fortune for them if I sold them, and God knows we could do with the money. But I won't. One day I will have to marry, my name will be extinct if I have no heir. Can you think of a more splendid apartment for a bride?'

Indeed I couldn't. 'It's like a jewel box!' I exclaimed. Three small golden rooms, the walls hung with yellow Chinese silk, the panelling and doors golden Chinese lacquer with a raised design of little men in big hats fishing among bridges and pagodas; all the furniture was Venetian eighteenth-century rococo, all in the most perfect condition, and there was a great golden bed, intricately carved, and so voluptuously wide and inviting that I sat down on it.

'Oh, please don't,' said Loni. Startled, I jumped up. Had I creased the embroidered silk cover? 'Forgive me,' he apologized. 'I just don't like to see anything touched here. I'm superstitious about these rooms. I take no women here.' He glanced briefly at the golden bed. 'I'm keeping it for the future.'

'You don't consider me a woman then?' I teased him.

He looked at me thoughtfully. 'Not really any more,' he said, 'I've grown too fond of you for that.'

Years later Loni was to find the flawless gem for that perfect setting. Of as great a Venetian family as was his own, a young girl who could have stepped straight out of a fresco by Veronese and whom Tiepolo would have depicted again and again, a true Venetian beauty with a complexion of peaches and cream, the small head so neatly furled in auburn gold, and neck, shoulders and breast the lustre of mother-of-pearl.

However, at the time I met him he was still involved with a married woman older than himself. He never spoke of her to me, he would have thought it most dishonourable to do so, but Niki hinted to me there was someone, although she mentioned no name.

It was obvious that some woman frequented his apartment. There were fashionable magazines that he never would have read, strange robes in his bathroom he never would have worn, and precious objects of modern make that he certainly could not have bought himself. Gold pillboxes and cigarette cases, a golden plaque with evening prayers engraved on it by his bedside, a woman's hand on his desk in gilded bronze, obviously cast from the plaster mould of a real hand.

One evening I held it in mine, looked at the distinct lines of the palm, and with a slight shudder put it back on the desk. 'Poor woman,' I said.

'What do you mean?'

'Well, she's dead, isn't she?'

'The nonsense you sometimes talk.' I saw he was very angry. 'Why?'

'Her lifeline. It's not a young hand. The cast must have been taken when she was over forty. It ends about then.'

I was proved almost right a couple of years later. The owner of the hand died suddenly in an accident. On the evening of my revelation the gondola which Celura called was announced much earlier than usual to take me back to the Grand Hotel. I had displeased Loni.

Poor Loni. His life wasn't easy at that time. He had had to give up his naval career and his independence for the sake of his family. A fortune recklessly depleted by his father could only be partially recovered by strict economy and frugal living; they all accepted this and tried bravely to be practical, but none of them really knew how. Loni took his responsibilities as head of the family very seriously. But being by nature generous, gentle and kind he was unable to enforce the necessary discipline. His health suffered under the never-balanceable weight of financial stress.

How often he must have longed for the freedom of the seas and for undemanding male companionship! Only too often I know he felt stifled by the female adoration that enclosed him. Not only that of his family, but that of the women that pursued him, attracted by his good looks and background, and whose appeal to his masculine vanity he could not resist. He had to possess them, and succeeded only too easily. They were more difficult to get rid of than to acquire, and often his family had to come to his aid to disentangle him from romantic involvements of which he had wearied.

Although of course there had been the usual amorous approaches which every Latin male feels it is his duty to make when he meets an attractive young woman, Loni and I had soon become friends. What he needed from me was sympathy and understanding, not sex, of which he had more than enough. He liked to talk about himself and his problems, and I was a good listener. More than that, I was gifted with much imagination and I had the capacity to mirror others as they wished to be seen. The picture I could give Loni of himself, even if somewhat exaggerated and overdramatized, satisfied him.

I often wondered what Granny and Countess Arrivabene thought of the long evenings I would spend alone with Loni in his rooms. I doubt they believed we were only talking, but they never showed any disapproval. In fact they were very kind to me. Sometimes Loni had to go to the mainland on business for a day or two and occasionally he left a message that he had guests and would I mind spending the evening with his mother or his sisters, if they were in Venice and not in Milan with their husbands. In a way it was all equally enjoyable. The girls and I had many interests in common, and we were never at a loss for subjects of conversation.

For my sake the radio was always turned on at six in case there might be news from Czechoslovakia. Leopold had written to reassure me that everything would be all right soon, but that I should wait. By then I didn't mind. Occasionally Loni would insist on listening to Mussolini's frequent speeches, his face grave, while Niki held her ears to shut out the sound.

Because the family disliked fascism, they tried to ignore it. Its crude vulgarity was distasteful to them and so was the opportunism that had tempted so many of their friends and relations into the party. They were Venetians, citizens of a sovereign republic, and even if it had ceased to exist, its ideals were still theirs. All the clamour about *Italia, Patria* seemed ridiculous to them. Like many other Italians they had great regional loyalty, but no general feeling of patriotism.

During the evenings when I was alone with Countess Arrivabene and Granny we played cards, three-handed bridge and other games at which I inevitably lost. I much preferred it when they talked to me of the Venice of their youth. I would question them about D'Annunzio, whom they had known well. He had expressed his admiration for Countess Arrivabene in several of his novels.

'Such a common little man, and so ugly, like a hairless monkey,' Granny said. 'Quite bald, even when young.'

'But what a great poet!' her daughter exclaimed, 'and such a beautiful voice, so seductive when he read or quoted from his works.'

'Yes, even great ladies . . .' Granny sighed, but did not continue, having met her daughter's eye. 'And how marvellously he wrote of Venice. You have read *Il Fuoco* of course?'

I admitted I hadn't. Countess Arrivabene started to quote in Italian. 'Like a weary courtesan bent under the weight of her jewels,' was all I understood.

'The Morosini?' I asked. I had met her, she was very old and bent and covered with gold chains and bangles, her reputation for past conquests legendary.

'Certainly not. It was the Palazzo Dario he was describing. Surely you've noticed it? It leans sideways and is encrusted with different-coloured marbles like jewels. It almost faces your hotel!'

'And did he love the Duse very much?' I would question them. 'Can artists ever really love? And both were great artists, but how splendidly they made each other suffer.'

'Finally he killed her,' Granny said. 'Threw her down from the rocks.'

'Only in his novels, Mother. I don't see him any more,' Countess Arrivabene added. 'It seems he's quite mad now, and writes speeches for Mussolini. He lives in a sort of museum to himself on the lake.'

'And the Marchesa Casati with her veils and leopards and negroes? Wasn't she very extraordinary?'

'Not really. She had a very white skin that freckled easily in the sun, that's why she wore veils. The leopards weren't leopards at all but cheetahs, that can be tamed like dogs and she only kept those Africans to look after them. She was quite a nice and rather ordinary person, fond of animals.'

When at last Leopold wrote that I could safely return I was unhappy to leave. I felt that if I could have been born into a family of my choice it would have been that of the Arrivabenes, and Venice my home. I think they too regretted my going. I promised to come back and visit them with my husband the following spring.

I had persuaded Leopold that he must meet the Arrivabenes, and he too felt he ought to thank them for all the kindness they had shown me. In March, half a year later, we motored to Vienna, intending to stay there for a couple of days before we flew to Venice. Although there had been a lot of unrest in Austria after the assassination of Dollfuss and a closer alliance with Germany seemed inevitable, the sudden brutality of the so-called *Anschluss*, the annexation of the country by Hitler, took everyone by surprise except for the Austrian Nazis who had helped organize it.

I will never forget the horror of the night and morning on which it took place, nor could Leopold. We had dined with Ulrich Kinsky and his second wife Mathilde. He had been one of Leopold's best friends for many years and I had grown fond of the beautiful, gentle Mathilde but I had never been able to learn to like him very much. I didn't know what to talk to him about. He was one of the best shots in the country, he flew his own private plane expertly, he was a good polo player, and the team he supported the finest in Austria. His country estates in Czechoslovakia were immense and very profitable, his palace one of the most splendid in Vienna. He was a good-looking, good-natured man, but to me he always seemed somewhat lacking in foresight and intelligence.

Nevertheless, what happened that night, after we had dined sumptuously at his house in Vienna where several members of the Austrian government had been present, with whom he was involved through being the head of various international sports organizations, came as a great shock to Leopold and to me as well as to them. Even if we had feared Austria's independence endangered for some time, none of us, except possibly Ulrich, knew how near the end was. After dinner we had turned on the radio. The news was threatening and grew even more so every hour until morning when there was no hope left. Austria was German. The despair on the faces of the members of the government before they hurried home, Mathilde's tears that she shed for a country that wasn't even hers and which had not treated her too kindly, and Ulrich's ever more open triumph remain unforgettable to me.

'Why?' we were to ask ourselves again and again. It couldn't have been opportunism, for Ulrich had a great position and vast wealth. Ambition? Did he hope to gain some supreme political power under Hitler? Or did he really think that Austria's loss of sovereignty would benefit its people? We had always believed him a patriot, why then did he turn traitor? Was he seeking perhaps some form of personal revenge on the class he belonged to because of their strict religious conventions that made his wife a social outcast because his former marriage had not been annulled by the Church? Did he believe Hitler would change all that?

We were never to know. We didn't see him again. Perhaps in the short time he was still to live his enthusiasm for Nazi Germany lessened after he had been in closer contact with its representatives. He died of a heart attack some months later. Mathilde took her children and her jewels to the Argentine.

After that night my husband refused to fly with me to Venice. He had many relations in Vienna who might be threatened. Our plane tickets were for the same morning and he urged me to leave, saying he would try and join me in a couple of days. 'Go to your Arrivabenes, better friends than some of mine, no doubt.' He was very bitter about Ulrich. I protested that I didn't want to leave him under the circumstances, not certain what sort of trouble he might get involved in, but he begged me to go.

It was easier said than done. The airport was in a state of total confusion, the noise of planes overhead deafening when I entered the building. As I had my tickets checked at the desk I suddenly saw Louis Rothschild beside me. I knew his brother Baron Alphonse and his sister-in-law Clarisse much better than I did him. They had always been great friends of Leopold's, Clarisse perhaps more so than I liked when I was first married. But I had often dined and danced in Louis's Palais in Vienna.

He was an elderly bachelor, a small neat-featured man, and very witty in a quiet way. Though I had met him frequently, I didn't know very much about him except that he had extraordinary physical courage. He played in Ulrich Kinsky's polo team. It was obvious that he could neither ride nor see very well, he always wore glasses. Only rarely did he hit the ball, and the cry 'Louis down' was frequent on the polo field. Quite unperturbed, he would pick himself up, remount his pony, and continue in the game.

'Where are you off to, Baron Louis?' I asked, delighted to see him. With all the confusion around me I knew he would be a help. 'Are you coming to Venice with me?'

'I hope so,' he smiled.

Two men in brown uniforms with swastika armbands approached us and one of them tapped Louis on the shoulder. '*Sind Sie der Jude Rothschild?*' he asked.

I saw him flush, but it was from anger, not fear. 'Baron Rothschild,' he said icily. They led him away.

I was so shaken that I started to cry, although I need not have shed as many tears for him as I did. We later heard from some of his fellow prisoners – scores of people were imprisoned in the first days that followed the *Anschluss* – with what courage, guile and humour he had confronted and confused his jailors. They were Austrian Nazis, and new to their profession. After the news spread through Vienna that Baron Louis had been arrested, his valet arrived at the prison in a van, which contained not only large amounts of luggage, but a bed and bed-linen, lamps, carpets and tapestries as well as orchids from the Rothschild greenhouses, peaches, grapes and wine from the Rothschild cellars, and a varied assortment of edibles of the most expensive kind. The prison guards were so amazed and impressed that, knowing no precedent, they let the valet in with all he had brought. He had explained that all he wanted to do was to make the *Herr Baron* comfortable.

Louis was soon deprived of most of these luxuries, but by then he had become popular with the prison guards. And when these were changed and replaced by German Nazis who were more brutal, he confounded these by quoting from Hitler's *Mein Kampf* which he had learnt by heart. Also, he was an expert at keep-fit exercises, and soon all his fellow prisoners and the bored guards were practising handstands and kneebends and goose-stepping under his command.

Of course he suffered insults and occasional brutal ill treatment. But he could take it. He was courageous, resilient and resourceful. The fate of Vienna's Jewish community and the thousands that had been employed and protected by the Rothschilds and whom he was unable to help caused him greater anxiety than his own survival. After less than a year, through the combined effort of members of his family in England and France, he was released in exchange for a large sum of money in foreign currency and allowed to leave for America.

But to return to the airport. Wondering what I could have done to help Louis, and badly frightened, I pressed through the excited crowd. German uniforms were in evidence everywhere, and I was told that the plane for Venice and Rome had been diverted to another runway. When I came out into the open I saw why. The sky was dark with German planes and the noise they made terrifying; one landed every minute.

I can't remember who finally guided me to my plane, nor how I got in. Its propellers were moving and it seemed ready to take off. Not that I knew anything about aeroplanes, this was to be my first flight. The pilot, or co-pilot (there were no stewardesses then), showed me to my seat. It was a very small plane compared to those of these days. I looked around, seeing pale and tense faces. There was an old man sobbing into his handkerchief; I wondered how many of these people were trying to escape.

'Why don't we leave?' I asked the young pilot who stood at the open hatch watching with evident admiration the precision with which the German planes were landing. '*Patienza, Signorina*,' he laughed, pointing to the sky. More and more planes were flying in.

But after another twenty minutes' wait the pilot's patience must have worn thin. The hatch was closed, the plane began to shudder and tremble, the noise of the engines deadened in the general uproar of sound. Had I known anything about flying I would have had every reason to be frightened as we took off. But I had no idea how short the runway was nor that we rose at an angle too steep for safety and only narrowly missed colliding with an incoming German plane. Then blue skies, blessedly empty except for a few clouds, the laughing young co-pilot who explained the danger that had threatened, only averted, he said, by superb aviatory skill and daring, and soon, below us, the sea crowned by Venice.

I went to the Grand Hotel, took a room that faced the Dogana and the Salute, and called up Loni. I told him from what I had fled. He sounded full of sympathy and concern. 'Come as soon as you can,' he said. 'We are all longing to see you and to hear all about it.' I slept for some hours then took the gondola to the palace. Nothing had changed, neither Venice nor the attics of the Papadopoli, nor the kindness, affection and understanding of my friends.

❧ 22 ❧

Three days later Leopold arrived, as I had hoped he would. 'There wasn't much I could do to help in Vienna,' he told me despondently. 'They've locked up the Hohenberg brothers, Schuschnig, Prince Carol Emile Fürstenberg, your cousin Balti Hoyos, members of the government, many others. I thought I might as well join you here. I don't want to see Vienna ever again.' It was a heartbreaking thing for him to confess. So much of his youth had been spent and happily mis-spent there, many of his closest relations still lived there, it was as much his town as Prague.

'You can't imagine,' he told me, 'with what enthusiasm the Viennese seemed to welcome the Nazis. German flags waving all over the town, and, like Ulrich, friends and even relations changing their shirts overnight.'

I told him about Louis's arrest at the airport. He hadn't heard. 'I can't think of anyone who has done more for Vienna than the Rothschilds. *Oh, das goldene wiener Herz* – Vienna's heart of gold – except for a few, all cowardly opportunists turning like weathercocks in whatever direction the wind blows strongest.'

There was no comforting him that night. He got very drunk, and I didn't try to hinder him as it seemed the only available anaesthetic.

Early next morning, being careful not to wake him, I went out on to the balcony that adjoined our rooms. It overlooked the sea, the Dogana, the church of Santa Maria della Salute, and the entrance to the Grand Canal. I breathed in the fresh clean air from the sea and the stench of sewage, mud and decay from the canal, which are both so much a part of Venice, with equal pleasure. The baroque convolutions that decorated the dome of the church of the Salute like great golden curls caught the morning light. In the past, Venetian women had washed their curls with urine to bleach them gold in the sun, I remembered.

I found Leopold awake when I returned to our rooms. He seemed none the worse for the night's excesses, and after having consumed a large breakfast, he said he wanted to go shopping. 'Let's buy some presents for your Arrivabenes,' he said, 'and let's invite them all for dinner tonight. And then let's leave, I want to go home now, don't you? I can't help feeling we'll be Hitler's next venture. Now Austria is gone we are surrounded by Germans on all three sides. All he need do is walk in.'

'Of course I want to go home,' I said. 'I've never left the child for so long, though I suppose she's all right with Dunkley.'

'Why not call them up?' Leopold suggested. 'I couldn't from Vienna, but we can from here.'

We did, and we talked to Diana who said hesitantly between long pauses that she had found a dead bird in the garden and that she and Nanny had buried it properly with flowers.

We bought some presents for the child and a pretty gold and enamel Victorian bracelet for Niki. I had to stop Leopold from buying anything more for the Arrivabenes. I tried to explain that they all had too much or too little to accept gifts readily, but I don't think he understood. 'It's a sort of pride,' I said. 'How odd, I would take anything anyone gave me with pleasure,' he laughed.

They all came to dine. Leopold had carefully ordered not only an opulent meal, but also a well-planned one, with all the wines to match the different courses. Knowing the Arrivabenes' frugal habits, I was not surprised to see that they neither ate nor drank very much.

Conversation was rather formal and stiff. I prayed Leopold would keep it so instead of trying to entertain Countess Arrivabene with the sort of jokes with which he usually amused his friends. However, on discovering that Granny spoke German, he turned to her with relief. They discussed Austrian families she had once known, and their descendants whom he knew, the sad end of the monarchy, and, I think, much else, because both were visibly enjoying each other's company and spent most of the evening together.

Loni, who sat beside me, was very silent all through the meal and played nervously with his napkin, folding and re-folding it while Niki watched with unconcealed amusement. After dinner Leopold and Loni retired to another table with their brandies. Countess Arrivabene and Granny had left us for some moments, and Niki and I were alone together.

We looked at the two men, Leopold leaning backward in his chair relaxed and comfortable, very much at ease. Loni leaning forward, tense and alert. I tried to view them quite impartially. Neither, I thought, gained or lost by comparison. My husband's physique fully expressed all the rough self-assured strength of the north, while Loni's Greek perfection of figure and face countered it with all the subtle civilization, expressible in the human form, of the Mediterranean south.

I unwrapped the bracelet. 'I tried to stop him,' I told Niki. 'But one can't. Please take it, he's so grateful to all of you for having been so kind to me. He wanted to buy presents for you all. You see, the only way he can express himself is by generosity.'

'I thoroughly approve,' Niki laughed. 'I think it's lovely.' She clasped it round her wrist. 'He rather dwarfs you,' she said. 'He's like a friendly fairy-story giant.'

'I don't think Loni likes him,' I ventured. 'He was oddly quiet and nervous at dinner. Did you notice?'

'Of course I did. But surely it's not too difficult to understand? You are lost to him now he has met your husband and he doesn't like it. You had become one of us – almost a member of the family. Now he has seen to whom you really belong, and it changes things. You don't know how difficult Loni became when I, and then Madina, got married. He's very possessive, he likes to be the only male in his harem of women.'

'I wonder what they can be discussing so intently?'

'Politics probably,' Niki said.

When they rejoined us, Countess Arrivabene suggested a bridge game. She and Loni played against Leopold and Granny while Niki and I watched. Mother and son played superbly, with much more skill, subtlety and finesse than the occasion merited. Granny, usually a reliable if not brilliant bridge-player, was completely carried away into reckless doubling and re-doubling by Leopold's erratic and exuberant game and encouragement. They lost heavily of course against their more sober and calculating opponents, but they had fun.

'What did you think of them? Aren't they extraordinary?' I asked Leopold after they had thanked us and gone home.

'Why extraordinary?' Leopold asked, surprised. 'I thought them rather nice, ordinary people. The young one's pretty. Niki? Is that what you call her?'

'What did you talk to Loni about for such a long time?'

'Race-horses.'
'But he doesn't know anything about them.'
'Well, he does now.'
We left for home the next day.

❦ 23 ❦

In the autumn of the same year the situation in Czechoslovakia worsened and war was only averted by the Munich agreement. Chamberlain declared peace for all time after visiting Hitler in Berchtesgaden. Czechoslovakia had been sacrificed; deprived of its most important line of defences in the Sudeten, the country was Hitler's for the taking.

In the following spring of 1939 German troops marched into Prague, unopposed except by snow. There had been a late and very heavy snowfall said to have been sent from heaven by our patron saint Wenceslas to deter the enemy. It didn't hinder the troops entering Prague except that a lot of tanks got stuck and many soldiers suffered frostbite. The troops had expected either resistance or welcome, and met with neither. It might as well have been a city of the dead, its empty silent streets blanketed with snow, the only footprints those of German boots. Every window was curtained, every shutter closed, like thousands of eyes that did not want to see the desecration of Prague. By autumn there was war.

Italy was still neutral and I was able to visit Eddie that winter; he had asked me to come, writing that he had problems and needed my help. On my way to Rome I stayed in Venice for two days; I had a special reason for doing so as I wanted to leave my jewels with the Arrivabenes. I was convinced that soon nothing would be safe from the Germans in Czechoslovakia. What securer place than Venice, and who more trustworthy than my friends?

There was also another reason that I didn't even dare confess to myself. I knew in what financial difficulties the family often was and, anti-fascists as they were, they might well be in serious trouble one day. At least by asking them to safeguard my small fortune I left them secure if it came to the worst.

Except for the sake of their easily convertible value, I have never cared for jewels. They didn't suit me; whatever looks I had were not enhanced by diamonds, flowers suited me much better. I had not written to the Arrivabenes that I was coming, I thought I would surprise them, certain of my welcome. I called Loni's number which I knew by heart, but there was no answer, so at six I went to the palace.

I found Countess Arrivabene alone in the drawing-room, laying a game of patience, just as Granny used to do. She was dressed all in black. Though she looked rather startled at my sudden appearance, she greeted me kindly. She enquired the reason for my journey, asked how my husband and daughter were, and how we were adapting ourselves to German rule.

I asked her if Niki and Loni were in Venice.

'Yes, they're both here, Loni's in bed, he's been very ill. Some germ or infection he caught on that absurd conquest of Albania. He had to rejoin the navy of course. They gave him a ship.'

'Is he seriously ill?' I asked anxiously.

'He has a constant temperature. Of course, my mother's death has upset him too. He did love her so.'

'Granny? I had no idea,' I stammered. 'I'm so sorry. Why? She seemed so lively and gay when I saw her last!'

Countess Arrivabene sighed. 'She was over eighty. One would not think that so kind and good a heart would ever tire, but it did. We all miss her terribly.'

'Poor Loni, it must have been terrible for him. Can I go and see him?'

'Perhaps another day?'

'I'm afraid I have to leave for Rome tomorrow.' I thought she looked relieved.

'But I have a great favour to ask you, Countess Arrivabene,' I then said.

'Anything within reason of course,' she answered with cool politeness. 'What can I do for you?'

'I want you to keep these for me.' I spilled the contents of my handbag on to the card-table in front of her, the three centrepieces of my tiara, two bracelets, several clips, and the huge ear-rings. Niki who had meanwhile joined us gasped, looking at the glittering pile of diamonds. 'You carry a treasure like that around with you in your handbag?'

'Not always,' I laughed, 'on the journey I wore them in a belt round my waist.'

Countess Arrivabene looked at me rather sternly, I thought. 'I don't quite understand,' she said. 'Why do you want me to keep these?'

'The Germans are threatening to confiscate all our property because of my husband's anti-German attitude. So I thought it would be safer to take my jewels out of the country, and I thought that if you were kind enough to take them, they would be safer here in Venice with you than anywhere else. Of course, no one must know,' I added, 'I am not allowed to take valuables out of Czechoslovakia, I could be locked up if anyone found out.'

For a long moment she contemplated the shimmering stones, and then looked at me. But I could read nothing in her impassive face. 'My dear child,' she said at last, 'it's too much of a responsibility for me to take. I'm an old woman, I might die; what then?'

'Mummy, don't say such dreadful things!' Niki exclaimed. 'We could put them in the safe,' she added. 'Not even Celura knows where it is. And even if it was found, only we know the combination. However long this war lasts, and even if we come into it, I doubt if they'll raid our attics or bomb Venice. The English and the Americans are much too fond of it to do that.'

'Does your husband know?' Countess Arrivabene asked. 'Does he approve?'

'Of course,' I said hastily.

'I do not like to risk the property of others. Anything might happen in the unforeseeable future.'

'That's just why I want to leave the jewels with you.'

She gave me a sharp and penetrating look. 'And if for some reason beyond my control they were lost? The palace might burn down, we might be robbed, what then? Would you expect me to replace them? You must know that I have not the money to do so?'

'I would never want anything back. I'd rather lose the jewels than that anything bad happened to any of you.'

She gave me one of her rare smiles. 'You're a sweet, foolish child,' she said. 'No wonder we all love you.'

I saw that she had understood. Niki, usually very perceptive, hadn't. 'You must take them, Mummy, they'll be quite safe here,' and turning to me, 'Coming back to fetch them will be a good excuse for you to return to Venice and us.'

Countess Arrivabene got up with difficulty but then stood very straight facing me. It was rather as if we saluted each other in secret. 'Thank you for your generous confidence,' she said with faint sarcasm. 'I don't think it will be misplaced.'

I put the jewels back into the leather bag and gave them to her. The next day I left for Rome.

24

I found Eddie in a bad mood.

Usually he was optimistic and cheerful even in adverse circumstances. Now he seemed very depressed, and his usual self-assurance was shaken. It was the parting from Mona of course.

'When will I ever see her again? God knows how long this war will last. Those bloody Germans seem very strong. What if she should forget me?'

What could I answer? I knew so little of what there really was between them, and I didn't like to ask. 'No woman ever forgets a real friend,' I said firmly. 'A casual lover maybe, but never someone she has learnt to trust and love as Mona does you. I'm quite certain of that.'

He seemed slightly reassured. 'She does write,' he said. 'They want me to come to New York.'

'Couldn't you?' I asked.

'With my name? Even here there is a lot of anti-German feeling growing among the Americans. I'd only be an embarrassment to Mona there and if America goes into the war, as it probably will, I'd be interned. Still,' – and I was glad to see him laugh again – 'they might make me an honorary citizen of Bismarck, North Dakota!'

'What about becoming an Italian? Surely you have lived here long enough for that to be possible?'

'Only too easy,' he said, 'but can you imagine anything more ridiculous than an Italian called Bismarck? I would have to change my name. I wouldn't mind in the least calling myself Signor Eduardo Campari or whatever, except for my mother. She has borne the burden of being a Bismarck so bravely. Still, I've been considering it, and I can't make up my mind. Help me. It would make things so much easier if I could change my name.'

I looked at him, remembering the many portraits of his grandfather that I had seen in Friedrichsruh. I saw the same-shaped head under Eddie's bright hair, the same large, clear blue eyes that had looked so compellingly out of the portraits, the same short blunt nose and sensitive mouth. I knew that in his youth the Iron Chancellor had looked very much as Eddie did now.

'But what about your grandfather?' I asked. 'Wouldn't it be a sort of betrayal? After all, he was a very great man.'

'Him? He would have changed his name like a shot if he had thought it politically advisable,' Eddie laughed. 'I wish I had known him though, and not just his legend. The Germans made him into a sort of Teutonic demi-god. All those pilgrimages to Friedrichsruh to see the rooms in which he had lived and died! Well, you remember.'

Indeed I did. The curtains that were always drawn, the bed in which Bismarck had died, the medicine bottles on the table beside it, the toothbrush in its glass on the washstand, and the clock that had never been wound since the hour of his death. The mere existence of these rooms, *Die Totenzimmer*, frightened me so much as a child that I hated staying in Friedrichsruh.

'Ghastly,' I said with a shudder.

'The greatest German that ever lived,' Eddie proclaimed. 'He just happened to have political genius. He could have been born anywhere and in any country and achieved the same, provided the time was right and the opportunity there for the taking. It just chanced that he was born in Prussia and that Germany was ready for unification.'

'But surely he was a great patriot?'

'About what?' Eddie asked. 'There was nothing there to be patriotic about. There was no German nation before he created it. I grant he was a genius, but he was as clever, calculating and ruthless as Talleyrand. And what a cynic! Do you remember Omama's story, when she came for her first visit to Friedrichsruh?'

I did, but I felt that all that Eddie was saying might be helping him. 'No, please tell me.'

'Well, he was a very old and disillusioned man by then, and rarely left the house. But in our grandmother's honour, he decided to take her for a drive through the Saxenwald.'

How well I remembered that forest, which had been presented by the grateful Emperor Frederick to his great chancellor, with its magnificent oaks and beeches, hundreds of years old.

News of Bismarck's planned drive had soon spread, and his admirers from all the surrounding villages and towns, even from as far as Hamburg, came to line the forest paths and acclaim and cheer him as his carriage passed. Our grandmother was much impressed, and turning to him said, 'How the German people love you, Prince Bismarck.' They spoke to each other in English, but then he spoke most languages fluently, Eddie remembered.

'I consider them no better than vermin by now,' was his answer. Omama was very shocked.

'Do you know how he died?' Eddie then asked.

'No.'

'Well, it was really because of a dog. He had these Great Danes that he loved. His favourite was called Tyras; it constantly escaped into the forest to hunt deer and was always in danger of being shot by game-keepers who had orders to kill any marauding dogs. One day Tyras returned with his muzzle covered in blood. It seemed quite obvious to my grandfather what he had been up to again. He decided the dog had to be punished and hit him hard with a riding crop. Then he saw that Tyras was dead. There was a bullet wound in his chest, and the blood on his muzzle had been his own. My grandfather couldn't forgive himself for striking his dying friend. His health declined rapidly, and a few weeks later he too was dead. His last words were, "Now I'll soon see Tyras again."'

For a while we were silent, thinking of the dog and its master.

'Have you ever read your grandfather's love-letters?' I asked. 'Those he wrote to your future grandmother when they were engaged. They were published in a little book.'

'Years ago,' Eddie said. 'I can't remember them.'

'I came across them recently by chance. There is nothing cynical in them. They are very beautiful, and written by a very sensitive boy, forever questioning himself if he is worthy of his young bride's love. There is a portrait of him at that age in the book. It's very like you. Shall I send it?'

'Yes, please,' he said.

After that conversation Eddie never mentioned wanting to change his name again.

He wanted to know exactly how things were in Czechoslovakia and what our situation was. I told him it was precarious because of Leopold's declaration of loyalty to Benes. Nevertheless, I had to grant that our protectors were not behaving too badly. After all, we were still allowed to have a president, Hacha, a very decent and patriotic old Czech lawyer. Even if he was quite powerless, he did give a semblance of independence to the country.

'No one has yet been persecuted for being Czech,' I told Eddie.

'At least Neurath is a gentleman,' he remarked.

'Did you know that his wife is a relation of the Larisches?'

'Are you on quite friendly terms with Neurath then?'

'Certainly not,' I replied indignantly. 'I've never met him, and her only once. She asked me to tea to discuss the qualifications of our gardener. He was a Sudeten German who had worked for us for years,' I explained. 'He was a quiet man until the occupation, then he started to throw his weight around. He was the only German in our village, and had to be got rid of lest he terrorize us all. We did not dare dismiss him, but hearing that the Neuraths were looking for a gardener to tend the terraces of the Hradcine palace I wrote to Frau von Neurath recommending him. She invited me to discuss the matter, probably as curious to meet me as I was to meet her.'

'What's she like?' Eddie asked.

'You'll see. When I arrived at the palace and was ushered into the drawing-room which had previously been Mrs Benes's, there was no one there but old Kosuth.'

'The painter? Wasn't he a student of Lembach's who painted my grandfather so often?'

'He was, and not bad at all. He has painted most flattering portraits of many members of the central-European aristocracy. He has a very grand studio in Prague in the Palais Nostitz and is doing the Neuraths and other German notabilities now. We are friends, sort of. He's as clever, mischievous and amusing as a monkey, and looks just like one.

'"Oh, what a beautiful hat!" he exclaimed as I entered the room. "Might it be for patriotic reasons that you wear the crown of St Wenceslas when you visit here?" I put my hands to my head, with no idea of which hat I had put on. Then I realized that the heart-shaped crimson velvet bonnet that rose from a beaded band was perhaps somewhat like the crown that our patron saint wears on statues and in pictures. "It's certainly quite unintentional," I said. I knew he couldn't be trusted an inch, and that soon every German in Prague would be told about my hat.'

Eddie looked very much amused. 'And Frau von Neurath?'

'She came rushing into the room a few minutes later. She was a middle-aged lady, with a kind and pleasant face, but it was flushed, her hair was dishevelled and she was out of breath. "I apologize for not having received you, dear Countess," she said, "but I was just listening to the news. Such good news too – six English ships have been sunk." As you can imagine, this left me speechless, while Kosuth grinned wickedly. Anyway, she has taken our gardener.'

I then told Eddie in what danger many of our Jewish friends were already. Some had been able to leave, others, knowing they were

146

Czechs, had trusted too long in President Hacha's government for protection.

'There's poor little Max Benies,' I said. 'I'm sure you remember him from Castolovice.'

'The jockey?'

'He wasn't a jockey, even if he did win over a hundred steeplechases.'

'Well, he looked very much like one. All I can remember about him is his wife Mimi and her sister Lisie Nostitz. They often came here – very good-looking women, and very social – I didn't know they were Jewish.'

'Well, they are not any more, except for Max. What with their fair hair and blue eyes, they are all that the Germans most admire – true visions of Aryan beauty. Besides, allegedly letters were found that proved they were closely related to an archduke. Anyway, thank God they are safe. I see Lisie almost daily in Prague and Mimi has found a German protector. He knew Hitler in Munich when it all started but since then has really only used this connection to help people in distress. But little Max has to go, so that Mimi can divorce him for desertion. There's a considerable fortune involved, if it were confiscated as Jewish property she and the children would have nothing to live on. Do you know the British Ambassador here?' I then asked.

'Of course, I dined with him only last week.' Eddie said.

'I'd like to go and plead with him for Max. Prince Schwarzenberg has offered him a job on his farm in Kenya. Max can still get out of Czechoslovakia and come here, but he would need papers to enter a British colony. Do you think the ambassador would help?'

'I'm sure he would. I'll call up and find out when he can see you.'

Eddie went to telephone while I thought of Max. Both Leopold and I had always been fond of him, Leopold mainly because Max amused him and because he admired him as a fine sportsman and a very courageous rider. Little Max Benies had been very popular and important on all our country's race-courses, even in Vienna.

Unfortunately, he was not so much so at home. Everyone adored Mimi. She was charming and a wonderful hostess. Max knew quite well how insignificant he must seem in comparison to her.

He felt that most of her aristocratic friends only came to Klecany, the very attractive and beautifully furnished baroque country house that was his home near Prague, for her sake. He became a reluctant and often disagreeable host.

He was intelligent and his wit could be as sharp as a knife-thrust. It was the only way in which he could attract notice.

Leopold and I, though we loved Mimi, couldn't help laughing and often applauding the cutting sarcasms with which he affronted some of her most distinguished guests and admirers.

When the persecution of Jews and the confiscation of their property began and Max was told that he must leave for his own safety and that of his family, he couldn't and wouldn't understand. He had never been an Orthodox Jew and he knew himself a good Czech. What was there to worry about? But if he really had to go, why couldn't his family come with him? 'It's all a plot to get me out of the way,' he insisted, 'so that Mimi can marry her German.' As a matter of fact she did later, thereby saving her own and her children's fortune, and much of Max's, as well as all of Klecany's furnishings.

My interview that Eddie had arranged with the British Ambassador had been successful. Sir Noel Charles was kind and sympathetic and when Max could finally be persuaded to leave he was given the necessary documents at the embassy in Rome. Tiny Max became an excellent manager of the large estate in Kenya with hundreds of seven-foot-tall Masai labourers, the tallest of all African people, under his command. Occasionally one or the other died a natural death, and he had to bury them himself single-handed since Masai tradition forbids them to touch a corpse.

Max liked his life in Kenya, but it didn't stop him from being home-sick and lonely and from hating the Germans. I think the happiest day of his exile must have been when he heard of the assassination of Heydrich.

Blutheini, as even the Germans called him since he was the most bloodthirsty killer of the Nazi hierarchy, had replaced Neurath as *Reichsprotektor*. Hitler had considered the latter too lenient towards the unsubmissive Czechs. Even if Neurath had condemned to death by execution students who had demonstrated against German occupation, his rule had been too mild for the Sudeten German Frank, his second-in-command.

Heydrich preferred sleeping in the country although the Hradcine palace was his official residence in which he worked. He had requisitioned Panensky Brerany. It was a small and charming country house, at a convenient twenty minutes' drive from Prague, close to Klecany, and had also belonged to Jews.

'Killed almost on my own doorstep,' Max must have triumphed when he heard of Heydrich's death. How well he must have known that sharp turn of the road as he always had to slow down on his daily drives to his office in Prague or on his way to the race-course. So well that I wonder if it wasn't Max himself who passed on the information about the only place in which Heydrich's heavily guarded car would have to slacken speed on its way to Prague, allowing the parachutists just enough time to throw their bombs.

I rather hope not. Max would have enjoyed personal revenge – after all, the monster was living in a Jewish house which used to belong to his friends, and Blutheini's extinction was a pleasure. But what followed would have caused him acute suffering had he been involved. The retaliations after Heydrich's death were horrible – thousands of Czechs were tortured, shot, hanged and imprisoned.

Max paid us a brief visit in Prague after the war had ended. Though he was justly proud of the position he had made for himself in Kenya, it hadn't left him any less bitter about what he had lost at home. Klecany was in ruins, many of his friends dead, and Mimi had remarried. Distrustful and pessimistic as he had always been, he didn't believe Czechoslovakia would keep its independence for long. He decided to return to Africa and took his daughter Rosie with him. She had grown into a pretty, intelligent young girl, and kept house for him in Kenya; I hope her companionship helped him forget much of what he had lost.

I had stayed with Eddie in Rome for a fortnight, then returned to Czechoslovakia. I never liked leaving the child for long, nor did Leopold and I enjoy being separated from each other, especially in wartime. I had noticed that Eddie lived much the same life in Rome as he had before. He had many old friends among the Italian aristocracy and he mixed freely with the English-speaking diplomats among whom he was very popular. Though he missed Mona desperately, they could still correspond and telephone.

However, all that was to change very soon. With Hitler winning on all fronts, Mussolini was encouraged to join the war, hoping to share in the spoils. Soon America declared war too. Eddie's position in Rome became very difficult. His brother, Prince Otto von Bismarck, was *chargé d'affaires* at the German Embassy. He and his wife naturally had to entertain and mix socially with the élite of Mussolini's fascists as well as to receive important visiting Nazis. Eddie could not affront his brother by never going near his house even if he didn't like the people he met there.

He had recently shocked the family by becoming a Roman Catholic. Even his mother had been deeply upset, for the Anglican faith she had been brought up in had remained her last link with the England of her youth and it was precious to her.

The fact that Eddie disliked Germany hadn't diminished his affection for his brothers and sisters. However diametrically opposed their loyalties were, they still had much in common. In truth, all of Bismarck's descendants suffered from one form of displacement or another. It was as if they had been reared in a nest in which a cuckoo's egg had been laid, out of which an enormous prodigy had broken, crowding them out of place and leaving them no space to develop freely. Throughout their lives the great wings of Bismarck's genius would overshadow them.

Eddie's pro-Western, anti-German and anti-fascist sympathies were well-known in Rome. He never tried to conceal them. Many of his Italian friends shared his opinions, yet the fact that he was so closely linked to the German Embassy through his brother's position and the fear that he was playing a double game lost him many old and trusted friends. Eddie persistently ignored the German colony and they grew equally suspicious of his loyalties.

Then came the allied victory at El Alamein and the defeat of both Italian and German forces in Africa. The invasion of Sicily followed, General Badoglio sued for peace, and Italy re-entered the war on the side of the Western allies. Mussolini was imprisoned. Eddie's brother Otto returned to Germany and strongly advised him to do the same. Eddie refused, convinced of a speedy allied victory, which didn't come. There was fierce fighting throughout Italy for many months, Mussolini was freed by the Germans, and his government re-established in the north. There were severe reprisals against those who had turned against the Germans or the fascist regime.

Eddie was arrested and taken back to Germany under guard. Otto was only able to help him in so far as an agreement was reached that if his brother joined the army, no further investigation into his activities in Italy would be made and he would be freed. Eddie had never done any military service, so he was sent to a training camp near Freiburg.

He wrote to me from there, in German of course, saying that he was quite well and looking forward to being able to reach the front soon. No censor could have noticed the small squiggle at the end of 'front' which turned it into frontier. So I knew he was going to try and desert – also that if he was caught doing so, he would certainly be shot.

Anxious weeks followed in which I had no news at all. I wrote to Otto who didn't answer. Then there was a rumour that Eddie had been killed on the eastern front. Somehow I couldn't believe it. Eddie and I were too close not to know if one of us had died. I wrote to Aunt Maggie expressing my deep sympathy and my sorrow, but so formally and stiffly that she would have certainly guessed that I was unconvinced of what I had heard.

She answered. She spoke lovingly and movingly of dear Albrecht, saying he had reached the front – there was the same odd twist at the end of the word. She said that she had heard that he had not suffered, and was safe in the hands of God. In spite of her sorrow, she remembered mine, and how great our friendship had been, even while I was still at school. Then she gave me news of the rest of the family.

So Eddie was safe, certainly in the hands of God, but alive, and since the only school I'd ever gone to was in Lausanne, he had reached Switzerland. Later I found out that all the family knew what had happened. The news had come to them through the Swiss Red Cross.

Eddie's escape had been quite undramatic. He had stolen a bicycle, changed into civilian clothes and pedalled into Switzerland where he gave himself up to the police. At his request they got in touch with relatives of ours who lived near Lausanne, and through their intervention he was granted asylum throughout the rest of the war, though he was semi-interned.

'It was all very dull,' Eddie told me later, 'but at least I could write to Mona again. She too had heard I was dead.'

Otto still had powerful connections, to whom he could point out that it was better for everyone to believe a Bismarck had died a hero's death than for it to become known that he was a deserter. Soon however the family had to face even graver troubles and more serious disgrace.

Otto's second brother, Gottfried, had been arrested for having taken part in the plot to assassinate Hitler; there seemed little doubt that he would be executed as Stauffenberg and the other conspirators were.

25

I have not mentioned Gottfried before because he is worth remembering at some length, and his tragic life needs explanation. Superficially seen, there was nothing very praiseworthy about his rapid rise to power in the Nazi party and his having been a member of the SS; nor even his having plotted to kill the leader to whom he had, after all, sworn allegiance.

It had always been intended that Otto, not Gottfried, should go into politics as had his father and grandfather before him. Although Otto became a member of the Berlin parliament, he was much too intelligent not to realize how little public appeal he had. He was small, dark, of undistinguished appearance, and wore thick glasses since he was very short-sighted. He was a brilliant speaker, but his quick wit and almost Latin temperament were not suited to the serious stolidity of a German audience. He was impatient of fools, devoid of illusions, rich and spoilt. He knew himself to be neither suited nor inclined to follow in his grandfather's footsteps. But he thought his brother was.

Gottfried had the presence and also some of the necessary qualifications. He was by far the best-looking of the three brothers, tall and dark-haired with a fine-featured face and deep blue eyes. He had been intended for the diplomatic service and educated accordingly. He had studied at Oxford as well as at German universities and had travelled extensively. He could be relied on to speak well in public without embarrassment. All the Bismarck children, except Eddie who was still too young, had been forced by their father to go through the terrifying experience of having to make political speeches at the dining-room table at an early age.

In spite of these advantages, Gottfried was by nature even more unsuited to a politician's life than Otto, but that was considered unimportant by everyone except his mother. She knew he had none of the deviousness, ruthlessness or genius of his grandfather, and yet he was the only one of her children who would put his country's welfare before his own. Gottfried was certainly not as clever as Otto, nor as charming as Eddie, and in character different to both. Gottfried was totally and absolutely good. Not that he was a paragon of moral virtues. Before his marriage he lived the life of any normal handsome young bachelor fond of women, but with one difference. He was the pursued, they the pursuers.

Women exploited his one great weakness. He was unable to hurt anyone voluntarily, least of all a woman, by saying no. He gave himself to them as generously as he handed out sweets and toys to children when they begged for them. He was a healthy young man, and his conquests must certainly have given him physical pleasure. But he had no male vanity, in fact no vanity at all. In some ways he was quite selfless, motivated only by gentleness of heart, love for his fellow men, and pride in his country.

When Hitler first came into power Bismarck was still a revered and almost magical name in Germany; Hitler wanted it among his adherents. Otto was approached first, but he was too wary to commit himself totally. All he conceded was that he might accept a future diplomatic post. But he strongly advised Gottfried to join the Nazi party. Otto thought the Führer common and rather absurd, and doubted that his leadership would last long, but meanwhile he felt that the more decent people that went into the party the better, so as to take over the government when Hitler could be ousted.

The National Socialist movement was rapidly gaining popularity. There was much that Gottfried liked about Hitler's ideas and the speed with which he put them into practice. Already there were far fewer unemployed and less poverty in Germany, for whoever wanted a job could find one. If the young were forced to work, they were also allowed to play, marching and singing and waving their flags. There was something joyful and springlike about it all, a spirit of renewal and rebirth seemed to be sweeping the country.

Gottfried decided to join and advanced rapidly in the party. He was given mainly administrative work for which he showed considerable aptitude, and was finally rewarded by being made *Bürgermeister* of Ruegen in the Baltic, that is governor of the island. He organized the sending there of thousands of underprivileged children from the slums of Berlin in the summer holidays, and he saw to their health and welfare. The island was near his country place in Pomerania, so he could look after both.

He should have been content, but by then Gottfried's enthusiasm for the party he had joined was waning. Even if his natural goodness made it difficult for him to recognize evil, he was neither stupid nor naïve. It began with the Jews. Gottfried had never taken Hitler's anti-Semitism seriously, nor the slogan-chanting youths, that proclaimed it. True, some Jewish shop-windows in Berlin had been broken, which was regrettable, but he believed that the hysteria would pass, and besides the Jews were intelligent enough to deal with the situation.

But when the persecution began in earnest, Gottfried was shocked. His grandfather had always protected the German Jews. What right had the little upstart Hitler to confiscate their property and send them out of the country penniless? Gottfried was not a member of Hitler's inner circle, but he had come to know most of its members through his work. He went to Goering, who was the most amiable and approachable of them, for information.

'My dear Bismarck,' Goering had laughed. 'Soon you and I will have to prove that our great-grandmothers were Aryans to satisfy the Führer. Anti-Semitism is his hobby horse. He rides it day and night. Liquidation of the Jews is an *idée fixe* with him.'

'Liquidation?' Gottfried asked.

'Oh, just a propaganda word like any other,' Goering said hastily. 'He wants them out of the country, that's all. We need foreign currency. Many of those who have relations abroad, who are ready to pay, can leave.'

'And the others?'

Goering shrugged his big shoulders. 'One will have to wait and see what the Führer decides . . . I wouldn't stick my nose into the Jewish question, dear Bismarck. Between ourselves, it stinks to high heaven already. What about a glass of champagne?'

There were other things that were beginning to stink, Gottfried realized. People were being arrested for no other reason than that they had written or spoken against National Socialism. There was growing suppression of those not entirely committed to Hitler and the methods that the Gestapo used to quell any internal resistance disgusted Gottfried.

He had also begun to fear that Germany was being rearmed to an extent that was inexcusable as a mere defence against Communist Russia. Were Hitler's real intentions to attack and risk a Second World War? He went to Friedrichsruh to consult Otto who was then first secretary at the German Embassy in London and had come home for a few days to visit his mother who hadn't been well.

I can of course only guess what passed between them, but I know that by then Gottfried was totally disillusioned with the party and that he wanted to leave it and retire to Rheinfeld. Also that Otto would have objected, pointing out that it had become dangerous to turn

one's back on Hitler. Otto had other reasons for wanting Gottfried
to remain in the party. He liked to be kept informed by someone he
could trust. He had no illusions whatsoever about Hitler and his
associates and was certain that they would destroy themselves either
by risking war or by the nation rising against them. There would be
some bloodshed of course, and one might have to send Ann-Mari
and the children to Sweden for a month or two. The question was
when? It was always good to be prepared, Otto felt.

Meanwhile, the more Gottfried could tell him about the idio-
syncrasies of the Führer and his intimates, the more delighted Otto
was. He would certainly never have considered being disloyal to his
country, but the absurdities of this gang would amuse his friends in
London. Because he could not understand that Hitler's ranting and
screaming and all the mumbo jumbo of pseudo-Wagnerian mysticism
with which he intoxicated the crowds could appeal to any sane person,
Otto misjudged its power. He reassured Gottfried that it was only mass
hysteria, and could not last.

In the afternoon Gottfried went to his mother who was having
tea in the drawing-room, resting on a chaise longue, dressed as always
in black. Like Queen Victoria, she had never gone out of mourning
after her husband's death. It was a very English tea, with thin slices
of brown bread and butter and hot scones and jam. Gottfried told her
frankly that he didn't like what was happening in Germany, what was
being done to the Jews and other equally innocent people, and that
he wanted to leave the Nazi party.

'My darling Gottfried,' she said, her small thin hands almost as
transparent as the fragile cup she was filling for him. 'Wouldn't it be
an escape from your responsibilities?'

'In what way?' he asked.

She glanced up at one of the portraits on the wall and met the
stern eyes of her father-in-law. 'You are the only one of my children
that really loves his country. You have an important position in the
party and you are to some extent protected by your name. Use these
advantages to try and right some of the wrongs you see.'

He saw the fear and courage for him in her gentle face. Then she
quoted. Aunt Maggie was never without Shakespeare or Goethe to help
her in difficult moments.

'This above all, to thine own self be true, and it must follow as
the night the day thou canst not then be false to any man.' She smiled
at him, but there were tears in her eyes.

Much later Gottfried was to tell me almost word for word of this conversation with his mother. He had every reason to remember it; it was the beginning of his secret crusade against the evils hidden behind the bright façade of Hitler's revival of German nationalism, and it was to lead him step by step towards the final decision that Hitler must be eliminated.

He remained in the party. In 1937 he married his and my first cousin Melanie Hoyos, a marriage for which I was partly responsible. He met her when he came to visit our grandmother in Vienna; we happened to be staying there too at the same time. He had only known Melanie as a child, since when she had grown into a very attractive young girl. She was small, rather plain, with a fascinating personality that made up for what she lacked in beauty. She had inherited all her French mother's brilliance and wit in conversation, although her imaginative gifts were entirely her own. If she set herself out to please, which was not always the case since she was often moody and wilful, the plain little girl could transform herself into a woman of such scintillating charm and attraction as to leave one spellbound.

There is no doubt that Gottfried was fascinated. He and his cousin became inseparable throughout the time he stayed in Vienna, but I'm sure he never thought of her as a possible wife. Their close relationship and the fact that he was fifteen years older than she was would have made it difficult for him to think of marriage, even if he had been in love with her. An enchanting child prodigy of whom he had grown very fond was all he remembered of her, I think, when he returned to Germany.

Soon afterwards Melanie paid us a surprise visit in Zasmuky where we were living then. She soon confessed why she had come. She had decided to travel to Rheinfeld, Gottfried's country place where he was staying, and persuade him to marry her. She had only used visiting us as an excuse to get to Germany without her parents' knowledge of her plans. I tried to dissuade her from going to him, but she wouldn't listen. Nothing would shake her from her conviction that Gottfried was the only man she would ever love, and that this was her only chance of winning him.

I could of course have stopped her by calling up her parents and warning them of her intentions. Leopold certainly felt that I ought to. 'The child's mad,' he said, 'you mustn't let her make a fool of herself.' If I didn't stop her, it was because I have always believed that even children should be allowed to make up their own minds as to what they want and that they learn more readily from their own mistakes than from decisions imposed on them by the advice of others. Anyway, I took her to Prague and found her a train that would eventually get her to Rheinfeld, but I insisted on her wiring Gottfried giving the time of her arrival.

Ten days later we got a telegram. 'Engaged. Love Melanie.' So did her shocked parents. There was indignation at first, and I was quite rightly blamed for my connivance, but in the end there was less family opposition to their marriage than might have been expected. Aunt Maggie infinitely preferred her favourite brother's child as a daughter-in-law to the stranger Gottfried might have brought her, and Uncle Alec, who appreciated Gottfried's integrity and goodness, was grateful to know that his daughter was in safe keeping.

Aunt Edmée however feared the possible effects of such a close relationship on her future grandchildren. 'Might they not be born lacking toes, or with too many, with crippled bodies or crippled minds?' Nevertheless, she accepted that her eldest daughter who was temperamentally difficult to control, had made a good marriage. Gottfried was wealthy, and the high position to which he had advanced in the Nazi party ensured some protection to those of his family who were less enthusiastic about Germanic revival than he was.

Hitler annexed Austria the next year and Gottfried came to Vienna soon afterwards. Melanie had stayed in Rheinfeld as she was nursing her first child and not able to leave. Gottfried, who didn't wear his Nazi uniform if he could help it, and never if he was staying with friends or relations abroad, came to Vienna in full SS battledress. He looked very lean and handsome in it, but his costume affronted his Austrian relations. They had not suffered the *Anschluss* gladly.

Gottfried, however, had his reasons. One of his first cousins, Balti Hoyos, was in jail for having joined in anti-Hitler demonstrations and so were others, imprisoned because of futile attempts to oppose the invaders. Only if he stressed his official status in the party could Gottfried help. His intervention certainly saved his cousin and several other members of his class from being imprisoned for years. Some of his grandmother's Jewish friends were still able to leave with a few of their possessions by following the instructions Gottfried had given her.

Next spring Hitler's troops marched into Czechoslovakia and by autumn there was war. Gottfried was beyond military age, married with three children by then and too useful to the party because of his administrative work to be expendable. Even if he would rather have served his country by soldiering than by abetting what he had come to abhor, he was not allowed to do so. By that time war had started in earnest and the bombardment of German cities begun, with the killing of civilians and the destruction of towns. He dedicated himself completely, using all his powers to organize adequate shelters and to aid the suffering civilian population.

After Neurath had been retired as Protector of Czechoslovakia and Heydrich had taken his place, Gottfried and Melanie came to visit us in Prague. Castolovice had already been confiscated. Gottfried had come to warn us; we knew very little about Heydrich. 'For God's sake be careful,' he said. 'He's one of the bloodiest killers of them all, he is totally without mercy. Tell all your friends.'

I hadn't seen Melanie since she had left us to meet Gottfried. I asked her if she was happy.

'If I loved him less, I would be happier,' she said. 'Often I'm so afraid. He's too good and brave. Sometimes I think he doesn't care for me and the children as much as he does for helping others, no matter what he risks.'

I was to see them once more, some time after Heydrich's assassination and the horrifying German reprisals that followed. Several of our friends had been executed and others were imprisoned. Day and night the Gestapo entered houses to search for weapons, and if they had orders to arrest or persecute for some other reason, a revolver discovered hidden under a bed or in a chest of drawers would be taken from its hiding place by the hand of the Gestapo agent who had put it there. For a Czech to have a secreted weapon was punishable by death.

Gottfried listened quietly to all we told him. He wrote down the names of our closest friends who had been imprisoned and said he would do his best but that things were becoming very difficult. Nevertheless, several were released through his intervention, including Uncle Franzi Kinsky.

I thought that Melanie was not looking well and seemed nervous and rather depressed; but when she rallied she enchanted us with her wit and humour as before. Almost too much so, I felt; it was as if she had escaped into a fantastic world of her own imagination. 'Gottfried is going to right all wrongs and save Germany,' she whispered to me before they left.

❦ 26 ❧

Some months later the attempt to assassinate Hitler took place. Stauffenberg, Peter Yorck, von Wartenberg and other young officers of the *Wehrmacht*, all with names famed for their fathers' and grandfathers' services to Germany in the past, were executed. Gottfried only survived through a direct appeal to Hitler by his mother. At first the Führer had refused to see her, but, frail as she was, she had great determination, courage and persistence. What she eventually told him, I don't know. She may well have warned him that neither Germany nor history would forgive him for killing Bismarck's grandson.

Gottfried was tortured, questioned and re-questioned by the Gestapo, and held in solitary confinement for many months. Melanie was imprisoned too and interrogated. She refused to speak, knowing that Gottfried's life was at stake. Not a word could the Gestapo get out of her. When one of them brutally hit her in the face he broke her jaw. She couldn't speak for weeks after that, even if she had wanted to. Otto, who had been able to clear himself of having been involved in any way in the plot, managed to have her released.

After several more months Gottfried too was allowed to return home on condition that he saw no one but his close family. Only gradually did Melanie realize how much he had changed. It was natural that what he had suffered in prison would have affected his health and spirit, but she was certain that thanks to her loving care he would soon regain his strength. If he preferred being left alone and didn't seem to take much pleasure even in his children's company, wasn't that just a habit acquired in his months of solitary confinement?

It was understandable too that he took no interest in the management of his estate any more since both of them knew that it was only a matter of weeks before Russian troops would be in East Germany and that they must be prepared to leave Rheinfeld. Melanie had started to pack. She had much of her mother's French common sense when it came to material possessions, and she was leaving nothing for the Russians to loot. Van after van was filled with household goods and furniture. Gottfried watched things he had once treasured being removed from various rooms with total indifference; they might as well stay where they were for all he cared, except that packing them kept Melanie and the children busy. Meanwhile he could withdraw more and more into himself and return to the brooding self-torture that had become such a habit in captivity.

His conscience gave him no rest. Had he done right or wrong? Millions of lives might have been saved and Germany kept from the total destruction it was now facing had the attempt to assassinate Hitler been successful. Yet was it not the act of a traitor to try and kill one's commander-in-chief to whom one had sworn allegiance, and for whom thousands were still loyally dying on the battlefronts?

He could not forget the faces of his dead friends. Had he dissuaded them they might still be alive. What right had he to live, saved only by his grandfather's name, when they had been so horribly executed? How could he look at his own children when those of Stauffenberg had been taken from their mother's arms and no one knew where they were or if they were dead or alive? Again, as so often, he remembered his mother's words. 'This above all to thy own self be true.'

He knew he had failed to do so. Compassion was the mainspring of his nature. By plotting to kill another human being, however evil, however certain he had been that by eliminating Hitler Germany would be saved, he knew that he had sinned against his true self and that guilt was destroying him as surely as he had wanted to destroy Hitler.

'And it must follow as the night the day?' Black indeed was the night that was falling over Germany.

'Thou canst not then be false to any man?' False to himself, false to his friends because he lived and they had died, false to his country by trying to change the course of history and not even succeeding.

The vans with the furniture reached Friedrichsruh safely. Gottfried, Melanie and the children arrived there soon afterwards, having joined hundreds of families who were fleeing west with their belongings. Friedrichsruh had been bombed and the main house had become uninhabitable. Otto, Ann-Mari and their children had moved into an apartment above the undamaged stable, but there was no room there for Gottfried and his family. They went to a nearby inn where Aunt Maggie joined them.

She had fled from Schoenhausen, the beautiful eighteenth-century manor house which was the ancestral home of the Bismarcks, in which she had lived since Otto's marriage. She left just in time; it was totally destroyed by Russian troops before they entered Berlin. There was a small dilapidated country house on Otto's estate in which his bailiff lived. The man was given other accommodation and Gottfried, Melanie, their children and Aunt Maggie moved into it.

The war was over. Hitler, who, if he wished for death, need only have joined the troops he had ordered to fight to the last in the streets of Berlin, committed suicide in his underground bunker. Admiral Doenitz signed Germany's unconditional surrender, but for months there was no peace for the German people. Those left in the East saw pillage, rape and total destruction of property. Those in the West were more fortunate with the English, French or American occupying forces. However, even under them arrests became as frequent as they had been under Hitler.

Whoever had been prominent in the Nazi party was then in almost as much danger as those who had not belonged to it had been before. Many of Gottfried's former friends were questioned, and some were imprisoned. But since three-quarters of Germany's population could not be jailed for having been followers of Hitler, soon only those who were known to have committed atrocities were arrested and brought to trial. The horrors of Auschwitz, Buchenwald, Belsen and other concentration camps were fully revealed and shamed every German.

Meanwhile a constant stream of refugees who had fled from the East flooded into West Germany. Ann-Mari, with the help of the Swedish Red Cross, and assisted by the two sisters, Melanie and Alice, and several other young people, Austrians, Germans and Swedes, organized shelters, distributed food, requisitioned housing for the homeless or found families ready to give them temporary accommodation.

Gottfried took no part in these charitable activities. His mother was dying of cancer, incurable by the time she had confessed to being seriously ill. Gottfried and Melanie nursed her with the utmost devotion, but all they could do to save her from the agonizing pains she suffered was to give her larger and larger doses of morphine. Her mind wandered, and she constantly asked for her youngest son Eddie before she died in Gottfried's arms.

Both Melanie and Otto believed Gottfried would become his old self again after he had recovered from the emotional exhaustion of his mother's suffering and death, as did the rest of the family. Never had there been such opportunities as there were now for someone known to have opposed Hitler. Gottfried could have any high office in West Germany for the asking, they pointed out to him. Surely he still wanted to serve his country?

He did not. He felt himself unworthy to do so. All he wanted was to be left alone to try and find the inner peace he had lost and to learn to forget the past. But in the years that followed he was never allowed to do so. Even if he only rarely left Schoenau he could not escape the many well-intentioned visitors, both friends and strangers that came to acclaim him as a hero, nor those that came to thank him for having saved their lives. There were also the others, still secretly as dedicated to Nazism as before, whom he knew must despise him as a traitor, but came nevertheless to appeal to him. Could he not just mention that they too had been involved in the plot to kill Hitler?

Melanie, unable to comprehend his disturbed state of mind, only added to his torture with her love and worship. The image of saint and martyr she was using all her imagination to build him into revolted him.

Then a young woman who had been a friend of theirs for some time and had worked with Melanie in the refugee assistance committee came to stay with them at Schoenau. She had been in love with Gottfried for years, and he had always been somewhat attracted by her vitality, intelligence and charm. With sure instinct she knew that at last he needed her, and that he was ready to seek relief from his lonely soul-searching in physical love. But all that Melanie understood was that Gottfried was being unfaithful to her. Passionately possessive, believing her marriage threatened, she made scene after scene and succeeded in putting an end to the affair, and with it Gottfried's last hope of finding a regeneration of spirit in the revival of his manhood. He sank back into apathy.

Finally Melanie freed his troubled soul, and with it her own. She had never been a competent driver; impatient and impetuous, she always drove too fast for safety. She lost control of the car on a slippery road, and Gottfried, though at her side, was too late to help. A lorry which was approaching hit them head-on. Melanie was killed instantaneously, Gottfried was taken to hospital unconscious and died a few hours later. They were buried together in the garden of Friedrichsruh.

27

When I arrived at the Grand Hotel in Venice I found Eddie waiting for me. We embraced; it was five years since we had been together. Then we glanced quickly at each other to see how much we might have changed. Eddie looked younger than ever, but then misfortune and suffering never would line his clear, bright face. He too seemed to approve of what he saw. I was wearing one of the dresses I had bought in Paris, and I knew it suited me.

We complimented each other on our appearance, surreptitiously wiped our eyes, and hugged each other once more.

'I guess we've both survived all right,' Eddie laughed. He often used American slang in moments of emotion, it was a form of understatement.

'I guess we have,' I answered.

There was so much for us to talk about, to ask and to tell, that we didn't know where to begin or end. It was to take all of that afternoon and night and most of the next day until towards evening Eddie had to leave for Rome to fly to New York. Only at the very beginning, when he told me he had had a recent letter from Mona and said what it contained, was there an unfamiliar and to me very disturbing unease between us.

He told me that Mona had written that Steinhardt had been to see her twice. 'Naturally she wants to help, if you and Leopold come to America,' Eddie said. 'But was it necessary to send a complete stranger to ask her to do so?'

'But Steinhardt's not a stranger!' I exclaimed indignantly, 'he's the kindest friend I've ever had. He practically saved our lives, and certainly many of our possessions. I wouldn't be here now if it weren't for him, nor have the chance to emigrate to America. Besides, I didn't send him to Mona. All I did was give him a list of names of people we knew in New York.'

'Which, it would seem, he took immediate advantage of to get into the house,' Eddie said reproachfully. 'Harrison can't have been too pleased, he doesn't see Jews socially. Anyway, he dislikes Mona being importuned by requests; she's so good-natured and kind-hearted, she'd give anything away to anyone if they asked for it. And think of my position with them,' Eddie continued. 'What excuse or right would I have to live with them if Harrison didn't employ me? And if his reason for doing so is my protecting Mona from herself and the undesirable people who might beg her for favours, what must he think if it's done on the behalf of one of my own relations?'

I understood only too well, but was also rather hurt. To have Steinhardt referred to as an undesirable person seemed to me inconceivable. 'But didn't Mona say she liked him?' I asked.

'You know very little about the exclusiveness of New York's rich upper classes,' Eddie remarked. 'But she said that though Steinhardt was rather brash and pushing she thought that he was an attractive man and she was touched by his fondness for you and his concern for your future. He asked her if she didn't have a spare house for you to live in.'

I blushed.

'Mona couldn't think of anything but a disused stable on their place on Long Island, but it's not got any bathrooms or anything. I wouldn't recommend it. She also writes that Clarisse Rothschild came to call on her, probably contacted by Steinhardt too, to ask her what could be done for you and Leopold. I know Clarisse is an old friend of yours, but Mona had never heard of her, and she is rather forceful and overwhelming as I can remember from Vienna. Besides,' Eddie added, 'I can't quite see why, if she's so anxious about you, Clarisse doesn't do something for you herself. She must be richer than ever now her Austrian properties have been returned to her. Why does she have to come to Mona for help?'

'I'm so sorry,' I said penitently. 'But how was I to know all this would happen? I never thought Mona would be bothered.'

'Well, she wasn't really,' Eddie said. 'She's anxious to do anything she can for you, if only for my sake, and so of course am I, but we don't really need go-betweens, do we? Now don't worry,' he smiled consolingly, seeing how upset and embarrassed I was. 'There's no real harm done. I'll be in New York all winter, I'll look after you. Now let's go and eat. What about that fish place we used to go to where we had the oysters?'

'And how sick we were!' I laughed.

'It was all your fault too. I told you they came straight out of the canals and that no one ever eats oysters in Venice and you said that was nonsense and that your parents-in-law had them sent in barrels of sea-water from here all the way to Czechoslovakia by train every week in the oyster season and that eating them never made anyone ill! And that canal water was very healthy to drink!'

'Well, Omama did arrange for it to be bottled here and sent to her. She always said it was the best of all laxatives.'

'I bet it was,' said Eddie, breathing in the rank smell of a small canal as we strolled towards the Piazza San Marco.

We lunched on the most typically Venetian dishes we could remember. *Gran' sevole*, a langouste-like shrimp fried in oil, followed by *zabaglione*, a sort of hot egg-nog. We also drank plenty of white wine. Then we wandered through the narrow streets, pausing now and then as they widened into squares to admire churches and palaces, but mainly laughing, chatting, remembering, glad to be together again.

Towards evening we became more serious. There was so much to talk about that we talked all night until dawn in my bedroom that overlooked the Grand Canal. First Eddie told me of the long, dull months in Switzerland after his escape, waiting for the war to end, and of the odd assortment of people, mostly Germans, that had been interned with him.

'I'm sure some were criminals who had fled from justice and not from political persecution as they declared. Others were genuine idealists who would have faced death for their convictions. But all of them were pathetic, uncertain of their future, fearful, lost and dis-placed. None of us had any money nor of course any clothes excepting those we had on us when we crossed the frontier. We shared everything. It was as close to communism as I hope I will ever get,' Eddie smiled, 'but it was also sort of Christian. All in all, it wasn't too bad. The Swiss fed us well and we were allowed to have books from the lending libraries. And at last I could write to Mona and tell her I was alive. The rumour that I had been killed on the Russian front had reached her in America.'

'How awful for her!'

'Yes, I think she minded,' Eddie said rather curtly. 'I couldn't write to Mama from Switzerland, but I'd made certain that she knew I was safe through the Red Cross.' Eddie continued, 'Had I only gone to her the moment the war ended . . . How was I to know that I would never see her again?'

There was no answer I could give.

'I somehow couldn't face Germany so soon after everything that had happened. Meeting my brothers! After all, from their point of view I had deserted and caused considerable inconvenience to them.

Mona asked me to come to America; naturally I longed for her, so I went. She had furnished a charming little house for me on their place on Long Island. It's a lovely property on the Sound. Well, you'll see it soon. Harrison made me his private secretary with a good salary, so I didn't have to worry about money. I can't say my duties were very arduous. All I did was help Mona in the garden and walk the dogs with her,' Eddie laughed. 'I couldn't have been more content!'

'Mama wrote frequently. She was living with Gottfried and Melanie then. She gave me all the family news and seemed to be enjoying her many grandchildren – and she said that she was very well. That alone should have made me suspicious. Her not complaining about her health as she usually did. Not that she didn't often feel ill,' Eddie added thoughtfully, 'but there was nothing really wrong with her except that she took her duties too seriously and she had to force herself to do much that was distasteful. In her married life too I think. Being ill was her only escape, and later it became a habit.'

I thought of the darkened room into which I was taken every morning when I had stayed at Friedrichsruh as a child.

'Don't talk above a whisper, don't remain longer than a few minutes, and above all, don't jump on her Highness's bed,' her maid would warn me.

As if I would have wanted to do any of these things! I was afraid of that still form, shrouded in lace, lying in the four-poster, Aunt Maggie's face a pale unrecognizable blur – even her low voice seemed disembodied and unfamiliar in the darkness. But the worst thing was the smell. Later, I was to know it was only the pungent scent of valerian which ladies took then as a medicine for migraine or nervous disorders; but then I thought it was the smell of death. I was always conscious that the frightening locked rooms called the death-chambers, in which the old Prince had died, and where for all I knew his corpse might still be lying, were directly under Aunt Maggie's room. In my childish imagination they were somehow horribly connected. When I had outgrown my fears I grew very fond of Aunt Maggie. I liked and admired her, but I never dared tell her how terrified I had been of her as a child.

'In none of her letters to me,' Eddie resumed, 'did she encourage me to come and see her.'

'Didn't you think that rather strange?'

'No, not really. She knew how happy I was with Mona, and she was much too unselfish to ask anything of her children which we didn't give her voluntarily, especially love. I believed too that she thought it better for some time to pass before I met my brothers again and also wanted to spare me the sight of Friedrichsruh which had been bombed. As for Schoenhausen . . . You know that the Russians destroyed it totally on their way to Berlin?'

I knew. For a while we sat in silence, remembering the lovely eighteenth-century house and its gardens in which flowers were more sweetly-scented and fruit seemed riper and tasted better than anywhere else in the world. I thought of the crumbling follies and pavilions in the park, of the clipped hedges and baroque statues and the high walls that enclosed so much enchantment, separating it from one of the most depressing landscapes I have ever seen. Flat barren marshland, often flooded by the River Elbe, treeless, grassless mudflats, criss-crossed by dykes and irrigation canals over which the unimpeded wind tore day and night.

Aunt Maggie had come to live in Schoenhausen after Otto's marriage. Eddie and I had stayed with her there several times for a month or two in summer. She rarely had guests except for close relations. The old house was haunted, and people were afraid to stay. Eddie and I didn't mind very much, although there were some nights when we crept into each other's bedrooms on some pretext or other, to borrow a cigarette or a book, and managed to frighten each other so much by talking about ghosts that we couldn't return to our separate rooms, much to the disapproval of Aunt Maggie's maid who also roamed the house at night.

Everyone called her Black Marie. She was indeed very swarthy; she came from Croatia and had been with Aunt Maggie for many years. She was a taciturn, morose and unfriendly person, but utterly devoted to Aunt Maggie. She gave us many dark looks in the mornings after we had spent a night together, but she never told on us. If she suspected we had come together for immoral reasons, she was certainly very much mistaken. All we did was sit and wait for the sound of a rattle which was said to precede the coming of the child.

Its portrait hung on the stairs. It was a rather stiff and primitive painting of the seventeenth century. The child had a funny little round face that peered out of a bonnet, and she wore a tight-waisted gown of pink brocade. In her hand she held a silver rattle. I doubt that Eddie and I ever really heard it. There are so many sounds in old houses at night that can be accounted for – creaking boards, mortar falling between walls, the wind rattling roof-tiles, the scurrying of mice. Nor did the child appear to us, though she frequently did to Aunt Maggie.

In the evenings Aunt Maggie would often read to us from her

translations of the Austrian poets into English or *Tristram Shandy* into German. There were occasions on which she would suddenly pause and seemingly smile at space.

'Is she here?' one of us would whisper.

'Yes.'

'Where?'

'Don't turn now, her hand is on your shoulder.'

I jumped up.

'Now she's gone. You startled her,' Aunt Maggie said disapprovingly. 'She wouldn't have hurt you, she was only trying to be friendly. Poor little lost soul, she was only five when she died.'

Then there was the inexplicable organ music heard at night by the few who ventured to stay in Schoenhausen. It was believed to come from the adjoining gothic church, the house was built on the foundations of a monastery which had been destroyed in the wars of the Reformation. 'A night service perhaps,' Aunt Maggie would suggest to her guests, refraining from disclosing that the church had not been used for many years as it was structurally unsafe, or that the organ had long since fallen to pieces. But all these were more or less benign spiritual manifestations. I don't think Aunt Maggie minded them at all, she had grown quite accustomed to them.

However, there had been one occasion on which, as she expressed it mildly, 'The child had been quite naughty'. At Eddie's request she had told me what had happened.

'Once a Bismarck of the secondary line asked if he could visit me since he had never seen Schoenhausen. I'd never met the man before. There was some sort of feud between the two families in the seventeenth century – a question of inheritance, I think, and it seems never to have been quite forgotten. Because of it we hardly knew these other Bismarcks.

'There was dry rot in this house then, and all of the bedrooms were being repaired, so I put this von Bismarck into the room in which the Chancellor had been born.'

I knew it well, I had even slept in it. It adjoined Aunt Maggie's private apartments and was rarely used, and was only occasionally shown to Bismarck devotees, as the death-chambers had been in Friedrichsruh. It was rather a pretty room, hung from floor to ceiling with eighteenth-century flowered material.

'I was awakened that night by a lot of noise,' Aunt Maggie continued, 'coming from that room. Thinking that perhaps the man had drunk too much wine at dinner and had gone berserk, I rang for Marie.

Together we opened the door.

'The wall-hangings stood straight out from the walls as if blown by some great wind, the room was ice-cold, the china jug and basin on the washstand shattered, and much of the heavy furniture moved from where it had been before. The unfortunate man was in his bed, clutching at the sheets, alive, but obviously in a state of the most abject terror.'

'I still think he must have opened the windows,' Eddie said. 'You know how it blows over these marshes on a stormy night.'

'The windows were both closed,' Aunt Maggie said firmly. 'I left him to Marie who boiled him some coffee. By morning he was gone. I've never heard of him since. There is no other explanation than that it was the child,' she said, 'and that it was some sort of revenge. Her tomb is in the church, but it doesn't tell us why and how she died.'

'Did they murder her?' I asked.

'We will never know,' Aunt Maggie sighed. 'Anyway, I'll never dare ask anyone of that line of the family to stay here again.'

'I wonder whom the child haunts now?' I asked Eddie.

'The Russians, I hope,' Eddie said bitterly. 'Do you remember those wonderful Chinese silk tapestries embroidered with flowering trees and birds that were in the big drawing-room? They were given to my grandfather by the Tsar when he was ambassador in St Petersburg. My mother couldn't take them when she had to flee though she was able to save some silver and furniture.'

'Of course I remember.'

'They were destroyed with all the rest.'

'Now the treasure will never be found.'

'It must lie very deep under the rubble of Schoenhausen by now,' Eddie sighed.

How Eddie and I had searched for it in the many vaulted cellars under the house. Aunt Maggie had insisted that it was there. All the documents in the archives mentioned that in the thirty years' war the monks had buried it before they fled. But although there had been many searches, nothing had ever been found. I'm not sure she didn't tell us about it to keep us happily occupied on rainy days. We spent a lot of time in the musty cellars tapping on hollow walls and digging, but all we found was a walled-in wine cache, forgotten since before the First World War, the old brandy and Tokay probably more valuable than any treasure we could have found.

Aunt Maggie never drank anything but mineral water. She felt herself quite incompetent to judge the quality of the old wines we had discovered, leaving it to Eddie and her two house-guests to do so.

One was Doctor Rudolph Kassner, a life-long Austrian friend of hers, the other her son-in-law Count Herman Keyserling. Both were frequent guests in Schoenhausen in the summer months. They were philosophers of some repute and did not mind the spirits that haunted the house nor did they object to those in bottles.

If they were haunted at all, it was by each other. No two persons could have been less alike, physically as well as mentally, in spite of both being men of learning. Doctor Kassner was a frail cripple and had been so since childhood. His useless legs dangled like a puppet's between the two sticks on which he supported himself. He was all head and no body. He had a rather marvellous face, albeit deeply marked by suffering, eyes that seemed to look penetratingly beyond the surface of things, a nose whose curved nostrils indicated a keen sense of smell and a large, very sensual bitter-sweet mouth.

Keyserling was all body, tall, exuberantly robust and strong, a man of insatiable physical appetites whose bearded face resembled that of a Russian peasant. Only his small alert and sparkling eyes revealed his formidable intelligence.

'Do you remember those evenings with Kassner and Keyserling? How brilliantly they talked!'

'Of course, and my poor mother always trying to keep them from quarrelling. Kassner's still alive, did you know? One of his admirers gave him a house in Switzerland to live in. I made enquiries, I felt Mama would want me to. It seems he's still writing his obscure stuff.'

Kassner's books were difficult for those not versed in philosophy to understand, and neither Eddie nor I were. Still, we had read most of them and had been enchanted by the poetry of their language and their evocative imagery. We did not doubt that he was a profound thinker even if we could only appreciate him as a poet equal to Rilke and Hoffmannsthal, both of whom had been his friends and admirers.

Keyserling's main book, *A philosopher's journey round the world*, had brought him fame and enough money to actually travel round it; it was quite comprehensible and very entertaining, and became a best-seller. His more profound philosophical writings were only read in academic circles. He later founded a school for wisdom in Darmstadt at which he lectured and taught.

'How they disliked each other!' Eddie laughed. 'Do you remember how they used to play hide-and-seek in the park on their morning walks? Keyserling always winning, poor Kassner unable to escape on his sticks in spite of hiding behind the statues and yew hedges? Keyserling usually the pursuer. Yet they couldn't leave each other alone. Even if they loathed each other physically, the delicate Kassner revolted by so much gross power, Keyserling disgusted by the cripple's debility, they knew themselves to be equals mentally and that they profited mutually from all exchanges of thoughts. Yes, those evenings were rather wonderful,' Eddie remembered, 'especially after we found the wine, though Keyserling soon finished most of the brandy.'

'You certainly helped.'

'Well, it was very good. My God, how Keyserling could drink, without it really affecting him much. He was as indestructible as Rasputin!'

'Poor Kassner could only sip. But what fun they were then, Keyserling playing the piano and singing Russian songs. Do you remember when he told us our characters in music? You were all Mozart, I was Strauss. And when Kassner analysed our faces! He really did believe in physiognomy. My ears were all right, he said, not large and standing out like some animal's alert for the sound of danger.'

'So were mine,' Eddie laughed, rubbing his flat ears.

'Not that he thought much of our noses. Only rather insignificant outcrops of your family trees, he said, I doubt you will have many descendants. And do you remember what he remarked about our mouths?'

'I've forgotten.'

'That they didn't close firmly enough at the corners.'

'And what did that mean?' Eddie asked, touching his mouth.

'That we had too little defence against what might enter into us. But he liked our chins, and he liked our eyes, good clear mirrors in which to reflect the world truthfully. And he loved my hair, he said it was like one of Leonardo da Vinci's angels, and then he quoted his friend Rilke, "*Alle Engel'n sind schrecklich*". It's out of the *Duino Elegies*.'

'Yes, he used to stay there often with Princess Thurn und Taxis and Rilke.'

'How frightening are angels? How can one ever translate Rilke into English?'

'My mother tried. Do you know, I've been to Friedrichsruh quite recently. I thought I'd have a look at her grave.'

'Oh, what's Friedrichsruh like now?' I asked, trying to distract him. 'I hear it's all been rebuilt since it was bombed.'

'It's rather pretty. In the Swedish style, I believe, but then I've never visited Sweden. And it's certainly in much better taste than all that former Edwardian grandeur. Still, I didn't feel at home any more. Nearly all the portraits of the old Emperor and of my grandfather are gone, some burnt, some sent to museums.'

'And the death-chambers?'

'Curiously they were the only rooms not destroyed in the bombardment. Ann-Mari has very sensibly converted them into nurseries for her many children.

'Everyone was very kind to me,' Eddie added. 'No one mentioned my desertion in the war, and Otto didn't seem to disapprove at all of my living in America, quite the contrary. I was asked for names and addresses of prominent and important people in New York.' He was silent for a while, clenching and unclenching his fingers, a habit he had when nervous. 'They had put my mother in the Bismarck mausoleum of course.'

I remembered it well. Like the death-chamber, it was a place of Bismarck worship to which pilgrimages were made from all over Germany. It rather resembled the Dôme des Invalides, in miniature. It had been built to glorify the remains of the Iron Chancellor and stood on a small hill adjoining a church, just across the railway line from Friedrichsruh, the peace of both constantly disturbed by the thunder of passing trains.

As children we had enjoyed watching them go by when we stayed there. So I think did Bismarck; there seemed no other possible reason why the house had been built so close to the railway track. It was a large Edwardian mansion erected on the site of a former wayside inn close to the Saxenwald, and there was equally no other explanation as to why Bismarck should have preferred it to his former home, beautiful old Schoenhausen. One of his great achievements had been the network of railway lines that connected all of the German states he had forged into one.

'Just one more tomb for the tourist to gape at,' Eddie said. 'I felt nothing on seeing it; not even her spirit would have wanted to linger there.' He buried his face in his hands. 'I will never forgive myself, never.

'I loved her more than anyone. More than I love you, more than I love Mona even, yet I hadn't the courage to go and see her die.'

'But if she chose to suffer so as to spare you suffering, why can't you accept her last gift to you, and be grateful?'

Eddie had no answer. He got up and went to the open window, looking out into the black night that had darkened the Grand Canal, only occasionally lightened by the lantern of a passing gondola. The silence only broken now and then by the call of a gondolier.

'Why then did she ask for me when she was dying?' Eddie questioned. 'They told me she did.'

I wondered how I could help him. 'For God's sake, come and sit down,' I said, 'and be reasonable. They had to give her so much morphine in the end that she was semi-conscious most of the time. She probably dreamt of you and called your name. Stop brooding. Your mother was over seventy. Did you think she would live for ever?'

'I suppose one does.'

'Anyway, all this feeling guilty is absurd. It's unworthy of her courage, and the last thing she would have wanted. She understood you better than you do yourself. Have you ever seen anyone die?'

'No.'

'Well, I have, and it's not pleasant to watch. Be glad she spared you that.'

'Perhaps you're right,' he said after a long silence.

28

'Now tell me about yourself,' Eddie demanded; he had regained his usual cheerful composure. 'How is Leopold? Is he very unhappy?'

'Sometimes, but it passes. You see, he lives very much in the present, like a child. On a day when he's enjoying himself, he forgets to worry about the future. Also poverty, which we may have to face, has no meaning for him; he has never known it, not even in the war really. There was always someone glad to lend him whatever he needed. He simply can't imagine what having no money might mean. If he was always generous to those who had less than himself, it was not because he understood the problems of poverty or felt any injustice in his having been born rich. It's just that he enjoys giving. I fear that this is going to be one of Leopold's greatest problems in the future. He will only know he's poor once he has nothing left to give.'

'What about those jewels?' Eddie asked. 'They might have gone some way to facilitate Leopold's generous impulses.'

'I haven't heard anything about them,' I confessed, 'but under the circumstances both Niki and Loni must have known that it might be

173

wiser not to mention them in a letter.'

'I very much doubt you'll find them,' Eddie said. 'Loni was in a lot of trouble towards the end of the war when Skorzeny scooped Mussolini from his hill-top prison and reinstated him. Like me, Loni was believed dead for some months. He must have gone into hiding somewhere. And his mother, Countess Arrivabene, died last year.'

'They know I'm here,' I told Eddie. 'I wrote to Niki from Paris. Let's leave it until tomorrow though, there's still so much to talk over.'

We ordered food and wine and went on talking, although it was past midnight.

'You never wrote and told me what happened when you had your own private war in Prague,' Eddie said.

'It only lasted four days, but I think they were the longest in my life.'

'And quite eventful, I gather. Czechs shooting Germans for a change, and welcoming in the Russians.'

'With bread and salt,' I remembered.

'Oh, is that the custom? Do tell me all. From beginning to end.'

'It's difficult, because you don't know the Maltese Palace in which we lived. So much was enacted in and around it. The palace is in the old part of town near the Charles bridge and the river, and it faces the French Embassy, which was closed of course in the war. Our entrance gates led into a large courtyard past Pan Rak's lodge. Rak was the porter and checked everyone who came in or went out. He was rather a clown-like individual with very short arms and a very large head, but he was no fool. He was also a patriotic Czech, and we had learnt to trust him in the war. He had a daughter who, fortunately for her, did not resemble him in looks. She was rather pretty and married to a fine-looking, upstanding Czech policeman called Port. They all lived together in Rak's two-roomed lodge. Port had been in jail for the last half-year, supposedly for having distributed communist leaflets, and his wife was expecting her first baby.

'Beyond the entrance of the palace, a wide and ornately carved stone stairway led to our apartment on the right. Through an arch beyond that was a large courtyard overlooked by tiers of balconied flats. These had two or three rooms and were mainly occupied by labourers and their families.

'Our apartment adjoined the very splendid state reception rooms of the Knights of Malta, all red velvet and gilded panelling, with some very fine tapestries. When we had first rented our small flat we were allowed to use these rooms occasionally for parties, but one day we found them locked and sealed. I peered through the key-hole. Where the tapestries had been there was bare wall. I went to Rak, who confirmed that some Germans had come in the night, warned him to tell no one, and taken the tapestries. It later transpired that Ribbentrop had heard of them and had them stolen for his newly acquired castle in Austria.

'Our flat consisted of only four rooms. We had rented it as a sort of *pied à terre* to stay in overnight when we went to Prague. We had of course never expected that it would be our only home through most of the war. Still, it was very pretty, with all the original eighteenth-century white and gold stucco ceilings and panelling, and I had furnished it accordingly.

'The child and her governess lived separately in one of the balcony flats, as did my maid. It was above the kitchen in which the cook Marina, a crazy witch of a woman who dabbled in black magic, had visions and told fortunes, slept in a sort of cupboard. Still, she performed magic too with the little food available, she was a very good cook.

'My bedroom was very small, all it could contain was a large canopied crimson bed, all embroidered, that had once belonged to an archbishop, two chairs and a chest of drawers. Yet when we had parties, twenty people found room there. It had a sort of hidden door that led into a large oratory that overlooked the nave of the church of the Knights of Malta. There was no other access to the oratory except through my room. I kept my trunks there, and food such as smoked hams from illicitly slaughtered pigs, tea, rice, coffee and flour, all bought on the black market. It was a good hiding place, and would have been so for people too.

'Our flat overlooked a walled garden which was for our use alone. We tried to plant vegetables in it during the war, but an immense plane tree cast too much shade for anything to grow under it. Perhaps most important, at least it became so to me, was the vast vaulted cellar underneath the front part of the palace. That, I think, is all.'

'Well, you've set the scene,' Eddie said. 'I know everything now except why you had your quite unnecessary war. I read at the time that over two thousand Czechs were killed in Prague alone.'

'And many more in the country,' I told him. 'It all started on May fifth in the afternoon,' I remembered. 'Adi Rotter had come to play bridge.'

'I knew them when they were at the Austrian Embassy in Rome,' Eddie interrupted. 'I liked them very much, I even helped Irma decorate her flat. How typically Viennese she was! I doubt if any other town in the world breeds more enchantingly frivolous yet essentially capable and intelligent women.'

'You don't know how wonderful she was in the war. Since there was no more Austria and Adi would not accept any position that involved him in any way with the Hitler regime, he found a small job in a bank in Prague as an accountant. He was paid just enough for them both to survive in a bedsitter with kitchenette. Yet Irma cooked meals there fit for the gods, to which she invited us, her friends and ours.'

'Like what?' Eddie asked.

'Like crayfish and *cèpes*, *Herrenpilze*. At the weekends they both went out by tram to roam the forests around Prague for food. The crayfish were easy to catch in the streams if you knew how, and Adi did. Irma gathered the *cèpes* under the old oak trees where they grew. She gathered herbs too, for although cigarette papers were still available, tobacco was rare. She dried the herbs and rolled them into cigarettes, they weren't too bad. And do you know what we all drank in the last two years of the war? Pure alcohol obtained from a friendly chemist. It was a hundred per cent proof, so of course we had to dilute it with water, but sometimes we made mistakes with the mixture and the consequences were often serious.'

'I'm surprised it didn't kill you!' Eddie exclaimed.

'Oh no, we'd grown quite tough.

'The Rotters were incredibly brave,' I remembered. 'They were in much greater danger than even we were, because at least we were definitely marked as Czechs whereas the Rotters might well have ended up in a concentration camp for being considered non-cooperative Germans, if of Austrian origin.

'Anyway,' I recollected, 'that afternoon Adi had come to play bridge with Leopold, Frenz Nostitz and a young Czech lawyer. We scarcely knew the latter, but he had been invited to make a fourth since he was considered a good player. All of us were feeling cheerful and hopeful for the first time for many anxious weeks. There had been a premature uprising in Slovakia which had been brutally quelled by SS troops who had burnt down whole villages and indiscriminately slaughtered civilians, and we had feared the same might happen in Prague. But now we had heard that the Russians had taken Bratislava and it was even rumoured that President Benes and members of his government were there and that Patton's troops had crossed the frontier at Asch. Surely, we thought, it would only be a matter of hours before the Germans holding Prague capitulated. After all, the war was practically over.

'They started their game. I sat and watched as I always did when Frenz played. It was a lesson in subtle strategy combined with daring, he was a brilliant bridge player. We saw a lot of him and Lisie all through the war, but never too much; they were dependable friends. In those years Frenz played a more dangerous game for even higher stakes than those he favoured at bridge.

'On the one hand he had to safeguard his beautiful Lisie, half Jewish by birth, by being on the best of terms with influential Germans; on the other he used these connections to gather information that might be of use to his Czech friends. It was a double game that demanded skill and courage and he played it superbly.

'It was a warm spring day and we were all sitting close to the open windows. Suddenly there was the sharp crack of a shot, followed by two more. "Damn," I remember Frenz saying, as he threw down his cards, "have they taken to executing some poor beggar in the streets by now?" We looked out into the walled garden but there was nothing to be seen. A volley of shots followed, deafeningly near. "They must be shooting from the roofs," Leopold suggested. "Perhaps it would be wiser to close the shutters," Frenz said. I did.

'Adi went to turn on the radio. There was the usual music, then the "*Achtung, achtung*" which preceded Prague-based German broadcasts. It ordered the population to keep calm and stay at home since there was some shooting in the streets because the traitor Vlasov and his troops had defected from the German army and were trying to fight their way out of Prague to join the Western invaders. The broadcaster said they were being dealt with, as well as those members of the Czech population who had so foolishly believed it an occasion to revolt.'

'But who on earth was Vlasov?' Eddie asked.

'He was a Russian general whom the Germans had taken prisoner early in the war. I'm not sure he wasn't a Ukrainian. In any case, Vlasov was easily persuaded that he disliked Stalinism, and so were many of his fellow prisoners. Told that they had been chosen to help liberate their beloved country, they joined the Germans. But their unit was never allowed near the Russian front. They fought here and there in France, and later in Italy, with great courage. Finally they were sent to help quell the uprising in Slovakia, but that was a mistake.

'You can't imagine how strong the feeling of brotherhood among all Slavonic people is. Under General Vlasov's command they turned against the Germans to fight side by side with the Czech resistance until

177

the Russians marched into Slovakia, from whom of course they could expect no mercy as deserters. Their arrival there coincided with President Benes's call for a general uprising of the whole Czech nation.'

'But wasn't it quite senseless of Benes? He must have known it was all over.'

'Of course he did, but he was a clever man and knew his people. He felt that for the sake of their self-respect, the Czechs who had been oppressed for so long needed this outlet, to be given the chance to fight. Unfortunately the liberation took longer and was far bloodier than he can have expected.

'The German resistance was fierce. They had machine guns, tanks and aeroplanes, and any amount of soldiers who, fleeing from the East, were trying to reach the West. The Czech population, poorly armed and disorganized, couldn't have put up much of a fight without Vlasov and the help of his four thousand men. It was really he who saved Prague. After three days' fighting in the city, which greatly diminished the occupation forces, they moved west and gave themselves up, trusting in the mercy of the Western allies. They were promptly delivered to the Russians. Vlasov and several of his officers were shot, the rest transported to Siberia.'

'What a grim tale,' Eddie remarked.

'There was still sporadic shooting towards evening, but it sounded farther away. Adi and Frenz wanted to hear the English news. I stuck the *Churchilka* into the radio, a piece of wire so named after Churchill. I must explain that the shortwaves on every radio in the country had been blocked by German police two years ago, and on each apparatus a tag had been stuck threatening the death penalty for listening to foreign broadcasts. But since almost everything was punishable by death by then, we didn't care. Our chauffeur Czerni had fixed the *Churchilka* for us. If properly plugged in and connected one could get the BBC. The wire could be pulled out in seconds and hidden in the palm of the hand if anyone not to be trusted came in.

'The BBC told us that Hitler was believed dead and that the Russians were in Berlin. It said the Americans had reached Pilsen and that German capitulation seemed imminent; it also mentioned that due to the national uprising in Prague the German occupation forces were still holding the town.

'Meanwhile the shooting went on. Frenz and Adi left, both saying they had to go back to their wives. Adi had discussed with Leopold whether, as an ex-Austrian diplomat, he shouldn't try and form a sort of interim centre of protection for Austrians still in the country. We agreed that it would be a good idea.

'After that Leopold insisted he must go out and see what was happening. I didn't like this, but as you know he can't be stopped, least of all by anyone's protests.

'I went to fetch the child, fearing she might be frightened. She was not in her room, neither was her governess nor my maid – even Marina the cook had vanished. I looked down from the balcony into the courtyard which was crowded with the inhabitants of the flats. They must have taken the day off work, because there were men as well as women. I saw my daughter and the rest of my household were there too.

'A large Czech flag, white, red and blue, was waving above them. Underneath it was Pan Rak. He must have secreted it for years, awaiting the occasion to unfurl it. "*Prijde den,*" one Czech had whispered to another throughout the war. "The day will come." Proudly he held up the flag, and then intoned the "*Kde Domov Muj*", our national anthem. An astonishingly sonorous bass rose from his barrel chest and soon everyone was singing with him the anthem which, for all I knew, could still bring the death penalty if sung in public. I joined in. It was quite a moment! But I couldn't help thinking that it was all rather dangerous and premature.

'I took the child upstairs with me. She said she wanted a flag of her own and I helped her paint one, not knowing how many more I would have to paint in a few days. I also told her she could sleep with me in my crimson bed for the night which pleased her. Although the shooting had died down with darkness, I felt I'd rather have her near me, though she didn't seem frightened. I suppose the pheasant shoots to which she had been taken at an early age had accustomed her to the sound of shots.

'Leopold had gone out, and hours passed. Pan Rak came up meanwhile to say that his daughter was in labour. He seemed to be more pleased than concerned. When I asked him if he had called a doctor he said that wasn't necessary and that one of the women living in the balcony flats was an experienced midwife. It turned out later to be our cook Marina. "My grandson will, with God's help, be born into a free country," Rak said proudly.

'I had put Diana to bed and still Leopold had not returned. At last I heard his familiar limping step on the stairs. I went to unlock the door and started back in horror. His face was covered in blood; I thought he'd been shot.

'"What's the matter?" he asked. "I'm sorry I'm so late, but they are putting up barricades against the German tanks that are starting to enter the town. I helped a bit."

'"But your face!"'

'"What's wrong with it?" He went to the mirror. "Heavens, no wonder you were startled," he grinned. "I must have cut my finger when I was lifting stones. I suppose I rubbed it all over my face in the dark." He showed me his hand – there was indeed a small wound on one finger.'

29

'The night was more or less quiet, but at dawn the shooting began again, hissing and whistling over the roofs, and there was a new staccato sound which Leopold told me came from machine guns.

'Our first visitor was Franzi Schoenborn.'

'Do I know him?' Eddie asked.

'I don't think so. You would not have forgotten his face. It was badly disfigured in his youth by an explosion and what is left of it is a featureless mask. But he is so intelligent and witty that one forgets. He was a great friend of ours, even if he remained a bit mysterious. However indiscreet he could be about others, he was very reticent about himself. He had been locked up by the Germans several times during the war, it was only much later that we found out that he had always been a member of the communist party.'

'Strange convictions for an aristocrat to have.'

'I think it was somehow connected with his burnt face. Anyway, that morning he was wearing the Czech uniform which we hadn't seen for so long, and he looked very smart and militant. He said that he had asked the Kinsky boys to meet him in our flat.'

'Those three young giants? I met them in Castolovice. Didn't you rather fancy one of them?'

'Well, yes, I did like Alphy best. He was incredibly good-looking and dear, but unfortunately he always really preferred Leopold to me. But I was fond of the others too. They were with us most of the time through the war, the Germans called them "The Sternbergs' bodyguards".'

'They arrived, Franz Anton, the youngest, in Czech uniform too. We gave them all coffee and they told us they were joining friends to try and take over the radio station. Leopold asked them where they would get arms from and they said they had plenty of guns that had been hidden in a cellar on the Hradcany almost under the Germans' feet which they had unearthed before dawn with their friends and transported in a stolen German car. "We've secreted that in a garage near the broadcasting house," Franzi said.

'We implored the boys to be careful, but they were too excited and elated to listen. They all left together.

'The cook Marina, wearing a very dirty apron, came in to tell us that she had safely delivered Mrs Port of a little girl.

'Puki Coloredo was our next visitor, and came in lugging a heavy suitcase. She said she'd come in from the country, that the Russians were rumoured to be very near, and asked if we would look after the bag for her since she didn't dare leave it in the hotel where she was staying. I asked her what was in it.

'"Everything of value that I could grab," she said, "even the golden vessels from our church, and my jewels of course." I hid the bag in the oratory, begging her to stay since the shooting was becoming continual. However, she said she had to get back to her husband and that she didn't mind the shooting. Poor little Puki. She had an incurable lung disease and perhaps knew that a shot would spare her years of suffering.'

'They had that beautiful Renaissance place near you, didn't they?'

'Yes, Opocno.

'There was a knock at the door and Rak poked his head in. We were just starting to congratulate him on the birth of his grandchild, when we noticed that his round clown's face was as white as powder, and that he was trembling.

'"There's a uniformed German downstairs," he whispered. "I think it's a general. He wants to see you, Pan Hrabe."

'You can imagine how we felt. Leopold ordered me to go to my bedroom and not to come out until he called me. "I doubt if he's come to arrest me, they always do that in twos, but perhaps they are short of men by now," he joked.

'A few minutes later I heard the sound of laughter and a voice that sounded familiar. "It's only Poldi Fugger," Leopold called.'

'Wasn't he Leopold's cousin?' Eddie asked.

'Not only that, but they were practically brought up together. However, we hadn't seen him for years. Poldi told us that the Russians were advancing so rapidly that they would be in Prague in a matter of days. He said that he was retreating with his troops towards the west, constantly harassed by Czech snipers, and that he had lost several men. He then asked Leopold if it would not be wiser for them to circumvent Prague, complaining that all hell seemed to have broken out in the town.

'"You wouldn't get through without considerable losses," Leopold told him. "I can only advise you not to try."

'The child came running to tell us triumphantly that the radio station was in Czech hands. "The Kinsky's have won," she said gleefully, then she caught sight of Poldi. She was only nine then, but she had learnt to recognize a German uniform when she was five.

'"This is your uncle Poldi," I hastily explained. She only shook hands with him very hesitantly. We turned on the radio as a Czech voice called on all the nation to rise against the Germans, then there was a sudden silence interrupted only by the ak-ak of machine guns, and the station went off the air.

'Leopold turned away, his face grim.

'"What's up now?" Poldi asked. "I've forgotten my Czechisch."

'"Nothing much except this. You won't get back through the town alive in that uniform," Leopold said. "Take it off; I'll lend you some clothes and we can hide you here until it's all over. Why, even now the porter who saw you may be telling someone that there's a German general up here. Angry Czechs might storm the flat and tear you to pieces, and us too for harbouring you."

'"We could always say he was our prisoner," I ventured.

'"That wouldn't help him much," Leopold snapped. "Just take off that uniform," he told Poldi, "and everything will be all right."

'Poldi seemed to hesitate, he looked so wan and exhausted that I felt very sorry for him. I brought him some coffee which he drank thirstily, then I took him to my room and showed him the oratory where he would be able to hide if it became necessary. The irony of the situation struck me. I had always hoped that a British parachutist would come to us and ask for help and that I would take him to the safety of the oratory; I had even put a mattress and pillows in it, just in case. Of course, he never came, and now I was as anxious for a German's safety as I would have been for his.

'"I'm rather tired," he confessed, "I can't think clearly any more. We've been on the march for three days and nights. If I might just rest for a while?"

'Leopold bundled together some clothes, gave them to him, and closed the door. The radio called "*Achtung, achtung*". So the station was in German hands again. It warned all Czechs to keep off the streets and proclaimed martial law.

'Poldi returned. He had tidied himself up, and brushed his uniform and looked refreshed and determined. "Your clothes were always too big for me, they never did fit," he said to Leopold with a wry smile, "but thank you both."

'I couldn't help noticing how well his uniform did fit. It must have been made for him by a first-class tailor.

' "I'll have to be going," he said.

' "Don't be a damned fool, Poldi!" Leopold exclaimed. "Don't you know the war is over?"

' "Perhaps, but as long as there has been no official capitulation I'm still a German general, and responsible for my men."

'He gave Leopold a friendly shove, and kissed my cheek and hand.

' "Hope to see you again soon," he said as he left.

'We never did. He is still in prison in Russia, though he's allowed to write to his family. Two days after he left us he was captured by the advancing Russians and so were those of his men who remained alive.'

'And all because of a uniform?' Eddie wondered.

By then I was recalling everything that had happened in those few days so vividly that I couldn't stop talking.

'Franzi Schoenborn returned,' I continued, 'he told us there was still a fierce battle for the radio station going on, it had been taken and retaken and there had been many dead on both sides. To our great relief the Kinsky boys were all right. "We ran out of ammunition," he explained, "so we quit."

' "And how's the rest of the revolution going?" Leopold asked.

' "Not too well, Vlasov's troops are fighting heroically, so are some Czechs. But the Germans are still holding key points in the town, and they have brought in the tanks."

' "Don't the barricades stop them?"

' "They did at first, and some tanks were destroyed by grenades or by fuel being flung at them and set alight. But now they march Czech civilians in front of them and make them take the barricades down at gun-point. There's no way to stop the tanks short of killing our own people. Also, there's a rumour that a German order has been intercepted that Prague is to be bombed in reprisal for what is happening now, once the Germans have left. But I don't think it can be true," Franzi added hastily, seeing my face.

'All our friends knew what a coward I was about our being bombed,' I told Eddie. 'It's something I can't explain, and will always be ashamed of. No one wants to die, but the question is, how? I don't think I would have minded so much being shot, I believe I could have held out even if the Gestapo had got me. It was the horrible impersonality of death dropping indiscriminately from the sky, the shrieking sound of the sirens, the crash of the falling bombs, the fear of being trapped in a cellar or shelter, and of being burnt alive or dismembered, or, worse, seeing it happen to others and having to hear their screams of fear and agony, that upset me. Even if I thought of England, and of what was happening there and with what stoical courage it was being faced, even if I remembered the German civilians, no less brave under bombardment, and tried to pull myself together, it didn't help me much.'

'Everyone is afraid of something,' Eddie said, trying to comfort me. 'But I thought Prague was never bombed?'

'Only once, and that was an accident. The allied planes that flew over Prague daily, so high in the sky that all one could see was tiny silver dots, made a mistake on their way to bomb Germany, and mistook Prague for Dresden. I suppose from the air it must look much the same, what with the river and the castle. It wasn't very serious, a few people killed, some houses burnt or destroyed. But you can imagine what the German propaganda made of it. Anyway, the Germans were furious that the Czechs knew themselves safe from allied air raids. Of course, the Skoda works, the big armament factories near Pilsen, had been bombed twice, but thanks to the *Churchilka* everyone had been forewarned of the raid by the BBC and there were no casualties.

'There was really no reason at all to sound the sirens every time allied planes flew over Prague, it was merely a German effort to intimidate our population. No one was really frightened, except me. I went down into the cellar with the child every time after that bombing when the alarm came. Because I didn't want her to become afraid too, I made a sort of treat out of it, keeping toys and sweets in reserve for these occasions, and telling her stories while we waited for the all-clear. Meanwhile Leopold would entertain the guests we always had for meals in our flat, too tolerant of human weakness not to let me indulge in mine.'

'Well, what happened next?' Eddie asked rather impatiently, although he didn't look at all bored.

'That morning? Toti walked in (my sister-in-law, Toti Radetzky).

Oddly enough, she was carrying a large black umbrella, though it was a bright, hot, sunny day. She lived rather far away from us in the outskirts of Prague.

'"But how on earth did you get here?" Franzi asked. "No trams are running, no buses, no taxis."

'"I walked, I simply had to see if you were all right," she said to Leopold.

'"You walked through all this shooting?" I asked, aghast.

'"Shot does rather fall from the house-tops like hail, I walked under this so as to be safe." She indicated her umbrella.

'"Aunt Toti, Pany Portova has had a baby," my daughter told her. She had been sitting quietly and unnoticed behind a Chinese screen which concealed a large and ugly iron stove that warmed our flat in winter, listening to all we said.

'"What a day to bring an infant into this world!" Toti exclaimed. "Is the father still in prison?"

'"Not for much longer," Franzi said. "We have planned to break into the jails next and to free the prisoners."

'Toti begged the child to go and bring her a cup of coffee from the kitchen. "I didn't want to talk about it in front of her," she explained, "but I saw some German soldiers lying dead in the streets, and a lot of other corpses, some of them women, Czech I suppose. I also saw one man being burnt alive. They had thrown petrol over him and set him alight. A German or a collaborator, I don't know."

'After she had drunk her coffee, Toti said she had to go, because there were a lot of friends she still had to visit. It was of course not real coffee we distributed so freely,' I explained to Eddie, 'it was made of toasted oak kernels which the foresters sent us from Castolovice.

'"I don't think it's the right time to pay social calls," Franzi told her.

'"She hasn't even a *legitimace*," Leopold said, which was true since my sister-in-law was Austrian by marriage.

'"I will have to see to it that the Prague *Narodny Vybor* gives her one," Franzi said.

'These cards,' I explained to Eddie, 'which all Czechs carried in the war, were issued by the Germans to mark one as a second-class citizen with only half the rights to food rations which Germans had, but in the days of our revolution and for months afterwards, their value became very great, especially if one didn't speak perfect Czech. Carrying one might mean the difference between life and death since they proved one's nationality.

'I begged Toti not to go; the shooting was by then almost un-interrupted.

'"I have my umbrella," she laughed. And incredible courage, I thought.

'After she left Brigide and Jozi Bromovsky came to gather informa-tion, almost as intrepid as Toti. Nothing would have induced me to venture out on to the streets by then.'

'Bromovsky? I don't think I know them,' Eddie pondered.

'Well, you did know Brigide's sister, only too well – Anthony Jenkins's wife.'

'Indeed,' he smiled; whatever he remembered must have been enjoyable.

'Brigide was the youngest of the Dunns. You probably never met her,' I said. 'She ran away from home when she was almost a child and married a German boy not much older than herself. He was killed in the first year of the war; there she was in Germany, a suspect foreigner, almost friendless, and very unhappy. She packed up and fled with her year-old baby son. How and why she came to Czechoslovakia, I can't remember now; one day someone brought her to our flat, introducing her as Countess Metternich, which she was by marriage. I knew nothing whatsoever about her then. In those days one was suspicious of every-one and very careful of what one said to strangers.

'Brigide was not. Her remarks about the Germans were such as I felt only a spy or an *agent provocateur* could afford to make, even if this one was just a slip of a girl. And yet she was obviously English and very appealing. "Here we go," I thought, and spoke equally unflatteringly about Hitler. Soon I realized how absurd my fears had been. While she was in Prague she married a very good-looking young Czech, Jozi Bromovsky, whom we all liked and whose family we knew well. He was a very kind and gentle person, and if anyone was worthy of her it was he. We saw a lot of both of them in and after the war. They are in England now, they managed to get out just in time. I don't know how, I think Franzi Schoenborn helped. I haven't seen them since. Really, the worst of all this business is the dispersal of all one's friends.'

'Well, continue your tale,' Eddie urged.

'I suppose we all had our highly alcoholic drinks as usual, and I think our guests left. Anyway, we were alone except for the child and had just started lunch when Rak reappeared, looking more frightened than ever, to say there was a large German car down-stairs. Czechs didn't have private cars any more then, and very few Germans did because of the scarcity of gasoline. Only members of the protectorate government, its military or police forces still drove.

'"Who is it?" we asked Rak.

'"I don't know," he said. "I think it is the Gestapo!"

'We went to the one window from which we could overlook the courtyard. There indeed it was, a huge, ominous, black Mercedes. And from behind the windows of the balcony flats, half-concealed by curtains, many eyes were observing it. A pair of very long sun-tanned legs were what first spilled out of the car, followed by the rest of a pretty fair-haired girl, and after that, Hansi Larisch. They waved when they saw us, and came running upstairs.'

'Another cousin?' asked Eddie.

'Yes, we hadn't seen Hansi for years, nor had I met his wife before. He was much younger than Leopold, and almost a child when we used to stay with his parents in Solza. His father, Uncle Hansi Larisch was my mother-in-law's eldest brother.'

'I know,' said Eddie. 'Stinking rich! Coal. He wanted to marry your mother, did you know?'

'Yes, he often told me so, but I'm not surprised she didn't take him. Anyone more parvenu, I have never met. And for no known reason. The family was just as good as any other. But his wife, Aunt Olivia, was sweet.'

'English, wasn't she?'

'Her father was Irish, Fitzpatrick, her mother American.'

'And Hansi's wife?'

'Silesian. Born Schaffgotsch.' Eddie always liked to know these things.

'Well, go on.'

'Hansi apologized for not having been able to telephone since there was such disorder everywhere, and asked if they could stay to lunch. He said they were on their way to Vienna where their parents were already.

'"Things were getting a bit hot in Solza with the Russians only a day's march away," he explained, "so we packed up and left."

'"And how on earth do you think you'll get through to Vienna?" Leopold asked them. I saw how irritated he was. The anti-climax of having expected arrest by the Gestapo only to be confronted by Hansi had shaken even his nerves.

'"Well, we got here all right, except for a few shots; fortunately they missed the tyres."

'"And us," the fair one giggled.

'But Leopold still looked grim. "Has your car a German number?"

'"I suppose so, it's one of Father's," Hansi said.

'"And what sort of papers have you?"

'"German ones, of course, Father thought they'd win the war."

'"And he didn't think of getting you a Czech legitimation card, just in case?" Leopold asked, with some irony.

'"No," Hansi said. "Why?"

'"Because by now you can't move a step without a *legitimace* and remain safe."

'"Can't we buy some?" Hansi asked.

'"I'm afraid that's one thing that is not for sale since it's worth a life. And without it, if you were stopped . . ."

'"But Hansi drives very fast," his young wife said with pride.

'Of course, we couldn't let them go, though we had no guest-rooms in the flat. I gave them my bedroom, and we warned them not to show themselves at the window that faced the courtyard under any conditions. Even if they had been seen, as I feared, their presence might be forgotten in the general excitement. I still don't know if their courage was sublime, or just foolish youthful disregard of danger, for the next two days and nights certainly tested everyone's nerves.'

30

'That day towards evening the shooting died down again as it grew dark. Alphy came, and looked at our guests with some amazement.'

'It's difficult to understand why all you rabid Czechs sheltered Germans in the end,' Eddie remarked.

'But you know how interrelated we all are. Even if those on the German side didn't dare go near us during the war, and we as Czechs were equally afraid to be identified with them, and both parties thought each other fools because of their convictions. You don't hate your brother or your cousin just because he's been stupid, and if he's in real trouble you help.

'Alphy told us that the Germans were withdrawing from Prague but that there was still a lot of shooting. "I've brought you these," he said, unwrapping a brown paper parcel. Czech flags fluttered all over the room. "People have become rather trigger-happy by now. They shoot at or smash any window that doesn't display a Czech flag. In consequence the whole town is decorated as if for Carnival."

'"Some carnival," muttered Leopold, "with thousands dead."

'I went up to say goodnight to the child and to hear her prayers as I always did. Svata Maria, the Hail Mary and the Our Father in Czech, Gentle Jesus in English, and God bless Mammy and Papi, Aunt Toti and Uncle Poldi and Uncle Hansi and the hedgehog in the garden and Milan. The latter was the son of a rather pretty Czech widow who lived in one of the balcony flats. He was Diana's age and used to play with her in our garden. The widow and I smiled at each other when we met, but I avoided further acquaintance as she had a German friend, a count, who frequently stayed with her, whom we neither liked nor trusted.

'I kissed the child goodnight, reassured her governess, who was rather excitable, that there was nothing to worry about, and told her that all was going well and she could indeed visit her parents the next day. Then I went to the kitchen to ask Marina what she could conjure up for our unexpected guests, and warned her not to speak about them to anyone. This was quite unnecessary since she had learnt to be secretive because of her sinister magical practices.

'Dinner was quite gay. Alphy had stayed, and the three good-looking young people laughed and teased each other as if no war had ever separated them. At nine we listened to the BBC. The news was good; most of the German forces had surrendered and the final capitulation was expected to be signed by Admiral Doenitz who had proclaimed himself Hitler's successor. Berlin was in Russian hands. Although the night was quieter I had to share Leopold's bed, which I hadn't done for years. Not that he noticed I was in it, he was much too tired by then, but I couldn't sleep at all.

'Next morning we heard President Benes on the radio, speaking from Bratislava. He praised Czech courage in the fight for freedom, but warned everyone not to risk lives unnecessarily since General Svoboda was marching on Prague with his troops to restore order. We left the radio on all day, of course. Meanwhile Hansi played card games with the delighted child and his wife combed and rolled up her long fair hair on curlers.

'The warning came towards evening, over the radio. As Franzi Schoenborn had told us earlier, an order of the German High Command had been intercepted, threatening the destruction of Prague by bombs as a final gesture of retaliation. It asked all the citizens to seek the nearest shelter and to remain there until further notice was given. Soon after the alert sounded.

'Through the courtyard window we could see a steady stream of people carrying pieces of luggage and featherbeds, coming out of the entrance which led to the various apartments, all making their way down the cellar stairs. Rak was standing by waving his short arms and giving orders. Several passers-by were also going into the cellar. Leopold told me to take the child and hurry, and said that he would send down the servants. He refused to go himself, promising, however, to come down when the bombing started.

'"I can't leave them here alone," he said, indicating the door behind which we could hear the Larischs talking and laughing, "and I can't risk them being seen by all those people in the cellar either. That damn car of theirs is conspicuous enough. If it comes to the worst I'll bring them down, but not before."

'It was a huge cellar built of great blocks of stone with stone arches and there were racks of slatted wood all along the walls on which I suppose the wines of the Knights of Malta rested in former days. They made quite good benches, even if they were rather high off the ground. There was electricity in the cellar, a small bulb hung from the ceiling, but it was still very dark. My maid, Marenka, came down with rugs and pillows, but she refused to stay.

'There must have been about forty people in the cellar, mostly women. Mrs Port was there with her newborn baby; Rak had made her comfortable on a featherbed but she looked very wan and pale. I sat down on the bench next to her and admired the small pink creature bundled in shawls. There were only a few familiar faces; an old woman who took in washing had piled six *periny*, the feather eiderdowns which are the dearest possessions of the working-class Czech, one on top of the other, and was lying on them, obviously prepared to spend the night; another had brought several saucepans; it wasn't clear whether she hoped to cook an evening meal on them or whether she just wanted to save them. A man sat clutching a violin-case and there was a remarkably good-looking and well-dressed girl holding a big bunch of yellow roses. Milan and his mother were there, and the boy came over to sit with Diana. They started some game together with a bit of string.

'A woman was hugging her cat, trying to keep it out of the reach of a dog who was struggling to tear itself free from its lead; there was a lot of hissing and growling and some laughter. No one seemed very frightened except me, but I hoped it didn't show. I asked the pretty girl with the roses where she came from. She was doing her nails with a manicure set she had taken out, and said she had just been walking by when the alarm sounded. She had been on her way to the American Embassy to welcome the Americans.

'"They will be here any moment now," she said, "my mother is from Chicago."

'Leopold came down, grinning at the Breugel-like scene, gave us some sandwiches and handed me a bottle of our alcohol mixture, but refused to stay. I asked how the Larischs were.

'"Making love in your scarlet bed by now no doubt. It's eleven o'clock."

'"Why don't they sound the all-clear?" I asked anxiously.

'"I suppose the threat remains," he said. "The German garrison has not capitulated yet, and they hold the airport."

'He went here and there, talking and joking, spreading warmth and reassurance in the cellar which was getting rather chilly by then. People took out loaves of bread and *Tlascenkas*, a sort of sausage, slicing off pieces with kitchen knives and sharing them with whoever wanted some. Then they settled down to sleep.

'Mrs Port fed the newborn child, baring her breast quite unashamedly. Then they too slept, as did my daughter wrapped in rugs beside me. I didn't dare sleep. The peaceful scene was absurd and yet somehow endearing. An old woman had put on her nightcap before she hid under her *perina*, the man embraced his violin as tenderly as he might a lover, the pretty girl lay beside her yellow roses. There is such trusting innocence in sleeping faces. And yet I knew that at any moment the scene might change into one of fear and horror.

'It came, but not from bombs. There was a sudden commotion as a man in prison uniform came pounding down the stairs. "The Gestapo are after me," he screamed, "they are coming to kill us." Although his head was shaven and his full-fleshed handsomeness gone, I recognized Port the policeman. Rak came running after his son-in-law, trying to calm him. I knew there would soon be panic in the cellar; people were picking up their belongings ready to flee. What were bombs compared to the threat of the Gestapo?

'I stood up. "Come here, Pan Port," I said. I took his trembling hand and led him to where his wife was lying with the child. She stretched out her arms to him, but he backed away. "They will kill her too," he sobbed, "and my baby."

'"It's not true," I said with all the authority I could muster. "There's not a Gestapak left in Prague by now, they've all fled. The war is over, Pan Port, the Russians will be here in a day or two. Don't you know?"

'I suppose he didn't, having broken out of Pancratz jail that night. He knelt in front of me and clung like a frightened child. "It's all over, Pan Port, it's all right, Pan Port," I repeated again and again as I stroked his shaven head. But still the tears flowed, and though at last he lay down beside his wife, we heard his sobs all night.

'At dawn the all-clear sounded. Diana and I went up to bathe and breakfast. Leopold told me that the German garrison in Prague had capitulated following the unconditional surrender of all German forces everywhere. We hugged each other; we had won our war at last, but there were still problems. Rak came up.

'"It's the German car in the courtyard, Pan Hrabe," he stammered. "There's a gentleman protesting at its being there. He is making a disturbance."

'We looked out of the window. There was indeed a small crowd gathered in the courtyard, and we saw that Count X, Milan's mother's friend, was gesticulating and obviously stirring up trouble. Leopold went down and I followed.

'"What is this German car doing here?" he asked Leopold aggressively. "Are you perhaps hiding Germans?" There were some angry murmurs; popular as Leopold was, Czech tempers were strained to the utmost by then. But the night had given me courage. The man was obviously trying to prove himself a patriotic Czech, which he certainly wasn't.

'"Have you a *legitimace*?" I asked him softly.

'He flushed. "I wouldn't want to hurt a woman, even if she insulted me," he said, "but I will hold your husband responsible for your offensive remark."

'"I'm quite ready," Leopold laughed. "Let's go into the garden and discuss the matter."

'Port, who seemed completely recovered from the night's ordeal and was dressed again in his police uniform, which hung round his emaciated form like a scarecrow's clothes, was the only one who noticed that Count X was armed. But so by then was he; revolver at the ready he followed them into the garden; I walked behind.

'"Well, what is there to discuss?" Leopold asked. "Some Austrian relations of mine happened to drive in a German car and they left it here. I can't push it away."

'The Count looked at Port's revolver. "Just a mistake," he mumbled.

'We never saw him again, nor did Milan's mother. She later committed suicide. She may have loved him.

'Nevertheless the problem of our guests and the car remained acute. Adi and Irma came for lunch. "Can't you make them Austrians and give them Austrian papers?" Leopold asked Adi.

'"But I have no authority whatsoever to do so," Adi protested. "I'd have to fake it all. They are Germans, aren't they?"

'"Oh come on, Adi," Irma said. "It's an emergency. We've risked so much we might as well risk this. Leopold needs help."

'By evening the Larischs had their Austrian papers and Austrian flags which the child and I painted and stuck all over the car. They reached Vienna safely.'

'You saved their lives!'

'Perhaps,' I said. What for? I thought sadly. That laughing fair girl was killed in a motor accident some months later.

'That morning our square facing the French Embassy suddenly became crowded with men in French uniforms or prison clothes. They were French prisoners who had been freed – some from concentration camps or slave labour units. They were being assembled at the embassy on their way back to France, but train services had of course been disrupted in the last few days and the French Embassy couldn't shelter them all. There they stood or lay in our square; many were ill, some dying. My sister-in-law Toti came to help. We carried out mattresses and pillows and whatever food and drink we could find.

'"You'll be in France soon," Toti comforted an old soldier as he died.

'Next day, in the early morning, the Russians came. Rak came to tell us that three truckloads of them had stopped in front of the palace entrance. Everyone from the balcony flats came down carrying plates of bread and salt to welcome them. So did I and the child, Leopold went back to sleep.'

'But weren't you terrified?' Eddie asked.

'Not in the least. My capacity for fear was too exhausted by then, besides they were just boys, some can't have been older than fifteen. Many lay asleep in their trucks; they had fought all the way from Berlin to Prague, and they were tired. They had taken off their uniform jackets, their shirts were torn and dirty, and their sunburnt chests exposed. To my surprise I saw that many of them wore large plain silver crosses on a string around their necks.

'Children soon swarmed all over the trucks, lifted on to them by the soldiers. Up went my daughter and her friend Milan too. I must bathe her immediately after this, I thought. The men were filthy, probably covered with lice, and carrying God knows what diseases, but I let her have fun. Russian and Czech don't seem dissimilar languages, even if the accent is quite different, but there are many words that have quite opposite meanings, and there was a lot of laughter as the children and the soldiers tried to communicate.

'There were similar scenes all over Prague on that warm and sunny morning on the ninth of May. Everywhere children and soldiers made friends; but then so many of those soldiers weren't much older than the children. Even the seemingly inexhaustible source of Russian man-power must have been depleted towards the end of the war.

'Russian troops were to remain with us for three more months. All in all, I can't say they behaved badly. Their square-built women in uniform directed the town's traffic quite efficiently, the young soldiers stood at street-corners fingering their short flute-like guns which they carried waist-high, but there were very few incidents. After all, we were friends and allies. Of course one would have preferred liberation by the West, but to be liberated at all deserved gratitude.

'The weeks after our war ended were a time of rejoicing and of mourning. President Benes was back. We could look up to the Hradcine, the seat of government, and at the many-spired cathedral that contained so much of Bohemian history with fresh hope and confidence, though they looked down on a city mourning its dead.

'Wherever one went among the streets and squares of Prague a pencilled note on a scrap of paper, or one more elaborately penned in ink with a name and a date was attached to a wall, or just laid between two stones on the street, and beside it a funeral wreath or a bunch of spring flowers. But it was the living more than the dead that one learnt to sorrow for. The survivors of the German concentration camps, now freed, roamed the streets of Prague. Not only Czechs, but French, Dutch, Jews, Poles, Russians, many in rags, some with shaven heads and in prison uniform, but all emaciated, many crippled, their eyes still abject with fear or ablaze with hate. Of course there were committees and organizations formed to help and advise all these displaced people; the diplomatic representatives of the various countries involved had reached Prague.

'But there was no protection for the Germans who were left. Small shopkeepers and tradesmen who knew they had never done anyone any harm and had stayed confident that their Czech friends would protect them were ruthlessly persecuted. Members of the aristocracy who had not declared themselves Czech, but had neither been actively pro-

Hitler, were imprisoned or at best allowed to leave the country with a suitcase, their estates confiscated and many of their beautiful castles looted and wantonly destroyed by angry mobs of Czechs.

Meanwhile the town was bright with flags. The Red Russian flag with its hammer and sickle so reminiscent in colour and design of the German one with its swastika flew side by side with our white, red and blue. The British military mission came. The first of the embassies that was reopened was the British with Phil and Phyllis Nichols. They came with their dogs and their children and their nanny. You can't imagine, Eddie, how good that old embassy smelt to me and what comfort being there brought me – the nursery smells of talcum powder and Pears soap, the doggy smells, even that of Phil's shabby old tweeds, the mess and disorder the happy children made with their tennis racquets, hockey sticks and gumboots. One evening Phyllis took me up to her bedroom before we dined. There were three large dogs on the bed, curled up in such secure and confident sleep that all I longed for was to join them; I'd had enough of trying to be brave, I was tired out!'

'And no wonder,' Eddie said. 'Thank you for telling me all that. I'm glad I didn't know at the time exactly what was happening or I would have worried even more than I did. Look, it's almost dawn.'

The sky was indeed silvering over the Salute. He left me, and both of us slept far into the morning.

After lunch I called up Niki and she asked me to come to the palace at six. 'As you always used to. We have something special to show you.' I thought she might be referring to the jewels. 'It's my new sister-in-law Graziella,' she said in her lilting voice. 'We all love her, and so will you. Bring your cousin of course, he's an old friend.'

'Palazzo Papadopoli,' I said to the gondolier once again and wondered why pronouncing what had seemed an almost magical invocation in the past had lost its power to stir my imagination.

The rickety lift had not changed, nor had the attics among the clouds, but the white stucco had gone rather grey and the gold had flaked from the ceilings. As I looked at my friends and they at me we knew we had aged and were not the same. Loni introduced his young wife to me with pride written all over his still remarkably handsome face. No wonder they all adored her. Half shy child, half self-assured woman, she had all the beauty and grace of her Venetian ancestry. It was she who poured the tea, offered sugar and milk and biscuits, making it quite obvious in her gentle way who was mistress of the Papadopoli by then.

I asked Loni what had happened to him after the African campaign in which I knew he had taken part.

'I believed you dead for several months,' I told him.

He said that after Marshal Badoglio had made peace with the allies he had found his way home to Venice and that when Mussolini had returned to power he had joined those who were fighting against the Germans.

'On foot and in the woods,' he said. 'And me a captain of the navy! Some of my men were captured and interrogated. One of them broke down and confessed, poor lad, I don't blame him. But after that I was high on the wanted list, and we dispersed and I went into hiding. Here, and do you know where?'

'In the secret golden rooms of course.'

'So you remember? Graziella has them now as I had always intended.' She gave him a shy smile. How like the lovely woman painted by Tiepolo she was, and how she must grace the golden bed in which no other woman had been permitted to sleep.

'I was kept locked up in there, Mother, Niki and Madina occasionally fed me.' Loni laughed. 'Of course they came looking for me. You can imagine how Mother confronted them. Because of Granny she spoke perfect German.'

I could indeed see the scene, Countess Arrivabene receiving the intruders with a polite but icy dignity that would have frozen even a member of the Gestapo.

'In any case,' he continued, 'they never found the secret rooms or me, though they searched all over the palace. The Americans had gone by then of course, and there was floor after floor of empty rooms.'

We talked for a long time; they wanted to hear all about what had happened to me and to Eddie in the war. But it had grown very late, and I knew it was time to leave. Eddie gave me a significant glance as I got up to thank Loni and Graziella. Of course I knew exactly what it meant, but I ignored it. I kissed Niki goodbye, and realized she was shaking with laughter.

'Haven't you forgotten something rather important here?' she asked. Loni left the room and returned with a large heavy white envelope which he gave me. My name was on it and in Countess Arrivabene's stiff and angular handwriting the words 'To be delivered at request of owner'.

'Well?' I asked Eddie triumphantly as we walked home from the palace with the jewels safe in my bag.

'Well,' he had to concede. It needed no further words between us. In the evening I took him to the airport. We embraced. 'See you in New York,' we both said.

31

Next day I boarded one of the motor boats at the Danieli that leave hourly for the Lido. They wait for passengers under the Bridge of Sighs – a prison and a palace on each hand – but since Byron's time the palace had become a hotel and the dreaded prison under the leads of the Signoria was no more in use. On the Lido I went to the Excelsior and asked at the reception for Madame Millesrois. I was told she was on the beach, and was given the number of her cabin.

I walked down the wide stretch of white sand with its rows of striped umbrellas and cabanas that fringed the sea. How familiar it all was! In the first years of our marriage Leopold and I had spent many a fortnight on the Lido. Not only was it the fashionable thing to do, but both of us liked swimming. However, the main attraction of the beach was to watch those that displayed themselves on it. It was like an exhibition ground on which only the most superb and expensive specimens of the human race were on show. What had happened to all those beautiful people?

I knew that Princess Jane San Faustino who had queened it over all of us had since died. But she was an old lady even then when she held court under her umbrella on the beach, always dressed in long flowing white garments, her sharp-featured face softened by the white crêpe widow's veil she wore. She would sit in front of her cabana morning and evening like a spider in the centre of her web, spinning threads of intrigue in which many got inextricably tangled. Although she did not devour her victims she quite often destroyed them. Those that had not shown her due respect or others whose morals she found objectionable soon vanished from the Lido. Princess Jane was American by birth and of Puritan ancestry. She was very witty and her sharp sarcastic remarks were repeated all over the beach; those of whom she disapproved never quite recovered from the bite of her humour.

I thought of all the handsome men who had roamed that beach, always in search of fresh prey; no half-way attractive woman had been safe from their attentions. Andi Robilant with his narrow brown hawk's face and golden hawk's eyes, Bebino Salina, dark and sleek as a black tomcat, the tall and splendid Duke of Spoleto, young Randolph Churchill and many others, equally attractive.

And the beautiful women! They came to grace that beach for a fortnight in August from every country, all of them ladies of wealth and fashion and secure social position. Mere good looks gave no entry to that exclusive set, and only very rarely did women who hoped to sell their favours penetrate that closed circle. Princess Jane saw to that. Nor would the men have been interested – why pay when so much was available at no cost at all?

Of all the famous beauties there, some of the Englishwomen were the most dazzling to Italian eyes. Their fair hair and complexions and cool self-assurance were irresistible to Latin males. I remember only a few of their names and faces; Lady Abdy, Lady Castlerosse, the two lovely Mitford girls, and the quite unforgettable Lady Diana Cooper, the most beautiful woman I had ever seen.

And those of other nationality? There was Princess Natalie Paley who was Russian, Tilly Losch, Viennese but married to an Englishman, Tiny Seilern, Leopold's cousin, also Austrian, the Venetian Madina Arrivabene, Eileen, later Countess Branka and Barbara Hutton, both Americans, and many long-legged Swedish girls and shorter-legged but seductive South Americans, all lovely. It was not easy for a woman less well-endowed to compete with so much beauty. If I didn't lose my self-confidence it was because people were kind to me; I was still very young and my naïvety probably was an amusement and novelty in that very sophisticated society.

Leopold was much too self-assured and certain of me then to resent the successes I had, even if they were mainly with men. The social life of the Lido didn't interest him much – he couldn't have cared less who was who or what they did, nor perhaps very much what I was doing. He had come to the Lido to swim, to lie in the sun, to eat good food, to drink quantities of wine and to observe the women who displayed themselves on the beach, marking their good and bad points much as if he had been judging horses. He made friends indiscriminately as usual, picking up most undesirable Czechs and Austrians in Venice and bringing them to the Lido.

What a silly snob I'd been then, I thought, with some amusement, always embarrassed by Leopold's choice of friends. Well, the war had cured all that.

I walked along the beach which had once been so white and swept clean every morning and evening with big brooms by small Venetian urchins. Now it was black in many places with oil or tar, empty cigarette packets and torn bits of paper had been discarded everywhere, and the people that sunned themselves on mattresses to the blare of transistors seemed of an altogether different species from those I remembered. But then nearly twenty years had passed since I first came to the Lido.

I found cabana number five. There was a powerful smell of scents and ointments, voluminous bathrobes littered the floor, but there was no Madame Millesrois in sight. In front of the adjoining cabin a man was reclining in a deck-chair, his face covered with a piece of newspaper. All that was visible was a huge stomach and two very hairy legs. I suppose I had disturbed his nap, because he sat up and stared at me. It was Maurice Rothschild.

'What were you doing in that cabin?' he asked gruffly in French.

'But don't you recognize me, Baron Maurice?'

'I really can't be expected to remember every woman I've known,' he grunted.

I think Maurice was not only the worst-mannered, but also the ugliest man I've ever met; he resembled a great, gross warty toad. I didn't know him as well as I did his Austrian relations, but I had met him occasionally in Monte Carlo and Paris. He was really revolting to look at, his rudeness proverbial and his behaviour with most women so crudely amorous that he caused scandals wherever he went. But because of Leopold's sometimes equally outrageous behaviour I had a fondness for *enfants terribles* and I was sorry for Maurice. I understood that, ugly as he was, he had to assert himself somehow, even if only by shocking and scandalizing people. His behaviour towards women was comprehensible too. He was very rich and could afford the cost, but the creatures he had to buy to satisfy his gross appetites had left him with very little respect for women. It had not been difficult for me to discover that imprisoned in that monstrous body there was a sensitive, intelligent, humorous although profoundly cynical and lonely Maurice.

'Ah, the little Sternberg,' he said, recognizing me at last. 'Where have you been all these years?'

'In Czechoslovakia,' I told him.

'Yes, the Germans got you. Well, they didn't get me, though they tried. Imagine all the soap they could have made out of my fat.'

I shuddered. 'But what are you doing here, Baron Maurice?' I asked. 'It doesn't seem the sort of place that you used to frequent in the past.'

'Returning to nature among the beasts. Look at those awful people,' he said, waving his hand. 'Yet it does give one privacy, since one cannot communicate with them. But would you explain,' he asked, 'what you were doing in my friend's cabana?'

I told him about Annicka, not mentioning of course that my anxiety for her had anything to do with Leopold.

'Never knew she had a sister, but then these women never talk of anything but themselves. Ah, there she comes! *Quelle femme!*' he exclaimed appreciatively, contemplating the enormous woman who was approaching us. If someone had told me she was seven feet tall I would have believed it, and her other proportions equalled her height.

A great fertility goddess was all I could think of to compare her with. I had never seen anyone in a bikini before – three postage stamps would have covered as much of that gleaming oiled flesh as what she was wearing.

'And who is this?' she asked Maurice in French, peering down at me through the division of those remarkable breasts.

'A friend of mine,' Maurice said. 'Countess Sternberg.'

She started to dry her mane of red hair with a towel. I couldn't help thinking of pathetic Annicka whose hair was also red, but that was the only likeness between her and this magnificent creature.

'She has something to ask you, Louisette,' Maurice said to her. 'It seems you have a sister in Prague in need of your help.'

When understanding dawned, the wide plains of her rather stupid face rippled into laughter, as did her entire body. 'This is too funny,' she gasped. 'This lady coming to plead for her husband's mistress. Letter after letter have I received from Annicka telling me of her affair with Count Sternberg, begging me to help her join him. She's a real bitch,' she said, turning to me. 'Do you know she was after my husband once too? But I'm not as tolerant as you are. I like to keep my home in order.'

'How very virtuous we are today,' Maurice sniggered.

'Madame,' I said with all the dignity I could muster, 'your sister is a great friend of ours. We are very worried about her.'

'Has she threatened suicide? She has to me. Always hysterical.'

'Just one letter from you,' I pleaded, acutely embarrassed, 'stating that you are ill . . .'

'Me ill?' she said, arching her splendid body.

'Just one letter,' I repeated, 'addressed to Monsieur de Jean, the French Ambassador in Prague, would allow her to leave Czechoslovakia. It doesn't seem too much to do for a sister,' I concluded.

I saw she was hesitating.

'One would expect somewhat more heart under all that,' remarked Maurice, contemplating her bosom.

'And what can you know of heart, Maurice?' she exclaimed angrily. 'You who have none!'

'Nevertheless, I think you'd better write that letter,' he rumbled.

The real Maurice enclosed in his monstrous form blinked out at me for a moment reassuringly, and I looked back at him with gratitude. Three weeks later Leopold was to confess that Annicka had arrived in Paris.

My family greeted me warmly on my return from Venice, but they didn't seem to have missed me very much. Our rooms were full of toys I had never seen before and there were flowers everywhere. Had Steinhardt arrived unexpectedly? I wondered, then remembered that he had never sent me flowers in the years of our friendship, thinking, I'm sure, that something so impermanent wasn't worth giving. Nor had he presented the child with toys, being of equally transient value.

'The Steinhardts aren't here by any chance?' I asked Leopold nevertheless.

'No, but there's a letter from Laurence for you. I hope you don't mind my having opened it?'

I did, very much, but I didn't say so.

'I thought it might be important. As far as I can make out they're coming next week, Dulcie and Dulcie Anne by air, he by boat. He wants you to fetch him at Le Havre.'

I took the letter. It was carefully worded and anyone might have read it. There was a lot about Mona. Rather too much praise, I felt jealously. He then said he had been obliged to undergo a small operation, nothing serious, the tumour had proved non-malignant. This rather shook me, for both his mother and sister had died of cancer and if he feared anything it was that. He said he had recovered completely but that his doctor had advised him to go by sea rather than air because it would give him a few days' enforced rest. He suggested I hire a car and pick him up at Le Havre the afternoon the *Queen Mary* docked there. Dulcie would join him in Paris a few days later.

'And the lovely flowers?' I asked.

'Chappy and Tiny and Antoine were here. They were so sorry to have missed you.'

'So am I,' I said with sincere regret.

'And look what they gave me.' Leopold showed me two large cheques.

I have had to omit part of a chapter here. It mainly concerned some of Leopold's Austrian relations of whom I had grown fond and whose life stories seemed of interest to me. I wanted to leave some record of their kindness, generosity and courage but since they objected to being mentioned in my memoirs I can only prove my gratitude to them by not doing so.

I'm free to speak of Kari Wilczek though, who died soon after the war had ended and who to me and to Leopold remained unforgettable, so good and loyal a friend had he proved himself through the most difficult years in which few Austrians dared associate with us because we had declared ourselves as Czechs.

When later the Austrian aristocracy was accused of either folding their hands in their laps or raising them high in the Hitler salute, Kari Wilczek's name would always be quoted as the great exception.

Oddly enough, I had met him for the first time in Coco Chanel's house in Paris. Though so much of my youth and Leopold's had been spent in Vienna, Kari didn't live the sort of life we enjoyed at the time, his interest being of an entirely different kind. I had heard about him of course. He was a relation and we knew his family well. A confirmed bachelor, he was considered eccentric. He had studied art. Excusable only because of an infirmity. He had suffered from tuberculosis of the bones as a child and though the disease had been halted it had left him with a crippled right arm. 'Poor Kari,' everyone sympathized, since he could neither shoot, ride, play tennis nor dance; all that was left to him was to become a professor of art.

A tall, heavily built, stoop-shouldered man, carelessly dressed, with the rough-hewn but distinguished face of an Austrian aristocrat, I wondered what had led him into such incongruous surroundings as

Coco Chanel's over-elegant salon in Paris, decorated with Coromandel screens, ornate mirrors and beige satin upholstery. It could hardly have been the simian charms of swarthy Coco herself, nor was it imaginable that he was interested in French *Haute Couture*. Leopold, who knew him, finally whispered to me who he was.

Obviously he must have come to view the pictures, I then thought. There were two very fruity Renoirs, a rather spinachy Monet and a magnificent Cezanne.

I was mistaken. A tall, fair, very beautiful woman walked into the room, smiled at Coco and sat down beside Kari. They talked together as if resuming a conversation recently interrupted.

Later I knew that her name was Lady Abdy, that she was Russian by birth and worked as a designer and model for Chanel.

Curiosity compelled me to make some remark. Since we were sitting on the same long sofa it would have been impolite not to include me in their conversation. I noticed then how very attractive Lady Abdy was. A sort of freshness and frankness about everything she said – and something strong and primitive and somewhat peasant-like about her beauty in spite of her fashionable clothes.

We spoke of Paris. 'Count Wilczek has taken over my artistic education,' she declared. 'Though I've lived here for years, I've remained unbelievably ignorant. He has become my guide through museums and churches. And how he makes my feet ache.'

She stretched out her smartly shoed feet. I couldn't help noticing that they were quite large and didn't look as if they would tire easily.

'I wish there was someone who would show me Paris too,' I said. 'I've seen hardly anything.'

'Then I most warmly recommend Count Wilczek. Sightseeing is his only passion.'

He smiled at her but it was a rather sad smile.

He turned to me. 'We are, I know, relations of some sort. Strange we never met in Vienna. But then I don't lead a very social life.'

'Except when you travel,' she laughed. She had magnificent strong white teeth.

He blushed like a boy. I wondered how old he was. Certainly over forty, I thought.

'I'd be delighted to show you whatever you would like to see,' he said politely. 'How long are you staying?'

'Only three more days.'

He looked away from me and at her questioningly.

'I'll be working every hour this week,' she murmured.

'Day and night?'

'I'm afraid so. Helping to get the autumn collection ready.'

'But it's spring,' he sighed. 'What about tomorrow morning, then?' he asked me. 'I have to go to the Louvre anyway. You've probably been there dozens of times but there's always something new to see.'

'If one has your vision – ' she said to him with affectionate warmth.

Next day we went. I knew I had a good eye for quality, much appreciation but very little learning then. Yet I think had I never seen a picture before nor been taught the names of famous artists I could have recognized a work of genius. So I believe can everyone, even if quite uneducated in the arts, who takes the trouble just to look, listen or read, for it also applies to what is truly great in music and literature. In all of us there is something that responds spontaneously to a masterpiece as it does not to minor art, however pleasing, fashionable, or entertaining. It comes as a shock of recognition, a shudder of joy and awe that seems to strike at the centre of our being. I do not know why this is so, except perhaps that what is immortal in art is proof of man's immortality too and genius makes us aware of it.

In the Louvre Kari led me from picture to picture, by-passing many and only allowing me to look at a few. These he explained to me in detail and I realized for the first time how one's vision can improve through understanding. It was as if I had been given magic glasses suddenly able to perceive what I had not seen before. Because to Kari, when he viewed a picture it was as if the artist was still at work in front of him, almost as if they became one, pondering composition and colouring together, rejoicing in every perfect brush-stroke, troubled where there was failure to fully express what had been intended, seeking the cause why hand and vision had failed each other, triumphing at difficulties overcome and finally viewing the completed masterpiece with equal satisfaction and delight.

I was not only amazed at his knowledge but at his patience and kindness. He took no notice of my ignorance, on the contrary praising the few perceptive remarks I was able to make. I knew even then that I had found a great teacher and how much I could learn from him if we became friends.

Next day he took me to Notre Dame, explaining the complex architectural beauties of the great church and telling me some of its history. On the next, we just strolled through the Bois de Boulogne together. It was spring and everything in blossom and as is often the case when a man is in love, his mood becomes all embracing and I felt included.

It was not yet a true transfer of affection, I knew. That was to come later when the beautiful Lady Abdy had either tired of sightseeing or perhaps had grown too fond of Kari to want to involve him in the anxieties and qualms of conscience that an illicit affair would have inflicted on someone as sensitive as he was.

At least that was what I myself felt when he later imagined himself in love with me, or perhaps was. Unrequited desire may ache but it does not disappoint and disgust as incomplete possession can. Even had I been in love with him and not with Leopold, I believe I would have respected his integrity too much to involve him in the secrecy, subterfuges and falsehoods which making love to a married woman entailed in those days. What I wanted was his friendship and he gave it generously for many years, perhaps hoping for more, but never demanding anything in exchange except to be allowed to enrich my mind and stimulate my interest in art and literature. He frequently came to stay with us, even travelled with us. Soon Leopold, though they had few interests they could share, grew almost as fond of him as I was. In Vienna Kari introduced some of his friends to me. Charming brilliant Doctor Wilde of the Wiener Kunsthistorisches Museum, Burckhardt, the great Swiss art historian, and many others. In short, he led me into a world of culture and intellect of which I had known little before.

After the *Anschluss*, when disaster struck, many of his friends who were Jewish or half-Jewish or had Jewish wives went to him for help. Not in vain. He protected their property and later their lives as best he could. His became a strange household. He had been forced to dismiss his valet because he believed him not entirely trustworthy. He had to go and forage for food himself, paying high prices for discretion. He had to carry heavy loads back to his flat to feed his hidden guests. There were always two or three, often more, who found at least temporary refuge there. Kari was comparatively well off but certainly not rich. He spent in those years almost all he had helping others and the risks he took for them might well have cost him his life too.

Several times he was questioned by the Gestapo but there was no real proof. When his flat was searched (he had been forewarned by a former female student of his whose boy-friend worked for the Gestapo) nothing was found.

Then a certain princess, a relation of his who knew of his activities, as I suppose did most of Viennese society by then, ruthlessly informed on him. She had her reasons. She was an amorous woman past her prime and wished to rejoin a Spanish lover, probably her last (she had grown old and fat), who had escaped to Spain from no other persecution but hers.

A travel permit was by then not easy to obtain. However she was offered one in exchange for information which she readily gave. She was a stupid woman, all for Hitler, as so many German and Austrian females were, often more enthusiastic than their men, power and cruelty appealing to their more primitive instincts.

Foolishly she boasted of what she had done. Soon all of the still powerful Austrian aristocracy knew. Nazi or non-Nazi they rose to Kari's defence. There was a death penalty then for harbouring Jews. Not only was he liked and respected but the most heinous of offences had been committed. A member of their own class and a relation had informed on another! Even the most staunch Hitlerites among them were incensed and went into action. The reason for the princess's accusations and the vagaries of her private life were convincingly explained to the Gestapo and Kari was saved.

Finally after the war had ended a British officer called at our flat in Prague. He said he was stationed in Vienna and had been given our address by Count Wilczek.

'He begged me to see if you are all right,' he said. He was a youngish man with a pleasant intelligent face.

'We've survived,' I told him and asked him to come in and have a drink, or tea, and to tell us all he knew about Kari, which he did.

'I had orders to look him up and see to his safety the moment we got to Vienna,' he explained. 'What with the Russians having taken over there was rather a mess and it was feared he might be in danger.'

'Who sent you to him?'

'I'm afraid I can't tell you that, except that it was someone pretty high up at home. It seems he made himself quite a reputation for helping people in the war.'

'And how is he?'

'Not too good, I fear.'

He then told us how he had rung and rung at the door of Kari's flat and finally banged at it, believing the bell out of order. Eventually it was opened partially though still latched by a chain, and an old man in dressing gown and slippers had stared at him and then let him in.

'"You're British, I see," he said, having recognized my uniform. "I feared you might be Russian. One has to be a bit careful these days."

'The room he led me into was rather grand, a library, the walls all books but everything was covered with dust. It looked as if it hadn't been cleaned for years.

'He offered me a chair and carefully wiping it before I sat down he apologized for the disorder, saying he lived all alone and had stopped bothering. I had several letters to give him from former friends of his who had safely got to England. He read these and his face brightened. I saw then that he was not as old as I had first thought – only very pale and thin. Then he thanked me and asked me if I wouldn't like something to eat since it was lunch time. It seemed impolite to refuse. He went to a cupboard and took out a tin which he opened and poured peas into a saucepan which he stirred on a small stove, adding some water. He also brought out a sausage from which he cut chunks which he threw into the broth and put some stale-looking biscuits and a half-bottle of wine on the table.

'"Not much of a meal," he excused, "but food is so difficult to get and has become so expensive. I've practically given up. After all there's only myself to feed now."

'I had my ration packet in my coat pocket and a flask of whisky. I put them on the table asking him to share.

'"You are very kind," he said. He didn't look the sort of man who would cry easily but he did, much to my embarrassment. Weak from months of starvation I think. I poured him some whisky and we ate his pea soup which wasn't all that bad and finished off with my chocolate and cheese and instant coffee. He ate very little. I've seen it before. Once a man has really stopped eating for a long time he can't start again all of a sudden.'

'But why?' I asked horrified. 'He has relations, surely they would look after him if he was in need or ill?'

'They may have their own troubles. Vienna's not a very nice place just now. Besides I had rather the feeling that he wanted to be left alone. Not that he was impolite, we talked for quite a while. The whisky helped. It seems he's very fond of art.'

'He's an expert!'

'He said some rather queer things, such as that he'd prayed for an allied victory all through the war but that things like the bombing of Dresden and Monte Cassino were unforgivable. I pointed out that we had to do it, that it shortened the war and certainly saved many lives.

'"What is a life?" he asked. "It's very brief. We are born to die and someone else will take our place. We are expendable. A great work of art is irreplaceable."

'This surprised me from a man who had risked his own life to save those of others.

'Before I left I told him I was going home on leave but would arrange for some army rations to be sent to him every week because his friends in England would want me to. He thanked me, but rather as if he didn't care if I did. "I envy you," he said as he led me out, "for having a country you can be proud of. I've lost all pride in mine and in my people." He shut his door and I heard him lock it.'

The young officer sighed. 'Well, that's all I can tell you except that he sent you both his love.'

'If only I could go to him,' I exclaimed.

'You'd find it very difficult to get through. They let in Austrian refugees, but no one else at present,' he said. 'Besides, forgive me for saying so, I think it would be no use. I think he's turned his face to the wall.'

However Kari did live another three years and came to see us in Czechoslovakia once more. Even if very frail and emaciated, his movements awkward and confused, his mind was as clear as ever and his convictions as uncompromising. He condemned Czech chauvinism as he had Nazism; he deplored the destruction of beautiful castles and works of art by Russians or Czechs just because their owners had been Austrians or Germans. He suffered with those now homeless and cast out as he formerly had for his Jewish friends. Retaliation he refused to tolerate or understand. He had become deeply pessimistic and warned us constantly what would happen to our country and us in the future. No one likes to be told they are doomed and we were rather glad when he left. It was the last time we were to see him. For a while he went to live in Lichtenstein as guest of his favourite niece who had been a student of his. Gina Wilczek had married the reigning prince. In Vaduz, sorting and rehanging and cataloguing the art treasures contained in the castle, he did, I hope, find some peace of mind and contentment.

Then we heard he was dead. Killed instantly in a street accident – in Vienna. When his body was examined it was found that he had no more than a few months to live. His system had been so weakened in the war that the bone disease that had afflicted him as a child had recurred and affected his spine.

33

After the visit of his Austrian relations, Leopold cheered up immensely. Rather too much so, I thought. Our emigration permits had still not arrived from America. If we had to wait too long I feared Leopold might well drift into the sort of life we had frequently enjoyed in the past, thinking it quite unnecessary to leave Europe, forgetful that he had neither wealth nor position to fall back upon any more, depending on friends to support him. That there must be limits to their generosity he was incapable of believing. There had never been any to his own.

The hot summer was over. People were returning to Paris. The Ritz bar was crowded again. More and more frequently former acquaintances and friends invited him to drinks, and listened to what he had to tell them with sympathy. Yet they all showed evident relief when he said we were emigrating to America.

Annicka had meanwhile arrived in Paris. Maurice Rothschild, faithful to his promise, had seen to that. Leopold thanked me for my successful efforts on her behalf but didn't tell me where she was staying. Not with her sister, I was certain. I wouldn't have been surprised if Leopold had installed her in the Ritz, it being such a convenient walking distance for him from our hotel. Still, I felt, the money his relations had given him was absolutely his to use as he pleased.

Contrary to Leopold, I didn't trust in friendships in which the balance of power had been shifted to our disadvantage. We used to have a lot to offer in exchange in the past. What now?

In need of distraction from my secret anxieties, I allowed him to persuade me to join him in the bar one evening because he said there was an English journalist who was longing to see me again. 'One of those that used to assemble like vultures every time before something unpleasant happened in Vienna as well as in Prague,' he told me.

'It must be Peter Rodd,' I thought. I had known his family in Rome and I used to rather like him. He had always been over-enthusiastic about something or other, or indignant and furious about something else, as the intelligent young are. He was no fool and I thought showed promise for the future. He had wanted to become a writer.

There had never been anything between us but casual friendship. But then I have rarely met an Englishman for whom I didn't feel immediate sisterly affection – anything else would have seemed to me almost incestuous. Besides the English attitude towards sex certainly wasn't mine. The urge seemed to come upon them inexplicably suddenly, often in the middle of an interesting conversation. There was no effort at courtship or of any of the polite preliminaries Central Europeans had accustomed me to. If the attempt proved unsuccessful, which in my case it always was, conversation was resumed without embarrassment or any evident signs of disappointment.

I found Peter in the bar. He had grown broader and fatter. His eyes that used to be a clear, light blue, puffy and rather bloodshot.

We had a round of drinks. I asked him rather anxiously what he was doing in Paris. 'No catastrophe impending here, I hope?'

'No,' he laughed. 'I live here now. I'm married to Nancy Mitford.'

'*The Pursuit of Love?*'

'Exactly.'

The book had just been published and I had read it with much pleasure and amusement.

'But, Peter, how wonderful. I'd so much like to meet her.'

'Well then, come along tonight if you're doing nothing else. I'll fetch you at nine and bring you back.'

Leopold didn't seem to be included in the invitation, nor did he seem to want to be. 'I have an important meeting tonight,' he said. I could imagine with whom but it sounded better the way he put it.

Peter came with his car at nine and took me to a charming eighteenth-century house rather like that of the Charles Roux. There was a big drawing-room with french windows opening on to the garden. A woman uncurled from the sofa where she had been sitting with a young man. Peter didn't trouble to introduce me, nor I think had he told her that I was coming, but she was quite friendly in a sort of absent-minded way. Knowing Peter, I could imagine that he often brought unannounced guests to their house.

She wasn't as fair and beautiful or as English-looking as the two of her sisters I'd met in Venice many years ago. She looked rather French, her dark hair very neat, her black dress simple, and there was that air of discreet elegance about her that only true Parisians have. Her face seemed to me rather mask-like, revealing none of the sense of humour which I would have expected after reading her book.

The meal was sketchy. We dined on a tray in the drawing-room. Peter didn't eat or speak, though he drank. The lanky young man only opened his mouth for food. He was obviously very shy and couldn't have been more than eighteen.

'He plays the oboe too beautifully,' Nancy said, 'he's studying at the Conservatoire.'

I told her how much I had liked her book. She smiled politely.

'I'd have thought it rather difficult for someone who's not quite English to understand.'

'Do I have such a foreign accent?'

'No, but you express yourself differently than we would.'

'Let's go and dance,' Peter demanded of no one in particular. I looked questioningly at my hostess. 'I'm rather tired tonight. Besides, I've promised Anthony,' she looked affectionately at the blushing young man, 'to hear his new piece on the oboe.'

'Do you think him good-looking?' Peter asked in the car.

'No, sort of gangling and dangling.'

Peter laughed. 'Nancy thinks him beautiful. Where do you want to go?'

'There used to be a place called the Poule or the Boule Blanche. It was rather fun. There were negro dancers . . . it's years ago. I'd like to see it again . . .'

'Good gracious, you do have low tastes.'

We went and the big, fat, old West Indian women, dressed in their wide flowered cotton smocks, toutous binding their hair, still swung their great hips and jerked their stomachs dancing the beguine to the rhythm of the tin drums.

We talked a lot, danced occasionally, and drank champagne. Peter made me tell him all about the happenings in Czechoslovakia in and after the war.

I asked him if he was still writing. 'Not much,' he said, 'Nancy does the writing now. She's started another book.' He didn't seem very anxious to talk about himself or her.

It was very late when we left. On the way home he suddenly stopped the car in a side street. He was rather drunk and there was a scuffle. It was, I suppose, what one has to expect if one goes out with a man alone, but I'd rather forgotten.

'Please, Peter,' I begged, 'don't spoil a most enjoyable evening.'

'What do you think I took you out for?' he asked angrily.

'To talk, I had hoped.'

'Then you're a fool,' he said.

Realizing how much stronger he was than I, the unpleasant possibility of being raped gave me an idea – not I grant a very nice one but then neither was my situation.

'I'm only trying to spare you, Peter,' I said, 'please let go. I was raped by a Russian soldier in Prague and I haven't been well ever since.' He switched on the light and peered at me. 'You mean?'

'Yes,' I nodded sadly. My disgusting lie had done the trick and certainly cooled Peter's ardour but I felt ashamed of myself. He was silent as he drove back to the hotel. The journalist recovered first. 'I could call tomorrow,' he said. 'I'd be grateful if you told me all about it. There might be quite a story. I wouldn't mention your name, of course, if you didn't want me to.'

Next day when Peter telephoned I refused to take the call. I had pleasanter things to think of. The morning mail had brought a letter from Anna. She had safely reached Vienna at last with her children.

Anna Linsky (this is not her real name) and her husband were great friends of ours. Anna had even come to the station in Prague to bid us goodbye when we left home. I had worried about her ever since. Her husband, Prince Max, had been forced to flee and to leave her to manage her own departure as best she could. He fled mainly because his younger brother, who had managed to reach the USA much earlier, had made a rousing, patriotic and virulently anti-communist speech on the Voice of America Czech broadcast, believing his family safely out of the country.

Max would have been arrested after that, had he not been forced by Anna to take one of the by then quite efficiently working underground night journeys, on which people were hidden in trucks and Czech guards, either sympathizing or bribed, would forget to shoot at those who crossed the frontier into Austria.

Anna had applied to be allowed to leave legally with her children. She was Austrian by birth. If her husband had deserted her and if she had no idea, as she declared, as to his whereabouts and her only means of support were her parents in Vienna, surely, she thought, they would let her go.

But it had taken her three months until she finally got the permission to leave. Steinhardt, who had known Anna and her husband well, having frequently stayed at their castle, had before he left made certain arrangements. He told her that if all else failed, she should go to an address he gave her and that there means would be found, if rather unorthodox, to get her and her children safely out of the country. She did not dare take advantage of this before she was certain she would not be allowed a legal means of exit. There were relations of her husband's still in the country, employees and old servants who might have been accused of conniving at helping her escape.

Finally she was allowed to leave. When she arrived at the Czech frontier her papers were examined and so were her suitcases. 'Too much luggage,' she was told, 'and their contents suspect,' though there was nothing of real value in them. She and the exhausted and frightened children had to return to Prague. They repacked at the railway station, squeezing everything into three bags and took another train. This time they were allowed to pass. She left, probably for ever, estates dutifully and efficiently administered, two castles in perfect order which she had refurnished and redecorated, people who had prospered in her employment or had depended on her generosity and whom she had never failed in supporting and helping.

One would have thought our new communist state, benefiting by all this, might have allowed its officials to overlook two surplus suitcases, mainly filled with children's clothes!

Anna was one of the very few real women friends I've ever had.

In general, I don't like women very much.

The truth is, I don't know what to do with them. I had married so young that I had accepted Leopold's and his friends' very old-fashioned ideas about them, which were that women were charming but unpredictable and incomprehensible creatures to be humoured, cherished and protected but not to be taken seriously as intelligent human beings. I had learnt to feel the same about them.

I could delight in a woman's beauty, like any man. However, since I wasn't one I was deprived of being physically attracted. In fact, rather the contrary. However *soignée*, elegant and well-washed a woman was I was always conscious of the smell of her femininity and it repelled me. It seemed to pervade even women's minds, their thoughts muddled and clouded by sex.

How clean was a man in comparison, I felt, with everything in its proper place.

The only woman I ever deeply loved was my Aunt Diana who took charge of me and my brothers after my mother's death. But she was almost sexless, a spinster and a recluse who lived in a self-created world of her own which was imaginatively so rich that she needed nothing else.

However, I had always been very fond of Anna. Though she was a few years older than I was we had gone out together in Vienna and attended the same parties and dances, she more reluctantly than I. Social life bored her. She thought it a waste of time. She was studying hard then trying to take a degree in History of Art.

She was the eldest daughter of Prince X who was imprisoned by the Nazis after Hitler annexed Austria. Her parents were not very well off. There was another daughter to provide for, and the charming and attractive eldest son, though he tried to work, was never quite as successful in business as he was with the ladies. The youngest was still at school.

Anna was devoted to her family. When Prince Linsky, who owned vast estates in Czechoslovakia, proposed to her she could not refuse, though it meant giving up her studies and leaving the Vienna she loved.

She married and moved into a large, neo-gothic, turreted castle that stood high on a hill overlooking dense, dark forests and a river equally dark. It was an impressive place but far from cheerful. Anna's husband was years younger than she was and very intelligent but somewhat eccentric. He lived entirely in the heraldic past, knew every coat of arms in Europe, and was an expert on genealogy and history.

He was more interested in writing on historical subjects than in the running of his estates. Gradually Anna took over some of their management and administered them with great shrewdness and aptitude. As was expected of her, she bore children. First a daughter and then the all-important heir. Another son followed and a second daughter.

Except for those who could read the intelligence, humour and goodness in her fine, strong face, Anna could not have been considered beautiful. Built rather square she was at best a handsome woman. Her looks were not enhanced by her being totally devoid of feminine vanity; her clothes always too long for fashion, her hair too short because it was less trouble to arrange, her boots too large, because she liked to walk in comfort. Even her jewels and furs, bought for her by her adoring husband, who liked to see her regally attired, were all over-sized.

'But why, Anna, darling,' I used to protest, 'must your mink coat be so enormous? It really doesn't look right.'

'Don't I know it,' she laughed, 'but divided in two it will. One half for each of the girls.' She really lived entirely for her children and for securing their future. She loved them so much that, reverting to some primitive instinct, even though she was a highly intelligent woman, she would disparage them if one praised their looks or their intellects.

'It's as if you feared the gods would hear and be jealous.' I teased her. 'Very pagan and you such a devout Catholic.'

Anna was indeed deeply religious.

Often she must have disapproved of my and Leopold's laxity of morals. The rules according to which she lived were very stern, though her sense of humour, which was acute, blessed her with great tolerance concerning others.

'I don't think you immoral,' she reassured me, 'just amoral, like an innocent animal.'

I often stayed with her in the castle, or in a lovely, small eighteenth-century country house, less formidable, which they owned, and she and her husband came to Castolovice almost as frequently.

Only once was she really angry with me. I had begged her to invite a young man of whom I was fond to stay overnight.

'As long as nothing improper takes place between you,' she admonished me severely. I reassured her and he was asked.

Next morning Anna's daughter, who was then six or seven, the same age as Diana (later they would go to the same convent school in Prague and become close friends), fell from her pony and, her face covered with blood, was carried home by the groom.

Anna, deathly pale, soothed the frightened child, washed her face clean, then turned to me in real fury. 'Now see what you've done! This is my punishment for condoning sin in my house!'

'It's only a very small cut,' I protested, which, thank God, was all it proved to be.

I was soon forgiven.

Prince Linsky, having declared himself for President Benes, had his estates confiscated by the Germans at the same time as were ours and Anna had to move to Prague with her family. All through the war I saw her frequently and her sane advice was of great value to me. We exchanged information, passed on warnings to each other, shared the same fears and anxieties.

When it was all over, Anna and her husband's return to their castle was more eventful than our own to Castolovice. A Russian general had chosen it as his headquarters and for the three months that Russian troops remained in Czechoslovakia, the General, his staff, and his lady (Anna could never quite make out if she was his wife or his mistress) occupied half of the house.

'But weren't you terrified of them?' I asked her later.

'A little uneasy at first,' she confessed, 'but really we got on quite well. I think the General's lady rather liked me. She had been an actress and briefly on the stage in Berlin and spoke some German. She tried to convert me not to communism but to her idea of how a princess should behave and dress. Also she disapproved of the way in which we treated our old servants and employees. I really think she felt I should occasionally have them whipped, as they used to castigate their serfs in Russia before the Revolution. As for my clothes . . .' Anna laughed. 'Of course I only wore old tweeds in the country. I really think she thought I should go about in ermine and with a crown on my head!'

One day, Anna recalled, the General's lady could bear it no longer. 'I teach you how to dress!' she told her. 'Give me name of good dressmaker in Prague.'

'As you remember,' Anna continued, 'Rosembaum had been taken over by the Germans in the war and I thought they might still have some clothes left. I was quite right. The General's lady had herself driven to Prague and returned with several extremely glamorous, long, spangly evening gowns, which she paraded in front of me from early morning to night. "This is the way a princess should dress," she told me.

'Both she and the General seemed very conscious of rank. Occasionally they would invite us to a cinema in our own ballroom, of which they had the use. The films were, of course, Russian, very long and very dull, sometimes lasting three hours. Four chairs only used to be placed in the middle of the room next to each other on which Max and I and the General and his lady sat.

'Far back stood the officers with their women. Some were wives, some female officers in uniform. They stood there for the duration of the show. I offered to provide more chairs. "Certainly not," the General's lady said. "It would not be right if they sat in our presence. We are first class, they second class."'

'So much for communism!'

'I don't think people realize how very Russian Russians remain in spite of communism,' Anna pondered, 'and how unpredictable and contradictory they are. Brutal, yet kind. Ours were so good to the children you wouldn't believe it, carving toys for them, singing to them – also the Russians have a sort of wisdom.

'For example, the General's troops were billeted in most of the villages around us. All in all they were quite well behaved and disciplined. But there was one lapse. A woman came to the castle to complain to us that she had been raped by a Russian soldier. It seems he had followed her, had watched and waited till her husband was out of the house and then forced her at gunpoint to comply. She was a respectable woman, there was no reason to disbelieve her. We took her complaint to the General.

'"Justice shall be done," the General said sternly. There were about forty soldiers billeted in the village from which she came.

'Next morning they stood lined up in front of the General, as well as the assembled villagers and the woman who had been attacked. The General went to her and put a loaded revolver into her hand.

'"Look closely," he told her, "and if you recognize the man shoot him." Of course, the poor frightened woman, even if she did recognize the man who had assaulted her, couldn't bring herself to shoot, as the General must have known.' Anna smiled. 'Solomon could not have been wiser, yet justice had been done for all to see.

'I can't say I ever got to like the General very much,' she continued, 'but I had reasons to be grateful to him. Do you know that I spent a night with him in a deserted house, just he and I alone?'

'Anna, how awful,' I said, shocked. 'How could that happen?'

'Well, I wanted very much to get to Vienna,' she explained. 'I knew, of course, that the Russians were there and behaving, since they considered Austria enemy country, rather less well than they did with us. I was worried about my family. I told this to the General's lady. She quite understood. "We go," she said.

'We went, in two Russian-type jeeps, each with three armed guards. For some reason the General's lady preferred going in the other car with two officers who, even if second class, looked extremely handsome. I went with the General. When we had crossed into Austria the car broke down, fortunately in a village. For an hour there were efforts at repairs but they proved futile. By then it was dark and the General's temper was growing short. Speaking Czech I could understand some Russian but not the words he used. In any case they made his driver cringe.

'"We sleep here," the General said to me. "It will take till morning before they can get spare parts sent and fixed in, or another car." Waving at a house that looked somewhat better than the rest he told the soldiers "Clear it!" It was very quickly done. The unfortunate inhabitants and their children, some of whom had already gone to bed, hastily draped in coats over nightgowns, fled to find refuge with the neighbours, or so I hoped.

'"Bring supplies," the General ordered, "and make tea." There was still a fire burning in the oven. The soldier found a saucepan and started brewing. The General unpacked a large wooden crate. A loaf of brown bread came out of it, a pack of butter, a sausage, a jar of caviar and a bottle of vodka.

'He pushed the latter towards me. "I have this for foreigners," he said, "makes for friendship! They like it, I don't!"

'He cut himself a huge slice of bread with a pocket knife, buttered it, smelt the sausage, shrugged and left it aside. "Tea!" he ordered. The dark brew appeared, served in the saucepan. "Cups!" he yelled. Two were found.

'I drank some of the strong tea gratefully but that was all I could face.

'"You sleep upstairs, is safer," he told me, "many Germans around. I stay downstairs and you . . ." he turned to the soldier ". . . get out and get the car repaired, or else!" The threat must have been terrible because the soldier left pale and shaken.

'I crept up into the bedroom recently occupied by those who had fled. I couldn't sleep. I lay down in my clothes. At five next morning there was a loud knock at the door and one of the soldiers gestured that the time to leave had come. The General and I bowed to each other formally in good-morning greetings and two hours later we arrived at my parents' house in Vienna.

'Of course, no one was awake. I rang the bell. I banged at the door. Not a sign of life.

'"Shall we break in?" the General asked.

'"Oh please don't," I begged. I had seen a shutter above open infinitesimally, someone was awake and watching. A Russian car, full of Russian soldiers, was the most dire threat to any house in Vienna in those days.

'I called out as loud as I could. The door opened and my father's old valet stood there, bravely facing death for my sake. He must have thought they had abducted me. I reassured him as best I could. I spent a very pleasant day and night with my family. They had not been unduly harassed themselves, though there was frightening disorder in the town.

'Next morning, at six, I was advised that the General was waiting to take me home. I excused not introducing him to my parents because they were still asleep.

'So, very soon, was he, and really slept all the way until we reached the castle five hours later.

'However, his lady did not return till noon. I saw him stamping around in the courtyard, obviously anxious. I think he loved her. To his evident relief, she arrived, then to my surprise I saw him make the sign of the cross. Instinctively, or because he still believed? Who can tell with Russians?'

34

Meanwhile I had wired Steinhardt that I would expect him in Le Havre. Three days before the ship was due I woke up with a violent toothache. Madame Poisson recommended a dentist who told me I had an abscessed tooth which he couldn't take out while it was inflamed. He gave me an injection of penicillin and told me to come back in a couple of days.

So with a swollen face and in acute pain I set off for Le Havre in a large chauffeur-driven Bentley hired from a firm also recommended by Madame Poisson.

I had not realized how far from Paris the port was, an over two hours long drive and every bump in the road hurt my throbbing tooth. Yet the valleys and forests through which the ever winding Seine flowed towards the sea were lovely and the joyful prospect of soon seeing Steinhardt again and the certainty that he had carefully planned his journey so as to have some time alone with me made up for much of my suffering.

We reached the docks where I hoped to find the *Queen Mary* either in port or due to arrive any minute. There were many ships large and small but none her size. I found a sort of office and enquired when she would be in.

'Not before late tonight,' I was told. She had been delayed by bad weather and had to wait for the next tide to berth.

What was I to do? I asked myself with some concern. Drive all the way back to Paris? Or wait?

I decided to wait.

'Is there a good hotel in the town?' I asked.

'Not what I think you would consider to be so, Madame,' the man said, eyeing me. 'Customers from the luxury liners go straight through by train to Paris. But there are several inns that have rooms to accommodate ships' staff and sailors.'

'Well, which would you recommend, since I have to wait for the ship? I'm meeting a friend.'

'I suppose the best is the Red Anchor,' he said dubiously.

'Can you telegraph the ship for me?'

'Certainly, Madame.'

AMBASSADOR STEINHARDT. WAITING FOR YOU RED ANCHOR.
I payed, called the chauffeur so that he could be given directions how
to find the inn and left the port.

Le Havre is not a pretty town though perhaps there are buildings
beyond the docks that are of architectural merit. The tall, grey, gaunt
houses near the port scarred and dessicated by sea and bombs during
the war among which I found my hotel were neither attractive nor
reassuring. There was something sinister about them I thought and so
did my chauffeur.

'Madame can't possibly stay here,' he said.

I explained to him that since I'd sent my telegram I'd have to.

We entered a sort of bar.

'Can I have a room for the night?' I asked what was obviously the
landlord. 'With a bath, if possible?'

Seamen were sitting round the counter drinking wine. They stared
at me and at the uniformed chauffeur.

'I do not have a room for two. We are full up. Will a single do?'
There was some laughter from the sailors and some remarks I did not
understand though I could guess their meaning.

'I am expecting a friend from the *Queen Mary*,' I said stiffly, trying
not to notice my driver's embarrassment. 'My chauffeur will seek his
own accommodation.'

'Indeed, Madame,' he said with evident relief. 'I have some relations
who own a farm near here. I can sleep with them. That is if Madame
is quite sure she should not return to Paris?'

I longed to, but I didn't see how I could after having sent the
telegram.

'No, I'll have to wait.'

'What time shall I come then tomorrow?'

If Steinhardt came at all he might want to sleep. 'At nine,' I said.

The room I was shown by the landlord's wife was small, dirty and
sordid beyond anything I had ever been in before. There was a narrow
iron bed covered with a grey blanket, a small washbasin, a brown trickle
oozing from the tap, a cracked mirror above it, a table, a chair and a
window.

'Have you really nothing else, I mean a little larger?' I asked. I
didn't want to hurt her feelings.

She regretted. There were so many ships delayed by the low tides
and all rooms taken by seamen glad of a night in town.

'Mind you,' she said, 'I keep a respectable house, Madame. There is nothing to fear. You will be quite private here. But since Madame has come without luggage, I would be obliged if she would pay for the room now.'

I did. She eyed my handbag with interest. 'We do not usually serve meals here,' she said, 'but if Madame would like me to bring her up an omelette.'

I thanked her. I said I didn't need food but asked her what facilities there were to telephone Paris.

'We have an apparatus downstairs in the bar but there's a lot of noise. I would recommend Madame going to the kiosk near the post office. It is quieter. I will direct Madame to it.'

We made our way through the street, riotous with sailors and their girls.

I reached Leopold. What relief to hear his voice. I explained about the ship and that I had thought it more sensible to stay the night than to make the journey twice, since Steinhardt could only arrive by morning. He agreed.

I bought some grapes at a stall and a bottle of wine. The street was crowded with sailors, most of them drunk. Darkness had fallen and I suppose I looked much the same to them as the women they were accosting or being solicited by.

My knees were shaking as I finally reached the inn and climbed up the stairs to my room. I felt dirty and soiled. There was no soap with which I might have washed my hands and nothing to cleanse me from my feeling of degradation either.

I opened the window to at least breathe in the fresh air from the sea and lent out over the sill. Other women were doing the same. Some were only partially clothed. All, I knew, waiting for the sailors and their urgent, brief, brutal embraces in rooms as sordid as mine.

I did not dare lie down on the dirty blanket that covered the bed. I sat at the table and drank some wine and waited. My tooth throbbed and so did all my body.

After midnight there was a commotion on the stairs. I heard loud voices and heavy bumping sounds. It couldn't be Steinhardt's steps – I knew he walked as lightly as a cat. Some drunken sailor, I thought with terror, and ran to lock the door. There was no key.

It was flung open and Steinhardt, lugging two heavy pigskin suitcases, plunged into the room.

'My God, what a place!' he gasped, 'I didn't dare leave anything downstairs.'

He put down his luggage and wiped the sweat from his forehead.

'Why are you crying?' he asked.

'With relief,' I sobbed.

He looked at me and at the narrow dirty bed with equal distaste, I thought, then covered the bed with the soft vicuna coat woven from the hair of those gentle creatures that live in the Andes. A coat I knew well since it had sheltered so many of our most valuable possessions when he had carried them out of our flat in Prague under its cover.

He made me lie down on it. He took a silver flask out of his pocket, unscrewed the cup-like top and gave me some of the brandy to drink. With a large, clean, white handkerchief he wiped my tears. Though his touch on my swollen cheek was agony, I didn't wince.

'I got off the ship as soon as I could,' he said. 'Were you afraid I wouldn't? The other passengers will only be disembarked tomorrow morning. The captain thought my leaving a bit odd. I had to commandeer his launch to get here. Urgent private business, I told him. And so indeed it is,' he said, smiling down at me.

Next morning my tooth had stopped aching, perhaps the penicillin had taken effect. Though neither of us had slept we weren't tired. It was a bright, fresh, clean autumn day, fields and woods through which we were driven touched with the first tints of gold. 'Is America as beautiful as France?' I asked.

'It's a continent, not a country. It has every landscape and every climate to choose from. Yes, it's beautiful. Wait till you see the Rocky Mountains, or Arizona, or the Great Lakes. I'd like to show it all to you one day. Meanwhile, even the country round New York is pretty in the fall. I must take you up the Hudson when you arrive. The autumn colours are wonderful.'

'And you think we'll have our papers soon?'

'Any day now. Of course there still are certain formalities. You will be called to the embassy and quizzed and grilled and have to fill out endless papers and there are the medical tests. Well, they will rather turn you inside out. It's somewhat tiresome, I'm afraid, but then considering you enter the country with almost all the rights and privileges that an American citizen has, with permission to work and live where you please, it seems worth it. Anyway, I have Dean Acheson's promise that there will be no difficulties to your entry. Leopold's political integrity is fully guaranteed and you – I told Dean how much you had done for America.' Steinhardt laughed.

'What on earth do you mean?' I asked indignantly.

'Have you forgotten your work for the American Institute?'

Almost! I had joined it on his advice. It was a sort of Czech-American friendship society for cultural exchange and better understanding, its members consisting mainly of women who arranged meetings at which Steinhardt spoke in the various towns. Dulcie disdained going on these tours with the ladies of the Institute and was highly suspicious at my doing so. 'I can't think what you have in common with those ordinary people,' she said. Not very much, I knew. Also that my position among them must have seemed rather incongruous. But beyond the opportunities that these expeditions gave me to see more of Steinhardt than I would have otherwise, I was rather touched by the enthusiasm of the ladies of the Institute, who sang 'America the Beautiful' at every possible occasion, and I agreed with their hopes and aspirations. Our Czech Republic had, after all, been created with American help, why should American-Czech friendship not be encouraged to continue?

'Do you remember Brno,' I asked, 'and how we fooled the guards?'

In whatever town Steinhardt stayed overnight he was given a Czech police guard that stood watch outside his bedroom door throughout the night but they could scarcely object to a lady of the Institute taking a prolonged bath! The bathroom had a second door that led into Steinhardt's room.

The villa in which our party had been accommodated was luxurious by Brno standards. It had once belonged to a wealthy Jewish family and had been taken over by the Gestapo as headquarters afterwards. Now they too were gone, but in the basement was left what the citizens of Brno had preserved as a showplace of German depravity.

It was really more absurd than obscene. The walls were crudely painted with scenes from the *Walpurgisnacht*, witches riding on broomsticks and being intimate with goats and in the middle of the room stood the life-sized figure of a naked woman representing, I suppose, some Nordic goddess. She was pale pink all over and had a wig of fair hair. We ladies of the Institute had shuddered appropriately when shown this room, or beer-hall, which I suppose it had been.

'Such atrocious bad taste,' I complained to Steinhardt afterwards.

'I thought it was rather fun,' he said. 'That doll looked rather like you.'

I asked him about Ottawa. 'We've really not properly settled in yet. You know how fussy Dulcie is about houses. We've been enjoying New York though. Seeing old friends and relations, going to the theatre and the Opera.'

'And Mona Williams?' I asked rather hesitantly, remembering Eddie's reproaches. 'You wrote to me that you had called on her.'

'First thing I did. She's by far the most important person socially on the list you gave me. She can be of great use to you.'

'Did you fall in love with her?' I asked anxiously.

'Of course I did. No normal male could resist such beauty. Were I not so tiresomely involved with someone else,' he smiled, 'I would certainly have sprung into action.'

At the entrance of the Ritz Steinhardt asked me to wait a moment until he could give me the number of his apartment. 'You can come back and have breakfast with me after you've cleaned up,' he said. 'Give Leopold my love and tell him I hope to see him soon.'

At the Cambon I paid off the chauffeur, tipped and thanked him. It had been an expensive journey, but those were the sort of costs to others I remembered from the past that one had as lightly ignored as Steinhardt did.

I kissed neither Leopold nor the child as I would usually have done on returning to them. 'My cheek's too sore,' I excused myself, 'I can't bear being touched.'

I bathed and even washed my hair. It was so short I could dry it in minutes. 'The ship only docked this morning,' I explained as I dressed hurriedly. 'I had to spend the night in a dreadful place.'

'Has Dulcie arrived?' Leopold asked. 'I don't even know,' I said. 'I think I'll go straight to the dentist now and have my tooth out.'

The ludicrous contrast between Steinhardt's luxuriously furnished and flower-filled suite at the Ritz (flowers with the compliments of the management) and the room we had left in Le Havre made me laugh. A large breakfast stood ready, even if it was only for one.

'I didn't dare order two but there should be enough for us both. Did anyone see you coming up?' he asked.

'No, I took the back stairs.'

'Good, Dulcie and Dulcie Anne arrive this afternoon.' He opened the door of the apartment and hung up the Do Not Disturb sign.

After my tooth extraction I returned to the hotel. Totally exhausted, I went to bed and slept.

I woke, there was someone staring down at me. It was Dulcie still in her travelling clothes.

'I had to rush over to see how you and Leopold are,' she explained.

'How kind of you,' I mumbled, 'sorry if I can't speak properly, it's the anaesthetic. I've had a tooth out.'

'Oh, you poor thing. Then you can't have seen Laurence yet, but I suppose he telephoned?'

'We don't have a telephone up here but he might have left a message at the desk.'

'Not much of a room, is it?' she asked, looking round and at my clothes lying about in scattered heaps, as were the child's toys.

'I suppose Diana sleeps here with you? Still it can't be very expensive, that's the main thing to keep in mind under the circumstances. And where is dear Leopold?'

'Usually in the Ritz bar at this time.'

'Well, I must hurry back. Laurence will be waiting. He'll be ever so sorry not to see you. I had hoped we could invite you to dine tomorrow night but I suppose you won't feel up to it. We are only staying a couple of days.'

'But I'm longing to see him,' I said, 'I want to thank him, to thank you both,' I added hastily, 'for all you've done for us.'

She smiled graciously.

'I'm sure I'll be all right tomorrow.'

'Then certainly come. Evening dress. But any little black dress will do, if you have nothing better.'

I'd show her, I thought. Though the dress was black, high-necked and long-sleeved, it was beautifully cut and the silk jersey it was made of so soft and flowing that it would have made anyone's figure look superb. And I had the jewels. The pieces of the tiara shaped like *fleur-de-lis* could be used as clips. I wore them and the enormous diamond ear-rings and all the bracelets. 'Goodness, Mummy, you look like a Christmas tree,' the delighted child exclaimed.

All lit up too, I thought, smiling at myself in the mirror.

We had drinks in the big drawing-room of the Steinhardts' suite.

Dulcie was looking rather splendid in pearl-grey satin. Dulcie Anne very pretty, as quiet and unobtrusive as ever, only her large almond-shaped eyes so like her father's, alert and full of secret amusement.

I wondered how soon she would go her own way. There must be plenty of suitors wanting to take her from her parents by now, I thought.

Steinhardt looked at me with frank admiration. He was one of those rare men whose interest revives quickly. We had greeted each other affectionately. There was no mention, of course, of Le Havre. I had warned Leopold not to speak of it. Both Steinhardt and Leopold had agreed long ago that Dulcie must not be upset because of her nervous disposition.

The men went to the other end of the room, sat down with their drinks and were soon deep in talk.

I remained with Dulcie. She looked at me rather critically.

'I see you've been shopping,' she remarked. 'They make such lovely costume jewellery here now. But quite expensive, I would imagine. Of course, I'm so absurdly old-fashioned that I do prefer the real thing, however small.' She contemplated the beautiful large diamond and emerald ring on her finger.

A table had been reserved in the main dining-room. It was in a most central position and had a spectacular flower arrangement. Both Steinhardt and Dulcie felt it their diplomatic duty to be noticed. But Leopold limping in drew more attention from the other diners, apart from the head waiter, than the Steinhardts did, and so for once did I.

'You found them after all,' Steinhardt remarked. 'Aren't your ears rather small for those ear-rings? They look heavy.'

'I had to have my ears pierced so as to be able to wear them. They were my mother's.'

'And the rest?'

'My mother's,' Leopold said. 'I don't know why she's put it all on at once.'

'For fun,' I said. 'Because I wanted to show off,' I added.

'You never wore them in Prague,' Dulcie remarked coldly.

'Because I didn't have them then. Friends kept them safe for me in Venice,' I explained.

On Dulcie's face I could read much that was passing through her mind. Relief that we had perhaps more financial reserves than she had expected, dispelling some of her fears that we might become an expense. Resentment that we were not as totally dependent on her and her husband as she had come to believe us to be.

In the two years of our friendship in Czechoslovakia we had undoubtedly been of use to both of them, not only as a source of information but by facilitating their entry into a society which, however near its downfall, had then still a lot to offer.

The fact that our positions were now reversed I knew didn't displease Dulcie and that it was she who now could dole out favours through Steinhardt gave her a sense of power that my vulgar exhibition of jewels had deflated.

'They are not very valuable,' I apologized. 'They may look rather good in the evening,' and indeed they glittered like the chandelier above, 'but in daylight much is yellow and flawed.'

'Well, all I hope,' Steinhardt said, 'is that you won't do what the Russian aristocrats used to who had escaped from the Revolution.

Our law firm with which they dealt once they had emigrated to the USA tried to keep their finances in order. Their wealth was mainly in jewellery, yet they would sell or pawn anything just to give a party, with caviar, vodka and champagne flowing like water and gipsies playing.'

Leopold and I looked at each other, knowing only too well we might become guilty of equal folly.

Two days later the Steinhardts left. I saw him once more in the privacy of a room Madame Poisson had kindly put at my disposal in the Cambon. I had told her that I had important, rather secret, matters to discuss with the American Ambassador. As usual, she understood.

Finally the letter from the American Embassy's Emigration Department came. It was addressed to Mr Leopold Sternberg, which made me feel we were titleless Americans already and that all that was needed was to fetch our first papers.

I was mistaken. For a whole week we sat in the large basement of the embassy, told to wait until we were called. The days of privileged treatment were obviously over for us.

Names were called according to the alphabet. Obviously, S was low on the list. We sat among people of the most varied European nationalities, all hoping for permission to enter the USA.

We made friends, of course. Leopold helped Czechs who spoke no English to fill out questionnaires; Diana played hopscotch on the squares of the stone-flagged floor with the other children; I tried to comfort and reassure some of the frightened women, persuaded by their more enterprising husbands to leave homes and familiar villages to seek greater prosperity in the New World.

Names were constantly being called but many, in their anxiety, didn't recognize their own. People went in and out, only rarely did one see a smile on the face of those that returned. The word 'Quota' was often mentioned. It seemed to have some ominous significance.

At last it was our turn. Only our Kafka could have aptly described what followed. The seemingly never-ending bleak corridors and the numbered cubicles as alike as the officials behind their desks, repeating the same questions: 'Where had we been at such and such a time? For what reason? Whom had we associated with then? What had been our loyalties at different dates? Why did we leave our country?' and so on. Soon neither of us could remember much about our past or ourselves. We were sent from numbered room to numbered room, the tired child bravely tagging behind. In vain did Leopold present papers which documented his political integrity. The identity card from the *Narodny Vybor* that proved him a patriotic Czech, the many 'To whom it may concern' letters written by Western diplomats, vouching for him, even the card that proclaimed him President of the Prague Jockey Club, none of it seemed to make any impression.

The papers were briefly glanced at and returned. The interrogations continued. The questioners behind their desks were not aggressive or cruel. Just totally indifferent, impersonal, as efficient and inhuman as machines. Or so I thought.

Finally Leopold rebelled. 'I am what I am,' he said, 'and to hell with you! I refuse to answer one more question.'

To my surprise, his interrogator laughed.

'To hell with you too!' he said, putting his feet up on his desk. 'Do you think I enjoy questioning people day after day?'

The medical examinations were no less harrowing and more embarrassing. I doubt that Leopold, even when he had enlisted forty years ago, had had to strip practically in public, only a small screen concealing his middle. His scarred thigh wound that still occasionally festered and the lack of circulation in his leg were closely examined. We were handed what looked like champagne glasses and told to fill them. We had no practice in this and spilled most of the contents. We were ordered to repeat but it was by then unrepeatable. Our blood was taken. Mine had never been tapped from the arm before. It took a dozen pricks until the vein was found. I fainted. We were tested for syphilis and X-rayed for tuberculosis and vaccinated against smallpox, typhoid and diphtheria.

Afterwards, sore in body as well as soul, we waited for the examination results, convinced we had not passed.

'Is it really all worthwhile?' Leopold questioned. 'Shouldn't we just stay here?'

'And how would we earn enough to live on?'

'Well, your ceramics. And why not Monte Carlo? Do you remember how much I won with that system? It's infallible.'

'Except when you forgot to double or redouble your stakes and lost it all. Darling, it would be at best a shabby, shoddy sort of life we'd have in Europe, always haunted by the past. In America we can start completely new, with every opportunity to succeed.'

'I suppose so,' he said dubiously, scratching his arm which was swollen and painful from the smallpox vaccination.

A few days later we were advised, with the compliments of the American Embassy, that our first papers were ready and that we had the right to enter the USA and remain and work there as long as we pleased, with possible citizenship ahead after five years.

We then booked our passage and started to pack.

I think Madame Poisson was sincerely sorry to see us go.

She gave us a splendid farewell dinner at her own apartment in a house some distance from her hotel. The flat was most opulently furnished in the style of Louis XV with elaborate draperies curtaining every window, already thickly covered with lace, ornamental figurines everywhere, and the rich odours of food cooked, no doubt, by Monsieur Poisson pervaded the rooms. He had dressed formally for the occasion in a frockcoat and striped trousers and came and went throughout the interminable meal (we had been invited for three o'clock and it lasted until five) serving, carving and slicing, full of pride and authority – the perfect host.

All I can remember was a marvellous light fish soup, truffles *en serviette*, a pot-roast that must have stewed for days in its aromatic herbs, followed by salads and cheeses and a chocolate soufflé, accompanied by wines, champagne and liqueurs and that we kissed Madame Poisson goodbye with profound gratitude and tears and that the child was sick in the taxi afterwards.

Our departure from Paris for Cherbourg next morning was highly emotional, thanks to Leopold's many Czech faithfuls. They came to the railway station to bid us goodbye. 'Our hearts travel with you,' they said, 'may Pan Buh [Mr God] grant that we too may follow soon.' They brought small gifts; loaves, of coarse ryebread, sausages and bottles of Slivovice to remind us of home; sweets and books for the child; at least three tattered copies of *Babicka* by Bozena Nemcova (tales of a grandmother and a Czech classic). They entrusted us with letters and messages to relations and friends living as far apart as New York and Chicago, California and Wisconsin. They handed us for safe-keeping things they still believed to be of such value that they were afraid to keep them in case they might be stolen by fellow Czechs. Paintings and drawings by Mánes, the original score of one of Dvorak's musical compositions, letters, mostly official, but bearing the signature of President Masaryk, and many other items precious only to nationalistic Czechs but by then only of sentimental value.

Though we were to keep it all carefully, none of it was later claimed, probably because it was unsaleable. Americans had lost interest in the democratic republic they had done so much to help create. Politically Czechoslovakia had to be written off and the Czechs who had settled in the USA did not want to be reminded of the past.

A very frail old man thrust a paper bag towards Leopold. His hand trembled. 'Take them,' he said, 'and plant them in the New World.'

Leopold examined the bag's contents. 'I am very fond of onions,' he said kindly, 'thank you.'

'Onions!' the old man screamed, 'they are *Sternbergia Lutea*, the golden lilies of the field mentioned in the Bible. Named after your ancestor who discovered them in those lands, Count Caspar Sternberg the great botanist, the friend of Goethe and of our famous historian Pallacki! The man who built us the Natural History Museum on the Vaclavske Namièsty in Prague. The finest in the world! Onions!'

'I'm sorry,' Leopold said, 'I am no plant expert, forgive me!'

'My grandfather was Count Caspar's assistant,' the old man, then somewhat pacified, explained. 'He was presented with a few of these rare bulbs. My family has nursed them through our winters ever since. This is all that's left. They are valuable. I didn't want the Russians to have them. No doubt you will find a sunny warm climate on that great continent of America where they will increase and flower.'

'But you, Pane doctore?' I asked. It was customary in Czechoslovakia to give this title, academically merited or not, as a sign of respect. 'Why not plant them yourself once you get to America or even grow them here in France?'

'They need a year till they bloom,' he said with a wry smile, 'and I have only a few more months. Please take them.'

I never see the golden autumn crocus bloom, obtainable by now in every good nursery, without remembering that old man. However, the small print on our emigration papers threatened dire punishments for bringing plants, roots, bulbs, even seeds, into the USA. Sadly we had to throw the *Sternbergias* into the sea.

The SS *Washington* on which we had embarked was one of the smaller American ships; Steinhardt had recommended our taking it. He had pointed out that on board her we could afford first-class accommodation, which we should not venture to do on one of the big luxury liners because of the expense. But he advised us not to go tourist class either. We didn't tell him that we had not considered doing so. We had travelled too much by sea not to know of the crowded discomfort of those herded together on the lower decks isolated from their superiors above.

'Not that tourist accommodation isn't quite clean and adequate these days on all American ships,' Steinhardt had said. 'But the press will be interested in you when you arrive and it might give the wrong impression if they found you down there . . . "Count and family

deprived of all by communism . . . Arrive in the USA penniless . . ."
etc.'

'Well, it's almost true,' Leopold said.

'Except for your help.' I had smiled gratefully at Steinhardt and he
had smiled back.

'It's not the sort of publicity we want,' he had then said firmly.
'It might bring you brief sympathy but it would harm you socially.
Not that Americans aren't kind-hearted and generous. But you see
ours is a country that offered such vast opportunities in the past, and
does even now, that poverty is slightly suspect. It simply means someone's no good. No American would ever confess to being poor and
neither should you. In fact, when they interview you, which, of course,
they will, I think you shouldn't make too much of what you have lost
but speak of your hopes for the future. You, of your ceramic art,' he
turned to me, 'and Leopold of whatever he plans to work at. It pays
to make a bit of propaganda for oneself. Optimism and enterprise
are what Americans admire most. A success story is much more popular
than one of failure and disaster in the USA.'

How often later was I to remember those words of Steinhardt's.

Once on board we saw to our belongings being safely stowed away
in the two cabins we had been given. Leopold's was an inside one, but
he didn't mind as long as he had a place to himself. His size would
always demand more space than other human beings needed. Afterwards
we went up and stood on the rain-washed deck to watch the coast of
France and of Europe dissolve and vanish in fog and mist, each of us
rather desperately conscious of what we were leaving, perhaps for ever.

'It's going to be rough,' Leopold remarked unnecessarily. The sea
was already starting to make itself felt and continued to do so throughout our journey. The SS *Washington* was a slow ship. It would take two
weeks for us to reach New York. It was the season of late October
gales. Soon the sea gave us no leisure for regrets. Keeping one's physical
balance became more important than mental stability; not breaking one's
bones more essential than not breaking one's heart. Also all sea voyages,
however rough, bring a sort of peace. The land one has left seems to
have ceased to exist; the land one hopes to reach is no more real than
a dream. Past and future become equally remote. With nothing in
sight but the sea, time itself seems suspended. A different element has
one in its care, against which all human strivings seem in vain. The
sea's power is absolute. It can sustain or destroy as it wills. The lands
are man's to use or abuse as he pleases but not the oceans.

Leopold and I were rarely seasick and to our relief the child (it was her first ocean voyage) did not mind the ship's rolling at all but seemed to enjoy it. Nevertheless, the first day and night out brought the familiar drowsiness, a sort of lassitude I knew only too well that made me prefer to remain in my cabin until I had grown accustomed to the rhythm of the waves. I left it to Leopold and Diana to explore the ship while I rested.

35

The first conscious memory of my life I thought was of the sea's movement beneath me.

I was three years old when we crossed the Channel from Dover to Calais. My brother, Hubert, was still a baby. Nanny Cass was with us but I have no recollection of my parents then or of the long journey by train through France and Germany that must have followed for us to reach Emkendorf, our future home.

My parents had lived in London and in Wiltshire in my grandmother's country place for the first five years of their marriage. Only when my grandfather died did my father return to Holstein. Hubert and I had managed to survive our birth in Goring-on-Thames. My mother was over thirty when she married, which was then considered rather too old for successful child-bearing. Perhaps she herself was afraid, or that her family feared for her, in any case a nursing home was chosen that offered 'Twilight Sleep'. What sort of anaesthetics were used I do not know, but in any case the mother slept all through childbirth, only to wake when her baby, washed and dressed, lay beside her in its frilly cot.

But all too frequently for the doctors' and the nursing home's reputation the cot remained empty. Too many babies did not wake from 'Twilight Sleep' and this method of painless birth had eventually to be discontinued.

Most women prefer their first-born to be a boy. In case they might not have another child, the son and heir is assured. So I was a disappointment to my mother from the start and I think she never quite forgave me for this, not even when Hubert was born two years later. He was beautiful, even as a baby, with huge violet-blue, darkly lashed eyes, very like her own, and perfect features. I had none of these assets and really couldn't compete then or later for her affection.

My father had to wait until he was nearing fifty to inherit Emkendorf. My grandfather's incomprehensible animosity towards him had debarred him from even visiting his childhood home for many years. It went so far that my grandfather had stipulated in his will that the place should be sold and the proceeds divided between my father and his sister Aunt Diana. He could not legally disinherit his only son, but he did try and deprive him of Emkendorf.

Even Aunt Diana, who had devotedly nursed the difficult old man for years, was shocked at this and left the considerable sum half of the property if sold would have given her, on Emkendorf as a mortgage, my father paying her the annual interest or not according to his changing fortunes.

Emkendorf was one of the most remarkable and curious eighteenth-century country houses in north Germany. Not its exterior; its neoclassical façade topped by architraves supported on columns was much like that of many other houses of equal size in Denmark and Holstein built in the same century. A large central block flanked by two wings, forming an open courtyard in the front, at the back a row of tall french windows leading on to a terrace that overlooked lawns, the lake and the park.

It was the interior of Emkendorf that was unique. In the later part of the eighteenth century painters and plasterers had been brought from Italy by Carl and Julie Reventlow to redecorate the house completely. The Pellicis came from Rome. There were several brothers, all good artists and craftsmen. They brought their wives and children with them and spent eleven years covering the walls and ceilings of most of Emkendorf's rooms with painting and plaster ornamentations. Much was reminiscent of Pompeii and Herculaneum, then rediscovered, much in the style of the *loggias* in the Vatican, though the most interesting and amusing frescoes were those on which the Pellicis had allowed their imagination full freedom in depicting mythological subjects.

In addition, Angelica Kauffman and her friend, Raphael Mengs, both fashionable painters of the time, had come to stay and contribute to the decorating of the house with panels and pictures.

The many marble busts and statues, some antique, some copies bought in Rome, were built into arches and niches recessed into walls, so were the large canvasses by Guido Reni, Salvator Rosa and Andrea del Sarto, painters much admired by the Reventlows.

The result of all this was an interior of amazing beauty, the like of which could perhaps be found in Italy but certainly not in Schleswig-Holstein.

Fortunately for Emkendorf my grandfather either had very little money or had disliked spending it. Even if parts of the house had fallen into disrepair the damage was not half as great as if Victorian efforts at modernization had been made by him. My father, who had great taste and knowledge, saw to careful restoration and soon the house regained its original splendour.

Emkendorf was soon mockingly to be called 'Engeldorf' or *Die Englische Colonie* by our Holstein neighbours after my parents had moved in. They had brought their entire household staff with them from London. A butler, two footmen and my father's valet, our cook, my mother's personal maid, house- and kitchen-maids. Mrs Donnalds, our housekeeper, came with her two daughters. One of them looked after the poultry yard, the other was in charge of the gardens. Both were spinsters. Piggot, the coachman, arrived with his wife and two children and my parents' hunters. They came even before the New Forest ponies my mother had bought – six mares and a stallion – which she felt could roam freely summer and winter, as they did at home, in Emkendorf's meadows and forests.

Three Jersey cows came too. They were not allowed to live with the Holstein cattle but were kept separately for the children's milk. Five dogs, all of English breed, arrived. Hens (Wyandots and Orpington) white and brown to provide English eggs for English breakfasts, and ducks and turkeys, all these animals reached Emkendorf safely, coming by ship to Kiel. Also thousands of bulbs and perennials. Though the beautiful old park needed no embellishing, the flower garden certainly did.

The Holstein climate was very like that of England. Mild, wet winters, followed by cool, wet summers. All that had been imported – vegetable, animal, and human – increased and prospered.

English engineers and architects came to install a large central-heating plant in the cellar. It devoured whole forests in the course of time. Eight modern bathrooms were built into the small powder closets that adjoined many rooms. One wing of the house was completely rebuilt inside, forming apartments for Piggot and his family. Mrs Donnalds too had hers downstairs, with new nursery quarters for us and additional guest-rooms on the top floor.

Furniture had to be bought – all eighteenth-century, of course. My father would have felt it almost a sacrilege to put anything of later date into one of Emkendorf's rooms.

All this cost a vast amount of money. My mother's fortune, like that of her sisters, thanks to the Whitehead torpedoes, was large but not limitless. Nearly all of it was spent on Emkendorf; first on rebuilding, modernizing and restoring, then on entertaining in it and displaying its perfection to friends and relations who came from all over Europe to marvel. But except for my mother's two sisters and their children who didn't count as such, Germans only rarely saw the interior of the house; a few princes, considered more or less possible because of their relationship to the British royal family, that was all. There were house-parties, dancing in the big ballroom and musical evenings, riding and boating in the daytime, though of course in all this we children had been too young to join.

The Emkendorf estate was not very large and except for its wealth of centuries-old timber didn't bring in much profit. My father loved trees and couldn't bear to see them cut. My mother loved animals and would not allow those bred on the farm to be slaughtered. Emkendorf's soil was sandy, light and poor. Heather and bracken grew profusely. Crops did not and potatoes were about its only produce. Most of the land was in pasture. My father was not interested in agriculture and farming at a loss didn't appeal to him. Finally Emkendorf's main farm was rented to a gentleman who payed a secure amount yearly, really only for the privilege of living in the former bailiff's house, a small eighteenth-century architectural gem. He farmed just as inefficiently and unsuccessfully as my parents would have done.

Diana came in to interrupt my thoughts.

'Are you seasick?' she asked, seeing me stretched out on my bunk.

'No, just resting and remembering. There won't be much time for that when we get to America.'

So Diana read in her bunk above me and my thoughts returned to Emkendorf.

The only Germans employed in those years were men who worked in the garden as labourers or in the forest as gamekeepers and women who came from near-by villages to do the washing, boiling our household linen in huge cauldrons and ironing sheets on long padded tables in the laundry. They also cleaned the kitchen and servants' quarters floors. We children couldn't speak to them since we knew no German. The only Holsteiners living in the house were a very old couple, Herr and Frau Yess. They had a small flat to themselves on the ground floor of one wing. She milked our Jersey cows and sometimes allowed us to try to do so too. She was a kindly woman with a face like a rosy wrinkled apple. He was the night-watchman and walked round the house after dark swinging a lantern, rousing all the dogs. But his main duty, even in my grandfather's time, was to wind the big clock set in the centre gable of the roof, activated by pulleys and lead weights in the attic. It pealed out the hours day and night, warning of the passing of time and, I believe, rang many happy hours for my parents.

Yet those five years were really all they were given to enjoy Emkendorf and each other.

I was six when the First World War started and I can well remember the extraordinary changes it brought to Emkendorf. Also the sad partings from all members of our household, several of whom Hubert and I had learnt to love and trust. No more teas with Mrs Donnalds; no more visits to the stable where Piggot showed us the new-born foals; no more running into the big vaulted kitchen, with its gleaming copper pots, for fudge and toffee, or to watch Cook throw big pats of butter into the fire to make it flame high. Soon there would not be enough butter even to put on bread, only carrot jam. However we could still go and look for newly-laid eggs in the poultry yard and soon roam house and park more freely than we had been allowed to do before.

Our mother, anxious for the welfare of the animals, and not trusting our new, and indeed very inadequate, staff to feed them properly, took over Mrs Donnalds's now deserted kitchen. There she stirred huge pots of mash for the horses, boiled game, which either my father or the gamekeeper had shot, for the dogs (by then they had increased to nine) and cooked hash for the chickens out of kitchen refuse. Corn was soon too scarce to be used for anything but baking bread.

Her hair tied up in a kerchief, her lovely face smudged with bran, wearing old clothes and a large apron, she looked much like Cinderella in her kitchen. True, there were no evil stepsisters to make her suffer, but her own two sisters' troubles at that time distressed her just as much.

Aunt Polly Plessen too was nanny-less, though that was the least of her worries. Her three eldest sons had been called up. Fortunately for them, two soon became British prisoners, safe and well looked after, even if condemned to years of boredom. The eldest, handsome Ludwig Carl, fought bravely all through the war, for Germany whatever his sympathies may have been, since he had studied at Oxford.

Aunt Maggie Bismarck's boys were fortunately still too young to fight but she too lost Nanny Rosser in whose care they had been.

However, the patriotism Aunt Maggie was expected to manifest as a Bismarck and which she thought it was her duty to inspire in her children, affected her health. Because of his ignominious dismissal of her father-in-law, she had learnt to distrust Kaiser Wilhelm and all his doings. His declaring war on his own mother's country seemed to her the last straw.

My parents had not faced the possibility that there might be war between England and Germany and had ignored the few warnings there had been. The assassination of the Archduke Franz Ferdinand, heir to the Austrian throne, and of his morganatic wife in Sarajevo that finally sparked off the conflict had been unforeseeable. But I think even had they known earlier what to expect they would not have left our home for England, or even Denmark, where my father could certainly have been re-accepted as a Dane. Their hearts and their fortunes were too totally committed to Emkendorf.

Later they were to learn to regret they had not escaped. The splendid isolation in which they had chosen to live had been, of course, resented by their German neighbours, not only by people of their own class but by the small tradesmen in the surrounding towns with whom they had never dealt. What edibles farm and gardens and forests had not provided had been shipped in large crates from Fortnum and Mason every month. Even the villagers, jealous of only foreigners having been employed, felt no loyalty towards my parents. Though both of them had never accepted that they were German, since neither of them were so by birth, they had not expected to find themselves treated as suspect aliens on their own land either, which is what then happened. Emkendorf was very near the Kiel Canal. My mother was accused of setting a lamp in her window at night as a signal and guide to British planes. My father naturally went to visit Piggot and the other servants in the internment camp, which was in a small town not far from Emkendorf, to see if he could help them in any way.

As a matter of fact, he did manage to get them later exchanged for Germans who had been interned in England.

His visits were noted. More proof of my parents' pro-British sympathies. As always in time of war patriotism and hatred of the enemy were more excessive among civilians than on the front – soldiers soon knew better.

Of course, there was never any proof of all the anti-German activities my parents were accused of and there were no official reactions. But they had to live in an atmosphere of petty animosity, of increasing small irritating pin-pricks, more wearing as time went on, than any real conflict would have been. In addition, there was no money. What was left of my mother's fortune was invested in England and blocked as enemy property. Only through my father selling some pictures were financial problems solved for the next couple of months.

36

To us children the war brought rather mixed blessings. The greatest and all-important one was that Nanny Cass had gone home. Small children cannot complain of cruelty except with tears and if they learn that cries and screams only bring further punishment they become silent and accept ill-treatment as part of life.

Our parents in the brief moments they saw us in the mornings and after tea, when we were brought to them befrilled and tied up with ribbons, clean, sweet-smelling, our hair brushed into curls with rose-water, marvelled at how quiet and well-behaved we were and always complimented Nanny on taking such good care of us. How should they have known how sore our bottoms were from her chastisements?

I, being two years older than Hubert, got the worst of it. Even at four I was a strong and wilful child not easily broken or subdued. What was then considered the right and correct diet and hygiene for children had been part of Nanny's training and was strictly adhered to. Fresh air was considered all important, however hot or cold, damp or icy the weather. Windows remained wide open day and night. The food she ordered had to be eaten, even if disliked. Spinach and milk-pudding reappeared cold for tea if refused at lunch. If not consumed, it was forcefully spooned into our mouths and if this made us sick we were shut into a dark cupboard.

Some instinct told me that only by refusing all food could I defeat Nanny. I was hardened to her punishments by then. Fortunately she didn't have much imagination and they never varied. Hubert bravely followed my example.

'Aren't the children getting very thin?' my mother asked with some concern.

'Only unhealthy children are fat,' Nanny declared authoritatively. However, I sensed she was worried because she started to try to coax instead of smack. It was too late. We had lost any desire for food. I doubt if the war hadn't come and enforced her departure we would have survived in her care.

Then, blessedly, Miss Jensen came. We called her 'Lenlen' and loved her. She was Danish and had been trained in London at a Princess Christian school for nannies. She wore a brown nurse's uniform and a brown veil. When I think of a gentle saint I remember 'Lenlen'. Placid and serene, she allowed us to eat what we pleased and to leave what we disliked. She shut the windows against the cold and her only punishments if we were naughty were far more effective than Nanny's had been. All she did was to turn her kind face from us and not speak to us for an hour or two.

We became happy, healthy, normal children in her care and would have continued to be so had our parents not shown a growing interest in us and our education. As the war progressed, the isolation in which they were forced to live and their financial troubles had begun to fray their nerves. Both my parents were extremely short-tempered but since they were still very much in love with each other they had means of reconciliation that we children lacked.

Nor had the servants much defence. My mother, furious at the inefficiency of the Holstein maids, threw a hairbrush or whatever came to hand at them. Screaming with fear they fled. Next day, my mother, in tears, would apologize and give them presents. She had the warmest of hearts, would help anyone in distress, her kindness and gentleness with animals was extraordinary but only with them did she seem able to control her violent outbursts of temper.

I suffered so much from them in my childhood that I learnt really never to lose mine later.

She had very large, long-fingered, very beautiful, strong white hands. These would descend in cracking blows on to the back of my neck whenever I had been naughty. Perhaps she didn't want to mark my face, but a blow on the neck is much more spine-shattering than a slap on the cheek or bottom. I believe I still feel the effects.

My father too, though he had somewhat more self-control, was irascible. He cursed the inefficient German butler daily, who was incapable, of course, of doing the work four trained English men-servants had done before. My father cared very much about polish in manners and behaviour, as well as on furniture and floors and silver and above all on his shoes, of which he had over fifty pairs. His appearance, good-looking as he knew himself to be even in middle age, was of great importance to him. His suits, all made in London to his great satisfaction, still fitted him, if rather tightly. They had to be brushed and the trousers pressed, his silk shirts carefully washed in soft suds, of which there were soon none available in Germany. In Holstein horse-chestnuts were ground to make soap. No wonder he kicked us children when we came to bid him good morning if we inadvertently stepped on the shoes he had, in despair, started to polish himself, or shoved us away if when kissing him we ruffled his rather sparse and carefully arranged hair or crumpled his trousers by leaping on to his knees.

My mother, perhaps confident in her beauty, had stopped worrying about her appearance. Since she had no maid to do her hair, she tied it up in a turban and day after day she wore the same old skirt and cardigan.

When my father protested, she said she couldn't be bothered and that she had no time to spare for vanity, which was true. If not feeding and tending animals she roamed garden, fields and forests, often with us, to search for edible weeds. We picked young nettles and sorrel for soup, dandelions for salads, wild hops and the roots of couchgrass as vegetables and blackberries, raspberries, wild strawberries or rosehips to be made by her into jams or desserts.

All these activities wouldn't have been necessary at all had she been less impatient with the slow, lethargic Holsteiners then employed. If properly directed they would certainly have fed the animals conscientiously. But my mother didn't trust them. None of them! The gardener would no doubt have been able to grow enough vegetables and fruit for our needs had my mother not accused him of selling the grapes and figs that still grew profusely in the by then unheated greenhouses, instead of bringing them to the house.

After their quarrel he only delivered what my father requested him to and since the latter always forgot what was needful we had practically nothing from the garden that we did not forage for ourselves.

There was trouble with the tenant farmer too, with whom arrangements had been made in the past that he was to deliver a certain amount of milk every day for our household. What milk the Jersey cows gave was just for us children, the thick cream used for desserts, or in the war shaken into butter in bottles by 'Lenlen'.

Herr Clausen was a patriot and when he found out that the milk he delivered was only used to feed animals he would not send any more, declaring it should benefit German children, not English dogs. My father managed to appease him but milk remained scarce while the animals in need of nourishment increased.

In our mother's bathroom with its Italian frescoed walls and ceiling, a duck hatched her ducklings in a cupboard. They were taught to swim in the marble bath. A wood-pigeon damaged by shot, minus one eye, and with a broken wing, was kept there in a basket too.

A fawn that had been found deserted in the forest by a gamekeeper and brought to my mother also lived in the bathroom, as well as a puppy, half-Alsatian, half-Labrador, the only survivor of a litter of nine. The rest had all been born dead, killing the mother, an Alsatian bitch. Both the puppy and the deer were bottle-fed by my mother. As they grew stronger they were to become her constant companions. Suzy, the deer, followed her upstairs and downstairs all through the house, slithering across the parquet floors on tiny hooves. Molly, the dog, galloped behind, barking fiercely, even at us children.

When I think of my mother now, I know how fond of her I could have become had I been old enough to understand her. I didn't envy the tenderness and affection she gave her animals. I knew that I felt much the same way about them as she. What I resented was that they could depend on her constant kindness while I could not and neither really could the more privileged Hubert. Her moods were as unpredictable as the weather: warm and sunny one day, dark and stormy the next. One never knew what to expect or be prepared for. Children fear uncertainty and insecurity much more than the strictest discipline. I still cannot read *Alice in Wonderland* without feeling the horror it inspired in me as a child when I was hoping to learn of a sane and reliable world in which everything was permanent and secure and in which things didn't grow larger and smaller, or vanish and reappear, and every word spoken seem to have a double meaning, as it does in *Alice* and in the world of childhood.

Really only 'Lenlen' and later Aunt Diana gave us some feeling of security. Our parents never did. We grew fearful of loving them, so unreliable did they seem to us. Yet how they could charm if in the mood. Both were very gifted people. My father drew beautifully, was a good pianist, and a master of the cello. My mother painted Turneresque watercolours and had a fine singing voice. Both might have become professionals at one or the other art had they been born into a different class. As it was they used their talents only for their own or their friends' entertainment. My mother even wrote rather well, highly romantic tales of love and death which I only read many years later, and a whole book on the lost continent Atlantis, a subject which had interested her for years and which she had carefully studied and researched. She was very imaginative. Occasionally she would share her fantasies with us, inventing strange tales and illustrating them with pencil and paint, keeping us spellbound. But these happy hours were rare. In general she hadn't much time for us. My father, Emkendorf and her animals kept her too busy. Often over-tired and irritable, all we could usually expect from her were reprimands and reproaches.

No doubt we had become rather naughty children. The change from Nanny's crushing discipline to 'Lenlen's' benign rule had restored our health and vitality and we were often uncontrollable. 'Lenlen', who was anyway rather deaf, didn't mind how much noise we made or how rough our games were as long as we didn't hurt each other. Placid and protective, she was really only interested in our physical welfare, dabbing Pond's Extract on cuts and bruises, rubbing sprains with Elliman's Embrocation and giving us castor oil if we hadn't been to the bathroom in the morning, which taught me regular habits for life. If we had a fever she gave us half an aspirin and for a high fever we were wrapped in cold, wet sheets. With these simple remedies she cured all our illnesses.

We were still thin but quite healthy and really very happy children, as long as we could escape our parents. We roamed the house freely. It seemed immense to us then. We hid in the park, not coming back when we were called, causing our parents constant anxiety lest we had drowned in the lake. If caught it was always I who was blamed, quite rightly, for having led Hubert astray.

When I was seven my parents decided I must have a governess.

This unpleasant decision was caused by something that upset my mother beyond comprehension. Only later was I to understand why. Emkendorf's attics under the roof were large and full of furniture, chests, old trunks and filled with odds and ends. It was a fascinating graveyard of unwanted and forgotten articles. We were not allowed to go there – told that the round windows were dangerous being so low from the floor that one could, if one opened one, step right out into the air with the courtyard forty feet below. But there were also other reasons as I was to discover, when we disobeyed and spent a happy afternoon there, having begged the key from Herr Yess. Because he had to wind the clock daily it was in his keeping.

In part of the attic someone called Mary Dameron seemed to be living. We never actually saw her but she kept all her things there in several old-fashioned trunks marked 'M.D.' They were unlocked. One was full of letters tied with ribbons, books with her name on the front page and photographs signed 'Mary'. One said, 'To my only beloved from his Mary'. Yellowed and not very distinct as these portraits were, they showed a young and pretty woman in a sort of fancy dress. She wore a blouse with big ballooning sleeves and her waist was tightly belted. Her hair was pulled straight back from her face, except for a fringe, and piled on top of her head. She seemed friendly. She was smiling.

The clock struck five, startling us by the clanging. We had never been so close to its big bells before. Hurriedly we closed the trunk, knowing it was tea time and that we might be searched for.

In the evening we asked our mother: 'Who is Mary Dameron?'

She looked frightened, I thought.

'Why do you ask?'

We knew we must not tell about the attic.

'I saw a book in the library with "Mary Dameron" written in it,' I said. It happened to be quite true, but I had taken no notice of the name before.

My mother seemed to breathe a sigh of relief. 'Many of the books are old. They could have belonged to anyone.'

We asked 'Lenlen' who Mary was but she said she had no idea – nor did she. A day later we crept back into the attic. Herr Yess hadn't remembered that we still had the key. We opened the other trunks. They were full of dresses of silk and satin and wool, gloves and fans, nightgowns of lawn, so fine you could see through them, edged with lace and ribbons, everything packed in tissue paper with muslin bags that still smelt of lavender. There was a dressing case with gold-topped bottles and jars, a large 'M' engraved on them, combs and brushes, hairpins in gold boxes, even a toothbrush and soap. 'Where can she have gone?' Hubert whispered. 'If she left everything here – ' 'Why did she come and not unpack?' I questioned. 'Perhaps she's here, hiding somewhere?' Hubert glanced at several large cupboards.

'You're silly. What would she eat?'

'Perhaps Herr Yess feeds her every day?'

The third trunk contained nothing but shoes and boots, all in flowered sacks. I drew out one after the other, tiny, narrow, satin slippers, embroidered with beads, boots of every colour, with pearl buttons. I tried on a pair. I was seven and they only just fitted.

At tea in the nursery Hubert put several biscuits in his pocket. 'For Mary,' he whispered. 'Lenlen' didn't notice. I shivered. Perhaps she really was somewhere hidden in the attics. We knew our grandfather had been an evil man; our father always said so. And Herr Yess was the only servant that still remained in the house since his day. Was Herr Yess Mary's jailer? Did our parents know about her? What crime could she have committed to have to be shut up for years? It was all a great mystery.

We did not know that there were mice in the attic. The biscuits we left for Mary were gone next day, certain proof we felt that she was somewhere hiding, too afraid to come out when we were there. We started to call to her gently but there was no answer. Next day we brought more food, which she also ate. I tried to read some of the letters tied in bundles. They were in English. 'St Louis' was written at the top of all the pages but the handwriting was difficult for me to decipher, except for 'My dearest daughter' and 'Your affectionate mother'. There were no envelopes.

'What's "St Louis"?' I asked 'Lenlen'. A French saint, she thought, a king.

We grew so accustomed to Mary and to playing with her things that I asked her if I could borrow her red boots for a day or two and Hubert wanted a little gold pocketknife and her nail scissors. She certainly didn't say no – to anything we asked her to lend us. I put on the red boots and pranced downstairs, Hubert behind me.

'Come here,' my mother called from the drawing-room, having heard us laugh. We stood quite still. Perhaps she would think we were gone. It was all right for Hubert. He could put the things in his pocket but I knew how long it would take me to unbutton the boots. My mother came to the door. 'I've told you dozens of times not to play on the stairs, they are slippery and it's dangerous. Come and have some tea with us,' she added, 'I never seem to see you any more. God knows what you've been up to this week!'

No escape was possible. Perhaps she wouldn't notice the boots. Our father was sitting on the sofa near the fireplace drinking tea. I plumped down on the ground hiding my feet beneath me. This startled my mother's favourite dog, Molly, who snarled. It was not very fond of children.

'Get up,' my mother said, 'it makes Molly nervous to see you squat like an animal.'

I had to obey.

'Where did you find those shoes?' my mother gasped, catching sight of them.

'Mary Dameron lent them to me,' I said brazenly. 'We asked her permission – we often talk to her.'

My mother's expression changed from anger to fear, even my father's face seemed to have lost all colour. He got up and put his arms around my mother's shoulders, whispering something to her, but she shook her head and I saw her eyes were full of tears. We crept away as silently as we could. Our parents did not seem to notice.

Next day the attics were locked. We hoped Herr Yess would remember to feed Mary, but since he and Frau Yess seemed to live entirely on boiled potatoes which she sometimes gave to us and which we thought a great delicacy, ours always being fried or mashed, we did not worry too much. Nor about keeping the things Mary had lent us. Neither of my parents mentioned the red boots or scolded us, which we quite understood. After all, it must be awful for them, we thought, to keep poor Mary locked up for ever, even if our wicked grandfather had forced them to do so.

A few weeks later, Aunt Diana came for one of her brief visits. Since we trusted her absolutely we confessed to our visits to the attic and about Mary.

She listened to us in silence, her ageing face still beautiful, but quite impassive. Then she asked us if we could keep a secret, even from our parents. We said we could. 'Will you promise?' she demanded. 'Cross our hearts,' we said, 'and wish to die.' It was the most binding of our oaths.

She smiled a little.

'I have never told you about Mary because your parents didn't wish me to. They had their reasons. They thought you were too young to understand.'

'Because of our wicked grandfather? He locked her up, didn't he?'

'My father? He never even met Mary. What absurd confusion untruths or half-truths can cause,' she exclaimed. 'Mary never even came to Emkendorf . . .'

'But her trunks, her clothes, her letters, everything?'

'Your father brought them here after her death. She was his first wife, an American.'

It took us a while to ponder these revelations.

'But why is it all such a secret, then?' I asked. 'Why didn't anyone tell us anything?'

'For a very good reason,' Aunt Diana said firmly. 'Your father loved Mary and to be reminded of her made him unhappy. So your mother felt the sooner Mary was forgotten the better for him. She didn't want you to know or worry him with questions. It's all very simple really.'

'What was she like?' I asked.

'Very pretty. Rather foolish, but then she was very young. Her waist was as narrow as this,' Aunt Diana joined index fingers and thumb of both her hands, as if encircling Mary's waist, 'and she had the smallest feet you've ever seen. She laughed and sang a lot before she began to cough. She died of consumption, like my sister, Constance.'

She then told us that our father had toured America as a young man. Good-looking, titled and hoping to inherit Emkendorf one day, he was certainly no fortune hunter. Nevertheless, since his father always kept him very short of money, he was not opposed to bringing back a rich wife from the USA should she please him. He found exactly the right person, a handsome widow who owned half of the city of St Louis. She was ready to accept him when he suddenly changed his mind. Instead of proposing to her he asked a poor relation of hers, Mary Dameron, who acted as a sort of companion and chaperon, to marry him instead. She was ten years younger and no doubt prettier than the rich widow.

They married in America. He could not bring her back to Emkendorf because of his father's opposition to the marriage. A penniless American of unknown ancestry seemed unacceptable as daughter-in-law to the old Count. However, my father had a charming small bachelor's cottage in which he had occasionally lived, situated on the shore of a lake, which belonged to his friend, Ludwig Plessen. He took Mary there. The honeymoon was brief. In the damp cold Holstein winter, with mist and fog hovering over the lake, Mary became ill and tuberculosis was diagnosed. My father travelled with her to San Remo, hoping sun and sea air would cure her, but she died after a few months. Since my grandfather even refused to have her coffin in the family vault, my father buried her in the Anglican cemetery in San Remo. A stained-glass window he designed on which she is depicted as an angel commemorates her in the English church there. Knowing the truth at last, Mary fascinated us no more nor did we ever speak of her again.

Nevertheless my mother didn't forget the fright I had given her and felt the time had come for stricter control. A governess was engaged, the first of many.

They came and went from then on and were to continue to do so for the next five years. I can count thirty-six of these unfortunate creatures. In the war they were, of necessity, German and it took some time until we could even learn to speak to them. Only a few knew any English. None of them stayed long. If they were young and pretty and my father eyed them with any interest, my mother found some pretext to dismiss them. If they were old and ugly, neither of my parents could stand the sight of them, and they went too.

After two years of war my parents decided they desperately needed a change of country. They planned first to visit my grandmother in Vienna and then, if possible, to go on to Fiume on the Adriatic where my mother had been born and spent much of her childhood. 'Lenlen' and Hubert and I were to travel with them.

Aunt Diana was summoned. Long before she was due to arrive we waited at the window that overlooked the courtyard and when at last the carriage which had brought her from the railway station came we would see first her two old Gordon setters jump out, welcomed by all the other dogs; then she descended, dressed as always in mannish tweeds, with a sort of Scottish tam-o'-shanter on her head. Afterwards the large, square leather trunk was lifted out. Remembering that she lived on an island we were sure it was full of treasures from the sea – shells and amber and spotted gulls' eggs. It quite often was.

We rushed down to greet her. Not that we dared embrace or kiss her, knowing how she disliked being touched. Hubert bowed, I curtsied, as she had taught us to. She answered with a gracious inclination of her head and the faint ironic smile which we recognized as approval. We saw her no more that evening. I suppose my parents had a lot to talk over with her since it was agreed that she was to remain in charge of Emkendorf until we returned. She was, as my mother well knew, the only person to whom she could with complete confidence entrust her animals. Aunt Diana and my mother had only three things in common: devotion to animals, to Emkendorf and to my father. Only the first could they share. Scrupulously polite when they met, which was rarely for more than a couple of days since Aunt Diana only came to Emkendorf when requested to do so, they never quarrelled but neither was there much evidence of affection between them.

Aunt Diana thought my mother crude, undisciplined, over-emotional and spoilt. My mother felt Aunt Diana to be arrogant, proud, cold and eccentric. Yet never did I hear a word of criticism spoken by one about the other. Family loyalty forbade that.

Two days after Aunt Diana arrived we had to leave. We travelled by train, completely filling a first-class compartment with picnic baskets, numerous trunks, bundles and a commode. The curtains towards the corridor were drawn. If anyone dared intrude we were told to cough loudly as if we were ill.

We spent a night in a hotel in Munich. Hubert got hold of 'Lenlen's' scissors and stuck them into the two holes of an electric socket. He got a screaming shock and all the lights in the hotel went out.

Of Vienna and our grandmother then I remember very little, only that she had six Pekingeses that looked very much like her and had as sharp a bite. She did not like undisciplined children and neither did her dogs.

But 'Lenlen' was with us and all the security she gave. She took us for walks in the Belvedere gardens close to my grandmother's house. She understood why I cried and cried after having seen the Imperial carriage, drawn by four snow-white horses with flowing manes and tails, when it passed us on the street. I knew I had never seen anything so beautiful before and perhaps never would again.

From Vienna we went to Fiume for the winter. We stayed in the villa which still belonged to my mother's family. It was close to the Whitehead Torpedo Works, still producing torpedoes for the Austrian navy, and living near it was not without danger because of Italian bombs. However, the sound of a plane was rare and slow-flying as they were then there was ample time for 'Lenlen' to hurry us into a sort of tunnel that went under the road and connected garden and beach, though I think my later fear of bombs must have originated in that dark and airless shelter.

A great change came over my mother in Fiume. Recollecting her childhood there with us, showing us the gardens, now overgrown, small plots of which had been tended by each of her brothers and sisters to grow what they pleased, weeding them with us and telling us stories about her youth, she herself became young and gay again. She wore pretty clothes she had bought in Vienna and seemed a different person – kind and sweet-tempered.

Accustomed only to mist and rain and sunlight which at best only filtered in through the clouds in Holstein, the radiance of the southern sky blazed above us like a revelation of how good life could be. Flowers blossomed all through the winter in the terraced gardens, birds sang and the sea never changed from blue to grey.

When we returned to Emkendorf my mother was pregnant, though of course we were not told about it. She was by then nearing forty and the specialist she had seen in Vienna had advised her not to have any more children.

It seems there were complications from the start, for she spent the next months in Emkendorf mainly lying on the sofa in the library, reading or writing, when not looking after the animals, or table-turning in the evenings. This was then very much in fashion, probably in an effort of those who had lost sons, husbands or friends in the war, to communicate with their spirits. My aunts and their children frequently came to stay and the older ones joined in this form of diversion. I was allowed to assist a few times and it was discovered that I was an excellent medium. From then on I was allowed to join the ring of hands hovering over the table in the darkened room and to tap out messages with the grown-ups. 'Are you there? One tap for yes, two taps for no.' There was no doubt that the table moved, tilted and turned without anyone cheating. But I had discovered that if I fixed my thoughts strongly enough on a name, a word or sentence it would invariably be tapped out. Children hear a lot more than their parents expect them to and my messages were well chosen and of great interest to the grown-ups. I enjoyed it all very much. It gave me a sense of importance which I usually lacked, but since I had to concentrate very hard I grew rather wan and pale and languid after these evening sessions and 'Lenlen' found it difficult to wake me in the mornings.

She protested to my mother. After that my occult gifts were ignored.

My youngest brother was born in Berlin. My mother needed a specialist's care so Aunt Maggie recommended her own obstetrician who still practised there and was a well-known professor and deliverer of the children of German aristocracy.

Poor Victor! As he grew older, he was never allowed to forget that we had been born in England and he in Germany. He had been christened Friedrich Victor, Friedrich implying peace in German, Victor for an undoubtedly non-German victory.

He was a fair, fat and bonny baby, whom 'Lenlen' from then on gave most of the affection she used to lavish on us.

My mother never really recovered from Victor's birth. She was always ailing and her temper more unpredictable than ever. The war was ending. Russian aristocrats, who had managed to flee the Revolution, flooded north Germany. Of course, my parents did their best to help them. Whole families found temporary asylum in Emkendorf but the tales of horror they told and the news of the Tsar and his family's execution shocked and frightened my parents. When the navy mutinied in Kiel and the German Republic was declared, they felt the same was going to happen as in Russia. Aunt Diana was hastily summoned to defend Emkendorf. No one ever questioned her courage. We packed whatever there was of value small enough to take and left very dramatically at the dead of night in the big barouche drawn by the Norfolk greys for the Danish frontier. It took us three days to get there. We slept in small inns on the way. The journey was quite uneventful. No *Spartakisten*, as the Revolutionaries were called, bothered us.

Once in Denmark we stayed with relations, first with the Rantzaus in Krengerrup, then with the Reventlows for Christmas in their beautiful castle Brahe Trolleborg.

It was a wonderful Christmas. We had not seen white bread and so much butter for years or, chocolate, and the abundance of good food, presents and the kindness and warmth with which we were received made us children feel so much at home that we soon started to behave very badly. So much so that the Reventlows began to fear our influence on their own strictly brought-up children.

Anxious to be rid of us they offered my parents a vacant country mansion near Sonderburg in Schleswig, which was gratefully accepted. It proved disappointing. It was a cold, damp, ugly house, very sparsely furnished, without any modern conveniences, not even a bathroom. We had to bathe in tin tubs and use the commode.

The landscape was flat, dull and uninteresting and the sea never reached the shore, great stretches of mud and sand separating it from the land.

My father tried to relieve his boredom by buying old Friesian chests and cupboards and stripping, sanding and polishing them; my mother hers by painting the walls of the grim-looking drawing-room with birds and flowering trees. A temporary Danish governess was found, a cook and a maid. But none of us were happy in Sonderburg, especially we children or 'Lenlen' because we had worms and had to be purged daily to remove them.

When Aunt Diana wrote that all was well, we returned to Emkendorf. We weren't allowed to stay there long. My mother was restless and felt ill. Though Victor remained there with 'Lenlen', my parents, Hubert and I, with whatever governess we had, and Molly, the dog, started to travel from one spa to the other. Almost for a year we stayed in rented villas or boarding-houses or cheap hotels. Though my father had begun to sell some of Emkendorf's more valuable pictures and furniture, the money soon bought very little because of inflation. Nevertheless he acquired a car and we went to Kissingen, Gastein, Franzenbad, Marienbad and to Baden-Baden in it. My mother felt no better. Strange as it may seem the doctors she consulted didn't recognize her illness. Highly emotional as she was, it was diagnosed as a nervous complaint and her frequent haemorrhages due to the change of life.

But I think she knew she was mortally ill and wanted us with her as long as possible.

When at last cancer was diagnosed it was too late for any cure. We were sent to her sister, Aunt Polly. She and Uncle Ludwig Plessen were spending the summer in Maruthendorf, a small country house, not as grand as Nehmten, which had the most beautiful park in Holstein, in which they usually lived. Billa, their youngest daughter, was my age and we knew each other from the time we were old enough to battle for each other's toys as fiercely as we were much later to compete for admirers. Yet we were great friends. We shared a Swiss governess. We rode a lot on fat Shetland ponies and everyone was astonishingly kind to Hubert and me, even the older cousins who usually ignored us.

We only saw our mother once more. She had been operated on in Kiel, really only to give her some relief. It was too late for any hope of her recovering. We were taken to the hospital to visit her.

We had not seen her for months. Pale and very thin she lay in the narrow, high, white bed. We had picked her some flowers which we gave her and put up our faces to be kissed, but she pushed us away. We saw she was crying. 'Go,' she said, 'I can't bear it.' And she turned her face to the wall, sobbing into her pillow. The flowers fell to the ground. We left the room also in tears. What wrong had we done that she should treat us like this?

We were deeply offended and because our last memory of her had been her denial of us we were more surprised than sorry to hear of her death. No one had told us she might die. It would have explained everything. We were naughty children but not entirely heartless. Had we known she was suffering we would certainly have tried to have been more docile and obedient and understood her moods and tempers for what they were, as part of her illness, and her despair at having to leave us and my father.

And known too that the agony of seeing us for the last time when she was certain of death had been too much for her to bear and that it was love, not dislike, that had made her turn away.

But no one explained and only much later was I to learn to feel regrets and to mourn her.

As it was, we quite enjoyed the funeral. Everyone sobbed over us and we felt important. Her coffin was carried by my cousins Plessen and Bismarck to the family crypt in the church of Westensee. Village children who had never known my mother joyfully scattered rose-leaves all the way.

Only my father's suffering disturbed us. He would not leave his room for days after the funeral, his eyes red from weeping when he finally did come down. He didn't mind any more if we rumpled his hair or stood on his shoes as we tried to comfort him with childish embraces. We knew no other way to show our sympathy and affection.

Aunt Diana who, to our delight, was now going to stay in Emken-dorf with us for ever, or so we confidently believed, and who knew our father better than anyone else, pointed out that the shooting season was drawing near and that he hadn't seen his relations in Scotland for years.

'Grouse, pheasants, then stags,' she said.

'But how can I leave?' he asked pitifully. 'Surely it wouldn't be right for me to go so soon?'

'Nonsense,' Aunt Diana said. 'Lilly herself would have wanted you to go.'

'Do you really think so?' my father asked, his face brightening.

'I'm convinced of it,' Aunt Diana assured him, lying probably for the first and last time in her life.

He left Emkendorf after that and only rarely returned there, knowing us safe in his sister's care.

37

'What are you reading?' I asked my daughter.

'*Gone With the Wind.*'

'How very appropriate,' I couldn't help exclaiming. Then, 'Isn't that rather too grown-up?'

'Not at all. It's just like us in the war. You sewing us clothes out of old curtains.'

'Red velvet,' I remembered, 'even Papi's dressing gown!'

'With white rabbit fur inside. It made him look like Father Christmas.'

'Or something out of *Boris Godunov*,' I laughed.

'Don't you think Rhett Butler is rather like Mr Steinhardt?' she then ventured.

'I'm afraid I don't remember the book very well,' I said, untruthfully. I had never dared ask myself how much she knew.

'Couldn't you go and see how Papi is?' I pleaded. She went reluctantly, only to return a few minutes later. 'He's in his cabin lying down,' she reported. 'He said it was too rough to stand up. He asked what you were doing. I said you were in your bunk, thinking. He said he had plenty to think of too. So I left him.' She resumed her reading.

Was he also, I wondered, recalling childhood and youth before our new life began? How different his memories were to mine. I got up and looked out of the porthole, clouded by spray. Beyond that grey, restless expanse of sea was Aunt Diana's island, where she still lived practically alone. She was nearly ninety and I knew I would never see her again.

Those morning visits to her bedroom in Emkendorf, when did they begin? When my brother and I were still too small to reach the brass handle of her door, I remembered. It had to be opened for us by 'Lenlen'.

Her rooms were always kept locked when she wasn't visiting us. My father insisted that they must remain absolutely hers and not be used for guests, knowing it was the least he could do to still make her feel at home in Emkendorf, half of which legally belonged to her.

Aunt Diana's apartment consisted of a drawing-room, a bedroom, a practically empty room in which only her dogs slept in two baskets, a breakfast-room in which she never breakfasted, and a large bathroom.

Her bedroom was dark when we were allowed to enter it but we were permitted to open the shutters and to let in the pale morning light.

The room had originally been intended as a small theatre. It was divided into two parts by a row of Corinthian pillars. The back wall of what must have been the former stage, since the floor was slightly raised, depicted a Bacchanalia – the god Bacchus, obviously too drunk to stand up, reclining on a sort of cart drawn by capering flute-playing nymphs and fauns, accompanied by goats, all festooned with garlands of grapes and vineleaves.

Facing all this, Aunt Diana – Ahna as we called her – lay at the foot-end of the bed instead of at its head, preferring the Bacchanalia to the light from the windows, her eyes always over-strained from too much reading.

The bed was enormous; a Victorian monstrosity elaborately carved out of shiny, bright red mahogany. It and the dressing-table and wardrobes to match had come from America with my father's first wife. For sentimental reasons he had not wanted to part with the furniture and had put it into the only room he knew my mother would never enter.

We were allowed to perch at the edge of the bed; Ahna's head with its neatly plaited hair rested on the white pillow and beside it lay a large and loaded revolver. This was the only one of her possessions we were not allowed to touch. Living all alone, as she generally did on her island, which smugglers, especially in the war, were liable to make use of as a hiding place for their wares, she needed some protection and it had become a habit of hers to take the revolver with her wherever she went. That she was quite capable of using it we were certain. My father said Aunt Diana was almost as good a shot as he was: the highest compliment he could pay anyone.

'If a robber came into the room, would you kill him?' we asked.

'Certainly not. I'd shoot him in the knee and then call the servants to take him away. But I doubt any robber will come up here,' she reassured us. We too thought it improbable. The big front door was heavily barred at night and the dogs slept in the hall, barking occasionally, even at the four marble Venuses that stood there when a ray of moonlight seemed to bring them to life. The thief would have to climb the wide stairs that even frightened us at times because of the banisters on which the Pellicis had painted hundreds of masks. With every step upwards different faces appeared expressing all human emotions: greed, lust and cunning, fear, anger and hate, sorrow and laughter. We knew it would take a brave robber to venture up those stairs at night.

Aunt Diana was in her fifties then, unmarried, and people said still beautiful. Small children really only recognize beauty in brightly-coloured objects scaled to their own size, not in human faces which, however familiar and dear, loom large and indistinct above them. Anyway we were, at such an early age, incapable of appreciating the pale perfection of Aunt Diana's features. But since she told us that she was beautiful, we believed her. Aunt Diana never told lies.

What we did admire was her hair, which we were allowed to unplait. It was dark, streaked with silver, curly and crisp. Sparks flew out of it when she let us brush it. Strangely she had hardly any eyebrows or eyelashes and no hair on her body at all. She told us that really well-born people had hair only on their heads. Since both Hubert and I, and even our baby brother Victor, were covered with soft fuzz all over, we felt some mistake had been made at our births.

We had at first tried to kiss Aunt Diana good morning as we did our parents. Gently, but firmly, she had pushed us away. 'I think kissing rather disgusting,' she said. 'Once a man kissed me and I was sick all over him.' We didn't try again.

After her breakfast, which never varied, consisting of tea, a soft-boiled egg, of which she never ate the white, and toast and marmalade, the fascinating ritual of her bathing and dressing began. She would rise from the bed, discard her voluminous white cotton nightgown and walk to the bathroom stark naked.

We were allowed to run her bath. 'As cold as it comes from the tap,' she would order. Then we would watch her immerse herself in the icy water without even a shudder.

She was the first and only grown-up we had ever seen in the nude.

I suppose she still had a very perfect body or she would not have washed, stood in front of her mirror, brushed her teeth and done up her hair without the slightest embarrassment, even in front of us children, with nothing on at all.

I must confess that after the first shock of surprise we grew quite accustomed to her nakedness, our aesthetic sensibilities still undeveloped and our sexual curiosity non-existent. All I can remember of my childhood impression of her was that she was very tall and white, with two odd bumps on her chest, and that her clothes and toilet articles and jewels and the pretty objects she allowed us to play with were of far greater interest to us than her body.

But in retrospect, considering her upbringing (her Scottish mother had even been lady-in-waiting to Queen Victoria), her lack of what was then called 'modesty' seems as extraordinary as was her independence of spirit.

Perhaps growing up in a house like Emkendorf where every wall and ceiling displayed nude gods and goddesses accounted for her lack of prudery; perhaps her name Diana brought some secret identification with that cool, chaste goddess of the moon – huntress, yet forever escaping the hunter.

Chaste, Aunt Diana certainly was. She frankly acknowledged that she lacked what she called 'the animal passions' and that the idea of being possessed by a man had always disgusted her. Not that she disliked men. She much preferred their company to that of women and confessed she had enjoyed being courted in her youth. My father said she had many marriage proposals as a girl. She quite liked telling us about these suitors, seeming to count her escapes from them a greater triumph than her conquests. Some of these admirers of hers I seem to know even now, so vividly did she describe them, mimicking their voices, gestures and mannerisms . . . The elegant, fastidious, rather sinister widower, Count Wallis, with his scented pointed beard . . . he lived in a castle near Meran which his Venetian wife, born Mocenigo, had filled with wonderful furniture and pictures.

'I liked the castle,' Ahna said, pensively.

'Then why didn't you marry him?'

'I think really because he always wore gloves. And when he took them off it was too obvious that he was going to try and hold my hand.'

Then there had been the languid Prince Carolath, the poet. Ahna could quote most of his poems – they were all about herself. They were beautiful. 'Indeed they are,' she said dryly, 'but he was not!' Another of her suitors had been a young Danish prince – 'As fine and mettlesome as his horse, but, alas, much less intelligent – I never really met a man I could have married,' she said finally, 'and even if I had, I wouldn't have left my family.'

'But didn't you want children?' we asked, believing that the point of marriage.

'Certainly not. I much prefer animals.' Irony of fate that she was to have the sole charge of us after our mother's death, a responsibility her sense of duty would never have permitted her to refuse.

My mother's family were too much in awe of Aunt Diana to dare voice their consternation to our father that poor Lilly's children should be left to the care of a cold, eccentric, frustrated spinster.

Nor would he have listened to their protests. If he knew his sister to be unemotional, unsentimental, and perhaps rather strange, he had witnessed too many examples of her courageous dedication to his family's welfare to believe her unfit to look after his children. She had sacrificed her youth to nursing first her sister, then her mother, and in her later years to looking after her difficult, bad-tempered, recluse of a father. She had been the kindest of sisters to my father, always ready to help with the little she had when he had been in financial trouble, and either abetting the love affairs to which he was prone, or finding some decent way out when he had wearied of his conquest. Finally, she had made the supreme sacrifice of retiring to her remote island and of leaving Emkendorf to his wife.

Besides, though he would never have confessed it to anyone, he couldn't help noticing that we children were happier, more manageable and better behaved when with Aunt Diana than we had ever been with him or our mother.

My thoughts returned to the Ahna of our early childhood. By ten o'clock she would be fully dressed in her tweeds, a white silk blouse, with a sort of stock round her neck, and walking boots. These morning costumes never varied through the years nor did what she wore in the evening, a high-necked, long-sleeved black velvet gown with a train, and for very special occasions a dress of black lace which was cut low. If these clothes became shabby or worn out she had exact copies made, though at longer and longer intervals. Contrary to my father, Aunt Diana disliked spending unnecessarily – probably the mixture of thrifty French and Scottish blood was stronger in her than in him – but her economies only applied to herself. She could be rashly generous with large sums that she could ill afford to give, first to my father and later to us children.

We were not allowed to accompany Aunt Diana on her morning

Above. My mother with me

Overleaf. A room at Emkendorf

Below. At Emkendorf with Nanny Lenlen and governess, Hubert, Victor, and me

Right. My father
Middle. Myself at the time of our engagement
Far right. My cousin Eddie
Bottom. Emkendorf
Bottom right. My grandmother, Countess Hoyos, born Alice Whitehead

Left. With Leopold and our daughter Diana, about a year before we left Czechoslovakia.
Above and Below. Castolovice. The courtyard and the drawing room

Above. Aunt Diana on her
ninetieth birthday

Right. Harry and Diana Phipps
on their wedding day

Bottom. Tan-Y-Bryn, our
house in Jamaica

walks with the dogs, our legs being still much too short to keep pace with her. She walked for miles. Both she and my father liked to roam the forests of Emkendorf.

They shared a great love of trees. Ahna preferred the beeches to all others. 'So like a Greek temple,' she would exclaim, in the groves where the tall, straight, silver-grey pillars carried their high canopy of leaves. My father was fondest of oaks. 'As beautiful in life as in death,' he declared, no doubt thinking of the great, solid beams into which they would be cut or the fine panelling and furniture they would provide, after having been felled.

Aunt Diana walked with her dogs and a stick, my father with a gun. Only rarely did he use it in Emkendorf after the war, meat supplies having become plentiful again. Though he never refused an invitation to shoot somewhere else, at home he preferred just watching the roe deer and the herds of fallow deer with their spotted fawns peacefully grazing in the early spring mornings, and in the autumn to see the rutting stags fight for the does, raising his gun now and then to take sight of an antlered head, and lowering it again without shooting.

Aunt Diana never killed for sport. She told us she had been able to hit the centre of a target nine times out of ten and down clay pigeons with only rare misses in her youth. She said she had never shot a live animal except from necessity, only seals on her island in the war when she had needed meat for her dogs, and any of her beloved animals – horses, sheep or dogs – if they were incurably ill and suffered. Then, tenderly we knew, she would soothe the distressed beast with her familiar touch and shoot it in the head with her revolver, trusting no one else to kill quickly, painlessly and without inspiring fear.

'I'd rather shoot a man than a horse or a dog any day,' she confessed to us, 'but thank goodness I don't feel it my duty to accord humans so much mercy.'

In the afternoons we were allowed to visit her once more. Impatient to spend as much time with her as possible we were often too early and she would take no notice of us whatsoever, continuing to read on her chaise longue. We had to wait until the big clock in the roof struck three for her to become aware of our presence. This taught us punctuality at quite an early age. Ahna was very strict about time and no wonder, because on her island being too late or too soon for the tide might mean life or death when crossing the inland sea.

Exactly at three she would put down her book without showing any sign of the reluctance I knew she must have felt. In the morning she read the newspapers, history or philosophy. Only in the afternoons and evenings did she indulge in novels. From then on she would give us her full attention until tea time. In those hours she tried to form our characters and to develop whatever gifts we had.

I regret for her sake, as well as ours, that we were very ordinary children in whom she couldn't wake genius or inspire moral perfection, though she did her best to try to do so. Nevertheless, I know how much I benefited from her teachings. In stimulating my interest in art and literature she prepared a constant source of pleasure for the future; in learning to share her knowledge of and love for nature we all of us profited and though none of us ever lived up to her high standards of courage and integrity, she did at least make us try.

Her moral teachings were far from conventional. Contrary to other grown-ups, she never reproved us if we were naughty, neither did she praise us if we were good. The only virtues she sternly demanded were politeness, honesty, fairness and courage. Only if we told lies, as children often do in self-defence, was she unforgiving, making us understand that to evade punishment through deceit was simply cowardice, destroying our self-respect and pride.

We had, naturally, been taught to believe in God and that good would be rewarded in heaven and wickedness punished in hell.

'Utter nonsense! There's neither the one nor the other, except in ourselves.'

'And God?'

She felt she had no right to totally undermine our faith.

'There's something of God in all of us,' she said. 'It's called a conscience. It tells us what is right and wrong.'

'I haven't got one,' Hubert said.

'You're quite mistaken. Is there nothing you're ashamed of having done?'

'No,' he said, sullenly, then bent his head and burst into tears. 'The mouse,' he sobbed, 'I caught it and then cut it in half with a piece of glass.'

Ahna didn't flinch. 'And why did you do this?' she asked, calmly.

'Because I wanted to see what was inside.'

'And do you feel that was right?'

'Yes.'

'Then what are you ashamed of?'

'It hurt the mouse, because it bled and died.'

'And that was wrong?'

He looked at her with tear-filled eyes, so enormously blue in his small face. 'Yes,' he said.

'And do you understand that no one could have told you that except your conscience?'

He nodded.

As usual there were no reproaches. On the contrary, Ahna took him to the piano and asked him to play one of the little tunes he occasionally made up and picked out with two fingers so she could write down the notes and play it to him properly. She taught us how to model things out of clay, her deft hands forming animals and men and women and recognizable likenesses of everyone in the house. Sometimes she would act for us. I don't know if she really was the marvellous actress I thought her, since she had never had any training, nor did I quite understand the meaning of the plays she knew by heart. Nevertheless, her Lady Macbeth sent shivers down my spine and her Portia moved me to tears. She was especially fond of enacting Ibsen's *Hedda Gabler*, though we felt that the realism of the last scene was rather spoiled by her not using her revolver on herself.

Or there were games. She had a lot of illustrated books on art. She would give us one or the other to look at. We had to memorize the illustrations of a picture or statue and remember whom it was by. If we could name the painter or sculptor while she concealed the text we got a prize. Aunt Diana's prizes were well worth striving for. In her cupboard she kept all sorts of exciting things: a coral crown that had been her mother's, embroidered shawls that had belonged to her great-grandmother who came from the West Indies. 'Was she black?' we asked. 'Certainly not!' Ahna said, indignantly. 'The Elliots of Antigua were a most respectable English family. The Seventeenth Earl of Errol would not have married a negress.' Strangely shaped stones and pieces of wood carved and smoothed by the sea, pieces of old lace, fans, tartan sashes, shells, small gilt pigs used to contain matches, silver fish with scales that moved, boxes of ornamental buttons and old coins, cameos and cairngorms – there was no end to the treasures those cupboards contained.

Often too she would take us through the house, teaching us the myths of the different gods and goddesses and of the Greek heroes, whose pictures adorned the walls of Emkendorf. A small guest-drawing-room upstairs illustrated all the adventures of Ulysses, in the next room a large and curious painting showed Venus splendidly nude by Raphael Mengs and Hera fully dressed by Angelica Kauffman. Ahna said they had worked on the canvas at different times for pro-priety's sake, each painting one separate half. Only Venus's arm crossed the gap holding out a belt to Hera which would ensure the fidelity of

Zeus, her husband, for ever. Nevertheless, in the next bedroom Danae was depicted, spreading her thighs to receive the god descending in a shower of gold.

Ahna preferred statues to pictures. 'Purer,' she said. Her favourite work of art in the house and certainly the most valuable one was a marble group of Eros and Psyche embracing. She said it was Greek, though some crude Roman copies existed. Even we could see that it was beautiful. The two figures were not quite life-size, which added to their youthful grace. The colour of the marble was a pale amber, slightly veined and almost translucent. She told us the sad tale of Psyche's curiosity and how the god of love, who only came to her in darkness, spread his wings and left her for ever when she lit a lamp to look at his face.

'Which proves,' Ahna said . . . but then, remembering we were children, fell silent.

After Emkendorf was sold, all the statues were temporarily stored in a furniture depot in Rendsburg. Ahna still hoped my brothers would one day earn enough to house them suitably. They were spared the trouble. A fire broke out in the warehouse, the marbles, crated in wood and straw, were pulverized by the flames. A most inadequate insurance was paid, 'Not even worth,' Ahna said sadly, 'a fragment of Psyche's head.'

On some days Ahna would take us from portrait to portrait, trying to teach us family history. It always started with Carl Reventlow and his wife, Julie, since together they had created Emkendorf. Carl's bust stood on the landing of the stairs. He wore a great, curled peruke and swirling draperies round his shoulders, the Danish Order of the Elephant round his fat neck.

Julie's portrait had been painted by her friend, Angelica, with much loving care and some genius. It showed a woman, no more very young, dressed *à la grecque*, a golden fillet binding her powdered curls. Her face was certainly not beautiful, the nose long and Roman, her features more masculine than feminine, but her outstretched welcoming arms were lovely and so was the practically bare bosom on to which one felt she was ready to draw her friends in fond, if austere, embrace.

Because of her intellectual interests and the poets, writers and artists who frequented Emkendorf, she had been called 'the Athene of the North.'

Klopstock and Schiller, both poets and dramatists, Pestalozzi, pupil of Rousseau and one of the first educationalists, Lavater, the famed Jewish phrenologist, the brothers Stolberg, Winckelmann, the classicist, all belonged to the famed circle to whom she was hostess and Egeria in Emkendorf.

Only Goethe, though she corresponded with him, was never invited. 'The divine Julie,' as her more intimate friends called her, though professing to be a free-thinker, was prudish about morals. Nor, judging from the curt reply with which the great man answered one of her letters, can he have been over-anxious to meet the long-nosed blue-stocking of whom he must have had an accurate description through his friends.

We were shown the portrait of our French great-grandfather, Julie's adopted nephew and heir. But not even Ahna seemed to know much about him. His wife was more interesting. She had been born a Countess Plathen and was our only German ancestress and had been famed not only for her beauty but for the variety of her love affairs. On her portrait she was dressed as a Vestal, a veil covering her head, and she was guarding a flame.

'Vestal, indeed,' we heard our father say, 'there is no doubt the services she rendered in her temple were available to all who came.'

Then we were hurried past the pictures of our grandparents because Ahna said they were bad paintings and bad likenesses. We hoped so. Our grandfather, a small, spare, insignificant-looking person, dressed in black, his face obscured by tufted sideburns and a large moustache, seemed very ugly to us – and so was our grandmother – she looked like a Dutch doll, carved in wood, her sleek black hair parted in the middle, her large black eyes totally void of expression.

'My mother was not at all like that,' Ahna declared, 'but then it was painted after her death from a photograph.' Ahna did not like to talk about her parents. We had to gather most of our information about them from other sources, less reliable but more intriguing. The Plessens had disliked 'the Old Count', as everyone, even his children, had called him, because of the shabby way in which he had treated my father. The Bismarcks had no cause to like him either as he had made it only too plain what he thought of Bismarck's Prussian invasion of Paris and the annexation of Holstein.

Bit by bit from conversations overheard, even from what our father said, we learnt what an evil old man our grandfather must have been and how cruelly he had treated his wife. There was no doubt that our Scottish grandmother had been very unhappy in Emkendorf.

Omama, my other grandmother, maintained that Queen Victoria's eldest son had paid young Isabel Wemyss too much attention when she was lady-in-waiting at Court and the Queen had arranged her marriage with the elderly attaché at the Danish Legation so as to avoid a scandal, pointing out that if my father had worn a beard and wasn't so slim he would look very much like Edward the Seventh. But then Omama would have relished the thought of her daughter being related to the British royal family, even if on the wrong side of the blanket.

The fact that my father was born two years after my grandparents' marriage was ignored, though there was proof that Queen Victoria had taken a certain interest in the couple because of the rather splendid wedding presents she gave them. Had Omama's story been true, it would have certainly explained my grandfather's dislike for his wife and son, which is otherwise incomprehensible. Yet had there been a scandal the Empress Frederick would hardly have been as intimate as she later was with my grandmother. In the summer months both she and my grandmother went to the island of Wyk with their children for sea-bathing. Ahna could well remember what a little terror the future Emperor William had been – even as a child. That island was the nearest my grandmother was ever allowed to her home across the sea, Wemyss Castle on the Firth of Forth. She was never to see her parents or her family again.

She had been brought up in a tradition in which ministering to the poor was obligatory for a lady. She tried to put this into practice in Emkendorf, visiting the villagers and bringing medicines and food to the sick or elderly. My grandfather soon put a stop to that. He was to all accounts extremely stingy and may have thought charity wasteful, or perhaps my father was right in surmising that he didn't want her to see certain children which bore a striking likeness to himself. My grandfather was known to have still taken advantage of the *droit de seigneur*, the village girls being taken to him before their marriages, to be sent away with a gift of a pig or a cow and occasionally something more personal.

My grandparents' rooms in Emkendorf had been as far apart as the length of the house would permit. Perhaps my grandmother had complained of loneliness or just from pure malice my grandfather had a large cage built in front of her rooms and filled it with apes which he bought in Hamburg's zoo, Hagenbeck.

He delighted in the antics of these beasts, their close resemblance to humans accented by the then keeper having orders to dress them in clothes. He must have savoured the mockery they made of mankind. Ahna said her mother had loathed and feared these apes always peering into her windows, through which she couldn't help seeing their obscene gestures and shocking sexual behaviour day after day.

They were only sent back to the zoo after one of them had become ill. Aunt Diana's elder sister, Constance, nursed it, but it died and soon afterwards so did she, having caught tuberculosis from it.

Since even then certain formalities accompanied death from a contagious disease, a doctor had to be called. My grandfather was grateful to him for making no difficulties about the death certificate and, as a reward, he was yearly invited to shoot a stag in Emkendorf. On one of these occasions the doctor was asked to lunch and noticed how very ill my grandmother looked. When they were alone together he told my grandfather that he feared the worst if nothing were done to help her. My grandfather told the doctor to mind his own business, assuring him that his wife was perfectly well.

The doctor went after his stag, shot at it, but since it could not be found believed he had missed and returned to town. A week later he got a furious letter from my grandfather, accusing him of having wounded the animal and not having taken the trouble to search for it, having left it to die in agony. It had since been found. Did he want the antlers? The postscript was 'By the way, you were right about my wife's health. She died yesterday.' The doctor happened to attend the Plessens too and the story of my grandfather's callousness spread through Schleswig-Holstein.

Yet he cannot have been quite as evil as he was made out to have been or surely Aunt Diana would not have spent the best years of her life nursing and tending him. For ten whole years, immobilized by a broken hip bone that would not set, he had kept her with him in Emkendorf, living in total isolation, refusing to see anyone but her.

'Did you love him?' we asked.

'No.'

'Did you hate him?'

'No.'

'Were you sorry for him?'

'Not even that – I felt it was my duty to look after him, that's all.' She would not be questioned further.

My father said that all the answers lay in my grandfather's trunk and had Aunt Diana allowed him to look inside all would have become clear, even the reason why his father had tried to disinherit him.

Aunt Diana had refused to let my father look. According to our grandfather's last request before he died, the large, black tin trunk, securely locked, was carried to the lake by two servants, Aunt Diana following. It was lifted into a boat and she and the trunk were rowed out to the middle of the lake and then the trunk was thrown over-board.

'The trouble was it floated,' Ahna confessed. 'It wouldn't sink and for days someone had to row out and try to thrust it to the bottom. At last it vanished. It got stuck, I suppose, in the mud among the stems of the water-lilies. My father's secrets – whatever they may have been – were safe.'

'But what could have been in it?'

'We will never know,' Ahna said, with evident satisfaction.

Many years later I asked her if it was because of her father that she had never married, fearing to suffer what her mother had, and if her retreat to her island wasn't a sort of escape from a world that had offered her nothing better than years of self-sacrifice.

'Not really,' she said, 'even my island is a world full of creatures as needful of attention and care as my family was. From these duties there is no escape.'

'Then you're a saint, Ahna.'

'If you knew how far from it! In the Christian sense I'm one of the great sinners, corrupted by pride and vanity – that alone was the reason for my retreat from the world after my father's death.'

'I don't understand.'

'Nor do I think could you. You are a perfectly normal young woman. I never was. Perhaps having grown up in Emkendorf and in the isolation in which my father chose to live had something to do with it. The house with its paintings and statues stimulated my interest in the Greek classics. I had a lot of time to read and I preferred history and philosophy to romantic novels. I liked the clarity of Greek logic. Plato's moral ethics appealed to me much more than the New Testament. Christian humility has never attracted me. The Greek ideal of a perfect soul in a perfect body seemed to make sense. Every mirror, every glance, told me I was beautiful. But that was not sufficient for my pride. I wanted to develop a soul to match the perfection of my body. Well, I failed.'

I looked at her sad, still beautiful, but ageing face, but though I loved her more than I ever would anyone else, I didn't understand.

'But to me you've always seemed perfect, Ahna – '

'That's what I believed too through the years in which I had practised all the recommended virtues which I most admired, courage, patience, self-control, charity and dedication to duty. My family gave me every opportunity to do so.' She smiled that faint ironic smile of hers.

'I worked at perfecting myself as a sculptor might have at carving a work of art, chiselling away the rough stone, removing all that was faulty, polishing and smoothing till there was practically nothing left of what had once been my normal human self. In a way I achieved a masterpiece. I had become void of all emotions. I felt neither anger nor sorrow, nor hate, nor love. I had made myself perfect. Perhaps my soul was flawless, but I had killed my human heart.'

'But that's not true, Ahna,' I said, deeply shocked. 'No one could have been kinder than you. Think how good you were to us children, how good you are to your animals – '

'They need my care, they depend upon me as you children did. That's all. I'm incapable of love.'

'Then I wish everyone was,' I said and bent to kiss her wrinkled hand, the only caress she would ever permit.

38

As small children we had been taken by our parents to visit Aunt Diana on her island. Though I went there several times later I will never forget that first visit. Her island was, and still is, what in Schleswig-Holstein is called a *Hallig*, one of many near or far from the larger populated island of Nordstrand, but only a few of the other *Halligs*, though the home of gulls and seals, were inhabited. And no wonder. I can't think of anything more unsuitable for humans to live on than those small, flat, sea-threatened windswept and, except for sea grass, barren islands.

To get to Südfall, which was the name of Aunt Diana's island, meant starting at dawn from Emkendorf, driving to the railway station, which took an hour, then three hours' train journey to Husum, one hour from there by steamer to Nordstrand and from there an hour and a half's drive until one reached the *Hallig*. This last part of the journey was by far the most exciting. Aunt Diana with her carriage had waited for us near the harbour and from there she drove the horses over some sandflats straight into the sea. For nearly two hours they splashed and trotted right through it, though I suppose its depth was no more than two or three feet. Nevertheless it was an eerie experience. 'It's quite safe,' Ahna reassured my mother, seeing her anxious face. 'The tide's out and there's neither quicksand nor deeper channels between these markers.' (At far intervals there were some wooden poles visible to left and right.)

After having reached the island, seeing the sea sweep back in full force burying our ocean-bed drive under fathoms of water brought a rather frightening realization of what we had escaped.

For the next six hours the only way to leave the island was by boat. This my father knew. He had ordered a fishing cutter in Husum to take us back in the event of not wanting to risk the discomforts of Aunt Diana's island overnight.

When she had bought the *Hallig* she had never intended to live there permanently, only for one or two summer months. The house was, she frankly admitted, inadequate and remarkably ugly, yet she never made any efforts to improve it.

'What did it matter how one lived if one didn't live in Emkendorf?' is I think what she felt. After my marriage she had paid me a brief visit in Czechoslovakia, very reluctantly because she didn't like to leave her dogs and it was too long a journey to take them on. Proudly I had shown her Castolovice to realize that the big semi-medieval castle which I thought rather splendid didn't appeal to her at all. I suppose compared to Emkendorf's elegant eighteenth-century perfection it was rather crude and barbaric.

The *Hallig* house had been built and occupied by an old sea captain who could not find his way back to land. It was constructed of slats of wood, like a boat, and roofed with tarred felt, its only ornamental feature a fretted wooden balcony that ran right round the upper floor of the house and from which the island and the grey sea beyond could be overlooked in every direction.

Inside the house was somewhat more comfortable than one would have expected. Downstairs there was a kitchen and a dining-room, upstairs three tiny bedroom-like ship's cabins and Ahna's sitting-room, walled entirely with bookcases but with enough space for a comfortable chintz-covered sofa in front of the brick fireplace, and her desk and some chairs. There was even a bathroom of sorts with a tub and a WC, though the water had to be pumped into both by hand and was salty.

There was a well on the island from which slightly brackish fresh water was drawn but this was used for drinking, cooking and for the animals – a herd of sheep, about twenty horses that roamed the island freely, two cows and several dogs.

The size of the *Hallig* varied since a large part of it came and went with the tide. When the dreaded high spring tide coincided with a north-westerly gale there was nothing left of the island but the small hill on which the house and farm buildings stood and into which the animals had to be herded for safety above the raging sea, waves splashing almost up to the kitchen and dining-room windows.

The house seemed of the frailest construction. How it withstood these violent storms was incomprehensible, though Ahna maintained that it was so draughty – many of the boards from which it was built joining no longer – that the wind could blow right through the house and, since there was no resistance, didn't blow it away.

In part of the farm buildings, Maschmann, a stocky Friesian, who looked like a seaman, lived with his red-haired wife, Dora. He drove Aunt Diana's carriage and fed her animals. Dora did the cooking and the cleaning. They had been with her for many years and were devoted to her, accepting all the hardship and dangers of island life without complaint for her sake.

In some bad winters the inland sea between the *Hallig* and Nord-strand, from which the food supplies came, would freeze and become impassable, the treacherous ice allowing neither boat nor carriage nor man on foot to reach the island, sometimes for weeks.

Once Ahna and the Maschmanns nearly starved, surviving only on boiled oats, of which there were always reserves for the horses, pickled gulls' eggs, and milk. Though Ahna would have shot a sheep under the circumstances, the herd always wintered in Nordstrand since there was not enough fodder for them on the island in the colder months. But these were only occasional hardships. In the First World War the island had been much better provided for with food than we were on the mainland. '*Gott segne unseren Strand*,' the island people prayed every night. 'God bless our beach.' He did in the war. Flotsam from sunken ships was almost daily washed up on Aunt Diana's beach. Chests filled with tinned food, ship biscuits, even smoked hams and barrels of wine. 'The last Bordeaux was a little salty,' my father complained, 'but the brandy excellent.' (Aunt Diana always sent him the barrels to Emken-dorf.)

My most vivid recollection of that first island visit was of the wild horses and seagulls. Aunt Diana was known to buy any horse too old for work. Since she paid a higher price than the knacker they were brought to her from all over the islands. Gaunt skeletons with sores from ill use, their pelts dull and lifeless, too weary to lift their heads when they first arrived on the *Hallig*, they recovered remarkably thanks to Ahna's and Maschmann's care. They had the run of the island and would come galloping towards one, jumping the narrow channels and waterholes as frisky as foals. We were accustomed to horses as children and to visiting them in the paddocks and stables but not to be charged by a herd of them. However, we had been taught not to show fear of animals and above all never to run from them.

Hubert and I held our ground, expecting to be trampled to death, only to discover that the horses were racing towards Ahna trying to be the first to nuzzle her pockets for sugar.

Thousands of seagulls – she would explain their different species and habits – nested on her island.

'I have to protect them with a gun when people come across the water to collect eggs and disturb the nests. Of course I only shoot into the air, but it does frighten them away,' she explained.

We thought the birds quite able to protect themselves. Wheeling and screaming they would dive for our heads if we got near a nest but never when Ahna was with us. They seemed to know her. She told us that in the nesting season farmworkers on the islands had to wear caps stuffed with straw to be safe from the gulls' sharp beaks. 'They know that no harm will come to their young from me,' she said. 'I take only one or two of the first-laid eggs from each nest. Seagulls can't count and they don't miss them. I never disturb them once they have started to hatch.'

The speckled eggs were a delicacy that fetched high prices, especially in the war. Crated by Maschmann they were sent to Kiel or Hamburg and were one of the few profitable products of Ahna's island.

Contrary to my parents in Emkendorf, whom the local population had never learnt to really know or trust, Aunt Diana was well liked among the island people. The dour Friesian fishermen and the hard-headed marsh farmers were not easily won. But when she had learnt to speak their language, the local 'Platt-Dütch', a mixture of Danish, German and English, the patois of the North Sea, they accepted her. She had, some time after she had acquired the *Hallig*, leased a small farm on the larger island of Nordstrand in order to grow food and to have a shelter for her animals in winter. On her visits there and when passing through to the mainland on her way to Emkendorf she would meet and talk to the local farmers and their flaxen-haired wives and children. She spoke their language in more ways than one. She could discuss the weather, storm damage, cattle prices, rheumatism (of which no one living on those islands was ever free) and its possible cures, or animal diseases as well as they did.

Like most aristocrats, Aunt Diana felt a much closer affinity with what she would have called the lower classes, people who worked on the land or made their living from the sea, than with members of the town-dwelling bourgeoisie. Their pretensions and aspirations were incomprehensible to her, whereas among the people of that bleak, storm-swept coast she recognized the qualities she herself most valued: endurance, courage and independence of spirit.

'*Unsere Comtesse,*' the island people called her and came to trust her implicitly in later years and in the last war even with their lives. These Friesians of the coast were not a lawless people as long as they were allowed to follow their own long-established customs and traditions, but they were stubbornly opposed to change and to any governmental interference in what they considered their independent rights.

Ahna shared their dislike of bureaucracy and took some pleasure in aiding and abetting their efforts to mislead and thwart governmental officials. In the First War many a boat would anchor at night off her island and men would climb up to the wharf carrying heavy sacks or boxes. If they were known to Maschmann they were allowed to go about their business with no questions asked and were helped to secrete the grain and food that was being requisitioned from the farms safely under the floorboards of one of the sheds or to take away what they had previously left when danger of confiscation was over.

If a stranger came who acted at all suspiciously, Maschmann and his wife, Dora, would invite him to the kitchen and treat him to *Köhm*, hot sugared tea, laced with rum, which was drunk as a stimulant on all the islands.

After three cups even a government spy would give himself away and be politely helped back to his boat by Maschmann.

When horses were being requisitioned for the army a sort of shuttle service was organized by Aunt Diana. The horses were herded from island to island at low tide. The puzzled military inspector would find nothing but a few foals, or animals too old for use, wherever he went.

However, all that Ahna could at that time have suffered for her varied anti-government activities was reprimands or fines. It was very different in the Second War when they were punishable by death.

Again the boats came at night, not unloading grain but human cargo – that was moved from island to island or from farm to farm as the horses had been. She was in her eighties then and what she demanded had become law on that coast. However great the risk to themselves and their families the islanders obeyed her without question. Ways and means were found to take these victims of Hitler's persecution to

Denmark from where they reached eventual safety. With the little money she had, the few old clothes she could spare and the food she mercilessly requisitioned, she helped as best she could but most of all I believe by instilling into those unfortunate, frightened people who rested briefly on her island some of her own indomitable courage and her never wavering certainty that the day of reckoning for Hitler would come.

I don't know how great were her personal risks. I doubt if even the most ruthless of Gestapo investigators would have adhered to his purpose on seeing her descend from her balcony in the trailing black velvet gown which she always wore, even on the island, in the evenings, to face him with all the dignity of age, the arrogance of her breed, and the loaded revolver in her hand.

'One has to be so careful these days,' she would apologize. 'An old woman living all alone – for all I know you might be a foreign spy – '

All through the war we had written to each other, outwitting the censors; she by a sort of intricate gothic script which she used when she wrote German and which was, except to me, as complex to decipher as a code. I was able to tell her everything that was happening to us in Czechoslovakia by referring back to childhood events. After the war ended I had frequently sent her parcels: recent English novels, books on politics, biographies, whatever I thought would interest her. And food chests, containing the things I knew she liked and had missed for so long. Twining's Earl Grey tea and English marmalade, ginger snaps and other biscuits, something called 'Gentleman's Relish', Colman's mustard and Worcester sauce and many tins of pineapples of which I knew she was fond. All this was by then available through friendly diplomats but certainly not in the shops of Prague.

Her gratitude was touching. Again and again she wrote to thank me, even giving me her opinion on many of the books, critical of some, appreciative of others, her judgement seemingly unimpaired.

Yet in none of her letters did she ask me to come and visit her and all suggestions that she come to live with us in Castolovice were politely ignored.

My brother, Victor, who then still lived in Glücksburg not far from her island and visited her occasionally, feeling it his duty to do so in spite of her having quarrelled with him, wrote that with old age she had become irresponsible and confused.

I did not want to see her changed or to lose the memory of what she had been to me before. Perhaps she didn't wish me to. In her letters – which as I was to know later she had painstakingly penned, her eyesight failing, her health weakened by frequent heart attacks – she had done her best to assure me that she was unchanged and not in need of any help.

I had of course written to her the moment we had reached Paris and freedom. She had answered typically, not wasting any words on what we had lost, only remarking that she trusted in my courage to start all over again. 'When Emkendorf went, other losses seem unimportant,' she said. In a way it was true even for me but much more so for my brothers. After it had been sold, it was heavily mortgaged and my father's large private debts had to be repaid, there was just enough left to give my brothers an education and a start in life and for Aunt Diana's frugal existence on her island to continue. My brothers had become as uprooted and homeless as Leopold and I now were.

I had not seen either of them before we left. We had lived in different countries for so long that being separated at even greater distance didn't seem to matter. They were both young and there was no reason to believe I might not meet them again even in America.

Hubert, when grown into manhood, was still of the most appealing beauty. But he had not been a good scholar. After having been sent down from several German schools, which he hated and where he failed all exams, he had started to develop considerable technical skill and inventiveness, possibly inherited from our great-grandfather Whitehead. But then, even as a child, there wasn't a clock or watch he hadn't taken apart or any other piece of machinery, and to everyone's amazement succeeded in reassembling in working order.

With a friend of rather doubtful repute he started to build light aircraft. A sort of hangar was erected on the flats of Ahna's island, with her permission. Interested and impressed by the work that went on there she was easily persuaded by Hubert and his good-looking young partner to invest considerably in the venture. Two planes were built. One flew just long enough for her to watch it rise and then crash-land in the shallows of the inland sea. Fortunately the pilot crawled out of its wreck unhurt and was rescued by boat from the sandbank on which he had climbed, but the plane was beyond repair and so was Hubert's partner's confidence in the whole enterprise.

He left the island, taking with him tools and instruments, and on his return to the mainland his signature sufficed in drawing out of the bank all that was still left of the money Aunt Diana had invested in the partnership. He was never heard of again.

Hubert dismantled the second plane since the first had proved unreliable and its parts were shipped to Hamburg where long and costly repairs had to be made which he superintended.

While waiting, he acquired an expensive flat, furnished it with whatever was still of value in Emkendorf, which my father hadn't sold, and installed a mistress called Rosa, twenty years older than himself. In his spare hours he put in sufficient flying time to get his pilot's licence. When his plane was at last declared airworthy he left flat and furniture to Rosa as recompense for her services and flew to Spain where civil war had broken out.

Hubert, all his life, was to be partial to lost causes. Romantic, sentimental, chivalrous, the country of Don Quixote suited him. Once in Spain, what he lacked in flying experience he made up for in courage. After two years of joining in the fighting there he was shot down, his plane a wreck. He was not expected to survive his multiple injuries and had such serious concussion that brain damage was feared. After months in hospital in Barcelona, deaf in one ear, nevertheless having made a remarkable recovery, he returned to Aunt Diana's island, bringing with him a Spanish wife, a native of Majorca. Since Dolores was well brought up, obviously what Ahna would have called a lady and could even boast some aristocratic ancestors, she received her graciously and did her best to make the unfortunate girl feel at home on the cold, grey, windswept island so unlike the sunny southern one from which she had come. Without much success, I fear.

Hubert, who never quite regained his normal health, was a difficult husband, but then I think both my brothers were. Only much later when they had emigrated to Canada did I meet their devoted, competent and self-sacrificing wives. Victor too had married in the war in defiance of Aunt Diana's wishes. She never quite forgave him for it. Renate was a perfectly respectable, very pretty young girl, daughter of the Mayor of the small town of Glücksburg, but she was not what Aunt Diana's generation called 'born', and however unorthodox, tolerant and free of prejudice Ahna was in other ways, marriage with a different class than one's own seemed to her as wrong as trying to mate animals of a different species.

She told Victor that if he insisted on the marriage she would refuse ever to meet his wife and, uncompromising as she was, she never did.

Much as I loved Ahna I thought this cruel and told her so. But she remained adamant, pointing out to me that the descendants of such unions were rarely healthy or normal.

Certainly she was quite wrong in my brother's case. Not only was his marriage very happy but his children quite sane, even if his son developed genius as a sculptor in later life.

But sometimes since I've wondered if she wasn't right. I've seen what happened when old, slightly degenerate families, inbred through centuries with members of their own class, mated with younger, healthier stock. Hereditary diseases, long dormant, suddenly erupting and becoming fatal. Mild eccentricity developing into madness or sexual abnormality. Even among my mother's relations there were signs of it. My grandfather Hoyos's family may have been too old and brittle for the stimulus of the strong plebeian Whitehead blood. One of my mother's sisters, poor Aunt Ella, if not a raving lunatic, was certifiably insane. One of my cousins became incurably mad and died in an asylum and most of my mother's family suffered from mysterious nervous or physical diseases, the causes of which no specialist could ascertain.

My brothers and I were more or less normal, but then our father's family had for centuries chosen wives which, even if of their own class, came from different countries to their own, which may have given us some immunity. Of the three of us, Victor was probably the sanest and healthiest. Since he had suffered the misfortune of having been born in Berlin and had German nationality and was of military age when the war started, he had no option but to join one of the services. He chose the navy, soon distinguished himself, became a captain, and received several decorations. Having proved his valour, he retired from the war after two years of service letting it be discovered that he was nightblind. He spent the last years in a shipyard in Kiel, superintending work on a new type of submarine that somehow was never completed.

Hubert, who had a British passport, had returned to Spain when war broke out. He requisitioned a large fishing boat somewhere, two diesel engines from somewhere else, and set sail with his Dolores. They arrived safely in Majorca, though Hubert was minus one finger, the diesel engine having exploded on the way. Aunt Diana remained alone on her island.

Was she, I wondered, thinking of me now as I was of her? She knew the date of our departure. I had written to her from Paris and had told her about Steinhardt, as much as I felt she might wish to know. Contrary to my father, who was vaguely anti-Semitic, frequently saying 'Damn Jews!' but really only referring to money-lenders, Christian and Jewish alike, to whom he was indebted, Ahna had taught us to respect the Jewish race, if for a rather odd reason, saying there were families like Menasse and Levi who could trace their ancestry back thousands of years, farther than we could, and so must be considered greater aristocrats than we were, and obviously more civilized and intelligent because of the antiquity of their race.

I was to receive the news that Ahna had died after we had been living in America for several years. She left me whatever money she could. It was not very much but it certainly was a help since by then we were almost destitute. She also left me everything that had belonged to her mother, things she had treasured all her life.

She died soon after her ninetieth birthday, which my brother, Victor, wrote had been an occasion for great celebration on her island. From near and from far, from Denmark, from England, from Schleswig and from Holstein, they had come to congratulate, acclaim and thank the *Hallig Comtesse*, the name by which she was known from coast to coast.

Journalists came, anxious to write her story, and the curious who just wanted to see the famous old lady of the island. A brigadier, whom she had befriended at the time of the British occupation of Holstein, came with several of his officers. So did a rabbi who had made the journey from Israel to thank her for what she had done for his people and, of course, all the islanders who had known her so well.

'Unbelievable,' Victor wrote, 'how they all cheered her. Strange, when one considers that she never loved anyone, how beloved she was – '

He sent me a photograph taken of her on this memorable birthday.

Ahna is standing on the balcony of her island house, gulls wheeling above her head, a dark, indistinct crowd of people below her.

She stands very straight, the old black velvet gown falls in regal folds, almost concealing how thin and frail she has become. Her hair, still abundant, is quite white. She seems to be looking beyond the crowd towards the open sea and smiling that faint ironic smile of hers. One hand is half raised as if in a gesture of farewell.

PART TWO

AMERICA

39

Leopold came stumbling into our cabin, tweaked the child's hair affectionately – she was still reading in the bunk above me – and bent to look at me.

'You're not really sick, are you?'

'No.'

'Then won't you dress for dinner soon? I'm getting rather bored, there's no one around to talk to.'

'No wonder, in this weather.'

'It's calming down. Do get up,' he begged, 'I'm lonely.' He would often say this, like a child, and it would always move me. I thought once more of Ahna. 'One could hardly call your husband beautiful,' she had remarked when she had first met him, 'except for his eyes – they are like those of a good and faithful dog, pleading to be taken for a walk.'

'What was lunch like? What's the Captain like?' I asked.

'Oh, we are not with him. The steward said we were at the Chief's table – whoever that is. He wasn't there. I was all alone,' he added reproachfully.

'An Indian Chief?' Diana queried, interested.

'Probably the Chief Engineer,' I said, recalling other voyages on ships. Odd our not sitting at the Captain's table but then I remembered that the ship's company would have seen our papers. As emigrants we must have fallen somewhat below former status, even as first-class passengers.

'What a blessing,' I exclaimed, 'not sitting with the Captain. We won't have to dress every evening and will have much more privacy –'

'Who wants privacy?' Leopold asked, indignantly.

At half past eight the three of us walked into the dining-room, adequately dressed. Leopold, who had a physical dislike of not bathing and changing in the evening, wherever he was, wore his dinner-jacket. The Chief Engineer rose politely to greet us. He was more broad than tall and his uniform fitted too tightly. His face was undistinguished, except for its ruddy colour due to years of life at sea, or drink, or both.

'Mr and Mrs Sternberg,' he introduced us, 'and their daughter – Mr and Mrs Gumps.'

The couple who were to share our table for the next two weeks scarcely looked up from their food. 'Evening,' they said and continued to eat. They were both very old, certainly in their seventies or eighties, and resembled each other, as couples who have lived half a century together often do. One can't expect a very attractive appearance from people at that age but the Gumpses' evident efforts to improve on their looks made them seem even more absurd and repellently ugly than they were. Both of them were very fat. Most old people shrivel and shrink towards the end. Not these two. As if in defiance of the inevitable they seemed to have swelled and distended and blown themselves up as do some animals when threatened, fluffing out furs or feathers to their utmost capacity.

Mrs Gumps was squeezed into red satin, draped in mink, and had a wig of ornately curled fair hair. Mr Gumps wore a flowered shirt and a scarlet cummerbund which in no way contained his stomach. Both Gumpses peered at us through ornamental glasses, their eyes strangely enlarged behind the thick lenses.

Leopold scanned the menu and asked for the wine steward, then turned to the Gumpses. 'Where do you come from?' he enquired with his usual friendliness.

'California,' muttered Mr Gumps, carefully dissecting the fish on his plate.

''Frisco,' said Mrs Gumps, wiping the hollandaise from her purple lips and leaving a stain on the napkin. 'We've been doing Europe – France and Italy that is – '

'And did you enjoy your journey?' I inevitably asked.

'Very interesting, but we'll be glad to get home, won't we, Papa?'

'Sure,' he mumbled, searching for fishbones in his dentures.

'Business is business,' she smiled brightly. 'We blame no one for wanting to make a profit, but they're a crooked lot over there. Especially those Eytalians. They tried to cheat us wherever we went. But Mr Gumps was not having any of that. He let them know exactly what he thought of them,' she said with evident satisfaction and pride.

Our soup came and the wine.

'Will you have some?' Leopold asked, proffering the bottle, unaccustomed not to do so.

'We don't drink,' Mr Gumps said.

However, the Chief Engineer readily accepted, politely pouring me, then Leopold, then himself, a glass.

'You come from England?' Mr Gumps asked, looking up from his plate now heaped with turkey breasts.

'No, why?'

'It's the accent.'

'Mr and Mrs Sternberg are from 'Slovakia,' the Engineer explained.

'Czechoslovakia,' my daughter corrected. It was the first word she had uttered since we had sat down.

'Sternberg?' exclaimed Mrs Gumps. 'Why, we know several Sternbergs in 'Frisco. Relations, perhaps?'

'I'm afraid not,' Leopold said. She peered at him closely through her thick glasses. 'You don't look it. Had your nose fixed?'

Leopold rubbed his blunt nose. 'What do you mean?' he asked, amazed.

The Engineer had a coughing fit.

'Don't tell me you don't know – our young people often have it done. There's my granddaughter, Sarah, as cute as a film star she would have been except that she had inherited Mr Gumps's nose. It looks fine on him but it didn't on her.'

We all gazed at Mr Gumps's large and bulbous nose.

'Why, now she's just as lovely as you are,' she smiled at Diana.

'Cut off?' the child asked.

'Well, sort of. Plastic surgery. Just a small operation. This part you see,' and Mrs Gumps pushed the end of her equally large nose from side to side with her finger as if it was a thing of rubber, 'is boneless.'

There was silence for a while. I looked around. The dining-room was only half full. There were several people, all elderly, sitting at the Captain's table but he wasn't presiding, first night out captains rarely left the bridge, I knew.

'Czechoslovakia?' Mrs Gumps queried. 'Do you maybe speak German?'

I admitted we did. 'Oh, so do Papa and I.' She said something guttural which sounded like German but which neither Leopold nor I understood. 'Papa's father came from those parts, Hamburg.'

'That's so,' old Gumps nodded. 'My family emigrated to the USA in eighteen forty-eight and they never regretted having done so.'

'We are emigrating too,' Leopold informed him.

'Same thing all over again. Glad you could make it.' Conversation stopped when the dessert the Gumpses had ordered came. It was an amazing concoction of whipped cream, ice cream, chocolate sauce, jam and bananas, pile upon pile of what must, I thought, have been leftovers from many previous desserts. Later I was to learn from my daughter, who developed a taste for this dish, that it was called a Banana Split.

The Chief Engineer rose from the table. 'Duty calls,' he said, 'meet you in the bar later?'

'Sure,' Leopold said, who had a liking for using and misusing expressions new to him.

'Do you and your missus play bridge perhaps?' Gumps asked. 'We like a little game now and then.'

'So do we.'

'What stakes?'

'Oh anything,' Leopold said, grandly.

'You're not professionals by any chance?'

'I'm afraid not,' I said. Both Leopold and I had played adequately well for many years but though we had once won an international competition in Vienna I knew it was only due to the confusion our erratic bidding had caused among the experts. 'Just ordinary bridge,' I confessed.

'Like Mr Gumps and me. Every Sunday we have our little "partee" with family and friends.' Mrs Gumps smiled.

'Well, we'll have to get together some time,' Mr Gumps said, rising from his chair. So did she. Standing up they were not much taller than they had been when sitting down. Supporting each other they trundled out of the dining-room.

'Really,' I protested, 'it's bad enough to have to eat with them but I won't play bridge with them too.'

'But why?' Leopold asked. 'It will pass the time.'

'Poor old things,' I said, 'it wouldn't be fair – I can imagine the sort of game they play – '

'We can always stop if we find they lose too much.'

We sent Diana to bed and went to the bar where we found the Chief Engineer drinking.

'What's your medicine?' he asked. 'Have some on me.'

We had two small brandies.

'Well, here's mud in your eye,' he said, lifting his glass. 'And in yours,' Leopold answered politely, though I saw he was puzzled. I hoped he was not recording the Engineer's toast for future use.

'I guess our table's not hilarious,' the Chief remarked apologetically. 'It's always so this time of year when we get the old ones coming back from Europe. They like a quiet trip home.'

'Quiet?' I said as the ship lurched and our glasses slid across the table.

'It will be all right once we're out of the Bay of Biscay tomorrow.'

'Is Mr Gumps in business?' Leopold asked.

'I guess he must have retired by now. Never heard of Gumps and Company?'

We confessed we hadn't.

'The old man owns half of San Francisco.'

The next morning the sea was indeed calmer. Reluctant to lunch with the Gumpses I persuaded Leopold that the food in the small restaurant called 'French', where one could order à la carte at extra charge, would be better, soon to discover that it was exactly the same as that which one got in the dining-room, only that it took longer to appear. Afterwards we walked the deck. The wind had died down and the weather had improved. Among other figures equally reclining in deck-chairs swathed in rugs lay the Gumpses, their stomachs ballooning under tartan plaids. 'See here, Mr Sternberg,' Gumps called, 'we missed you at lunch. We were scared you were sick.'

'Just a little,' I said.

'I'm sorry,' said Mrs Gumps. 'Papa and I aren't that way or we wouldn't travel by boat.'

'What about our bridge game,' asked Mr Gumps, 'or aren't you up to it?'

'Of course we are,' Leopold said.

'Would four o'clock suit you? In the card-room?'

'Isn't it enough to have to dine with them,' I protested again, 'without having to spend the afternoon with them too?'

'There's not much else to do. Why not make some money? Seems they can well afford to lose it.'

At four we met them. We had the card-room to ourselves. 'We don't usually play with strangers,' Mr Gumps said, carefully shuffling the cards, 'especially not on boats – No necessity to cut for partners I take it? It don't make much sense to split up the families.'

'Of course not,' Leopold said with evident relief.

'You play the Blackwood Conventions?'

'I'm afraid we just play rather old-fashioned bridge,' I said hastily. Leopold and I were good average players when teamed together, since we knew each other so well, but we hadn't counted with the Gumpses having spent almost double the amount of years with each other. They played incredibly slowly, deliberating each card as if reluctant to let it go. But they played well – *Jouez mal mais jouez vite* we had been taught since childhood by impatient parents. Leopold became bored and didn't concentrate and we lost the first game and rubber. For the next two deals we had hopeless cards and the Gumpses won. In the final game our cards were too good for caution. We overbid and were doubled. I foolishly redoubled and that was that.

Mr Gumps counted up the score. 'That will be a hundred and twenty dollars that you owe. Try again tomorrow?'

'Sure,' Leopold said, pulling out a wad of money from his pocket and counting out the crumpled notes.

'You should get your husband a wallet,' Mrs Gumps said reproach-fully. 'He'll lose it this way.'

'He often does,' I laughed.

'I don't think we should play with them any more,' I told Leopold when we had reached our cabin. 'I had no idea the stakes were so high – besides even if they are slow they play better than us. We can't afford to lose like we did today.'

'Nonsense, we'll win it all back tomorrow. Besides, I didn't under-stand the way they were bidding. They seemed to tell each other every-thing by calling what they hadn't got. Maybe there's a book on Black-wood in the library – '

I found one and brought it to him. He studied it for a while. 'Seems to me to take all the fun out of the game, everyone knowing exactly what the other has. Might as well lay all one's cards on the table.'

We did no better at bridge next afternoon nor in any subsequent games. I grew very anxious about money. Of all that Leopold's relations had so generously given him there had only been a thousand dollars left after we had paid for our passage and settled various debts in Paris. Annicka had not been able to take more than a suitcase out of Czecho-slovakia. She had needed clothes and since winter was coming, a fur coat. All I could be grateful for was that it hadn't been mink but modest lamb. Not that I had enquired how Leopold spent his money, after all it was his, but the bills had arrived at the hotel and he had left them all over the place, including the largest for her ticket to the USA. She would, I knew, have no difficulty in obtaining a visitor's visa and would soon follow, though I appreciated Leopold's tact in not allowing her to travel on our ship.

I had not met her in Paris. Leopold was strictly old-fashioned, believing wife and mistress must be kept apart, and though this didn't displease me I couldn't help but feel a certain pity for this woman, con-demned to non-existence where I was concerned and not permitted to join in our social life, though Leopold did occasionally, I knew, intro-duce her to some of his male friends. Secure that Steinhardt would fly over from Canada soon after we had arrived to bring us the money he had kept for us, as well as our valuables, we had believed a thousand dollars ample for our journey and for the first week or two in New York.

By now the Gumpses had half of it. I didn't doubt they would take the rest if Leopold continued to insist on trying to win it back, his pride forbidding him to give up the game.

I began to hate the Gumpses and to evade them as much as I could by making us late for dinner and speaking to them as little as possible. I thought I saw triumph on their ugly old faces every time we met. Since all the ship's staff believed us firm friends because of our games, we were invited to all social occasions together; to the Captain's cocktail party in his cabin; to the cocktail party in the lounge; seated together at the horse-races where, in an effort to recoup our losses, we lost another fifty dollars, whereas the Gumpses won.

No wonder they had made a vast fortune. I have never seen luckier people. Not only at cards did they win but on every occasion for gambling the ship offered. Twice Mr Gumps won the sweep on the ship's daily speed, Mrs Gumps the bingo contest. Even at the fancy dress ball did they get first prizes for the most original costumes, though I must say they merited them. They appeared as two bulky parcels, wrapped in brown paper tied up with string, inscribed with their names and address in California. They looked incredibly funny!

Added to our financial troubles, Diana had started to cause me considerable anxiety by vanishing for hours and giving no explanation on her return as to where she had been. At last the always friendly Chief warned me that she was spending too much time in the tourist class where she had found friends and that this was contrary to ship's regulations. I had to scold her, whereupon she not only sulked but, knowing how much I disliked the Gumpses, spent the rest of the day with them.

I couldn't reprove her for this but I did ask what she could possibly talk to them about.

'Us,' she said, 'and the war and Castolovice. They were very interested.'

Next afternoon, as usual, we played bridge. We owed the Gumpses eight hundred dollars by then. They lost, and, for the next five days before we were due to land, we won almost every rubber.

They played as deliberately as ever, concentrating on each card and making mistake after mistake, grinning at each other wryly occasionally.

'I knew we'd win it all back,' Leopold triumphed, 'it just took me a while to learn their Blackwood.'

I understood by then, only wondering what tales of loss and tragedy Diana had told them. But I didn't ask her nor did I enlighten Leopold. I didn't want to hurt his feelings though I think he guessed towards the end too. Because when on the last evening before we were due in New York Mr Gumps checked the score and showed it to him we had regained all we had lost, plus ten dollars. Mrs Gumps drew an expensive pigskin wallet out of her bag, such as one could buy in the ship's shop, and gave it to him.

'Just a little memento of our games,' she said. 'We've enjoyed them so much. Mind you keep your money safe in it from now on,' and her double chin quivered with suppressed laughter.

Thoughtfully and carefully Leopold put the ten-dollar note into the wallet. 'I will always keep this. Thank you both,' he said. And he did. I've still got the wallet somewhere with the note in it.

There had been the usual rounds of farewell drinks, 'hope-we-meet-agains', in the bar the night before we landed that conclude all ships' voyages. There was no one from whom we minded parting. Our pre-occupation with the Gumpses had kept even Leopold from making many friends.

We had been told that it was well worthwhile to get up at dawn next morning to see the famous skyline of the harbour. I decided to do so. Leopold refused, saying, quite rightly, that we had seen it before. But those had been very different circumstances. We had been tourists then, now we were approaching a land that I hoped would become our own.

I woke Diana at six and we went on deck to see the distant towers seeming to float among clouds in the morning mist like a mirage between sky and sea, with the Statue of Liberty guarding the harbour.

I thought of the many millions of emigrants who, like us, had stood on the decks of so many ships through the years and with how much emotion, how much hope, they must have looked first on this land that promised freedom, happiness and prosperity to all.

'Can one walk up into her head,' Diana asked, indicating Liberty, 'or is there a lift up into it?' 'I suppose so,' I said, slightly shocked, not having viewed the statue from that point of view.

There was a loud hooting of tugboats approaching our ship from different directions. We returned to our cabin. Leopold was still asleep. I woke him. We had been told to be ready for passport control at eight.

Anxiously we waited in the lounge where everyone was assembled. We waved to the Gumpses. Mrs Gumps was adorned with one of those enormous orchids that, wrapped in cellophane, with mauve ribbons to match, seem to come unblemished out of ships' refrigerators even at the end of a voyage.

There was every reason, I thought, to feel as nervous as I did. We were the only emigrants among the first-class passengers. If there was anything wrong with our papers I knew it meant Ellis Island and perhaps even being forced to return to Czechoslovakia. My fears were unnecessary.

Our documents were checked and stamped. There was no questioning this time, only smiles and 'Good luck to you, hope you'll like our country'.

Relieved, we went to assemble our belongings which were already packed, had a large breakfast and returned to the deck. Great white ships were berthed one next to the other in the docks. The towers of Manhattan Island rose, tall and splendid, the glass of their thousands of windows glittering in the morning sun. The air was fresh, cold and crisp.

The pier at which we eventually docked was crowded with people come to welcome relations or friends. They waved and called. I looked for Eddie but he wasn't there, though he'd promised he'd meet us. For a moment I thought I recognized Steinhardt's narrow dark face among the crowd but I knew I must be mistaken. He had written he couldn't possibly leave Ottawa before a week or two after our arrival.

❀ 40 ❀

We walked down the gangway into the vast customs shed. For the next three hours we waited there, sitting on our shabby old trunks watching the most luxurious of luggage being practically torn apart, everything opened and examined, clothes, shoes, hats, watches, cameras, bottles of scent and underwear exposed to everyone's view and checked by the customs officials.

'They seem very strict,' I whispered anxiously.

'Don't bother,' Leopold said, with the confidence of all Central Europeans who evade customs duties as a sort of sport.

Our turn came at last.

'Anything to declare?'

'Nothing but personal belongings,' Leopold said.

Our trunks were opened. Bed-linen, embroidered with stars and coronets, by then crushed and slightly yellow, emerged; Leopold's old suits, tarnished silver racing cups he'd won twenty years ago, the old teapot and – unrecognizable as new – even the clothes I had bought in Paris, crumpled, since I was a very inefficient packer. The other trunks and suitcases contained much the same assortment of shabby odds and ends.

'OK,' said the customs man, as he kindly helped us to thrust things back into the bulging trunks and to lock them again. 'You're emigrants, I take it?'

We said we were. 'The best of luck.' How friendly Americans are, I thought happily. We were allowed to pass the barrier and there was Eddie smiling and waving.

'You haven't waited all these hours?' I asked with concern, as I hugged him.

'Certainly not. I've only just come. I know how long the customs take. I've been through it with Mona dozens of times.' He turned to the uniformed chauffeur beside him, 'Bridges, will you see that the luggage is put into a van and taken to the Devon Hotel?'

'But mustn't we go with it?' Leopold asked rather anxiously. 'It might be stolen.'

'I doubt anyone would want to,' Eddie said, eyeing the battered old trunks that were being carried out. 'Besides, people don't steal in this country. There's organized crime, yes, but not petty theft. Did the press bother you?'

'No,' I said. 'I think some journalists came on to the boat but they did not seem interested in us. After all, we are just ordinary emigrants, presumed to be Jewish.' I told him about the Gumpses.

'Come, I've got the car waiting.' We took the lift. 'My, haven't we grown!' Eddie laughed down at the child.

He walked us to the big cream-coloured Rolls-Royce.

'Mona thought you'd be more comfortable in this than in a taxi because of Leopold's leg.'

'How kind,' I said, sinking back into the luxurious upholstery, 'but won't she need the car?'

Eddie shrugged. 'We've got three more. She's longing to see you. She wants you to come and dine tomorrow night.'

The chauffeur came back. 'Everything's in order, sir.' He was as English as the Rolls, I realized.

'Now, I have to warn you,' Eddie said, 'the Devon is only a small hotel but since it's on the wrong side of Fifth Avenue it's cheap, yet it's only a few steps from Central Park and the Plaza. Mona and I found it when we were walking the dogs.'

'Darling, I'm so grateful.' It was a lovely sunny day and though we passed through the garish hideousness of Broadway, soon we were on Fifth Avenue, wide and bright. To left and to right the great towering buildings that really seemed to scrape the sky –

'There's our church,' Eddie showed Leopold. 'St Patrick's. There's a twelve o'clock mass every Sunday.'

'How beautiful New York is!' I exclaimed, feeling happier than I had for many months.

'Yes,' Eddie said, 'but also rather frightening. Fantastic and somehow inhuman. It's like Xanadu. Do you remember that poem?'

I did and knew what he meant. The towering domes and spires and the dark caverns beneath them, the river and the sunless sea –

'Even Central Park,' Eddie said, quoting:

'So twice five miles of fertile ground
with walls and towers girdled round,
Enfolding sunny spots of greenery.

'Well, here we are.' We stopped in a narrow side-street. The hotel was small, as Eddie had said, striving for no further height than five floors. He took us to our rooms. There were flowers everywhere. Great white lilies, sprays of white and yellow orchids like butterflies, long-stemmed chrysanthemums.

Mona? I didn't need to ask.

There were three rooms, two double bedrooms and a small sitting-room, all pleasantly furnished with semi-antiques, and a large bathroom.

'Look into your cupboards,' Eddie laughed. He opened one. 'This is Leopold's,' (it contained a bar complete with every imaginable drink) 'so he can entertain all his friends – and now to yours.' We went into the other room. 'Mona thought you might need some clothes.' Suits, day-dresses, evening dresses, nightdresses hung in rows in the wardrobes. Below were many pairs of shoes and on the top shelves hats, gloves and handbags for daytime and evening use.

'Now don't think it's all new,' Eddie said brusquely, 'but since Mona rarely wears anything twice it's as good as.' He saw I was close to embarrassing tears of gratitude. 'And don't think you've been forgotten either,' he said fiercely to the child, concealing his own emotion at the pleasure he was giving. 'Open your cupboard,' he ordered. There were toys and books and rows of pretty frocks.

'How can I ever thank Mona enough, and you, Eddie?'

'I really don't know. It was all her idea. She's like that. Only don't call her up. She hates being telephoned. You'll see her tomorrow night. I've got to leave now. We're going to the Metropolitan to hear Jarmilla Novotna in *Traviata*. She's too beautiful. Isn't she Czech? Do you know her?'

'Of course we do,' Leopold said, 'she is married to one of my oldest friends, Jiri Daubek.'

We thanked Eddie once more and he left us. There was a packet of letters on the desk, the top one I could see was from Steinhardt. I tore it open.

'They are coming very soon – !' I exclaimed, unable to conceal my delight. 'They want to show us New York, take us to the theatre and out to dinner. Isn't everything too wonderful? I'm so happy! Everyone is so kind!'

Leopold poured himself a large whisky. It struck me that he had been strangely silent ever since we had arrived. I looked at his unsmiling face with sudden concern. 'Anything wrong, darling?'

'No. It's only that I hope I will not have to depend entirely on the generosity of your friends in the future.'

'But they are your friends, just as much as mine.'

'Really?' he asked almost bitterly.

'Don't spoil everything on our first day,' I pleaded. 'Soon we won't have to depend on anyone but ourselves. In any case what is there to resent in a kind welcome, a few presents? Why, we would have done the same for friends at home under the same circumstances.'

'That's just it. What have we to offer in return now? I don't want to spoil your pleasure,' he added, 'but don't rely too much on friendship. I have a feeling . . .'

Was it pride or jealousy, I wondered? He had never been jealous before. Still, whatever he felt it could not be ignored. In a superficial way I was cleverer than he was but he had much surer and deeper instincts than I and his knowledge of human nature was far more profound. 'I only don't want you to be disappointed, that's all,' he said.

'But Eddie loves us as much as we love him!' I did not dare mention Steinhardt.

Leopold did, though indirectly. 'It would perhaps be wiser to consider what we now have to offer Mona or Dulcie – nothing! Please give me my letters!'

I handed them to him. He put on his glasses and started to read while I pondered his words. Was he right? He gave the letters to me, one after the other. The first came from Austria from my sister-in-law, Toti, uncomplaining as usual, though it was obvious how hard up she was, having to take care of an old bed-ridden relation in exchange for board and lodging, in an isolated country house where Leopold's youngest brother had found refuge too.

Franzi, Leopold's other brother, who had lived in South Africa since before the war, wrote to say he'd lost his job once more and did Leopold know of anything suitable for him in America.

There was a letter too from Annicka. I recognized her childish writing. Leopold put it in his pocket, unread.

The last letter was from his elder sister and somewhat less depressing. Attractive Fanny, one of the most courted of girls in her young days, had, after a disastrous first marriage which had been annulled, married my cousin, Mogens Plessen. He was a doctor of medicine, a most unusual profession for a young aristocrat to have chosen in those days. He had specialized in tropical diseases and, still quite young, had gone to practise in Africa, only returning to Europe on a few rare occasions. On one of these he had persuaded Fanny to join him. Passionately anti-Nazi, she wanted to leave Austria; as much in love with my cousin as he was with her and tempted by the romantic adventure of starting a new life on the Dark Continent, she agreed to marry him.

I don't think she ever regretted it but her life with him was not to be an easy one. Mogens had one great fault. Though a good and conscientious doctor, he was incapable of accepting any authority but his own. Hospitals had to be run according to his ideas, staff had to follow only his orders and he invariably quarrelled with his superiors. Practices where he could be in sole charge were hard to find and he had to earn his living. They moved from place to place, never remaining long anywhere. Mogens worked for fruit companies, coffee plantations (in charge of the health of native labour), in leper colonies, in places remote from all civilization, and Fanny, who had been so spoilt in her youth, had often to live in jungle huts frequently alone all day, while Mogens was at work, wild animals and primitive black people her only company. Or she had to aid him as nurse and accustom herself to the poverty and diseases from which many of the African labourers and their families suffered.

Yet like all my in-laws she had great courage and never complained. Now she wrote there was hope they might be coming to America. Mogens would have to retake his medical exams to practise there.

Through a friend with whom he had worked in Africa, he had been offered a well-paid job as head of a small hospital in Connecticut should he qualify. He had inherited some money from an old Danish uncle and could now afford to be without an income until he got his American degree. The hospital would sponsor the Plessens' entry into the country.

'But this is wonderful news,' I said to Leopold, knowing how glad he would be to have his sister near him.

'Yes,' he said. 'I was thinking if they really do come, perhaps we could buy a house together in the country and have the rest of the family come to live with us too. Land can't be very expensive here since there's so much of it. I could farm. After all, it's the only thing I know how to do. And the brothers – well, they'd all help and they'd have somewhere to live.'

'But I thought you wanted a job here, in New York?'

'Of course I do, but it would be nice to have a piece of land just the same – and to be with one's family.'

Heaven preserve us! I thought, not from the land and house for which I longed just as much as Leopold, but from living with my in-laws.

Though I was fond of each one of them individually, when they were all together they were overpowering; strong, opinionated and, though they loved each other, quarrelsome. All of them had been bred never to have self-doubts or fears. They were in their own way as absolute as the God they believed in, whereas I had no faith in myself or the Deity.

'I think I'll go to bed,' Leopold said. 'I'm tired. All that standing around at the customs, I suppose.'

'Does your leg hurt, darling?'

'A little. Will you order some food?' I telephoned down. I poured him another whisky, unpacked what I knew he would need and made him comfortable in his bed and kissed him. 'It's all going to be all right, darling,' I said, 'don't worry!'

I went to my room. As usual, since our emigration, I had to share it with Diana. I disliked sleeping with her intensely. Not because I didn't love the child, on the contrary I loved her too much. Her comforts seemed more important than mine. I couldn't read in bed because she didn't sleep when the light was on. I couldn't smoke, at least not as much as I liked to, since she complained of the smell. I coughed in my sleep, and when at all nervous even more so, and the sound frequently woke her. All efforts to stifle my coughing in the bedclothes only made it worse.

It embarrassed me to dress and undress in front of her or to paint up my face before the looking-glass. It was no use telling myself she was still a child, her intelligent, critical and sometimes mocking gaze belied it.

Of all the benefits riches had ever conferred on me, privacy, I knew, had been the greatest of them all.

'Would you mind very much,' I asked her as we dined in the small drawing-room off the indifferent food that had been sent up, 'if I slept here for once on the sofa? It's been such an exciting day. It will take me hours to get to sleep.'

'Not if you leave the door open between us,' which of course I did. I collected a pillow, sheets and blankets and lay down on the sofa, having poured myself a stiff drink. I hoped it would induce sleep. It did not.

I thought of Leopold's warning not to depend too much on my friends. I felt confident that nothing could ever change between Eddie and me. We had never demanded anything of each other except the happiness of being together and never would. Mona knew it, of course, and since she was fond of Eddie accepted me as she might have his favourite sister.

With Dulcie things were very different. I doubted even her affection for Leopold would survive our present circumstances. And she certainly had no reason to be fond of me. I had been able to offer her enough in the past to keep the balance even, between what was opportune for her and what suited me. What, I wondered, could I do to tip the scales to my advantage again? It had suited Dulcie not to notice what she called 'the goings on' between her husband and myself in the past. Now she had no reason to remain complaisant. If she insisted on an end being made to the friendship, or even threatened divorce, all I could hope for, at best, was occasionally meeting Steinhardt in secret. He was as fond of his family as I was of mine. If Dulcie started making unpleasant scenes it was not her he would give up in the end but me. Besides, his position made it almost impossible for him to risk stealthy rendezvous in hotel rooms or boarding-houses, nor did I enjoy that sort of brief meeting. I thought of Le Havre and shuddered at the memory. I wanted things to remain as they had been in Prague. Not even the greatest passion, I knew, could survive long without mutual interests, friends in common, the pleasure of meeting in public as well as in private, in surroundings worthy of whatever occasion. No, I had to find something that would persuade Dulcie that it was still advantageous to share our lives. Had I any important friends socially or politically prominent enough to impress her with? I couldn't think of anyone.

At last I fell into a troubled sleep.

At nine Eddie rang up to say that it was a lovely morning. He and I were both early risers. Like most people whose pleasures are mainly visual we preferred day to night. He told me to meet him at the Plaza, saying he was walking the dogs in the park and that I could bring the child.

We found him at the edge of the fountain in front of the hotel holding two white woolly bundles. The sun was bright on his face and hair and he looked young and happy. 'Oh, can we go in one of those carriages?' Diana asked. Some horse-drawn cabs that took tourists round the park were drawn up near by. 'I've never been in a carriage before,' she added. 'What a lie,' Eddie laughed, 'I took you for drives myself in Capri and Rome – though I suppose you were too small to remember. Come, hop in. You can take Micky on your lap but be nice to him.' She cuddled the woolly dog. Eddie held the other one on his knee as we started off. 'What breed are they?' I asked. 'Capri terriers, the only two in the world. An unrepeatable species. They have no father and their mother is dead.'

'How sad,' Diana sympathized.

'They are brothers. They have each other. How I love the smell of horses,' he exclaimed, as we trotted through the park, 'it reminds me so much of childhood. Do you remember the time when, except for the railway, this was our only form of transportation?'

'Of course.'

'How do those dresses fit, child?' he asked.

'They are lovely, Uncle Eddie, but I got stuck in some. They are rather small.'

'How was I to know how big you had grown? Take them to Sacks and change them – and yours?' He turned to me. 'I know they fit. Mona and you have almost the same figure.'

'I wish I had her face too,' I said.

'Well, one can't have everything. You'll have to wear one of the dresses tonight. She will be disappointed if you don't. What about that dark blue heavy silk that ties over one shoulder? I remember it because it went so well with her sapphires.'

'Will I have to remain alone in the hotel?' Diana asked, only a slight quivering of her lips revealing what she felt.

'Gracious!' Eddie exclaimed, 'that's something I hadn't considered. Why not bring her along? She can't dine, of course, but she can stay with one of Mona's maids upstairs. The English one is just like an old nanny anyway. She'll give her tea and find her somewhere to sleep till you go home. Would you like that, child?'

'Very much, Uncle Eddie.' We had arrived in the middle of the park. He told the driver to stop. 'Now you have a good run with the dogs but don't let go of their leads,' he admonished. 'See they do what they ought to.

'She's a nice girl,' he remarked, 'pretty too and the dogs seem to like her – always a good sign – but you can't have her hanging around all the time, unable to go out at night because of her. Seems to me a boarding-school is the only solution. I'll make enquiries.'

'But wouldn't that be very expensive?'

'Probably, but you can scrimp in other ways. After all, she's your only child and having her well brought up is important.'

He pointed. 'Over there is Mona's house on Fifth Avenue. No, that's the Metropolitan Museum. It's not quite as large as that and it's much farther to the left towards Harlem.'

'How nice to be near Harlem,' I remarked. 'We used to spend night after night there when we first came here, though it's thirteen years ago. It used to be such fun.'

'No one dares to go there at night now. White people aren't welcome. Even the park has become unsafe. Mona wants to sell her house. You won't like her house here very much, though you will love the one on Long Island. That's quite extraordinary. This one is full of good pictures, furniture and things, but it's sort of boxy, all the rooms are as square as cubes. Architecturally it's very ordinary. Well, you'll see tonight. Oh, by the way, Mona has asked as many people whom she and I could think of whom you and Leopold knew – including an old friend of your family's, Gabriella Grey. I don't know who she was – Countess something or other – but her husband is American, not only rich, but nice and of good family and liked by everyone. She and Mona are friends and shared their anxieties for you in the war.'

'I can't remember anyone I've ever known called Gabriella,' I said, 'except for Gabriella Lichtenstein.'

'Well, it's certainly not her. You will be sure to recognize this one when you see her. She's a mighty good-looking woman. Don't you love this park?'

I looked across the wide expanses of green, at the trees, vivid in their autumn gold, the small lake reflecting the blue sky and the shining towers that enclosed it all.

'Very much, it's almost like being in the country.'

'Not at all! It's as marvellously artificial as a theatre decoration – I wouldn't be surprised if some of the trees and flowers weren't made of paper or plastic . . . Well, I've got to go. Harrison is not coming down tonight. Big dinner parties bore and tire him. Besides, he's in a bad temper. He's had trouble with the tax people. He always wanted to make a billion and now he can't. Still, he did manage nine hundred and twenty millions, but I see his point, a billion is a nice round sum. I'll have to do the seating. Mona's stopped bothering, which is a pity. The combinations she thought up were much funnier than mine.'

We called Diana and the dogs back. He gave the cabby some notes, told him to drive us home and walked away, the little dogs pulling at their leads towards Mona's house.

41

I found Leopold in a much more cheerful mood when I returned.

'I've been out too,' he told me, 'and look what I bought. Now we can make tea.' It was an electric kettle. Leopold drank tea every time he wasn't drinking something stronger. 'And do you know who I met coming out of an antique shop? Erich Goldschmidt, as elegant as usual. He was delighted to see me.'

'And how's Biene?' I enquired. Erich and his beautiful German wife had always been inseparable.

'Seem's she's farming with her brother in California. I asked Erich if he farmed too, thinking that really unimaginable. He assured me he didn't. I asked him what he did. "Nothing much," he said, in that languid drawl of his. "In the morning if it's fine, I walk up and down the Avenue and admire the girls, then I go home for lunch and rest. In the afternoon I visit the antique shops and in the evening I go to the theatre or the Opera,"' Leopold mimicked Erich's lazy voice. 'Nothing seems to have changed for him at least. He is staying here with his cousin, Renée Bekér.'

Erich and Biene had been very much part of our social life in the past. Though they had a house in Berlin they were equally at home in every other capital city, knowing everyone who was worth knowing, their good looks, good manners and good taste appreciated by all.

'He said we must come and lunch with him and Renée soon. I asked him for some decent restaurant near here. He said the Twenty One was quite good and the Plaza not bad. We'd better go there, it's the nearest. Oh! and Clarisse called me, she is coming to see us this afternoon.'

We ate in a rather shabby old-fashioned dining-room at the Plaza Hotel, which might as well have been in Prague or Vienna, the decorations red plush and tarnished gold. The food was very good but the bill enormous. It was to take us a long time to learn that the more old-fashioned-looking a restaurant was in New York, the more expensive it proved to be.

Clarisse Rothschild was waiting for us in the drawing-room. She hugged all three of us, one after the other, clasping us to a breast that once had been so large and full and now seemed to have shrunk. She has aged very much, I thought, sadly, recollecting with some shame how I had hated this once so overpoweringly voluptuous-looking woman in the first years of my marriage. She and Leopold had been friends for a very long time and she saw no reason why a child like me should prove an obstacle to the intimacy continuing. Neither did Leopold, who assured me, I think quite truthfully then, that there had never been more than mutual affection between them.

Whenever we stayed with her or were invited together to various country houses, or when she came to visit us in Zasmuky, she completely ignored the fact that a newly-married couple might like occasional privacy. Morning, noon and night she would walk into our bedroom as if it was hers, without knocking, stretch out on our beds, and start to laugh, joke and gossip with Leopold about their mutual friends, many of whom I then scarcely knew, making me feel I was non-existent.

But it was even worse when she did suddenly notice me and saw fit to give me good advice as to how to run a house, how to deal with servants (all of which Leopold did anyway, then), where to buy my clothes and which people one could receive and which not.

It was all well and kindly meant but Clarisse's friendship was as generously overwhelming as her physical proportions and she lacked tact.

She was English by birth and never did she let the Austrians forget it. Though of a Jewish family (Sebag Montefiore) of such distinction that intermarriage with the Rothschilds was acceptable on both sides, she had grown up and been educated like any other English girl of good family. She was still quite young when she married Baron Alphonse. He was many years her senior. But even then she was a big handsome woman, of the type Rubens would have enjoyed painting. She had everything: good looks, wealth, not so much in terms of money, but translated into magnificent possessions – palaces, country houses and estates, rare works of art and fabulous jewels. Courted by most of Vienna's society, flattered by numerous sycophants, no wonder she had become rather domineering, autocratic and spoilt.

Yet she was devoted to her husband. His was the only authority to which she submitted. We were a very gay group of young people then and our behaviour not always exemplary, but when Clarisse said 'Alphonse has put on his glasses,' and he calmly glanced at one or the other of us, we all knew it was a call to order. There was no one in Vienna who hadn't liked and respected him. Small, quiet, modest and self-effacing, he was nevertheless a personality: as gentle and wise and learned as an old rabbi, yet keenly observant, if humorously tolerant, of human frailty.

I looked at Clarisse, so changed and aged since we had seen her last in Vienna, and thought of the irreparable losses she had suffered. Her only son, still a schoolboy when the family fled from Vienna, had died of a throat infection in Switzerland and now Alphonse too was dead.

'I couldn't save him,' Clarisse said, wiping the tears from her still remarkably beautiful eyes. 'It was his heart. It must have broken. It wasn't the material losses he minded, it was the treachery of so many whom we had believed our friends and of a country which he loved. And the sufferings of our people.'

'Poor old Clara,' Leopold said (he had always called her that in the past), kissing her wet cheek. 'It's all over now. If you went back to Austria you would be welcomed by all your old friends. There's not a Nazi left among them.'

'Turned their coats once more?' Her eyes flashed blue fire. 'I never want to see them again!'

'Don't be unfair, Clara,' Leopold remonstrated, 'some were just mis-guided, stupid and certainly not all of them were for Hitler.'

'I can count those of my friends that weren't on two hands – and when I think of Ulrich . . .'

She and Ulrich Kinsky had been inseparable for many years before his remarriage and the *Anschluss*.

'Perhaps he too would have learnt to regret had he lived longer,' I ventured. 'Many have.'

'Regret? All they really regret, even now, is that Hitler didn't win the war – you can't imagine, and probably don't know since you were in Czechoslovakia, how our friends and even some of your relations be-haved after the German takeover, rushing to get hold of our properties cheap. Houses in Vienna, land – anything – even our china and silver.

People who had dined in the Palais hundreds of times eating from our plates. I wonder the food didn't stick in their throats and choke them.'

'Surely it can't be true?'

'It certainly is. I do have a few old faithfuls left who were able to spy for me and the Rothschild coat of arms was on all of it. Oh, I won't rest till I get the last teaspoon back!

'And do you know what their excuse is now, since our lawyers have started to trace things that were practically stolen? That they only acquired them so as to keep them for us!

'And the governments! They'll have to repay too, for what was confiscated. The Czechs for Vitcovice and Schillerdorf and the Austrians for our ruined looted palaces in Vienna and for the forests of the Langau.'

'Don't be so bitter, Clara,' Leopold protested, 'it's no good.'

'And so would you be if you'd lost all that we have,' she said angrily.

I couldn't help thinking that even if our losses were smaller, she had every chance of claiming compensation. We had none.

'Meanwhile,' she continued, 'I have to live in this horrible country where all that people care about is how rich you are, while I'm practically penniless! I scarcely know how to find the money for the rent of my flat, maintenance, even food. Poor Eugene lives in a two-room cottage on Long Island. He had to give up the big house there because it was too expensive and Louis [both were her brothers-in-law] is trying to farm in Vermont, dressed in red . . .'

'But for goodness' sake, why?' Leopold asked, puzzled.

'Because in the shooting season here anyone who pleases can buy a gun and shoot at anything that moves. If one's dressed in red there's a chance of surviving.' Clarisse's indignation was comprehensible, accustomed as she had been to the strict shooting conventions of Europe.

'However, Louis is the only one of us who seems quite happy. He's married. Did you know?'

'No, I always thought he was such a confirmed bachelor. To whom?' I enquired.

'Hilda Auersperg. You knew her in Vienna, of course.'

'Nice woman,' Leopold said, appreciatively.

'Yes, but I'm all alone now. Betty and Gwen think only of their husbands.' She was referring to her daughters whom we had only known as children. 'I'm too old to make new friends. I miss Vienna terribly and the Austrian countryside, the shoots – all our way of life as it used to be before Hitler.'

'Then pack up and go back, Clara.'

'What, and live among those traitors? Never!'

'But aren't there a lot of nice people here?' I asked. 'Americans seem so kind.'

'Don't you believe it. They have snobberies that would even have made your grandmother blush.' Omama and she had been friends in Vienna.

'But what on earth can they be snobbish about?'

'Each other, and when they came over and who made his money first and how, as if anyone cared, and to which clubs they belong and whom they can keep out. They seem to try and prove something by discriminating. I really can't be bothered with what goes for society here. Imagine, I wanted to join a country club on Long Island because I like playing golf and they wouldn't have me!'

'But why?'

'Because I'm called Rothschild. Have you ever heard of anything more absurd?'

I had not. It had been an almost magical name in the past that had opened every door in Europe, the family not only honoured for their wealth and financial genius but for the integrity, generosity and culture of all of its members.

'Which reminds me,' Clarisse said, anger still plain on her face, 'your friend Steinhardt came to see me. He wanted money, I think. I'd do anything in the world for both of you, you must know that, but financially I really can't help.'

'But, Clara, we never expected you to,' Leopold exclaimed, obviously very embarrassed.

'That's what I thought,' she said with evident relief, 'or that you would have sent me anyone like Steinhardt! It must have been his own idea.'

'But didn't you like him?' I asked, surprised.

'Oh, it's a type you meet here very often, always trying to get something or somewhere.'

'It seems to me he's got quite far.'

'Because he's an ambassador? All you need to do is to contribute to party funds to become one.'

'Well anyway, he's a wonderful person,' I said indignantly, 'you don't know how many people he helped get out of Czechoslovakia. We wouldn't be here except for him, nor have anything to live on. He brought out all our valuables.'

'Has he returned them?' Seeing my face she apologized. 'I'm sorry. You wouldn't believe how I've been cheated and swindled by people who promised to safeguard valuables for us. I trust no one any more. But I'm glad you've found such a good friend, even if he won't be much of a social asset.'

'But why?' Leopold asked.

'Because he's Jewish, that's all.'

We fell silent. What was there to say? I thought of a story I had heard in Vienna in my youth of how the first Baron Rothschild and Prince Schwarzenberg, both connoisseurs of art, frequently met in picture galleries and became friends.

'I wish I could show you my collection,' Prince Schwarzenberg said with regret, 'unfortunately . . .'

'I know you don't receive Jews in your Palais.'

'No, but as I hear, neither do you, Baron Rothschild, in yours.'

It had been true even in my days. I remembered when the entire Austrian aristocracy went to the Rothschild dinner parties and balls there had rarely been, except for some of their own closest relations, any Jews present.

Yet the family had never neglected helping the Jewish community of Vienna and had remained strictly Orthodox, taking their religious duties as seriously as we took ours. We respected each other's faith. It was perfectly normal for Clarisse to say: 'Come and lunch after mass,' or teasingly to Leopold: 'When did you go to Confession last?' or for Leopold to commiserate with Alphonse because the synagogue had been badly heated and he had caught cold, or to ask Clara how the goose had tasted after she had fasted all day on the Day of Atonement. Clarisse even came to several Christian weddings, though Alphonse didn't, and we went to a few Jewish ones when relations of theirs married, though at the first Leopold, having politely taken off his hat, as he would in church, had it hastily thrust back on his head by Alphonse, the top-hatted congregation watching disapprovingly.

The reason why the Rothschilds (in the Vienna of the past) rarely invited Jews to their palaces was quite simply because being members of the aristocracy they followed the customs of society as they were in those days. People in trade – and many Jews were – could not be received. Prominent intellectuals or artists – yes, but what were then termed shopkeepers still only entered by the back door.

'Shall I make you some tea, Clara?' Leopold asked, swinging his kettle.

She laughed her old throaty laugh for the first time that afternoon. 'You'll set the house on fire.' Prophetic words. Some time later he nearly did. 'Where's the teapot?'

'I haven't unpacked yet,' I said, looking at all the luggage that crowded our rooms. 'I don't know what we are going to do when Steinhardt brings the rest of the stuff. Is storage very expensive?'

'Incredibly. I ought to know,' Clarisse said.

'Wouldn't it be better,' I asked, 'to take it straight to an antique dealer, unpack and sort it there and he could sell what we don't want to keep? We have to sell most of it anyway.'

'But what is it?'

'A lot of china, prints, silver, silver plates, some pictures.'

'The usual country house stuff, I imagine. Probably all nineteenth-century,' Clarisse said, rather unkindly I thought, but then with Rothschilds only the Renaissance and French eighteenth century counted.

'Don't you know of a decent antique dealer here to whom we could take it to?'

'Decent? They are all thieves!' She thought a while – 'Perhaps old Rosenblatt would do, though a robber too at least he's from Vienna and perhaps for old times' sake won't skin you alive.'

'But I remember his shop,' Leopold said, 'my father used to buy a lot there – any furniture that had a star in the marquetry or painted on and which Rosenblatt made him believe had belonged to Sternbergs.'

'Just like him,' Clarisse said, though whether she was referring to my father-in-law or Rosenblatt was not clear. 'We never bought anything there but I go to see the old man sometimes, just to talk over the past. He will probably remember you.

'Well, I've got to go. How good it is to have you here, Leopold. We must see a lot of each other. You must come and lunch whenever you can. You'll have to take pot luck, I'm afraid. I have to mind even my grocery bills these days.'

Later we were to lunch and dine with her quite frequently. She had a beautiful apartment on Fifth Avenue overlooking the park, superbly furnished with first quality eighteenth-century furniture, fine pictures and china, and the food was as delicious as only a French chef can make it.

'But what's it all about?' we asked Erich, whom we met after our first lunch. He was not only Clarisse's cousin, but one of her most devoted friends. 'Surely she can't be as poor as she says she is?'

'Of course not. It's all in the mind. Why, what's in her apartment alone is worth a fortune and she'll be immensely rich when she's repaid for what she's lost in the various countries. It's pitiful really. She clings to money as if it were life itself. But then I'm afraid it's all she has left to cling to now.'

42

In the evening another Rolls came to fetch us. This one appropriately was as black and silver as the night. A black chauffeur would have added the ultimate in elegance, I thought. However, ours, as I could tell by his looks and smile, was unmistakably Italian.

I would have liked to have spoken to him of his country. Hearing a friendly Latin voice with the accents of Rome or Naples would have reassured me. I was feeling as nervous as if I was going to my first party. But a pane of glass divided us from the driver and I didn't dare press one of the row of silver buttons which I thought would slide it open in case Leopold would start amusing himself by trying them all, with embarrassing consequences.

Of my daughter I had no such fears. Her behaviour was always reliably correct. Sitting bolt upright so as not to crush her new dress she stared out of the window at the high towers now ablaze with lights.

Would the dinner party be very formal? I wondered. If so, the prospect appalled me. I knew how very unconventional my and Leopold's behaviour had become in the war and that it had not improved much afterwards.

Also, as Dulcie had frequently pointed out, our manners at table were 'unAmerican'. At embassy dinners or luncheons either given by the Steinhardts or members of their staff in Prague she would reprove us for having started the first course before our hostess and for using both fork and knife while eating, instead of cutting everything up neatly and then laying the knife aside on the plate. Steinhardt had laughingly explained that these customs were still those of early American days when a woman, by testing first, proved to her guests that the food was fit for consumption and a man, by laying down his knife, that he had no intention of killing anyone.

But even more than to our table manners did Dulcie object to our frequently disrupting all conversation at dinner parties by ignoring our neighbours if they were dull and speaking across the table to anyone we pleased.

However, the worst offence habitually came later. Based on English custom the ladies left the dining-room before the gentlemen, but according to American custom they rarely met again until it was time to go home. Though I realized that Americans much preferred talking to their own than to their opposite sex, I did not enjoy this and neither did Leopold. After a good dinner he liked to relax with some pretty woman, while I wanted to talk to Steinhardt. So, to Dulcie's horror and to the amazement of the embassy staff and much I think to the ambassador's secret relief, I used to join the men and Leopold the ladies.

After all we were Czechs and had a certain position in our country. Let Americans think what they pleased.

It would be different tonight. Though I knew there would be no rigours of etiquette at Mona's house, she was much too cosmopolitan for that, nevertheless I feared the evening.

It was, I knew, our début in New York society. I have always lacked self-confidence. My parents had convinced me at too early an age that I had neither brains nor beauty. When my Aunt Diana had tried to reassure me as to the contrary it was already too late. Yet a certain amount of appreciation is necessary to one's well-being and self-respect. It didn't take me long to discover how to gain it. I had one valuable gift. I could charm.

Perhaps because I had no personality I was allowed free access to that of others. I could so respond to their thoughts and feelings that I became a welcome extension of themselves and since each man loves himself above all else I was often included.

I had learnt to practise my arts quite early on those that seemed worthy of attention and with whom I could establish rapport, gaining strength and self-confidence from every conquest. My gift had very little to do with sex though I would later use even that if it was the only key to another's personality.

Whatever my magic was, it worked on most sympathetic human beings, providing I could isolate them from others. In a crowd I had no powers at all. There was nothing spectacular about my appearance nor was I good at general conversation, my voice was low and didn't carry and if I felt lack of interest I could become tongue-tied with shyness.

Still, Eddie would be there to give me courage and Leopold was with me. I looked at him. Light and darkness intermittently flashed across his face as the car moved forward; his hair that he always believed if smoothed down by water would remain tidy, springing into the most unruly grey waves as usual. He certainly didn't share my rather snobbish nervousness. To him all men were equal anywhere and if no worse certainly no better than himself.

When we had arrived at the house a footman took our coats, a tall gaunt woman with a tired face who had been waiting in the hall led Diana away and the butler showed us into the drawing-room.

Though a large room it seemed scarcely big enough to contain its wealth of flowers and people.

Eddie who was standing near the door came to greet us. 'I'm waiting Morfona,' he said, 'she's even later than usual.'

What a crowd,' I whispered.

Now don't be nervous,' he warned. 'They are all old friends of yours and Leopold's.'

'Do I look all right?'

'You look exactly what you are, charming,' he reassured me. 'All you need is a stiff drink.' He called the footman. Gratefully I gulped my Martini.

When Mona finally swept into the room Eddie's admiring glance was the first to meet hers. They smiled at each other. She wore a green gown that enfolded her like foliage, baring only her flower-like head, neck and shoulders.

'I suppose everyone knows everyone by now. Sorry I'm late,' she apologized, evading the boredom of introductions. Then she joined us. 'Welcome to America, darlings,' she said. 'I'm so glad you are here at last.' She kissed me and looked up at Leopold affectionately. 'Adverse events have at least not depleted your stature, my dear Sternberg.'

We tried to thank her for all she'd done to make us comfortable in the Devon Hotel, for the flowers and presents. She shrugged her lovely shoulders, then scanning my dress she started to laugh. 'You've got it on back to front, darling. How like you! Not that it matters. It's just as pretty that way.'

'Gabriella,' she called across the room. 'Here they are at last – our refugees. Come and welcome them!'

Rather hesitantly, I thought, a remarkably good-looking woman separated from the man she was talking to and joined us. She was superbly dressed and groomed. Her hair, cut very short, was red-gold and curled all over her head like the petals of a chrysanthemum. Her pretty face was perhaps somewhat over large but her complexion flawless and the big velvety brown eyes very appealing.

'I'm so happy you are safe,' she said, stretching out a hand on which the largest of diamonds shone. She spoke with a pronounced French accent.

'Gabriella and I worried about you a lot in the war and have really ever since,' Mona explained.

Leopold and I looked at each other, ascertaining that neither of us believed we had ever seen Gabriella before.

There was an awkward silence. And yet, I thought, her eyes now as pleading and panic-stricken as those of some gentle animal led to be slaughtered seemed somehow familiar.

'Well, don't you recognize each other any more?' Mona asked, puzzled.

Then, as if in desperation, the woman turned to Leopold and whispered something to him. All that I could understand was that she was speaking Czech. Whatever she said it had the most startling effect. To my amazement he bent down and hugged her as if she had been a long-lost sister or daughter.

Peering at me over her bent and curly head he said one word – 'Gabi'.

Then I knew.

I did not want to be outdone by him in kindness.

'It's been so long, Gabi,' I said, taking her hand after he had released her. 'I almost didn't recognize you at first. You've cut off all your lovely hair!'

Mona, satisfied as to our happy reunion, moved on to greet some of her other guests.

'*Zaplat Pan Buh!*' Gabi exclaimed, her eyes shining with tears of gratitude. Czech words used by the humblest to thank for alms. 'May God repay you.'

She had not lied when she had told Mona that she had known our family intimately for years. In a sense it was quite true.

Gabi Kroll had been discovered in a small Czech town when she was sixteen by one of those enterprising gentlemen who lived on the fringes of our society. Anxious to belong, they curried favour with the wealthy young bachelors of the aristocracy by finding them attractive and complaisant girls.

The story was always the same. Seduced by one of these men, often promised marriage, the girl would leave her respectable home to join her lover, then finding all her hopes deceived, she feared to return to her parents. Totally at the mercy of her protector for support and help, promised if nothing else social advancement, pretty clothes and a gay life if she was nice to one or the other of his aristocratic friends, she usually complied.

It was to the advantage of procurer and receiver alike that these arrangements were handled with utmost discretion. Any girl who made trouble was cast out by her protector to earn her living as best she could. Many of these ended up as ordinary prostitutes. Gabi had been more fortunate than most.

Recommended to Leopold in his bachelor days by one of his more disreputable friends as an attractive, healthy and obliging girl, all of which proved true, he had kept her for several months and then passed her on to his brothers. There were four in all. The youngest had lived with her longest. I don't doubt that each of them had treated her as well as custom and circumstances in those days permitted. The Sternbergs, if ruthless womanizers, were kind-hearted and generous.

I had of course never been allowed to meet her but I had seen her frequently in restaurants, bars and nightclubs with one or the other of my brothers-in-law. She was, I knew, no older than myself. Sometimes our eyes had met, hers seeming to plead for affection and acceptance.

But what a transformation! I remembered her then, her wealth of chestnut-coloured hair piled in a big chignon that had made her head seem over large, her plump figure and the flashy tasteless clothes –

Incredible that this slim, elegant, sophisticated-looking Gabriella had evolved from pathetic Gabi!

As was natural to him, Leopold asked her frankly how she had been able to change so advantageously for the better.

She told us without any false modesty. After the affair with Leopold's youngest brother had ended she had met a Frenchman who had come to Prague on business. He had taken her with him to Paris and eventually married her. 'A real aristocrat too,' she said with some relish. 'I owe him everything. He was cultivated, generous and kind. He had me educated, taught me how to dress and how to behave.'

'But you left him, since you've remarried?'

'He left me, he died. He was an old man. He provided for me as best he could. He was not very rich but there was enough for me to be able to live independent of men for some years. When the war started an American woman friend of mine persuaded me to leave with her for the United States. We came here and thanks to Xenia's connections and my being a genuine French Comtesse I was soon accepted in New York's best society. And then I found my wonderful husband – '

Once more her big eyes pleaded. 'I have told him so much about you.

He knows of course that I am Czech by birth. I have allowed him to believe that we are – well – relations.'

'As indeed we are,' Leopold declared gallantly.

A tall, thin, round-shouldered man who looked scholarly and intellectual was introduced to us by the now radiant, happy Gabi. For a few moments we discussed the tragedy of Czechoslovakia. He was well-informed and sympathetic. Then dinner was announced.

Because of the interlude with Gabi I had not been able to meet any-one else nor had I had time to look at the place-card in the hall to see where I was seated. I wandered round the dining-room table until Eddie came to my aid. 'I've put you next to the President of the Audubon Society. He's at Mona's left. With your liking for birds you should have a lot in common. He's an ornithologist.'

Mona was already seated, Prince Serge Obolensky whom I had met years ago in Vienna on her right. We smiled across in recognition. My neighbour was an elderly man with very white hair, very black eye-brows, and a clever animated face. I had no trouble in talking to him at all, since he obviously liked best to hear himself speak. He had travelled extensively all over the world, knew the Arctics as well as the tropics and one witty anecdote about his adventures followed another. Occasionally he looked beyond me from right to left accustomed I thought to lecture to larger audiences. Soon he had not only my attention but Mona's and Prince Serge's too. He was telling a story about the rapacity of a species of penguins in New Zealand so tame that they had rifled his pockets. Mona looked round the table scanning the men immaculate in their black dinner-jackets and white shirts and started to laugh. 'Aren't they exactly like penguins?' she asked. 'People so often remind me of various birds. Women of peacocks, parrots and geese, men of birds of prey. What bird do I make you think of, Serge?'

'An angel.'

'But that's silly. A real bird – '

'Well, angels have wings – a bird of paradise.'

'All that's nice about them is their fine feathers,' Mona protested. 'Can't you do better, Professor?'

She flashed upon him the incredible turquoise blue of her marvellous eyes.

'A kingfisher?'

'More applicable to my friend Wallis, Duchess of Windsor than to me,' she laughed and turned to Serge once more. He and she were old friends.

'What about yourself?' I asked the ornithologist. 'What would you like to be?'

'A phoenix.'

'But it never existed.'

'Unfortunately not. I'm an old man,' he sighed. 'And you?' he questioned politely, continuing to play a game which must have seemed childish to him. 'What bird do you choose?'

'A skylark, I think.'

He looked surprised and amused. 'Hail to thee, blithe Spirit!' he quoted, 'but do you often rise at dawn to sing for joy?'

'I have neither voice nor wings, but yes.'

'So did I when I was young – ' He fell silent and then quoted the last lines of Shelley's 'Ode to a Skylark'.

'Teach me half the gladness that thy brain must know,
Such harmonious madness from my lips would flow
The world should listen then as I am listening now.'

What a charming man, I thought, feeling confident that I had made a friend, then Mona asked him some question and I remembered that politeness demanded that I speak to my other neighbour who had taken no part in our conversation and whom I had scarcely looked at. I glanced at his place-card. 'Tennessee Williams' it said. I looked at him. He was fair-haired, rather stout, had light blue eyes and an indifferent nose. A large pendulous moustache obscured his mouth and chin.

Since what was visible of his face seemed rather young the formidable moustache looked stuck on like a disguise.

'Are you a relation of Mona's husband?' I asked.

'No, why?'

'Because of Williams – '

'It's not an uncommon name.'

'But surely Tennessee is? Isn't that a state? Would one not be either a foundling or a very important person to be so named?' I asked, thinking I was being amusing.

But whatever took place under his moustache didn't look like a smile at all. He reached for his wine-glass and emptied it in one long gulp.

'Are you in business?' I questioned then, thinking he looked it and believing it was the right thing to ask every American male.

'No, I write.'

It was the last thing I would have expected by his appearance. 'Such as?'

'*A Streetcar Named Desire*. Perhaps you might have heard of it?'

'I'm sorry, I haven't. But do tell me what is a streetcar?' I was in no way tempted to discuss desire with this rather unfriendly young man.

He looked at me with such round-eyed amazement and distaste that I felt very uncomfortable. 'I've only just arrived in America,' I apologized.

Quite rudely I thought he turned away from me and started talking to the woman on his other side.

My friend the Professor was conversing with Mona. What I had feared might happen had – no one was paying me the slightest attention. There was nothing left but to appear cheerful and as if I didn't care. I looked across to where Leopold was laughing with Anita Lobkowtiz. I thought guiltily of the trick we had played on her and her husband in Paris where we had seen them last before the war started.

Returning from a journey and passing through Marseille we had bought two attractive-looking small monkeys intending to take them home with us to Czechoslovakia. From the very first they proved unmanageable. When let out of their cage in our Paris hotel they made the most awful mess of our room and bit ferociously when we finally managed to catch them. We decided it wasn't worth taking them home. We were leaving for Prague that afternoon. What better way to dispose of them than to present them to the Lobkowitzes where we were lunching? A gift for their children.

Prince Edi Lobkowitz was of a junior line of that large Czech family. He had always been a friend of Leopold's and remained so when he started to earn his living as a stockbroker in Paris. When he eventually married an American we had become as fond of Anita as we were of him. Whenever we came to France we would look them up. On this occasion we wisely left the presentation of our gift to their children until after lunch. If the catch of the cage door slipped or Leopold intentionally opened it, knowing exactly what would follow, I never knew. The Lobkowitzes, justly proud of their newly decorated flat, had watched with horror as the monkeys skimmed up the curtains to settle on the ornate pelmets, chattering with rage or fear, their droppings striping the blue satin with brown, while the children shrieked with delight. We made futile efforts to help catch the creatures but had to excuse ourselves since our train for Prague was leaving within an hour.

We were later to hear that the monkeys had totally wrecked the flat and that the Paris Zoo had to be called in to remove them, after which, since it proved the animals were of quite a rare and valuable species, the Lobkowitz children were allowed to visit the zoo free of charge, which may have been of some consolation to their parents.

Obviously Anita had forgotten or forgiven. She was, I knew, by nature tolerant and generous and she had a great sense of humour. She was a big flaxen-haired handsome Swedish American who had been as popular in Paris as she was in New York. She rather towered over her small dumpy husband, but only physically. Edi had outsized himself in the war. Having joined the free Czech forces under Allied Command he had proved himself a hero at Tobruk, holding a strategically important desert outpost with just a few men for eight weeks, attacked again and again by air and by land, short of food and water, until relief came.

After the war had ended Edi with the Czech brigade marched into Prague as decorated as a Christmas tree. I looked across to where he sat. His round amiable face was very ordinary. How little one really knows of people, I thought, until they are put to the test. He was sitting next to Gerda Czernin and there was no doubt about his enjoying her company. Gerda's humour was as tip-tilted as her nose, I knew. The only imperfect feature in an otherwise flawlessly beautiful face it added a sort of piquant charm to her good looks.

She had not changed I thought since I had seen her first nearly twenty years ago in Monte Carlo at the Hotel de Paris. She was then married to a Mr Stiasny, a rich Czech industrialist, and all over the Riviera the couple were known as *La belle et la bête*.

Poor Stiasny was indeed remarkably ugly and she of such beauty that the contrast made everyone stare. So did I then.

'Couldn't we meet them?' I had begged Leopold. Since they were Czech he didn't think it would be too difficult and always tolerant of my whims he invited them to dine with us.

That Stiasny worshipped his wife was very evident. Perhaps he believed in some magical transformation through her beauty, hoping, like the beast in the fairy story, to be changed into a handsome prince by love. On closer acquaintance, he proved to be well-educated and intelligent and we grew quite fond of the strangely assorted couple.

We never saw them again since they lived mainly in the South of France and when Hitler came to power Stiasny, who was Jewish, could not return to Czechoslovakia. Later we heard he had died.

After the war had ended Meggy Lobkowitz (her husband of another line of that family) came to us very perturbed to say that her favourite brother, Hans Czernin, had suddenly married someone called Gerda Stiasny in Paris. Had we ever heard of her?

We reassured her we had, and that she was lovely. I felt glad for Hans of whom I was fond. He had been one of my earliest admirers and we had always kept in touch even when he had moved to work in Paris before the war.

'But what sort of family? Stiasny? She can't be born? Is she at least a Catholic?' Meggy cared very much about these things.

'I wouldn't worry, Meggy,' Leopold laughed. 'Hans is lucky to have got her. As for Stiasny – surely you know what it means in Czech?'

'Happiness,' she admitted.

I wondered if she later remembered when Hans and Gerda did everything their limited means permitted to support and help Meggy and her children after they had fled from Czechoslovakia.

I looked at her again. Still the small head held so high, the long strong white neck rising from broad shoulders, the generous breasts and narrow waist. She was dressed all in white and remembering the bird game reminded me of a beautiful billowing swan.

Now Hans was working in New York. I looked to where he was seated. He caught my glance and waved. He had broadened a bit and no wonder (we later discovered what a wonderful cook Gerda was) but his open boyish face had not changed.

He and Gerda were to prove invaluable friends while we were living in New York. Regularly once a week they would invite us and Diana to dine in their tiny flat, Gerda cooking delicious meals, which by then we were very grateful for, and giving us much better advice on how to economize than any of our richer friends could.

I turned to Tennessee.

'We must be at least thirty at this table,' I remarked, 'do you know everyone?'

'No,' he said and averted his face once more.

He actually dislikes me, I thought with some surprise. Usually the worst that could happen to me was indifference.

My Professor was still talking to Mona. I continued to contemplate her guests. There were several more familiar faces. Nin Ryan whom I had known in Vienna. Princess Boncompagni, Viennese by birth. Laurene Shevlin, whose mother and stepfather, Princess and Prince Orsini, had stayed with us in Castolovice (he was a distant relation of mine) – all outstandingly attractive women, though Mona outshone them all. There were several men I didn't know. Two looked quite unAmerican. One, very young, had the wide eyes and curving smile of an archaic Apollo, another with marked Slavonic features had a completely shaven head, such as I had only seen on people that had escaped prison or concentration camp.

Some of these in Czechoslovakia (mainly communists) kept their heads shaven even long after the war had ended as a reminder to all of what they had suffered.

My curiosity got the better of my resolution not to try to talk to Tennessee any more.

I turned to him. 'Please tell me who is the unfortunate man with the shaven head?'

'I wouldn't call him particularly unfortunate,' he muttered, 'his name is Yul Brynner.'

Mona rose. 'Don't be too long in joining us,' she smiled as the females trouped out and the men regrouped around the table.

In the hall Mona tucked her arm into mine. 'We must hurry,' she whispered, 'or the women will want to come up too. There's a perfectly good powder-room for them down here. I don't like to have them in my bedroom or bathroom. They mess around with my things, look into my cupboards, examine everything on my dressing-table – creams, scents, bath oils, soaps –

'Of course, they are all old friends,' she added as she shut the lift door and pressed the button, 'but they do presume rather – '

Her bedroom was much as I would have expected, knowing her taste and Eddie's. Large, serene, uncluttered, mainly white except for a few superb pieces of Chippendale furniture. The bed was wide with a high canopy and back of embroidered Chinese silk, birds and flowers entwined in pale muted shades. The bed was prepared for night. The immaculate freshly-ironed sheets were folded back. They were neither flowered nor coloured as had become fashionable. Edged and interset with lace they were of the finest thinnest linen. How rare their quality was I knew. Only in Ireland and in one factory in Czechoslovakia had they been able to weave so fine. A sheet like that, lace and all, could be drawn through a wedding ring.

The two shaggy white Capri dogs slept in their separate baskets surrounded by their toys. They barely raised their heads as we entered, confident, I think, that Mona would take no stranger into her bedroom.

Again there were flowers everywhere. In pots of jade and lapis and rock crystal, their stems gold and enamel, their blossoms and leaves carved from gems.

'All Fabergé?' I asked, amazed.

'Most of it. They are pretty, aren't they? Harrison has old-fashioned ideas about flowers in bedrooms. He thinks the scent is unhealthy. So he gave me these instead. The bathroom's over there, darling, if you need it.'

That too was full of enchanting objects, animals and birds cut out of semi-precious stone. On the dressing-table whatever jars of cream there might have been defied inspection, encased as they were in pots of pale tortoiseshell and gold.

Not that I was in the least bit interested in what cosmetics Mona used. None, I would have thought, since no improving of what nature had blessed her with was imaginable.

'Come, let's rest for a moment,' she said when I returned, drawing me down on a sofa beside her in front of the fire that was burning brightly. 'It will take at least half an hour till the men have finished gossiping in the dining-room.'

She looked at me approvingly.

'You haven't changed at all, darling. Still ever so young. Extraordinary after all you've been through and considering all you have lost. But I know how brave you are. Steinhardt told me.' She hesitated for a moment. 'I'm so glad you sent him to me – he has your welfare very much at heart and so have I!'

'You liked him?'

'But of course.'

'He's fallen desperately in love with you, but then who doesn't?' I said as casually as I could.

She stiffened and sat up rather straight. 'Surely you can't think that. I – ,' then she smiled. 'Darling, I thought him good-looking and intelligent and quite a man. But so does he – rather – '

'May I come in?' Eddie called and walked into the room. He was laughing. 'You won't believe it,' he said, 'I went to see if Harrison wanted anything and found him in his dressing gown playing piquet with the child! It seems she couldn't sleep and that they met on the corridor.'

Seeing the concern on my face Eddie told me not to worry and that they were quite happy together.

'Dinner was all right, I thought,' he said to Mona.

'Except for the pheasants,' she sniffed.

'Stank to high heaven,' he laughed, 'don't know where the chef gets these English ideas that they must hang till they drop.'

'Write it down, darling, or we'll forget.'

Eddie scribbled into a small gold-encased notebook.

'As for you,' he said to me with mock severity, 'what did you do to poor Tennessee? He was absolutely shattered. He asked me who that unpleasant foreign woman was who'd made fun of him. When I told him you were my cousin he nearly fainted. What on earth did you say to offend him?'

'I can't imagine, but he was most unfriendly. I asked him what business he was in and he said he wrote – does he?'

'Do you mean to say you've never heard of Tennessee Williams?'

'No, should I have?'

'But, darling, he's only the most famous young American playwright we have – and his *A Streetcar Named Desire* is the greatest hit ever. It's playing in every theatre all over the world by now,' Mona said.

'Though obviously not known in Czechoslovakia. It doesn't matter,' Eddie added kindly, 'I explained to him how shut away you've been for years from everything of importance and made him understand that it was just ignorance, not malice. He's very sensitive and plagued by self-doubts like all artists, in spite of his success.

'You'll like Gore Vidal much better. He's well on his way to fame too. I must give you his novels to read and I'll bring him to talk to you later. He's brilliant, but in a way more like us. Suffered as much from family tradition as we did in our youth. These things still exist in this country in isolated patches and since things grow bigger here, if not better, than anywhere else, so does family pride and eccentricity, but he's certainly risen above it.'

'Is he by any chance the boy who looks like an archaic Apollo?'

'Why so he does, rather,' Eddie laughed, 'though his wits are far from archaic. Come, darling, we've got to go down,' he said to Mona.

In the drawing-room on the ornate wide staircase in the brown and gold library where some, including Leopold, had settled down to bridge, people grouped and regrouped without formality, laughing and talking, very much at ease with each other and at home in Mona's beautiful house. So was I by then. Many came up to me, remembering when we had last met, to say friendly but ordinary things which I knew were totally non-committal. 'You must come and lunch or dine whenever you are free – Just telephone – ' One never does.

Anita Lobkowitz, more sincerely anxious to be of help, came to tell me, since Leopold had asked her advice at dinner, about a school for the child that she knew of. 'It's in Loredo Park,' she said, 'quite near here. It's a bit old-fashioned and exclusive but that's all for the best these days. And no more expensive than the few good private schools are. It's rather a nice place. Loredo Park used to be very fashionable as a country retreat in my childhood. People had houses there. Even now there's a country club, golf, tennis and riding. I'm sure I could get you in.'

Not being adept at any of these sports it was the last thing I wanted, but the school sounded promising, especially because of its proximity to New York. 'Only an hour's drive,' Anita said, 'and they allow the boarders to come home for weekends.' This in Diana's case, I knew, was all important. Totally uprooted as the child was, any lengthy separation from us was unthinkable for the present.

Anita promised that she would take us out there early next week to see the school.

Eddie came to introduce Gore Vidal to me. His face was indeed curiously of the antique world, like a Greek mask, but by no means a tragic one. The wide eyes were alive with humour and so was the smiling mouth. We talked for a while and I thought him as charming and amusing as Eddie had told me I would. The Professor had obviously not been bored by me at dinner because he rejoined me and even Mr Tennessee Williams gave me a forgiving look. Hans Czernin came to ask me about Czechoslovakia (he still had relations there) and I felt surrounded by friendliness.

Later, we all sat at Mona's feet grouped round her on cushions on the floor. Yul Brynner of the shaven head – I had meanwhile discovered that he was a famous actor and film star, sat cross-legged and sang Russian songs, accompanying himself with a guitar. It was all very pleasant.

But my best moment came towards the end of the evening when Mona called me to her once more.

'Now remember, darling, anything I can do for you I will. I've been thinking. I've always known you were talented but Steinhardt told me you've really become quite an artist in ceramics and that you want to make a living of it here. I know many shops, which I could probably persuade to take whatever you can produce, but what is it actually?'

I didn't dare refer to buttons any more. 'Figurines mostly – statuettes.'

'Portraits?'

'Not really.'

'But why not?'

'Why not indeed?' I asked myself, looking at Mona, so lovely in her green dress, thinking what an exquisite figurine she would make.

'I haven't even bought my kiln yet or clays and glazes,' I said hesitantly, 'but once I'm ready would you pose for me in that green dress?'

'But of course,' she smiled. 'I'd be glad to. We might give the statue to Harrison for Christmas. I never know from year to year what to give

314

him. And if it's any good,' she added, 'I'm sure all my friends will want to be portrayed in ceramics and you will make a fortune. We might even have an exhibition here of your work and have it written up in the papers. Though I loathe publicity, I'd bear it for your sake, darling – now you just go ahead and get yourself fixed up. You'll have to find some sort of studio to work in, I suppose, and I'll do the rest.'

Though I knew I was no artist, at best a gifted amateur and almost totally devoid of technical knowledge, so great was the encouragement that Mona's kindness and confidence gave me that fame and fortune seemed already within reach.

Eddie, when Mona called him to tell him about our plans, tried not to look as sceptical as he must have felt. Not wanting to curb her enthusiasm in case it might upset my hopes, not wanting her to be eventually disappointed in me, he thought it best to joke.

'I thought you only made baroque saints,' he laughed. 'You won't find many models for those in New York. Not among the women anyway. Morally, I wouldn't know, but physically? They all diet till they are as thin as sticks, not a voluptuous curve left anywhere. You'll have to change your style.'

'But you won't want to do them nude, will you?' Mona asked, rather anxiously.

'Of course not. That wouldn't be the point. Either in their favourite dress, jewels and all, or in a sort of fancy dress that stresses their individuality and character.'

Mona looked delighted.

'How would you dress Nin over there? She'd make a neat little figurine.' Nin Ryan was tiny, very dark with large languorous eyes and expressive gestures, her trim boyish figure encased in stiff cloth of gold.

'She makes me think of a Persian miniature, some young prince – I think I'd give her a turban, a tight coat of brocade and those pantaloon trousers. Oriental dress in any case.'

'I doubt she'd appreciate that,' Eddie said, 'even if she is Otto H. Kahn's daughter, she feels very Anglo-Saxon.'

'What about Mita?' Mona asked. 'I'm sure she would pose for you.' I had known Countess Corti in Rome. She and her husband were great friends of Eddie's. She was at present in New York to show and model the famed clothes of one of Italy's best-known designers. She displayed them to perfection.

We watched her as she walked through the room with the grace of a dancer, her tall willowy figure more expressive than her pale face, dark hair severely drawn back from it and pinned on top of her head. Her features, though exquisite, had a sort of dreaming remoteness as if she were listening to the rhythms to which she moved.

'Pavlova or Karsavina, though I've never seen either dance – one of the great Russian ballerinas.'

'Funny you'd say that,' Eddie exclaimed, 'her mother was Russian, though certainly no ballerina, one of the ducal families.'

'Darling, I think we are going to do splendidly,' Mona laughed, 'you are so observant and perceptive.'

It was after two o'clock before I collected Leopold and the sleepy child was brought down.

'I won quite a lot at bridge,' he said, cheerfully crackling bills in his pocket as we were being driven home.

'So did I at piquet,' Diana remarked. She was by now quite wide awake. 'But Mr Williams said he didn't like playing for money, so we played for these, look!' She thrust out her palm. It was full of shimmering shells.

'He collects them. He has thousands, millions perhaps, of them in glass cases and boxes in his rooms. He showed them to me.'

'You know you shouldn't have bothered Mr Williams,' I said, severely. 'How did it happen anyway that you met? I thought you'd been put to sleep in one of the maids' rooms.'

'So I was,' she giggled. 'Miss Rose was very kind. She brought me tea and cake and made me comfortable on her sofa with a rug. She has a very pretty room.'

'And then?'

'She told me to go to sleep and left me. But no one could have slept with the noise coming from downstairs. I could even hear Papi – and someone was singing, I thought, in Czech. Well, I walked out on to the landing just to see what was happening and underneath was this old gentleman in a dressing gown doing the same, leaning over the balustrade also looking down. I suppose he couldn't sleep either. I thought it was only polite to call "good evening". He seemed rather startled.'

'No wonder,' I said. 'Had you any idea who he was?'

'How should I have had?' she said indignantly. 'No one ever told me Auntie Mona had a husband upstairs.'

Leopold laughed. 'And then?' he asked.

'Well, we made friends,' she said. 'I told him who I was and he said his name was Harrison Williams and then he invited me to his rooms full of pictures of sailing ships and beautiful models of yachts. I spent a very pleasant time with him,' she said, 'and he has invited me to visit him at his home in the country on Long Island. He has a beach there full of shells!' She put her head on my shoulder and was soon so fast asleep that the chauffeur had to lift her out of the car when we arrived at our hotel. He carried her in with all the respectful tenderness Italians have for the very young.

Leopold rewarded him with one of the notes he drew from his pocket. Startled at the chauffeur's effusive thanks, I asked Leopold while we were going up in the lift how much he had given the man.

'How should I know?' he laughed. 'They were all green, all the same size and shape. It was too dark to read what was on them.'

Once in our rooms and the child put to bed we poured ourselves quite unnecessary drinks, as one does when one's already slightly drunk.

'What a wonderful evening!' I exclaimed enthusiastically, feeling very cheerful. 'Everyone so kind and anxious to help and advise. Anita even knew of a good boarding-school for Diana.'

'Yes, she told me. But surely you don't seriously want to send the child away?'

'She needs an education.'

'Why? As long as a girl is pretty and pleasing? Do you want her to become a schoolteacher?'

'She will have to earn her living, darling.'

'Nonsense. She'll find a man to support her like every sensible and attractive girl does – as you did.'

There was no arguing that point.

I changed the subject and told him of Mona's plans for my ceramic portraits.

He looked even more dubious than Eddie had. Leopold had never taken my past artistic efforts seriously. Even if I had occasionally sold one or the other of my statues of saints it had been mainly to friends. He probably, quite rightly, believed they bought them out of kindness.

'I will need a studio, of course – a place where I can work undisturbed. Clay makes an awful mess,' I added hastily, not liking the look he gave me, 'and they'd never allow a kiln to be installed in a hotel room. It would be impossible to work here.'

'Surely we won't live in this place for ever? We could get a house or a flat in time. We've only been in America for two days. Aren't you rather hurrying things?'

'I have to,' I declared. 'Otherwise Mona might lose interest. To-morrow I'll go to the addresses the woman in Paris gave me to order a kiln and the materials I will need. The sooner I start the better. I'm sure it won't be too difficult to rent a cheap room near here which I can use.'

'I see,' he said, and I feared that as usual he saw too much, since though I did need a studio I also desperately wanted somewhere I could meet Steinhardt in private when he came to New York. Attack is the best form of defence, I had learnt. 'You've never believed I have any talents,' I accused him.

'Many,' he smiled.

'Well, I'm going to prove that I'm an artist whatever you think. I'll make a fortune, you'll see – ' I knew I had drunk too much and was talking foolishly but I couldn't stop. 'Anyway you know nothing of art, you and all your kind!'

'How true,' he grinned, amused at my outburst.

This infuriated me. 'You seem to take pride in being as ignorant as a savage. All you can do is mock at what you don't understand.'

'All I know is that you are going to have a Godawful hang-over tomorrow,' he said, getting up. 'Goodnight. I'm going to bed. I have an important appointment with the Czech Committee before lunch.'

Was he angry? Even I, who had known and loved him for so many years, could only guess at what he really felt since, in general, he concealed all his emotions behind the mask of a clown. Hardly ever did he lose his temper or quarrel with anyone but on the few occasions on which I'd seen him really angry his rage had been as sudden and terrible as an earthquake. Once I too had felt its force. It was in the early days of my marriage and I had deliberately made him jealous. He wrecked the entire room piece by piece in the hotel in which we were then staying, smashing everything, including me. Next day he had taken me to the hospital to have my broken arm X-rayed and put in plaster, kind and gentle, full of sympathy yet totally ignoring the fact that it was he who had caused my injuries.

I went to wash and undress and crept into the darkened room where the child slept to lie on my bed and think over what I had said to him.

My accusations had been true, for he was indeed not interested in any of the arts except for that of the theatre and that probably only because he knew himself as good a comic actor as any seen on the stage.

To all other art forms – literature, painting, sculpture and music – he remained almost stubbornly indifferent. Partly because most members of his class thought any display of intellectual interest ungentlemanly, but also for personal reasons. He was guarding his image as entertainer. He knew quite well that the comic impact of his seemingly naïve primitive personality would be lessened by any signs of culture.

If asked what books he preferred he would declare he had only read one: *The Bloodsoaked Sandwich on the Cemetery Wall*. The title, of course, his own invention.

If someone rashly enquired as to what poetry he liked he would happily oblige by quoting the most obscene rhymes and limericks. He had an extraordinary memory for anything he thought funny or rude. If questioned as to his taste in paintings he would solemnly mispronounce well-known names like Pisano, Pisanello, stressing a double S, Sodoma, or Archibaldi. Anyone who knows German can guess what he could make them sound like.

He was not unmusical. That is, he could remember a tune correctly but the words of his songs were not those the composer would have chosen.

He delighted in startling and shocking people. Yet he rarely offended. He never attacked anyone personally or mocked their weaknesses or absurdities. And he never overplayed his Rabelaisian role, judging, with canny accuracy, just how much his audience could take. Nor did he become repetitive. Ad-libbing as he always did, even if his jokes were crude, they were original. Of course, his spectacular appearance helped. Giants as well as dwarfs tend to make one laugh.

Why, I thought, had I dared speak as I had, asserting my artistic superiority when I knew he was in his way a better artist than I could ever hope to be? For the simplest of reasons: envy.

He had always overshadowed me. Even if I had been allowed to grow and develop freely in his care it had been as a sapling does under some great tree nourished by its roots and sheltered by its crown. I now wanted to grow on my own.

Steinhardt's affection in the years after the war had given me self-confidence and a taste for power. The goodwill and protection of the American Embassy had been of inestimable value then and much of it had been mine to dispense.

Now in the New World and starting a new life I hoped to prove that I could achieve some personal importance and independence from Steinhardt as well as from Leopold. Not that I could ever imagine wanting to part from either.

But in Leopold's case, what triumph if it should eventually be me who would support him and the child by my work – reversing the past. Could I do it? And, if so, dared I? Would it not mean undermining his pride and self-respect?

I could not sleep. I got up and went into his room. He was in bed but the light was on and he was playing patience, the cards spread out on his blanket.

'I'm sorry I was so aggressive,' I said.

'Probably the effects of this climate. It's supposed to be over-stimulating. That's why all Americans are so restless and always in a hurry. Goodnight.'

I had been dismissed.

❈ 43 ❈

At the end of our first week in New York we had just enough money left to pay our hotel bill. But much had been accomplished. Leopold had been welcomed warmly by the Czech Refugee Committee. Though offered no paying job he had been asked for help in collecting money, clothes, finding work and accommodation for Czechs already in the USA and sponsors for those who hoped to reach it.

'You have such important connections, dear Count, as we all know,' ex-Minister Zenkl had flattered him. 'We need your assistance.'

'I'll have to go to the office most mornings, I suppose,' Leopold said. 'They will give me a secretary. All I will have to do is dictate appeals and sign various petitions for funds. They seem to think my name is still worth something.'

What could I say? That soon we might be in desperate need of help ourselves? But since involvement of some kind with our lost country and responsibility for its people were essential to Leopold's well-being, all I could do was to congratulate him.

I too had in a week's time achieved more than I dared hope. Certainly not due to my own efficiency but thanks to that of a country where it seemed it was only necessary to express a wish for anything and there it was as if by magic delivered at one's door – all one needed was to sign one's name on the bill!

'What a great country,' I thought, 'where business was based on such trust and confidence.'

And with what speed and efficiency requests were understood and satisfied.

It had taken me just one hour, though the taxi drive had been unexpectedly long and expensive, to reach 'Downtown' and to buy everything I needed at Wenger's representative. It was a rather grim-looking district where dark basement store-rooms in narrow dirty streets remained lightless below the shining towers of the office blocks.

Confessing that I was just an amateur I was given expert advice by a gentleman who introduced himself as Mr Adams. I was to deal with him for years to come but I do think that first time he took some advantage of my ignorance, selling me more than I needed. A large kiln, firebrick shelves to go with it, stilts and thermostat were certainly necessary but not the vast amount of glazes and underglazes, colours, liquid gold and silver and large sacks of different clays.

When did I wish delivery? This afternoon or would tomorrow do?

I had to tell him I hadn't even found a studio yet.

'I think I could help you there,' Mr Adams smiled. He was old but his teeth were obviously new. 'I know of one or two studios in Greenwich Village that are available. We meet so many artists here.'

I gave him my address and told him that I wanted something near it, knowing how far the Village was from the Devon.

'Can't I just rent a room?' I asked. 'I don't need much working space since I only make figurines.'

He looked at the kiln. 'You'll need special wiring for that.'

'I thought one just plugged it in like a lamp.'

'You'd blow every fuse in the place.'

'I couldn't have it in an apartment building then?' I asked anxiously.

'Well, it's a bit unusual. Still, I don't really see why not. I guess our electricians could fix it up for you and connect it to the mains. You'd have to have a special meter of course. Sure, it can be done. This is still a free country. One can get away with most everything if one's ready to pay for it and keep one's mouth shut.'

'Do you mean I shouldn't tell the people I rent the place from what I'm going to use it for?'

'I guess not before we've installed your kiln. They might think there was a fire hazard. But once it's all set up according to regulations no one's going to expect you to take that out again. It weighs a ton.'

I thanked him and asked for the bill.

'No sense in paying before we deliver. If you just sign here.' He handed me several pieces of paper.

'But couldn't you tell me the total?'

Purposely I hadn't enquired as to the prices of what I had bought. What would have been the use? It all seemed essential if I was to start work.

The sum I had spent frightened me. 'Of course, if you'd care to pay a small deposit, say a couple of hundreds? You're from the Old Country. I can tell. My father came from Stoke-on-Trent – England.'

I gave him the money.

'Installing the kiln will, I suppose, be extra?'

'Sure,' he said, 'but it won't be much. We do all we can to help our customers.'

As he bowed me out flashing his teeth I thought of the smile on the face of the tiger.

Just a necessary investment, I tried to comfort myself on my way back again by taxi. I had not yet learnt that even millionaires took the subway to get to and from the city. And later when I did use it I was to suffer agonies of claustrophobic fears. Anything underground would always terrify me. If it was a childhood memory of the dark tunnel in Fiume where we had sheltered from imaginary Italian bombs in the First World War or the cellar in the Maltese Palace in Prague to which I had fled so often with the child from the presumed danger of allied and German planes, anything below the earth's surface was to me closely associated with death.

Next day Leopold had gone early to what he was in future in true American fashion to refer to as The Office, and I went in search of my studio, promising the child I wouldn't be away longer than an hour. Understandably she got bored when left alone in the hotel. I walked west towards Sixth Avenue, enquiring in every apartment building I passed for a room to rent. In the third building I tried they said a small apartment was available. Should they telephone the agent? He'd be around, they told me, in no time, which proved true.

A youngish man, over-smartly dressed, took me up by lift to a fifth-floor flat.

'Everything you will want here, honey, and more.' I had grown accustomed to being called 'Honey' in America by complete strangers, on the telephone and in shops, and rather liked it, but somehow I didn't from this young man.

We entered a narrow dark corridor.

'Your kitchen,' he said. There was a two-burner hotplate, a sink and an icebox.

'And this is the lounge. Large, isn't, it?' Since it was completely empty it seemed so and it had a big window.

'Does it face north?' I asked.

'Sure,' he said, 'if that's what you want, honey.'

The floor was covered with shiny linoleum in a pattern imitating parquet and the walls were primrose yellow.

'I've kept the best for the last,' he sniggered. 'This will really surprise you!' He flung open a door and we now contemplated an enormous bed, quilted in the shiniest pink satin, mirrored walls reflecting its voluptuous vulgarity. The light he had switched on glowed rosily from an imitation shell suspended above it.

The room was small and except for some shelves and the built-in cupboards there was nothing but bed. Adjoining was a tiny bathroom also done in pink.

'And all brand new and unused,' the agent declared. 'The chick who decorated it sure had taste – unfortunately she couldn't complete the lounge.'

'She moved somewhere else?'

'You could say so. She passed on.'

'Do you mean she died here – ?'

'No fear. She never even moved in. The bed's not been slept in since it was installed. Nobody claimed it and we saw no reason to pay for removal. It's yours for free if you want the apartment.'

I enquired as to price. It cost per month as much as the Devon did in a week. Central heating was included, only electricity would have to be paid. I gave my address and name, signed some papers. Where it said 'Profession', I wrote 'Artist'. The agent leered. 'Well, you'll find this a very convenient location for your work. Perhaps a small deposit of two weeks' rent in advance?'

I paid and he handed me the keys.

'Glad to have met you,' he said. 'Maybe you'll let me come round and see you some time.'

I inspected my rashly acquired property more closely after he had left. Though the sitting-room window was large it faced other windows across a narrow street. There was no view. I would need some furniture, of course. A large table to work on, a comfortable sofa or two, something to eat on and some chairs for my guests. There was certainly room enough for these and the kiln. Some pots and pans for the kitchen – though I had never cooked anything in my life before, surely it wouldn't be too difficult to learn to make a risotto or a soufflé if I had a guest for lunch?

I returned to the bedroom. This had only a very small window. With difficulty I opened it and looked down a lightless grimy shaft from which unpleasant odours of drains and garbage rose. I shut it quickly and sat down on the bed. The mattress was clean, firm, resilient and undented by use. The walls of looking-glass reflected and re-reflected an ocean of pink and myself at such unfamiliar angles and in such mirrored multitudes that I jumped up, frightened, and fled from the flat.

Arriving at the Devon, I found Leopold and Diana waiting.

'How was the office?' I asked him.

'Expensive,' Leopold said. 'They begged me to contribute to funds for refugees if I possibly could. Well, I gave them a hundred dollars which was all I had in my pocket. I'm broke. How much have you got left?' Since Leopold was liable to be careless with money, always leaving it around, I usually kept larger sums for him.

'Practically none,' I had to confess.

'But how is that possible?'

'Well, buying the kiln and all that and the studio.'

'Do you mean to say you've rented one?'

'It's quite near here and ever so cheap.'

'Well, I'll be damned! Do you, at least, have enough to pay for our lunch?'

I looked in my bag. There were only five dollars left. How could I have been so rash?

The child, disturbed by the concern on our faces, looked from one of us to the other.

'Do you mean we haven't enough money left to even eat?' she asked plaintively.

'Just an accident, darling, just for today.'

She blushed bright red. 'Then be my guests,' she said. 'I've saved twenty-five dollars. I've noticed a place near here called an Automat. Every kind of food in glass cases. All one does is put some cents in the slots and out it comes. We could eat an awful lot there for twenty-five dollars – maybe there's even a jackpot.'

Leopold kissed the top of her head. 'Of course we'll go,' he said, 'and thank you. The time will come, I see, when your mother and I will have to depend on you.'

Meanwhile he turned to me. 'There's no alternative but for your calling Steinhardt and now – '

'But he'll be at lunch,' I demurred.

'Nonsense, it's not even one.'

'Then you'll have to do it,' I said. Even in Prague I had only ventured to call Steinhardt when it seemed imperative to do so. He didn't like

being interrupted when he worked and he had warned me that Dulcie
had friends among the embassy staff who would report that I had
telephoned.

'Besides, it embarrasses me to ask him for money,' I added.

'But why, when it's ours? All right then, I'll call,' Leopold said
impatiently and had the American Embassy in Ottawa on the telephone
within minutes.

I went out of the room. I did not even want to hear what he would
say.

'No trouble at all,' Leopold came to tell me. 'Laurence quite understood. He said he'd wondered how we had managed for so long on so
little. He explained he had only waited with sending it because he had
thought it easier if he helped me open a bank account here. They are
coming next week. Meanwhile he's mailing a cheque for two thousand
this afternoon. He sent you his love –

'And now,' he said to the child, 'will you take us out to lunch?'

We walked through the same street as I had in the morning.

'That's where my studio is,' I pointed up at the dingy apartment
building, having seen how much Leopold's temper had improved,
'and imagine, it even has a tiny bedroom and a bathroom.'

'What on earth for?'

'Well, my models must have somewhere to tidy up and wash their
hands – and at last we can store some of our trunks. You're always
falling over them in the Devon.'

'This is it,' Diana said with pride, guiding us into the large hall of the
Automat. It was indeed an amazing place and its fascination dispelled
my anxiety about Leopold's reaction to my flat. For there in many
hundreds of individual glass cases that formed a long wall every
imaginable delicacy was indeed displayed ready prepared on a plate.
Portions of lobster and crab and prawns and fish fillets and cutlets and
huge steaks, egg dishes of every description and sumptuous creamy
desserts and strawberries, raspberries and cherries in November.

And each dish costing only a few cents. We settled down at an
empty table that had not been easy to find as the place was crowded
and joined the queues foraging for food.

We opened case after case, tempted by what we saw to carry it back;
Leopold, awkwardly balancing because he didn't have his stick and
trying to carry two plates, dropped one but no one seemed to notice.
There were no waiters in sight, only a man at a desk where Diana went
to change her dollar notes into silver and some women in aprons
pouring coffee at the far end of the hall. We heaped our table with

more and more plates and finally sat down to eat, Leopold grumbling that there was no wine, but nevertheless delighted at the great variety of foods.

But alas, like on the ship everything tasted not only the same, because of some preservative, but worse! The meat must have lain too close to the fish, so had the desserts. The lobsters' convincing scarlet appearance in the cases when turned upside down revealed faintly greenish flesh. The steaks were underdone only on their surface, the rest was tough rubber, and the beautiful strawberries were only a layer on top, below was a mouldy mush, and so on.

'I'm afraid I can't eat any more,' Diana sighed, looking at the plates arranged in front of her, 'yet it seems such a waste.' She had learnt to value food in the war.

'Oh, I don't think they'll be wasted,' Leopold said. 'I'm sure they put what one leaves back in the cases. Don't worry if you can't finish it all. Someone else will next year.'

Relieved she smiled. 'But it's a wonderful place, isn't it? We haven't even spent all I had.'

'We are very grateful to you, darling, and have enjoyed it very much.'

'But you've eaten so little, Mummy.'

'I didn't want to mention it, but I've had a rather upset tummy for days,' I excused myself.

'And now indeed you will,' Leopold's mocking glance told me.

Nevertheless we managed to survive the meal.

Next morning Steinhardt's cheque arrived, much to our relief.

For the time being all was well, except for Diana's either sulking or bursting into tears whenever school was mentioned. Only with great difficulty could she be persuaded to at least look at Loredo Park with us.

Edi Lobkowitz drove us there, Anita having excused herself because of a bad cold, but feeling we should apply as soon as possible.

'It's a bit of a snob school but it does make for a better class of children,' Edi said, driving us out of New York in his sports car at a speed that bespoke of the courage he had shown in the African campaign.

Diana sat quiet and fearful but I knew it was not the pace we were being driven at that she minded. I pressed her hand. 'If you don't like it I certainly won't send you there. We will find some other place.'

'I don't want to be sent anywhere,' she answered bitterly.

'It's run rather like an English school, except that it's co-educational,' Edi remarked.

'What, boys and girls together?' Leopold grinned. 'I wish I'd been sent to a school like that in my youth!'

'I know what you think,' Edi laughed, 'but American children mature later than we did. Must be all the milk they drink – Pretty here, isn't it?'

We were indeed passing through what, if one didn't look too closely, seemed like real country, woods and green meadows, small hills and valleys but all as carefully planted, tended, pruned and mown tidy as in a well-kept park.

'You'll be able to ride for miles,' Edi told Diana, turning round when he should not have without slackening speed, 'and there's a fine golf course over there, tennis clubs, swimming pools – everything.'

Because of the war years in which we had not been able to keep horses, Diana had not learnt to ride nor had she ever shown any aptitude or liking for any other sport. She frowned.

He drove us up a steep hill, the road narrow and twisting in hairpin bends between fortress-like crenellated stone walls.

We stopped on a terrace in front of a small castle of astonishing architectural diversity – medieval, gothic, Tudor or Jacobean! A bit of them all.

'It's a little like Castolovice,' the child said, showing some interest.

'It used, of course, to be a private house,' Edi Lobkowitz explained. 'There are several of these pseudo-castles built in the European style in the last century round about here. Not as splendid, of course, as the imitation Rhine castles on the Hudson. They are really amazing and so are the palaces in Newport. Such a pity people are starting to give them up and beginning to prefer those shabby little white wooden houses of an earlier date which was all they could afford to build here before – I mean, if you're rich, and most of them still are, why not show it?'

'I quite agree,' Leopold said.

We passed through a stone portal on which stone lions couched into a courtyard where children were playing a noisy game lying on top of each other on the ground. They rose as we entered. They had been covering a football. They were dressed in grey flannel uniforms, their white shirts soiled, their ties awry, their hair unkempt, but their ruddy faces shiny with sweat and radiant with good health were pleasing.

One taller than the rest blew a whistle. They dispersed. He was a good-looking boy with a ready smile and showed no trace of schoolboy embarrassment as he came to greet us.

'I guess it's the Head you want to see. I'll take you.' On the way he questioned us as to where we were from. I suppose it was obvious to him that we were foreigners. Leopold's large hat and stick alone must have looked unfamiliar. 'Czechoslovakia? My, that must be very far away. What's it like?' Amiable and curious he continued asking us questions.

Diana gave him a sidelong glance.

'It's your turn to tell us something about the school,' I said. 'Do you like it?'

He had led us into a large, rather imposing hall in the Tudor style. 'I guess I wouldn't be here if I didn't.'

'And the Headmaster?' Leopold asked.

'Old Snobby? He's OK. He doesn't bother us much. And if he did, he wouldn't stay long. After all, it's our school, not his.'

Edi Lobkowitz made a vaguely apologetic gesture. 'It's the New World,' he whispered.

'Seems rather like ours used to be – in more privileged times,' Leopold remarked.

Our guide flung open a door, said, 'Hi there – folks to see you,' and left us.

Diana looked after him, if with disapproval or admiration I couldn't judge. So did I. Only later was I to learn how typical of American youth such self-confidence and lack of respect for authority was.

The Headmaster rose from behind his desk, shook hands with us and patted Edi Lobkowitz's shoulder in a chummy way, making it obvious that they were old friends. He poured us sherry out of a cut-glass decanter.

'I think I'll just run down to the club for a minute while you have your talk,' Edi excused himself.

'Yes, of course. You have so many friends there,' the Headmaster smiled.

He was in appearance and speech all one would have expected and hoped for in a man of his position, so much so that he reminded me of a distinguished actor. Everything was just right, his greying hair neither cut too short nor too long, the straight gaze behind simple plain horn-rimmed glasses, the healthy complexion, his rather shabby well-cut tweed coat and his baggy flannel trousers.

He had a fine, deep voice and spoke with practised fluency, occasionally with some humour.

He informed us at first that the school had been bought and was still more or less supported, controlled and owned by what, with a slightly apologetic smile, he called 'our local aristocracy, people of inherited wealth. Families long established in and around Loredo Park, even if many of them now live in New York.' The school had been founded so that the offspring of this élite could be educated without being sent too far from home and housed and cared for in surroundings like those they were accustomed to among children of equal background, wealth and distinction.

'Because of all this, you see,' the Headmaster explained, 'it is only very exceptionally that we venture to take in pupils who do not quite belong to the same category. It's not that we are undemocratic – but neither children of the newly rich, however great their fortunes, nor the children of those, however worthy, who cannot afford a certain living standard are happy here. They don't fit into the family.'

He cleared his throat. 'And there's another thing. Though our educational standards are high, most of our boys go to college from here a too brilliant child might feel itself somewhat held back. We cannot give preferential tuition to those above average intelligence. It would not be fair to the rest of our pupils to be made to feel themselves mentally inferior. Do you understand?'

'Certainly,' I said and had to refrain from adding, 'Only too well.'

'Of course, they have to work hard, but as the old saying goes "All work and no play makes Jack a dull boy." Modern educational methods have proven that children benefit more from learning through games and play than they can from books – but then I must confess that I'm a great believer in sport – a healthy body – '

'*Mens sana in corpore sano*,' Leopold intoned, tapping his stick. I saw he was getting bored by the lengthy monologue.

'Exactly what I was going to say!' the Headmaster exclaimed, not looking too pleased. 'You still have your Latin, I see.'

'Don't!' my eyes pleaded, fixed on Leopold, fearing what might come next. I knew his extraordinary retentive memory for anything rude, even in Latin.

The Headmaster turned to Diana, who had been sitting quietly, her face impassive, staring out of the window, listening, I knew, to all that had been said.

'What is your name, my dear?'

'Countess Diana Sternberg,' she answered coldly.

'Well, perhaps you will allow me to call you Diana – we Americans aren't very good at foreign titles. Do you know Latin too?'

'Only a very little, I'm afraid. Mostly from prayers,' the child said.

'Oh, of course.' The Headmaster's brow wrinkled momentarily but he smoothed it with his hand. 'You would be RCs of course. But we have several children – '

I thought he'd say 'Equally afflicted' but instead he said, 'There are facilities for them to go to the church of their choice – on Sundays. How old are you, Diana?'

'Nearly twelve.'

'Well, perhaps you'd like to see some of the children coming out of class? By the noise they are making it must be "break". If you go through that door there you will probably find them sliding downstairs by way of the banisters and you might meet some of the teachers.'

She didn't budge from her chair.

'We'll be with you in a minute, darling, but please go now.'

Leopold, who hated to see her frightened, got up. 'I'll go with you,' he declared. But this for reasons I well knew, embarrassed her even more.

'Thank you, Papi,' she said with pathetic dignity, 'I'll manage,' and walked out.

'A charming girl. Where did she learn to speak such good English?'

'It's not only taught in America,' Leopold remarked, his patience, I knew, exhausted. 'She speaks German, Czech, some French and Russian.'

'And Latin? Quite a scholar then? Might make our children feel like little dunces – eh?'

He contemplated us both one after the other, the shrewdness of his gaze in no way concealed by his reassuringly schoolteacher-like spectacles.

'I'll be quite frank with you,' he said and laid his hands on his desk. He wore a gold signet ring. 'We now only very rarely accept children here of non-American parentage. We did so in the war for compassionate reasons and have done so occasionally since, but it was not a success. Much as one sympathizes with what some of them have had to endure and suffer, we have found that they were, compared to our clean-minded, healthy, uncomplicated American kids, precociously mature, often uncooperative and unappreciative of our American ideals, in short, a bad influence in the school. Several even needed the attention of expensive analysts – However much one wishes to help those less fortunate we are not a charity institution.'

Leopold rose to his full height and towered over the Headmaster. 'Obviously not,' he said. 'If there should be anything further to discuss I'll leave it to my wife to do so.' He limped out.

'I hope I haven't offended your husband,' the Headmaster said, looking slightly shaken. 'I was just trying to make things clear.'

'So will I then,' I said with some asperity. 'My daughter is perfectly normal, neither precocious nor immature. She suffered at having to leave her home but she is adaptable, sensible and certainly not in need of an analyst.'

'Exactly what I thought when I met her. One learns to size up a child at a glance in my profession. I'm sure she would be a credit to any school. It's just – ' he hesitated ' – well – Princess Lobkowitz has informed me of your misfortunes – and seemed to expect us to reduce our fees in a special case like this. I'm afraid, much as I'd like to help, that's impossible. Our charges are extremely reasonable compared to those of other much less prestigious and famous private schools.'

So that was it.

'Princess Lobkowitz is very kind,' I said, 'but naturally we would expect to pay what everyone else does if we decide to send Diana here. We are not entirely destitute yet.'

'Then forgive me for even having mentioned it. Well, all I can say now is that I will warmly recommend your application to the members of the School Board should you choose to apply for – Diana, wasn't it?' He pushed a large number of papers towards me. 'These forms will have to be filled out and sent in as soon as possible before term begins. I do wish there was time for me to show you round the school,' he said, rising, 'and to introduce some of the teachers to you but most of them will be taking classes now. However Mrs Elliot is acting as housemother for the moment. Though her husband is from Oxford and teaches English, she comes from Vienna. She will certainly make your daughter feel at home. Do ask for her. She'll show you all there is to see of this splendid old house and of our happy family of children.'

He escorted me to the door which I noticed was padded and no wonder, the sounds that met us were ear shattering.

I found Leopold and Diana watching the children, some sliding down the banisters with wild shrieks, others thundering upstairs. Attractive, healthy looking boys and girls, if noisy, I thought. A bell rang and they gradually dispersed.

'*Gottseidank*,' a thin, nervous-looking woman exclaimed, who had been standing next to Leopold. 'A moment's peace! I'm Lotti Elliot and this is Tom, my husband.' He was shortish, a young man, much younger than she was I would have thought, with an ugly, forceful, clever face and a shock of untidy black curls.

'Aren't they hell? No discipline whatsoever,' he said, 'though really they are not a bad lot. Some even have vestiges of brains if one could teach them to use them. But no! It's sport and more sport and nothing but fun and games, lest they complain to their bloody rich parents at being overworked. If their grandparents climbed up the hard way, their descendants are sliding down the softest way they can find – Late for class as usual, Marc!' he called to the tall boy who had welcomed us. Marc grinned amiably, in no way perturbed as he sauntered upstairs.

'What would you like to see?' Mrs Elliot asked. 'Excepting for the classrooms I can show you everything else. The dining-room with refectory tables of solid oak and genuine pieces of linenfold panelling and a great stone fireplace in which no fire is ever lit; the library in which no one ever reads a book; the gym, more popular, where they climb and hang like monkeys most of the time, or the dormitories?' We said we'd like to see these.

She led us upstairs. The girls' dormitories were all one would have wished for even in a well-run country house. Large and very clean and with no more than two beds in each room, bedspreads and curtains of flowered chintz, befrilled dressing-tables with mirrors above.

The rooms were gay with toys, Teddy bears and other stuffed animals and dolls of all sizes.

'The boys' dormitories are higher up, in the hope that they won't climb out of the windows,' Mrs Elliot laughed. 'We live right at the top in the attics, but come and see. It's rather *gemüethlich*, and I will make you some coffee. It's been a long time since I've seen anyone who knows Vienna and Prague. My grandmother came from Czechoslovakia.'

In the large beamed attic that ran the full length of the top of the house, part of the roof had been replaced by glass windows through which the sun poured on to flowers and herbs in pots and boxes. There was scarcely any furniture in the big room except for a desk and a large couch covered with an Indian rug. Books and pillows littered the floor and the white-washed walls were covered with a great variety of prints, reproductions of old masters, maps, pictures of animals, birds and flowers and a few primitive paintings, obviously done by children.

'Tom teaches some of his more intelligent pupils up here. They learn much better, of course, when separated from the others.'

She went to a small stove and brewed coffee, then served it in a hand-painted little pot with matching paper-thin china cups.

'*Alt Wien?*' I noticed.

She smiled. 'I still have a few things left to remind me of home.'

'Are you happy here?' Leopold asked, who had seated himself in the only chair available while we lay on what must have been the Elliots' bed. 'That is perhaps too big a word – content would be better.'

From then on we spoke German. She told us that she had met her husband in Vienna where, being a qualified language teacher, she had given him lessons. 'He was so young,' she said, 'so innocent. He insisted we must get married. He took me to Oxford but life was hard there. He had so many friends and I saw so little of him and we had no money. What we earned by teaching was not enough to live on. Then this offer came, they pay well, and we thought we'd try it for a year or so – and here we are. Tom misses Oxford terribly at times. There is no one to whom he can talk here. The other teachers are nice friendly people, but – '

'And the Headmaster?'

'Oh him! He doesn't bother us much as long as we don't bother him. He doesn't even live here. He has his own house near the country club. We really only see him on special occasions when the School Board meets or for the end of term prize-giving when he makes a fine speech. But he deals with the parents, the school's finances, engages the teachers and dismisses them and decides which are suitable school applicants. Tom and I are virtually in charge of the children by now. The other teachers are only too glad of someone who can impose some sort of discipline. You wouldn't believe it how intimidated American parents and teachers are by children and no wonder. A child of ten will stand up and frankly tell his parents what he thinks of them and their views and principles and refuse to co-operate if in any way his wishes are not indulged or if he feels in any way frustrated.'

'They must be monsters,' I said.

Her brown eyes crinkled with amusement. 'Not really. I've never met happier, more self-confident or more contented children. Since no one dares impose anything on them they don't like, they have never learnt to hate or fear. Since they get everything they want they are devoid of envy and kind and generous towards each other as European children have never learnt to be.'

'But surely that would only apply to those of the richer classes who can afford to indulge their children in every way?'

'Not really because all American children have the same tastes, rich or poor, which are easily satisfied and quite cheap: Coca Cola, chewing gum, ice creams, hamburgers and frankfurters and an occasional movie or ball game – that's the lot.

'If I had a child I would like it to grow up here – so free of all the complexities and frustrations and even the tortured intelligence of Europeans.'

She drew Diana towards her, encircling her and holding her close.

'You'll be happy here, I know,' she said.

Whatever surprise the child may have felt at this unexpected embrace I could see she liked it. She did not draw away. It was not the first time either that I'd noticed how she didn't mind being kissed and cuddled and now, as always, it made me feel guilty. Like every only-child she had needed the reassurance of tangible affection of love expressed by touch and caress. But once she was no more a baby but a growing girl, a kiss on the forehead in the morning and evening was all I had given her. It had not seemed right to me to indulge myself in physical, if maternal, tenderness with which I'd seen many mothers overwhelm their children beyond babyhood. And yet I knew she missed it. All I could hope for was that one day she would understand that it had been respect for her as a person and not lack of love that was the reason for my physical coldness.

'You must be very fond of children,' Leopold remarked, watching the tender embrace with some surprise.

'But of course,' Mrs Elliot said, 'I would have given anything to have a daughter of my own just like yours. She's so pretty and sweet –'

A girl with flying hair rushed into the room.

'There's a man who says he's a prince downstairs. I couldn't understand his name.' She was either very much out of breath or choking with laughter. 'He's looking for a count and countess.

'We'll be down in a minute. Diana, this is Peggy, one of our best pupils and the untidiest girl in school. You'd be in the same classroom, I imagine.' The children shook hands and by the time we got downstairs must have achieved some degree of intimacy.

'Look here, Mrs Elliot, couldn't Diana and I be room-mates, please?' the tall fair girl asked.

'But what about Veronica?'

'She's leaving.'

'That's the first I've heard of it.'

'I guess it won't be the last. She's convinced her parents she will grow a brain tumour from overwork – so home she goes.'

Mrs Elliot made a helpless explanatory gesture. We thanked her and told her we would let her know our decision as soon as possible but by the warm look she and Diana exchanged as they parted I knew it had already been made for us.

44

The Williamses had left for Long Island. So had Eddie. Mona needed a fortnight there to see to the replanting of the gardens before it grew too cold, he told me. He telephoned every day though to enquire if we were all right. He was amazed when I said I had rented a studio and would soon start work.

'Mona wants you to come and see this place. What about Wednesday for lunch? I'll come and fetch you with the car. We might have a quick look at your studio. I could meet you there and then pick up Leopold and Diana afterwards. What's its address?'

'No. 134 58th Street.'

'East or West?'

'West, I think, since it's quite near here.'

'Oh dear!' Eddie exclaimed. 'I should have warned you to go no farther west!'

'But why?'

The telephone made odd sounds. 'It's only Micky barking. It's just that it's not a very respectable district. It's where most of the call girls live – so, convenient for the park and Fifth Avenue.'

'That's what I thought too.'

'Well, after all, how should you know? I'll be there at eleven.'

It was not without anxiety that I waited for him that Wednesday morning in my studio. That he must not see the bedroom I knew. But there was no key with which to lock it. I pushed a packing-case against its door. In the primrose-coloured lounge in which there was not a chair to sit on and certainly no facilities for lounging, the big black kiln stood like an upright coffin. It had been connected to the mains in the basement and wired up through five floors in a day. How the small lift could have sustained its weight and why the lounge didn't collapse under it was beyond my knowledge. Still, there it was in working order. I had even ventured to turn it on, having carefully studied the instructions. But the moment there had been a red glow visible through the peephole I had been frightened and had switched it off. Bags of clay and tins of glazes, boxes full of a vast assortment of small jars and bottles all neatly labelled as in an apothecary's shop filled the apartment.

There was a sudden startling buzzing sound. No warning from the kiln, I ascertained. The main switch was off.

A bang at the door and Eddie's voice reassured me. I didn't know I had a doorbell. My first visitor, I thought.

'Well, this is it, darling!' I led him into the lounge, hoping he wouldn't notice the so-called kitchen in the corridor.

'The window faces north, giving the best light possible.' It happened to be rather a dismally grey day. The primrose walls had turned a dull mustard and the window was dark with rain or dirt.

'As you see, I'm fully equipped to start work. Look at the kiln!'

Eddie did. 'It's large,' he remarked.

'Not really.' I opened the heavily hinged door. 'Look, the firing chamber is just big enough for a human head.'

'Gracious,' he said, drawing back to a safe distance, nevertheless peering with interest into the wired cavity with its shelves.

'I'm going to do Mona first, or so I hope.'

'There isn't any danger, is there?' he asked anxiously.

'Not if one's careful.'

He contemplated the room. Bare, except for the kiln and the packing-cases. 'Does one make ceramics sitting on the floor?' he asked puzzled.

'No, of course not. I will need a table and some chairs. Just ordinary – '

'Oh, you can find those, even extraordinary, in second-hand shops here quite cheap. When things get a bit outworn or faded or shabby whatever their quality once was, Americans throw them out, just when they have reached the mellow condition in which Europeans start to appreciate them. You've got running water I see,' he said, having discovered the sink. 'But where, may I ask, will you pee? In it? After all, you can't rush back to the Devon Hotel every time – '

'There is a bathroom – '

'In there I guess. Let's have a look,' and Eddie had shifted the cases and opened the bedroom door before I could think of some way to stop him.

'Oh my God!' I heard him exclaim and the thump with which he must have landed on the bed. I found him doubled up on the pink satin cover so convulsed with laughter that he couldn't speak. 'Oh, ho, oh,' he moaned, wiping the tears from his eyes and sat up to see the multitude of laughing Eddies reflected in the mirrored walls. He collapsed once more. 'I've only been in a brothel once to oblige a friend who was scared,' he gasped, 'I never went to the bedrooms but – Has Leopold seen this?'

'No,' I had to admit.

'Well, I hope he never will or anyone else. Not only is this the tarts' district as everyone knows, but this room – You ought to be ashamed of yourself. Look at that obscene lamp casting its rosy glow!' He burst out laughing once more.

'Well, I know it's not in the best of taste,' I said defiantly, 'but I intend changing it.' (I had no intention of doing so whatsoever.) 'After all it's not me that decorated it.'

'Where is the girl that did? Did you meet her?'

'No, I only saw the agent. He told me she had passed on.'

'Passed out I would have thought. I like large beds but this is big enough for ten. One can imagine monstrous orgies.' He grimaced at himself in the mirror.

'But no one's ever lain in it, Eddie – not even me.'

'Well, it will have to be removed. What do you want a bed for anyway?'

'I thought if Leopold ever travelled, he may have to, you know, for the Refugee Committee, and the child was at school, it would be senseless to keep the expensive apartment in the Devon. I could live here.'

'All it needs is a red light over your front door. Darling, seriously, this won't do at all. For how long have you rented it?'

'For a year,' I confessed. 'It wouldn't have been worthwhile having the kiln installed otherwise.'

'So you are stuck with it! I always knew you were crazy but this really is the limit! How could you have imagined Mona or any of her friends for that matter coming to a place like this to pose for you?'

'They don't have to see the bedroom.'

'And what if they have to go to the bathroom? I suppose that's it?' He swung himself off the bed and opened the mirrored door. 'More pink,' he exclaimed, 'also the bidet! Come, let's get out of here. It's starting to give even me lewd ideas. Besides, it's late – '

We took the lift down. In my nervousness I pressed the wrong button and we landed in the cellar.

'Most unfortunate that you ever had to leave Czechoslovakia!' Eddie said unkindly, pressing a knob that brought us into the narrow entrance hall and finally out into the street.

The cream-coloured Rolls was waiting with Bridges at the wheel.

'We will be late for lunch, sir,' the chauffeur warned.

'I'm sorry, Bridges. Slight family problems. Now just to the Devon and we can go home.'

'I'll have to drive round the block, sir.'

'But it's only two steps – '

'I can't reverse in this street, sir.'

Once in the car Eddie said, 'Now that you're stuck with the ghastly place all we can do is get a lot of chintz or cotton and drape it over those mirrors and the bed. Mona has lots of stuff stored which she ordered and then didn't like. I know she'll let you have some. You can sew, can't you, and tack things up with a hammer and nails?'

'Darling, why do you ask when we've done all those things together dozens of times? Remember when we had to rehang your grandfather's room in Schoenhausen?'

'True. One rather forgets one's manual gifts in this country where everything is ready-made. Most Americans can't even sew on a button or hang up a picture.'

We found Leopold leaning on his stick in front of the Devon and Diana very smart in her new blue dress and coat and little hat to match, all from Sacks.

The sky cleared as we drove out of New York, the wide, smooth, shiny roads curving, circling, bridging, by-passing and overpassing each other. There were heights from which one could see it all like a gigantic map or a game of snakes and ladders, bright streams of multi-coloured cars flowing smoothly in every direction but never meeting.

'It's like in dreams,' Diana said.

'Or nightmares,' Eddie said. 'I never drive here myself if I can help it. I'm too afraid to fall asleep.'

He asked Leopold about his new job.

'It makes no sense to me,' Leopold told him. 'All we do in that office is sit around and talk about the past and of who did what and of why everything went wrong. Nothing but recriminations and accusation, everyone blaming someone else for the disaster. There's no money. However many letters we send out to Americans of Czech origin appealing for help only one in a hundred brings in a few dollars, just enough to keep the Committee going, but not sufficient to assist thousands of refugees not only here but in Europe. I get cramps in my hand from signing my name so often. They believe I have an inter-national reputation! Well, so I once had – but it was for giving not for begging. Besides I need a paying job.'

'Oh, we'll find something,' Eddie said, comfortingly, though I knew he didn't believe we would. He was very fond of Leopold, amused by his originality and in a way impressed by his total lack of inhibitions and the fact that conventions that restrained lesser human beings didn't seem to exist for him.

Still both Eddie and I knew that because of his unique personality no subordinate position would be able to contain him and for a job at the top he was equally ill-equipped through his lack of education.

'Perhaps you could manage a hotel like Serge Obolensky does,' Eddie suggested. 'He's made a great success of it. It can't be more difficult than looking after Castolovice.'

'I don't think my leg would stand up to it any more, but I wouldn't mind being a barman. I could sit most of the time. My arms are certainly long enough to reach the bottles.'

'Or you might go into the films,' Eddie laughed. 'I'm sure you'd make a fortune.'

'What with my ugly face?'

'Well, not all comic actors are beauties.'

Leopold pondered this. 'The trouble is that I'm not funny in English.'

'Only rude, Papi,' Diana said primly.

'As a matter of fact I have been offered a very well-paying job.'

'But how splendid!' Eddie exclaimed, surprised.

'You never told me, darling,' I reproached him.

'Because I was too ashamed to tell you. It was offered to a colleague of mine in the office and even he – with four small children to keep – refused to accept it. He was approached by a man from the CIA. It seems they want someone reliable to befriend recently-arrived refugees from communist-ruled countries and to report on how far they have been indoctrinated, what their real loyalties are and so on. He thought I'd be just the right person since I inspire confidence.'

'But that's like spying!' I exclaimed, shocked. 'Poor people. Haven't they suffered enough? Even if they became communist either from fear or opportunism or even idealism they must have been horribly dis-illusioned to leave their country and to risk escape and come here expecting freedom, not investigation or persecution.'

Leopold grinned. 'I'm not certain I won't take the job. That I'm a brilliant misinformer I know from experience.'

'I wouldn't touch it,' Eddie said, looking worried. 'You'd get into awful trouble. Once there is a witch hunt on in this country all one can do is try and not get involved.'

'I was only joking,' Leopold said. 'I'd rather be shot than become an informer. There's another possibility, equally profitable, more so perhaps and less unpleasant. I met an old friend of mine on Fifth Avenue, Veruska. She used to work in Prague. She must be over forty now, but in splendid condition and doing very well. She told me she makes three hundred dollars for two to three hours' morning work, has the rest of the day and the night free.'

'At what?' Diana asked, her interest in money having grown with our complaints at the lack of it.

Leopold looked slightly disconcerted. 'She's a masseuse,' he said after a moment's thought, 'and exercises elderly gentlemen before they go to their offices in the morning.'

'Leopold, really,' Eddie warned, shaking with laughter.

'She offered me twenty per cent of her earnings if I'd look after her affairs, just advise her and cheer her up. She's homesick and so are all the Czech girls in the office. They would, I know, be only too grateful for the same arrangement. Now, if I had only five girls working at three hundred dollars a day under my protection at twenty per cent, why we'd have – ? Count it out, Diana, you are better at it than I.'

'Three hundred dollars a day, Papi,' she said, joyfully.

'Leopold, you are terrible,' Eddie said, thinking he was joking. I was not so sure.

When we reached Long Island the roads narrowed into lanes and there were many trees, though bare of foliage, still beautiful, the intricate lace of their branches silhouetted against the clear sky. It smelt of autumn, of dead leaves and wet earth. All of us, country born and bred, sniffed appreciatively.

Beyond wide expanses of smooth lawns big houses surrounded by trees and shrubs shone whitely at intervals.

'Do you know all the people that live around here?' Leopold asked.

'Only a few,' Eddie said, 'mostly old friends of Harrison's, but they are very old by now. Also, however social Mona's life is in town, here and in Capri she tries to escape.'

'Look!' Diana cried, 'the sea!'

There was indeed a brief glimpse of blue beyond the trees.

'It's called the Sound,' Eddie told her, but noticing her look of disappointment he reassured her. 'It is part of the sea.'

We turned into a lodge gate, cottages, stables and greenhouses to right and left, into parklike grounds, the drive walled by tall, clipped yew hedges.

'It used to lead to the house,' Eddie explained, 'but the house has been pulled down. Mona grows lavender in what is left of its foundations. It was a nice big Edwardian country house.'

'Beyond repair?' Leopold asked, interested, since he had been used to spending a good part of his annual income on restoring castles and churches at home.

'Not at all,' Eddie laughed. 'There was nothing wrong with it, except that Mona didn't like it and wanted to enlarge her garden, so Harrison had it removed. I warn you, where they live now is no house at all. It used to be the old indoor squash and tennis courts and swimming pool, all under a tin roof, over which Mona has persuaded so much ivy to grow that the whole thing looks like a green mountain. Inside – well – you'll see.'

We stopped at a door set in a high wall overgrown with creepers.

'There are really only two big rooms. Mona and Harrison's bedrooms and bathrooms are tiny and the servants live in the cottages,' Eddie told us, 'and so do I.' He led us through a small hall into a long narrow room, its walls and ceiling dim silver metal, interpersed with painted panels that reached from floor to ceiling, opening like windows on to a world of fantasies.

'Goya? Tiepolo?' I asked, confused.

'No, Sert,' Eddie explained. 'He made a fortune in America as a decorative artist. But I like his paintings. An equally fasionable French designer did this room. Very "Art Nouveau".'

On the panels acrobats and dancers, tumblers and wrestlers, monkeys and clowns were at play painted in rich deep colours. Curtains of linked silver chains draped the windows and a door opened on to a small terrace with steps leading into a garden entirely roofed with glass.

High walls were covered with climbing plants. Orange and lemon trees in ornamental pots were grouped round a blue pool over which a fountain played. Brightly coloured tropical birds flashed in and out of the foliage. Gardenias and camellias and orchids bloomed everywhere.

'But this is paradise!' I exclaimed.

'I thought you'd like it,' Eddie said. 'We often sit here in the evening and watch the birds.'

'Oh, may I go down and look at them?' Diana pleaded, equally enchanted.

'Of course.' He gave her a bag of bird seed. 'They are quite tame. They will feed from your hand.'

We left her and Eddie led us into the largest room I think I've ever seen, larger than the ballroom in Emkendorf and wider, if not longer, than the great salon in Castolovice.

'What marvellous colours, Eddie!'

'Yes, I know. I think it's the most successful room Mona's ever done. There's nothing to equal it even in the Palm Beach house. She has an incredible gift of combining colours, learnt from the flowers, I suppose, that she's always arranging. But usually she likes things more muted. Only here, where it can be very grey on winter days outside, she wanted the room to glow. For colours she simply picked all the shades of the rainbow.' It was true, merging in perfect harmony were orange and rose and violet and blue, yellow and green.

'Of course, the carpets help,' Eddie added. 'They are Chinese. Aren't they wonderful? They are supposed to have come from the Old Summer Palace in Peking before it was burnt down. So does some of the furniture – ' Richly carved chests, cabinets and screens with the satiny sheen of old lacquer, coral and gold stood between wide sofas and comfortable chairs and many that looked less comfortable but were enchanting, eighteenth-century pieces of *chinoiserie*. An enormous table that didn't even seem big, so large was the room, was heaped with books and magazines, a smaller one, laid for lunch, stood in front of french windows that overlooked lawns, beach and the sea.

'Have a drink, Leopold?' Eddie offered, opening a cabinet. 'We can have another later but we've got to go and undig Mona out of the garden now or we'll never have any lunch.'

We found her on all fours in a rock garden, the two dogs barking defensively as we approached. She jumped up, her face rosy with exertion, her silver hair standing on end. 'I was trying to plant some bulbs,' she explained, 'but these brutes dig them out the moment I put them in. They think it's a game.'

She waved her gloved hands. 'I can't even kiss you, darlings, I'm so dirty. Let's look for Harrison. Micky, go find! Go find!' The dog did indeed lead the way to a long stretch of closely mown lawn where Harrison's tall thin figure was visible swinging a golf club.

He greeted us. He looked old and frail, I thought. He had aged a lot since I'd seen him last.

'I've got to clean up,' Mona called and started to run. With her narrow hips, tight blue jeans and the rough fisherman's jersey she was wearing she looked like a boy.

Both Harrison and Eddie watched her sprinting towards the house with equal amused tenderness, I thought.

We had more drinks and a delicious lunch but its gaiety was marred by Diana saying she had found a dead bird in the winter garden. She was pale and shaken and wouldn't eat. She had, I knew, a horror of dead birds since one of her pets had died.

'Poor little thing,' Mona sighed. I wasn't certain if she was pitying Diana or the bird.

'Probably died of old age,' Eddie said cheerfully. 'After all, it's natural to do so.'

I don't know if Harrison resented this remark. In any case, he was very silent at lunch. Efforts of Leopold to interest him in the problems of Czech refugees, which I felt to be rather embarrassing since they hinted at assistance, were politely ignored by him. I talked to Mona and Eddie about Capri and heard with a pang of disappointment that they were going there in March.

'I simply can't bear to miss the spring there, darling, but I'll be back for a while in June – Come, let's have coffee near the fire.'

We rose.

Harrison looked down at the child with an expression of wry humour.

'Do you drink coffee, Countess Diana?'

'I do not, Mr Williams.'

'Then may I escort you to the beach and show you some of our local shells?'

'I will be delighted, Mr Williams,' she answered as formally, and off they went.

Mona laughed. 'Harrison's not easily charmed,' she said. 'All his life he's had to defend himself from being taken advantage of. I think that's why he is so fond of children – they need so little to be made happy. Darling, now what about our portrait? We've to get it done before Christmas and the exhibition before March. Can you do it?'

'Of course,' I said. 'I'm fully equipped. I have a kiln and a studio.' I evaded Eddie's anxious glance.

'And when must I sit? I warn you, I'm the despair of portrait painters, photographers and dressmakers. I get so impatient.'

'But you don't have to sit for me, Mona. I know your face by heart. All I need is to make a few notes. I could do it now if Eddie will bring me a pencil and paper.'

'Leopold, if you'd like to rest in my cottage for a while, it is the first one just round the corner. I'll join you when this is over,' Eddie said.

Leopold went, looking pleased. I think he was glad to escape. He was rather awkward with Mona, thinking her perhaps too delicate for his earthy humour.

'I thought you'd make a drawing,' Eddie said, looking over my shoulder. 'What on earth are those dots and squirls for and why do you hold up the pencil and squint at Mona like that?'

'Making measurements. It won't take long,' I reassured her and was rewarded by a smile of relief.

'And what's that you're writing? "Left eyebrow slightly higher than right! Ears, remarkably small and flat," ' Eddie read. 'What does that line mean?'

'It's how the jaw curves. I can't explain now, I have to concentrate. Please stop talking.'

After half an hour I thought I had memorized enough.

'Is that all?' Mona exclaimed, delighted, 'and I can go back and work in the garden?'

'I might need a few photographs.'

'Oh, Eddie has hundreds in his rooms. He will give you whatever you want. I'll say goodbye now, darling. I must get those bulbs in before it's too dark.'

'I didn't even thank her properly, or Harrison,' I complained to Eddie.

'Don't worry. I'll tell them. Anyway, he's gone to sleep. I heard him go to his room.' We found Diana outside. She was carrying a large basket of pale yellow and pink shells and looked happy.

We found Leopold equally content lying on Eddie's bed, leafing through some magazines that looked like *Men Only*. The cottage was as attractive and as perfectly furnished as everything in which Eddie lived always was. There were drawings and photographs of Mona everywhere.

'The best are by Cecil Beaton,' Eddie said. 'He's a great friend of ours and since he's such fun Mona doesn't mind sitting for him. I think he brings out most of what's so flower-like about her beauty. Here, take these! I don't want to hurry you but Bridges is waiting and I've got to help her in the garden.'

✖ 45 ✖

I had written to Steinhardt several times in the last weeks, reporting the little we had achieved, but telling him how many kind and helpful friends we had found.

I had written carefully. I knew Steinhardt only worked at the embassy and lived in a house of Dulcie's choice in the suburbs of Ottawa. I wasn't certain the mail might not reach her first. He had answered my letters, enquiring why I wrote so coldly, saying he was doing all he could to get to New York as soon as possible but that since Dulcie insisted on coming with him and had not been able to travel because of not feeling well, they had been delayed.

He said it was quite safe to write to the embassy or even to telephone. 'Ottawa is not Prague where everything was bugged and letters photostated,' he wrote. 'However, more passionate declarations of affection for which I very much hope, might be better given personally next week,' he added. 'One can never be quite sure about letters.'

I answered briefly, giving him the telephone number and address of my studio, saying I worked there most mornings, which was true by then.

Often I took the child with me. She would read or listen to the radio or play the patiences Leopold had taught her while I experimented.

At first I only fired pieces of clay to ascertain their colour and degree of hardness after they came out of the kiln, the same with glazes painted on them later and re-fired at a lower temperature.

Then I started on the figurine of Mona. It was about twelve inches high, looked remarkably like her and was graceful and pretty, but I knew only too well the difficulties ahead – the clay would shrink as it dried and distort the likeness, the figure, if not sufficiently hollowed out, would crack in the kiln and I'd have to start all over again. I had bought a table and chairs, some kitchenware and had several of the trunks from the Devon with things we didn't immediately need brought over so as to make room there for those of our more valuable belongings Steinhardt had promised to bring.

Leopold disliked my absences, especially in the early morning, when he depended on me to make his tea.

For a couple of days he seemed to manage quite well, then he called me at the studio. His voice sounded hoarse and strange.

'Please come immediately.'

'What's the matter?'

'The kettle's caught fire and so did the room.'

'Oh, my God! Are you hurt, darling?'

'No, it's just that the smoke is unpleasant and so is the hotel manager.'

'What's wrong?' the child asked, seeing my face.

'Only that Papi has set the hotel on fire!'

We rushed over to the Devon. Several fire engines were drawn up in front of it, a ladder and a hose were being lowered from our rooms through the windows, but there were neither smoke nor flames visible.

We found our sitting-room crowded with hotel staff trying to mop up while the manager contemplated the charred sofa, the tattered, blackened remains of the curtains and the sodden carpet.

He turned to Leopold who though covered with soot seemed unharmed and quite unperturbed.

'You might have burnt the whole place down – lives might have been lost – and all because of a cup of tea! Well, it may prove to have been the most costly one you've ever hoped to drink.'

This was very worrying. 'But isn't the hotel insured against fire?' I asked him.

'Naturally, but not against people cooking in our rooms. It's against all regulations.' He stalked out, the staff followed with pails and mops.

'But what did you do?' I asked Leopold.

He looked mildly penitent, then started to laugh.

'I plugged in the kettle,' he said, 'just as you told me to, then went back to sleep. When I woke there was an awful lot of smoke coming from this room and the curtains were burning. But it was me who put the fire out, not the fire brigade,' he added.

'How?' I asked. 'Did you find an extinguisher?'

'No, but at least thirty large soda syphons in Mona's bar. All I needed to do was squirt – '

'Oh, darling,' I didn't know whether to laugh or to cry 'at least you are safe.'

'Yes, but the kettle's ruined. Its bottom was burnt right through.'

Except for that there was, on closer inspection, not very much damage done.

Our bedrooms though reeking of smoke were untouched. What with all our trunks it would have been disastrous had the flames spread.

'Will they want us to leave?' Diana asked anxiously.

'I don't think so,' Leopold grinned. 'After all it was me that saved their hotel.'

As a matter of fact the management was very decent, gave us a new sofa and curtains and only insisted that no more tea should be brewed. On the day the Steinhardts arrived in New York everything was in order again. They had come in their private plane and were staying at the Hotel Plaza. There had been a telephone call from Ottawa saying their Excellencies expected us for lunch.

Not much to my surprise, knowing Dulcie's liking for unannounced visits, she walked into our sitting-room at twelve that morning. 'I've just arrived,' she said. 'Laurence declared he had to go straight to his office so I thought I'd come and see how you live.' She was bundled as usual in furs and her small face peered foxily out of the hood. Her gaze went to the bedroom doors which were closed.

'No, Laurence is not hiding in there,' I would have liked to have reassured her. How often in Prague had she come to our apartment unexpectedly too but since she couldn't get in without ringing the door-bell there had always been time for me to hide anyone I didn't want her to meet.

Leopold hugged and kissed her as he always had, genuinely pleased to see her again. So in a way was I.

I knew from my own observation and from what Steinhardt had told me that though suspicious Dulcie did not want to know the truth even if she guessed it.

If there were times when she implied that she knew all, it was because intimidating me gave her a sense of power and superiority, but never would she have risked a direct accusation for fear I might not deny it.

In the years in Czechoslovakia in which we had seen each other almost daily she and I had been bound to each other like opponents in an interminable chess game in which neither could win or lose. We were too well matched. All moves had their countermoves, each of us trying to foresee and forestall the next. Both of us rather enjoyed the game but short of upsetting the board by carelessness or anger which neither of us could risk it had always ended in a draw.

'And where is little Diana?' she asked.

'In here,' I said opening my bedroom door. The child was lying on her bed reading. She jumped up politely.

'And how you have grown!' The usual inevitable and unanswerable comment that children are accustomed to.

Diana, though I knew she liked Steinhardt and Dulcie Anne, was not fond of the ambassadress. For an unfair reason. Dulcie long ago in Castolovice had stepped, certainly unintentionally, on Bibi's paw. Bibi, Diana's beloved little pug, had protested loudly and feigned lameness for days.

'And so you sleep here with your dear mother?'

'Yes, not with my dear father.'

Leopold's bedroom and the bathroom were inspected next. Satisfied, Dulcie returned to the sitting-room with us.

'Have a drink, Dulcie,' Leopold offered, opening Mona's cabinet.

'But I drink nothing but Vichy water, don't you remember?'

'And champagne,' Leopold said, taking a bottle out of the icebox.

'Just a glass now and then,' she protested, sipping hers with relish.

'Mud in your eye,' Leopold said, lifting his glass.

Dulcie giggled. 'You are awful, Leopold! One doesn't say that in polite society and certainly not to a lady.'

'But I thought it was the usual American toast.'

'Only among the lower classes – Well, well, orchids and champagne,' she commented. Since orchids last longer than any other cut flower, Mona's had survived.

'Not bad under the circumstances.'

'People have been very kind to us since we've arrived in New York. We've found many friends,' I said hastily.

'No doubt you will soon be forgetting the Steinhardts,' she answered with feigned regret I thought.

'Never,' I exclaimed fiercely. 'We owe you everything.'

'I suppose that's true,' she said pensively. 'Doesn't this apartment cost rather a lot?'

'Of course it does,' Leopold said, 'but one must live somewhere.'

'Laurence always thinks you both would be much happier if you settled in the country. It would be so much cheaper too. A small farm in Pennsylvania or New York State or Vermont. You could well afford to buy one with what he saved for you.'

Could she be telling the truth? I doubted it.

'Yes, a farm would be nice,' I countered, 'but I was rather thinking of Canada.'

Dulcie looked startled. 'Why that?' she asked.

'Because it would be nice to be near you,' I said, 'and for another reason. My mother bought some land there long before I was born. It was confiscated in the two world wars and the taxes were never paid but there might be something left. I thought I'd ask the ambassador to help me put in a claim for my two brothers and myself.'

'You never mentioned this in Czechoslovakia,' Dulcie reproached.

'It didn't seem very important then but it might be now.'

'It's true, Dulcie,' Leopold said, seeing her disbelief.

Slightly ruffled she adjusted her furs. 'Well, I'll be seeing you in half an hour,' she said, rising from her chair.

'Shall I call a taxi?' Leopold asked.

'No, I walked here and I'll walk back,' she declared bravely. Though I knew Dulcie never put a foot to the ground if she didn't have to I also knew how much it would have upset her to pay a taxi for such a short distance.

She left.

The Steinhardts' apartment in the Plaza was what in Europe would have been called the Royal Suite. Dulcie Anne, looking very pretty, greeted us with her usual quiet grace and took charge of Diana.

Steinhardt gave me the briefest of friendly hugs and from then on talked only to Leopold. That it had to be so I knew. Both he and I didn't like meeting in public after a long separation without having managed some hours in private before. Otherwise even the most casual glances became fixed, searched too deep or too long. Even hands had to be kept under stern control lest they touch and clasp. All very ridiculous, we knew, but so is passion.

I told Dulcie about Mona's party and house and kept her interested all through lunch which, thanks to oysters almost too large to swallow without a shudder of delighted disgust, rare roast beef, and enormous strawberries, was enjoyed by all of us.

Over coffee plans were made for the week. 'I'll be busy in the mornings,' Steinhardt said, 'I've found a lot of work waiting for me at my office and I guess Dulcie will have some shopping to do, but at night I want to show you New York. I've got tickets for *Kiss Me Kate* and for *South Pacific* for all of us and we'll dine and dance after the shows.'

'How wonderful!' Dulcie smiled benignly at my gratitude.

'And then,' Steinhardt added, looking directly at me for the first time, 'I want to take you to my cousin, Judge Irvin Untermeyer. I think he must have one of the finest collections of china in the world. His figurines might be an inspiration for your work.'

'Oh dear,' Dulcie exclaimed, 'must we really go there? He always frightens me. He looks at people as if he was condemning them.'

'Just a professional habit,' Steinhardt laughed.

When it was time to leave he took us down in the lift and in the hall when Leopold and Diana had stopped to look at a showcase, said, 'Tomorrow at ten then?'

'How else?' I asked. 'You have the address!'

The week that followed was exhausting, if enjoyable. Every morning Steinhardt came to my studio. He paid more attention to me than to its bizarre decor, though the mirrors amused him. By eleven when Dulcie started telephoning I was back at the Devon and he in his office. Every evening we all met to go to one or the other musicals and afterwards they would take us backstage where, much to Diana's delight, we met several famous actors and actresses and, even though I can't remember which, either Rogers or Hammerstein, or both.

Usually, Diana having been dropped back at the Devon, we dined at Sardi's. Steinhardt knew a lot of show-business people, having been the legal representative of many in his young days as a lawyer. Afterwards we always ended up at El Marocco, welcomed by the proprietor and shown to the best table.

'The man has always remained grateful to our family,' Steinhardt explained. 'He was in serious trouble once and my uncle, Sam Untermeyer, Irvin's father, who was New York's most famous criminal lawyer, got him out of it.'

Steinhardt liked dancing. Though not particularly musical – he had once confessed to me that he couldn't even tell one national anthem from another which was awkward for him as ambassador – he had a sense of rhythm, was a good dancer and enjoyed displaying a pretty woman in his arms. If he was somewhat vain of his appearance, as he moved on the dance floor, appreciative glances reassured him that he had every right to be so.

He took pleasure in showing off his women too. I remember one of the evenings at El Marocco on which all of us had made every effort to look our best. Dulcie very regal in grey satin and pearls, her grey hair piled into a high pompadour. Dulcie Anne, who had a beautiful figure, clothed in ivory velvet the texture and colour of her skin. I in Mona's green dress still fragrant with her scent. She had given it to me since she thought it would help in completing the figurine.

But as usual Leopold attracted more attention than any of us. Of the many well-dressed, indeed beautiful, women and good-looking men present one or the other frequently came to our table, barely asking to be introduced to the Steinhardts, to talk to him.

'What a lot of people you know, Leopold,' Dulcie said rather enviously. 'But then it's all café society, isn't it?'

'I don't know about cafés,' he said, 'I've spent half of my life drinking in nightclubs all over the world – so have they. One always meets again.'

Since Leopold couldn't dance, Steinhardt, as when we had gone out together in Prague or been at embassy parties, danced first with Dulcie, her small hesitant steps not matching his, then with Dulcie Anne, who was a practised dancer, and last with me, the rhythm of our bodies so attuned that we moved as one person.

As we returned to our table I noticed an expression on Dulcie's face I knew only too well from the past.

'A very pretty dress,' she remarked, 'but isn't it cut a trifle low?'

I tried to change the subject, enquiring about Ottawa. She said it was restful, Steinhardt that he found it rather dull after Teheran, Moscow and Prague.

'Even in Lima we had a revolution when I was there, but in Ottawa all I can do is to work for closer unity between Canada and the United States. After all it would be natural if they joined. It's one continent. But it's a slow process. Otherwise there's nothing but the usual social round of cocktail and dinner parties.'

'Oh, Laurence, don't say you don't enjoy them. Having all those women make up to you!' and with a sidelong glance at me Dulcie added, 'especially that pretty English girl you are always with.'

Dulcie Anne, though strictly loyal to both her parents, had a kind heart.

'Oh, the one Daddy says has no more brains than a chicken.'

Steinhardt too had seen my face. He gave Dulcie a sharp look.

'As a matter of fact,' he turned to Leopold, 'I was very much hoping you would come and visit us soon. I don't know what you are doing for Christmas. Following ancient customs I suppose, midnight mass and all that, but why not spend New Year with us? We are having a big dance for Dulcie Anne. You will find quite a few friends among the diplomats, several of them were in Prague. It wouldn't be the first time we spent New Year's Eve together. We always came to you – well now you must come and stay with us.'

'Oh, Laurence, the guest-rooms aren't ready,' Dulcie protested.

'Well then, they'll have to be by then.'

'Of course, I always meant to ask you,' she stammered, confronted by Steinhardt's stern gaze. 'I just wanted to make sure you would be comfortable in our house.'

'What do you say, Leopold?' Steinhardt asked.

'Thank you,' he answered, looking pleased, remembering, I knew, several Czech friends in Canada whom he wanted to see.

'Well, that's settled then.'

I looked at Dulcie's forced smile. I felt sorry for her, knowing exactly what she must be feeling. For a whole week she had joined with Steinhardt in giving us a good time at considerable expense to them both, she hoping this was the last confirmation of friendship necessary, a sort of farewell party – the final pay-off. Generous, considering how much we were indebted to them. And now? No end – but another beginning?

I took her hand. 'You are very kind,' I said, and really meant it. To my consternation and shame I saw tears in her eyes.

46

Next day before they left they took us to lunch with Judge Untermeyer who was later to become one of the kindest, most sympathetic friends I have ever had.

A smallish man, who even if he was Steinhardt's first cousin didn't resemble him in the least, received us. He was plumpish and of rather porcine appearance. His hair stood up in white bristles, his skin was very pink, his nose long and snout-like, his eyes small and bright. But if he looked rather like a pig, it was a very clean, well fed and intelligent pig.

He greeted us with great politeness but rather stiffly and formally. There was something of past centuries in his manners.

'Perhaps you would like to look around before we have lunch,' he said. 'Larry tells me you are interested in antiques and porcelain.' I'd never heard Steinhardt called Larry before.

'Do you think you can manage the stairs?' he asked Leopold, glancing at his stick rather anxiously I thought. Later I knew he had feared not so much for Leopold's safety but for that of his porcelain.

'Now don't tell me, Larry, that you've become interested in my collection?' he said smiling at his cousin affectionately. The Judge had a very nice smile. 'Go down to Ida. She will give you some goose liver and champagne. She's so looking forward to seeing you. You do remember her, don't you?'

'How could I forget! My first love. Those golden plaits.'

'I'm afraid they are very white by now. Ida must be over seventy. She's my cook,' the Judge explained, 'and worked for Larry's parents when he was a boy.'

'She used to bath me every night.'

'Now, Larry, don't start reminiscing here,' the Judge warned, 'go to her.'

I could see on what easy terms he and Steinhardt were but with Dulcie the Judge was merely very polite. 'I have added somewhat to my collection since you last saw it years ago but then you and Larry have been away so long,' he said.

He had a low pleasant speaking voice and practically no American accent. He then enquired about Dulcie Anne, regretting she hadn't been able to come and led the way up the beautifully polished Jacobean stairs that must have originated in some very grand English house.

From a long gallery filled with glass cases full of china he led us into at least five rooms containing beds of rare beauty, not slept in, I was sure, since the centuries in which they had been created and used – Italian Renaissance, English sixteenth- and French eighteenth-century, all with their original velvet hangings, needlework tapestries, or silk or satin draperies.

And everywhere on consoles, tables and on carved wall-brackets were porcelain vases or figurines. Often I knew their origin, quite often I didn't, but my comments pleased the Judge.

'Nymphenburg?'

'No, Hoechs. You're right. Vienna.'

'Du Paquier.'

'Yes, that's a vase painted by Herold. No, those are Chelsea,' and so we continued from room to room.

'Irvin, I'm just a little tired today,' Dulcie said, 'and with beautiful things like yours one has to concentrate. Will you forgive me if I go down and rest a little now and see some more after lunch? Leopold, I know, feels the same and will take me down.'

Leopold, who was not the least bit interested in china, but had dutifully contemplated one object after the other trying to seem knowledgeable, not daring to comment, looked relieved, put his arm through Dulcie's and they went.

The Judge's small blue eyes crinkled with amusement but he said nothing.

'I don't think I've seen any Meissen anywhere. Do you dislike it for some reason?' I asked.

'I like it more than I can afford. Come and see – ' he smiled. He led me into a small room. The walls were shelved with glass or held carved brackets, and there it all was from the beginnings of the Meissen factory in Dresden in the early eighteenth century till its great period ended.

Boettger's first ventures in manufacturing true porcelain (its secret so jealously guarded through centuries by the Chinese). Small figures and ornaments and teapots still in red stoneware, then with the addition of kaolin to the paste the great discovery had come, and the translucent pure white chinaware had emerged from the kiln.

After that, vases and bowls copied from the Chinese – decorated with Oriental motifs – but soon replaced by work of much greater quality and originality. The small room contained samples of them all. Dozens of Kändlers, beautiful lifelike birds. All the colourful figures of the Italian *commedia*. Harlequins and Columbines, Pantalons and Scaramouches at play, dancing, drinking or making love. Then the groups and statuettes, charming, intimate portrayals of courtly life. A gentleman bending to kiss a lady's hand, a lady in a negligée and nightcap fondling her pug while a beturbaned blackamoor serves the morning coffee, another having her hair dressed. A couple in hunting costume with guns and dogs under a green tree, every porcelain leaf perfect. A cavalier in court dress bowing to a lady who flirts her fan at him, a gentleman at the barber's – and the more pastoral scenes with their veiled eroticism. Shepherds playing their flutes or presenting birdcages or cockerels to shepherdesses. Rustic couples embracing or pursuing each other, kisses exchanged in flowered grottoes. And all decorated in the most lovely colours, every detail of dress as perfectly moulded and painted as were the small faces and hands.

But that was not all – exquisite boxes set in gold, scent bottles, needlecases, cane handles, ornamented with miniature scenes or flowers and great vases and bowls of superb quality.

I sat down on the sofa. I had forgotten the Judge. The inexplicable feeling that I had lived in the eighteenth century overcame me once more. I do not believe in reincarnation nor that ancestral memories can haunt one or descend from one generation to another. Yet as a small child from the day I had discovered that I could draw, I had pictured people in crinolines and farthingales, even rabbits, cats and dogs dressed in the same style. I stole cotton-wool to make my dolls white wigs and perukes – Why? Perhaps I had seen pictures and recorded them unconsciously. But there is no explanation for a nightmare that recurred frequently from the time I was five until I was seven.

Again and again I would wake screaming with fear to tell my terrified brother and 'Lenlen' that two soldiers had cut off my head and thrown it into a basket. 'Lenlen' tried to soothe and calm me, explaining to me that it was just a bad dream, so did my parents.

But so vividly did I remember the dream long after it had occurred that I could describe exactly how the two men had been dressed.

Only much later Aunt Diana confessed to me that I had, to my parents' amazement and consternation, accurately described the uniform worn by the executioners who served the guillotine at the time of the Terror in France.

Fortunately as I grew older the frightening dream ceased but not my feeling of belonging to the eighteenth century. Its paintings, its architecture, its music and literature all seemed more familiar and comprehensible to me than that of my time.

'Forgive me,' I said to the Judge, whom I felt my long silence might have offended and who was indeed looking at me with some concern. 'It's one of the most beautiful collections I've ever seen. It recalls so much – was there ever a century like it?'

'I suppose not. Though Greece and the Italian Renaissance were, from the point of view of great art, more important. Yet only in the eighteenth century did all the arts combine to pleasure man and beautify even his most humble functions – Look at that chamber-pot!' The Judge waved his small, plump, well-kept hand. 'It is as ornately decorated as a dinner-plate! Contemplate the sofa you are reclining on,' (I was by then) 'and this chair' (he was sitting facing me). 'Note the framework, the feet and arms as finely carved and with as much dedication as things were formerly made for use in churches to glorify the Almighty. Now they are shaped and curved and cushioned to embrace the human form. Even the beds. Well, you have seen my few examples, their canopies, their plumes and ornate curtainings remind one of the baroque draperies and heavenly clouds that used to surround the high altar or the ark in churches or synagogues. Now they give splendour and dignity to what we share with all animals: copulation, birth, sleep and death. Yes indeed, in no other century did the art of beautiful living reach a higher peak of perfection and in none could man indulge his tastes and appetites with happier results and more terrible consequences.'

'The Revolution?'

'Was it not inevitable, with a single ruling-class having indulged itself at the expense of the under-privileged masses for so long?'

'Oh, I don't know,' I said looking around, 'see those enchanting porcelain beggars in their rags, the shepherds with their lambs, that old woman crouching over her fire and the ornamental black slaves.'

'Portraying the picturesqueness of the poor so charmingly didn't solve their problems or fill their empty stomachs,' the Judge said severely.

'So then you blame the ruling classes in – oh – let's call it Our Century, for having brought on the Revolution?'

'To a great extent, yes.'

'Well so do I. But it was not their immorality, their extravagance and frivolity and total disregard for the welfare of their fellow men that caused their downfall. Far from it. The masses don't rebel against what they vicariously enjoy. The scandalous behaviour of their betters has always delighted them.'

'As every gossip column still proves,' the Judge admitted wryly.

'It was something else,' I added hesitantly. 'I believe that a century can follow the pattern of the life of a man. Certainly the eighteenth does, that of an aristocrat who indulged himself to excess and suffered from surfeit towards the end. With it came the stirring of conscience.'

'When the devil grows old the devil a saint would be,' the Judge quoted.

'Exactly, and what would this aristocrat or ruler, knowing he could take none of his worldly goods with him, finally do, but remember his immortal soul and try to acquire benefits in heaven by good deeds.'

'I am not religious myself,' the Judge said, 'but it is a reaction that comes to all of us who have had the fortune to live too well.'

'So my aristocrat starts to think, which no aristocrat ever should for he does so at his own peril, on how to benefit his fellow men. Not only by charity but by reforms.'

'Too late to stem the tide of revolution,' the Judge said.

'Or too soon! The masses do not rebel readily, however great their grievances. They are too fearful. But let their rulers show the slightest sign of weakening or self-doubt in their right to oppress and suppress by concessions and reforms, the floodgates open and bloodshed and terror is the result.'

The Judge looked at me thoughtfully. 'You are rather reactionary,' he said mildly.

'Perhaps, but with some reason. Our class in Czechoslovakia lived as much for pleasure as had the French aristocracy in the eighteenth century, though in a less grandiose style and with somewhat more moral restraint. Yet we welcomed socialism even if it was to our disadvantage, feeling it was what the people had decided and that at last, instead of a privileged few, all would benefit. Oh, we were quite idealistic about it! And what did it achieve? We had merely opened the door wide to communism – the silent terror that is as cruel as bloody revolution. Now our people are more brutally suppressed than even in the days of monarchy.'

I looked round the lovely room with all its portrayals of courtly life, so full of grace and charm.

'I do not defend the frivolity of the aristocracy,' I said, 'except that without the pleasures they took in all the arts in the past the world would be very much poorer.'

'And so would I,' the Judge said. 'Come, we must go now. Lunch will be ready and Larry will wonder what's happened to you. I hope,' he said as we went downstairs, 'you will come back. I lead a very quiet life since my wife died. I rarely even see my children who have families of their own. I meet very few people. Those worth talking to are rare. Larry has told me how gifted you are. Whatever might be of help to you in my collection as model or inspiration is yours to use. Now that I've met you, I'm not surprised at his devotion.' So the Judge knew – I must have looked embarrassed.

'You can depend absolutely on my discretion,' he said, his small eyes twinkling with amusement. 'I think I'm the only person Larry confides in. We are very old friends.'

We found them in the drawing-room, as full of museum pieces as had been the rooms upstairs, mainly English early-eighteenth-century furniture, chairs and sofas, all with their original tapestry or needlework covers.

Steinhardt gave the Judge a quick questioning look and seemed pleased by what he read in his cousin's face. They were drinking champagne and spooning *pâté de foie gras* on to toast.

The Judge poured me and then himself a glass. 'To Our Century,' he said, raising his.

Lunch was rather stiff and formal. The meal was served by two elderly parlourmaids in starched caps and aprons, the food, though cooked to perfection, oddly Germanic or such as we might have had at home when there were no guests. A creamy potato soup, followed by boiled beef with dumplings, vegetables and pancakes as dessert filled with redcurrant jelly and browned in sugar. The Judge ate more than he talked. Dulcie talked more than she ate. She was an expert at French cuisine and I think did not appreciate the heavy nostalgic meal that the rest of us enjoyed, as well as the wines on the quality of which Leopold complimented the Judge.

'They are still from my father's cellar. I saved them,' he explained to Steinhardt, 'when we sold the house on the Hudson – but I'm no expert,' he added quite untruthfully, I thought, considering with what appreciation he was sipping vintage Rhine wine.

'I've always felt it to be a great pity that that splendid medieval castle had to go,' Dulcie said and to Leopold, '–It was not unlike Castolovice.'

'A pretentious and vulgar fake,' the Judge declared, pouring horse-radish sauce on to his beef from a George the First sauce-boat. All the magnificent and highly polished silver on the table and sideboards was Georgian.

After lunch we had coffee in Meissen cups in the library. Later I was to know all those rooms so well and become familiar with what they contained but all I could do then was divide my attention as best I was able. I had to keep Leopold from falling asleep after his meal, Dulcie from feeling neglected, Steinhardt from confusing me and the Judge interested.

'What marvellous bronzes. You've deviated from Our Century,' I told him.

'Well so did eighteenth-century collectors. Most of these are of the Italian Renaissance, some a little later. I rather like that satyr by Riccio and that muscular Hercules attributed to Rizzi, but this is my favourite,' and he took a nude female figure down from a shelf. 'What elegance and manneristic grace. "Giam Bologna" of course.'

Steinhardt had joined us. 'Unlike with china figurines,' the Judge said, 'which might, God preserve us, be dropped when handled, bronzes should be touched and fingered to be appreciated. Here – hold her, Larry. Not like that,' the Judge protested. 'Take her in your right hand and feel her with your left, since you have used it less it's much more sensitive. It will tell you how beautiful she is more so even than your eyes can.'

'Never thought of that!' Steinhardt said, gently fingering the smooth curves of the bronze.

'Or why we Jews have a much more highly developed sense of touch than other races?' he asked, eyeing Dulcie wickedly.

'I really wouldn't know,' she said primly. Dulcie had often told me that she had been christened a Presbyterian and didn't consider herself Jewish.

'Because for so many centuries coins have passed through our fingers that we learnt to recognize their value from the raised surface by touch even in the dark. And this sensitivity of the hand soon applied to works of art too. I can often tell a fake just by touching an object.'

'You liked my cousin?' Steinhardt asked as we descended in the lift.

'Very much,' Leopold said. 'A nice old gentleman.'

'For all his wealth I rather pity him,' Dulcie sighed. 'He leads a very lonely life since his wife committed suicide.'

'No one knows if she did,' Steinhardt said sharply.

Next morning they flew back to Ottawa.

47

After the Steinhardts had left I completed Mona's figurine and set it aside knowing how completely it must dry before I dared fire it. Inspired by the Judge's Kändler Harlequins, I tried to model one. But there were difficulties. Clay has to be shaped when wet and a figurine formed all in one piece, unlike those of porcelain of which the separate parts are poured into moulds and then reassembled – arms, hands and fingers are almost impossible to be left unsupported in clay, since the more fragile pieces dry and crumble before the main body. Still, by placing the Harlequin's one hand on his heart and the other on a tree I managed.

Mona had withstood the first fire without cracking and the second, for the glaze of her green dress and silver hair, without any mishaps either. There had been very little shrinkage and the likeness was remarkable. I hadn't dared glaze the face for fear of obscuring the features, the rosy clay was not unlike her skin and I had only touched up eyes and lips lightly with watercolour paints.

What I didn't know then is that unglazed clay remains porous, collects dust and grows grey after a certain length of time.

I called up Eddie on Long Island. 'Mona's cooked,' I said, 'come and see.' He motored down immediately.

'It's a bit like a doll,' he said, 'but it's very like her. Really, I think it rather charming.' I hugged him delighted. Eddie rarely said anything just to please. I felt very happy. If my first portrait was a success what might not follow – ?

'Well, how have you been?' he enquired. 'How were the Steinhardts?'

'Pleasant,' I said, 'and very kind. They took us to all the shows and restaurants and they've invited us to Ottawa for a New Year's party.'

'I'm so glad,' Eddie exclaimed. 'Mona feels awful about not being able to have you for your first Christmas here or for the New Year either, but Harrison has insisted we all go to Palm Beach. He wants to fish and try out his new boat. Also they've decided to sell their house there. One has to see what things to keep and which to leave. So I guess I'll have to hang the Christmas tree ornaments on a palmetto palm for them this year. I'm sorry, darling. But perhaps it's all for the best. It may be easier for you and Leopold under the circumstances. If we were together we might become too sentimental and nostalgic on Christmas Eve. What about having lunch with me today?' he added.

'I'm sorry, I can't. We are going to Renée Bekér's.'

'Strange woman that,' Eddie remarked. 'I've never been able to make her out. In fact she rather frightens me. She has the most perfect manners of anyone I've ever met yet she seems as cold as ice. Perhaps it's because she thinks I'm German. What with her being Jewish I can't blame her. Lovely things she has, though. The deceased Monsieur de Bekér must have been stinking rich. Those Tiepolo panels alone – '

'I felt rather like you about her when I first met her,' I told Eddie, 'but then I saw how kind she was to her cousins, Erich and Biene, who after all are as displaced as us. And to Leopold too – And I discovered something else about her by chance. What do you think she does in the mornings?'

'Probably reads Voltaire or dusts the French furniture.'

'She was late for lunch one day and Erich let slip that she must have been detained in the cancer ward and then begged us not to speak of it since she didn't want anyone to know.'

'She's not dying, poor woman?' Eddie asked, shocked.

'No, but she goes every morning to try and comfort those that are – the incurables.'

'Shows one can never tell about people,' Eddie said after a prolonged silence.

'Well, if you won't come with me I've got to go,' he said, rising from his chair. 'You wouldn't have anything like a clothes brush?' he asked, contemplating the dust that had collected on his suit and shoes.

I went to fetch one. 'It's the clay,' I apologized. 'I don't quite know what to do about it. I sweep and I mop but it doesn't seem to go away.'

'What you need of course is a vacuum cleaner.'

'And what's that?'

He sighed. 'One would think you'd lived on a desert island for the last years. It's an electric machine that sucks up the dust.'

'And where can I get that?'

'I'd think they'd be advertised in any newspaper – Can I take Mona with me? I'll be very careful. Have you some tissue paper or something soft I can wrap her in? I'm sure she will be pleased with it and so will Harrison.'

With the statuette bundled under his arm, wrapped in one of my scarves, he left.

Towards evening Mona telephoned. 'Darling, it's lovely,' she exclaimed. 'Such a pretty doll! I'm going to do something about it too. Wait and see.'

A few minutes later Eddie called. 'Imagine what Mona is going to do for you. She hates publicity yet she's going to call up Jerome Zerbe, he's a famous photographer, to come and take a picture of her with your doll and will allow an article about you and your work with the photographs to be published in one of the daily papers.'

'Isn't that rather embarrassing?' I asked.

'What do you mean?' he said indignantly. 'Obviously you have no idea what advantages that sort of publicity can bring you in this country. And if, as she wants to, she has an exhibition of your work in her house later, well, your fortunes are made!'

'But, Eddie, surely you realize what an amateur I am?'

'Of course I do. But with Mona's help you might just make it. It doesn't pay to be too modest in America. One has to beat one's own drum a bit if one wants to succeed. By the way,' he added, 'Mona has persuaded Diana Vreeland to sit for you. *Harper's Bazaar*.' (Later she was to become editor of *Vogue*.) 'She's very important in the fashion world.'

'I've never met her.'

'You will – I must say portraying her should be a bit of a challenge,' he laughed. 'But I do think,' he then warned, 'that you will have to clean up that sordid place of yours before you invite anyone in. It took my man hours to clean up my suit.'

I had from the beginning of our stay in America subscribed to the *New York Times*. Its weight and volume was impressive. Its standard of reportage high on those rare pages which contained articles squeezed in among the advertisements and in any case the wealth of paper it provided could be put to all kinds of uses, such as covering my studio floor to protect it from clay.

Now I searched its pages for vacuum cleaners and to my delight found an ad that offered one for nineteen dollars. All the others seemed to cost ten times as much. Though Steinhardt had deposited several more thousands into our bank account I knew that the money and what we might still obtain for our valuables would probably, except for some extraordinary stroke of luck, have to last us for the rest of our lives. In spite of Eddie and Mona's encouragement I knew I had every reason to doubt my artistic abilities as I did Leopold's qualifications for earning a living. I must be careful I knew.

I dialled the telephone number given and asked if I could see the vacuum cleaner.

Two men came. They were dressed in very tight-fitting suits. They sat down on my studio couch without being asked to do so. They kept their hats on their heads and their cigarettes in the corners of their mouth, dropping the ashes just anywhere.

They looked like gangsters. I was rather frightened.

'Have you brought the vacuum cleaner you advertised?' I asked.

'Sure, it's outside.'

'Then please bring it in.'

One of them went and returned with a large box. He took out a domed object like something from outer space with a long tube attached.

'Please show me how it works.'

One of them plugged its flex into a socket and with a hum its snake-like end slithered over the floor, indeed miraculously removing all the dust.

'I'll take it,' I said and asked them for the name of their firm and wrote out the cheque.

'Say, lady, you've forgotten a zero. It's a hundred and ninety bucks – not nineteen.'

'But that's surely what you advertised it for in the newspaper?' I asked, puzzled.

'Not this one.'

'Then which?'

He brought a smaller packet and took out something obviously made of cardboard with a paper bag attached.

'It might work for a week or so with luck, but in this dirt of yours it would blow in a day. In any case it's not for sale. This model is merely for advertising purposes.'

'And if I wanted one just the same, could I have it for nineteen dollars?'

'Sure, but you might have to wait a long time. It's out of production.'

'What a dirty trick!' I said angrily.

'Lady,' one of them grinned, 'all that's dirty here is your floor. As for tricks, have you never heard of salesmanship? And what's more, we've allowed you ten per cent off the model we showed you.' 'Just try and buy it for the same money in a store!' the other one sneered.

'Please go,' I said, 'and take your machines with you.'

Quite unperturbed they did.

A few days later I bought the domed cleaner identical with that they had shown me in a department store. It did indeed cost fifteen per cent more. Still I felt I had gained a moral victory.

I started to spend more and more time in the studio. Mainly because I was fearful to leave it when the kiln was red hot, high firing took at least eight hours. Diana often came with me or joined me for lunch. I was trying to teach myself to cook. Though the big kiln could have roasted a large joint I had no kitchen oven and most recipes demanded one. Of course I couldn't mess up my valuable kiln with food. All my problems were solved when I bought something called a 'pressure cooker'. Though it hissed and whistled ominously and exploded on two occasions staining the ceiling with its contents, nevertheless meat and vegetables and herbs thrown in indiscriminately together produced in half an hour a quite edible and healthy stew, better I thought than that served in the sort of restaurants we dared afford.

Only rarely did Leopold join us. He had seen the studio by then of course, the mirrored pink glamour of the bedroom decently veiled with a brown and white chintz that Mona had let me have.

He didn't seem to mind my working there early and late any more. He still drove to his office every morning but mainly I think to hear the latest news from Czechoslovakia and often went out to lunch or dine without me. He had acquired a circle of friends of whom he seldom spoke. One day, not much to my surprise since I so rarely saw him, he told me Annicka had arrived in New York.

'She's aged terribly! Not at all attractive any more, poor thing! I feel sorry for her,' he said with his usual ingenuity, knowing I would be pleased to hear this, even if I doubted its truth. She was younger than me.

'How sad!' I said, equally tactfully. 'By the way, what happened to her husband?'

'He couldn't get out. There's a rumour he's hanged himself. I do hope it's not true.'

I remembered the little man so amiable and friendly and so proud of his wife's social success, thanks to Leopold's attentions, and felt rather sick.

'Where is she staying?'

'Oh, I found her a room somewhere. She's working.'

'Gracious! At what? Not with Veruska, I hope?'

Leopold flushed, if with anger or embarrassment I couldn't tell.

'She's making hats. You won't remember but I once had a friend called Lily, before we were married.'

How could I ever forget, I thought. I had suffered years of jealousy retrospectively about Leopold's long affair with that beautiful Viennese.

'I thought she lived in Paris?'

'She did but her husband died and she has a dress shop here now. She's been very helpful about Annicka.'

'No doubt they have a lot in common!' I couldn't refrain from saying.

Leopold wisely changed the subject, reminding me that Clarisse was expecting us for lunch.

We found her brother-in-law, Louis Rothschild, there. I hadn't seen him since his arrest at the Vienna airport. He remembered it only too well. 'I'm not sure you don't bring me bad luck,' he joked. 'Our last encounter was far from fortunate for me.' Yet he was obviously glad to see us again, wanted to know how we had escaped and what our future plans were. Leopold told him about his problems and I of my hopes for my ceramic work.

'Mona Williams has promised to have an exhibition at her house once she's done enough portraits,' Clarisse said impressively.

'Men or women?' Louis asked.

'I've only thought of doing women up to now,' I confessed. 'Men's clothes aren't very picturesque – Still,' I stared at Louis, struck by his face. It was neither beautiful nor ugly but there was something rare about its expression. Where had I seen such serene and smiling composure before?

'You look rather like a Buddha, Baron Louis,' I exclaimed. 'Would you sit for me?'

'In the nude? You forget, I've recently married. I doubt Hilda would approve.'

'Just your head,' I pleaded.

'But I'm only here for the day. I have to go back to Vermont tomorrow.'

'I could do it after lunch here, if Clarisse lets me. It won't take me more than half an hour.'

'After lunch I sleep!'

'All the better,' I said, 'if your eyes are closed.'

'How most unflattering!'

'I was thinking of your glasses. I can't make those in ceramics.'

'Let her do it, Louis,' Clarisse begged. 'It will help her to have your statue for her exhibition.'

'It would certainly be unique. No one even in better days has wanted to eternalize my looks.'

After lunch I called a taxi and was back with my lump of clay wrapped in a wet cloth within minutes. Clarisse looked at the dirty bundle dubiously. 'Don't make a mess on the Aubusson. It's worth a fortune,' she warned, leading us into a small sitting-room. Louis sat down in an armchair. 'You should do Eugene instead of me,' he remarked. 'He was always the best-looking member of the family. Still is, though quite deaf.'

'I only met him in Paris once when he was married to Kitty and she was so glamorous one rather forgot him.'

'Poor Eugene,' Louis yawned. 'He's still not got over her death. He never leaves Long Island and weeps on her grave every day.'

I begged him to lean back, to take off his glasses and to loosen his collar and tie.

'So you are forcing me to undress after all,' he sighed but did as I ordered, baring a remarkably strong, smooth and youthful neck, though he must have been over sixty-five.

I took my lump of clay in my hands and started to mould it into the shape of a head. For a few moments he watched then leaned back, contemplated a picture over the fireplace, a cupid in flight displaying its plump rosy bottom, and murmured, 'I wonder why Boucher was so fond of po pos,' closed his eyes and slept, a benign smile curving his well-shaped mouth.

Next door I could hear Leopold and Clarisse laughing and joking. They were always happy together discussing the past. In half an hour I had enough of a likeness to be able to do the rest in my studio. The heavy closed eyelids reminded me even more of a meditating Buddha.

When Louis woke I held the head out to him.

'I'm going to glaze it jade green,' I said.

'Won't it look rather like a frog?' he asked, peering at it through his glasses.

'Not after I've finished.'

'And how much will you charge me for it?'

'But, Baron Louis, I never thought of that,' I said, truthfully as he knew.

'Have you sold anything here yet?'

'No.'

'Then let me be your first patron.'

He took out his wallet and carefully counted out fifty dollars.

'I hope your profits will increase with fame,' he said, handing me the bills. It was the first money I had earned in America. I could have hugged him except that there was a sort of calm remoteness about him that forbade such familiarities. I thanked him as best I could. 'Now may I continue my afternoon's meditation undisturbed?' he asked and was asleep again before I had left the room.

48

Really ever since we had arrived in New York it had been Christmas. In the shops, in the streets and the squares illuminated trees decked in gold and silver, stars, angels and Santa Clauses, holly and mistletoe ornamenting every department store, loudspeakers shouting carols or songs about 'Jinglebells' or 'White Christmasses' non-stop.

Perhaps fortunately for us, because this premature excess of good cheer took the edge off whatever seasonable nostalgia one might have felt, it even blunted one's appetite for traditional Christmas food.

Everything that had been so rare and precious at home in the war and even for a long time afterwards because it was almost unobtainable was here displayed in all the food departments of the big stores in incredibly lavish abundance.

I remembered the meagre turkey, fed in secret in some friends' backyard so that we should not be without this traditional dish on Christmas Day.

Here the birds flaunted their plump breasts by the hundreds or thousands wherever one looked. On the bread and cake counters the shiny brown-sugar-glazed plaited 'Stritzels', spiked with almonds, and rich dark round plum puddings and Christmas cakes lay heaped into mountains.

I looked at the great piles of sweets and chocolates and mince pies and gingerbreads and marzipan and though I knew I should be grateful to be living in a land of such plenty I could have cried for the poor country we had left. But it was the wonderful display of toys in all the shops that in a way disturbed me most. How much I had been obliged to deprive the child of at an age when she would have still enjoyed toys so much! It was too late now I knew. She had been very fond of dolls unobtainable towards the end of the war, like so much else, so I had made her one, moulding it out of wax. Candles could still be bought since they were indispensable in the blackouts imposed when allied planes flew over Prague on the way to bomb Germany.

However dreadful their mission, these planes provided us with most lovely Christmas tree ornaments, like strips of silver foil (something to do with radar). All of Prague's children went out to collect this angels' hair, though it was strictly forbidden by the German authorities to do so.

'We are invited out for Christmas Eve,' Leopold told me, much to my surprise since most of our closer friends had left for the holidays to stay with relations in the country. This was two days before Christmas.

'It will be easier with strangers,' he declared. 'Nothing to remind us of home or the past. Just a quiet dinner. I don't think they'll even have a tree. They are not that sort. And bridge afterwards.'

'But who are they?'

'Oh, someone introduced me to them. He is the manager of one of the best hotels here – They are awfully kind people. They've been very good about Annicka.'

'And now they'd like to meet the rest of your family?' My irony was as usual quite lost on Leopold.

'Of course. What's wrong with that?'

'Oh, nothing. Will Annicka be there too?'

'Certainly not. They know quite well *Was sich schickt*', (translatable as 'what's proper') 'even if they are Americans.'

'What tact – and is Diana included in this invitation?'

'Naturally, or I wouldn't want to go. Can't leave the poor child here alone on Christmas Eve! Besides they have two very pretty daughters, schoolgirls about her age. It will be nice for her to meet someone young.'

I hesitated. 'Will it be a big party?'

'No, only us and them. Just a quiet evening. It will save us sitting here all alone together till we have to go to mass.'

'I thought we only had to go to midnight mass at home?'

'I don't see that it makes any difference where we are as far as the Church is concerned.'

I couldn't answer this.

'If we go to your friends',' I conceded reluctantly, 'we will have to give Diana her presents first.'

His face brightened with relief. 'So then I can telephone that we're coming?'

At six on Christmas Eve I asked Diana to leave the sitting-room. 'Really, Mummy,' she protested. 'I've smelt that tree that you keep hidden for days and seen most of the presents. I'm not a child any more. Let me do the tree, Mummy, this year!'

'All right,' I conceded. 'There it is – ' pulling it out of a wardrobe.

'That's not a tree. That's a shrub,' she exclaimed.

Every year, as of course she remembered, one of the tallest of fir trees to be found in our forests had been chosen and felled for Christmas. Even when Castolovice had been confiscated, our head forester had managed to have one transported to us in Prague.

In its decoration Diana had been allowed no part. Confined to the nursery with whoever was in charge of her at the time, only when the candles on the tree had been finally lit on Christmas Eve and the Christmas bell rung, had she been allowed to join us. Possibly she had resented missing all the fun of unwrapping the ornaments carefully stored from year to year, all the marvels in blown glass for which Czechoslovakia had been famous: birds, angels, glittering balls of every colour and size, as well as the almost ritual decorating of the tree. First the Star of Bethlehem (and our coat of arms) attached to its top shoot, then the polished red apples and the oranges, if available, tied to its branches to weigh them into perfect balance, then the various ornaments, the smallest above, the largest below, finally the sweets and candles. Everyone helped – there were always members of Leopold's family present for Christmas – standing on ladders so as to reach the highest branches.

Only Diana for whose pleasure and surprise it was all intended was not allowed to join in the laughter, the arguments and the quarrels caused by differing opinions as to how and where every item should be hung.

Finally she had been led in to view the tree in all its glory but had had to wait before she could look at her presents till every servant had been given his, or hers, and wished A Happy Christmas.

'There isn't very much to put on this bush,' she complained, 'except for chocolates.'

'And there won't even be any of those left if you start eating them now,' I remonstrated.

Nevertheless, unhelped by me, she carefully and precisely, after a certain amount of deliberation using the meagre supplies of ornaments

I'd bought, managed to transform the small tree into something beautiful. She had even then an uncompromising desire for perfection, which both Leopold and I lacked.

She went to dress and we arranged her presents around the tree. Not wrapped, as they do in America or England, a custom I was only to adopt with great reluctance later. I was bad at wrapping and unwrapping and disliked the rustle of paper.

Leopold and I had decided it was silly to give each other presents under the circumstances but of course we did, though just small things. I had found a beautiful tie which he immediately put on. It lit up in the dark, miraculously displaying a bosomy naked lady. He gave me patience cards, address books and a hairbrush that played 'Jinglebells' when used and some very pretty beads that I later found out Lily had chosen for him.

For Diana he had bought a roulette wheel, no doubt wanting to try out one of his systems on it himself, and an enormous Teddy bear, compelled by some childhood memory, I suppose.

'It looks very like you, Papi,' she said, 'large and cuddly!' I had chosen mainly books I hoped she would like, puzzles which I knew she loved and some pretty frilly grown-up underwear, the reason for that being that she had been horrified at the contents of the boxes containing her school outfit when they arrived. And no wonder. I had ordered everything that had been listed by the school as necessary at the place recommended. There was enough to clothe at least three children I thought and nearly all of it grey, coats, uniforms, berets, blouses and T-shirts and, by the dozen, socks and stockings and scarves and ties, underwear and remarkably ugly grey striped flanelette pyjamas.

'They look like what people in prison wear!' had been her indignant comment. 'I'd rather sleep naked – You must have made a mistake, Mummy,' she declared after she had looked at all the clothes. 'Except for the three skirts, the rest is for boys not girls.'

Yet I had correctly stated her age, measurements and sex. Had they just sent me whatever surplus they wanted to be rid of regardless? It looked very much like it. As it had all been very expensive I called up the school and asked for Mrs Elliot. Out of breath, I knew, from what attic height she had descended to get to the telephone, she said of course she remembered me and Diana and was looking forward to seeing us soon. She said it didn't matter in the least what the child wore as long as she had a school uniform for special occasions.

'I should have warned you that list was made twenty years ago,' Mrs Elliot laughed, 'and no one took the trouble to have it reprinted. The tailors you went to are quite out of fashion now. One can get everything ready-made in the department stores much cheaper.'

I called up the firm, asking if I could return most of what they had sent. They refused to take anything back, saying it had all been specially made to measure and that boys and girls wore the same coats and blouses and ties even if their lower garments varied slightly.

There is nothing more upsetting for a child than to be made to feel ridiculous through not wearing what others do. For months Diana was to remind me of my dreadful mistake and demand replacement of the things she refused to put on because the other girls wore pretty dresses, silk stockings and had chiffon nightgowns edged with lace.

My only surprise present which gave her pleasure was a portable gramophone with records of all the songs from the shows we had seen with the Steinhardts. It would have been cruel not to let her play them. 'Some enchanted evening,' Enzio Pinza's rich velvety voice throbbed.

'Stop that noise,' Leopold demanded. Obediently, if reluctantly, the child tried to turn it off. The needle caught, repeating the refrain again and again. 'Never let him go – go – go – go – '

I succeeded in turning it off.

'Happy Christmas,' he said, bending to kiss each of us in turn formally as parents did their children under the Christmas tree at home.

Then the telephone rang. Though I was delighted at Eddie's calling from Palm Beach to wish us Happy Christmas too, I had hoped it might be Ottawa. Had we got Mona's hamper? Eddie asked. 'I chose it all myself,' he said, 'everything I knew you'd like for dinner, champagne and all, so you would not have to go out on Christmas Eve.'

I told him it hadn't arrived yet.

'Well, it's still very early. It's sure to come. Here it's like summer, most unsuitable Christmas weather, and nothing but crimson Poinsettias that look like paper flowers all over the place. I hope we come back soon. How I long for Capri.'

The hamper arrived just before we left and an enormous bunch of flowers, anemones, narcissi and freesias, flowers that grow wild in Capri in the early spring, from Eddie.

'Let's take some with us,' Leopold suggested. 'Americans always bring flowers or a present when they are invited to someone's house.'

Not having moved in the circles with which Leopold seemed to have become familiar I did as he told me, reluctantly dividing off half of the flowers and tying them with a ribbon.

'Should I add a Christmas card? What's her name?'

'I really don't know,' Leopold said. 'I've only been there once or twice for a drink. He calls her "Baby Doll"!'

We went. Not only was the hall and lobby of the hotel bright with fairy lights and ornately decorated but even more so the manager's large apartment to which we were shown by the lift-boy.

In its ante-room Santa Claus received us. Snowy beard, fur-lined cloak, hood and all. There was an embarrassing moment. Was this our host or a hired hotel Santa Claus? We had seen so many lately on the streets and in the shops.

It was rather like one of those awkward occasions when one's invited by friends to the house of a stranger and doesn't know if one's shaking hands with the butler or one's host.

Safer not to shake hands, I thought. Leopold too was puzzled and Diana retreated behind us. Mumbling something incomprehensible under his beard, Father Christmas ushered us into a room in which a vast tree blazing with electric lights reached from floor to high ceiling.

'Fooled you,' he said, pulling off his beard. 'Guess you didn't recognize me.' I could hardly comment since I'd never seen him before. 'It was the girls' idea,' he laughed as he dismantled and emerged in a well-cut dinner-jacket, carnation in buttonhole. 'They thought it might make your little daughter feel more at home if she was welcomed by Santa. After all, he is your patron saint, is he not?'

'St Wenceslas is,' Diana said firmly. 'St Nicholas is the patron saint of Russia.'

'Oh, that's where the confusion must have arisen. Still I guess it's all one country by now.' He smiled benignly, an elderly rather hand-some man, who reminded me of the advertisement in which identically well-fed and well-dressed men drink whisky or brandy in front of fake Tudor fireplaces.

'Good King Wenceslas,' he started to hum not unmelodiously, interrupted by the spectacular entrance of his wife.

She was small and rather stout, encased from head to foot in silver spangles, her golden hair crowned with one of those lesser imitation tiaras that are crushed on to the brows of aspiring beauty queens who get the third prize.

'Doesn't she look just like the Christmas Fairy!' her husband ex-claimed. 'All it needs is to set her on top of the tree.'

Involuntarily we looked up to where some small and gauzy creature floated, and back at her.

Leopold was trying hard not to laugh.

371

I proffered my flowers. 'Baby Doll's' blue eyes widened with surprise as she contemplated the by then rather untidy and wilting bunch. With embarrassment I realized that she'd probably never received a flower that was not wrapped in cellophane and certainly not such as these, evocative as they were to me of Italian spring, which could be bought at every street corner for practically nothing in New York.

Nobly she rose to the occasion. 'Oh, you poor dears!' she said, referring to us, I think, not to the fading flowers, embraced me and kissed me full on the mouth, did the same to Diana, who I saw surreptitiously wiped hers afterwards – and no wonder. The Christmas spirit exhaled was strong. Then her generous impulse to hug us all was momentarily defeated by Leopold's height, but he gave her a hand up.

Champagne was served. Then two tall angels appeared and curtsied to us. They wore identical long white silken gowns, flowing in gothic folds, their hair as golden as their mother's, if perhaps more naturally so, curling about their beautiful impassive faces as carefully painted on as any features on fresco panel or canvas had ever been.

Presents were taken from the tree and given to us. There was some confusion. Leopold carefully unwrapping his parcel found he had received a gilt vanity case from Elizabeth Arden, Diana a pair of cufflinks from Cartier and I a small transistor radio intended for her.

It was soon sorted out with much laughter and considerable embarrassment on our side, since we had brought no gifts.

Dinner was stupendous. The hotel was one of the best in New York and so was its food. Tactfully – I couldn't help wondering if it was Annicka who had warned them that we were Roman Catholics – there were no meat dishes. Only caviar, lobster, à l'Americaine, followed by fresh asparagus, a savoury and a rum flaming plum pudding. Hotel waiters served with speed and efficiency under the critical eye of their master. The wine waiter adorned with his chain of office proffered glass after glass for our host to taste and after his approval filled ours. Conversation was rather haphazard, restricted mainly to the doings of members of New York society whom we didn't know. However now and then we too dropped a name or two, of people we really had met, which seemed to burst upon our hosts as startlingly as the bangs made by the crackers Diana and the angels were pulling. Paper hats emerged from these which we put on. We rose from the table. 'Baby Doll' took me to her bedroom, which rather reminded me of the blissful vulgarity of mine in the studio, though much larger – more in the 'style Louis' as they say in America, though which of the French kings it refers to doesn't seem to matter much.

Unashamedly 'Baby Doll' relieved herself in the adjoining bathroom, leaving the door open and continuing our conversation as if we were still at table.

Afterwards coffee and brandy were served, the latter in such ballooning glasses that even my nose, which is small, hit the rim every time I tried to get at the contents.

Then the lights were dimmed, only the tree remained lit and Leopold's tie shone in all its naked glory. There was much laughter. Then our host demanded silence. 'The girls have prepared a little surprise,' he said.

The angels stood up and sang – '*Adeste fidelis*' and 'Noel', 'Hark the Herald Angels Sing' and '*Stille Nacht*', all the old Christmas hymns we had always known, the strong American accent making the words almost incomprehensible, but the angels' voices incredibly sweet, true and moving.

I burst into tears. It was almost as bad as when we had heard our national anthem in the Czech church in Paris. Even Leopold took out his handkerchief. Only Diana who had of course drunk very much less than we had remained unmoved.

Afterwards there was more champagne and merry-making to counteract the spell of emotion. Confetti was thrown and streamers – the angels perched on Leopold's knees, who looked delighted. One of them was at least sixteen. 'Baby Doll' caressed me and Santa fed Diana sweets.

When before twelve we excused ourselves for having to go to midnight mass it was quite understood.

After the final embraces, while we tried to thank them, and then by taxi back to the Devon, even Leopold realized that for once he was in no fit state to go to church.

Neither of us could stop laughing.

'What's so funny?' Diana asked. 'I thought they were very nice and kind people.'

Indeed they were. I still don't know their name. I never saw them again, though I suppose Leopold did.

✖ 49 ✖

Ottawa was deep in snow when we arrived and it was very cold. The
embassy car came to fetch us at the station. The town centre through
which we were driven with its spired Houses of Parliament (ostentatious
Victorian baronial style), and the immense Château Laurier Hotel
(indeed like the imitation of a French Loire château) were transformed
and beautified into medieval splendour by their mantle of snow and
reminded me of Prague.

The Steinhardts' residence, so-called, was in a suburb of Ottawa;
Rockcliffe Park, a large villa of semi-classical appearance, as comfort-
able, luxurious and as overheated and overdecorated as whatever
Dulcie chose for them to live in.

We only stayed five days and they were so filled with social events,
luncheon parties, cocktail parties and dinner parties that all we seemed
to do was eat and drink, dress and undress and dress again and
try to rest in between. It wasn't very suitable for the child, I knew, but
she didn't complain, in fact seemed rather to enjoy the attention paid
her by grown-ups and certainly the food.

We met several old friends who had been in the diplomatic service in
Prague or Vienna. We were introduced to the Prime Minister, Saint
Laurent, who had recently replaced Mackenzie King, and I spent a
pleasant evening talking to an extremely civilized and witty gentleman
called Lester Pearson who was to become Canadian Prime Minister
some years later.

Rarely did I meet Steinhardt except in public. Dulcie or Dulcie Anne,
Leopold or Diana were always by my side. The few occasions on which
we could talk for a few moments were at cocktail parties or after
dinner. Even then someone would always come and interrupt. I saw
once more how popular he was, not only with his own staff but with
the Canadian government officials and the diplomatic corps, his
electrifying vitality seeming to stimulate and spark off even the dullest
into wit and animation.

Dulcie had not been slow in pointing out a fair, very pretty young
woman to me. 'That's Laurence's new girl-friend,' she said.

'She's attractive,' I remarked lightly, 'but then he has such good taste in women.'

This silenced her, since she didn't know to whom I was referring.

Later when I could talk to Steinhardt for a few minutes I asked him about his new girl-friend as casually as I could.

He seemed rather puzzled.

'Which?' he asked.

'Over there,' I said.

He glanced across briefly. 'Oh, she – Do you know, I think she's fallen in love with me. At least Dulcie says she has – Physically I find her very attractive,' he added with devastating frankness, 'but then these northern girls have such a terrific sex urge. Southern women for all their romantic approach are in the end much less co-operative. It stands to reason that the reproductive instincts are stronger in a climate where the survival of the species is more threatened than in the south. It's as simple as that – '

'And so – ?'

'And so – nothing – ' he laughed. 'I really haven't the time. Besides I'm quite satisfied with what I've got – '

'Not much, under the circumstances,' I complained.

'Yes, what the hell are we going to do? I can't possibly get to New York before next month. With the elections here so much work has piled up and Dulcie's getting a bit difficult.'

'I'll think of something,' I assured him. Convinced of my circumspect ingenuity in the past he gave me a warm and grateful look.

However, what he believed to be an effort of mine to ensure us an opportunity to be alone together, a plan of which in this case I was totally innocent, angered Dulcie more I think than if she had caught us embracing.

It happened on New Year's Eve on which there was a large party and dance given by the Steinhardts with all of Ottawa's eligible society present.

The villa's ballroom, which I hadn't seen before, was decorated with ornamental objects which the Steinhardts had collected at their various posts or had been presented with – Turkish rugs and brass, embroidery from Peru, lacquer boxes from Russia and Slovak pottery, all exhibited in glass cases.

I was dancing with the former Danish Ambassador from Prague, now accredited to Ottawa, an old bachelor whose caustic humour I knew only too well. He halted in front of a glass box.

'Interesting, isn't it?' he asked, 'if rather unexpected in a ballroom.'

I looked at the small brown head with distaste. 'Poor little monkey! Wonder why they thought it worth stuffing?' I asked.

'That's no monkey, that's a human head.'

'Nonsense, it's much too small.'

'They shrink them like that in Peru.'

I looked more closely at the little face, the whole thing was no bigger than a fist. Though its eyelids were closed (sewn up I could see and so was its mouth) it did look very human. It had a lot of long fine black hair.

'But this is too revolting!' I exclaimed. 'Do you mean the Peruvians do this to their dead?'

'Oh yes. In the early days it was only the heads of enemies killed in battle. Now they use whomever they can find to shrink. Mainly members of their family who have died or people who have been executed or murdered. Tourists pay a lot for these heads. It's quite an industry in Peru. The skull you know is carefully taken out, the skin of the face resewn over stuffing and the whole thing dried in hot sand.'

'Thank you,' I said, feeling quite ill, 'please, no more details.'

But when Steinhardt came to ask me to dance I voiced my disgust quite vigorously. 'How can you and how dare you display the unburied dead in your ballroom like this?'

'What do you mean?' he asked, amazed. I showed him. 'Oh that, I'd quite forgotten about it. Dulcie must have hung it up. She bought it in Peru. I guess it is a bit gruesome-looking.'

'It's not only that, it is very unlucky.'

'But why?'

'Believe me, I know. A friend of ours in Czechoslovakia brought back a mummified leg, probably stolen from a tomb. When he returned with it from Egypt he broke his own. It never healed and he became a cripple.'

'I never thought much of your doctors in Czechoslovakia,' Steinhardt remarked but I could see he was slightly disturbed. Like all irreligious people he was superstitious.

'Come,' I said, 'take it down and we'll go out and bury it.'

'What, in the snow?'

'I don't mind where as long as we do it.'

'Oh, that's it then! As good an excuse as any,' he laughed, relieved. 'Not that I've ever made love in the snow before, not even in Russia.'

He unhinged the glass box. Dulcie's eyes which were always everywhere took note. She swept across the room towards us. 'What are you doing with that head, Laurence? I've only just hung it up.'

'We are going to bury it, Dulcie,' I said. 'It's New Year's Eve and it must not stay in your house a minute longer. It can do terrible harm, I know.'

'I've no idea what you are talking about. I paid two hundred dollars for that. I won't have it removed or buried. Put it back immediately, Laurence, and go and talk to the French Ambassadress. She has something important to discuss with you.'

Rather shamefacedly he obeyed.

'How dare you!' Dulcie exclaimed, turning to me, her pale face pink with anger. 'Haven't we done enough for you without your trying to walk out with what's mine?'

What could I say? She would not have understood.

'Just a joke, Dulcie,' I tried to appease her.

'A very bad one then. What you need is some strong black coffee.'

Even the following day she let me feel her displeasure. On the next I left. Leopold had decided he might as well fly to Toronto to visit members of the growing Czech colony there. Several of our former neighbours were settling in and around the town. Diana had pleaded to be allowed to go with him. She knew some of the children whose parents he wanted to see and she had never flown before. She begged for this treat before she entered school. I had every reason to hurry back to New York and work on my portraits. Yet letting them go off alone like that worried me. I disliked being parted from them, was never quite certain what Leopold would be up to and I had a guilty conscience. It suited me only too well to have a day to myself in Ottawa.

I had told Dulcie that I would leave in the early morning by Greyhound bus for New York, explaining that I wanted to see something of the country and that I'd discovered it was cheaper than to go by train, which she thought very sensible. I had told Steinhardt that when I reached the bus station I would walk out again, find a taxi, go to the Château Laurier Hotel, book a room and telephone him at the embassy.

It seemed a perfect plan. But I hadn't counted with what was either Dulcie's vigilance or Dulcie Anne's kindness.

The latter insisted on driving with me to the bus station, helped me buy my ticket, saw that my luggage was properly stored in the bus's insides, found me a comfortable seat and sat down beside me, chatted for a while and only got off when the bus was ready to start, waving me goodbye as it left.

What was I to do? Greyhound buses go as fast as express trains and we were out of Ottawa in minutes. By the time I had tried to collect my wits we were in open country. It was snowing heavily.

I got up and staggered forward. It was not easy at the speed at which we were going to get to the front of the bus, I had to cling to the seats of startled passengers on my way to reach the driver.

'When is the next stop?' I asked him.

Not unnaturally he didn't turn round.

'Two hours, maybe more. Can't tell in this weather,' he mumbled, his eyes fixed on the road.

'I want to get out,' I demanded.

'That's impossible,' he said, not slackening speed. 'You'll have to wait until we get to the frontier. There's rest rooms there.'

'*Est que c'est que vous, vous sentez malade, Madame?*' a kindly French-Canadian enquired.

'*Non, mais je dois retourner à Ottawa, j'ai oublié quelque chose. Mon passe-port!*' Speaking French had reminded me of frontier difficulties. I didn't even have a passport, neither had Leopold. Our Czech ones were invalid but we had American travel documents. There had been no difficulties in getting into Canada, nor would there be any in re-entering the USA, I knew.

'I've forgotten my passport,' I repeated to the driver. 'They'll not let me into America.'

'Well, that's your problem, not mine. I'm paid to get these folks to New York.'

'If you would please just stop for one moment.'

Reluctantly he slowed down and the bus stopped.

'And now please let me out!'

He turned and stared at me, so did the passengers.

'Here?' he asked. We were in a forest, high snowbanks on the sides of the road and not a house in sight.

'Surely there must be buses that go back to Ottawa?' I asked.

'Not on this route, lady,' one of the passengers said, all of them interested in my problem and behaviour by now.

'Guess you'll have to thumb a ride,' an American girl giggled, raising her thumb and skirt. Cars were occasionally passing.

'See here,' said the driver, 'there are some farms about a mile back if you can make it. You can probably telephone from there and get a taxi to take you back to Ottawa. It will cost you plenty, even if it's only fifteen miles, but I guess if you can afford to lose your ticket to New York you can manage that too.'

'Can't I get a refund?' I asked as he helped me out into the snow and pulled out my suitcases, dropping them beside me.

'I wouldn't know. Maybe you can sort it out at the office in Ottawa.

If you ever get there. Here's your stub and good luck to you.' He boarded the bus. Some of the passengers waved, then I was alone in the drifting snow. It was bitterly cold after the comfortable warmth of the bus. Though I wore my fur coat I had on ordinary shoes and nothing on my head. I looked at my watch. It was only ten o'clock. I started to walk, knowing I must not stand still, carrying my two suitcases, hoping to reach the farms. Blinding gusts of icy wind, spiked with snow, hit my face. Because of the high drifts I had to walk in the middle of the road.

Car after car passed, swerving and skidding when they caught sight of me. None stopped. Probably they thought I was mad or drunk, sliding and stumbling as I did.

And indeed only madness could have compelled me, I thought angrily, responsible as I was for the child and Leopold, to risk my life in the wilds of Canada for the sake of a few hours with Steinhardt. 'Damn him!' I said every time I slipped. 'Damn him!'

Then a car did mercifully stop. A frosted window was wound down and a man in a knitted cap peered at me.

'Thought you was a bear,' he said. 'They sometimes come south for food in weather like this. What with that furry coat and the snow. Where you heading for, Missus?'

'Ottawa,' I managed to say though my teeth were chattering.

'Well, hop in. This is not walking weather.'

It was a sort of van. He flung my suitcases into the back and I crept into the front seat beside him. When we had started I told him about my getting off the Greyhound bus because of my lost passport.

'I guess St Peter wouldn't have asked you for it. Still they say it's quite a pleasant death in the snow,' he reassured me.

He seemed a friendly man, even if he had an unpleasant smell.

'Could we just open the window a little?' I begged.

'Oh, sure! I guess they stink a bit but nothing like they do in summer.'

'Fish?' I asked unnecessarily.

'Sure. I deliver them in Ottawa every week.'

By then we were approaching the town. He dropped me at the Château Laurier. I offered to pay him for his kindness but he refused to take any money. He hauled my suitcases out from between the boxes of fish.

'Nice to have met you,' he said.

'Even nicer for me!'

I booked a room. My dishevelled appearance may have caused some surprise but every good hotel receptionist recognizes mink, even if dripping wet. I was asked to sign my name. I knew I mustn't put my own. My brain as numb as my fingers, I wrote 'Mrs Fish'.

Not that I was allowed to forget them. My suitcases smelt so strongly that the porter looked at them curiously.

I had a hot bath, pouring half a bottle of scented oil into it, and felt I might survive. Life returned to my frozen limbs. I ordered some whisky, drank it and telephoned Steinhardt at the embassy.

He seemed surprised. 'However did you make it? I feared you were gone for good. Dulcie Anne said she'd seen you off.'

'Well, I'm here. The room number is fifty-six and my name is Fish, Mrs.'

'I'll be right round.'

When he came I told him nothing of my adventures, knowing from experience that he disliked hearing of the difficulties involved in our meetings.

'Wise, not to give your name, but why Fish?'

'Oh, I saw a van delivering some downstairs, that gave me the idea.'

'Can't have been very fresh by the smell in the corridor,' he sniffed, taking off his hat and coat. 'I met several people in the lobby that know me. Bit risky coming here. Ottawa's a small town and people gossip. Got to be a bit careful.'

I thought of what I'd risked to be with him and couldn't help remarking with some asperity, 'You didn't worry about such things in Prague.'

'No, why should I have? There everything could be explained as being of political importance. Here visiting Mrs Fish in a hotel bed-room is not. Still, I guess it's worth it.'

I was exhausted and my nerves were on edge. 'Is it?' I asked. And then asked the foolish question with which all women seek verbal reassurance of affection.

'Seems I'll have to prove it,' was his only answer.

'Haven't you rather overdone the scent business?' he remonstrated later. 'I seem to reek of it. I've got to go home for lunch.'

'You might say you are trying out a new aftershave lotion,' I said, feeling more cheerful. 'Will you be back in the afternoon?'

'Wish I could,' he sighed. 'But I was so sure I'd seen the last of you I agreed to speak at an exhibition in Montreal. Dulcie's coming with me and we are spending the night there with friends.'

Sensing my disappointment and trying to appease, he said, 'By the way, I forgot to mention, if you want me to do something about that land you think you might still have some rights to in Alberta, I'd have to have yours and your brothers' permission to deal with it – and all necessary documents pertaining. I'm still a good lawyer, you know – There may be nothing in it – but it will be an excuse to keep in touch.' He smiled significantly.

He put on his coat and hat. 'Now be careful,' he warned, 'don't roam the hotel. Lots of people have seen you in our house in the last days – I suppose you'll have to stay the night so as to take the morning bus since you already have a ticket?'

'Yes.'

'Sorry to have to leave you like this. Seems an awful waste – but I'll be in New York as soon as I possibly can.'

'Not the only waste,' I thought after he'd slipped furtively out of the door, his hat pulled down over his face like gangsters do in films. 'What about that bus ticket?' I knew I was very tired, too tired to drive to the Greyhound station and argue about refunds. 'Let it go,' I thought, besides I felt I never wanted to board a bus again. But neither did I like remaining closeted in my hotel room a minute longer than necessary.

I called the desk, said I had been obliged to change my plans. When was the next train leaving for New York? In an hour, they told me. I got out of bed, drank the rest of the whisky, dressed, counted my money. I had spent nothing in Ottawa except the bus fare, I had enough I knew. I paid my hotel bill and left for the railway station.

From the train I gazed with distaste at the monotonous snow-covered, uninhabited landscape beyond Ottawa through which we were passing, wooded plains, low uncared-for forests of scrub and saplings, tree-stumps proving that anything large and tall had been ruthlessly felled. A cold, inhospitable and unlovely country, I thought. Not even the sight of the wide St Lawrence river as grey as the grey sky above roused my interest. I closed my eyes and tried to sleep. I had no premonition whatsoever that the desolate landscape through which I had passed was to be the scene of a tragedy that would alter my life completely in the future. I arrived in New York late at night.

❈ 50 ❈

On my return from Ottawa, I found a large parcel addressed to me in Eddie's writing. I opened it. It contained twenty identical copies of the *Sunday Mirror* magazine with a large photograph of Mona on its front page holding my figurine on her knee.

'Now the famous beauty is a doll!' said the headlines.

There followed much in praise of Mona's finely chiselled features captured on canvas by the world's leading artists, her loveliness even translated into stone and marble and the many photographs by famous men which recorded her beauty.

'But never has a china doll been made of her before!'

Then it mentioned me '. . . With her family wealth gone down the drain of European politics a Countess turns to art as a livelihood.

'The Countess Leopold von Sternberg is herself both a beauty and a fashion plate. With her twelve-year-old son she managed to flee their homeland when the red tide of war spread over Europe. She was possessed of great wealth from tremendous holdings in Czechoslovakia but the Russians swept that country behind the Iron Curtain and all her riches vanished. Today like so many displaced blue bloods the Countess is faced with the task of supporting herself by her own efforts in this democratic country. She should do well if the work she turns out is all as artistic as the little china doll she presented to the Harrison Williamses.'

Then there was a photograph of the doll itself.

'Dearest,' Eddie wrote, 'I know it's going to make you and Leopold and your friends laugh so I sent you as many copies as I could find. Sorry they turned Diana into a boy and never mention Leopold at all. It's partially Mona's fault. She dislikes publicity so much that she told the man to just go ahead, giving him only a vague idea what it was all about except that she wanted to help you. Well, he did his best as you can see. And so has she. You may think it an insufferably vulgar article but then, so what? If one wants to succeed in this country being advertised is one of the things one has to face. Now just work hard at your other dolls and don't worry. Should be back in New York in six weeks or so.'

I was not as shocked as Eddie expected. In fact rather pleased. After all what the paper said was partially true and flattering.

I immediately sent a copy to the Steinhardts, hoping they would be impressed, enclosing it in my letter of thanks for our stay in Ottawa.

Leopold and Diana, back from Toronto, read it with interest. None of us were accustomed to see our names in print.

'I'll take one to the office,' Leopold declared. 'It will interest them. After all, you are *Umelecka Narodna*,' he laughed.

I had indeed during the war, more through the kindness of friends among Czech artists than there having been much merit in my copies of baroque statues, been given a card that identified me as an Artist of the Czech Nation. It was to have unforeseeable value in the confused and hectic days after the war ended. I had never learnt to speak Czech fluently. I might easily have been mistaken for a German in the streets of Prague had not my Artist's card been a sort of passport that even the Russians respected.

Diana decided she might as well take one of the magazines to school with her.

'It will explain something,' she said.

Poor child! How she disliked going. There had been too many recent changes in her life for her not to dread another.

'But we'll see you every weekend,' I tried to reassure her.

'And if you don't like it come back,' Leopold said cheerfully.

'We'd only have to find another school,' I warned, hating myself for having to say so.

For the next two months I worked hard at my ceramic portraits. I knew I was neglecting Leopold but it simply couldn't be helped. I had to concentrate on my subjects and if he came to the studio as he often did at first he would make a joke of the whole proceedings, so I had to beg him not to come which hurt his feelings. He was still trying to find work and one disappointment after another was sapping his optimism and self-confidence. His stay in Toronto too had disturbed him. Though he had not liked the town itself the vast orchards around Beamsville close to Niagara Falls where most of his friends were settling had left a strong impression. By selling whatever valuables they had been able to save when they fled, or helped by relations outside of Czechoslovakia, they had bought small or larger fruit farms in that area from which they hoped to make a living and assure future prosperity for themselves and their children.

Most of them were country-bred members of our former aristocracy who knew themselves unfit for office work in the cities or any form of business not connected with agriculture or farming or forestry. Their ancestors had lived off the soil for centuries. If they had to start a new life in a strange country it could only be on the land, even if it was only a few acres.

'They do all the digging, fertilizing, pruning and fruit picking themselves,' Leopold told me. 'It seems it's almost impossible to hire workmen in that part of Canada and even if it were possible they couldn't afford it. They help each other as best they can. They begged me to join. Urged me to try and buy a fruit farm too. But what good would I be at manual labour? I'm older than all of them and a cripple. Perhaps I could sit on the road at one of those stands and sell fruit for them in summer.'

'Oh, darling, don't be absurd. There are still endless possibilities open to someone of your intelligence. You must just have a little patience,' I tried to reassure him.

'I don't know,' he pondered. 'I really don't know what to do. There at least one would be among friends. If we sold the pictures Steinhardt brought we would probably have enough to buy a farm. Still, I don't see you slaving as those wives do,' he added, 'cooking and cleaning and washing sheets and underwear and looking after the children – nor would I like you to.'

'I'm sure I would be quite hopeless at it!' I said, all unknowing that a time would come when I would have to do all that and more.

'And the houses they live in,' he continued. 'Just square little wooden boxes in which you hear every sound. No gardens, no real trees, no woods or meadows, just mile after mile of orchards. Still, I suppose it must be lovely in the spring,' he added. 'Do you remember the hundreds of cherry trees I planted in Zasmuky?'

I did and how we had watched them grow and blossom and bear fruit. Sadly I thought that whatever might befall us, good or bad, Leopold's longing for his lost lands would never cease.

I knew myself much more adaptable than he was but then women generally are, having in any case to leave their homes when they marry. Though I had never lived for any length of time in a big city before I was growing fond of New York.

Surely in no other city in the world do people of such different racial origins live in such close proximity or is the contrast between the very rich and the poor so evident on so small a circumference of ground.

Yet Central Park belonged to them all. Children of every complexion and kind seemed to play there together without much animosity. Lovers of every species embraced there undisturbed. Old people of all nationalities sat on benches enjoying the spring sunshine. Smart English nannies pushed their American charges in high-wheeled shining perambulators. Young negro mothers not to be outdone, with prams almost as expensive-looking, exhibited the enchanting black faces of their babies, peering out of freshly laundered, ironed and starched pillows and bonnets. Italian men strolled proudly carrying their offspring high on their shoulders for all to see and admire while their wives walked humbly a few steps behind. Ancient Jews, some still with ringlets and wearing the black kaftan of the Orthodox, guarded grandchildren or great-grandchildren, feebly admonishing them in Yiddish not to stray.

Clarisse Rothschild had been knocked down by a thief there and her bag stolen. I didn't heed any warnings. Though a coward when it comes to catastrophic events like fires, floods, storms, earthquakes or war against which the individual is powerless, I was not particularly afraid of men, black or white, or even of criminals.

We are all animals of the same species, even if some of us are more ferocious than others. There are set rules in the animal world which apply to humans just as well. To show fear provokes pursuit, threatening behaviour invites attack. The animal that does neither is rarely endangered. Even the worst criminals, except such as are mentally ill, do not kill their fellow men for pleasure, they do so from fear. So I continued to walk in the park often with Diana and never met with any unpleasantness or danger.

However Harlem was different. I had been told that if I went there alone I would be robbed, insulted and probably raped and murdered. I didn't believe it. Even if it was fourteen years ago since we had spent night after night there laughing, dancing, drinking with its people and listening to jazz, there had been no question of having to be careful with one's money or of risking one's virtue or one's life. We had been treated as honoured guests.

I wanted to see for myself what it was like now.

Of course I didn't go at night. I went in the morning, plainly dressed with just a few dollars in my bag.

Once there I walked through street after street, crowded with black, brown and almost-white-looking people. They were even more smartly and flashily dressed than I remembered and the houses and shops looked clean and prosperous. No one insulted me or tried to rob me or attack me. How could they since they didn't even see me? It was as if I didn't exist. Those that stood in groups gossiping, laughing or arguing didn't pause in their conversation or move to make way for me to pass. I had to step out into the road to circle round them. Not even the children at which I smiled spared me a glance. It was like being invisible and it was very frightening.

Finally I went into a drugstore that had gaily striped awnings and sat down at one of the little tables. There were black men in working clothes, youths in blue overalls, drinking soft drinks through straws and children running in and out for ice cream cones or packets of gum sold by a big powerful-looking negro standing behind the counter. Obviously the owner of the place.

Again no one took any notice of me. I felt so disembodied that I wondered if I still had a voice.

'Can I have a cup of coffee, please?' I asked. It came out much louder than I had expected.

There was a sudden silence.

All eyes were fixed on the man behind the counter. Would he refuse to serve me? I wondered. He seemed to deliberate, then shrugged his wide shoulders. 'How do you want it?'

'Black and strong, please,' I said, as I'd done hundreds of times before. Only the roar of laughter that broke the silence made me realize what I'd said. 'Then come and get it!' the owner called, grinning from ear to ear, showing splendid white teeth. There was more coarse laughter.

I knew I was blushing but hoped people of a different complexion wouldn't notice. I got up and with what dignity I could muster approached the counter. At least I wasn't invisible any more.

'Say, you're not American. I can tell from the way you speak,' the big man said as he poured my coffee.

'No, I've only just arrived here. I'm from Czechoslovakia.'

'Been as far as Pilsen myself,' he said, surprisingly, 'never got to Prague though.'

'You were in the army?'

'Sure, France, Germany. Must have been bad those years for you Czechs.'

'They would have been worse if we hadn't been sure you Americans would win the war,' I remarked. I couldn't have said anything more effective had I tried.

There was a murmur of appreciation. People drew near and looked at me as if I was a human being at last.

'What brought you to Harlem, ma'am?' someone beside me asked politely.

'I used to come here years ago when we visited New York,' I explained. 'I always remembered how friendly everyone was.'

'Well, I guess you've noticed a change,' the big black man said, polishing some glasses.

'Yes,' I said, 'but why?'

Everyone drew even closer. Obviously he was a man of some importance among them, whose words counted. He looked at me not unkindly, I felt, but who can tell what goes on in the mind of those forever masked in black?

'Suppose you have a right to know coming as you do from Europe,' he said. 'It's like this. We don't want whites here any more. They cause nothing but trouble. Politicians, or agitators, or preachers, or do-gooders, or tourists that come to stare at us as if we were some kind of strange animal, or those that cotton up to us full of brotherly love, or those that come here for thrills or drugs or black sex! We cannot stop them from coming. We don't want to use no violence against them either, so all we can do is make as if they weren't here. Ignore them. It's a sort of passive resistance but it works. It scares them stiff.'

'It certainly frightened me,' I said. 'It made me feel like a ghost!'

He threw back his head and clapped his big black hands together. 'Thought you was a spook?' he laughed, obviously delighted. 'No offence meant to you personally, miss,' he then said. 'You can't help your colour no more than we can ours and you not being American it ain't none of your fault that things are as they are.'

'But I thought you people had everything you wanted by now – equal rights and all that.'

'Sure, on paper. And the right to fight their wars and do the dirty work!'

I tried to pay for my coffee but he wouldn't let me.

'I'm real sorry, miss.' 'So am I,' I said. We shook hands. 'Hey there, you no good lazy niggers,' he called. Two stalwart youths stood at attention. 'Escort this lady and see there's no trouble.'

They did as ordered, clearing the streets through which we passed by shoving people aside and handing me into a bus with cold courtesy.

I didn't tell anyone about my expedition, fearing to hear 'I told you so', but it left me with a feeling of unease whenever I looked towards Harlem just across the park.

Meanwhile Diana had started school. At first she complained bitterly, saying she hated it but could really give no valid reason for doing so.

'Has anyone been unkind to you?' 'No. Mr and Mrs Elliot are very kind.' 'And the children?' 'Some are quite nice,' she conceded, then burst into tears. 'Is it the food?' I asked, knowing how particular she was. 'It's all right,' she sobbed.

387

What then was wrong? Only gradually did I understand. She had lived for months with us, sharing our life almost as if she were grown up, doing more or less what she pleased, getting up when she felt like it, sleeping only when she wanted to, telling us what we ought to do more frequently than we told her. What she really resented was the discipline that even the most lenient of schools must impose.

Also she disliked sport. The Headmaster had made it quite clear that he thought sport more beneficial to health, morale and the development of team spirit than study. Diana did not share his opinion, mainly I think because she was unable to excel in any games. Though she had long straight legs and there seemed nothing wrong with them, she could neither run fast nor jump without frequent, perhaps not quite unintentional, accidents. Rarely was there a weekend when she didn't appear with a bandaged knee, ankle or foot which after anxious investigation by me seemed not to have suffered any visible damage.

'She has not what they call "the team spirit",' Mrs Elliot told me in private when I had come to see how things really were. 'Diana is very much an individual. If she personally can't win she doesn't care which side does. But she is an exceptionally good scholar, attentive, intelligent and ambitious and will soon be head of her class. And that surely is all that matters,' Mrs Elliot smiled.

'And her behaviour?'

'Exemplary. But then she's so well brought up in comparison with most American children who behave like little savages. Such marvellous manners! Though, if I may say so, perhaps a little over-conventional and too serious for her age. One cannot help noticing her disapproval of others who really don't know what it's all about, not having had as strict and careful an upbringing as your daughter.'

I felt I had, in all honesty, to contradict this assertion.

'That's not true,' I declared, 'what with the war years and what came afterwards she couldn't have had a more unsettled or difficult childhood.'

'But not one of parental neglect?'

'I don't think so. She was always with us.'

'Which goes to prove what an important influence the manners and morals of her parents must have had on Diana. Whatever the circumstances, giving a child a good example is so important in the formative year.'

Could she be joking? She was an intelligent woman.

'It's not thanks to our example,' I said hastily, 'that Diana is as she is, rather the contrary.'

I had for quite a while had my suspicions that her correct behaviour and extreme conventionality were due to her resentment at our lack of both.

'In any case, you have a daughter to be proud of,' Mrs Elliot said. 'Tom and I have grown very fond of her.'

Satisfactory as some of this was, the school was proving even more expensive than I had anticipated. There were so many extras I hadn't foreseen – dancing classes, art. Diana drew very well and it seemed wrong not to have her taught to paint. That a girl should have piano lessons seemed obligatory. Then there was all the sports equipment she was expected to have, however little she used it, and, of course, as much pocket money as the other children were given by their wealthy parents, spent as far as I could make out mainly on expensive food-hampers that provided clandestine midnight feasts.

We were, I knew, living far beyond our means. Two apartments in an expensive district of New York. Taking taxis wherever we went. Eating in restaurants where the food was indeed better than in Automats but also much more costly. Even my work (I didn't know then that there was something called Industrial Current that might have halved my electricity bill for the kiln had it been properly installed) was proving unexpectedly expensive.

Something I knew had to be done. I telephoned the Viennese antique dealer Clarisse had recommended, gave my name, which brought friendly immediate recognition in German, '*Ach der liebe Graf Sternberg so ein Freund*,' presumably referring to my father-in-law, certainly not to Leopold who had rarely shopped for antiques.

I explained the situation. That we had fled from Czechoslovakia, had been able to save a certain amount of valuables, some of which I would have to sell as I desperately needed money.

He quite understood. 'Bring whatever you've got,' he said, 'and I will see what I can do.'

Next day I had the various crates and boxes containing practically everything but the pictures delivered at his address.

I followed by taxi. The shop was small and somewhat too far on the East Side to still be part of the large area of internationally famous antique dealers. Its owner was a rather charming dapper elderly gentleman who looked like a benign Mephistopheles. He had a small pointed black beard, oddly slanting eyebrows and a persuasive manner. The shop contained mainly china and Austrian refugees, who didn't come there to buy or sell but to drink coffee and talk. Mephisto worked with his son, a youngish man who suffered from a nervous disorder. Even when I got to know them both well I never dared enquire what had caused his trembling. It was a sort of palsy, I suppose. He shook all over. Yet amazingly the china he handled so precariously never broke and I never saw him drop a piece.

He and I unpacked the crates together. First a large collection of *Alt Wien* coffee sets on little trays, these and pots and cups hand-painted with landscapes or flowers, a collection made by my father-in-law.

Mephisto watched as we worked, unwrapping and listing one thing after another, occasionally exclaiming '*Hübsch sehr hübsch,*' but more often frowning when a handle was missing or a piece cracked or chipped.

Then came the flowered Meissen dinner-service of a hundred and fifty pieces, plates, dishes, sauce-boats, soup tureens and salvers. He was not impressed by this. 'Mostly twentieth-century reproductions,' he said, turning round plate after plate to scan the mark and setting a few aside with a more satisfied air.

Of the silver too there was almost an equal amount, engraved with our coat of arms, which didn't please him much. 'Easier to sell if it had the Star of David!' he remarked. (Ours had eight points instead of six.) 'In any case modern silver like this is only worth its weight.'

There was a rather bizarre collection of table ornaments, drinking cups and jugs in the form of knights in armour made of silver gilt, studded with mother-of-pearl and what I believed were precious stones.

'Copies,' he shrugged, 'of Renaissance originals inset with glass. Still, who can tell? They might appeal to American tastes.'

It was strange and rather painful to see all those things that we had valued and cherished in the past and that had added splendour to our dinner parties littering the floor of the dingy shop like so much junk.

There was a large box of English prints too. They had been very fashionable in my parents-in-law's days. I had in the last hours before we left Castolovice surreptitiously removed them from their frames and replaced them with illustrations out of English magazines, mainly for the servants' sake, who had been warned that everything now belonged to the state and that they must see to it that nothing was taken by us.

I could have saved myself the trouble. Most of them proved quite valueless reproductions.

'You must understand that I can't buy all this myself,' Mephisto said, 'but I will try and sell it for you as best I can. It will take some time, of course.'

'But I do rather need money now.'

He glanced briefly at his son who seemed to nod, though perhaps his head was just shaking as usual.

'I could certainly advance you a reasonable amount if you leave this here on deposit. Five hundred?'

Seeing my disappointed face he increased his figure to eight hundred. I agreed and he wrote me out a cheque.

'We will have to list everything, of course,' I said, 'and keep accounts of the things sold for both our sakes,' trying to sound businesslike and polite at the same time.

'Naturally. I will do my best for you, be assured of that.'

Perhaps he did but certainly not in a very orderly fashion, but then neither was I capable throughout the two years of our business association remembering which items had been sold and which hadn't or what china in the shop was mine or theirs. Both father and son seemed as confused as I was when it came to checking lists or finding anything.

However, they usually had some money for me, smaller or larger sums, when I visited the shop about once a month.

I grew fond of the palsied son, who though very absent-minded was intelligent and well read. He was a great admirer of the poet Rilke as I was and confessed to writing poems himself, though he never showed them to me. I liked the atmosphere of the little shop. Though I rarely saw any customers, it was as Clarisse had said a sort of meeting place of Austrian intellectuals, writers and artists who came to discuss their problems over innumerable cups of coffee. I remember meeting Kokoschka there and that he spoke as brilliantly as he painted.

And then there was *Die Mamma*. Though she remained invisible she seemed a person of great importance. There were always polite enquiries as to her health and respectful greetings of *Handküsse* to be relayed to the *Gnädige Frau Mamma* through husband or son. She never came into the shop, at least not when I was there but often the presence of someone behind the tapestry curtains at the far end was evident, a muted female voice could be heard which was not that of the black maid who carried in the coffee.

'Couldn't I call on your mother?' I asked the son one day. 'Now I know the rest of the family so well I would so like to meet her too.'

'I will tell Mamma. It will please her,' he said, 'but she can't see anyone any more. She is blind and very ill. She has a brain tumour.'

'I'm so sorry!' was all I could say, knowing how inadequate it was.

When a few weeks later, again in need of money, I came to the shop I found it locked and shuttered. But seeing a gleam of light through a curtain I rang the bell. The son let me in as he obviously had a lot of other people, elderly men and women who were sitting around somberly dressed. A single candle lit the shop, the mirrors were covered with sacking and the curtains drawn. '*Die Mamma ist uns gestern gestorben,*' the son whispered, tears running down his face. He was unshaven and his coat was torn.

Someone was reading out of a Bible, the others joined in the words, they were speaking Hebrew I think.

'It's the psalms for Mamma. "The Lord is my shepherd".'

'Forgive me for intruding,' I whispered as I moved towards the door. 'Please give your father my most sincere sympathy.' He caught hold of my hand, mine shaking in his. 'Friends are such a comfort in times of bereavement. My father will be glad you came, only he can't leave Mamma. She looks so beautiful. Come!' There was no escape, his trembling hand was remarkably strong and I didn't dare struggle in front of the praying people. He drew me through the tapestry curtain.

There Mamma lay in her open coffin. A candle burnt at its head. It smelt of honey. A face narrowed and blanched, revealing nothing but the austere dignity of death. Bending over her, his sparse grey hair and beard dishevelled, his clothes in disarray, crying, moaning and perhaps praying was a distraught old man.

When I returned to the shop a fortnight later everything was much as usual. Mephisto's hair and beard were a youthful black again. He looked as neat and dapper as ever and even managed a smile when I tried to express my sympathy. 'The Lord giveth and taketh away. Blessed be the Lord,' he said.

The son trembled no worse than he always had and told me he had written a new poem. 'In Memoriam' of course. After that I was handed a hundred and fifty dollars but didn't feel it right because of their recent bereavement to enquire what they had sold, nor, I knew, would they have been able to give a coherent answer.

They could have cheated me out of almost everything in those two years had they been as shrewd and rapacious as antique dealers are supposed to be, by taking advantage of my ignorance and total lack of business sense.

But I know they didn't. If anyone cheated it was I, reclaiming things for which I had long since received payment.

One thing is certain. No one could have been kinder and more helpful in the first years of our emigrant life than Jews. I don't mean people like the Rothschilds and their relations who had always been friends or even the Steinhardts to whom we owed so much.

It was the Jewish dentist who had managed to escape from Prague and was trying to earn his living in New York and repaired our teeth and never sent a bill. It was the doctor, once famous in Vienna, who treated Leopold's leg free of charge – there were many others who gave invaluable advice and tried to help in every way they could. Why? I asked myself again and again. We were not Jewish. What we had suffered was as nothing compared to what they had. And yet loss of home and country we shared and that which had been so comfortably and humorously understood in Austria, *Juden und Aristrokraten gehöeren zusammen,*' remained true, even in exile, to our great advantage.

🎕 51 🎕

The first portrait I completed was of Diana Vreeland. Tall and thin with more angles than curves, her jet-black hair uncompromisingly drawn back from her high forehead, her eyebrows like French accents above quick lively dark eyes, nose long and broad and a wide scarlet mouth. She wore the plainest of black dresses so well cut that it gave her a sculptured appearance. She looked not only elegant but competent and self-assured. One of those women who are their own masterpiece.

What must she think, I wondered, not only of my shabby studio, scarcely worthy of the name, but of what I was doing? She had come, of course, only because Mona had begged her to. She sat very quiet, not moving, not talking, patient and incurious, knowing, I'm certain, that I was no artist but giving me every opportunity to be one. If you have to stare at a face for any length of time in silence and it looks back at you, the essential personality penetrates the concealing mask and you know the truth about each other better than if you had spoken. I knew she saw me exactly as I was, a rather frightened beginner, but I didn't mind. I felt her sympathy and understanding. Perhaps she too in her youth had struggled to succeed and perhaps her fame in the fashion world had not been easily won.

Jarmila Novotna who was my next sitter had also worked hard to succeed. True she had a lovely voice and a beautiful face but that is not sufficient to make a famous opera-singer. It had taken years of dedicated study till she achieved her spectacular début in opera. She came to me out of pure kindness wanting to help. Her husband, Jiri Daubek, had been a lifelong friend of Leopold's and was now working in New York. I didn't know her very well as she had always been *en tour* and the couple had left Prague before the war. She had a classically perfect face but was a very vivacious, rather restless and impatient sitter. I let her go after I had done her head and we agreed I would dress her as the Bartered Bride in Smetana's opera, a ribboned wreath of flowers in her hair, wearing the wide skirts and the many petticoats of our national costume. The statuette had succeeded quite well, I thought, except for a large crack. I had been too impatient to take it out of the kiln before it cooled.

Then came Mita Corti, doing Eddie a favour. He and she were great friends. Because she moved like a dancer I had wanted to do her in a ballet costume but when I saw how perfect her figure was I draped her in a sarong of brown and white cotton, leaving her arms and shoulders bare, and with her little head on its long neck, slanting eyes and full mouth she looked like a dancer from the island of Bali.

I made a bust of Dulcie from memory, I knew her face so well, draping her hair with the sort of snood she always wore and one of Princess Boncompagni, just magnificent proud head and shoulders.

Afterwards I sketched Nin Ryan in her own house (I don't think she would have appreciated my studio), and worked on the statuette afterwards, dressing her as I pleased in a turban and Oriental costume. One more of Mona from memory posed against a flowering tree and a few smaller figures, fantasies in the eighteenth-century manner.

The latter I took to the Judge. I had since lunched with him several times. We had always been alone except for the two ancient starched parlourmaids. I enjoyed every hour spent with him. Only to him did I dare speak freely about Steinhardt, boring him, I'm sure, with endless questions about Larry's family and childhood.

'What was his mother like? Beautiful?'

'I wouldn't have called her that,' the Judge said tersely. 'Minny Guggenheim liked her food. She was in fact very fat.'

'And his sisters?'

The Judge shrugged expressively.

'Larry took after his father who was good-looking.'

'And were they all as brilliant and clever as Steinhardt is?'

The Judge looked at me quizzically. 'Larry's an awfully good fellow but I wouldn't call him particularly clever. Too impulsive, too anxious to please. It's Dulcie who is the shrewd one.'

'Don't I know it,' I sighed. 'Will she make him President, do you think?'

'That will be the day,' the Judge cackled, much amused. 'Larry, the first Jew in the White House. I thought I'd gone far when I was made Judge of the Appellate Court!'

'Do you mind being born Jewish?' The Judge was the only person I'd ever met of whom I could ask such a question, knowing it would not offend.

'No,' he said without hesitation. 'I have never regretted it. But then I am by nature a rather lazy man and having been blessed with a considerable inherited fortune I might have overindulged myself had I not been a Jew. Being one is a challenge, you see. One is responsible to one's people to achieve the most one can so that others may follow. If I took my education seriously and worked hard at my legal career it was not because I particularly enjoyed doing so. I wouldn't have minded at all in my youth being what is now called "a playboy",' the Judge said, his small blue eyes crinkling with amusement. 'I worked for the sake of fellow Jews. Even my collection which will eventually go to the Metropolitan Museum is proof of what a Jew can achieve.'

'Do you think Larry feels the same?'

'Dear, dear,' said the Judge. 'Is he never out of your thoughts?'

I blushed. I blush very easily and he noticed and chuckled. 'Obviously not –

'Yes, instinctively Larry feels the same,' he conceded.

'Now come, there are several of my things you haven't looked at yet.'

Obediently I followed him, knowing there was no collection or person from which I could learn more.

When I brought him several of my smaller figurines somewhat in the style of his Meissen ones he was appreciative but not enthusiastic.

'The modelling is graceful but alas what coarse material! What thick and ugly glaze compared to the soft lustre of porcelain. There is a saying which applies to sculpture – "Clay is life, plaster death, marble the resurrection" but only being cast in pure porcelain would bring resurrection to your figurines. As for the decoration,' (which was done in overglaze painting which I found very difficult) 'well, it's somewhat lacking in precision,' the Judge remarked. He took one of his Kändler Harlequins down and held it next to mine. 'Do you see the difference?'

Indeed I did.

'I tell you what. There's a factory that makes very fine china in New Jersey. Lennox. I sometimes have things repaired there. They might be glad to cast your clay models in china and even pay you for it. I could recommend you to them if you wish.'

Grateful as I was for this suggestion I soon forgot all about it. The great exhibition of my work was drawing near and I felt extremely nervous at the prospect. Eddie kept me informed from day to day about the invitations sent out to art critics and journalists as well as to all and everyone who counted socially in New York. He and Mona had ordered half of the books in the library to be removed, the shelves being used to exhibit my statuettes. Everyone portrayed was, of course, invited and whatever friends I had of any kind would be welcome. But I had not dared risk asking the Steinhardts or the Judge. What if the whole thing proved an embarrassing failure?

Ranged on the shelves among orchids and gardenias with which Mona had not been able to resist filling the empty spaces stood the small figures, each of them, except for the first one of Mona I had made, which had turned a dusty grey, highly glazed and because of that all of them looking very much alike.

The party started after six in the evening and lasted until nine. There was a lot to drink and everyone seemed to be enjoying themselves. Occasionally someone glanced briefly at my figurines and then moved on in search of more interesting objectives.

Leopold, conscious of the importance of the occasion and wishing to help, dragged reluctant guests to view the exhibits. Eddie, equally trying to assist, introduced several people to me with stage whispers of 'Might be useful to you', or proclaimed loudly for anyone to hear, 'Oh, she only charges five hundred dollars per portrait.'

'But, Eddie, you can't!' I said, trying to stop him. 'It's too much – they are not worth that.'

'They will be once people know how expensive they are – you don't understand Americans.'

Finally Nin Ryan brought a man to me, saying, 'Howard wants to meet you.' I think his surname was Dietz and that he was a theatre producer. In any case he looked like one. 'He is the wittiest man in New York,' Nin told me, then turned to him – 'Well, and what do you think of our famous sculptress, Howard?'

'Quite a chiseller, isn't she?'

'That was not very funny,' Nin said indignantly, trying not to laugh as she drew him away.

I didn't at first understand, after all sculptors use chisels, but Nin had made me feel something uncomplimentary had been implied. I went up to Eddie who was talking to Mita. 'What's a "chiseller"?' I asked him. 'It's a slang expression. It means a cheat, I think,' Eddie said. 'Or someone who tries to get something out of people for nothing,' Mita explained. 'Why do you ask?'

'Just something I overheard,' I said. I was much too ashamed to confess I had been called one. So that was what they probably all thought, that I was a cheat taking advantage of Mona's kindness and social position to sell my worthless products.

After that whenever I heard someone laugh or saw people whisper together I knew it was about me. Even the kindly-meant praise of my portraits by friends sounded like cruel mockery.

'Wasn't it a success, darling?' Mona asked, her lovely face glowing with enthusiasm as I came to thank her and say goodbye. She and Eddie, the two dogs, her maid, the dogs' maid and Eddie's valet were leaving for Capri that week. 'When I come back you will have made a fortune!' she added happily.

Several papers mentioned the fact that Mrs Harrison Williams had given a large party in honour of an artist (they did give my name) who specialized in ceramic portraits but the rest was all about who had been there and with whom and what they had worn.

Not one of the people who had sat for me, except for Louis Roths-child who had already bought his little jade-green head, seemed to want to buy their portraits. I couldn't blame them. After all they had only posed out of kindness. So I just let them have them, though Nin didn't even want hers as a gift.

I had one order, thanks to the exhibition, from a very wealthy woman who lived on Fifth Avenue in an apartment as pink as her complexion and as pale blue as her hair. The whole effect was rather sugary. She was an elderly lady. If there was to be any resemblance I could not make her look seventeen. She objected to my having aged her and refused to pay the five hundred for the bust so I let her have it for fifty.

My last venture in ceramic portraits came through the Judge. The Linskys were friends of his. They too were collectors. They wanted themselves portrayed sitting on a rococo sofa holding hands, in front of them a table and on it the most precious objects of their collection, the whole thing to commemorate their devotion to each other and to art. It was a challenging order. They lived outside of New York in a smart modern suburban house in which I felt the many fine antiques they had acquired did not look quite at home.

I visited them several times to sketch their faces and figures. They were middle-aged. Mr Linsky was small, spare and lean. Mrs Linsky the contrary. They were kind and friendly people and showed great patience, sitting for hours holding hands. Back in the studio I worked hard at the group. The technical difficulties were enormous. Either the sofa or the table legs collapsed before the rest had dried. Yet I wanted so much to create something *à la Kändler* or Bustelli which I knew was what they wanted.

When the group was finally completed, glazed and decorated it had turned into a marvellous caricature of them both. Had I been able to do them in eighteenth-century dress they might not have looked as funny as they did in modern clothes on that very elaborate sofa. I can't blame them for not having been pleased. Very kindly they gave me a hundred dollars for my trouble, said the group hadn't turned out quite as they had expected and would I please take it away. After that I knew my days as a ceramic portraitist were definitely over.

Steinhardt had come to New York several times in those months, flying there and back to Ottawa in his private plane in a day. As long as he didn't stay away a night he said Dulcie suspected nothing.

Strange, I thought. Were there really people who could only make love in the hours of darkness?

Of the failure of my exhibition and of the collapse of all my hopes I, of course, told Steinhardt nothing.

On the contrary, I boasted of my success – artistic, social and amatory – and did a lot of vulgar name-dropping. I think he believed me. He had no reason to doubt. I had always been truthful with him in the past. But then I had nothing to conceal. However I did tell him that I might give up ceramic portraits, however profitable, for a much bigger and artistically and financially more rewarding enterprise to sell models for figurines to all the big china manufacturers in America. I lied, saying I had made contact with Lennox in New Jersey already. The Judge, I knew, would not give me away.

'Why they make all our embassy china,' Steinhardt remarked. 'Eagle and all in gold. I seem to have eaten off it half my life and constantly have had to reorder more. You might sell thousands of figurines through them.'

I thought it wiser to change the subject. 'It's Leopold's problems that trouble me most now,' I said. 'You see, it hurts his masculine pride to see me so successful while he can't find a job. You have so much influence here and in Washington,' I pleaded, 'can't you find him something that at least sounds important and that will give him some-thing to do even if it doesn't pay very well?'

Steinhardt sighed. I knew he was genuinely fond of Leopold. 'Finding Leopold a job is like trying to fit a square peg into a round hole.' He thought for a while. 'Didn't you know George Kennan when he was in

Prague?' he asked.

'Yes, very well.'

'He might be of use. He has quite an important advisory position in the State Department and is very highly thought of there I hear. Of course he's only a career diplomat but seems intelligent, writes well and knows a lot about Russia and its Slavonic satellites. He would be just the right person to help Leopold. Why haven't you contacted him?'

I knew exactly why not. George and Annelies, his Norwegian wife, had been friends in days when we still had a lot to offer. They happened to be the sort of people who would feel compelled to give us their last shirt if they thought us destitute. We were not yet in that condition, nor capable at the time of deliberately trying to exploit real friends for help.

'I've never met him,' Steinhardt said, 'but I hear he's an attractive man. Were you and he lovers when he was in Prague?'

'Certainly not!' I exclaimed indignantly. 'He was much too nice!'

'I don't quite know how to understand that,' Steinhardt said, not looking too pleased. 'Surely the one doesn't exclude the other?'

Totally, I knew. 'Of course not,' I said hastily.

'Not interested in sex perhaps? Too intellectual?'

I had to laugh, thinking of Annelies and her warm, ready, happy smile.

After Steinhardt had left I tried to remember when I had first met George Kennan. He was one of those rare people whom you think you have always known. Even when you meet them for the first time you just go on talking as you had before.

I tried to think when he had first come to Prague. Was it before the Germans came? Certainly he and Annelies remained there till well into the war. I remembered his invaluable advice when so many Czechs had come to feel, however reluctantly, that all that was left to them was to submit to German rule, calmly explaining to us and others the issues at stake and warning that soon no compromise would be possible.

Dear George, I thought, and dear, always cheerful and optimistic Annelies. How good it would be to see them again! Should I write?

I wondered if they knew we were in America. Yet they certainly would have enquired about us and perhaps have heard through diplomatic gossip that I was well kept by Ambassador Steinhardt, which I knew many people thought.

That this was not true I could not have explained, not even to George nor anyone else, without sounding like the lady who protests too much. How was he to know that Steinhardt was not the sort of man to look twice at a woman who cost him anything? And that all Stein-hardt had done for us, facilitating our escape and that of many of our friends, was only partially due to my feminine charms. If he had helped us and others it was mainly because he felt in a way guilty, knowing he had been over-confident in his powers to save the country for the West. He had felt responsible for those of his friends reassured by his optimism when he should have warned them to sell out while it was still possible to do so.

52

Summer had come and it was getting insufferably hot in New York. Neither the Devon nor my studio had air-conditioning. I had more or less given up working, disheartened by the exhibition. The child was back from school, bored, listless and tiresome. Leopold complained bitterly of the heat, and all our friends had left the city to go to the seaside, the mountains or the country.

It was then I thought of the Kennans. They had come to see us and warmly invited us to stay with them on their farm in Pennsylvania.

So I wrote and they answered they'd be delighted to have us for as long as we could stay, all summer if possible – but that we must not expect great luxury. Life on the farm was simple but they thought we'd like to know what real American country-living was like and that Gracie and Joan, the Kennans' two daughters, were looking forward to meeting Diana.

Leopold and I studied the map of Pennsylvania to find East Berlin in Adams County where the Kennans lived. An odd name, but half of the state seemed dotted with German names, all too familiar to me from the time of my childhood in Holstein: Hamburg, Altona and Hanover. Much more fascinating and mysterious were names like Palmyra, Egypt, Lebanon and Paradise.

In any case we ascertained that East Berlin was not so far from New York that we could not return to it within a few hours if we needed to.

We telephoned the Kennans the time of our arrival and left next day by train.

It seemed only a short while later that we were out of the industrial districts and in open country. What an extraordinary contrast! Land as verdant as a well-tended garden. Neatly squared fields, green with crops, others dug or ploughed, the brown soil open ready for seeding or planting. Men dressed in solemn black, big hats shading their heads, were digging or guiding fat glossy Shire horses behind what looked like wooden ploughs.

'Look,' Leopold exclaimed, 'it's like hundreds of years ago. Why, not even at home in my youth did I see such primitive methods of agriculture. What a strange country America is.'

Who on earth could they be, these solemn-looking people in black with their big biblical beards? Orthodox Jews?

There were no women in sight and no houses.

'I think I know what they are,' Diana said. 'We learn about these sects in school. I think they are called Amishes. They have a religion that forbids them to use any machines. They weave their own clothes on wooden looms and only marry each other. But what they believe in I've forgotten.'

The country became less cultivated and more wooded. We crossed a big river, its shores fringed by dense forests that looked almost tropical. The trees were of no species we could recognize, nor had we ever seen such birds – bright blue or scarlet, flashing through the foliage. Small white herons waded in the shallows.

'Do the Indians still live here?' Diana asked.

I don't know, I thought, but surely their ghosts must haunt this land that was once theirs.

Even where the trees had been cleared it looked lush, green and fertile. There were orchards and flowering meadows and neat stone houses with gabled roofs unlike any I had seen in America before. They looked as if they had been built long ago by people firmly decided to stay and take root in this country. They were quite unlike the New England white wooden houses that seemed to me like ships ready to sail away in the slightest breeze.

At the station when we arrived was George lean and sunburnt in a singlet and jeans to welcome us and drive us home in his ramshackle-looking car.

'It's a hideous house,' he said, 'and not even comfortable yet. It's only recently we bought the place. Still, I hope you will like it. We certainly do!'

George's eyes were as bright a blue as I remembered and they shone with the pride of ownership when he said, 'This is where my land begins.'

We had crossed a small stream on a bumpy country road, passed through fields and pastures, farm-buildings, a big barn, then stopped at the strangest-looking house I think I have ever seen. It looked like a very large white cardboard box, as tall as it was wide, in fact perfectly square. It reminded me of boxes which I had used to house my dolls in as a child, cutting windows out anywhere with scissors. So too had the architect who had built this edifice. Not only were there windows in the most unexpected places but there were small balconies and porches attached at random. To complete it all there was an effort at Colonial elegance, a pillared portico, not as is usual at the front of a house, but at the back where there was nothing but fields and a faint view of distant mountains to impress.

But though the house was ugly outside, its interior was pleasantly spacious. There were three floors of quite large rooms with a decent staircase connecting them and well-polished pine-board floors. The house was still sparsely furnished. It looked cool and airy even if it wasn't.

What heat! Leopold and I had never known the like of it, not in Italy or even in the Tropics yet there was no searing sunshine, the damp lush country with its many streams steaming generally under a blanket of clouds that would be torn apart now and then by the most violent of thunderstorms bringing some hours of relief.

When we had first arrived George had taken us straight into the kitchen where Annelies was sitting shelling peas, scattering them all as she leapt up to embrace us. Her two daughters who were helping her came forward more shyly. They were pretty, graceful girls and soon Diana was talking and laughing with them as together they picked up the peas from the floor.

The kitchen was quite large and for some unknown reason the coolest room in the house. It was also the cosiest because Annelies was usually in it. So was a baby in its cot, gurgling contentedly most of the time and smiling when inspected but what sex it was I've forgotten or how many more children Annelies later had. When I think of her it is always surrounded by children, ministering to them, cheerful, kind and patient and treating grown-ups in much the same motherly way as she did her babies.

Life started very early on the farm. George got up at five in the morning to tend the animals and labour on the land. Though he had a hired man to help he seemed to do most of the work himself, driving the tractor, cutting the grass, raking and turning and stacking it, sometimes helped by the girls. Leopold took advantage of the dawn coolness after the sweltering nights to sleep and I wandered out barefooted through the dew-soft grass to bathe in the small stream. There was not a soul about, even the birds were not quite awake, only the ducks quacked indignantly when I joined them in the water. How I loved those early mornings.

At eight George came back for the large breakfast Annelies cooked for all of us. There was bacon and eggs and porridge and cereals and waffles and fresh milk; strangely, to us, no butter, but margarine that Annelies squeezed in a bag and plenty of bread.

George would return to work. Annelies would often take the car, I or Leopold accompanying her, to do the shopping in the adjacent small town. It didn't take us long to realize how carefully she chose and bought, comparing prices, rarely taking the more expensive cuts of meat and that nearly all the vegetables we ate were grown by her in her small garden.

Yet neither Annelies nor George were people to economize on food unless it was strictly necessary.

And she did all the housework herself! Neither Leopold nor I had ever lived in a place where it was our hosts and not the servants that worked for our comfort and it embarrassed us.

'I can't stand it,' Leopold protested. 'Why should Annelies cook for me? I am going to help her!' From then on he was often to be found in the kitchen trying to make himself useful in one way or another, lumbering here and there, breaking eggs into the wrong dishes, up-setting pots and pans, chopping onions, tears and sweat streaming down his face, messing up a quite unnecessary amount of clean plates, ignoring that they would have to be washed afterwards. Even if it must have rather tried Annelies's patience she accepted his wish to help with her usual kindness.

In the morning I made our beds and tidied our room. Lunch was usually just salad and cold meat. In any case it was by then too hot for anyone to want to eat. Afterwards the house grew silent. Even George and Annelies rested and the children slept. So did we, if we could. It was quite simply too hot even to move. Towards the evening George would either drive us around the countryside and show us some of the small towns which had many attractive old buildings, or we would sit in the big drawing-room downstairs, the doors wide open to catch any breeze wafted from the twilit mountains and talk and drink gin and tonic. That is we drank the gin and George the tonic. Since we knew the amount we consumed was indecent we always hid a few bottles we had bought in our rooms to replace those we had emptied. George didn't notice and Annelies who liked a drink or two occasionally on those evenings when she could spare the time from cooking dinner didn't seem to mind.

After dinner George would go to his room, not to sleep but to write, often all night long, Annelies complained.

'What are you doing to yourself, George?' I asked him one day, looking anxiously at his face, drawn and narrowed by exhaustion. 'Surely it isn't necessary to work so hard at farming when you can make much more by writing?'

'One has to try things,' he said.

I looked at his distinguished, rather delicate face and thought of that of another writer, one of the greatest ever, coarse-featured as any Russian peasant, who had had the same idea.

'You're just trying to do as Tolstoy did and turning poor Annelies into Sonia,' I teased him. George didn't seem to mind.

Happy as I was in East Berlin I soon longed to see Steinhardt again.

Should I write and ask him to meet me in New York without his having begged me to do so? Never, I thought, remembering Aunt Diana.

Once, after I had been married for several years, she had quite calmly as if enquiring about the weather asked what physical love was like. 'Is it pleasurable?'

'Very much so,' I said.

'But is what you do any different from what animals do or the lower classes?'

'No, I suppose not,' I had to concede. 'It's an urge common to all.'

'No wonder I was never interested,' Aunt Diana said, 'imagine having to behave like a bitch in heat or a housemaid in love.'

It had taught me not to idealize my emotions.

How was Aunt Diana? I wondered. By then nearly ninety, I knew. Though I wrote to her for birthdays and for Christmas and kept her more or less informed about us, I thought of her as little as possible and if so only in connection with childhood and past. I dreaded her death so much that I tried to part from her even before I had to.

Perhaps she felt the same. She wrote only very rarely and briefly as if already from a far distance, saying the least possible about herself and her health. She had, however, sent me all the documents concerning the land in Canada and I'd also had my brothers' legalized signatures permitting me to deal with the matter as I thought best which I had forwarded to Steinhardt.

Would anything come of it? I wondered. Hoped. Perhaps just

enough to buy a small farm like that of the Kennans?

How country bred I really was I had discovered once more in East Berlin. Even Leopold seemed to be reverting contentedly to a more primitive form of existence, untroubled, living from day to day with no thought of past or future.

Once I went to New York to meet Steinhardt for the day. Leopold went more often for reasons of his own. Annicka was still there, though it seemed having difficulties with her working papers. Leopold was hoping to solve these complexities for her through friends.

Steinhardt seemed pleased at our prolonged stay with the Kennans. 'It will certainly be an economy,' he said. 'By the way,' he added, 'you might as well enquire a little from him as to what they think of me in the State Department. Just casually, of course. I couldn't really care less. I'm getting so bored with diplomacy. It leaves one no initiative these days, all orders come from Washington. I'd return to my law office gladly but Dulcie's next step is Paris and after that God knows what! It's a relief to be with a less ambitious woman for a change,' he smiled.

'All my ambition by now is to have a small farm,' I confessed.

'Not a bad idea,' he thought, 'just look around for one and I'll help you get it. Not too far from New York, mind. I don't want to lose you.'

'And what if you go to Paris?'

'Well, I could always fly over for a couple of days.'

After I returned to the Kennans I enquired discreetly, I thought, as to what those in power thought of Steinhardt. But in discretion George was more than a match for me. He wouldn't commit himself or anyone else. So I had to invent a flattering answer to put into my next letter, which I hoped would sound convincing.

The summer was ending. The child had to return to school and we to New York but we kept in touch with the Kennans even when they moved to Princeton, where George at the Institute for Advanced Study at last had leisure to write and to earn more and the farm was no longer needed as a source of income, though they kept the place for rest and holidays.

We later visited them in Princeton where they had a little house, Annelies as always surrounded by children, though not, I think, all of them her own, and George took us to the Institute where we met his very attractive friend, Oppenheimer, and even saw Einstein walking around looking with his big mane of unkempt hair and untidy clothes like a tatty old lion.

Then George was appointed Ambassador to Russia and the family moved to Moscow. Their kindness to us always remained in our memories though we saw them no more.

Eddie and Mona were back and we spent several pleasant weekends with them on Long Island, also visiting Eugene Rothschild who lived close by. Though his house was just a white wooden cottage it had a lovely garden and the house was full of pictures, furniture and objects such as only Rothschilds possess. He lived in it with his housekeeper, a small, plump Irishwoman. She had been his wife's nurse and companion in her last illness.

Now she was cherishing Eugene rather as if he too was an invalid and in need of constant attention, though he looked perfectly healthy to me, a tall, robust, handsome man showing no signs of old age except for being rather deaf. The housekeeper, whom I was later to get to know well, lunched with us, rather to my surprise, and joined chirpily in the conversation, more or less playing hostess. I wondered if she was his mistress, but knowing how much he mourned his wife I thought it improbable.

Many friends were back in New York who frequently invited us and had it not been for the ever recurring worry about our future, life would have been quite pleasant.

To Eddie, of course, I had to confess that in spite of all Mona's help I had achieved nothing as a portraitist.

'Don't you worry,' he said kindly. 'We'll think of something else. But whatever gifts you have,' he added severely, 'you have none for selling yourself.' He looked me up and down. 'You are still a very pretty woman. I can think of many men who'd be only too ready to help you if you were a bit more forthcoming. I'm sure Leopold wouldn't mind, since he doesn't seem to bother about Steinhardt.'

'In short, you want me to become a tart?'

'Certainly not,' Eddie said, indignantly, 'but what's wrong in marrying someone with money and safeguarding Leopold's and the child's future as well as your own?'

'Wouldn't it be a rather complicated household?' I asked, laughing at the idea.

'Not at all. In this country anything is possible. By the way, Etti's in town. Remarried again. Never heard of the man, Davis or David, an American this time once more. She called up Mona, asking for your address. I guess you'll hear from her soon! She didn't sound quite as cheerful as usual.'

'This is her fifth marriage, isn't it?' I asked. 'What with all the engagements in between I've rather lost count.'

🎀 53 🎀

Next day Etti called and urgently begged me to come and see her as she was in bed with a bad cold. She gave me the address of her hotel.

How vividly I still remembered when I had first met her. We had been staying with one of Leopold's brothers on his property in Moravia. One of his neighbours was old Countess Mitzi Baltazzi, a great friend of my father-in-law. She was the widow of one of two Baltazzi brothers, rich Greeks, who had settled in Austria, well known in the sporting world for the horses they bred and in society for the style in which they lived. They were friends of Edward the Seventh and internationally as popular as they were in Vienna. They were also the uncles of unfortunate little Marie Vetsera, whom Etti was supposed to resemble. If so, it was only a family likeness. Etti would never have died for love of a man.

Countess Mitzi was by then very old but still one of the most rewarding gossips about her contemporaries, now old ladies as venerable as she was herself. She had frequently come to stay in Castolovice and I had delighted in her frankness when she reminisced with my father-in-law.

'Do you remember when that Pole, I forget his name, came to have tea with Norah,' (Princess Fugger, a close relation of his) 'and he attacked her with a butter knife?'

'Did he want to kill Aunt Norah?' I had asked.

'Oh no,' said Countess Mitzi, 'all he wanted was to slit her *dessous*. And then, dear Betka, do you remember her blue hair ribbon that so many gentlemen wore proudly in their buttonhole?'

'I do not,' lied my father-in-law, who was rather prim.

'She had tied it – well, you know where – a fresh one, of course, every night.'

It was a hot summer's afternoon when we went to Napajedle, a large imposing baroque château. Countess Mitzi gave us tea. She was delighted to see Leopold again whom in any case all old ladies adored because he treated them as if they were quite young.

Looking mysterious she handed him a bottle, warning him not to

407

drink but to smell its contents.

'Petroleum,' he said, putting it down with disgust.

'And on my property,' she exclaimed with triumph. 'We have started drilling. It is costing quite a lot but they promise me I'll make millions once the well is deep enough. I wouldn't believe it's oil,' she added, 'if they didn't bring me a bottle to prove it every week. And such pleasant people. They've even taken me to see where we drill. Not that I understand about machinery,' she said, 'but there was a sort of wooden box. I suppose the rest is underneath.'

Leopold and I looked at each other with some concern. Poor Countess Mitzi!

'Now where is that child?' she asked, struggling with the heavy silver teapot. She banged hard on the table with the sugar bowl. A footman came. 'Please fetch Countess Etti,' she demanded.

'Totally useless in the house, my grandchild,' she complained. We didn't even know she had one. 'Nothing but horses day and night. She certainly takes after my husband's family – always in the stables or in the paddocks!' Part of the Napajedle estate was by then leased as a stud at which the famous white horses of the Spanish Riding School in Vienna were bred.

After a while a young girl appeared. She was small and thin, yet proportionally perfectly shaped and rounded. She wore a pink cotton dress, her hair was brown, long and somewhat tousled and her pointed childish face enchantingly pretty.

'I'm sorry, Granny,' she said, 'but the Empress has foaled. She's all right and so is her son.'

Silently she helped her grandmother pour tea and served whatever of sandwiches and cake there were. She seemed very shy. Leopold, not unaware of her innocent yet feminine charm, started to talk to her about horses. She flushed with pleasure.

Hesitantly at first, then encouraged by his interest, she discussed with him the Arab ancestry of the Lipizaners, how they had originally come with the Moors to Spain, then with the Habsburgs to Austria, and their pedigrees. 'You can trace them back for many hundreds of years,' she said, 'and breed accordingly – May I please show them after tea, Granny?' she asked.

'If you must,' Countess Mitzi grumbled.

We had to plod, led by Etti, from paddock to paddock in the blazing summer heat to see the yearlings, then through the vast, cool stable blocks to view mares about to foal or with foals just born, staggering on spindly legs. Etti, totally unafraid, entering every box, soothing the nervous mares, helping the foals to their feet.

Grooms stood at attention wherever she went.

'Shall I bring out the stallions?' she asked. 'There are only three here now, but they are the best.'

She gave a brief order and one after another the powerful white stallions of heraldic beauty were led out of their boxes by the grooms.

'I'll put them through their paces, if it doesn't bore you too much,' Etti said politely to me, having probably noticed by then my lack of knowledge of or interest in horses.

Nevertheless I think I have never seen anything more beautiful than this small girl running beside the huge white stallions as they trotted and cantered to her orders. The virgin and the unicorn.

When we returned to Countess Mitzi we asked her if we might invite her granddaughter to a house- and shooting-party in Castolovice which we were having next month.

'Of course she's not out yet. Still the time has come when she should start to consider *epouseurs* not horses,' the old lady deliberated. 'What with her Greek blood she should marry as early as possible. Poor child, she never knew her father and my daughter lives the life of a merry widow in Monte Carlo and Paris, most unsuitable places in which to bring up a young girl. I hope you will find her an eligible eldest son.'

We did, with disastrous consequences. Count Vladschi Mittrovsky was extremely eligible – besides being one of the best shots in the country – handsome, I suppose, in any case, tall and well built, rather inarticulate but at that time, because of her youth, so was Etti.

Vladschi's parents owned one of the most beautiful and uncomfortable medieval castles in Moravia which he would one day, inherit.

Etti with her sweet child's face and promising figure, dressed demurely in the latest Paris *jeune fille* fashion, clothes sent by her mother for the occasion, made every other girl at the party look coarse and dowdy.

For the three days the house-party lasted Vladschi never left her side. On the fourth they became engaged. Etti was as radiant and proud as she had been when she showed off the big stallions she had tamed. We were pleased, knowing her grandmother would approve, though I was rather surprised that Etti should have fallen as much in love as she had with someone as ordinary as Vladschi.

They left for Vienna together, Etti to be introduced to his family.

However, soon there were difficulties. Everyone knew that Countess Baltazzi had drilled away most of her fortune in her futile search for oil, also that Etti's mother spent more than she should, without being able to afford to do so. All Etti could bring into a marriage was a trousseau and her charming person.

It didn't seem sufficient to the parents Mittrovsky. Vladschi was entirely dependent on his father. All he had was a small monthly *appanage*, three fine guns, a lot of smart suits and a sports car.

Knowing he could not marry without his parents' consent, Vladschi broke off the engagement.

Poor little Etti! Feeling in a way responsible we tried to comfort her as best we could, pointing out how young she was and how many men there would still be in her life, more attractive than Vladschi. Prophetic words but she would not listen. She felt disgraced, deceived and deserted. Above all, her pride was deeply hurt.

'I'll show them,' she said and she did ever after.

She remained in Vienna with her mother for the next month then she became engaged once more. Baron Charles Buxhoeveden was a young man everyone liked. He was of Baltic origin and had through his German mother, born Siemens, inherited a large fortune. He was good-looking, cheerful, friendly and a generous spender. I was delighted for Etti, thinking she couldn't have found a nicer or more suitable husband.

But this engagement too was broken off, if by mutual consent.

I fear Etti was still seeing too much of Vladschi. Finally her mother, Countess Wurmbrandt, who had friends in New York, decided a complete change was necessary. Besides the trousseau had been expensive, why not put it to good use? So exquisitely dressed and maturing into real beauty Etti arrived in America.

After a few weeks of social success she married a member of the large, immensely wealthy, Irish Catholic Ryan family of New York.

There was a splendid, much publicised wedding, followed by a honeymoon on his yacht. Etti, who always in spite of her fragile appearance was able to stand any physical hardship on land, became terribly seasick and unresponsive towards her husband.

Naturally he was disappointed but when on returning to town things did not improve the robust, red-haired Irishman felt he had made a bad bargain. He decided to get rid of Etti. It was only too easy. She had done as foolish a thing as only a very innocent girl would have ventured to do. She had bought from her husband's money, which she not unnaturally believed was also hers to spend, the most expensive wristwatch she could find at Cartier's and had it engraved with the damning words 'Vladschi, my love, I think of you every hour'. Her husband discovered the watch in her bedroom before she had been able to send it to Vienna.

This was evidence enough. Not only did he declare, seeking Catholic annulment, that the marriage had never been consummated but produced the watch in the divorce court, proof that Etti had a lover in Europe to whom she was still faithful and to whom she sent expensive presents.

The Ryans were a powerful family. Etti hadn't a chance against them or against the press campaign that made her out to be a predatory foreign adventuress of the corrupt Austrian aristocracy and niece of notorious Marie Vetsera who had seduced the heir to the Imperial throne and been killed by him in a fit of jealousy before he shot himself. (Nothing could have been more untrue. The real reason for his death was political and that the girl had voluntarily agreed to die with her lover though kept secret as long as the Austrian court existed, should have been known to everyone by then.)

With an album of most uncomplimentary newspaper clippings carefully cut out and pasted in, Etti returned to Europe. She seemed quite proud of it. Never having seen her name in print before or so many photographs of herself she showed it to all and everyone with childish delight.

But after all this Etti did finally grow up. She had lost most of her illusions but none of her pride. If her reputation was somewhat tarnished she managed to give it shine and glitter by marrying one eligible man after the other. First Count Pally Palfy, much older than herself, already twice divorced, a well-known womanizer and one of the handsomest men in Hungary, then Count Tommy Esterhazy with whom she remained longest, even bearing him a daughter, after that Count Zsiga Berchtold and in the intervals brief engagements to others.

Why did nothing ever last?

That Etti attracted men was in no way surprising. Not only was she very pretty but she was the best of companions, gay, witty and tolerant. She could share in all the pursuits men of her class enjoyed, shooting and riding as well as any of them, minding no discomfort when it came to outdoor life or adventure, displaying courage and endurance incredible in so small and fragile-looking a person. Besides she was a marvellous hostess and housekeeper. Wherever and with whomever she lived the food was delicious, the house comfortable, the servants perfect and conversation, thanks to her, bright, lively and gay.

No man could have wished for a better wife, except in one respect. Etti had a curious attitude towards sex. She thought it unimportant. Once established and dominating a household and husband she couldn't have cared less where the man went for his pleasures as long as he didn't bother her.

It was, I think, partly a sort of revenge on all males for what Vladschi had done to her, because never afterwards did she permit herself to fall more than superficially in love with any man. In consequence she moved from one to the other without regrets.

I cannot count her many admirers but all in all she had six husbands. Only the last became permanent. It was then that Etti came home. She had never known her father, now she finally found the sure guidance and protection she had always missed. Arpad Plesch was an old man, kind and wise. He was also a financial genius. He had amassed a great fortune, had a house in Paris, a villa surrounded by one of the most famous botanical gardens in the world which he had created in the South of France, a house in the Bahamas, but more important than all this to Etti he had race-horses.

He was rich enough and fond enough to indulge any whim or wish she might have had. Etti had only one, to return to her first and greatest love, the horses among which she had grown up so happily and who had never failed her in affection. He bought her a stud in Ireland where she could breed race-horses and I'm certain the proudest day of her life was when she won the English Derby with her horse, Psydium.

But all this was still in the future when I went to visit her that evening in New York. I found her in an inexpensive-looking hotel in a small room and on a narrow bed huddled in pink *crêpe-de-chine* sheets, the by then rather old-fashioned equipment which elegant European women used when travelling on trains or ships or staying in hotels.

She still looked like the child I had first met in Napajedle who among the big white stallions had so much reminded me of the virgin and the unicorn, her brown hair flying as she leapt out of bed to hug me. She wore no nightgown and her body was still like that of a very young girl. She snatched a bathrobe much too large into which she vanished except for her child-like face peering out at me with eyes that seemed to have lost some of their innocence. There was, I thought, a hard glitter in them. 'I'm so glad you've come,' she said, 'I've been so miserable and lonely and I'm broke.'

'What's wrong, Etti? I though you were happily remarried. I was hoping to meet Mr Davis or David.'

She shuddered as she drew the white robe around her.

'He's gone,' she said, 'it was only a temporary arrangement,' and then with a smile, 'Perhaps he didn't like sleeping in the cupboard.'

'What do you mean?' I asked, puzzled.

'I'll show you,' Etti said, with unmistakable triumph in voice and gesture as she pushed open a large clothes closet. In it hung a lot of her dresses and suspended from the wall a sort of camp bed. 'One pulls it down at night,' she explained. 'Most convenient. Come, you must have a drink.' She mixed me a Martini, carefully measuring the ingredients and stirring them as I somehow felt she had learnt to measure and mix as to quantity and quality many things – 'And now for dinner!' She opened a tin of hamburgers, put them on a hotplate to warm, then flamed them in brandy. 'You see, I've even had to learn to cook.'

We ate and talked.

'What happened to Zsiga?' I asked.

'Oh, he's remarried.'

She told me of the war years they had spent together in Switzerland. 'We had no money and then I became very ill. I had to be operated on. What they took out I don't know. Perhaps it was my gall-bladder. Men will tolerate anything but illness.'

How true I knew. Even Leopold's affection for me, kind as he was, had markedly waned every time I had been ill and Steinhardt wouldn't come near me if I had a cold.

I asked Etti about her plans for the future.

'I'll have to stay here until I can get a divorce. You can't imagine what trouble all these divorces are. It would be so easy to remarry except for that.'

'Have you someone in mind?'

'Of course,' Etti laughed. 'But sometimes I get very tired of it all.'

A few weeks later I found her comfortably established in a pretty, modern flat, two coloured maids in attendance. 'Friends lent it me,' she said vaguely. Then she suddenly left for the Argentine.

54

Winter had passed. Steinhardt had come to New York occasionally, too rarely for my liking, too frequently for me to doubt his continuing affection. Towards spring he brought good news. The claim to the land in Canada was proven and I was at liberty to sell it if my brothers agreed.

'You are a hopeless lot, you aristocrats,' he complained. 'Had your parents or even you or your brothers bothered to pay the taxes or let someone else do it for you in wartime, that land would be worth a million. Now all you'll get is a few thousand for what is left. Still, I suppose it's better than nothing. In a couple of years there wouldn't have even been that. Besides it was so complicated a case that prolonged legislation would have cost you more than the land is worth.'

In spring I had every excuse to travel to Ottawa. It was to meet my brother, Hubert. Pending completion of the sale and having decided to settle in Canada on the proceeds he had taken a job as a mechanical engineer in a factory in Ontario.

I did not stay with the Steinhardts but with Hubert in a small hotel, only calling on them once to introduce him so that he could thank them, hoping he would make a good impression. There was no doubt he was still very good-looking. Even in the strange clothes he wore, which were a mixture between a battle-dress and workman's overalls, he looked slim and distinguished. When I mildly asked if he had nothing more conventional to wear he opened his heavily lashed dark blue eyes wide with astonishment. 'I feel more comfortable in these,' was all he said.

Hubert was in some ways very much like me. He had in fact all my faults in exaggeration. Being with him was like seeing myself in a distorting mirror. If I was sensitive and romantic, he was so in the extreme. If I felt money was there to be spent, he simply gave it away. I had always had a taste for travel and adventure. Hubert had it to such a degree that he was incapable of settling anywhere for long. Always planning something new, living in fantasies that were unreliable, he had drifted from place to place, from one job to another, never making more money than just sufficient for survival.

So it was with some trepidation that I took him to lunch with the Steinhardts. Like me Hubert when shy would either not speak at all or say far too much. In this case he never stopped talking all through lunch about himself. That the Steinhardts couldn't make him out at all I read in their faces. He told them practically his whole life story of how he had built aeroplanes on Aunt Diana's island, of his adventures as a pilot in the Spanish Civil War and that he had flown for a gold-mine in Brazil, crashed and survived ten days in the jungle, living on parrots he had shot with a self-made bow and arrow and drinking water out of plants, and of how he had sailed a small boat single-handed from Husum (in Schleswig-Holstein) to Majorca. After that he told them about the factory in which he was now working and that he was expecting to be fired any day, because he had incited immigrant workmen to strike, as he declared they were under-paid and badly treated. Not that he minded losing his job, he said, since he had been looking around for a place to buy and had found one near Calgary.

'But that's in Alberta,' Steinhardt remarked, surprised. 'If you wanted to live there you might as well have settled on your mother's land.'

'I didn't like the look of it,' Hubert said. 'Too civilized round about there. But I've found exactly what I want. It's a place where it never rains.' Hubert had always suffered from rheumatism. 'It's on a lake, it's irrigated by streams and it's a fruit farm. All I and my family will need to do is pick once a year. Besides the Dukhobors are all around. That's one of the reasons why I want to live there.'

'Who are they, Count Reventlow?' Dulcie asked. She hadn't been able to get in a word before thanks to Hubert's monologue. 'Czech relations of yours?'

Steinhardt laughed. 'Dulcie, the Dukhobors are not a Czech family but a Russian sect that causes the Canadian government endless trouble. They obey no laws but their own, they refuse to pay taxes or to send their children to school or to church.'

'I have much the same ideas,' Hubert remarked. 'Living with them will suit me fine. By the way,' he turned to Dulcie, 'please do not call me Count. I have long given up my title.'

Steinhardt came to see me at the hotel next day. He asked me about Hubert. 'Are his stories true? It all sounded a bit too fantastic for belief.'

'So is he. It's all true.'

'And he has a wife and children?'

'Yes, though I've never met them. She is Spanish. I hear she's a saint.'

'Well, I guess she'd have to be. He seems quite a rebel, your brother. Well, I must say you are an original family. Leopold so totally unconventional. You – well, I guess they broke the mould when they made you, but your brother – remarkably good-looking though, better-looking than you.'

'So I've been told from early childhood,' I said bitterly.

Then we talked of other things, I mainly of the farm I now, thanks to the Canadian money, felt I could buy. 'It will have to be in Pennsylvania,' I told him, 'with one of those old stone houses.'

'I wouldn't be in too much of a hurry,' he said. 'After all your work in New York has become quite profitable. Irvin tells me you are doing very well.' Kind, always loyal, Judge Irvin who knew exactly what a failure I was. 'He seems to think the world of you,' Steinhardt added. 'It's not like him. He hasn't looked at a woman since his wife died.'

'Perhaps I'll marry him,' I teased, thinking of Eddie's suggestions. 'He's very rich.'

Steinhardt didn't seem to think this at all funny. 'Don't you have enough with one member of the family?' he asked, almost angrily.

'I was only joking.'

'Look here, if you really want that farm and you find something you like I'll help you. That's a promise.'

I thanked him and we then discussed summer plans.

'Why not come here?' Steinhardt asked. 'You can't possibly stay in New York all summer. There's a nice little place in the Gatineaux Hills just above town. It was a hotel, well, I guess it's a sort of summer camp. Dulcie and I found it one day when we were driving around. It's sure to be quite inexpensive and I could come up now and then to visit you.'

'It sounds wonderful.'

'Dulcie will, of course, have to know, but you can say you discovered it with your brother and that he will join you there. The child will like it. There's even a small swimming pool and if Leopold gets bored he could always visit friends in Montreal or Toronto.'

It seemed a very pleasant prospect, so on my return to New York I wrote to the Gatineaux Hill Lodge and booked rooms for July when Diana's holidays started.

But I had reckoned without Dulcie. I had written to her telling her of our plans. She had answered kindly, saying she would be delighted to have us so near throughout the summer.

Then a brief note of Steinhardt's followed, saying that though he hoped we wouldn't change our plans, Dulcie had arranged for a rather VIP tour of the National Parks as a surprise. They would be guests of the government, that Dulcie Anne was longing to go on this trip and that he saw no way out of it. 'In any case we will be back in Ottawa in two or three weeks,' he wrote, 'I hope you can wait that long.'

It was too late and seemed too complicated to make other arrangements. Though Leopold had not been very enthusiastic about the prospects of a summer in Canada, he had his reasons to comply with my wishes.

The moment the Canadian money had been paid into our joint bank-account in the spring, he had left for Spain to visit relations who had invited him to stay. I doubt the Hohenlohes, his cousins who lived in Marbella, received Annicka. Nevertheless she had accompanied him on the journey.

He had returned with a badly upset stomach, not, I felt, due to drinking water or, as he claimed, the rancid oil with which the Spanish cooked, but too much cheap wine. He was I knew as glad to be back with me as I was to have him safely back. Whatever he may have felt for Annicka or I for Steinhardt, nothing would ever change the fact that Leopold and I needed each other most.

However, confessions had to be made on both sides. His that he had spent half the Canadian money on his journey, there had – it seemed, been some gambling in Marbella too; mine that I had bought a farm in his absence.

'I've made a down-payment on it. It's practically ours. It's a lovely place.'

'But we haven't enough to buy a farm and live.'

'Oh, it was quite cheap. And Steinhardt has promised to lend us whatever we need.'

Leopold's thoughts were easier to read in his face than when expressed in words. I didn't like what I saw.

'And where is this farm?'

'It's Nowhere. That's its name. No train goes near it and no bus line either. But it is in Pennsylvania. The nearest big town is, I think, Scranton.'

'I sometimes wonder which of us is more irresponsible,' Leopold said.

I had found the farm in a magazine that listed properties all over America. There were two of these published every month. One very glossy with photographs of expensive country houses and estates, the other just a newspaper advertising what was cheapest. It was in the latter that I had found it.

'Eighteen acres, woodland, orchard and pasture. Small stone Pennsylvania Dutch house, large barn, stream and spectacular swimming pool. Price $2500.'

It was almost the least expensive in the magazine yet it seemed to offer a lot.

I had immediately written to the agent and next weekend taken a rather reluctant Diana with me to view the place. She was not at all interested in country-living by then, only in Mr Elliot's Shakespeare class in which she had come first.

It took us three and a half hours by bus to get to the small town where the agent lived. He had booked us rooms for the night in a sort of boarding-house. It had a sign up, 'Modern comfort', and traditional Pennsylvania Dutch food. It was a wooden house with a large porch on which stood innumerable rocking chairs and many old car wheels, perhaps as ornaments.

The comfort consisted of a very clean modern bedroom and the most delicious and plentiful food. At least to me it seemed so since it reminded me of that of my childhood in Holstein: smoked sausages and ham, sweet fruit soups, spiced baked potatoes, kraut and dumplings and jams and jellies accompanying every meat dish.

A very old couple owned and managed the place. After our dinner we rocked with them on the porch that overlooked a road and other wooden houses.

Any moment I felt the cowboys would come galloping into town raising clouds of dust and shooting.

However, nothing happened, at least not of that kind. Our hosts talked an almost incomprehensible language. It was a mixture of German, Swedish and American as far as I could make out, but they seemed anxious to communicate. It was obvious that they were curious about us. The agent had probably told them of the property I had come to see.

'So you are nudists?' the old lady said.

I thought I had misunderstood. 'We are from Czechoslovakia.'

'But you go without clothes?'

Diana and I looked at each other in amazement, knowing we were quite properly dressed.

'Of course not – why?'

'*Ach, Wilhelm*,' she screamed at her husband, who was obviously very deaf. 'They say they don't go naked. But the place you've come to buy,' she queried, 'didn't you know it was a nudist camp?'

'I thought it was a farm.'

'Really, Mummy,' Diana said, looking at me with stern disapproval.

'It used to be quite a good farm,' the old man mumbled. 'A lot of fruit on it too. Was all the nudists had to eat in the end. Apples,' he added with grim satisfaction. 'We are decent folk around here. We did not want them to walk naked among us. So we starved them out by not selling them food or drink.'

Next day very early the agent came to fetch us in his car. For a couple of miles we drove on the highway towards the distant mountains, then along a country road densely shaded by trees.

We enquired about the nudists. 'So you heard,' the agent laughed. 'People here are still absurdly old-fashioned. But it's all to your advantage. Only because those people gave the place a bad name, is the price so low. Well, this is it!' And indeed it was. On a small hill among flowering apple trees stood a little grey stone house. Adjoining it a large wooden barn silvered by age and all around rolling land undulating between groups of trees, meadows very green with the young spring grass sparkling with dew and in the distance a ridge of hazy mountains.

'Well, you'll want to look around,' the agent said, 'before you make up your mind.' By the expression on my face he must have been reassured that it was already made up. 'Here are the keys to the house. It will need to be repaired, of course. The nudists didn't bother with it. They camped in the barn. Oh, and don't forget to view the swimming pool. It's just under the house. It's quite something! Used to be their main entertainment area. Guess you'll want to stay awhile and explore?'

'Of course.'

'If I come and fetch you towards evening will that be OK?'

I thanked him and he left.

We wouldn't have needed the key as the door of the house swung open at the first touch. There were two rooms downstairs, not large, but well proportioned, good Georgian windows, if covered with spider webs, even a small stone fireplace. An enclosed staircase and two more rooms above in which swallows nested and in which mice or rats had nibbled the floorboards. There was no bathroom, no plumbing of any kind and no electricity.

Then we inspected the barn. It was large and lofty with big beams supporting the roof and would I thought eventually extend our living quarters, the house being so small. Its floor was littered with straw mattresses and tattered blankets. There was a strange and very unpleasant smell.

'There may be someone dead in here,' Diana shuddered.

'No, very much alive – look!' Two small furry black animals with white feathery tails scuttled away, lifting them as they ran.

Skunks!

We went in search of the pool. Underneath the hill on which the house stood there was a rock-strewn valley through which a clear stream flowed cascading into what probably had once been the quarry from which the stones for the house had been dug. It was now a large deep pool, the water so transparent that one could see the rocks below. From it the stream continued flowing more gently among blue and yellow irises down into the meadows.

We went down to the pool and with some trepidation drank water out of our cupped hands. It tasted mountain cold and quite pure.

'I'm going to buy this place, darling, if I can. I've fallen in love with it.'

'Mummy, you're always in love with something or other,' she said, which I knew was quite true. How many houses or gardens or properties all over the world had I not passionately desired to own, only deterred by Leopold's shrewdness. 'Of course you shall have it, if you really want it so much, but remember we can't afford more than one place abroad. You might see something you like better.'

Inevitably I always had.

But Leopold was in Spain with Annicka and there was nothing to deter me now.

The sun was setting its last light, painting the mountains pale gold. It grew chilly and soon it was dark.

'What if the man never comes back?' Diana asked plaintively. 'He may have forgotten or had an accident.'

It was with great relief that I saw the lights of an approaching car soon afterwards. The agent apologized cheerfully for being late. 'An important deal,' he said, 'and then I thought I might as well go home and have a bite to eat.'

I'm glad he couldn't see Diana's indignant face.

'Thought I'd give you plenty of time to look around – Well?' he asked as he drove us back, 'it's a fine place, isn't it? Real unspoilt country too. And a gift at that price.'

'Would a small deposit secure it?' I asked.

'Oh, I guess we can arrange that, provided the full price is paid as soon as you take over.'

'All right. I'll buy it.'

'You couldn't do better,' the agent said.

'By the way, what's its name?' I asked.

'Well, it's been called "the Nudist Camp" around here for quite a while but in the books it's listed as "Nirgends Farm". Must have belonged to Dutch people.'

Since he pronounced Nirgends the English way it only slowly dawned on me what it meant in German – Nowhere.

I went there once more alone to meet the builders and to tell them exactly what ought to be done – where the bathroom should be and so on. It seemed there were difficulties to get electricity to the place because the posts would have to cross someone else's land and a pump would have to be installed to bring water up to the house from the stream. I didn't ask for an estimate. The agent had assured me it was a most trustworthy firm and after all these installations were essential if we were to live at 'Nowhere'. So what was the point of enquiring about price? If it came to the worst I still had my jewels and the pictures to sell. And seeing the place again I had been just as enchanted as I was that first time. Of course it was rather far from New York but in a country as large as America one had to grow accustomed to greater distances, as I explained to Leopold, saying people thought nothing of driving three hours to a party, which was quite true.

'And far from where, anyway?' I asked, making him laugh. 'Nowhere.'

❧ 55 ❧

In July we left for Ottawa and the Gatineaux Hills. Leopold very reluctantly, only persuaded to do so because I had explained to him that I by now had to borrow the promised money from Steinhardt for the farm and that these things could only be transacted personally.

The Lodge was a large log cabin with accommodation for about ten people in tiny bedrooms under the eaves, the ceilings so low that even I hit my head against them occasionally and Leopold, because of his height, daily. There was a big dining-room and a bar, these mainly frequented by people from Ottawa who came up into the hills for a breath of cool air or to eat or drink. The food, cooked by a French-Canadian chef, was remarkably good. One could walk in the wooded hills, look down on the spires of Ottawa, seeming to vibrate in the summer heat, and there was a small shallow pool to swim in. But these were the only distractions except for the bar that the Lodge offered. It would have been a nice enough place in which to spend a weekend but not, as we eventually did, nearly two months.

After two weeks there was still no news from Steinhardt. I called the embassy. 'No, their Excellencies were only expected in ten days.'

There was nothing to do but wait. The Lodge belonged to and was run by a young red-haired couple of Scottish descent. They were nice friendly people but over-worked and under-staffed. They had a new-born baby that lay in its pram unattended all day in the hot sun where no one could hear its cries and a four-year-old daughter called Heather who was supposed to look after it and the two dogs. She had the face of an angel and was an absolute fiend. I sketched her again and again, hoping to portray her lovely face when I got back to New York, holding her attention with the most lurid and cruel tales I could think of. At least it kept her from hitting the baby and pulling the dogs' tails some of the time. I must say Diana gallantly assisted me in keeping Heather under control by teaching her to swim in the pool and ducking her whenever she became vicious.

I grew rather fond of the harassed and over-worked young couple. Leopold was by then so bored and anxious to leave that I knew there was only one way to hold him. An appeal for help was something he would not refuse even if it only benefited strangers.

'Look here, darling, they are charging us practically nothing for living here. Why not let's help out a bit? Besides it would be fun.'

I knew it was essential to wait for the Steinhardts and that Leopold must be kept busy somehow. 'Why not offer your services as barman on weekends? And I'll serve at table as a waitress.'

He was delighted at the idea as he always would be at anything out of the ordinary.

So on the weekends when the Lodge was crowded I would dress in one of the waitress's uniforms. I was not very competent, I admit. I remember spilling sauce all over a man's shoulder and having to apologize abjectly and clean up afterwards.

Leopold took turns as barman. He invented his own system rather like that in English pubs. Everyone who wanted a drink had to pay when he was handed it. He also, because it was less complicated to add up, fixed the same price for a Coke, beer or whisky or gin. Only a few customers protested. Canadians aren't fussy or stingy people, especially not when it comes to drink and his gifts as an entertainer made up for those he lacked in keeping accounts. In fact never, we were told by our grateful landlords, had the bar made such profits as when he served in it.

Time passed slowly, however. Day after day I waited for a call from the American Embassy. At last it came.

'We're only just back,' Steinhardt said. 'I have been longing to see you!'

'So have I for quite a while,' I said bitterly.

'Forgive me, I know, but it simply couldn't be helped. Can you manage the Château Laurier tomorrow afternoon at four?' What an impetuous-sounding warm laughing voice he had, I thought. 'Telephone me your room number at the embassy.'

'The Steinhardts are back,' I told Leopold. 'He wants me to come to the embassy to discuss the loan tomorrow afternoon. I'll have to go.'

'And can we leave then?'

'I'm afraid it would look a bit strange if we did, going away the moment they arrive, after all he's done for us. I can't just pocket the money and go.'

'No, I suppose not,' Leopold said but there was something unfamiliar in his voice, a sort of weary resignation which I didn't like.

Next day I left by bus for Ottawa in the early morning. I booked a room in the hotel for overnight. I knew it might look suspicious if I did not. I went shopping in the town. There were things the child and Leopold needed. I stopped at a snack-bar for some indifferent-tasting food, returned to my hotel room and waited. At 3.30 I called the embassy and gave Steinhardt my room number.

I tried to read the newspapers I had bought. The beginnings of a poem by Rilke haunted me. '*Immer warten nur die Menschen welche wirklich lieben.*'

'Those always wait that really love.' It sounded very ordinary in English.

At last Steinhardt slipped into the room, carefully locking the door behind him. I thought he didn't look very well. His narrow face was not its usual golden brown but rather pale.

'How was your journey?' I asked resentfully. 'Enjoyable I suppose?'

'Not really. I got a bit bored. All those lakes and parks one much like the other. I don't think I have much of an eye for natural beauty, except when expressed in the female form.

'Look here, I can't stay very long. Dulcie's arranged a welcome-back party at our house at six for all the diplomatic corps.'

When I later confessed that I had found a farm that I'd made a down-payment on and needed him to help me with the rest he looked rather startled.

'How much?' he asked.

'It cost two thousand and five hundred dollars,' I said. 'If you can manage that I think I can deal with repairing, modernizing and furnishing the house and stocking the farm.'

'Anything you want, of course, but I would have thought what with one thing or another you didn't need any more money.'

I didn't dare explain at what rate Leopold and I spent it or why.

Instead I went to the desk, took one of the Château Laurier's notepapers provided for its guests, carefully wrote out 'I owe Ambassador

Laurence Steinhardt $2500 to be repaid at request plus %', signed and dated it and brought it to him. He had meanwhile written out a cheque.

He scanned my piece of paper. 'Scarcely a legal document,' he said. 'Still, if it makes you feel better.' He put it in his briefcase and handed me the cheque. 'No word of this to Dulcie, mind.'

'Of course not, if you don't want me to.' But I didn't quite understand, after all he had 'Nowhere' as a security. It was a plain business deal I thought with nothing to conceal.

'Will you come and visit us soon in the hills?' I asked. 'I've spent my time looking for places where we can be alone together in the woods.'

'I'll do my best,' he said. He wiped his forehead with his handkerchief. 'Is it very hot in here?' he asked.

'No, but you are,' I said, touching his face.

'Truth is I don't feel too well. Maybe I have caught cold.'

He left rather abruptly.

All the way back to Ottawa, having cancelled my room for the night for which, of course, I had to pay, I wondered uneasily if I had done something wrong. Steinhardt's manner had somehow implied I had.

I remembered the many promises he had made us in the past, all of them fulfilled but others more lightly made to me and intended as mere signs of affection – offers of vicuña skins from Peru, sables from Russia and emeralds, prayer rugs from Istanbul, anything I wanted. All I wanted was himself, as he well knew.

But surely this was different, or was it?

Leopold left me in no doubt when I presented him with Steinhardt's cheque.

He quoted something in Czech that sounded very like 'Love and money make bad bedfellows' but I didn't dare ask him to translate it.

A week passed and we heard nothing from the Steinhardts. 'You have got to call up Dulcie,' I urged, 'after all, it's only polite that you should and she's *your* friend.'

Reluctantly he did, calling Rockcliffe Park.

'Her Excellency is out.'

'And the Ambassador?'

'Absent for a week or two. Do you wish to leave a message?'

Two more weeks passed. There was only one telephone in the Lodge. I stayed close to it day and night. Not wanting to look entirely idle I answered every call and noted down bookings for rooms, dinner or luncheon parties. Now and then I telephoned the American Embassy, always the same polite evasive answers.

I was in despair by then. What other reason could there be for this prolonged silence than that I had, by borrowing money from him, offended Steinhardt, or Dulcie, or both?

I thought of all they had done for us. How dared I have expected more? And yet it seemed such a small sum. I remembered all the presents I had given them in the past, valuable old books, silver figurines which I'd had cast after my models, surely of as much monetary value as these few thousands which would give us a home and security for the future?

But all that was as nothing compared to the fear that I might have lost Steinhardt's affection for ever through my stupidity.

Finally I forced Leopold to call Dulcie once more, thinking if he gave his name she might answer. Very reluctantly Leopold did.

Surprisingly he reached her. I stood beside him as he asked what had happened, why had we not heard from them for so long.

He turned to me, 'I can't understand a word she is saying. I think she is crying. Something about Laurence. Here, you take it – '

He handed me the receiver.

Surely she couldn't now make believe that she had found out what she must have known for over four years? I heard sobbing sounds but felt no pity, I knew how easily she cried. Suddenly I felt furiously angry, all my frustration and anxiety of the last six weeks exploding.

'What on earth is the matter, Dulcie? Here we have been waiting for months in this miserable camp, hoping to see you and Laurence and not a word from you. I never would have come if you had not written how much you were looking forward to having us here,' and with rising anger, 'Every time we telephoned you were out, no message we left brought an answer. Is that a way to treat old friends? At least you might have the decency to explain if we have offended you in some way.' I heard her blow her nose.

'It's Laurence,' she stammered, 'he's been in hospital ever since two days after we came back. Pneumonia. And he's allergic to penicillin. They had to try other drugs which only made him iller. He nearly died. He's just a little better now.'

'But for God's sake why didn't you let us know?'

'I was too worried to think of it,' she sobbed, 'and then there are things one has to bear alone.'

Oddly after the first shock I felt no anxiety or fear for Steinhardt. Had there been any real danger surely I would have sensed it?

'I am so sorry,' I said penitently. 'Forgive me for having been so cross but how could I have known?

'He will be all right,' I added, 'people with such zest for life as he has don't give up. Where is he?'

There was a longish silence.

'He is not allowed visitors except for family and still needs complete rest,' she finally said.

'I would certainly not want to disturb him but I thought I could send some flowers.'

She gave me the address.

'I'm sure Laurence will want to see you and Leopold the moment he is out of hospital,' she said graciously. 'How long are you staying?'

'As long as necessary,' I couldn't refrain from saying.

She hung up.

I telephoned the private clinic and asked to speak to the nurse who attended Ambassador Steinhardt, knowing that Dulcie might have given orders at the desk that all enquiries should be relayed to her.

I gave my name, said I had just spoken to Her Excellency and how was the ambassador.

She giggled. 'Well on the way to recovery,' she said, 'in fact we have trouble keeping him in bed. Such a handsome gentleman and what a charmer.'

'When will he be home?' I asked.

'Next week I believe, but we sure will miss him.'

Indeed, I thought. Even the nurses felt as I did.

I knew I had to wait. However impatient Leopold was to leave, he liked Steinhardt and was grateful to him. Once he heard he had been seriously ill he too felt it would be inconsiderate to go before we could see him again.

A week later Dulcie invited us for tea. 'Laurence is still very weak,' she warned, 'he must not be excited in any way.'

After the nurse's reassuring report I though Dulcie was just being fussy and officious, but when I saw Steinhardt I realized that he had been seriously ill. He was wearing a dressing gown and slippers in which he shuffled around like an old man. He had lost weight, not that he had ever had much of it to lose, and I saw his hand tremble noticeably as he lifted his teacup.

Though the smile he gave me was as warm as ever I suddenly felt cold. What if I had lost him? And why had I not known he was ill? But even if I had, what could I have done? It was his wife and daughter's privilege to nurse and attend him, not mine.

He thanked me for the tree I had sent him.

It was standing in the drawing-room on the window-sill. It was an orange tree bearing both fruit and blossoms.

'I thought you'd like it better than cut flowers,' I said.

'You were right. They die too soon. Now a tree like that can last almost for ever given as much care and attention as these women shower on me,' and he looked with amused affection at his wife and daughter. 'Besides orange blossoms might come in useful soon – '

'Oh, Laurence, it's still a secret,' Dulcie protested.

I looked at Dulcie Anne. She had always been pretty but now there was, I thought, a sort of transparent luminosity in her face and her large Oriental eyes, shaped like her father's, flecked like her father's with gold, seemed to shine with a new lustre.

I had always liked her and come to value her discretion.

'Are you thinking of getting married, Dulcie Anne?'

'Nothing is settled yet,' her mother said hastily, sparing Dulcie Anne an answer.

'And how was your brother?' Dulcie asked, changing the subject.

I had to collect my wits quickly.

'He didn't stay with us very long. He has bought his fruit farm among the Dukhobors. And we too have bought our farm – ' I saw Steinhardt's quick warning look ' – from the Canadian money,' I added hastily.

'What a surprise,' Dulcie exclaimed. 'Why was I never told?'

'You were not very easy to reach for the last two months,' I said with some bitterness.

She made a helpless gesture with her pretty hands.

'Where is it?' she asked.

'In Pennsylvania,' I explained and described the place with all the enthusiasm I felt for it.

'And how much did it cost?' Dulcie asked. I told her.

'That doesn't seem excessive. There must be something wrong somewhere if it's as attractive as you say.'

'Well, of course it will cost more in the end. It needs repairs, there's no water or plumbing at present. But I can sell my diamonds for that.'

'I always thought they were rather too large to wear in your ears,' Dulcie commented, 'still, I'm glad you've found a home wherever it might be,' she added. 'When will you move in?'

'Next spring I suppose.'

'Oh, only by then,' Dulcie said with obvious regret.

'And what about your ceramic work?' Dulcie Anne asked.

'I can do it there, once I have electricity, just as well as in New York and send my figurines to the different firms with which I have contacts.'

427

'I'm so glad for you, Leopold,' Dulcie exclaimed. 'A home from home at last.'

I didn't dare look at his face.

Dulcie Anne had gone to ask for some more tea. Dulcie was talking to Leopold.

'What about the Château Laurier in a day or two?' Steinhardt whispered.

'Impossible, you've been much too ill.'

'Just try me.'

'We are leaving for Toronto tomorrow,' I said, loud enough for Dulcie to hear. Leopold, though perhaps surprised at this sudden announcement, not that we hadn't planned to visit the Colloredos there some time ago, didn't flinch.

'The Colloredos are expecting us.'

'So then it's goodbye? How sad!' Dulcie said. 'Still, I hope it's *au revoir*.' Dulcie prided herself on her excellent French.

'See you in New York,' Steinhardt managed to whisper before we left.

56

Leopold and I had known the Colloredos for a long time, that is the three elder brothers. The youngest lived in Switzerland. They had remained staunchly patriotic Czechs in the war and had bravely faced the dangers this entailed in the time of the German occupation.

I had been fond of their father too. He had been in the Austrian navy as a young man and had sailed across the Atlantic to New York in a small boat with a crew of two. He was old when I knew him but he delighted me with seafaring and hunting stories. Not that he was a great talker. He was a shy, solitary sort of person. He could have been a painter of merit had he studied, as it was he drew and sketched charmingly in the romantic manner. I used to come upon him in odd places busily painting. On a hilltop in Capri, among the ruins of Paestum and in Pompeii, always alone, a bottle of Chianti by his side.

But that was after his beautiful and extraordinary wife had left him and her four small children to live in self-imposed exile in the South of France.

No wonder, I often thought, that the brothers grew up to be unlike other people. And what made them even more so was that they lived in magnificent castles and on great estates which they would indeed inherit one day but which they merely administered at that time for their uncle, Prince Colloredo Mannsfeld, who preferred to live in Paris. He had married a lady socially unacceptable in Prague or Vienna or even Budapest. I may be mistaken but I think she was a sharp-shooting ex-barmaid from Texas.

Through some strange coincidence each of the three young Colloredos inhabited castles that accurately expressed their own personalities.

Joseph, the eldest, lived in Opocno in a medieval tower instead of in the magnificent adjoining castle, a marvel of Renaissance architecture in the Italian style. Joseph preferred the austere tower reminiscent of the times of knighthood and chivalry. It was built of great blocks of rough stone and it still stood firm, strong and proud, overlooking the park, river and forests, Colloredo land as far as the eye could see.

Dobris, Kata's castle, was as different from Joseph's tower as he was from his brothers. A big, light, sunny pale pink baroque palace among terraced gardens with clipped hedges and geometrical parterres. Stone statues of gods and goddesses everywhere, fountains playing, water cascading from stone basins decorated with Nereids and Tritons. It was, if on a small scale, a park like that of Schönbrunn or even Versailles.

Kata was the most worldly of the brothers, also the best-looking. A charming, gay bachelor and a wonderful host. It took little imagination in such surroundings to picture him as a young *grand seigneur* of the eighteenth century.

Last but not least came Honome, short for Hyronimus. Highly intelligent, gifted and witty he was certainly the most eccentric of the brothers.

Brilliant as he was, he could have achieved anything he pleased in the arts, in business or politics. If he did not it was because his critical faculties were more highly developed than any other of his talents.

His castle, Spirov, partially early gothic, with a top dressing of baroque flamboyance, neo-gothicized later and modernized in the twentieth century in the English fashion, was as diverse as Honome's personality.

Even more so the surrounding park with its maze, its artificially created wilderness, its tree house, Gothic chapel and Chinese bridge.

After the communist takeover only Joseph and Honome emigrated to Canada, helped to some extent financially by their uncle to start a new life there.

Kata was spared the loss of beautiful Dobris. He died in the war, still quite young, of cancer.

Joseph chose to live on the land. Honome settled in Montreal. The French-Canadian atmosphere of semi-continental sophistication appealed to him more than agricultural pioneering. He bought an apartment house, then another. When it came to business matters Honome had no perfectionist qualms. He did as best he could and being brilliantly clever of course succeeded.

The youngest brother too was doing well in Switzerland. But money was needful. Not only because they all helped each other whenever some new investment was planned or made but because since their father's death they had had to support their mother and their half-sister in the South of France.

Countess Berthie Colloredo's story is such an extraordinary one that I hope she won't mind my telling it as best I know it. She had caused one of the greatest scandals in my young days in Vienna, even more spectacular than when two well-known young aristocrats had been caught making love in the men's lavatory at the Jockey Club.

I had met her first in my grandmother's house in Vienna. One of my uncles Hoyos was a great admirer of hers. But then who wasn't? She was a dazzlingly beautiful woman; not only that but the best of wives and mothers, her reputation blameless and her only fault that she showed slightly more intellectual interest than was thought suitable in a woman in those days and that she was over-fond of music.

Then something incomprehensible happened. An American concert-singer called Ronald Hayes who was touring Europe came to Vienna. He was black with a wonderful voice and all of musical Vienna ecstasized over his performances.

Persuaded to do so by Berthie, who had heard him sing, my grandmother, always anxious to get hold of celebrities, however exotic, invited him to tea. He came. He wasn't even very black. A small, quiet unassuming man. Berthie towered over him protectively in all her fair splendour, pleased, it seemed, at exhibiting this gifted specimen of a different race to my grandmother. Blacks were a rare sight in Vienna in those days and I think Mr Hayes must have been the first to have entered a drawing-room as a guest.

The problems of coloured people in America or Africa were remote and uninteresting to Austrians compared to the curiosity their complexions aroused.

Even when Berthie started to travel with Ronald Hayes from concert to concert all over Europe, people noted that she had always been eccentric and musical. That she might have fallen in love with a black man was quite simply beyond imagining.

'Nor did she really,' Phil Nichols, who had worshipped her when he was a young attaché in Vienna and who had always remained her friend and defender after her disgrace, told me, when he was British Ambassador in Prague many years later.

'But why then? She had everything: beauty, wealth, a charming husband, four children,' I said.

Phil tried to explain. 'Berthie had very high moral standards. She could not accept what must have frankly been no more than a sensual lapse. Oh no,' Phil said, wrinkling his nose as he always did when amused, 'something great and dramatic had to be made of it, to save her pride. Yet the child need never have been born, her husband need not have known, or anyone, more than that she had been, for a while, infatuated with a beautiful voice.

'But that was too shabby for Berthie. So she idealized the affair, not as a great love which it wasn't, but as an act of God, believing in the end in her own invention that she had been chosen to give birth to a child that would unite all that was best in the two races. Her aristocratic blood mixed with that of a black genius would surely produce a sort of Messiah who would save the world from racial conflict for ever. You see, though a beautiful woman, Berthie didn't have much common sense or even sense of humour. Only a lot of imagination and a great gift for self-dramatization. Though her husband, who loved her, stood by her as best he could the scandal was sparked off by American publicity. It happened because of an interview Hayes's mother gave the press – "Austrian Countess leaves husband for black lover by whom she is with child" – This made it impossible for Berthie to remain in Austria. A separation was arranged and her husband bought her a small property in the South of France to which she retired, leaving her four children in his care.

'Hayes didn't behave too well. Fearful that his mother's indiscretions might harm his musical career and arouse racial indignation he returned to America to tell the press that he had no intention of marrying anyone not of pure black parentage.

'Poor old Berthie. She is still beautiful and proud, though as worn as the rocks she lives on. We went to visit her in her tumbledown castle near Toulouse last year. No electricity, water has to be fetched from the well, fowls running in and out of the rooms, dirt and disorder everywhere.'

'And the child?'

'A buxom young woman by now. Only slightly *café au lait* – a languid beauty. Very gifted. Writes poems rather *à la Baudelaire* but scarcely the hoped-for Messiah, I fear. She has produced enchanting twins and Berthie adores them.'

'And the husband?'

'Not present as far as I could ascertain,' Phil Nichols said.

On the flat lands around Beamsville the fruit trees, mile upon mile of them, stood in orderly rows like an army of trim soldiers on parade. The ground on which they grew as tidy as they were. I thought of the tangled moss-covered old trees of our orchards at home and the green unkempt grass spangled with dandelions beneath them. Not a weed to be seen on this vast plain.

Joseph Colloredo's house was no different from most that at intervals dotted this orderly landscape. Small and low, built of slats of wood. But its interior was surprising. He had from his father, who had lived mainly in Austria, inherited and been able to bring over to Canada a quantity of magnificent baroque furniture, immense bow-fronted cupboards and chests of drawers, their opulent curved forms and marquetry making a mockery of the mean pine walls of the box-like rooms.

Puki, Joseph's wife, who was by then too ill to move out of bed, lay in a monumental baroque edifice not unlike an ornate tomb. Her small, sad, sweet face smiling bravely as it always had in the past, more like that of a frightened child oppressed by a nightmare than ever.

I had grown very fond of Puki. Both she and Joseph had come to stay with us in Castolovice and we had visited them in Opocno and even in the war when both of us had been deprived of our homes we frequently met.

But even then Puki had suffered from an incurable disease, a gradual calcification of the lungs. It had progressed very slowly. Through the years she had been able to lead a more or less normal life while still in Czechoslovakia, now I knew the end was near.

She didn't seem to mind very much. 'I've never been anything but a burden to Joseph,' she gasped with every short breath she was still able to take.

'You know that's utterly untrue,' I protested. 'Not only does he love you – why, he's never looked at another woman – but Joseph was born to bear burdens. All his strength and goodness demands it.'

She knew I was right, as her faint smile told me.

Puki's life had not been easy. Born of a respectable Austrian middle-class family she had, quite young, married a famous tennis champion called Menzel. He had treated her very badly and Joseph, who knew the couple well, always chivalrous, had come to her rescue. She was a small, gentle, very appealing person and he fell in love with her. She divorced Menzel and became engaged to Joseph.

Berthie who by then often saw her grown-up sons, staying with them in Czechoslovakia, her past forgiven if not forgotten, did everything she could to stop the marriage. One would have expected, considering the scandal she had caused and the harm she had done her family, that she would have been more tolerant. Not at all. She was and always had been a strict Roman Catholic. From a religious point of view her sin, once confessed, had been absolved by three Hail Marys and three Our Fathers penitently said.

She had certainly not transgressed against the laws of the Church as Joseph was trying to do by marrying a divorced person, as Berthie frequently pointed out. She further emphasized that Joseph was heir to a great fortune and would be Prince Colloredo after his uncle's death and that an alliance with someone of as humble origin as Mrs Menzel was unsuitable. And worst of all, what heirs could Joseph expect from this puny delicate creature?

Berthie had dwarfed her future daughter-in-law in her full-bodied splendour and arrogance, trying to dissuade her from marrying. But Puki clung to Joseph as tenaciously as she did to life itself. And Joseph who had sworn allegiance to a damsel in distress could not be moved from his knightly vows. He married her in spite of all family opposition.

Contrary to all predictions, Puki bore him a child, though it took the last of her strength. Though robust and healthy it was a girl. Not the all-important heir.

Heir to what in the end? I thought, a small orchard in Canada, as I watched long-legged fair Christina, already resembling her grand-mother Berthie, as she ran like a young colt among the peach trees with Diana.

When Leopold and Joseph went visiting the many Czech friends that lived around Beamsville, I remained with Puki. She could not move from her bed. A Slovak woman who lived in the neighbourhood came daily to attend her wants and cooked the meals. In the nights Joseph took over, cradling her in his arms for hours, holding her up so that she could breathe more easily. Her courage was as extraordinary as was Joseph's patience and devotion.

She talked quite calmly of her death. 'Christina will be all right,' she said. 'Perhaps she took all the strength out of me. Now she will give it back to Joseph. They will look after each other. But I hope he will marry again. He's a strong, healthy man. It was not right that he should have had to nurse an invalid wife for so many years.'

'But if it's what he wanted to do most of all?'

As far as her short breath could permit Puki giggled. 'Men are funny,' she said.

It was the last time I saw her. We had stayed only two days in Beamsville. A month later Honome appeared in New York on one of his sudden but always welcome visits.

'Puki's dead,' he said cheerfully. 'Thank God. At last Joseph is free.'

'Free of what?' I asked. 'Love?'

'Oh, he will recover,' Honome said with his usual cynicism but then averting his face to look at the narrow strip of sky from our window he surreptitiously wiped his eyes.

'She died rather well. With serenity and dignity,' he said. 'Somewhat like a saint. She blessed us all, even my mother.' Honome left as abruptly as he had come.

Joseph never did remarry.

When Eddie returned from Capri that autumn I had to confess some of my follies to him, though none of the emotional ones. Not because he was unfeeling or unsympathetic about anything that concerned me but because we had both long come to the conclusion that love was something best left undefined and unexpressed in words even among intimate friends.

However he showed great interest in the farm, though grumbling that a place which was 'Nowhere' couldn't be a wise investment.

I showed him drawings and plans I had made of house and barn, telling him I must do the furnishing and decorating as cheaply as possible and asking for his advice.

'Pennsylvania Dutch?' he pondered. 'Of course, you could paint it all up that way. Tulips and daisies and interlaced hearts and birds. But too colourful, I think, to live with for long,' he decided.

'Why not, since the house is so small, make it all blue and white — sort of delft? Tiles and vases. And since you say it has a stream, willow pattern and all that. And simply paint the furniture white (off-white, of course),' he added, 'with blue lines and rococo squirls – cheap, pretty, rustic and appropriate. Let's go shopping tomorrow.'

We did, buying anything pleasing that was blue and white as to plates and ornaments. They were quite unfashionable then and cost very little. More expensive were the carpets. 'Difficult to find these colours in rugs other than Chinese and one can't scrimp on everything,' Eddie warned. Also bales and bales of blue and white patterned or striped chintzes and cretonnes.

After that I had to confess to him that the time to sell my mother's ear-rings had finally come.

'Such a pity Mona can't wear them. They are even too large for your ears. Imagine them on hers! Besides Harrison won't allow her to wear ear-rings.'

'Why?'

'Because her ears are like small seashells and he loves shells. Still, you can't go hawking those enormous diamonds on your own. You would be sure to be cheated. I think I know who could help. Maurice Sandoz. Do you remember him?'

Vaguely I did. A tall, very good-looking Swiss who had a splendid villa that Eddie had helped build and decorate for him above Rome.

'He may not want to buy them himself. The jewels he collects are somewhat rarer. Renaissance, occasionally eighteenth-century or Fabergé. All he cares about is craftsmanship and clockwork. Easter eggs out of which birds fly singing. He has a peacock that even Mona hesitated to buy, so incredible was its price. All blue and green, enamel on gold. It struts, unfolds its tail and walks around. I'll send him to you.'

Two days later what I supposed was Sandoz's secretary called on the telephone. Would I receive Monsieur at twelve that day?

I said I would be glad to do so and tidied my studio as best I could.

Precisely at twelve my doorbell rang. Punctuality is considered the virtue of princes, I thought, as Sandoz swept regally into my humble flat in a cloak lined with sables. He was at least six if not seven feet tall, his face of classical perfection, as brightly painted as we are told Greek marble statues were in the past.

His entry was followed by that of a young gentleman-in-waiting, who was not introduced to me, to whom Maurice flung his furs, his hat and his gold-headed diamond-encrusted ebony cane. '*Attends dehors, Pierre. And shut the door!*'

Monsieur Sandoz's clothes too were of unfamiliar cut and material with gleams of jewels here and there.

He towered above me in all his magnificence. After having cast a brief look around my studio he had obviously decided not to sit down. Scents delightful and strange made me sneeze.

'I hope you don't have a cold?' he asked in a tone of voice as if it was *lèse-majeste* to sneeze.

I handed him my ear-rings. He looked at them briefly. 'Not I'm afraid quite in my line. Still, I will see what Harry Winston can do about them.' He put them into his pocket as casually as if they were pebbles.

'Pierre,' he called. 'Cloak please.' Redraped in his sables he bowed from his great height and left.

I immediately telephoned Eddie to tell him all about it.

'He was very splendid,' I said.

'Greatest queen there's been since poor old Naps died,' Eddie laughed. 'But he won't cheat you, that's for sure.'

A few days later I was summoned to Harry Winston's famous jewellery shop on Park Avenue where stones the size of crown jewels lay around on beds of velvet.

Mr Winston himself received me.

He was polite and friendly, apologizing that he could not give very much for the ear-rings mainly because of their colour.

'You have perhaps like many ladies only worn your diamonds at night?'

'Why, of course.'

'And not looked at them in daylight?'

'No, I don't think so.'

'Come,' he said and led me out on to the street, holding up the big stones one by one against the light.

'Funny,' I said, 'they look yellow.'

'And more. One has a large piece of coal embedded in it. It will have to be entirely recut to be of any value.'

His offer was much less high than what I had hoped for. Nevertheless I thought it would pay for the farm repairs and keep us for at least a year. I gave the diamonds one more look, thought of my mother, who had, in spite of all financial difficulties, not sold them. Of my father who had kept them for me. Of the Arrivabenes who had guarded them all through the war and of Diana who I had hoped would wear them on her wedding-day as I had done on mine.

'Thank you very much, Mr Winston,' I said and took the cheque.

Walking along Park Avenue I paused here and there to look into the shop windows. Though thanks to Mona's kindness I had lovely clothes, I did not possess an evening coat and winter was coming. I bought one of snow-white fox fur.

After all, fine furs kept their value almost as much as diamonds, I felt. 'A sensible investment,' as I explained to Leopold.

He was happier in those days than he had been for a long time. His eldest sister had come to live in Connecticut where he could visit her frequently. Leopold was deeply attached to all members of his family but I think most of all to Fanny who was closest to him in age and most like him. Her husband, Mogens Plessen (my cousin) was working in a hospital in Hartford. Though a qualified doctor, American laws required him to retake his medical exams before he could practise in the USA.

I had started to work again. Thanks to the Judge's introduction I had taken some of my figurines to Lennox in Trenton, New Jersey.

It was an unimpressive-looking place, just a group of large, low, shed-like buildings. I was disappointed until I saw how high was the level of craftsmanship of what was produced there. The firm had been founded and was run by six old Englishmen, three of them born in Stoke-on-Trent. They still took an active part in the work. In true English fashion they thought any exterior display to advertise their wares vulgar and quite unnecessary. Let their products speak for themselves.

They had made one concession to modernity. They had hired a brash young American sales manager who did their accounts and hurried around the display rooms trying to prove himself important.

The old gentlemen took scarcely any notice of him as they pondered designs, superintended the casting and saw to it that the decorations painted on by hand by well-trained girls and women were perfect. Any piece that had the slightest fault was not sold (as it is in most factories as second-class ware) but smashed, the shimmering shards piled high in the yard.

The dinner-plates and tea and coffee cups were almost translucent, so fine was the porcelain. All ornamentation discreet and in the best of taste.

As for the figurines, they were small works of art. However it was just their fragility and delicacy that gave me my chance to work for Lennox.

The old gentlemen admitted that figurines were expensive to cast and that there was constant trouble with breakages in packing and transport. They wanted to start something simpler and more robust on the same lines and, if possible, pieces without undercuts that could be moulded in one.

They suggested a series representing different operas: *Carmen, Don Giovanni, Madame Butterfly, Mephistopheles* – and so on. I was to make the clay models. They would do the rest.

I worked very happily on these subjects in my studio and once a week I drove to Trenton to whittle away at the plaster casts according to their advice.

Only 'Madame Butterfly' reached the porcelain stage. When she was cast we all realized we had made a mistake.

Though certainly suitable for cheap mass-production, I had made all the figurines too flat to have the lively grace and charm of those more complexly moulded.

'Not quite up to our standard,' the old gentlemen regretted. 'Our fault not yours,' they apologized. They paid me a thousand dollars for my work, with which I was well pleased and we parted as friends.

57

The Steinhardts only came to New York once before Christmas. He had completely recovered from his illness but seemed somewhat preoccupied and depressed. It was Dulcie Anne, of course. She was definitely getting married to a young Canadian suitable in every way, but that Steinhardt disliked losing her was obvious.

'I guess I'm very much a family man,' he said. 'I don't like change.'

Dulcie was busy choosing the trousseau and he had work in his law office. I didn't see much of him but he promised to return soon and alone when the wedding was over.

But though I wrote to him frequently in the next months ever more urgently and in the end rather despairingly, reproaching him for neglecting me, only in March did he at last write that he was coming to New York.

Leopold was by then in Europe, staying with Austrian relations for a month. The child was still at school. The rooms in the Devon Hotel had been given up for the time being and I lived in the studio.

In preparation for Steinhardt's arrival I had put champagne in the ice-box and a small tin of caviar. He was fond of both. I expected him at ten. It was a grey, dull-looking day, so I pulled the curtains back into place, turned on the lamps, tidied up both rooms, had my bath and went back to bed.

I didn't feel in a particularly welcoming mood. Why had he delayed so long and why as minutes ticked away as I watched my clock was he so late now?

Perhaps it was slow. I turned on the radio to check the time. The ten o'clock news had passed but they repeated the headlines.

'USA Envoy's plane crashes in flames. It is feared there are no survivors. Further news will follow.'

Quarter past ten. I rewound my clock. Well, he should be here any minute now.

What, I thought idly, are envoys, as I lay back among my pillows? Some sort of courier? Poor people all dead. But then I had always been afraid of flying. So, strangely, because he flew all the time, was Steinhardt.

'It's the odds,' he had said. 'They mount up.'

'But surely one's just as prone to have an accident the first time one flies as the hundredth?'

'I never thought you knew much of mathematics,' he had laughed.

The telephone next to my bed rang.

Let him ring a while, I thought, before I accept his apologies for being late.

Finally I took it but it wasn't Steinhardt, it was the Judge.

'Oh, how are you, Judge Irvin? How nice of you to call.' There was a pause –

'I wanted to tell you before you saw the newspapers,' the Judge said. 'There's been a plane crash.'

'Yes, I heard it on the news. The envoy's. Tragic.'

'It was Larry's plane.'

'How awful,' I exclaimed. 'How upset he'll be. No wonder he's late. I've been expecting him all morning.'

'Larry's dead,' the Judge said. 'Come here as soon as you can,' and hung up.

'Larry's dead,' I repeated like a sort of jingle. It made no sense. Any minute now he would come in, moving as silently and with as much smooth grace as the big cats do when they stalk their prey. Tiger, tiger, burning bright –

My mind seemed to explode. Flames were all around me and the fear and pain was so great that I screamed.

After that nothing. I dressed slowly and carefully, did up my face that looked back at me strangely, read a letter of Leopold's that had come in the morning mail without understanding a word and like a sleepwalker took the lift, called a taxi and arrived at the Judge's apartment.

'Oh, my dear,' he said, taking my hand. 'Why, you're as cold as ice.' It was true, my teeth were chattering and I was shivering.

'Come to my room, it's warm there.' We went upstairs. I saw the leaping flames in the fireplace. 'Oh, for God's sake put it out,' I pleaded. Perhaps the Judge understood. He took a priceless Herold vase, filled it with water in the adjoining bathroom and poured it over the fire. Steaming, hissing and smoking it subsided into charred embers. There was a bottle of brandy and two glasses standing prepared on the table. 'Drink,' said the Judge. I did.

But I remained in my cold, trance-like state. I looked at the Judge. His small eyes were glistening with tears. Why, I wondered, does he cry?

'I too was fond of Larry, you know,' he apologized, wiping his eyes.

On the table in front of me among other precious objects was a fifteenth-century bead-embroidered box that had probably once contained relics.

Unconsciously I picked off bead after bead. Frequently the telephone rang. The Judge went into another room to take the calls, so that I should not hear, I suppose.

What did it matter? The brandy was taking effect.

'What's it all about?' I asked the Judge angrily. 'Please kindly tell me.'

'Are you quite sure you want to know?'

'Yes.'

'They are not certain if it was sabotage or an accident,' the Judge said. 'Larry, because of Czechoslovakia, was not too popular among communists. Investigations are being made. In any case the plane caught fire near the St Lawrence River, a short distance from Ottawa. One man, the co-pilot I think, jumped. Though his legs were broken he survived. The deep snow broke his fall. They have been able to interview him. He said that the ambassador being an experienced flyer, after having ascertained that they were only five hundred feet from the ground, thought it too low for a parachute to open and hesitated to jump, so did the others. Seconds afterwards it was too late. Farmers living around there saw the flaming plane plunge into the snow and heard the final explosion. Though they ran to help there was nothing to be done, except assist the sole survivor. The other bodies were thrown clear by the explosion. Though badly burnt, Larry's has been identified.'

'Dulcie?' I gasped, the unbearable searing pain seeming once more to consume me.

'I've spoken to her. Of course, she's terribly upset, poor woman. She has asked me to help about the funeral.'

'Where?'

'Here in New York. In the Brooklyn Jewish Cemetery, where the Steinhardts have a family mausoleum. Dulcie said she would prefer Arlington in Washington. No doubt she'll get him there in the end,' the Judge added with a faint trace of sarcasm. 'The funeral is in three days. There will, of course, be a lot of people. Are you planning to attend?'

'How can I? Even if I ought to! You know I can't,' I said desperately.

'I've been considering that possibility. Why should you have been here at all when the accident happened? You might have been, say, in North Carolina with your daughter. After all, it's spring and it's worth seeing the camellias there in bloom.'

I stared at the Judge, wondering which of us was still sane. 'Camellias?'

'Charleston would be best. How soon can you get hold of your daughter? I don't want you to go alone.'

'By tonight, I suppose, if I telephone now.'

He called up the number of the school for me. I reached Diana and told her to take the next bus for New York.

'But, Mummy, I can't. I'm invited to spend the weekend with Sarah Ball. Don't you remember? They are having a party.'

'We are leaving for Charleston tonight.'

'But, Mummy,' she said angrily, 'I've been looking forward to this for months. How can you be so mean? I don't want to go to Charleston!'

'Steinhardt is dead.' I heard her startled exclamation as I put down the receiver.

'It is the most sensible thing you can do,' the Judge said who had been listening. 'Just for a couple of days till after the funeral. Have you enough money?'

I nodded. I couldn't speak. Because I had said he was dead my mind had accepted it at last and I had started to cry.

'Come, lie down,' the Judge said, guiding me to his bed. I lay on the velvet gold-embroidered coverlet and stained it with my tears. He hastily brought me a clean white pillow and a box of Kleenex. Slowly the frightening pain seemed to drain away.

'Rest awhile,' the Judge said. 'Shall I read to you?' He often had in the past. He rather prided himself on his indeed fine voice and histrionic gifts.

'It will calm us both.'

'Please, not Gilbert and Sullivan!' Odd how one can laugh and cry at the same time. He had all the librettos of the operettas. They amused him and he often read from them.

'Dickens then? No? Really I think Shakespeare would be best under the circumstances.' He went to his bookcase and took out a large, well-worn volume, settled down in a chair, put on his glasses and read the great speeches in the tragedies that mourn and glorify the dead: Antony's for Caesar, Cleopatra's for Antony. He read for an hour.

'She died nobly,' the Judge remarked, closing the book, 'not that I suggest – ' he added with sudden anxiety.

'Why, where would I find an asp?' I asked, starting to laugh. 'In Central Park?'

Reassured he asked me if I wanted something to eat, suggesting he might find some tins since poor Ida had collapsed because of the tragedy.

The very mention of food made me feel sick. 'I must go home and pack,' I hurriedly said.

'Well, look after yourself.' With great tenderness he kissed my brow. 'And remember to call on me if there's anything I can do to help – '

That afternoon we left for Charleston. At the station every news-stand showed pictures of Steinhardt, smiling and confident and below his photograph several of the charred, blackened, dismembered plane and things covered by tarpaulin lying in the snow. There was no escaping the big sensational headlines in the papers either since every-one on the platforms was reading them. So were most people already seated in the train.

I bought sandwiches for the child, fruit and ice cream, knowing I could not face the dining-car, and comic magazines and books to keep her amused on the journey.

As soon as the train had started moving, I rang for the Pullman porter, asked him to fetch me a bottle of mineral water and to make up the top bed of our compartment. 'But it sure is early, ma'am,' he drawled.

I tipped him. Leopold had taught me always to tip before and after a night train journey.

'I don't feel well,' I said. 'Please – '

He did as I asked.

'Now listen, darling,' I said to the child. 'Tell them to do your bed whenever you please. Have you everything you want?'

'I think so, but, Mummy, it's only six o'clock. You can't go to sleep yet.'

I told her I was very tired and would take a sleeping pill, begged her not to wake me, except in case of an emergency, before morning, crept into my top bunk, swallowed three of the tablets instead of one and soon drifted into unconsciousness.

A jolt of the train must have woken me. I couldn't think where I was or why. I didn't remember anything.

The swaying movement, the rhythmic throbbing sounds and the narrow bunk convinced me I was on a train. Had we then finally crossed the frontiers of Czechoslovakia, were we free at last, were we on our way to Paris and to America? Soon I would see Steinhardt again.

I started up, opened my curtains and looked down straight into his smiling face. Diana was sitting underneath me, the newspaper she was reading on her lap. Several more were stacked beside her on the seat.

She looked up startled, then she blushed.

'I'm sorry, Mummy, I thought you were asleep,' she stammered. 'I bought these at the bus station and hid them in my bag. I had no chance to read them earlier. I didn't want to in front of you. Nor did I like to ask you what really happened. But I thought I ought to know. Poor Mr Steinhardt. It's all very horrible, isn't it? Being burnt alive. Still, they say here it can only have taken seconds.'

I retreated behind my curtains.

'Are you all right, Mummy?' I heard her ask anxiously.

'I'm going back to sleep,' I managed to say. 'Goodnight, darling. Time you went too.'

I heard her talking to the Pullman attendant, the sounds of her bed being made, the rustle of paper as she unwrapped sweets or gum, then silence.

I lit a cigarette. 'Only seconds,' I thought, but there are sixty seconds to the minute. I pushed my watch forward and pressed the burning cigarette against my wrist. The pain was excruciating but I held it there for a full minute, the flesh smoking and curling as it burnt. When I finally took the cigarette away there was a deep blackened hole.

I felt sick and faint but the much greater pain that had suffused my entire body before was gone.

I found a Band-Aid in my bag (the child always demanded one for the smallest hurt) and covered the ugly wound, took two more tablets and slept.

Diana had to shake me awake when we neared Charleston. In my

443

drugged stupor I couldn't remember the name of the hotel the Judge had recommended.

'It's an old Southern mansion furnished with antiques,' I told the taxi driver. 'Do you know it?' 'Sure, it's the best hotel in Charleston and the most expensive,' he grinned. 'All genuine old Colonial style.'

We were shown a room with an enormous four-poster bed and a wooden cot.

'I can't sleep in that,' Diana quite rightly declared. 'It's for a child of five.' She was given a room next door.

By then not only my wrist but my whole arm ached, even my fingers were swollen. Serves me right, I thought, disgusted with my hysterical self-mutilation. I forced myself to undress and wash and then, not able to keep my eyes open, I climbed into the high bed with some difficulty and fell asleep once more.

I woke at noon. Diana was perched on my bed staring at me. 'Mummy, is there something wrong? Are you ill? You look funny. Your eyes are all puffed up.' I winced as I moved my left hand and quickly put it back under the covers.

'I had some breakfast. I hope you don't mind. Don't you want some?'

'Just coffee,' I said. 'Black.'

'It's a funny sort of place, this,' she informed me. 'Everything old and shabby and tattered and torn. They say it was a famous mansion before the Civil War and that everything is still of that period but surely there would have been time to redecorate since? Look at your curtains.' They were patterned cotton, yellow with age and indeed in tatters.

She went to order my coffee.

A handsome black woman appeared with a tray. She wore a flowered dress and her head was neatly tied in a kerchief.

I knew by then that I had to do something about my arm. It was aching and throbbing and I felt hot and cold as one does in fever.

'Would you do me a favour?' I asked. 'Sure, ma'am, anything you want,' she smiled automatically. 'I've sprained my wrist very badly,' I explained, 'perhaps even broken a bone. Lifting a heavy suitcase.'

'Sorry to hear that, ma'am.'

'Will you please ask the manager to send me a doctor as soon as possible?'

I had meanwhile managed to tie a handkerchief round my wrist and showed my swollen hand to the child.

'Mummy, it looks awful.'

444

'Just a bad sprain,' I said, 'but I've asked for a doctor to come and bandage it properly. And please stay in your room when he appears. I don't want you to hear me complain the way you do when you've hurt yourself. Or go and have lunch – '

'All alone?'

'Why not? No one will steal you.'

Unwillingly she went when the doctor came. I wondered if he wasn't part of the hotel's decor. His grey locks and moustache, his old-fashioned dress, courtly manner and speech were rather too much like the Southern gentleman as portrayed on the stage.

There was of course no concealing what had made the ugly circular wound once it was uncovered. Only a red-hot poker or a cigarette thrust into the flesh could have caused it.

The doctor looked shocked. 'That's a third degree burn,' he said, 'and it's already started to go septic.' I looked at it and shuddered and tried to smile at the doctor.

'A silly party game,' I said. 'We all held our cigarettes to our wrists to see who could stand it longest.'

'I guess you won,' was his dry comment. He cleaned the wound while I clenched my teeth so as not to scream, put some powder on it and pads of gauze which he took out of his black bag and bandaged it. Then he gave me an injection. 'Just in case,' he said.

'It will heal but I must tell you your wrist is marked for life. Keep the dressing on and wear your arm in a sling, a scarf will do, for the next fortnight.'

I thanked him. 'Glad to have been of service,' he bowed. 'If you have any further parties let me know.'

I cannot remember very much about the days that followed, only that I rarely left my room, that I cried a lot and wrote Dulcie a long, rather hysterical letter. Though I thought I wrote with most moving sympathy, trying to express on page after page my sorrow for her and Dulcie Anne, I knew I was to a great extent indulging my own and putting myself in their place.

Diana, though concerned for me and kind the first day, soon grew bored and impatient at my prolonged despair. She pointed out that she had given up everything she had looked forward to by going on this futile journey, only to be shut up in a hotel bedroom. Finally she brought me my hand-mirror. 'Just look at yourself, Mummy,' she demanded angrily.

I did. My eyes were red and swollen, so was my nose. My matted lifeless hair stuck to my head as if it had never been combed or washed. I turned away in disgust. Still, what did it matter? There would never be a reason to try and look pretty any more.

'I don't care,' I said.

'Well, I do. What will people think? After all, you are my mother!'

I knew I had to pull myself together if only for her and Leopold's sake.

I bathed and dressed. Though my arm was still very sore the swelling had gone down. We had lunch in a sort of courtyard where ornamental ironwork, former balconies and gates, stood around like stage props.

A wisteria dripping scented blossoms roofed the patio. Diana said the food was good but I couldn't eat. Afterwards we went for a drive to see the famed gardens of Charleston which were open that week. Several times we got out to walk among big trees from which grey moss hung like weeping veils of sorrow and under which camellias bloomed, their fallen petals carpeting the ground, red and white like blood that had dripped on snow.

I grew tired. I sat down to rest on a bench. A very elegant little black snake with pink markings approached my foot, its forked tongue vibrating.

I watched it with pleasure. It was so pretty. Like an enamel ornament. I have never feared snakes. Even poisonous ones do no harm if one keeps still, I knew. It inspected my shoe and then zigzagged away into the long grass.

Diana who had been walking around while I rested had caught sight of it before it vanished. 'For God's sake, that was a coral snake,' she gasped. 'They told us in school that their bite is instant death.'

'An asp?' I laughed, thinking of the Judge's reading. 'Anyway, it's gone.'

I had, I knew, at last regained some composure and that the time had come to face the truth.

What after all had I lost? Someone who had never belonged to me like Diana and Leopold did. Someone whom I had feared to own, yet dreaded to lose. It must have been the same for him. How long could it have lasted? I was nearly forty.

Passion cannot continue at fever heat year after year. Inevitably we would have drifted apart, he sooner than I because he was a man. Oh, I would have fought and regained his affection time after time, I knew, but with ever more loss of self-respect, more deceit, more make-believe. And the harder I would have struggled to hold him the less my chances

446

to keep him would have been. Even in this last year how many signs had I ignored that he had become less anxious to be with me than I with him?

Now he was dead. But what more did that mean than that I might now keep him alive in my heart as long as I pleased? No one could take him from me any more. Not even he himself.

My life I knew would change. It would grow quieter and more serene with nothing to look forward to but also nothing to fear. Soon we would be moving to the farm. I thought of the peaceful countryside with longing and of the little grey house that would be all blue and white like a willow pattern plate.

58

On my return to New York I found many letters. From Mona, from Eddie, from other friends expressing their tactfully worded sympathy, discreetly referring to the tragic event.

Even Leopold didn't seem quite to know what to say. His telegram was brief. 'Shall I come? Love and kisses.'

I sat down and wrote back immediately, telling him I was longing to see him, which was true, but that there was no need to hurry since the funeral was over, that Diana and I had been in Carolina when it happened, that of course I was very sad but that I was looking forward to the farm. Better he didn't come just yet, I thought, the temptation to weep on his broad and comforting shoulder would still be too great. Such self-indulgence, common decency and my respect for him forbade.

Then I called up the Judge.

'So you are back,' he said, I thoughs rather coldly. I wondered if it was because I hadn't written or telephoned from Charleston.

'Yes, and the first thing I want to do is to go to the cemetery. Please tell me how I can get there.'

'You will have to take the subway. It's miles away in Brooklyn. What on earth do you want to go there for? It's all over!'

'Just to be near him for a while.'

'Near what?'

'Well, surely we have souls that live on after death.'

'I very much doubt it. But if so, I wonder what use to you Larry's soul would be without his body?'

Though prone to sarcasm I had never heard the Judge speak like that before.

'What's wrong?' I asked.

'Just a few small matters I want to discuss with you. I'll expect you for dinner tomorrow night.'

'Of course I'll come, but what – ?'

He had hung up.

I was very puzzled. He had been far from friendly. What on earth could I have done to offend him?

Next morning the child went back to school.

When the mail came I saw to my surprise that there was a letter from Dulcie. So soon, I thought, but then I knew how punctilious she was about her correspondence, probably because of her diplomatic training, always answering immediately. I opened it with some trepidation. It was quite short, formally thanking me for my kind sympathy and regretting not having seen me at the funeral. 'But then there must have been hundreds of people. Laurence had so many friends,' she wrote and then came something rather strange. 'It has of course been a great shock to me and a tragic loss to the world but I can get over it. I doubt you ever will!'

What did it mean? Generous understanding? A hint that she had always known? A threat?

I couldn't make it out at all.

I went out and bought some flowers, a large bunch of freesias, hoping their scent would sustain me, as, terrified, I descended into the underground station. Only once or twice had I ventured to use the metro in Paris but this was infinitely more frightening, a labyrinth of tunnels through which with sudden roars speeding monsters flashed past or stopped briefly to spew out or suck in a stream of people, doors opening and closing upon them as mercilessly as devouring teeth.

Americans are friendly even underground. I was told which train to take to Brooklyn's cemeteries. It happened to be a fast, non-stop one. Through abysmal darkness it sped, hissing and roaring and swaying. Very few people seemed to have braved this journey and those there were tried to read newspapers in the dim electric light in an effort to conceal what I thought must be abject fear.

And then suddenly daylight, as the monster rose hissing out of the bowels of the earth. Sunlight even, shining on gardens of the dead. To left and right cemeteries, crucifixes, marble angels, tombs, statuary among tall cypresses and trees in blossom, every grave bedecked with flowers. Crowds of people walking along the paths, bending here and there over a grave as if to greet a friend or a relation, gaily, as devout Catholics do to whom the dead are not dead but just resting. But why were there so many people? Suddenly I remembered it was Easter week. The Death and the Resurrection.

The train stopped.

'How do I get to the Jewish cemetery?' I asked the man who sold tickets in a little booth. 'Just down those stairs, honey, and it's all before you.'

From the platform I looked on to what seemed a walled village of tiny houses, many with domed roofs, green lawns, regular paths. I climbed down the stairs, crossed a main traffic-laden road with some difficulty and entered the iron gates which stood open. I walked along a drive. All around me were strange, small edifices, Greek be-pillared temples, gothic pavilions, marble obelisks. As far as I could see the extraordinary medley of miniature architecture stretched for miles. And not a single human being in sight. How would I ever find Steinhardt's grave?

Surely there must be a caretaker? At the end of the drive was a crenellated cottage that looked like a Victorian castle lodge. It had curtained windows so it couldn't be just another tomb. I rang the door-bell. A shutter opened and an old man peered out. Grey-faced, grey-haired, a small black cap on his head.

'Are you in charge here?' I asked.

'Yes, but not today.' He looked at me curiously. 'Are you not Jewish?'

I neither denied nor assented.

'I've come from far,' I pleaded. 'How can I find Ambassador Steinhardt's grave? He was buried three days ago.'

A flicker of interest animated his old face.

'A fine funeral,' he said with some relish.

'Would you please take me wherever he is?'

'What, on the last day of Seder? Don't you know that it's the Passover? Oh, the young these days.'

He closed his shutter and reappeared at the door. He was dressed all in black in a tight-fitting coat buttoned up to his neck rather like that of a priest. Together we walked along a path edged by violets growing like weeds among the unkempt grass, he and I all alone among the tombs.

'Does no one ever come here?' I asked.

'Only for funerals and they are getting rarer. People prefer cremations these days.'

'But does no one visit the graves?' I asked anxiously, fearing I might perhaps encounter Dulcie.

'What for? Everything is well looked after here and dead is dead. As for man,' he intoned suddenly, 'his days are as grass, as the flowers of the field so he flourisheth. For the wind passes over and it is gone and the place thereof shall know it no more. But the loving kindness of the Lord is for ever and ever.'

Was he a rabbi? I wondered. I didn't dare show my ignorance. As usual I excused myself by saying I came from Czechoslovakia.

'In the old cemetery in Prague,' I told him, 'we used to put little stones on the graves just to say we had been there and had prayed and remembered the dead.'

'An ancient custom, no more in use in this country.'

We had come at last to a small building in the gothic style. Piles of ribboned wreaths and bouquets of flowers surrounded it. All wilted, browned, shedding petals, a soggy, evil-smelling mess of decay.

'We haven't, because of the Passover, had time to clean up yet,' he apologized.

'I want to go in,' I said, trying to open the iron door.

'Only close relations are allowed into the vaults.'

'Which I am.'

He unlocked the gate.

An oriel-shaped stained glass window illuminated the small square interior. Its walls were lined with black marble slabs. They had handles like drawers, one ranged above the other inscribed with names and dates in gold lettering – 'Steinhardt, Steinhardt' again and again. Through the stained glass multi-coloured rays of light flooded the tomb. I looked at the window more closely. Why was the design so familiar? A ship in full sail on a blue sea, a rainbow arching above, a dove with an olive branch in its beak and the words 'Super Sum'.

'Not a bad family motto,' I heard Steinhardt saying, 'if rather arrogant,' and my laughing answer that I thought it referred to God not to members of his family or himself, as according to his instructions I had sketched the ship and all the rest he had described on a piece of paper to be later engraved on a silver barometer I was giving him for his birthday in Prague.

And here it all was. The emigrant ship crossing the ocean, the dove that returned to Noah's ark bringing its message of hope after disaster, the rainbow, God's promise that all would be well.

Tears blurred my vision.

The old man shuffled his feet impatiently. 'I can't stay here all day,' he said.

'Where have they put the Ambassador?' I asked. He indicated a still unlettered slab of marble.

I stared at it, concentrating. Surely he must hear the inner voice with which I invoked his spirit.

'Time to go, miss,' the old man said and rattled his keys.

'I will come back,' I promised silently. 'I won't leave you ever.' I was still holding my bunch of freesias. 'Where shall I put them?' I asked then saw there were two little vases attached to the wall on each side of the window.

'Will you pour in some water?' I begged as I thrust in the flowers.

He shrugged. 'Tomorrow,' he said, 'after Seder.'

From then on I travelled to the tomb twice a week, as to a secret assignation. Soon the old man let me have the keys whenever I asked for them. Though I still dreaded the underground journeys it was the price I had to pay for the strange happiness and peace I seemed to find once I was in the cemetery.

I bought a grave from the caretaker. It adjoined the Steinhardt tomb. It cost five dollars. It was covered with weeds. I cleaned and tended it as I did the tomb and the grass around it. It gave me a feeling of belonging.

I had gone to the Judge the day after my return from Charleston.

I had found him alone as usual. He led me into the drawing-room, stressing I thought that this was a formal occasion, since we usually sat in the Meissen room surrounded by all the delightful porcelain frivolities of the eighteenth century or in his more austere tapestried bedroom in front of the fire.

There had always been goose liver and champagne before a meal. There was again but offered with cold politeness.

'Well, did you enjoy Charleston? It should have been very pretty this time of year.' He didn't even look at me but at a big vase. He got up to adjust it on its stand as if it had threatened to fall.

'Enjoy? But, Judge Irvin, what can you mean? I've managed to survive – that's all. What has happened?' I then asked anxiously. 'Why are you so changed? Is it because I didn't write? What have I done wrong?'

'Your letters,' he said, looking at me at last. 'Larry left them in the embassy safe. Dulcie has read them all. I cannot imagine why a trained lawyer like Larry kept them,' he added. 'Perhaps they were too difficult to dispose of. Probably there was no fireplace in the embassy.'

Joy flooded me. So he had cared enough to keep my letters. 'But, Judge Irvin, there was nothing in them that not even Dulcie could have read. They weren't love letters. It would have needed a lot of decoding to recognize them as such. Mostly just gossip about people that I thought would amuse him.'

'Indeed,' said the Judge bitterly.

'Of course, I did constantly urge him to come to New York. That may have angered Dulcie.'

'Angered? She blames you for his death. She says he would never have flown on that day except for your insistence.'

I shuddered. Perhaps it was true. Yet I had never thought of it, weakened as I still was by shock. There were some things my mind could not accept yet if I was to remain sane.

The Judge looked at me more closely. Moved to sudden pity, he put his hand on mine.

'It's nonsense, of course. It could have happened any time, anywhere. For that you are not to blame. However, if you will forgive me for talking about myself for a moment,' he added sternly, 'unimportant as I am in this tragedy – Why did you, in your letters, have to mock my affection for you? Dulcie told me when she came to see me here after the funeral that in them you had said things so cruel and dreadful about me that she didn't dare let me read them. Not that I wanted to. But I do demand the truth from you now. What did you say?'

I searched my mind. I couldn't think of anything disparaging I had ever written about the Judge. Suddenly I laughed, remembering.

'Go on.'

I blushed. 'It's embarrassing to tell you. I wanted to make Larry jealous. I wrote I thought you were falling in love with me and that if he was not more attentive I would marry you.'

The Judge pondered this. 'I think that rather more of a compliment than an insult,' he said with a wry smile.

'Surely that can't be all. Please think carefully.'

I did and suddenly remembered with shame and horror. It had been when we first came to New York. I had told someone about meeting the Judge and about his collection and the man who knew him had said, 'It's all very well but I don't like going there since his wife flung herself out of the window on to Fifth Avenue from his apartment.'

I had then written to Steinhardt about it, asking him what had really happened in a sort of gossipy, frivolous way, saying had the Judge been so bad a husband that his wife had to commit suicide in such a spectacular manner, whereupon Steinhardt had written back to tell me it was all not true. I had forgotten about it since. 'I remember now,' I said. 'Something quite unforgivable.'

'That is for me to judge.'

Then I told him the whole story, knowing that even if I hurt him I owed him the truth.

'And is that really all?' he asked.

'As if it weren't bad enough, but I know there's nothing more.'

He looked at me in silence, his face sad. 'My wife didn't jump out of the window. She died in her bed,' he said at last. 'She was not only a beautiful woman but a very cultured and intelligent person. She was a niece of the writer Feuchtwanger whose strange books you probably know. She was rather highly strung, over-imaginative and prone to melancholia, but very lovable, gifted and talented, if not sufficiently so to reach the heights she aspired to. Yet I believed ours was a happy marriage. We had children, now all grown up. We seemed ideally suited to each other. My common sense and realism tempered her leaning towards fantasy, while she stimulated my interest in the arts and in literature.

'And then one morning she didn't wake. She had always had difficulties about sleeping and she took tablets. She died from an overdose, if by accident or intentionally I will never know. It is a question I will ask myself for the rest of my life. It has made me a very lonely and rather unhappy old man.'

I took his hand and pressed it against my cheek. 'Forgive me, Judge Irvin,' I pleaded.

'There is nothing to forgive, except for you listening to and repeating ugly, cruel gossip. I would have told you everything had you asked me.'

He got up. 'You are acquitted,' he smiled. 'Now let's go and dine. Ida will be becoming impatient.'

Next day a Mr Brown called me on the telephone. I knew all about him. He had been Steinhardt's partner and a personal friend of his for years. 'A good lawyer and the most decent and reliable man I've ever known,' Steinhardt had praised him. 'I'd trust him with anything, even my most private affairs.'

'Something has come up that concerns you, Countess Sternberg,' Mr Brown said. 'If it's not too inconvenient I would be grateful if you came to my office as soon as possible.'

I looked at my watch. 'At half past eleven?'

'That would be very kind.'

What could he want? Then I remembered that Steinhardt still had kept all my documents which he had needed to put through the Canadian land sale. My birth certificate, marriage license, first papers and Czech passport. Probably they had found them in the office.

I shook hands with Mr Brown. He was older than I had expected but he had a nice, firm, healthy face as if he spent much time out of doors. He gave me a chair and reseated himself behind the big desk. So this had been Steinhardt's office, I thought. It looked rather old-fashioned and cosy, mahogany panelling, comfortable leather-covered armchairs and thick carpets. From adjoining rooms came the clicking sound of typewriters.

'Mr Brown, I'm so sorry. You too have lost a great friend. The ambassador spoke of you so often with so much respect and affection.'

'Thank you,' he said, quietly.

'I suppose you have asked me to come and fetch my documents?' He looked surprised.

'I am almost sure we have nothing of the kind here,' he said, 'but I'll check the safe just in case –

'Meanwhile there is this little matter Mrs Steinhardt has asked me to settle for her.'

He pushed a piece of notepaper, on which I recognized my own handwriting, towards me. It was the IOU I had written in the Château Laurier Hotel.

'It was found among Laurence's personal papers.' Mr Brown turned away and gazed out of the window, seeming to watch a pigeon that perched on a ledge preening its feathers.

'She expects immediate repayment,' he murmured, 'and I'm sorry to say she has every legal right to collect debts owing to the deceased, plus percentage. Perhaps if you pleaded with her – ' he shrugged.

'How much does it come to?'

'Two thousand, eight hundred and fifty dollars.'

Pride and anger made my hands tremble as I tore out my chequebook and wrote out the cheque.

'Here is her pound of flesh,' I said, handing it to him.

Faint amusement flashed across his face, but was instantly controlled. 'Well, now that's settled,' he said, 'let's have a look and see if we can find those papers of yours.'

He went to the safe concealed behind the mahogany panelling and searched among piles of documents. 'They are definitely not here and

I know they are not in Ottawa,' he said at last. 'I've been through all the papers in the embassy with Mrs Steinhardt. Might it not have been possible that Laurence was bringing them back to you himself since he was coming to New York?'

It was, I had to admit, quite probable.

Mr Brown and I looked at each other, each of us remembering, I think, the burning plane.

'There was very little left,' he said.

I repeated his words as I returned from the city. What was there left? I wondered. Steinhardt was dead. I was without identity, neither born nor christened, nor married. I had no proof of nationality. I belonged nowhere and even 'Nowhere' was gone. The farm would have to be sold immediately. The cheque I had written Dulcie must have taken almost everything we still had in the bank.

Left was only a lot of blue and white second-hand furniture and household equipment stored in a warehouse, almost unsaleable, I knew.

On my return to the studio I telephoned the agent through whom I had bought the farm, telling him I must sell. He said he regretted this but that he didn't think it would be too difficult now that electricity and plumbing had been installed and that he had had several enquiries. How much was I asking?

'As much as I can get,' I said, 'provided the buyer takes over the builder's bills.' Three days later he telephoned to say he had an offer for two thousand, five hundred and that since building costs had been considerable and still unpaid he advised me to accept it, which I did.

The Judge, with whom I was on the best of terms once more, was shocked when I told him the whole story.

'But why such haste?' he asked. 'What could she have done if you had refused to pay because you might not have had the money?'

'Sent me to prison, I suppose.'

'I doubt she would have dared to do that. Still, "Hell knows no fury like a woman scorned."'

'No one ever scorned Dulcie. Certainly not Larry nor did I. I did everything in my power to keep her content through the years, short, of course, of giving him up.'

'What a vengeful act,' the Judge pondered with distaste. 'Surely she knew how much you and your husband had come to depend on the farm for the future?'

'Oh, she knew. But perhaps in her place I would have done the same. You see, my IOU was written on the paper of the Château Laurier Hotel on the day Larry got so ill. It must have been pretty obvious that I had been there with him and she need only have checked with the reception to find out that I had booked a room.'

'But do you mean to say that she didn't know about you and Larry before this?'

'She never had any definite proof.'

'Larry should not have kept that note.'

'Well, it's too late now,' I sighed. 'I'm going to try and leave New York for a while. Perhaps I can stay with my sister-in-law in Connecticut with Leopold and the child over the summer. I'll have to see – '

'I would miss you very much,' the Judge said.

'Oh, I would always be back here once a week to go to Brooklyn.'

'You still haven't given that up? What on earth do you do there?'

'Well, sort of talk to him – I can't explain.'

'There is a name for that sort of madness.'

59

Next day Clarisse Rothschild called me up to say that she was back from Austria.

'I thought you never wanted to go there again?' I said, surprised that she had.

'Oh, one learns to forget and forgive. And it was good to see old friends once more. People like Leopold and I do, after all, have our roots there. I found him in better form than he's been for a long time. Chappy and Tiny are very kind to him.' (The Seilerns, his cousins, with whom he was staying in Kitzbühel.)

'He will be back here next week. He asked me to call you up to see if you were all right. I'm sorry about Steinhardt. He must be a great loss to you. Wish I had known him better but then I somehow don't get on very well with American Jews. What about driving out with me to lunch with Eugene tomorrow? The garden's lovely just now, all the lilacs in bloom.

'Poor Eugene really does need cheering up,' Clarisse said as we drove towards Long Island. 'I do my best but that woman Gerty's only thought is to remind him of Kitty. Every morning she forces him to visit the grave, she talks of nothing else but Kitty to him day and night.

She wears all Kitty's clothes – she seems to try and impersonate her in every way. It really is revolting. Maybe she thinks he'll marry her in the end. But not Eugene. He's lazy and she's a good housekeeper but he's much too shrewd to be caught by a person of that class.'

'And he still only thinks of Kitty?' I asked with sympathy. 'He must have loved her very much.'

'Oh, I suppose so or he wouldn't carry on the way he does. His latest is a sort of cross on her grave. Though she was a Roman Catholic when she was married to Wemper'le (Count Schoenborn) and what a charming man that was, if constantly unfaithful to her, she became a Jewess after the divorce. She had to. The family would have not permitted the marriage with Eugene otherwise.

'The cross is a sort of compromise, I suppose. It's Celtic, carved with snakes and things. Neither Christian nor Jewish as far as I can make out. And he's planned on leaving all his money (mind you, he's richer than all of us since the Czechs paid) to found a home for crippled or under-privileged children as a sort of memorial to Kitty, instead of leaving it to the family as he should.'

Small, plump, her blue doll's eyes wary, the housekeeper received us dressed in smart tweeds, a diamond clip sparkling on her collar, and led us into the drawing-room. 'The Baron has slept rather long today,' she said, 'but then no wonder he has such troubled nights. He dreams of her constantly, you know.'

'Really,' Clarisse said and stared at the diamond brooch. 'Didn't that belong to Kitty?' she asked. 'I seem to remember it.'

'But of course,' Gerty smiled. 'The Baroness left me all her jewels. I have it on paper in her own handwriting. But then – ' she took out a small pocket handkerchief into which she sniffed – 'I did nurse her faithfully till the last.'

Eugene appeared. Kissed his sister-in-law and greeted me.

He was looking remarkably healthy I thought, if slightly bulging round the waist. A handsome man still though I knew he was nearing seventy.

We lunched. The food could not have been better. Conversation less so. Clarisse talked incessantly about Vienna, about the family, about friends and relations. Gerty chipped in now and then, obviously well informed about Rothschild affairs, only to meet Clarisse's icy glance and to fall silent.

Eugene spoke very little, using his hearing-aid which he constantly adjusted as an excuse not to join in the conversation.

After coffee he suggested he show me the garden. Borders of peach-coloured peonies under the lilacs, beds of tulips and dogwood trees in blossom.

He took me to see the big house in the grounds. 'I could not live there any more without Kitty,' he said. 'It's rented now. I prefer my little wooden hut, my retreat, my *hermitage*.' Though it was not quite that, furnished as it was with beautiful French period pieces and price-less pictures, I understood what he meant.

'I can't tell you how I miss her, but then one cannot explain these things to people who have not lost someone they loved. She is ever present. I seem to hear her voice, even to see her at times. Yet I do not believe in life after death,' he sighed.

We passed a rather pretty cottage.

'Who lives there?' I asked.

I noticed he seemed to have no trouble hearing me without his aid at all.

'It used to be the gardener's but he's moved to his wife's house in the village. It's empty. I suppose I should rent it to someone but it's so near my house I don't like the thought of strangers so close.'

'Rent it to me,' I said on the spur of the moment. 'I wouldn't bother you. I need somewhere desperately to put furniture I bought for a farm I've since lost and somewhere to live through the summer.' Appalled by my cheek I added, 'It was just an idea. Forgive me for mentioning it.'

We walked for a while in silence.

'I might let you have it rent free,' he surprisingly said, 'under certain conditions. That you and Leopold would respect my privacy, never call on me unannounced, that you would only walk in certain parts of the garden where I don't go – Our establishments would have to remain entirely separate. You would pay for electricity and heating, of course,' he added, 'keep the cottage in good order and furnish it. But you must accept that it's not a permanent arrangement, that I have the right to ask you to leave whenever I want to.'

'But Baron Eugene!' I didn't know what to say, feeling gratitude so immense that it left me speechless. 'Do you really mean I can have the cottage?'

'Well, that's what I said, isn't it? Provided you keep your part of the agreement. We had better go back. I doubt Clarisse and Gerty are enjoying each other's company. As to Gerty – if you decide to come and live here – she has her uses but she also has a temper. It would be wiser to befriend her than the contrary. Is that understood?'

On the way back to New York I told Clarisse about the cottage.

Though rather surprised, she seemed to approve.

'Anything better than the way he lives now. If nothing else, Leopold will cheer him up. After all they were in the same regiment.'

By the next week I had all the furniture moved to Long Island in one big van. It was a charming cottage, two rooms below, kitchen and drawing-room and three bedrooms above and a bathroom. It took only a few hours to install and arrange the furniture. All blue and white, everything harmonizing as intended, the carpets laid, the curtains hung.

My kiln and the rest of our belongings would follow.

No one, neither Eugene nor Gerty, came to interrupt my day of installation. But that I felt was as agreed. How pretty it all looked. I was as happy as I was still capable of being. I couldn't wait to show our house to Leopold and Diana.

When Leopold finally arrived from Austria, I had booked a room for him in the Devon, I had to confess to him about our having lost the farm and why. He was, I think, more relieved than disappointed. Perhaps since he had never seen the place he had not looked forward to living there as I had. We did not talk of Steinhardt's death, except in connection with 'Nowhere'. Dulcie's name was, after what I had to tell him, never mentioned by Leopold again. He was like that. Once disappointed in some-one they ceased to exist for him. 'How small and mean,' was all he had said at the time. Lack of kindness and generosity, whatever the circumstances, was something he could not forgive.

After we had been established for a week, keeping strictly to ourselves, only walking in the part of the garden we had been permitted and doing our shopping by taxi, Gerty called, no doubt curious about how we were living. She blinked with amazement as I took her from one prettily furnished room to the other.

'Why, you've made it really nice,' she had to admit. 'But then I've always liked this cottage. I would have taken it for myself if the Baron hadn't needed me closer.' She then asked if we needed any help and gave me a list of tradesmen who would deliver if I telephoned, which proved very useful. Two days later the doorbell rang. It was Eugene. 'May I come in?' he asked. He looked around appreciatively. 'You seem most comfortably installed,' he smiled. 'What good pictures.'

I had hung up the last valuable possessions we had left. A Flemish Madonna supposedly by Memling; a small, rather over-painted Nativity by Cranach, and another rather strange picture attributed to the Austrian painter Rueland Frueauf, Our Lady robed in white, stretching out her arms to a crippled child.

Eugene looked at the paintings with grave appreciation.

He had studied art, was an expert on Titian and a connoisseur. 'Some-times I regret my religion,' he said, 'it deprives me of the pleasure of having such subjects in my house.'

I showed him all the blue and white rooms, the willow pattern kitchen and told him how happy and grateful we were for being allowed to live in his cottage.

'I never see you,' he grumbled, 'you don't even seem to walk in the garden.'

'But, Baron Eugene, surely that was one of the conditions for you permitting us to live here?'

'True,' he said, 'but I'm allowed to change my mind, am I not? Do walk wherever you please and let the child run around. It can't be good for her to be shut up in the house all day.'

I thanked him.

'I like gardening,' I said. 'Perhaps I could do a bit of weeding for you.'

'Very useful, but you had better discuss that with the gardener. Perhaps you would like a plot you could grow your own vegetables in. It would be an economy, wouldn't it?'

'A great help,' I said.

'Are you a good cook?' he then asked.

'You must come and dine one day and see.'

'I certainly will whenever you ask me. I am often very lonely, you know.'

Gerty came towards evening, as if Eugene's visit had given approval of more neighbourly contacts. Leopold poured her a drink. He was just back from New York.

'It's so nice having you here,' she exclaimed. 'The Baron and I are often very lonely since the Baroness died.'

'Come in any time,' Leopold said kindly. From then on she was in and out of the cottage every day, watching me cook or sweep with great curiosity. I didn't really mind. I had nothing to conceal, except the hour when I locked myself up in my room to think of Steinhardt. I had not given up the hope to communicate with him somehow. I was trying automatic writing but though the pencil moved at great speed over the pages what it wrote was indecipherable. There was no doubt that something compelled me to do this and that some unexplainable forces were unleashed in my trance-like state. The furniture in my room cracked ominously, once, a chest of drawers moved several inches away from the wall and back. It didn't frighten me. I had recognized I had certain powers as a child when my mother had allowed me to join in table-turning which was then a fashionable form of entertainment.

However my séances gave me terrible headaches afterwards and since there was never a sign that these manifestations had anything to do with Steinhardt's spirit which I was trying to reach I gave up, feeling much closer to him on my visits to Brooklyn.

I don't think Leopold ever knew I went there. I had every kind of excuse to go to New York once a week to ask my friends the Viennese antique dealers for money and to visit the Judge.

Then one day when I had gone to the cemetery as usual and asked the caretaker for the keys of the tomb he had said he thought I wouldn't need them any more. 'He's gone. They have taken him away to Arlington to bury him among the Goys.' So I went to Brooklyn no more and tore up the document that proved me owner of a grave there.

In the hot summer weather the pleasantest time was evening and either Gerty or Eugene were always to be found near our cottage, walking round it, peering into the windows, calling to Diana or me to come for a stroll and enjoy sunset or moonlight in the garden. Soon we had no privacy at all. Gerty amused me with her dramatic tales of the great love that had been between her and the Baroness (she never called her Kitty). Eugene's sorrow moved me, since it was like my own, and we had long philosophical discussions about life and death. But as time passed a certain *joie de vivre* seemed to reawaken in both of them. Gerty wore scarlet teagowns in the evenings when she came to us for drinks. Eugene, looking very handsome in his green velvet dinner-jacket, seemed to have forgotten all conditions under which he had let us have the cottage, invited us nightly for dinner, invitations which, since it spared me cooking, I was only too glad to accept. However, he left me in no doubt that he was recovering at last from his years of mourning.

Gerty only accepted this very reluctantly. 'I don't know what's come over the Baron,' she complained. 'He doesn't even want to visit the grave any more. It must be the hot weather.'

'I do think he rather needs to see a few more people. No one can live in such isolation for ever. He seems even to enjoy our company.'

She looked at me suspiciously.

'I have a feeling the Baron is falling in love with you.'

'Not with me,' I protested, 'with life. After all he's still a healthy virile man in spite of his age.'

'You may be right,' Gerty pondered. 'Perhaps he needs some distraction.'

461

Some weeks later the distraction arrived, much to my relief. Gerty had a small dress-shop in Glen Cove where she sold second-hand models of first-class clothes. One of her customers and friends was a young English woman. Not quite a film star – a starlet let's say.

She begged Eugene to invite her friend for lunch. I too was asked. I thought I had rarely seen a prettier face, a more ravishing *décolleté* and more voluptuous curves draped, rather unsuitably for lunch in the country, in pale pink chiffon.

She didn't speak much, which was to her advantage since Eugene was so deaf, but her looks did. From then on she became a frequent visitor.

All in all it had been a pleasant summer. We had been able to have guests. The child her friends. Leopold his. Eddie who was staying near by with Harrison and Mona came over again and again to mess around in my kitchen, inventing new dishes, rearranging the furniture, doing everything he could think of to cheer me up, though we never spoke of Steinhardt's death.

Frequently he drove me and Diana over to see Mona. She was, though as kind as ever and as radiantly beautiful, worried about Harrison who after a heart attack had to keep to his bed.

The Judge came from New York to lunch or dine with us several times.

Nevertheless, the ever closer intimacy with which both Gerty and Eugene seemed to expect us to live with them was starting to cause me some concern. How and where would it end?

One day Leopold brought Honorka for lunch.

I knew him from Prague where his visits before and after the war had always been an event. A Chicago-born Czech, rumoured to be immensely wealthy, he had played the role of the typical rich uncle from America in Czech circles, giving generously to all sorts of charities, even invited by our President and leaving no doubt as to his importance.

Though he amused Leopold I had never been able to like him. He was a large man with a broad, red, coarse-featured face and a very loud voice. He used to hold forth in the bar of the Ambassador Hotel when he was in Prague. 'Free beer for all – ' of which he consumed large quantities himself. Boastful and vulgar, yet never lacking an appreciative audience.

He seemed now somewhat more civilized than I had remembered him, quieter, less self-confident and opinionated, as we had lunch and talked mainly of home.

'Honorka has something he wants to discuss with you,' Leopold said when we were having coffee.

'Indeed, Mrs Sternberg.' (Honorka always stressed his Republic-anism, American or Czech, by not giving us titles.) 'I have a proposal that might interest you. I know you make figurines. Well, so do I. Only I mass-produce them. I have a factory in Chicago and a smaller plant in St Petersburg, Florida where I spend my winters. It is there I would need you and your husband's help.'

'China figurines?' I asked, interested.

'Well, not quite,' Honorka said. 'It's a patent I bought of a special mixture from which we cast the figures. It's harder and more lasting than china clay and needs no firing. Yet I can reproduce even most complicated models taken from porcelain, wood, bronze or ivory in this material. I have,' he smiled ingratiatingly, 'read of course all about your exhibition in the papers and about your artistic gifts. You have, I know, great taste and knowledge. Your advice would be invaluable. I'm just a plain, simple, ordinary self-made man,' he said, looking from me to Leopold as if for a denial but since none was forthcoming he continued, 'I'm no artist.'

'And what would my work be?'

'Oh, just some help in the decorating and perhaps we could start a new line in figurines, but mainly advisory.'

'And how much would you pay?' Leopold asked – quite un-embarrassed.

'I wouldn't venture to suggest a salary to your wife but I can do better. I will make her a partner in the firm. That will give you thirty per cent of the profits. I made over sixty thousand bucks last year and hope to double it in this. Moreover, I can offer you a small house rent free, near the factory. The best climate in the world, flowers, the sea –

'Well, take it or leave it,' he said nonchalantly, leaning back in his chair. 'What do you say?'

I looked at Leopold, wondering at the doubt I saw in his face. It seemed a wonderful offer.

'It's for my husband to decide,' I said. 'I don't know if he wants to move to Florida.'

'Think it over. I'll be in New York for the next three days, at your disposal.'

He left.

'It sounds very tempting,' I told Leopold after Honorka had gone. 'He offers a lot.'

'If it's all true. I don't entirely trust the man, even if he's made a fortune, no one knows how.'

'So you don't think we should accept?'

'I didn't say that.'

'Is it that you don't want to leave New York? Is it because of Annicka?'

'No,' he said, looking surprised. 'I suppose she could just as well make hats in Florida. Look here, do what you think best. I'm going to have my afternoon nap.'

As usual the final decision was up to me.

Next day I telephoned Honorka saying we accepted.

Soon I had to tell Eugene that we were planning to leave.

'But why?' he asked, not at all pleased I could see. 'I've tried to do everything in my power to make you feel at home. And living here must have saved you a lot of money.'

I tried to express my gratitude for his kindness and generosity as best I could.

Gerty too was shocked and uncomprehending. 'Do you mean you'll leave everything just like that after all the expense you've gone to? What about the furniture?'

'I will have to sell it before I go.'

She thought for a moment.

'It's all second-hand?'

'Some of it, not the bedding of course.'

'Would you take five hundred dollars for the lot?'

'Excepting some sheets, blankets, towels and pillows, the three pictures and my kiln – yes.'

'Done!' said Gerty, slapping down her hand like a horse dealer and writing me out a cheque.

I often wonder if she moved into the blue and white cottage when Eugene, much to his family's surprise if not to mine, married the pretty young English woman Gerty had so rashly introduced to him. Contrary to expectations it turned out to be a very happy marriage.

'If we go to Florida I will need some money,' Leopold said. 'Whatever Honorka promises, his won't be available immediately.'

'Debts?'

'Sort of – a private obligation. I thought we might sell the pictures.'

They were the last of the valuables we had left.

'They belong to you, darling.'

'I have asked Clarisse's advice,' he confessed, 'since she knows all the big dealers. But she says there are few private buyers who want religious pictures these days. She thinks it would be better to get in touch with some of the smaller museums. She knows several of their directors.'

Soon serious-looking gentlemen came out to Glen Cove to scrutinize the paintings, questioning provenance and attribution but nevertheless anxious to buy. Finally we sold all three. One to the Hartford Gallery, two went to Washington. We did not get very much for the pictures. Prices for old masters, excepting for those with great names, were then still comparatively low.

I regretted parting with the paintings more than I had minded selling anything else. If they had even beautified Castolovice, how much more so our rooms in the Devon, my studio and finally the Long Island cottage. They had transformed our surroundings wherever we took them. They were like windows opening on to another more magical world.

It was losing the Madonna, attributed, falsely it proved, to Memling, that saddened me most. She was seated on a hillock, little flowers blossoming at her feet, her scarlet cloak spread wide in gothic folds. On her knees she held the Christ-child and from it flowed light that touched her pale sad face, her narrow hands and her golden hair and swept beyond, over hills and valleys, castles and towns, all bathed in the magical radiance that seemed to emanate from the child.

'Don't you mind losing the Madonna?' I asked Leopold. 'After all it must be hundreds of years that she has blessed and protected your family.'

'Well, now she is helping us once more. After all, it's only her picture we are selling.'

When I visited the Judge for the last time to say goodbye before we moved to Florida he handed me an envelope. I opened it. In it was a cheque for two thousand, eight hundred and fifty dollars.

'But, Judge Irvin, how can I accept this?'

'I would resent it very much if you didn't. It's in repayment for what should never have been taken from you. I'm only sorry I couldn't give it to you before you so hastily sold the farm.'

Or before we sold the pictures, I thought as I said goodbye to my kind and generous old friend.

'Annicka has decided not to move to St Petersburg just yet,' Leopold told me. 'She thinks in a small place like that you and she might meet, which would be awkward. She's a good girl. She doesn't want to embarrass anyone.'

I couldn't help but feel sudden pity.

'I wouldn't really mind.'

'But I would,' Leopold said. 'However, I would like to give her a nice present before we leave. She earns very little making hats and I think now after we've sold the pictures we can afford it. Don't you agree?'

60

It was in early January that Diana and I travelled to St Petersburg. She was by then as reluctant to leave her school as she had at first been to join it. Only the promise of a house of our own near the sea, a wonderful climate where one could swim all the year round and future riches persuaded her to accept my decision without violent protests.

Leopold had felt it wiser to let us go ahead to put things in order before he joined us.

Honorka had written that he regretted not being able to meet us, being delayed in Chicago but that we should just drive to the given address where we would find everything prepared. The house would be ready and his foreman, Jan Veverka, and wife would see to all our needs. They lived close by.

We left our main luggage at the railway station and hailed a taxi. The driver was black.

'Sure you want me, ma'am?' he asked. 'There are white drivers around.'

'Of course we do if you will take us.'

I gave him the address. He peered at it.

'Don't right know where that is but I guess we'll find it. Town's growing every minute. North, you say?'

'Number five, Palmetto Drive, off the Clearwater Road.'

He drove through the town centre, a few tall buildings, banks, shops and offices all looking very new, clean and prosperous, but the rest of St Petersburg seemed one vast rambling garden that went on for mile after mile, dotted with low-built white bungalows, surrounded by orange, lemon, grapefruit and trees with blue or scarlet blossoms.

'Isn't it lovely?' I asked Diana.

'Yes, but where is the sea? You said our house was on it.'

'Will we soon get to the sea?' I asked the driver.

466

'Opposite direction,' he said. 'Miles back now.'

We had been driving for over half an hour, the meter jumping ominously all the time, the driver slowing down now and then to look right and left and then shaking his close-cropped black head as if puzzled. At last I got worried fearing he had either lost his way or was driving us around in order to collect a bigger fare. The district we were passing through seemed almost wild – jungle-like. Big patches of tangled vegetation, scarcely any houses and it was getting quite dark.

I begged him to stop, which he did.

'Surely there must be a policeman around who can tell us where the place is?' I said.

'What are you up to, lady?' he asked. 'Trying to frame me or something?'

'I don't know what you mean.'

'Ma'am,' he wailed. 'I'm taking you straight back where you came from before you call the police.'

'But what on earth's the matter?' I asked.

'That I'm scared stiff, that's what's the matter, at being caught driving around two white girls so far from town after dark. This is a black taxi as anyone could have seen by its colour,' he added.

'But it's green,' Diana said.

'Sure and the white ones are blue. It's not my fault,' he almost sobbed. 'I hadn't had a fare for days. You spoke foreign-like. Well, I thought I'd risk it for once driving whites. And now, ma'am, I just simply don't know what you are planning to do to me out here – ' he gulped, rolling his eyes.

Poor man, I thought, trying not to laugh. 'All we want is to get to that house,' I reassured him. 'Look, it's so dark no one can see us or the colour of your taxi or of our skins by now. Drive to the nearest gasoline station, take this address and find out where the place is.'

It didn't turn out to be far from where we were. We drove about half a mile back and distinctly legible by the street light it said 'Palmetto Drive'.

He stopped once more.

'Better leave you here. Don't want to stay in front of no house this time of night. Man at the station said it was a new street. Guess that's why I couldn't find it. Only a few houses. You won't need to walk far.'

We picked up the two heavy suitcases. Palmetto Drive was narrow and dusty, lit only by an occasional street light. We passed one or two houses as we trudged along.

'This is worse than "Nowhere",' Diana complained. 'Mummy, I'm frightened and I'm cold.' The temperature had indeed dropped as it does at night-time in winter in Florida.

'That's Number five,' I exclaimed with considerable relief. It was a small house. We rang the bell. Nothing happened but we could see light behind the curtains. We rang once more and a tall man stood silhouetted in the open door.

'Pan Veverka?'

'Come in, we've been expecting you but we heard no car. How ever did you get here?' a female voice called in Czech.

'We walked all the way from the station,' I joked feebly.

'Gracious, you must be tired,' Mrs Veverka exclaimed as we entered the living-room, 'please be seated.' She was a small, thin, anaemic-looking woman, still young, but lines of worry or discontent had marked her face. We shook hands and sat down. I could tell they were working-class people by their manner and by the way the room was furnished, by their accent she was Czech and he Slovak. He was a rather handsome dark man with gipsy eyes. I thought how fine he would look in embroidered Slovak peasant dress instead of in his ugly ready-made suit. He didn't seem particularly friendly, his swarthy face sullen, as his wife offered to make us some coffee.

I thanked her but said we were very tired, would they just show us how to get to our house.

Both Veverkas inspected us in silence as if trying to make us out. Perhaps it was our clothes. Thanks to Mona we were simply but no doubt very expensively dressed in a fashion probably strange to them.

'The house may not be quite what you are accustomed to,' Mrs Veverka said at last. '*To neni Zámek.*' (It's no castle.)

'Could we now perhaps go?' I begged. 'It's not very far I hope?'

'Oh no, it's in our yard. I'll just tell Jan to stay with our son while I take you round or he won't go to sleep.'

A minute later she rejoined us. We picked up our suitcases. She didn't offer to help. She led us out to what in the light of the street lamp looked like a small garden shed of unpainted wood, roofed with corrugated iron. 'It was our first home here after we came from Chicago,' she explained. 'Jan built it all himself. He's a good carpenter,' she added as she opened the door and switched on a light.

We walked straight into a tiny kitchen. There was no hall, not even a place to hang up a coat. 'And this is the bedroom.' It led out of the kitchen and was too small to contain anything but a large bed and a cupboard. 'Toilet and bath,' she showed us with pride. 'Well, it's not large.' Indeed it wasn't. The tub was dwarf size. 'Running water,' she pulled the flush. 'Hot too for the hands and bath if you light the gas but be careful. I better show you how.' She turned the handle of a metal container, held a lighted match to its spout and jumped back as far as she could in the narrow space. There was a hiss, a roar and a flash of blue flame which, however, subsided into a flicker. 'When you want no more hot water just turn it off. It's quite easy.'

We returned to the kitchen. She opened a cupboard. 'Bread, milk, butter, sugar, tea and coffee for your breakfast. The bill's on the counter. You won't find it difficult to shop here. There's a store just across the street.'

I thanked her. She opened another door. 'The lounge.' It was somewhat larger than the bedroom, had a sort of couch, four chairs, a table and a lamp with a yellow silk shade. There was also a small iron stove with a tin pipe that went up to and presumably through the ceiling.

'Shall I light it?' she asked. 'The house gets rather cold when not in use.' It had indeed.

A cloud of smoke swirled through the room. 'That's just at first,' she said. 'It warms up quickly. It's a good little stove. We've arranged the rooms as Pan Honorka ordered us. I hope you find it to your taste. I've cleaned it all thoroughly, put fresh sheets on the bed.'

'It couldn't be nicer,' I said politely.

'Well, I hope you'll feel at home. Mr Honorka was very anxious that you should. *Dobro noc.*'

She left.

Only then did I dare look at Diana.

'It may not be quite what we expected,' I said hastily, not liking what I read in her face. 'These things do occasionally happen.'

'Only to you and Papi,' she said bitterly. 'Where may I ask do you expect me to sleep?'

'Well, with me I suppose.'

'What, in the same bed? I'd rather sit up all night. You toss and you turn, you cough and you snore.'

'Really, aren't we getting a little spoilt?' I asked, nettled. 'It's a big bed. I'm sure all three Veverkas slept in it together.'

'And won't Papi be pleased at doing that! Though I doubt he can even get through the front door and if he manages to squeeze in he will certainly get stuck in the bedroom or bathroom later.' Though I knew it was true I ignored this.

'Let's go next door. Perhaps you can sleep there.' The adjoining room had grown very warm and the stove was glowing bright red.

'With that,' she protested, pointing at it. 'It will explode any minute.'

'And so will I,' I said, finally losing my temper. 'I want to hear no more complaints. Go and unpack what you need and bring me the gin.'

She brought it. I gulped it straight out of the bottle. She watched with disapproval. 'There are glasses,' she said.

I soon felt somewhat better and calmer.

'The trouble is you lack all spirit of adventure,' I declared. 'Lots of children go on camping trips and live in huts like this and enjoy it. Why, I have slept in tents and shooting boxes much more primitive and never thought of complaining.'

'Perhaps you hadn't been promised a house near the sea – '

Finally I bedded her down on the couch. I had found clean sheets in the cupboard. The stove had meanwhile gone out. I covered her with my fur coat, brought her milk and bread and butter, conceded I didn't think we could remain in Honorka's hut for long. 'Just till we find something else,' I assured her and was rewarded with a triumphant smile.

I crept into the big bed and slept wrapped in my dressing gown, my travelling pillow under my head, not wanting to come into too close contact with the Veverkas' former connubial couch.

Some sound must have woken me at dawn or the pale light that fell from the uncurtained window on to my bed.

I got up and walked out in my dressing gown. It was cold but the air was fresh and sweet with the scent of orange blossoms. Not that there were any trees or flowers around our hut or the Veverkas' adjoining house, just some spiky-looking grass and the dusty road.

No effort had evidently been made at creating a garden. But then as I knew Czechs of that class eat no vegetables except for cabbage and potatoes and though Slovaks painted flowers on their pottery and embroidered them on their clothes, they rarely grew them.

There was a small fenced yard in which I heard hens clucking and another tin shed somewhat smaller than our house that looked like a workshop.

How drab and ugly it all was, yet beyond the road great clumps of feathery bamboo swayed and bent in the morning breeze and the sky was turning from pink to blue. I returned to the hut, washed with cold water and some warm that I boiled on the two-plate electric burner much too fearful to use the gas, and made myself tea.

Diana was still asleep. I dressed and went out once more, taking last night's road. I passed several small houses, one larger and more prosperous-looking standing in a big garden, obviously a nursery by the amount of small trees and flowers in pots it contained, and found the store. I was surprised to find it was already open, less so when I saw it belonged to Italians, remembering how they worked from dawn to dusk in southern Italy. The Signora, I was to get to know her well, seemed to have forgotten the language of her country or perhaps my accents didn't remind her of it; plump, short-legged, sprightly and vivacious and speaking a sort of Italian-American slang she sold me marvellous fruit, gallon bottles of wine, pasta, a chicken, cheese, olives, salami – in fact whatever I or she could think of and promised her son would deliver it – '*Presto!*'

Indeed he did, racing up to the hut some minutes later on a bicycle with my parcels, giving Diana still in her nightgown an appreciative smile, showing superb white teeth, proving he was born in America and not in the slums of Naples and greeting her cheekily with 'Hi there, beautiful.'

I had passed Mrs Veverka who was sweeping her doorstep, her head tied up in a kerchief, on the way. 'My, you're up early,' she had exclaimed, amazed.

'It's a lovely day,' I remarked.

'It's always the same here except in summer when it's hotter,' she said without enthusiasm.

'Oh, I forgot to tell you, Mr and Mrs Palice are coming to show you the workshop at eleven,' she added.

'And who are they?'

'He's Mr Honorka's partner and the manager. They work here.'

'How many people does Mr Honorka employ?'

'Depends,' she said. 'They come and go. Well, I'll have to cook breakfast.' I saw she was not very anxious to talk to me.

I found Diana having hers in a somewhat more conciliatory mood than the night before. At eleven the Palices arrived. 'May we come in?' they called through the open door. They were a nice-looking youngish couple. He had a fine featured, rather tired-looking, face. Hers was more vivid and expressive and very attractive. Both wore jeans and flowered cotton shirts.

'I'll come out,' I called. 'I haven't tidied up yet.'

'Welcome to Florida,' Palice said as we shook hands.

At the end of the drive was another corrugated iron shed larger than ours into which they led me. First into a small room with many shelves on which stood hundreds of brightly-coloured figurines. 'These,' Palice said, 'are the finished products ready for sale.' They were I could see plaster copies taken from all sorts of models: Chinese gods and goddesses and pagodas, tortoises, rabbits, frogs, lizards and birds, Indian dancers, nymphs and fauns, crinolined ladies and naked ones. They were coarsely and crudely reproduced and seemed to me quite hideous.

I suppose it wasn't difficult to gather from my face what I thought.

'Enchanting, aren't they?' Mrs Palice smiled sweetly. I was only to find out later what a sense of humour she had.

I picked up the figure of a dancer only partially dressed, her body bright pink, with draperies of orange and purple, the whole thing covered with thick shining glaze obviously sprayed on.

'That's one of Mr Honorka's favourite models,' Mrs Palice remarked. 'He likes bright colours.'

I was taken into another room where an equal amount of objects were ranged on shelves, these still in the white plaster stage and undecorated. 'The drying room,' I was told. 'Here the casting is done.'

'Morning, Jan,' Palice said in Czech. To me they had spoken almost perfect English. We walked into another room. Veverka mumbled something but didn't look up. He was dressed in stained overalls and was pouring liquid plaster into a rubber mould.

I went closer, interested. 'I suppose the moulds are quite flexible,' I asked, 'once the plaster has hardened you can pull them off like a glove?'

He didn't answer, only gave me a sullen look.

'You're quite right,' Palice said politely. 'It's one of the advantages of our casting method.'

The air was thick with plaster dust.

'Well, I think you've seen everything there is to see.'

'Then let's go back to the hut and talk,' I suggested.

Once there I sent out Diana to delay them while I took the sheets off her bed. I then asked them in and opened a bottle of wine. They had been talking Czech to her. She spoke it much more fluently than I did.

'We have been telling your Diana that we have a daughter, though younger. I hope they become friends,' Mrs Palice said.

'Well, to our partnership in Honorka's company.' Palice raised his glass with a rather ambiguous expression on his face.

'How many partners are there?' I asked.

'Excepting Honorka, there's me, Jan Veverka and now your husband or you, I suppose – there was another but he left.'

'Have you signed a contract yet?' Mrs Palice enquired.

'No, Honorka wanted me to but there wasn't time.'

The couple looked at each other with relief I thought.

'And what do you think Mr Honorka expects me to do here?' I then asked.

'Well, I believe he wants you to advise and help decorate, as my wife does, and your husband to do the rougher work with me such as mixing and pouring. That's at least what he implied.'

'Do you mean there are no other workers?'

'No.'

I couldn't believe what I was hearing. I stared at Palice's tired face.

'And how long have you done this?'

'For the last two years.'

'And does it pay?'

'For the first few months the company did quite well. As you perhaps know by now Americans are like children, they snatch at anything new and grow tired of it as soon. We sold quite a lot of figurines in the beginning. Honorka is good at advertising his wares. As partners, of course, we shared in the profits.'

'But surely you are also paid a salary?'

'Oh no, not as partners, though my wife gets a small amount for every figurine she paints up.'

'Franta, tell her!' Mrs Palice exclaimed impetuously. 'Mrs Sternberg has a right to know the truth about us and others that Honorka has cheated and deceived before it happens to her.'

'I would be very grateful if you did,' I said as I poured the Palices some more wine.

'Well, take our case,' he said. 'I was first secretary in the Czech Embassy in Washington. When our country became communist almost overnight I knew I would be recalled to Prague. We decided to try and stay in America. Permission was granted. I had to find work but it wasn't easy. My studies had been in Czech and my diplomatic training was of little practical use. Finally I worked as a translator and Lisa took in typing but even together we earned scarcely enough to support ourselves and our daughter. Then Honorka, whom we had frequently met in the embassy where he threw his weight around – he was a very active member of the Czech American Friendship Society and it was through this organization that he discovered our address, called on us and offered me a partnership in his factory in Florida. A rent-free house (it proved to be rather like this) and a share in the considerable profits he said he was already making. "Just light, artistic work," he promised, "and the sky's the limit to what you will earn." Who would not have accepted gratefully? Besides,' Palice continued, 'we wanted to leave Washington. All our friends were diplomats; even if unwillingly, they had to associate with the representatives of the new Czech regime whom we did not want to meet.

'So here we are. We work hard all day for practically nothing by now, while Honorka sits in his fine villa on the beach.'

'– And cooks the books, I'm sure,' Mrs Palice burst out, her face flushed with indignation.

'Not that we are his only victims,' Palice went on. 'He has a factory in Chicago too into which he lures emigrant Czechs with false promises and partnerships to tempt them to work for him for nothing.

'Take Jan Veverka here. Well, he's not very intelligent. He comes from a small Slovak village. I don't even know where Honorka found him. He has a sort of spy network by which he traces emigrant Czechs. He promised Jan literally the earth, that is a fine piece of land, you can imagine what that means to a Slovak peasant, and partnership in the factory. Of course Veverka accepted. He came here with his wife and child and built himself this little house, Honorka kindly paying for all the materials. He was then encouraged to build a larger one in which they now live, only to finally discover that the land on which the houses stand belongs to Honorka. He can't sell, he can't escape, he is enslaved for life and now Honorka has even demanded that he gives you this shack.' Palice looked around with distaste. 'Renting it has been one of Jan's few sources of income of late except for carpentry work which he does after hours.'

'Poor man. No wonder he resents our presence here and shows it.' I exclaimed, 'Oh, thank God I delayed signing that contract. Exactly the same would have happened to us as it did to you, without your warning. But can't you free yourselves, just walk out?' I then asked.

'It's not so easy,' Palice said. 'I've been offered a well-paid job in a tourist office. We like living here, the climate's wonderful. We have found a good, quite inexpensive, convent school for our daughter too but I'm under contract to Honorka and though I am seeking legal advice we are not American citizens yet. He can denounce us, perhaps even have us sent back to Czechoslovakia. He's a powerful man, thanks to his wealth, and quite ruthless.'

Diana had been listening intently to our conversation. I could see she had liked the Palices from the first.

'Just wait till Papi comes here,' she said. 'He's afraid of no one. Why, he will make such a laughing stock of Mr Honorka that he can't show his face anywhere any more. Don't you know Papi?' she asked Palice.

'Well, I know something of his reputation,' a shimmer of hope brightening his face. 'He must be quite a personality.'

'Diana's right,' I said, 'I think Leopold will be most useful in solving your problems. I will write to him and explain and when he comes we'll let him deal with Honorka.'

Agreeing that we must meet again soon we parted.

✤ 61 ✤

Though shocked and indignant at what I had heard I did not feel particularly disappointed at the failure of our hopes. To me, since Steinhardt's death, nothing seemed very important any more and I had become more liable to simply leave things to fate.

Besides, thanks to the picture sale and the Judge's gift, there was no immediate urgency to find work, and time to look around. I might even start ceramics again, perhaps rent a little shop, I thought. Even if Honorka's offer had been genuine and we could have earned a lot, whatever artistic talents I had would have been totally wasted massproducing plaster figurines. The only thing that was essential immediately was to find somewhere decent to live before Leopold arrived.

'I'll just go over and ask the Veverkas to telephone a taxi for us and then let's go to the sea,' I told the delighted child.

By the rich smell of stewing onions I could tell Mrs Veverka was cooking lunch.

'Could you telephone me a taxi, please,' I begged, 'and ask how much the call is so I can repay you? We want to go to the beach.'

'All the way by cab? Why, it will cost you a fortune.'

Nevertheless she telephoned. 'We love your little house,' I said, 'but I think we will have to find some other place to live in as soon as possible.' Fear and relief seemed to alternate in her face.

'May I ask why?'

'It's because now that I've seen the factory I know it's not the kind of work either my husband or I would be any good at. And to live so near the plant and accept your house rent free from Honorka wouldn't be possible if we didn't work for him – which we are not going to do.'

'But what if he blames us? He might think that we'd said or done something to put you off.'

'Well, you haven't. Which is what I'll tell him. Don't worry, Mrs Veverka, I think I understand the situation by now.'

She gave me a grateful look.

At least Honorka's deception had given us the impetus to come here, I thought happily, as we drove through orange groves and past lovely gardens down to a sea as blue as the sky. There was a long, wooden pier and at its end a sort of domed pavilion. On one side of it stretched a sandy beach crowded with tanned young people and children, on the other was a yacht basin with boats large and small tied to the pier. They looked clean and trim, paint and brasswork gleaming in the sunlight.

'How I wish we could live on a yacht,' Diana said as we walked along the pier.

'Only millionaires can,' I said.

'It wouldn't have to very big. Look at that one. It's marked for sale.'

I did. It measured I thought about thirty-five feet. It was unpainted but its mahogany planking shone with polish or varnish. On its bow the name *Margaret* was painted in gold letters. It had a spacious deck, a large deckhouse and portholes that proved there were cabins below.

'I've never seen the inside of a big boat like that,' Diana said. 'Couldn't we sort of make believe we want to buy it and look? There is someone inside, I'm sure. There's smoke coming out of that chimney.'

We climbed down the steps that led to slippery sea-washed planks from which the boats were approachable.

'What now?' I asked Diana.

'Now you call "Ahoy there", loud.'

I did my best. Surprisingly it met with success.

A man in a yachting cap, a singlet and blue trousers answered my call. 'Welcome aboard,' he said. 'I'm Captain Barker.'

With his help we stepped down on to the deck.

He was an old man, browned by sun and wind to the mahogany colour of his boat. His round bald head shone like a polished coconut, most of the rest of his face, except for bright little eyes and a big nose, was sun-bleached beard.

'May we look around?' I asked, as one does in shops, implying one is not going to buy.

'Sure.'

He took us below where there were two neat cabins with double bunks and a lavatory, above was the deckhouse, a long, narrow room with windows, couches and chairs ending in the raised bridge with its steering wheel and instrument panel. Boxed in, forming a sort of bench, were the engines which he uncovered.

'Brand new diesels,' he said, 'both of them – had them fitted last year.'

He showed us the galley with its stove and orderly array of pots and pans, crockery and cutlery, then took us astern where the ropes lay neatly coiled, tins of fuel and paint, anchors and fishing rods.

'Why, it's like a little house,' Diana exclaimed, amazed, 'and much better than ours!'

'Better than any because when you get tired of a place, off you sail to another.'

'And why are you selling?'

'Wife wants to live ashore. Wants a garden. Damn fool thing to want if one has the sea.'

'And how old is the boat?'

''Bout thirty years.'

'But isn't that very old?'

'No more than is a woman of thirty. The *Margaret*'s good for another twenty years if she's treated right, her bottom scraped every winter and given a new coat of paint and varnish.'

'And is she sea-worthy?' I asked, trying to sound expert.

'Ma'am, I've sailed her for ten years now and never a mishap and she's had to weather quite some storms. Ask anyone along the coast about her. She has quite a reputation, the *Margaret*. Tell you what, I'll take you out on her now.'

'But we shouldn't waste your time.'

'There ain't no better way to live than wasting it,' he laughed as he jumped nimbly on to the planks, untied the rope and was back on the boat again in seconds. With a long pole he pushed us from the pier, ran to the bridge, pressed a button and the engines started as he took the wheel.

Slowly we edged past the pier and out of the harbour, threading our way between buoys and boats and then greater speed and we were out in the bay. The water was very calm, there was scarcely any motion and I felt all my love for this most unpredictable and dangerously seductive of elements reawaken.

He cut the engines. 'Quite safe to let her drift for a while in this weather. Saves oil.' Silence, only the wash of little waves against the bow.

He restarted the engines. 'Want to take the wheel?' he asked Diana, pulling her up on to the bridge and seating her in the raised chair. Her face scarlet with excitement she clung to it. 'You don't have to hang on for dear life,' the skipper laughed, 'take it easy, you're not on the highway steering a car – Now try to turn to starboard. To the right!' seeing she didn't understand and neither did I. 'No, you've got to swing around much farther till she moves.' He helped her revolve the wheel almost full circle. 'See, it's quite easy,' he said. 'You'll do fine with a bit of practice but I guess I'd better take us in now myself.'

They changed places.

'Oh, Mummy,' she whispered as she sat down beside me, 'if only we could buy this boat.'

'It would be utter folly,' I said.

'Why? Papi would love living on a boat.'

'I very much doubt it. Look, we don't even know what it costs.'

'Well then, ask.'

After we had landed I did.

'Two thousand, five hundred.'

Why not more, why not less? I thought with a shiver. Why did it have to be the exact sum the borrowing of which had caused me so much anxiety and final disgrace and had then been so surprisingly restored to me by the Judge? What did it mean? Was it a sign that I should buy the boat?

'You will have to give me some time to think it over,' I told the Captain.

'I'm in no hurry,' he said. 'Truth is, I don't like to part from the old girl one little bit even if my Mrs wants me to get rid of her.'

We walked back along the pier.

'How could I ever make ceramics on a boat?' I asked Diana. 'We've got to earn a living somehow.'

'We could take people out fishing and for trips round the coast.'

'And how do you think Papi would manage at sea with his bad leg in rough weather? And you, my dear, will have to go to school.'

'I wouldn't mind so much if we lived on the boat.'

This was a concession indeed.

'And think what fun Papi would have talking to all those yachting people and all the naked girls on the beach!'

We crossed the road. Facing us was a row of shining new shops with big plate-glass windows, obviously quite recently completed, all of them unoccupied and with 'For Rent' signs on them.

They overlooked the harbour, beach and sea.

'Just what you want, Mummy, for your ceramics.'

I remembered with regret having reproached the child the night before for her lack of adventurous spirit. 'We live on the boat and you work here. It's perfect,' she declared, 'and every morning and evening we can just cross the road and swim.'

We took a bus back to Palmetto Drive.

'I'll have to do something about our luggage,' I said. 'It can't remain at the railway station.'

I found Veverka in the yard, prying open some tins of paint or plaster.

For the first time he greeted us with a smile. Obviously he had been told the good news that we were not staying long.

I asked him if there was anywhere where we could store our luggage, my kiln and my crates of clays and glazes for the time being.

'There's only my workshop,' he said, 'and I need all the space there is.' He unlocked the little shed. It was full of tools and a large carpenter's bench. 'Still, I might make some room if it's only for a week or two.'

'Certainly no longer,' I said, wondering where we would go.

'Come and have a glass of wine, Mr Veverka. We missed you yesterday when the Palices were here.'

'Wife doesn't like me to drink,' he said. Nevertheless he gulped down two glasses hurriedly, his gipsy eyes anxiously scanning the yard.

'Glad you're not staying. No good here,' he said and left.

It was only three weeks more that we remained with them. Almost daily we went to the beach to swim in the cold but exhilarating waters of the bay and to look longingly at the *Margaret*. Also to see the signs on the row of shops, one after the other, change from 'For Rent' to 'Rented'. Finally there was only one, the largest, left. Then I called the agent whose name was on the doors and made an appointment to view the shop.

It was quite a long building, if rather narrow, stretching from its glassed front on Beachdrive for thirty yards I was told to another glassed door that led on to a paved backyard.

There was running water, a lavatory with washbasin and an extra sink.

'Would I be allowed to partition?' I asked the agent, explaining I was a ceramic artist and would have to divide it up into studio and shop.

He thought that could be arranged though, of course, at my expense.

I enquired as to the rent. It was exorbitant. It would have been so even in New York.

'Best position in town,' the agent shrugged. 'Customers from the yacht basin, the beach and all those that stroll along. You'll have to make up your mind pretty quick, ma'am. All the rest were snapped up soon as we advertised them.'

'All right, I'll take it,' I said.

On the same afternoon I agreed to buy the *Margaret*.

I remember the reckless folly of that day even now with amazement. But like a gambler who having lost and lost again throws all he has left in the world on the table, challenging fate once and for all, I felt the time had come to risk all or nothing.

So there we were owners of a yacht with no experience whatsoever in handling a boat that size and the most expensive shop in St Petersburg with nothing to sell in it.

There are certain legal formalities that apply to the sale of large boats as they do to houses or land in America.

When the Captain and I met to sign the necessary documents in the office that dealt with such matters I filled out a form giving my name, place of birth, permanent address, which I had to leave blank, and handed it to the gentleman in charge.

'You are a US citizen I take it?'

'No, not yet, though I hope to become one in two years,' I smiled.

'But, ma'am, whatever made you think you could buy a boat under the circumstances? It's against the law for any alien to own an American-registered boat that size, especially in these waters.' This was indeed shocking news.

'But couldn't I get permission somewhere – perhaps through friends in New York or Washington?' I pleaded.

'It's not even worth trying. Believe me, I know.'

The Captain and I looked at each other.

'Well, I guess the deal is off,' he said quite calmly.

'I'm so dreadfully sorry and you went to so much trouble for us.'

'Was a pleasure,' he said and then exploding into laughter, 'Wait till I tell the wife that she's not rid of the *Margaret* yet!'

Outside the office I apologized once more.

'Don't worry. Come aboard any time.'

'Would you – do you – take people out on trips and to fish commercially?'

'For dough do you mean? Sure.'

'Then I promise I'll send you every friend I have that comes to visit us here. It's the least I can do. I'm staying in St Petersburg, boat or no boat.'

Where? I wondered. Perhaps we should try and buy a house now that the fateful two thousand, five hundred had remained unspent.

'But why not live in the shop?' Diana asked, though bitterly disappointed at the loss of the *Margaret*. 'At least it's on the beach and we can swim every day and watch the boats.'

'I don't think we'd be allowed to.' Still, the shop was big enough to be divided into three rooms I thought and since my installation of the kiln in the New York apartment house I remembered much that would not have been permissible in other countries was so in America.

Through the Palices' help I got in touch with a building firm. There would be no difficulty with the partitioning they thought but the bath was another matter. Because of some inexplicable plumbing difficulties the tub would have to stand raised on a platform to be reached by a small staircase, but since the ceiling of the shop was very high there seemed no reason why this couldn't be done. So a partial second floor was built for the bath. From it one had a magnificent view through the glass front of the shop on to the street, beach, harbour and sea.

Once more I bought furniture. Three sofas that opened out into beds, display cabinets and shelves which I lacquered black and decorated with gold in the Chinese manner, white carpets, sea-green curtains and scarlet cushions, spending too much as usual but telling myself as so often before that it was all absolutely necessary.

In two weeks we moved in. The front of the shop consisted of the selling area divided by curtains from a sitting-room that turned into a bedroom at night. In the studio, somewhat larger, my kiln had already been installed and a long table on which to work, the bath was on its platform and underneath a large hot-water heater, the third bed-sofa and cupboards for our clothes. Since the door to the backyard was also glass there was plenty of light to work by.

I had a few figurines and ornaments left, our silver tea and coffee sets and various pretty small objects to which I was attached and that hadn't seemed worth selling. I put these on the shelves.

Though the place didn't look the least bit like a shop, more like a stage set with its many draperies, it was very attractive I thought.

There were, however, as we soon discovered, certain disadvantages to living in it.

Though we had curtains to draw over the glass front at night, with the lights on in the shop we were silhouetted against them especially when on the bathing platform and our outlines plainly visible from the street. Whereas, with our lights off, people promenading Beachdrive were equally silhouetted against our curtained windows. It was like a shadow play visible from both sides.

In addition, every step on the pavement could be heard approaching, halting and continuing along the drive, snatches of conversation, arguments, even violent scenes enacted in front of the shop at night, while in the daytime since we kept it closed and curtained, the curious came to stare through every chink they could find and to rattle at the door.

A certain amount of activity had started in the adjoining shops. Crates and cartons were carried in and people came and went. A sign saying 'Jeanette Chapeaux' was put up on one side of us, which considering Annicka's hat-making endeavours seemed rather too opportunely close for comfort.

However, I needn't have feared. Jeanette herself turned out to be a plump, matronly widow with two buxom daughters. Together they ran the shop and trimmed the hats. It was very much a family business and certainly too small for there being any danger of them employing anyone else. I was to grow very fond of these three hard-working but always cheerful and friendly women. They came from Ohio. They were to prove a great help to me, giving advice, and sending me customers, once I had started making and selling ceramics.

On our other side was the Cashmere Shop in which a languid, not at first very forthcoming, young man sold expensive cardigans, twin-sets, jerseys and coats all of the finest cashmere wool. Beyond was a flower-shop and a liquor store.

Meanwhile Leopold had arrived. We had fetched him at the railway station and with some trepidation taken him straight to the shop, not knowing what he would say at having to live in it. However, a perfect morning, the sun shining on sea and beach, the air still fresh and cool, had its desired effect and as always when we had been separated for any length of time he was glad to be with us again.

Though he admired the shop and approved its position he complained at having to sleep with the kiln, even if not yet in use, and protested at the drawn curtains which he immediately opened.

'But now everyone can see us!' I objected.

'And what does that matter?'

He then insisted he must bathe. We filled the tub for him, helped him up the steps and left him.

'Nice view from up here,' he called.

So had the passers-by who stopped to stare, since his head and naked torso as he stood up to scrub himself were plainly visible above the partitions through the windows on street and beach.

All I could do was redraw the curtains hurriedly.

After that he lay down to rest, fortunately choosing the one sofa-bed that wasn't to be seen from the street. I brought him tea, which I had boiled on a hotplate.

He lay back content, sipping it, and listened while I told him the entire story of our arrival, our stay in the Veverkas' hut, Honorka's perfidy, our buying and losing of the *Margaret* and our renting of the shop.

Leopold always laughed readily at human folly, even his own, but I'd seldom known him to laugh as much as he did that morning.

I then confessed I had invited the Palices to come for drinks in the evening, since I felt I owed them a lot for warning me, and also Honorka who had telephoned asking to see me several times but whom I had not dared confront unaided.

'But please don't quarrel with him,' I pleaded. 'He can still do the Palices a lot of harm.'

'Have you ever known me to quarrel with anyone in all these years we've been together?'

'No,' I had to admit.

'Only fools piss against the wind.'

We lunched in St Petersburg's best restaurant.

Afterwards we showed Leopold the beach, the harbour and the *Margaret*.

That evening the Palices were the first to arrive. Leopold liked them as I knew he would and soon they were talking of mutual friends of the ex-Czech government now dispersed all over the world, as they sipped their whisky.

I think we had all almost forgotten Honorka as he came blustering in, nearly as tall as Leopold, though he had a stomach like a beer barrel.

He shook hands with us and the child but he only gave the Palices a brief nod.

'Good to see you again, old friend,' Leopold said, patting him on the back and mixing him a drink as stiff as those he took himself.

'Nice little place you have here,' Honorka remarked, looking round with evident surprise. 'Must cost you a lot though. Had I known it was a shop you wanted I could have got you one cheap. I have good connections in this town.'

'Rent free like the Veverkas' hut?' I asked gently. Honorka's face turned an ugly red.

'Seems I never could have fitted into it,' Leopold said. 'You must have rather forgotten my size, old friend.'

'All I wanted to do was to help you as I have other homeless Czechs,' Honorka stammered angrily. 'But then I suppose what I had to offer was not grand enough for the Countess?'

The Palices sat quietly listening, expecting, no doubt, that either Leopold or Honorka, or both, would explode into insults. Diana too watched for the coming battle with interest. But Leopold only looked amused as he said, 'On the contrary, my wife liked your *châta* very much,' (Czech name for a poor hut) 'and we are both grateful to you for your kind intentions.

'But then who doesn't know of your generosity?' he continued. 'When I worked in the Czech Refugee Committee everyone was praising your heart of gold.'

Honorka seemed to swell and grow even larger at this compliment and an almost pleasant smile widened his face.

'But you know how the world is. The greater the man, the more envy and unkind gossip,' Leopold said in a tone of regret, 'even in the Committee – of course, I didn't believe a word of it, knowing what a gentleman you are.'

'What do they say?' Honorka's hand trembled slightly as he lifted his glass to his mouth.

'Well, it seems there were some quite unbelievable complaints about your exploiting emigrant Czechs. Persuading them to become partners in your companies and enslaving them by making them sign a contract to work for you, profit or no profit. Of course, I assured everyone it wasn't true – '

Honorka glanced at Palice for the first time that evening. It was not a pleasant look.

Leopold saw.

'Palice has been telling me how good you've been to them,' he smiled, though his grey-green eyes were hard as he stared straight at Honorka. 'But since they have found a job that suits them better I told them there was no doubt you would not insist on holding them to their contract, generous as I know you to be, nor will you mind, I hope, that my wife feels that she would be no good at the work you expected her to do –

'Have some more whisky, old friend,' he offered cheerfully. 'It's nice to think we will be living in the same town from now on,' and he poured and handed Honorka another glass.

I felt almost sorry for the man. Nevertheless he rallied.

'This comes as a relief to me,' he said to Palice. 'I've long wanted to close down the business here. I only kept it going to help people like you. Of course the profits might have been great had there been somewhat more efficiency and harder work – Well, no use crying over spilt milk. My businesses in Chicago are far more important than this.'

Then he suddenly turned to me. 'Since we have quite a surplus of figurines that I could let you have cheap, it might be a help to you to sell them here – in your shop.'

I thanked him, murmured something about ceramics not being combinable with other wares. I don't think he heard, as, with a rather forced smile that included even the Palices, he bowed and staggered out.

'Well done, Papi!' Diana exclaimed. Palice took Leopold's hand and clasped it gratefully. 'And to think I believed myself a diplomat,' he said.

62

Diana had meanwhile allowed herself to be persuaded to go to school. It had not been easy. Her memories of the strict Ursuline nuns in the convent she had gone to in Prague, of the big vaulted, cold, dark schoolrooms and the icy chapel in which mass was said every morning at seven and which all pupils had to attend, had left her with a horror of convents as well as fear of the strict discipline and high standards of behaviour and learning demanded by the Ursulines.

The school was housed in a large, square, very modern building, all plate-glass and white walls, standing in well-tended grounds. Inside there was none of the mysterious magic with which all centuries-old European convents seem impregnated. There was no atmosphere of austerity nor total dedication to God. If He was worshipped, as I'm sure He was, it was in the open air and sunlight. The Mother Superior was a fresh-faced, cheerful, humorous Irish woman, her nuns, though plain, looked as happy and healthy and uninhibited as the girls they taught.

'Academic standards aren't very high,' Lisa Palice admitted, 'but it's the only good day-school in St Petersburg and no undue importance is given to religious teaching. We ourselves are Protestants and so are three-quarters of the girls' parents. There is no pressure towards conversion. In fact very little pressure of any kind. Spoilt American children may be, but at least they grow up free and uninhibited.'

Diana's schooling settled, I went to work in my new studio. I had by then ascertained what would sell best in St Petersburg. It was in one way quite a unique town. To it from all over America the elderly came to retire, many persuaded by children and grandchildren who wanted to be rid of them that in the warmth and sunshine of Florida they would recover their lost youth. Lonely, homesick and forsaken by their families, these old people herded together for companionship, gallantly trying to forget the inevitable end by joining in all the amusements and distractions the business-conscious city of St Petersburg offered them.

There were bridge clubs and bingo clubs, dance clubs and come-together clubs. There was communal singing and prayer meetings, fancy dress-balls and barn dancing, sightseeing trips by bus to the Everglades or to the various other towns along the coast. Above all there were the marriage bureaux where widowers or widows or those unattached could find a companion for the few years, sometimes only months or days, left to them. Frequently some enterprising young woman came to St Petersburg to make a quick profit by charming an infatuated old gentleman into marriage, to be left a rich widow in the shortest of times.

There were, however, only very few young men who risked doing the same, American women being, except for those of some Eskimo tribes, the most long-lived in the world. A Czech whom we knew tried and managed to persuade a wealthy seventy-five-year-old widow to marry him. She outlived him by twenty years.

As if by mutual consent death was totally ignored in this strange community. If someone collapsed on the beach or in one of the clubs or dance-halls, which frequently happened, no one took the slightest notice, except for the attendants prepared to deal with these emergencies. The corpse was stood up and walked out between two of these as if still alive.

Next day on enquiring where so and so had gone, one was not told that he had 'passed on' but told he or she had moved to Palm Beach or Miami. It was perhaps a polite way of implying that the deceased had moved up, not down.

In dress youthfulness seemed to be all that mattered. The lame, the blind and the deaf paraded, adorned in the brightest of colours, especially the men who wore flowered shirts, large be-ribboned straw hats and shorts that exposed their withered shanks. The women dressed in the palest of pastel shades, blue or pink like babies, their hair or wigs dyed to match, their sagging painted faces brightly upheld by perpetual smiles and, most important to me, their persons adorned by a vast amount of what is called costume jewellery.

Why not mine? I thought. It was not difficult to find inspiration for jewels in Florida, on land as in the sea – varied flowers and fruits, colourful birds and the white seagulls, shells and starfish and seahorses. I moulded all these in clay, fired them applying coloured glazes and refired and then attached to them earclips or pins with glue, linking the necklaces together with gold links.

Soon shelves covered with black velvet displayed my glittering jewels in the shop window.

I had also put up a sign: 'Countess Sternberg. Hand-made ceramics.' So what? I thought. We are far from home. If it helps in attracting customers who cares about the vulgarity of using one's title for advertising purposes?

To my surprise – the shop was sold out in two days. I had to draw the curtains, write on the windows 'Closed for repair' and lock the doors until I could make more jewels to sell.

Meanwhile Leopold, though impressed and pleased with this unexpected success, declared that living in the shop had become impossible and so did Diana. The kiln had to be fired all night, which made the studio unbearably hot. Diana could find nowhere to do her homework without it becoming covered with clay or glaze and there was no privacy at all for any of us.

'The Palices tell me houses are quite cheap here,' Leopold remarked. 'All one does is make a small down-payment and the rest is like rent.'

My two days' success had gone to my head. But I was also tired and nervous and knew I couldn't continue to work and sell with my family always around clamouring for food and attention.

'Then for God's sake go and buy a house, darling, but the cheapest you can get, and as close to the school and the shop as possible.' I gave him the name of the agent from whom I had rented it. 'Doesn't matter what it looks like. Anything will do, as long as it's furnished. Just somewhere to sleep and eat,' I told him, as I pressed flower petals into moulds and assembled shells into necklaces. 'I leave it all to you. I simply haven't time just now to bother.'

By evening he had bought a house, or at least committed us by making the down-payment on it. It was in the poorest, if not quite the negro quarter of St Petersburg. It had a front porch, netted in by mosquito wire which faced a car repair and gas station, a sitting-room and a kitchen, two bedrooms, a bathroom and a glassed-in back porch which overlooked a small strip of garden enclosed on two sides by other houses, on the third by a corrugated iron garage.

'Ours too,' Leopold said proudly.

There was a strange mewing sound. He bent down and picked up a small, very thin, black cat. He held it to his face.

'They simply left it here to starve,' he said. 'This must have been its home.'

'And that's why you bought the house?'

I needn't have asked.

All in all, it was not too bad. The beds looked clean and unused. Whatever furniture there was was unpretentious, functional I think it's called. There was even a certain amount of pots and pans and china-ware.

'We could sleep here tonight,' Leopold said, cuddling the purring cat. 'I borrowed some milk for it next door. Very friendly people. I don't think it would be really fair to leave it tonight now it has us to look after it, do you?'

Within a couple of days we had brought our trunks and most of our belongings to the house. Leopold and Diana each had a room to themselves. I slept in the glassed-in porch at the back, usually with the cat snoring and purring on my chest all night.

A routine began that was to continue more or less the same for the next two years of our stay in St Petersburg, only occasionally interrupted when Leopold went to New York for a week or two, charging himself to buy the materials I needed. A mere excuse, I knew, since I might just as well have had them sent, but as always we tried to maintain each other's self-respect as best we could. I got up at six every morning, worked for an hour in the garden, then made my bed, cleaned the kitchen and sitting-room, made Leopold his tea and Diana her break-fast before she left for school, and took the bus to the shop. Once there I switched on the kiln to fire whatever had dried overnight, turned on the radio to hear the news and the following serial, an ever continuing story about the adventures of a large American family, which made my moulding, gluing and linking of the jewels less monotonous.

At nine thirty I opened the shop and sold whatever I had been able to make the day before. I then took the bus back at twelve thirty to cook Leopold's lunch, if he hadn't done so for me by throwing meat, veg-etables and herbs all into a pot together. Back to the shop again, usual-ly with him, where he did the selling in the afternoons, which he rather enjoyed, while I tried to work, constantly interrupted or called by him, upon which I had to leave the most delicate pieces I was assembling till they became too dry to work on and had to be thrown away.

'Meeting the Count' had become one of the main entertainments of St Petersburg. Had we been paid for every story Leopold told the amazed and fascinated old ladies we would have indeed made a fortune. As it was they sat around on our bed-sofas listening spellbound to the incredible tales about life in Europe that he invented. But he was not a very good salesman. I simply couldn't spare the time to mark the prices on every item separately so each morning I laid them out in groups according to what they cost. People came, picked up things, put them back in the wrong place, whereupon Leopold sold the jewels either for too much or too little, which caused endless confusion, arguments and complaints.

Also the ladies naturally wanted to try things on before they bought. Leopold had to put on his glasses and bend from his great height to assist them in clipping ear-rings and closing necklaces. Frequently an old woman whose withered neck he tickled or whose ears he fumbled with as he tried to adjust or clasp the jewels started to giggle or to protest, startling him so that he dropped the piece which of course broke as ceramics do if they fall.

Another difficulty was that he was not only asked to wrap the items bought but to gift-wrap them. Leopold could barely tie his own tie but certainly not rosettes of pink paper ribbon.

It was a relief when towards evening he made his round of visits in the adjoining shops, either to buy the cheap California Rhine wine we had started to drink, a gallon of it a day, or to discuss what subjects I never quite knew with the languid young man of the Cashmere, or to exchange pleasantries with the ladies of the hat-shop, who by nature prone to laughter went into hysterics at his jokes.

Then back to the house to feed the cat and ourselves and Diana. I cooked dinner. She, if in a gracious mood, would help with the dishes afterwards. Then I worked once more in the garden. Though this was small it was soon to be transformed into a most exotic flowering tropical jungle to which the neighbours objected, saying it deprived them of light and air and was breeding mosquitoes.

I remember with amazement the energy I had at that time. The harder I worked the less tired I seemed to be and I wasn't at all unhappy.

Certainly I hadn't forgotten Steinhardt but I had to admit that his death had freed me of all emotional preoccupation and strain and so given me greater strength than I'd ever had.

Till the summer heat came –

Suddenly all of St Petersburg was empty. The old people had either travelled north on their once a year visit to children, grandchildren or relations, or remained in air-conditioned houses afraid to venture out. A hundred and five degrees day after day. Never had I known such heat! I still went to the shop, still worked, sold then not necklaces but pins representing the different yacht-clubs of America to my rare customers, by then only young people from the boats. Jeanette's shop was closed. They were summering with relations in Ohio and the Cashmere Shop was shut. It was indeed not the season for selling wool.

Leopold suffered most, so much so that I feared for his health. An ugly heat rash covered his entire body. He came no more to the shop, he seemed to have lost all interest in it. He sat on the front porch, on the walls of which I had painted flowering trees, in his underwear and drank iced wine and studied the Constitution. He had decided he wanted to become an American subject and had been told that it was obligatory to know the Declaration of Independence by heart. With the sweat pouring from him he tried to learn the English words for the truths that had been self-evident to him all his life.

Diana had holidays. She was doing well at school and had made a lot of friends. Most of their parents, if they hadn't left St Petersburg for the summer months, lived on the other side of the city facing the Gulf of Mexico where there was always a cool breeze. She persuaded us that our small beach on the bay was dirty and the water stagnant, which indeed it had become, and forced us to join an expensive beach club on the west coast where she could meet her friends.

We spent quite a lot of pleasant evenings on that long windswept white beach, swimming or watching the dolphins play or the absurd-looking, quite tame pelicans, so awkward on the ground, so beautiful when they spread their great wings soaring into flight to dive for fish.

People came to visit us. Leopold's sister and her husband for a while, then Eddie, enjoying everything as he always did, taking us to Tampa to eat hot Mexican food and to visit the colony near Clearwater where the Greeks who had settled there still followed the traditional method of diving from fishing boats for sponges.

❧ 63 ❧

It was with Eddie too that we went to Sarasota, the winter quarters of the famous Ringling Circus, to view the museum, an imposing and rather beautiful palace of golden stone in the Renaissance style though built only a little over twenty years ago to house Mr Ringling's picture collection. It overlooked the sea.

'Now this is the sort of place you should live in,' Eddie remarked, 'instead of slumming as you do.'

'Tell me how?' Leopold asked.

Eddie contemplated the old guide who led us from room to room, attributing pictures to artists who had certainly not painted them, mumbling sentences wearily that he must have repeated from the time the house was built.

'Nothing could be easier,' Eddie whispered. 'Mona and I have endless friends in museum circles. Obviously the place needs a new and more entertaining guide. We recommend Leopold – and all of you move in.'

'But I know nothing about paintings,' Leopold protested, nevertheless looking at Eddie hopefully. Poor Leopold. How tired he was of helping in the shop though he considered it his duty to do so. The high cool rooms and the arcaded courtyard of Ringling's castle reminded him of Castolovice, I knew.

'You won't have to!' Eddie eyed several pictures marked Rubens and Rembrandt. 'It couldn't matter less who you attribute these to and you would certainly make a more entertaining guide than this poor old idiot. And just think of the tips you'd get!'

'And what about my shop?' I asked.

'Well, you live here and drive there every morning. It's only a short distance – there must be a bus.'

'And Diana's school?'

Eddie glanced at her appreciatively. She was indeed becoming prettier every day and since she had always been very fond of her uncle, unsparing with the charm she kept in reserve for those she liked.

'Why,' he said to me, 'you weren't much older than she is now when you got married. High time she left school. What's the good of educating a girl anyway? She'll never find a husband if she becomes an intellectual. Still, I suppose you should send her to Europe soon, to sort of finish her off. After all we still have some decent relations in several countries who'd look after her and see to it that she meets the right people.'

Diana was too polite to respond to this, except with a vague smile.

'Meanwhile,' Eddie added, 'she could help Leopold here showing the gallery and maybe learn something of art.'

Much to my surprise, since I thought Eddie had been merely joking, a few weeks after he had returned to New York we received a letter from the director of the museum, asking us to come and see him.

He proved to be a pleasant-looking, youngish man.

'Look here,' he said, 'I've only just arrived and am charged with putting this place, its accounts and above all its pictures into some comprehensible order. The former director has retired – and here, I get this – ' he indicated a large pile of letters ' – they are from friends and colleagues and people much more important than I am, recommending you – ' he looked at one of the letters to read the name ' – Count Sternberg, as a guide and further demanding that you should be housed in the museum, which is impossible. This is a public gallery. It has offices but no living quarters. Besides, frankly, great as your qualifications as museum guide may be,' he laughed, measuring Leopold's giant size and scanning his flushed and embarrassed face and glancing briefly at me who, thanks to Mona, was dressed in the most recent of Paris gowns, 'I hardly think – though living here might suit you – that you would enjoy guiding the type of tourists that tramp through these rooms all around the museum during the winter season when the Ringling Circus is here.' He escorted us out with polite words of regret, expressing the hope we would meet again. 'Perhaps I would have done better to apply for a job in the Circus,' was Leopold's comment as we drove back home.

More successful than this effort of Eddie's to help us was when he sent me a welcome order for fifty pot-pourri bowls which Mona had persuaded Mary Chess, the well-known New York perfumers, into taking.

'Of course you can make them!' Eddie wrote when I voiced my doubts to him in a letter. 'Just cover the lids with the same flowers and shells and things you use for the jewels.'

It succeeded better than I thought and the twenty dollars I got for

each, though I heard the pots with their scented contents were sold at
Mary Chess for a hundred and fifty, tided me over the summer season.
But only just. The rent of the shop and the payments for the house
swallowed nearly all the profits.

Had I had help, there would, I knew, have been no limit to what I
could have sold in the winter. One pair of hands was simply not enough
to produce what was needed to stock the shop for the season. I begged
Diana to find me some of her schoolmates who would like to earn
extra money. Only one came. She was very fat and grew more so on the
sandwiches and ice creams Diana insisted she must have in order to
work at all. She showed no artistic talent whatsoever.

Leopold, always trying to be helpful, started mixing clay and pressing
it into the moulds I had made. The moulds were small and delicate, his
hands big and strong. Usually only dust was left. I considered employing
black girls but was told by the owners of the other shops that it
would not be proper.

That at least one-third of the population of St Petersburg was black
was only noticeable in the early mornings when they went to work and
their enchanting children, their tight little plaits tied with gay ribbons,
hurried to school and at sunset when they returned to their districts.
Black women could occasionally be met working as maids or char-
women in the more opulent houses and men cleaning rubbish from the
street or beaches. In the buses which I then took daily these women
were allowed to sit at the back and if the bus became crowded with
whites they had to get out. Public conveniences in the town were
strictly separate, so were the drinking fountains. But I doubt these forms
of discrimination were as sad as the intangible wall that separated the
two races, causing to both a sense of unease and guilt.

Most of the whites in St Petersburg came from the North and had
more liberal ideas than those still held in the South. Nevertheless, even
to them, any social contact with blacks seemed out of the question.

Since Leopold too by now had managed to learn to travel by bus,
usually helped up the steps by the conductor, he would if he saw a
tired-looking old negress get up and offer her his seat. If there were
protests, really remarkably rare, he would answer in Czech. Fortunately
no one understood what he said, only I blushed at his obscenities.

He was less kind to the gawky white schoolboys that ever more
frequently came to sit on the front porch in the evening waiting to take
Diana to the movies or a ballgame.

'Who are you and what do you want?' he would invariably ask them
sternly, an imposing but slightly comical figure, since because of the

heat he was only partially dressed.

Stammering they would explain as best they could, whereupon, adjusting his white underpants, embroidered, since they still came from Czechoslovakia, with the eight-pointed star, crown and his initials round his waist, he would storm into the house calling loudly to Diana, 'The dogs are sitting on the porch again, wagging their tails.'

His indignation that these fourteen- or fifteen-year-old Americans dared to court his daughter was extreme.

Naturally she resented his behaviour. She was at that difficult stage of development, half child, half woman, and fearful of being treated like one or the other. Because her background and upbringing had been so unlike that of American children she dreaded to be thought different by them and did everything she could to conform with their standards. If she went out with boys it was not because she was attracted by them but because it was considered the thing to do by her schoolmates. Very little sex was involved in these immature romances – but much giving of fraternity pins, badges and rings which were collected by the girls like trophies.

Poor Diana. No doubt she loved us but again and again she remonstrated at our being so different from American parents. She was ashamed to bring her friends to the house, usually the daughters of well-to-do middle-class business people, who lived in better districts and tidier, better-kept houses than ours. She was embarrassed by our obvious poverty and couldn't understand why we weren't too. Not that we liked the discomfort in which we were forced to live but people who have known inherited wealth never feel they have sunk as low when deprived of it as people who have had to struggle to make it. To be honest, as long as our strength and health lasted we thought it all rather a joke.

Diana, rightly proud of the position she had made for herself at school, liked by the nuns because of her good manners and by her schoolmates because she was always ready to help them with their homework, lived in perpetual fear that we would disgrace her by our unorthodox behaviour. Our having become members of the beach club instead of pleasing her caused her acute anxiety. She scarcely dared go and swim or play ping-pong with her young friends for fear of what we might do or say when she wasn't present.

To her surprise we became quite popular, even if Leopold, trying to conform and be very American and jovial, cheerfully hailed acquaintances in the bar as 'Old Bugger', slapping them on the back, forgetting both his physical strength and his English.

But the worst incident occurred after she had returned to school and we had started working in the shop again.

One day on his way to it Leopold stopped at the bank for some money. Beside its entrance was what he mistook to be a mail box. Trying to insert some letters he found no opening but written on it was 'Pull', so pull he did.

Sirens shrieked, I could even hear them in the shop, and within minutes big fire engines thundered through the town to surround the bank. There was panic and commotion everywhere, people came running by calling out that the bank was on fire. I walked in its direction but there were such crowds I couldn't get through and seeing neither flames nor smoke I returned to the shop, wondering what had happened to Leopold. Probably caught up in the traffic, I thought.

Only in two hours did he appear. I asked him where he'd been. 'At the police station,' he said. He then very shame-facedly told me what had happened. 'When the alarm went off I tried to flee,' he said, 'but what with my leg I couldn't go far and two women recognized me. "That's the foreign Count!" they screamed, "he's set the bank on fire." One stayed with me while the other called the police. Well, they let me go in the end but there were reporters and photographers. I suppose it will be in all the newspapers.'

When Diana returned to the house in the evening she held a paper in her hand. She laid it down in front of us, too angry to speak.

There indeed was a large photograph of Leopold and the caption in big letters: 'Count reads "pull", so he pulled' and the whole story. Diana was in tears.

'You have made me the laughing stock of the school – I will never forgive you,' she sobbed, went to her room and banged the door.

A few days later she had obviously relented, buying Leopold a bottle of scotch, from the small amount of pocket money we could give her. It was always so after she had made a scene. She would try to show her affection for us by presenting us with whatever gifts she could afford.

Soon we were to embarrass her once more. She was helping Leopold to close the shop for the evening. I was working at the back but could see what was going on in the front. A youngish-looking man entered. He was of medium height, rather good-looking, with curly dark hair, very large, round, black eyes and a full mouth. He looked Spanish, I thought, perhaps Cuban. So many of them lived in Florida then.

'Can I help you?' Diana asked, the usual phrase with which we offered our wares for sale.

He shook his head, smiling at her, then turned to Leopold.

'It was your name that brought me in,' he said, much to my surprise in German with an Austrian accent. 'You are Leopold Sternberg, aren't you? We have never met but I think you knew my father.'

Leopold stared at him, then bowed very low. 'Majestät,' he exclaimed. 'Curtsy to the Emperor, Diana.'

She burst out laughing. 'Papi, have you gone mad? There are only two emperors left in the world, one is a Jap and the other is black.'

She looked at the good-looking young man apologetically. 'My father's always making jokes – '

'This was rather a courteous and loyal one, even if my name is now only Otto von Habsburg.'

I wiped the clay from my fingers, hurried into the shop and curtsied low.

I then remembered that I'd read in the papers that he was on a lecture tour through America. There had been nothing but praise for his brilliance as a speaker, his knowledge of history and his modest and unassuming manners.

'May I sit down?' he asked and with a gesture that was, I think, quite unconsciously royal permitting us to do the same.

'One meets in strange places,' he said. 'We are all of us far from home.' He then turned to Leopold to question him closely about the war years in Czechoslovakia and the communist takeover later. He was obviously well informed and deeply interested in all that Leopold could tell him.

I begged Diana to close the shop, draw the curtains and to bring cold drinks.

They talked for a long time. 'The unfortunate Czechs -- ' I heard the man who might have been their emperor say with a sigh – 'after all they have suffered, what they have to endure now must make Austrian oppression seem mild. And there is so little hope except for the lesson history teaches that its wheels never stop turning.'

I had gone to rummage in a drawer where I kept all sorts of things we had brought from home. I held out to him a small picture depicting a head of Christ crowned with thorns. It was rather awkwardly and pains-takingly painted on vellum. On its back was written in the spiky German gothic script of the time – '*Justitia et Clementia* 1743. *Meinem lieben Sternberg dies Bild soll Dier zur beständigen Erinnerung dienen das allzeit Deine gnädigste Frau verbleibt, Maria Theresiv.*'

He turned it round and round. 'This certainly is the Empress Maria Theresia's writing. I think she must have painted the picture herself.'

'Our family always thought so,' Leopold said.

'Quite an honour but your ancestors served her well. This was, I think, not her only reward?'

'Oh no,' Leopold replied.

'But perhaps the most charming and now it's all you have left.'

He rose. So did we.

He stared for a moment at the display of ceramics.

'I am married as you perhaps know. May I buy something for my wife? How pretty that necklace of fruit and flowers is. I think it would suit her. She is very fair – the few jewels we had left are, of course, long sold – '

'Wrap it,' I told Diana.

He drew out his wallet.

'Please not, your Majesty – it's all we have to give.'

He understood. 'I'll take it in exchange for the trouble my ancestress took in painting that picture of yours,' he laughed. 'Thank you.'

Even Diana curtsied as he left.

❦ 64 ❦

The all-important winter season came and once more I sold as much as I could produce. But since this was limited, so were the profits. We made just enough to survive and I was beginning to fear at too great a cost to myself. I was working too hard; I never had time to relax, even to read a book. When I came home at nights there was still all the house-work left to do. Nervous and exhausted I drank more than I should, snapped at Diana and was irritable with Leopold.

He at least had a small circle of friends, most of them Czechs, nearly all of them destitute, homesick and unhappy, whom he tried to comfort and advise as best he could. If he gave them hope for a better future, it was certainly not because he believed in it any more himself.

The only people I saw were my customers and they were of quite extraordinary sameness in speech, manner and looks, nearly all of them old ladies. Men only rarely entered the shop. Again and again I had to repeat the same phrases. 'Yes, genuinely hand-made – just your style. How that colour suits you. Just a little too large, I think,' and so on. Would I have to go on doing this for ever? I wondered. If so, it would eventually drive me mad I knew. I couldn't even take any pleasure in my designs any more because Mrs Jones wanted exactly what she had seen on Mrs Smith, which meant nothing new and original appealed. My need for some sort of change was getting desperate. In the summer at least there had been enough time and leisure to drive to see parts of Florida still wonderfully unspoilt, remote uninhabited beaches and stretches of land covered with dense jungle-like vegetation full of rare birds. If only I could buy a piece of land I thought, remembering the farm we had lost. Yet the two thousand five hundred the Judge had given me was long spent.

Then surprisingly Aunt Diana came to my rescue. She had died several months earlier but she had not forgotten me. She had very little to leave except her island but a part of the proceeds of its sale, after several bequests to people who had served her had been paid off, was to go to me, the rest to my brothers. Also a large trunk appeared after several months. It was old and battered and one of those with which she had always come to Emkendorf when we were children. She must have packed it herself, for it contained everything I had admired and coveted as a child, things she had cherished herself because they had belonged to her mother. Embroidered shawls, tartan sashes, laces and fans, a crown of corals, a dressing case, a gift of Queen Victoria's with gold-topped boxes and bottles, family miniatures, drawings of Scottish castles, a small picture of the Madonna kept, not for religious reasons, but because the calm, pale, oval face was so exactly like her own and a black lace evening dress covered with jet with a long train which I had designed and sewn for her when I was fifteen in which she had so regally swept down the stairs at Emkendorf on festive occasions so long ago.

One morning when I thought I had reached the limit of my endurance and would have done anything not to go to the shop the mail arrived with a cheque for me from her lawyer. The island had been sold. I had my two thousand five hundred.

Once more I suppose the sensible thing would have been to pay off the mortgage on our house with it. None of us even considered this. Leopold went on a prolonged visit to New York. Diana got the new gramophone she had wanted for a long time and numerous records, also enough money to buy all the dress materials she fancied. Spoilt as we were by Mona's gifts of clothes, she would not have deigned to wear anything available in St Petersburg. She designed and sewed all her dresses herself and finished and ironed them so they were as fresh as anything from the best of dressmakers, leaving the house every evening immaculately attired and her room in a state of such disorder that I shed tears when once a week I felt I had to clean it.

Needless to say, after the cheque had come the first thing I did was to go in search of land.

I found it near a place called New Port Ritchi, an hour's drive north of St Petersburg. Just a few houses and a store on the main road, beyond, to right and left, flat, uncleared land covered with palmetto palms. A mile farther on the agent, who had driven me out to view the ten-acre property, stopped the car in front of a small, recently built frame house.

Some efforts at clearing and planting around it had obviously been made.

'Is this it?' I asked, disappointed. 'If so, we might as well drive back to St Petersburg as fast as we came.'

'I must confess I haven't had time to see the place. Believed it was on the Gulf – though we'd better enquire.'

We walked into a clean modern kitchen where a young woman was sitting peeling potatoes.

'Are you Mrs Hegg?' the agent asked.

'Thank the Lord not,' she laughed. 'His place is about half a mile from here on the bayou. There's no road but if you follow that path,' she pointed, 'you'll find it. Be careful, there's lots of rattlers. We always wear high boots when we go down that way to the water.'

We started to walk in the direction she had indicated, picking our way among the spiky green, fern-like palm fronds that rustled ominously as if they were full of rattlesnakes, safely reaching a narrow stream in which a half-submerged rowing boat lay. From there a house was in sight, shaded by several large trees. It was nothing but an old wooden shack that could not have contained more than one small room. Some hens scratched in the dusty soil around it and then two starved-looking mongrel dogs approached us, barking fiercely.

A man came out of the hut and called them back. Though his yellow-white hair and beard were unkempt and all he wore was a pair of tattered trousers, I have rarely seen a more splendid-looking specimen of a man. Tall and immensely broad in chest and shoulders and fair skinned, he looked like some Norse God, Thor or Wotan – his eyes were pale blue and oddly child-like though his big rough-hewn face was lined and weathered and showed his age in spite of his still superb physique. I later learnt that he was a Finn, an ex-sailor who for reasons only known to himself and never revealed had settled on this remote peninsula, building his hut on the only spot on his ten acres where trees and scrub concealed from him one of the loveliest views I have ever seen. A wide expanse of water of a clear translucent pale green and as calm as a lake surrounded and enclosed by mangroves. Beyond a white sand beach and the deep blue Gulf stretching to the horizon. And not a house in sight anywhere nor any human beings, only sea-birds by the hundred, fishing undisturbed along the water's edge.

The Finn when asked by the agent if he was Mr Hegg had mumbled a sort of '*Ja*'. Either he had never learnt to speak much English or didn't want to. Silently he showed us the chicken coop and outhouse, its use obvious by its smell, and his living quarters that contained a bed covered by a dirty blanket, a seaman's tin trunk, an oil lamp and a gun and old clothes hung on hooks. One half-full and several empty rum bottles littered the floor. Outside he pointed out some orange and lime rees and a patch of ground, netted in against the fowls I suppose, where a few vegetables grew.

He then showed us a well, letting down a bucket and winding it up. The water seemed quite clear.

'Why are you selling?' I then asked him directly. 'Are you going back to Finland?' He shook his head, his blue eyes wary. 'No,' he said. I then realized that most of his taciturnity was probably due to his having no teeth at all.

'Well, I think we've seen everything,' the agent said. 'I'll let you know in a few days what the lady decides,' he told Hegg.

I shook hands with Hegg. His child-like eyes seemed to plead – 'Good fishing around here,' he mumbled.

We returned the way we had come. 'Well, I guess it's not quite the sort of thing you want, though it wouldn't be a bad investment. His land goes right down to the Gulf. As a matter of fact, I have a firm of developers I could interest. There would be room to build about twenty chalets and a motel with sea view on the place once those trees are cut down.'

'Never,' I said to myself. At all costs I had to save that lovely unspoilt stretch of beach. A small, white, arcaded house standing among orange groves and a garden of gardenias facing the sea I would build on it, nothing more.

'And he definitely asks two thousand five hundred?'

'It's cheap at that. Prices for land with sea view are rising every minute in Florida. But perhaps he'd agree to a mortgage.'

'You see, I can't afford that much if I want to build. I was wondering – he seemed such a good type – these Scandinavians are usually reliable and honest – if he wouldn't mind if I pay a half down and the rest monthly and he agreed to stay and look after the place as caretaker.'

'He doesn't seem to have done much about it up to now,' the agent remarked.

Why should he have? I thought. Fish from the sea, fruit and vegetables from his own garden. Eggs from his hens. What more did one really need to survive?

'I think I must warn you that if he agreed to that he would remain part owner till you had paid the full price – it might be impossible to get rid of him should he prove unsuitable as a caretaker.'

'Oh, I don't think it would ever come to that. He may not talk much but he looks all right to me. I was planning to camp there in the summer with my family. One would feel safer having him near.'

Two days later the agent telephoned to say that Hegg had agreed to my conditions and would stay, provided I bought him a truck so he could get to market, which seemed quite a reasonable request. I sent the agent a cheque for half the price and the first monthly instalment for the rest, which was to be paid off, plus percentage, in two years.

The property in New Port Ritchi was mine, or so I thought. I described its beauty to Diana and Leopold with the enthusiasm which I felt and the fact that I owned it had restored all my energy and interest in my work. Everything I produced and every item I sold brought me closer, I felt, to eventually saving enough to build a house for us on the bayou.

Though I doubt Leopold shared my enthusiasm, he was glad to see me happy. Only when I told him I was going to buy a truck did he show some concern.

'But you know nothing of cars or trucks. You can't even drive – what on earth do you want it for?'

'It's for the caretaker.' I had told him all about Hegg. 'For taking fruit and vegetables and fish to market. Obviously he can't carry it all for miles on his back.'

It was not the only thing I bought. A tent, a Primus stove, a plastic bathtub, several buckets, an Elsan toilet, two cots and sleeping bags and a first-aid kit for snakebites, all of which I had been told in the shop were essential if one wanted to camp in Florida.

Leopold watched as a battered-looking truck arrived that weekend, already loaded with our equipment. I had persuaded Diana to come with me to New Port Ritchi. Leopold excused himself by pointing out that there was no room for him, which indeed was true. Diana and I could only just squeeze into the narrow front seat next to the driver. 'Back on Monday,' I called as we set off.

'Are you sure the car's all right?' I asked the driver as we bumped along and I started to feel my bones ache. 'It doesn't seem to have any springs.'

'It's a truck, ma'am, not a luxury limousine. What did you think you'd get for that price? Feather upholstery? Main thing, she holds together and doesn't fall apart on the way.'

'You mean it might?'

'No. I'm just fooling. We've given you six months' guarantee. She's OK.'

Diana was very quiet.

'Aren't you looking forward to seeing the place?' I asked.

'Of course, but I was rather thinking of the snake kit. You see, I read the instructions. If one is bitten one has to slice the spot open with a razor blade and suck out the poison.'

I shivered. 'It's not as if we were going on a jungle expedition. I'm sure Hegg knows all about snakes and keeps them off the place.'

'It will be a bit scary at night though, us all alone in the tent.'

'Nonsense! We'll camp close to his hut and be quite safe.'

I had telegraphed Hegg we were coming and to expect us at a given time near the farm on the main road.

The farmer and his wife were working in their garden when we arrived. They gave us a welcoming wave but there was no Hegg.

'I suppose we'd better drive on to the bayou,' I told the driver.

The driver contemplated what was nothing but a narrow footpath.

'What, straight through the palmetto? Ma'am, you are crazy. You need a tractor for that.'

'Glad to be of any help I can,' said the young farmer who, with his wife, had joined us.

Smiling at Diana and then at me he continued, 'Considering we are neighbours now. Won't take me more than a couple of hours to clear a way. If Hegg doesn't cause trouble. I hear he's staying?'

'To look after things, till I can build. I wonder where he is, though? He was supposed to meet us here.'

'There he comes!' the farmer's wife said, trying to stifle her laughter. Swaying from side to side, balancing like a sailor on a tilting deck, Hegg, only recognizable by his giant size, was making his way through the palmetto. He wore a straw hat, a flowered shirt, new trousers and as he approached closer he displayed a set of shiny white teeth. His beard was gone, obviously shaved off very recently as the sun had not had time to brown his chin or neck to the ruddy colour of the rest of his face. Not that much of that was visible, his eyes were obscured by large black glasses. He carried a stick. 'Smartened up quite a lot since he's come into money,' the farmer whispered.

Poor Hegg! He looked utterly ridiculous, but how pathetic, I thought, probably he'd longed to be able to afford these adornments for years.

Hegg stared at the loaded truck.

'Will you give us a hand, Mr Hegg?' I begged. 'I'm afraid we will have to carry our things.'

'What's the truck for then?' he asked.

'The driver says it can't go through the palmetto.'

'Guess I'll show him,' he exclaimed angrily. Stumbling and nearly falling he managed to get into the front seat. The driver who had meanwhile got out, watched with some concern as Hegg, after several vain efforts, managed to start the engine, tried to shift into first but went into reverse instead.

'Hey, that's my garden!' yelled the farmer. Hegg managed to stop, grinning sheepishly. 'Bit out of practice,' he mumbled. He started the truck once more and with a crashing of gears and the engine roaring he ploughed into the palmetto.

'Is the man mad?' the driver asked.

'No, only drunker than usual,' the farmer remarked.

'Well, he'll wreck that truck for sure.'

Hegg almost succeeded in doing so. The truck shuddered, swayed and lurched as if it was going to turn over and then stood still.

'Guess he's broken the axle,' the driver said. 'Well, it's none of my business any more. Got to catch my bus home. 'Bye –' He walked away towards the main road.

Hegg got out of the truck very red in the face. We joined him. 'Next time I'll see she makes it,' he screamed, hitting the car with his stick. 'Nothing but an old wreck anyway. Must have found her in a junk yard.' Muttering and cursing he staggered through the palmetto towards the bayou.

'What now?' Diana asked.

'Well, we'd better unload our things.'

Finally the farmer, who had been watching, came to our aid, shouldering the heaviest of our equipment, while we carried the rest.

'Does he get as drunk as that frequently?' I asked anxiously.

'No, only occasionally but more often now since he can afford it.'

'And I thought him such a reliable, decent type – is he dangerous?'

'Never heard of him causing trouble and he's lived here for the last twenty years. But he's a loner, never speaks to anyone if he doesn't have to. I guess he's a bit loco.' The farmer touched his own head.

Two dogs came racing towards us, barking and snarling. The farmer calmed them with a word and patted them. 'Poor brutes,' he said, 'they come to us for food. All Hegg gives them to feed on are the contents of his stinking privy.'

'But do you think we dare spend the night here?' I asked when we were in sight of Hegg's hut.

'I'll make sure.' He went and peered into the one small window. 'As I thought, lying on his bed dead to the world. He won't stir till morning.'

He helped us put up our tent, finding a spot beyond Hegg's hut and behind the belt of trees that concealed it on a ledge of clean white sand overlooking the bayou and the bay. He drew us some buckets of fresh water from the well, marvelled at all our equipment and told us we could sleep 'As safe as a bug in a rug'.

'What about snakes?' Diana asked.

'Well, don't bathe in the river. It's full of water moccasins and they are deadly. The rattlers rarely leave the palmetto. Still, if you get into any trouble, it's not far to our home,' he smiled. 'You'll always be welcome.'

'Bless you,' I said, with all the gratitude I felt. I doubt he'd ever heard the expression before except perhaps in church. He looked puzzled.

'I mean, thank you for your kindness.'

'Why, what sort of country would this be if not even neighbours helped each other?'

He left. The dogs followed him. We sat on our cots in the open tent. Sky and sea were darkening, except where the setting sun had left a wide wake of shimmering gold. The bayou glowed a faint pink purple, the twisted shapes of the mangroves mirrored in the still water. There was a smell of salt and seaweed and mud, a pleasant, cool breeze came from the Gulf. It was very quiet except for the occasional cry of a sea-bird and the splashing of a fish.

'Could anything be more beautiful?' I asked Diana.

'Yes, a nice comfortable house with doors one can lock.'

I went to inspect our food supply. We had brought enough with us for three days. We ate some ham sandwiches and drank some wine and lit the oil lamp. The latter was a mistake. In minutes the tent was full of moths, small, large, some as big as bats, beating their velvety wings against the glass trying to get at the flame.

We had to carry the lamp outside to clear the tent. They followed in swarms. Finally we put it out, secured the flap and went to bed. There were two small netted openings for air but it became very close and hot and neither of us seemed able to sleep.

Some time later there was a scratching and scraping sound and our tent shook.

'It's Hegg,' Diana whispered. 'Where's that knife for snakebite?' I pointed my flashlight through one of the flaps, trembling with fear, but it was only the poor hungry dogs eating the paper in which we had wrapped our sandwiches.

I pushed some of our cold meat through the flap and a hunk of cheese. They fell upon it, then, sated, lay down against our tent as if to guard us or our food supplies.

'We're quite safe now,' I said, 'they certainly won't let anything in, not even Hegg.'

Reassured we finally slept, to be wakened by fearful growls followed by the sound of kicks and yelps.

I opened the tent flap to see the dogs running away, their tails between their legs and Hegg standing in front of me. Over his arm was the tattered blanket I had seen on his bed and he was carrying a basket full of live fish, crabs and shrimps. He was not wearing his sunglasses or his fine new clothes nor his teeth. His blue eyes were still slightly puffy and bloodshot but as gentle and innocent as a child's and he was obviously quite sober and trying to be friendly.

'Remembered you might be cold at night so I brought you this – ' he proffered the filthy blanket. 'Caught these for your breakfast,' and he handed me the basket of fish.

But I felt in no way appeased. Cruelty to animals, as a matter of fact, is one of the few things that makes me furiously angry.

'Why did you kick those dogs? They kept us safe all night, while you lay in a drunken stupor.'

'Thought they were bothering you.' He shook his big head from side to side. 'Guess I was a bit under the weather yesterday. Can't really remember. Something about a truck?'

'Yes, it's in the palmetto where you wrecked it.'

He passed his hand over his forehead. 'Hurts,' he said, 'better go and see,' and lumbered off.

I carried the basket of squirming fish, crabs and shrimps to the stream and watched them swim away.

We boiled some coffee.

'We are not going to stay here another night, I hope,' Diana said.

'No, we will take the afternoon bus home,' I decided. 'Come, let's walk to the beach.' We went along the stream that flowed into the bayou and out on to the wide stretch of land.

'Look at the shells,' Diana said, entranced. All along the water's edge they lay in iridescent heaps, shells of every different shape and size. We started collecting. I could use many of them for my work, I knew.

We were carrying them back to our tent when we saw Hegg come out of it. 'Snug in there,' he said, not at all embarrassed. 'Coffee sure smells good.' I lit the Primus, heated what was still left in the pot and handed him a cup. He looked for all his size so humble and gentle and penitent that I felt I might have judged him too harshly and felt rather ashamed at having feared him. After all it wasn't the first time I'd seen someone drunk.

'How's the truck?' I asked.

'Soon get her going again.' He showed all his gums in a wide smile.

'I think there are a few things we ought to discuss before we go,' I told him. 'We have to leave this afternoon.'

He gave me a sidelong glance. I'm not sure it wasn't one of relief.

'Is it agreed that you look after the place for us?'

'Sure.'

'Well, I'm planning to build in time but meanwhile I want you to do some planting for me. Trees take longer to grow than houses. Let's walk around and I'll show you what I plan. I'll buy the plants, of course, and have them sent. The house will stand here,' I indicated the site of the tent. 'Behind it I want several ornamental trees and borders of croton hibiscus and gardenias, beyond that towards where you live an orange grove – you'll have to prepare the ground a bit, of course, dig in the plants and water them daily.' He looked at me, his blue eyes vacant of comprehension I thought.

'Do you understand? Can I trust you to do it?'

'Sure, you can trust old Hegg with anything.' He arched his broad shoulders and blew out his chest, as with pride. 'You taking the tent back with you?'

'No, but I'm going to padlock it. I don't want to leave it open in case we find snakes or scorpions in it when we return.' Or him sleeping in it, I thought.

We had some lunch, cleared the tent of food, which we gave to the dogs when Hegg wasn't looking, fearing he might have wanted it himself, put everything in order and locked the tent flap. We shook hands with Hegg, his honest grip making me wince, and we walked towards the farmhouse. The truck stood where it had the day before. We thanked the young couple for their kindness. I pressed ten dollars into the woman's hand. 'It's to feed those poor dogs,' I begged.

'How was Hegg this morning?' the farmer asked.

'Sober and repentant,' I laughed. 'I felt almost sorry for him. I think you are right. Coming into all that money suddenly must have been too much for him not to go on a binge! I've asked him to do some clearing and planting for me and to look after the tent.'

The farmer said nothing but he looked far from optimistic. We returned by bus.

Leopold laughed as we told him our adventures but then grew serious. 'I'd better come with you next time and have a look at this Hegg of yours. I don't quite like the sound of him.'

🎴 65 🎴

It was quite a while until we went back to New Port Ritchi because of something that was going to worry me infinitely more than what Hegg was up to or even what happened to the place.

Mona's husband, Harrison Williams, had died in the early spring. Though he was old and had been ill for a long time, I knew it must have come as a great shock to her and that she and Eddie would sincerely mourn him. Difficult and autocratic as the old man had been, cynical and ruthless when it came to business, he had been the kindest, most loving of husbands, a good friend to Eddie, whom he trusted, and even kind to me on the few occasions on which we had met. To a greater or lesser degree we had all been sorry when he died.

I was surprised when only a few months later I got a letter from Eddie, briefly announcing that he and Mona had married. Almost secretly it seemed, just a Catholic priest and two witnesses. Delighted as I was at the news I wondered a little. It was so unlike them both to flaunt all conventions. Why this hurried marriage too soon after Harrison's death for decency? Why couldn't they – since except for the war they had rarely been separated for the last fifteen years – have waited a little longer? And why did Eddie write so curtly? True, he rarely indulged in emotions or sentimentality but that in this case, surely his moment of greatest happiness, he should express none seemed totally incomprehensible.

Nevertheless I wired them both my most ecstatic congratulations.

There was no answer.

Then a letter came. It was in unfamiliar handwriting. Only when I read the signature did I realize it was from a young Austrian, a distant relation of Eddie's, who had been staying with Mona. I had never met her.

It was as emotional and dramatic a letter as only could have been penned by a very Catholic member of the Austrian aristocracy, in whom tragedy evokes the most intense religious fervour.

'Our poor, dear, beloved Eddie – may God spare him – I pray for him day and night.' Kind of her, I thought, since she scarcely knew him. What on earth was it all about? I asked myself.

The next sentence told me. 'He has cancer. Only an operation, the New York professors say, can save him. I am writing on Mona's behalf. She couldn't face telling you the awful truth. He is in Germany now. It seems there is a doctor there who has had some success in curing the disease with X-rays, but the specialists here doubt it will do any good.' She then gave me the address in Germany, 'in case I cared to write'. Cared to write?!

Eddie ill! Eddie's life perhaps threatened? Why, it was impossible. He was one of the strongest, healthiest people I knew. Also the person I loved most in the world after Leopold and Diana. It simply couldn't be true. There must be some mistake. I immediately telegraphed Eddie to the given address of the *Clinique* in the Black Forest. 'What's wrong?'

'Plenty,' was the answer, 'but don't worry. Writing.'

His letter brought little comfort. Yes, the doctors had diagnosed cancer of the colon but he doubted the treatment in the *Clinique* was doing him any good. 'It is unpleasant, the nurses hideous, the food lousy. Mona wants me to face the operation, so I'm leaving for Lausanne where she will join me for the great occasion. If I don't survive it, don't grieve. I've had a good life up to now,' he added.

Desperately I questioned Leopold, who, because of his long years in hospital, had more medical knowledge than I about the operation.

'Is it very dangerous?'

'No it's not and many people have lived a more or less normal life for many years afterwards free of cancer.'

'But then he'll be all right?'

Leopold who was fond of Eddie gave me an odd look. 'I hope so,' he said and left the room.

A week later I got a telegram from Mona. 'Operation successful. Eddie recovering splendidly. Love from us both.'

And indeed when he came to see us some months afterwards he looked wonderfully fit and well.

He only stayed a couple of days. On the last evening we remained up late in the shop together. Leopold and Diana had gone home.

Eddie rarely drank excessively but that night he did. We had talked much as usual about the past, about friends and relations, about what he and Mona were planning to build or redecorate and about New Port Ritchi. Suddenly he said, 'You are the only person in the world I can ask. Have you noticed anything different about me since my operation?'

I had. He had acquired an odd habit of suddenly pressing his hand to his hip. Often there were rumbling sounds as if from his stomach and an unpleasant smell.

'Nothing at all,' I lied.

He sighed. 'That's what Mona says too but then she's so kind. One can't quite trust her not to tell one what one hopes to hear. Didn't you wonder why we married so suddenly and soon after Harrison's death?' he then asked.

'Yes, I did rather.'

'It was because they had discovered I had cancer. She married me out of pity.'

'But, Eddie, how can you say that after the years in which you've loved each other?'

'Because it's true. When I learnt all about this operation I decided I preferred death, yet I wanted a few more months of happiness and Mona belonging entirely to me as my wife before I died. Of course she agreed to marry me. She is like that. Afterwards she insisted on saving my life by persuading me to be operated on after all. I'm cured of cancer so they say. They cut away most of my guts and made a stinking large hole in my side that will never close. I'll spare you the revolting details. You can read them up in any medical book.' I saw the despair in his face. I could have cried with pity for him, would have given anything to embrace and comfort him, but that was not our way with each other, nor would it have helped him.

'Do you suffer any pain?' I asked.

'Some discomfort at times but it doesn't hurt.'

'Do you feel ill?'

'Not really, except that I often wish I had died.'

'What a tragedy – when I think of all the wonderful life you're still going to have, gifted and creative as you are, popular with everyone, friends all over the world and married to Mona, it really shocks me to hear you complain, instead of thanking God you're alive.'

'Maybe you're right.'

I walked him back to his hotel.

In later years we always corresponded and saw each other as frequently as possible but the subject of his health was never again mentioned between us. Fastidious as he was, I knew what he suffered and so did Mona. But neither ever complained. I saw them in the marvellous houses and surroundings they were forever creating, in Capri, in Rome and in Paris, Eddie looking as young and as handsome as ever, the perfect host and the most devoted of husbands, Mona's radiant beauty unchanged, their wealth permitting them anything they might desire, envied by all, except for the few of their closest friends who knew the truth.

But to return to New Port Ritchi.

I had bought a variety of fruit trees and shrubs and sent them there. I had heard nothing of Hegg, though I had written him instructions on how to plant and excused my having not been able to get to the place for so long. Even if he could read, I doubted he knew how to write, so I had expected no answer.

When I finally got there, a neatly cleared drive on which I walked to the bayou reassured me. The truck was standing at the edge of the little stream. Obviously it had been put in working order since it had got there, though I saw with some consternation that its headlights were smashed.

I approached Hegg's hut expecting to find the beginnings of an orchard and a garden surrounding it. Nothing but dead, withered trees and plants. I inspected the tent. I needed no key to unlock it. The flap was torn open and it was quite empty.

I went and hammered at the door of Hegg's hut. I was furious.

It took a while until he came out, blinking at the sunlight, his eyes puffed from sleep. He was stark naked.

I retreated. So did he. He returned with his trousers on, carefully shutting the door behind him.

'Didn't expect you,' he muttered.

'Obviously not,' I said, pointing to the desert that should have been a garden by now.

'No rain,' he said.

'And couldn't you have watered?'

'No, my back's bad.' He rubbed it. 'Aches something awful – been abed most of this month. Getting too old for such hard work.'

I felt no pity this time.

'And where are the things in the tent gone?'

'Dogs must have torn it open. Moved everything into my place. All safe in there. Want to come in and see?'

'No thank you,' I said, turned my back on him and walked away.

'Hey there!' he called, 'where you going?' but he didn't follow.

At the farmer's house the dogs welcomed me. They were looking sleek and fat.

'You been there, I see?' the farmer's wife said, reading in my face the despair I felt. 'All going to ruin. It's a real shame.'

'He says he's been too ill to work.'

'Him sick! Not too sick to drive to town every evening, now Tom's cleared him a road and repaired the truck, all dressed up and only coming home in the mornings. They say he's keeping a woman there with whom he spends his nights drinking. He's becoming a menace on the road. He don't know how to drive. He will either kill himself or someone else and then there'll be bad trouble! Smashed his headlights the other night and came home in the dark without them. Get rid of him, ma'am, if you can. He goes around boasting the property's still half his and that he needn't work for no one.'

I begged the couple to let me pay for the drive they'd cleared and the repairs of the truck but they would take no money.

'We feel real sorry for you, ma'am,' the little wife said. 'If it wasn't for us having more land than we can manage and me expecting we'd look after the place for you if you can get rid of Hegg. But I guess we simply can't spare the time and labour.'

'Maybe we should have warned you,' the farmer remarked, 'but you so trusting, wanting to give the man a chance.'

'Well, he's had it,' I said indignantly.

When I came home to Leopold I was in such despair that, much as I knew he disliked tears and complaints, I started to cry.

'I'm such a fool,' I sobbed. 'Everything I've done since we've come to this country has been a failure or ended in disaster. All my hopes, all my ambitions.'

'And what about mine?' Leopold asked gently.

I didn't heed him. 'My exhibition. Steinhardt's death. The loss of the farm. This reckless move to Florida, the expensive shop and horrid house, both of us working ourselves to death just to survive, the child becoming more and more of a stranger to us and now my last hope of our building a home on that lovely land where we could have settled for the rest of our days gone too, because we'll never have enough money to pay off Hegg. All folly and failure – Sorry you married such an idiot, darling' I added, wiping my eyes.

'I am not,' he laughed, giving me a brief hug. 'At least you are never a bore, except when you cry. There's no reason to despair. Something is sure to turn up,' he comforted me. 'You have forgotten how many friends we still have.'

That this was true struck me forcibly. However unsuccessful we had been in other ways, we had rarely failed in inspiring friendship. All through our long journey from place to place since we had left home it had been the encouragement, advice, help and generosity of others that had made our survival possible, not our own futile efforts to succeed.

Proof of it came once more when one of Leopold's oldest friends paid us a surprise visit, coming from Jamaica where he and his wife were spending some weeks. He and Leopold had shared a gay bachelor life in Vienna in their youth, then he had married Leopold's most favourite cousin. The couple had as frequently stayed with us in Castolovice as we in their castle near Vienna. They were attractive people to look at and to be with and we were very fond of them. I hadn't seen either for years, though Leopold had paid them a brief visit at the time Steinhardt died.

Count C – or 'C' as I will have to call him (he does not appreciate his good deeds being publicized.)

In any case 'C' was one of the most kind-hearted and generous of men and still much attached to Leopold. He was, I think, appalled at the conditions in which he found us living. The summer heat had set in. Leopold had grown very thin. He looked far from well. Neither did I, I suppose, tired and disheartened as I was and having grown careless of my looks. The contrast between our former and our present appearance and our past and present way of life must have shocked 'C' deeply.

Even the shop, though he kindly admired my jewels (never, I think, had he seen any that weren't family heirlooms or set by Cartier), seemed to depress him.

'You actually sell here yourself?' he asked Leopold, aghast.

'Yes, and gift wrap too,' Leopold grinned.

In the evening 'C' took us to the best restaurant in St Petersburg – Diana was spending the weekend with some friends on the Gulf – and over a highly enjoyable, well-chosen meal started protesting at our way of life.

'I can't understand,' he said to Leopold, 'what sort of false and stubborn pride keeps you here, struggling to make a living in a country where you will never be understood or appreciated as you once were and still could be if you came back to Austria. How everyone would welcome you! Political differences of opinion are long forgotten and people live in their castles again, even if not on the same grand scale as one did before, in quiet comfort. There's not a relation or friend who wouldn't be anxious to give you a decent home and any help they can.'

Leopold forked an oyster, of which he was very fond, into his mouth. 'I'll have to think about it,' he mumbled, not daring to look at me.

And I knew why. Next day I managed to talk to 'C' alone for a moment. 'Please don't try and persuade him,' I begged. 'I know how gladly he'd go by now but for one reason only and that is that Vienna is so near Prague.'

'Surely he wouldn't be so foolish as to venture into Czechoslovakia?'

'Leopold's not foolish, he's worse, he's foolhardy and he'd have no difficulty in being let into the country. He would think he could depend on his former prestige and popularity for his safety once he was back among his own people. I wonder how many days before they'd lock him up or kill him?'

'I thought he was an American subject by now?'

'No, he's still a Czech. They would even have a legal excuse to imprison him for having left the country without returning, taking out valuables – and so on.'

'I hadn't considered that danger.' 'C' looked at me anxiously. 'If I could only help him somehow,' he pondered. 'I can't afford as much as I used to in the past, but a small monthly – *appanage* or would it hurt his pride?'

I had to laugh. 'He has no pride at all about money. He takes it as easily as he gives it away. He's careful about what I earn because he feels it's mine. Had he any money of his own every impecunious Czech would benefit. Not he.'

'But then what can one do?'

'Only find him a responsible job. But you know his limitations.'

We sat for a while in silence, then suddenly 'C's' handsome face lit up.

'I believe I have an idea,' he exclaimed, 'but I'll have to think about it overnight. You're taking me to the beach club tomorrow?'

'Yes, we thought you'd like it. It's a pretty place.'

Next day when we sat with him in deck-chairs, sipping our iced drinks on the beach, shaded by umbrellas from the summer sun's

merciless rays, he started to tell us all about Jamaica, about its mountains, streams, forests and beaches, its old Colonial houses and estates.

'All,' he said, 'incomparably more beautiful than anything in Florida.'
And the climate – 'In the hills the temperature is always like that of
spring at home,' he declared, wiping his forehead. In spite of the sea
breeze it was indeed almost insufferably hot.

'Yes, it is a wonderful island,' he continued. 'I wouldn't be surprised
if it wasn't to become one of the world's most famous tourist resorts.
Already hotels are going up all along the coast and land prices are rising.
Property is sure to triple in value in the next few years. I am very much
tempted to make a small investment there myself.'

'A house or land?' I asked.

'Well, a combination of both. I was really thinking of a small hotel or
guest-house. Somewhere for us to stay for a few weeks once a year, we
can't leave home more often. A place that is self-supporting – obviously
I couldn't look after a hotel myself.'

He glanced at me briefly to see if I understood his intentions.

I hoped I did.

'I would need a manager, a gentleman, of course – someone I
could really trust and who knows how to deal with guests as well as
servants.'

'Sounds quite a pleasant job. I'd think anyone would take it, even me,'
Leopold remarked jokingly.

'I rather hoped you'd think that.'

'You mean – ?' Leopold looked genuinely startled and amazed.

'Of course. You have all the experience necessary. You always were
a wonderful host and no household could have been better run than
Castolovice. You'd have all the servants you need, native labour is still
very cheap in Jamaica, and a decent home to live in. Besides,' he said,
turning to me, 'you'd make a fortune there with your ceramics, what
with all the thousands of tourists that are starting to flock to Jamaica
now, buying anything in sight. Why, you could even start a factory.
There's no lack of young natives who'd work for you for practically
nothing.'

'C' paused for a moment to scan our faces. What he read in them
must have satisfied him.

'It would be doing me the greatest of favours if you took the job,
Leopold,' he pleaded. 'If you agreed, all that's necessary is that one of
you flies over and finds the right sort of place. Not too expensive. Mind
you, I don't think I can afford anything on the beaches, prices are soaring there. A house in the hills, perhaps, where it's cooler and with a view

of the sea, anyway big enough for a guest-house and some land, of course, where you could grow fruit and vegetables. I trust your judgement. I know you'll find what we want. Once you have, just cable me and I'll buy it and let my lawyers see to the rest.' He thought for a moment. 'I couldn't afford to pay you a salary but any profits you can make from the guests would be yours and whatever surplus there is should go into improving the value of the property – could you agree to that? Think it over and let me know.'

What was there to think about? It was too kind and generous an offer. It had come at so exactly the right time when I had started to despair our ever achieving anything in America, when Leopold's health was failing and both of us sick and tired of the shop, when Diana, much to our concern, had declared she was 'going steady', which sounded much like becoming engaged, with a student from Florida University. His future ambitions were to become a jet pilot, and though a pleasant-faced and well-mannered youth he was certainly not what we had hoped for in a son-in-law. There was every reason to leave and none to stay.

Of course we accepted with gratitude.

Next day 'C' left.

The first thing I did was to ascertain the name of the main Jamaican newspaper. It was called the *Daily Gleaner*. I wrote to its office and asked them to place the following advertisement, enclosing ten dollars.

'Small hotel or guest-house wanted. Some land. Sea view.'

I quoted the approximate price which 'C' had thought we shouldn't exceed, gave my address and waited for answers.

There were not very many. One offered a house in the Blue Mountains above Kingston with an 'English climate and fine sea views'. Checking the map of Jamaica and the height of the place where the guest-house was situated I could doubt neither. From nearly two thousand feet the entire Caribbean was probably visible and I had been told it either rained and occasionally even snowed on those high peaks.

Another was in Port Antonio, a prospering tourist resort on the North Coast, so it said, but there was no mention of any land.

The third, in the hills of St Anne, offered twenty acres and a house large enough to accommodate many guests but no sea view.

The last letter seemed to be written by an English woman. Her name was Mrs Cradwick. Her address Tan-Y-Bryn near Mandeville, a small town in the centre of the island as I discovered from the map.

Tan-Y-Bryn? Perhaps she was Welsh?

She wrote she had run her guest-house successfully for the last fifteen years when, widowed, she had been forced to seek an income from a house too large for her needs by renting rooms. She said her paying guests were mostly English people who returned year after year in the winter months, and young engineers needing accommodation since bauxite had started to be mined near Mandeville. She was selling because she felt she was growing too old for the business.

'Tan-Y-Bryn is in the hills with sea view. There are ten acres of land, mostly landscaped. I'm a great gardener. The climate is excellent, the temperature rarely rising above eighty and seldom falling under sixty in the winter months. The house, if not quite what is called here a "Great-house", has a pleasing appearance and is in good condition, adequately equipped and has, if I say so myself, one of the most beautiful views in the world! There is also a cottage, servants' quarters, various outhouses, catchment and two large tanks sufficient for our water supply. In case you are interested I would be only too glad to have you come as guests and I will have a spare room ready when you let me know the date of your arrival.'

I showed the letter to Leopold.

'This sounds very much like it,' I said.

'Well yes, but I do think you should look around, get to know the whole island before you decide. Your decisions are often somewhat hasty.'

Which I knew was only too true.

'But won't you come?'

'No, since you are sure to find something, it seems a waste for us all to fly there and to have to come back to wind things up here. I can see to most of that as long as you do the packing ready for shipment. You must take Diana, of course, high time she forgot all about the jet pilot, and I'll come when everything is settled.' I looked at him with some surprise.

'You see I really think it would be foolish for me not to stay these last three months, because of American citizenship, in case I ever need it in the future,' he explained.

'Well, do as you think best. The only thing that worries me is that you'll be awfully lonely here. Who is going to feed you and clean for you?'

He had the grace to blush. 'I feared that might bother you, so I thought I'd have Annicka come down for a while to look after me while you're not here. She has her uses you know – '

'I've never doubted it!'

'I mean she's a very good cook – '

I had no right or reason to object to this arrangement. All I resented was his devious first excuse for staying.

Though it was true that it now needed only a couple of months for us to become eligible to apply for American citizenship, having remained in the country nearly five years, we had decided against doing so.

Perhaps had Steinhardt not died, had we been able to settle securely on our farm on land we owned we might have grown roots, instead of drifting from place to place like tourists.

Yet true citizenship, which means total commitment and loyalty to a country, can, I think, only be acquired by birth. Much as we liked and admired America, its progressiveness, its freedom, its opportunities for all and its democratic ideals, we never felt it to be our country and to swear allegiance to a land that would always remain strange to us seemed morally wrong.

It was very different for Diana who was firmly decided on becoming an American as soon as she could. For all purposes she was one already. Her memories of Europe were not like ours. All she had known of it as a child was war, danger, fear and loss. It was only too natural that she wanted to forget and disassociate herself as much as possible from the past, even from us, not from lack of affection, but because we were a constant hindrance to her in the process of Americanization.

Our decision to move to Jamaica shocked and disturbed her, though I pointed out all the opportunities and advantages settling there would offer us, she saw none for herself.

'I will get a job here after I've graduated,' she threatened. 'I might even get married – '

'You are much too young to even think of marriage.'

'You weren't much older,' she countered.

Not in years, I thought, but certainly in worldly experience. Vienna, Rome, Berlin, London and Paris – I had known them all when I was Diana's age.

'I don't want you to think I will try and force you to stay in Jamaica if you don't like it. If you want to return to America to become a USA subject you can.' Her face brightened. 'I have some friends in Washington with a daughter your age. He is the Spanish Ambassador and his wife is Viennese. They assured me they would take care of you. And then there are the Palices,' (they had since moved to Washington) 'and you'll find many friends among the diplomats and their children.'

'You seem to have worked it all out.'

'Only in case you don't like Jamaica.'

'Why Washington?'

'Well, it happens to be a somewhat more interesting and important town than St Petersburg. And if we sell the house here and New Port Ritchi I can spare you enough money to support you there, though perhaps you can learn to type and find a job as a secretary?'

She gave me a strange, frightened look.

'You seem quite anxious to get rid of me.'

'Oh no, I just thought because of the way you have been behaving these last two years that you would be rather glad to be rid of us for a while.'

It was, I knew, a cruel thing to say but it was as effective as it was true.

'Mummy, I never meant to be. Only you and Papi are so different. It's difficult sometimes. Of course I'll come with you to Jamaica.'

That decided, it nevertheless took three weeks for me to get my British passport. I had to write to Somerset House in London for a copy of my birth certificate, to Vienna for proof of my marriage, since all my documents had been destroyed with Steinhardt in the flaming plane. The British Consul in Tampa finally gave me my passport. I had managed to sell New Port Ritchi and though I made no profit I was at least rid of Hegg. The lease of the shop was in any case expiring in a month if I didn't renew it. A shipping company packed my kiln, my materials and the furniture, agreeing to send it and our trunks to Jamaica on demand.

I left Leopold very little. I had even packed most of his clothes. The house was to be sold furnished as we had bought it but only on condition the buyers agreed to take good care of the black cat, to which we had become much attached. Leopold begged me to leave him the large stewpot in which we had cooked so many meals. I hoped for his sake that Annicka would provide a more varied menu. My only regret on leaving St Petersburg was parting from my fellow shopkeepers on Beachdrive. All of them had been kind and helpful, also many of my most faithful customers had become friends. 'See you in Jamaica,' I said, though most of those were so old I might as well have asked them to meet me in the beyond.

Diana and I travelled by bus to Miami, amazed to find a skyscraper city that looked like a mirage of New York, suspended between the incredible blue Florida sky and the Caribbean Sea.

From there we took the plane. It was my first flight since Steinhardt's death and I was certain it would be my last, except for the reassurance of having Diana with me. Surely she was too young to die?

And gradually as I forced myself to look down into the clear, many-coloured depths of the sea beneath us I became less fearful. At least there would be nothing left, nothing to be covered by a tarpaulin, nothing to be burnt or buried if we plunged into the sea.

PART THREE

JAMAICA

🎔 66 🎔

Kingston Airport seemed much like any other except that on our arrival thermometers were thrust into our mouths by a black nurse, glasses of rum punch into our hands afterwards and that calypso music blared from many loudspeakers.

Customs inspections were brief and polite.

'How long do you intend to stay?' one of the uniformed officials asked with a friendly smile.

'I hope for ever.'

He laughed as at a pleasant joke.

The drive by taxi to Kingston took us across a long stretch of tarmac over which planes zoomed. The Blue Mountains were partially visible, they seemed more green than blue and their peaks hidden among clouds.

Half-naked children ran behind our and the other open taxis, trying to hang or climb on, begging for pennies.

We passed some factories, obviously producing cement by the dust that blew across us from them, then through a shoddy-looking district of mainly wooden houses, huts, open-fronted shops and bars from which came more loud calypso music. The road was crowded with people of every imaginable complexion and dress. Black women in oddly old-fashioned clothes, wearing elaborately trimmed hats high on their fuzzy heads or sheltering under sunshades, some to my surprise even wearing gloves. Girls of paler skin exposing most of it in brief, low-cut cotton frocks, their curly heads bare. Black slim-hipped youths in tight trousers and gaudy shirts. Tall, stately Sikhs in turbans. Small pale Chinamen. Dark men with long, plaited hair and beards, strings of beads round their necks. White sailors and tourists of every nation. The crowd was a kaleidoscope of colour in constant movement and with the additional clamour of sound and variety of smells and the hot sun, somewhat overwhelming as a first impression of Jamaica's capital city.

The Myrtle Bank Hotel where we had been advised to stay and had booked rooms seemed a blessed quiet oasis with its palm-shaded grounds, its swimming pool and cool arcaded patios overlooking the harbour.

I had planned to stay there overnight and for us to tour the island the next day to look at the various properties offered.

We bathed and changed and felt it was time for lunch. We were early though. Only a few tables were occupied by rather loud-voiced American tourists, some of whom had been on the plane with us. They waved in recognition. We waved back but sat down at a table as far from them as possible and ordered our food. There was everything available on the menu one might have wished for. The Myrtle Bank was famed for its international cuisine.

A man obviously of some importance, since all the waiters sprang to attention when he entered, looked briefly round the big dining-hall that was open on to the garden and then, much to my surprise, approached our table. He was of medium height, the width of his shoulders perhaps slightly exaggerated by the tailor who had fashioned his smart, cream-coloured suit. But it was his face that was interesting. His big, powerful nose sloped in an uninterrupted curve from his forehead and his eyes were set sideways like those of birds. Had he worn a beard he might have sat for the portrait of an Assyrian king carved in stone thousands of years ago.

His glance rested on us both but only very briefly. He would, I felt, need only seconds to assess the worth of anything, including ourselves.

'May I sit down?' he asked. He had a slight, what we later knew was a Jamaican accent. 'I am Abe Issa,' and reading in our faces, to his surprise I suppose, that this meant nothing to us, smiled and said, 'Welcome to my hotel.' A waiter pulled up a chair.

'I hear you are planning to settle in Jamaica?'

'But how could you possibly know?' I asked, amazed.

'It's a small island,' he said, 'and it's part of my business to be informed. But I'm not omnipotent. I must confess in this case it was just by chance that I heard about you from Mrs Cradwick whose letter you answered. She and I are old friends. So you think of buying Tan-Y-Bryn?'

'Why, nothing is decided. We are going to look at several properties tomorrow.'

'I wonder which? I'd be only too glad to be of assistance and I know most of what is for sale in Jamaica.'

'There's a place in the Blue Mountains – ' I took the various letters out of my bag.

' "English climate", indeed,' he snorted through his big nose, 'it's as cold as the Arctic. You'd never get a guest to stay up there. Port Antonio? Why, I even know the house. It's a ramshackle ruin in the middle of the town, shut in and not even a garden.'

He flipped the letter away, also the one from St Anne. 'Used to be a military camp. They haven't been able to sell it for years.' He looked at me searchingly. I couldn't help wondering how his sidelong eyes focused in so direct a glance.

'Much wiser, if you're thinking of an investment, to pay a little more and buy something near Montego Bay or along that coast. Hotel after hotel is going up there, including one of mine. Still, I know some property for sale, quite reasonably priced if you can afford to build.'

'I'm afraid we can't.'

'Well then, all I can advise is Tan-Y-Bryn. My mother often stayed there when it grew too warm down here in the summer. It has an ideal year-round climate. It's not a very luxurious establishment but Mrs Cradwick, Joe, never seems to lack guests. Of course she can't charge much, the place is too remote, but she manages to make a living none the less. Surprised she's selling. Feeling her age at last, I suppose, because now with the bauxite people needing accommodation all around Mandeville she should be making plenty of money.'

'What are bauxite people?'

'Managers, mining engineers.'

'And bauxite?'

'A mineral from which aluminium is made. Some parts of Jamaica have rich deposits of it in the soil and several large companies, American and British, have concessions to mine. Good old Joe!' Issa mused, 'she's as shrewd as they come but honest in her way. Quite a personality.'

One of the waiters came running in. 'Mr Bustamante just arriving, sir,' he gasped. Our new friend rose. 'I suppose I have to go and greet him. Well, good luck.' He bowed. 'I'm sure we will meet again.'

We would indeed. Not only was he to be of assistance to us on getting permission to settle on the island permanently but he was even to arrange Diana's wedding festivities some years later in his hotel.

The Issas were of Syrian origin, their family long established in Jamaica where they had acquired wealth, influence and power.

Mr Issa returned quite soon with Bustamante, then chief minister. He was a tall, spectacularly handsome man of bronze complexion with a leonine mane of white curls. A party of Jamaicans followed. They all sat down at a large flower-decked table. They were somewhat obscured from sight by the quantity of waiters that flocked around them but their speech and laughter could be heard – it was not in the least subdued.

'Just listen to them!' An indignant American female voice was nevertheless audible above the cheerful noise the party made. 'Most of them black and behaving as if the place belonged to them.'

'And so indeed it does,' Issa, who had turned in his chair, said mildly but loud enough for everyone to hear. It silenced the American lady and her companions.

'Interesting, isn't it?' I asked Diana as we went to our rooms. 'Very different from Florida.'

'Yes, but there don't seem to be any young people around, only middle-aged tourists,' she complained, meaning, I was sure, lack of what she called 'boys'. To comfort her I took her shopping. We didn't have to leave the hotel grounds to do so. All along its entrance front were boutiques selling every sort of tropical clothing. I bought Diana a white bathing suit she fancied and several colourful dresses of Indian cotton, which were quite cheap, for both of us.

Later I telephoned Mrs Cradwick. She had a rather shrill, strong, not in the least elderly voice. Yes, of course, we could come and stay tomorrow. She would send down a car to fetch us. 'The man's name is Selvyn,' she said. 'Black as the ace of Spades.'

Towards evening Diana, who wanted to try out her new bathing suit, suggested us going to the pool. At first it was almost empty as she swam, then one or two undoubtedly 'boys' dived in, followed by dozens of others. They were naval cadets off a training ship that had come in to dock in the harbour. They flocked around her in the water like fish nibbling some tempting morsel. Diana got out and fled, much to their vociferous regret, whistles and catcalls.

I couldn't have laughed more.

Later, as we dined, it was obvious that the ship's officers were making a night of it in the bar and felt they lacked female company. In their search in and around the hotel for it not even I was spared several invitations to join them, as for Diana she was so overwhelmed by proposals that she became frightened.

'Seen enough young men?' I asked, meanly, as we went to bed. 'All of them Americans.'

Next morning we left for Tan-Y-Bryn. Mr Selvyn was not very talkative but no wonder, since it must have needed all his skill and concentration to get us safely through the crowded streets of Kingston and as much for most of the drive. The main road was almost as congested with traffic of every kind as the town. Not only with cars but with carts laden with sugar cane, fruit or vegetables, drawn by briskly trotting mules, often three of them in a row; trucks closely packed with passengers piled on top of each other, and men and women on small donkeys, squatting between two huge baskets, the animal practically invisible under them. Others making their way to market on foot, bunches of bananas or other fruit carried on their heads. In addition, children, dogs, goats and pigs continually running across the road.

Soon we began ascending towards green hills visible in the distance, passing through small settlements, groups of wattle huts, shaded by the rich, dark foliage of breadfruit and avocado trees, then through banana groves, their big, tattered leaves flapping in the wind.

It was growing markedly cooler. We reached Mandeville, already high in the hills, a pretty, clean, rather English-looking town. 'In fifteen minutes we arrive,' Selvyn informed us, smiling for the first time. Probably he was as pleased as we were to reach the end of our journey. We had been driving for over two hours.

He accelerated and with a roar the car shot up one of the steepest hills I've ever seen. On its top perched a village of neat little houses.

'Walderston,' Selvyn said, 'my home.' We turned left into a stone-walled drive, woodland on one and pasture land on the other side, catching a glimpse of a large house behind tall trees and shrubs.

'That's where Miss Elsie lives with her auntie. Very good old English family the Walders.'

'Is Miss Elsie young?' Diana asked.

'Same age as me.'

It's very difficult to tell the age of black people but Mr Selvyn looked about fifty.

The drive continued through an avenue of tall trees in flamboyant scarlet blossom. To the right was a small cottage and to the left, beyond a terrace of well-kept lawn, lay the world as it must have looked when God was creating it.

'How beautiful!' Diana exclaimed.

'Can we please stop a moment?' I begged our driver.

He did. 'Finest view in Jamaica,' he said. Indeed it was.

Under an immensity of sky and swiftly passing clouds, mountains, hills, valleys and plains far below seemed to appear and vanish, changing shape and colour as in dreams. There was an illusion of constant movement as if the earth was still in the process of being created as shadows of clouds and brightnesses of sun perpetually transformed the landscape. Even the sea, visible in the far distance, a narrow, silver line, would suddenly vanish, seemingly absorbed into the sky.

'You can on some days even see Kingston from here,' Selvyn commented as he drove on.

The house that faced this stupendous view was surprising to say the least. Separated as it was by only a narrow terrace from a precipitous drop of many hundreds of feet, one would have expected something more solid-looking than this airy building with its tier upon tier of balconied arches, all of elaborate lattice work, painted green. It looked like a large neo-gothic folly set up for some garden fête.

Selvyn stopped the car at the entrance of a sort of conservatory, equally built of lattice, its roof partially glazed. Orchids hung in baskets from the ceiling and African violets bloomed among ferns.

'My mistress will be in the drawing-room.'

'Mrs Cradwick?' I asked, rather startled. Though the word was familiar, it had to me implications that I hoped were misinterpreted in this case.

My doubts were dispelled when we entered a rather sparsely furnished sitting-room. From one of the wicker chairs, putting aside some knitting, a tall, grey-haired woman rose slowly and awkwardly, supporting herself with a stick. But once she stood, she was dignity and morality personified.

'Welcome to Tan-Y-Bryn,' she said with a faint smile and a voice in no way resembling the strong, shrill tones I had heard over the telephone. We shook hands and I introduced Diana.

I started to thank her for having sent the car to fetch us in Kingston.

She looked puzzled for a moment. 'But I'm not Mrs Cradwick,' she then said. 'My name is Beatrice Noble. I'm just a guest here. A most natural mistake,' she added, sensing my embarrassment. 'Joe's been working in the garden but she will be here any minute. Do sit down.'

She asked us politely about our first impression of the island. We agreed that Kingston, though colourful, was hot, noisy and overcrowded. She then told us that she had lived in the hills above Montego Bay ever since she had married fifty years ago and explained that she spent a month in Tan-Y-Bryn every year to drive down to Milk River with Selvyn three times a week to bathe in its radioactive springs.

'Though there is a sort of boarding-house there, it really is too primitive for comfort,' she said, 'but the waters are considered miraculous in curing rheumatism and arthritis and they do ease my crippled back a little.

'I will be sorry to see Joe leave Tan-Y-Bryn. She's such an old friend,' Mrs Noble added with a sigh as she resumed her knitting. 'Still,

I hope you too will allow me to come and stay should you take over the guest-house.'

Was it then an accepted fact that we would buy the place? I asked myself with some surprise.

Mrs Cradwick's appearance spared me an answer. Preceded by a brisk patter of high heels on the stairs she hurried into the room, apologizing for not having received us and giving 'cleaning up after garden work' as an excuse. She spoke with the same strong, shrill voice we had heard on the telephone and with an accent which I thought to be Welsh. Mrs Cradwick looked neither old nor young nor middle-aged. Her face was smooth and unwrinkled, sunburnt a reddish-brown, so was her straight, short hair. Her eyes were small but of the brightest greenish-blue, the colour of the Caribbean, her nose rather flat, her cheekbones high and her mouth wide and humorous. She had a neat, slim, youthful figure and wore a short cotton dress.

She sank into a chair and out of an embroidered bag she was carrying took a small paper fan and fanned her flushed face.

'Now you must tell me all about yourselves,' Mrs Cradwick said briskly, 'your letter revealed so little – only your name told me you must be German or Austrian.'

'Czech,' Diana said ' – at least we once were – before we emigrated to America.'

'Fancy that,' Mrs Cradwick pondered. 'And your husband was unable to come with you? Such a pity.'

'Of course you will know Austria?' Mrs Noble said. 'My son once stayed a whole summer with a Count and Countess Hoyos when he was quite young. I think the castle was called Soos.'

'But that belonged to my uncle, my mother's brother,' I exclaimed, surprised. 'What an extraordinary coincidence!'

'It's a small world!' came from Mrs Cradwick.

'Even stranger that Count "C" who has charged me to buy a property for him on this island lives quite near Soos in Austria,' I said.

Mrs Cradwick straightened alertly in her chair, though her impassive, smiling face didn't change. 'Then it's not for your husband and yourself?'

'Well, in a way it is, because if we find a suitable guest-house or hotel we are to be the managers and even if we don't own the place my husband's cousin, who is a very kind and generous man, wants it to be our permanent home. He is only buying a property as a future investment. He does not mean to live here himself.'

Mrs Cradwick could not conceal her surprise. She looked at Mrs

Noble as if for help.

'If I were selling a place,' the old lady deliberated, 'I would, being only a woman, be delighted not to have to argue about price and so on with a buyer. It would be so embarrassing! In a case like this all it needs is lawyer to communicate with lawyer to settle matters to everyone's satisfaction.'

There was no doubt that these wise words reassured Mrs Cradwick. She jumped up. 'How time flies,' she laughed, 'and I haven't even shown you your room and you must see the rest of the house while the guests are out.'

She led us upstairs. Ours was quite a large room, its walls and ceilings of slatted wood painted white as were the two iron bedsteads and the furniture, of which there was not much. There were neither curtains nor rugs but the floorboards gleamed with polish as did the rather fine, heavy mahogany doors. Everything looked very clean, if rather austere. However, any disappointment I might have felt as to the room's decor was instantly dispelled when I walked out on to the covered balcony to contemplate once more that marvellous view.

'If you want to wash your hands, your private bathroom is in there,' Mrs Cradwick indicated. 'I'll wait for you on the landing.' She discreetly shut the door behind her.

The bathroom was very small, in fact part of the verandah walled off. Still, it contained everything necessary, if slightly rust-stained. The taps ran rather brown.

'Look, a fish,' Diana said, peering into the basin.

'Nonsense, how could there be?'

But she was right. A very small dead fish was floating in the water.

Mrs Cradwick then showed us the six bedrooms, some small, some large, all equally plainly furnished, but all of them very tidy, the beds made, the guests' varied possessions arranged in perfect order and symmetry.

'Of course everything needs a bit of modernizing,' Mrs Cradwick admitted. 'The house is sound but except for new paint applied whenever necessary not much has been changed since it was built eighty years ago. At first I couldn't afford to make changes,' she continued, 'and later I discovered it wasn't necessary. My guests were quite content with things as they are. You see, here most of one's life is spent out of doors. All one needs is somewhere to sleep or shelter from the rain.'

'And does it rain very often?'

'Almost every afternoon,' Mrs Cradwick admitted cheerfully. 'Oh, just for an hour or two. It's a most convenient arrangement of the

Almighty. It waters the garden, fills the tanks and gives everyone an excuse for a pleasant afternoon siesta.'

'How far is this place from the beaches?' Diana, who had been ominously quiet, asked.

'The North Coast? A good two hours to Montego Bay but through wonderful country and to the South Coast, which is less developed, about an hour. But that's driving rather fast I would say. You see we are right in the middle of the island here,' she proclaimed as if it was an advantage. 'You will, of course, need a car wherever you settle in Jamaica,' she added hastily. 'I'm sure you both drive.'

'Neither of us do,' I had to confess.

'Oh, one can always learn. I only learnt a couple of years ago and now I whisk around as if born to it. I go to market twice a week. I've found it more economical to do the shopping myself than to let the servants go. Now I will call Mrs Noble and we will have lunch. Viewing the cottage and my garden can wait until afternoon.'

The dining-room was not quite large enough to contain its five tables and numerous, what I learnt were called Windsor chairs.

The centre table shone with polish and was prettily laid with starched snowy napkins, gleaming cutlery and a bowl of yellow and red hibiscus blossoms. Two black maids served.

'I thought it would interest you to have a real Jamaican meal,' Mrs Cradwick laughed, 'such as the natives enjoy.'

Mrs Noble gave her what I thought was a rather sharp look.

'So do you and I, Joe,' she said with a tinge of sarcasm.

We were served what I thought were rather lumpy scrambled eggs, to find they had a most unfamiliar taste and texture.

'Akkees,' Mrs Cradwick explained. 'It's those pretty pink fruits you will see growing on the trees all over the island.' She then explained the next dishes, 'Saltfish and rice and peas.'

The fish was indeed very salty, though soaked in a milky sauce, the rice soggy and the peas some sort of beans as far as I could make out.

Suddenly there was a rumble as of thunder and the room darkened.

'Ah, here comes the rain, as regular as clockwork,' Mrs Cradwick exclaimed, evidently delighted. 'And would you believe it in two hours the sun will be out again.' I didn't. There was a bright flash of lightning, immediately followed by thunder so loud that the house seemed to shake. Rain poured in torrents, beating against the windows like hail.

'Don't worry,' Mrs Noble said, probably having noticed my frightened look as bright flame hissed past the window, 'it's only the lightning conductor. I myself always think they are a mistake. They seem to attract more than they repel.'

'I don't share your opinion, ever since I was struck I've been grateful for Mr Cromevan's having erected it. I feel quite safe now.'

'Struck?' I looked at Mrs Cradwick, aghast.

'Yes, while gardening here. Right across one cheek.' There was no visible mark.

'It must have been a great shock,' I murmured, trying to eat my fruit salad, angry at Diana's amused look, regretting all the trouble I had taken to teach her not to fear thunderstorms as a child.

After having swallowed my coffee scalding hot, I begged to be allowed to go to my room for a brief rest. 'We all do, after lunch,' Mrs Noble said kindly, knowing, I'm sure, that all I wanted was to get away from the proximity of the lightning conductor.

Diana followed me.

I threw myself on to one of the beds. 'If this happens here every afternoon I don't think I can face it,' I said.

She had gone out on to the verandah. The thunder still rumbled but more faintly and the downpour had stopped.

'Mummy, come and look,' she demanded. 'There are rainbows everywhere.'

Still fearful I obeyed. The whole immense panorama of mountains, hills and sea still partially veiled in clouds and curtained here and there by dark, slanting sheets of rain was re-emerging into light, sparkling in all the iridescent colours of the rainbows that arched above.

God's promise after the Flood, I remembered.

67

'I suppose you want to buy this place,' Diana remarked, watching me, 'just because of the view? The house is hideous inside –'

'Pretty curtains, some decent carpets and furniture, some repainting and our things from St Petersburg – it would only take a few weeks to make it attractive.'

'And what about Papi? Will he like living up here so far from everything and everyone?'

'You forget it's a guest-house. Always full of people to keep him amused.'

'Well, if they are all as old as Mrs Noble I doubt it.'

'Wait till tonight. We haven't met anyone yet.'

In the late afternoon Mrs Cradwick took us to see the cottage. It was rather dark inside, due to the tall trees that surrounded it and the creepers that shaded its verandah. Still, there were four medium-sized rooms and quite a big bathroom. It seemed to me, like everything else, to have possibilities.

'Just right for a family running the guest-house and yet wanting some privacy,' Mrs Cradwick commented.

Then with great pride she showed us what she called her garden. Since everything else with its flowering trees, lawns, borders of tall, pink begonias, croton and hibiscus seemed like a garden to me, the tidy plot of roses, delphiniums, lilies and sweet peas on trellises did not impress me very much.

'I couldn't live without my English flowers,' she explained, 'though they are difficult to grow here.' We passed a wooden building with an adjoining small water tank. 'It used to be the stables when we still kept horses, now we just use it for garden tools and as a workshop.'

'May I see?' I asked. It was quite roomy and lofty inside. It would make a perfect studio, I knew.

'Now what about a cup of tea?' Mrs Cradwick suggested. 'I'm dying for one myself.'

We sat in the shade of the verandah facing the view. The air was pleasantly cool after the rain. A maid brought tea on a tray.

'So the house and the cottage could accommodate about twelve people comfortably?'

'Oh, more if they sleep double. I've often had fifteen,' Mrs Cradwick declared.

'I hope you don't mind my asking, but how much do you charge your guests?'

'Not at all, you have every right to know, but it rather depends on the length of their stay. My usual charge is seven pounds a week, all included, but in case of old friends and more permanent guests I give a special price.'

This seemed astonishingly reasonable to me. 'And you actually make a profit?'

'Oh yes. The servants cost very little. They find their own food.'

'And how many have you?'

'My permanent staff consists of eight.'

'I will have to write to my husband,' I said.

'Of course,' Mrs Cradwick smiled. 'The final decision would naturally be his – or does it depend on your friend, Count "C"?' Then with slight hesitation she said, 'Don't think that I doubt for a moment what you have told me about his generous intentions but with what I hear goes on in those continental countries and all the political changes since the war could the vendor be certain that Count "C" will pay?'

'I would naturally give "the vendor",' I laughed, 'the address of his most reputable law firm in London. I think their report would be in every way reassuring.'

'As shrewd as they come!' I remembered Issa's saying about Mrs Cradwick. Was it true? She seemed more naïve than cunning. That she was anxious to sell and I tempted to buy was obvious and that knowing nothing of us she wanted to make certain she would be paid if she sold Tan-Y-Bryn was mere common sense of which I felt in any case she had a lot.

She had been quite frank, I believed, in answering all my questions. I saw no reason not to be equally so.

I told her that though managing a guest-house successfully was important to us, I hoped our main profits would come from my ceramic work which I would continue wherever we settled on the island.

'Pottery?' she asked rather dubiously.

'Not quite.' I begged Diana to go up and fetch some of my samples.

Mrs Cradwick looked at the glittering pile of jewellery which Diana had deposited on her lap, evidently fascinated. She examined one piece after another. 'Why, they'd sell like hot cakes all over the coast!' she exclaimed, 'even in Mandeville. A great friend of mine, Rhoda Jackson, has just started a gift shop there. She's an artist herself. She paints. You must meet her. But didn't they sell well in America?' she questioned, fingering a pair of ear-rings. 'I would have thought – '

I explained I hadn't been able to produce enough without help and that in Jamaica I was hoping I could find local girls whom I could teach.

'Why, you'd find plenty!' Mrs Cradwick exclaimed enthusiastically, 'and do some good too. Just between ourselves,' she looked around in an odd way as if fearful to be overheard, 'it's pitiful how hard it is for young Jamaicans of the more educated class to find any job at all if they happen to have been born black, even in the tourist industry.' She contemplated the jewels once more. 'Please do wear some tonight. All my guests will be so interested. We will be dressing for dinner. We don't usually but since it's your first evening – '

At half past eight when we came down the drawing-room was

crowded. The first thing I noted was the barely concealed amazement on every face turned towards us as we entered. We wore the trailing, exotic-looking, low-cut cotton dresses we had bought in Kingston and I as well as Diana glittered with jewels.

A big, burly, good-natured-looking, elderly man with a red face was measuring rum, lime juice, sugar water and ice in a jug assisted by a lady in a flowered silk dress too tight for her ample form, nor did the bright gold of her hair and a lot of make-up convince one of anything except that once long ago she might have been pretty.

'Major and Mrs Reynolds,' Mrs Cradwick introduced, 'they are so kind helping with the drinks. I would have no idea how to mix them.'

The Major certainly did, I thought, as I drank from the tall glass I had been handed. It was a most potent concoction.

'Mr Edmeade and Mr Baker. Two of our bauxite engineers, both Londoners,' Mrs Cradwick explained, bringing two young men to join us. One had a beautiful, distinguished, dreamy face. He looked like a young poet. The other was a coarse-looking, heavily-built youth with pimples. 'And this is Norah and John, Mr and Mrs Jenkins. They come from Liverpool and are my permanent guests. So is Mr Peters. He has a very important job as superintendent of native labour at the bauxite plant,' she said, smiling up at the tall man she was introducing. 'We are old friends, what with his having lived on the island for nigh upon twenty years.'

'Twenty-three to be exact,' Peters corrected. There was, I thought, something Germanic about his appearance. His head more square than round, covered with close-cropped whitish-blond hair, his eyes a pale Nordic blue, his expression hard and uncompromising, even when he smiled.

'Will you act as host, please, Mr Peters?' Mrs Cradwick pleaded rather coyly. It was obvious that she admired the man.

He bowed.

She seated the Major to her left, Mrs Noble to her right, Mrs Reynolds and myself on each side of Peters, who was facing her, and Diana next to the Major. To my surprise the other guests sat at separate tables, the two men together at one and the young couple at the other. Probably there was not enough room at ours.

'So you are considering buying Tan-Y-Bryn?' Mrs Reynolds remarked loudly to me. I could see she was one of those unpleasant women who pride themselves on being outspoken.

Mrs Cradwick gave her a warning look. It had no effect.

'Nothing is in any way decided,' I said.

'Well, I'd think twice before you settle in Jamaica. How we have come to regret that we bought a place here after we left Kenya, instead of going back to England.'

'But why?'

'It's the natives. They are really getting quite out of hand, especially down near the coast where we live. One simply doesn't feel safe any more.

'As for the servants! I have to keep everything under lock and key, you wouldn't believe the thieving that goes on,' Mrs Reynolds declared, flushed with rum and indignation. 'And they are so clever at it. For example, I had bought a new, very expensive pair of shoes. Suddenly one of them vanished. The maid and I searched high and low for it. Nothing to be found. So finally, since it was useless, I threw the other one away. A week later I met my maid in the market wearing both.'

I glanced surreptitiously at the two maids. The dish of curried chicken trembled slightly in the hands of one but her face remained quite impassive. The eyes of the other were lowered but she was biting her lips, obviously trying hard not to giggle.

'Driving becomes more dangerous every day,' the Major mumbled. 'On every road one encounters men or children who jump in front of one's car, sticking out an arm or leg and yelling "Mash me, man", since they've found out that the insurance pays if they can prove the slightest damage to themselves.

'The trouble with the natives here,' he boomed, 'is that there simply are too many of them. They should be deported back to Africa where they belong.'

'They are nevertheless British subjects,' Mrs Noble said.

'Yes, more's the pity. Well, soon they will have self-government and a fine mess they will make of it.'

'We will have to clear out then, of course. It wouldn't be safe to stay,' Mrs Reynolds declared. 'Even now they are becoming the privileged people here. All the Governor is interested in is their welfare, not ours. Why, we've never even been asked to Government House. Not that I'd care to go since I hear one meets nothing but Jamaicans there, however white some of them manage to look.

I had a letter of introduction to Sir Hugh and Lady Foot sent to me by the Nicholses when I had written to them that we were planning to settle in Jamaica. I thought it better not to mention it in this company.

I looked surreptitiously at the other two tables. Their occupants sat close enough to have heard every word. I wondered what they must think of the conversation. But except for glancing now and then at

Diana, who was looking very pretty, they seemed to pay little attention. Perhaps they had heard it all before.

Mrs Cradwick, however, seemed to have decided to put a stop to it. She straightened, one could almost say she uncoiled like a snake ready to strike. There was a sharp glitter in her eyes as she looked at Peters, who grew rather red and contemplated the pudding on his plate.

'I fear we are not giving our guests too good an impression of our island or ourselves,' she said. 'Washing our dirty linen in public.'

There was a sudden silence.

'Have you noticed the beautiful jewels Countess Sternberg and her daughter are wearing?' she added in a more conciliatory tone. 'She makes them herself and wants to start a business here.'

The diversion was welcomed by everyone, and equanimity seemed restored among these oddly assorted people.

When we left the dining-room Norah sidled up to Mrs Cradwick, whispering something to her.

'Why, by all means, let's have some music in the loggia. Do bring down your gramophone and records.'

Deck-chairs had been placed in a circle in the conservatory. Through the open lattice one could see the garden, as alight with flitting fireflies as was the sky with stars. The night air was heavy with the scent of flowers.

We all sat around. Mr Jenkins put on the first record.

'There are different forms of calypsos, though all accompanied by the beat and rhythm of drums and all sung in a high falsetto. They record important events that have taken place on the island, often in a spirit of mockery and derision, sparing neither white nor black. Some are tales of village life in all its aspects and some are frankly lewd.'

This certainly was one of the latter.

Mrs Noble rose. Mrs Cradwick followed. The Reynoldses excused themselves for having to go to bed because they were leaving early next morning.

A second record was put on as obscene as the last. I glanced briefly at Diana. She was tapping her sandalled foot to its rhythm, her face expressing faint amusement.

Mr Peters got up. 'Well, I will say goodnight. I'm not too fond of calypsos of this sort.'

'Got rid of the whole bloody lot of them,' little Mr Jenkins chortled triumphantly, after Peters had gone. 'Hope you weren't too shocked,' he turned to me.

'Just a little,' I smiled, not wanting to disappoint him.

We had been put to the test I knew. But if they had hoped to scandalize me or Diana it had proved a failure. Leopold's jokes had immunized us both to all forms of verbal or rhymed indecencies.

'We might have some Bach now they've all buggered off,' the beautiful young man said. It was the first time I had heard him speak. I wondered at his strong Cockney accent.

The crystalline harmonies of a Bach fugue followed. When it was over the young couple drifted out into the dark garden hand in hand.

'What about going down to Mandeville for a pint?' Baker asked.

'Nighty night,' Edmeade called to us. They drove away in their car and finding no one left in the drawing-room we went to bed.

There were no curtains to our windows and I woke at dawn to watch the sun rise over land, mountains and sea. Then I walked in the garden. A flock of screeching parakeets rose from a tree, a flashing streak of emerald green as they vanished into the sky. Tiny iridescent humming-birds with long tails trembled over flowers, their wings almost transparent. One hovered so close to my face, its sharp beak so near my eyes, I had to defend myself by brushing it away.

An hour later we were, excluding Mrs Noble and Mrs Cradwick, assembled for breakfast in the dining-room, all seated at different tables. Except for bidding each other good morning no one spoke. Coffee or tea, porridge or eggs, baked beans and sausage, toast, butter and marmalade were available.

Peters, who had a table to himself, scanned the *Daily Gleaner*, then passed it on to the Reynoldses, unfolding *The Times* instead.

The Jenkinses and the two engineers read the *Sun* and the *Mirror*. Except for the locally published *Gleaner*, the English papers were almost a week old before they reached Tan-Y-Bryn.

Within the shortest time all the guests had left the house.

We found Mrs Noble alone in the cool drawing-room, knitting as usual.

'I am allowed the privilege of breakfast in bed,' she smiled. 'Well, how did you enjoy your evening yesterday?'

'I thought it very interesting,' I said carefully. 'Especially the conversation. All in front of the servants too. But then I suppose they don't understand very much English?'

'As well as you or I,' Mrs Noble said.

I suppose she noticed how shocked I looked.

'It's the sort of talk they have grown accustomed to hear from a lot of Mrs Cradwick's guests.'

'And are the servants really as difficult as Mrs Reynolds said?'

'Not at all. Trust them and they will trust you. Jamaicans have a strong sense of justice and fairness which is the best heritage we English have given them. Treat them right and they will be honest, loyal and devoted, Only if they feel distrusted, disdained, can they be very difficult indeed – devious, cunning and dangerous. Mrs Reynolds has never been able to keep a servant longer than a few weeks.'

'And Mrs Cradwick?'

'Oh, she's wonderful with them, but then she understands them so well, being Jamaican – '

'But I thought she was English, she looks so white – surely she can't have any negro blood?' I stammered, embarrassed.

Mrs Noble laid down her knitting. 'I have lived on this island for over fifty years and it's a question I have learnt never to ask about anyone here. You would be wise to follow my example.'

I thanked her for advice that was to prove to be the greatest advantage to us in Jamaica in the future.

'Good morning. I've got all the servants assembled in the yard ready to meet you,' Mrs Cradwick ran up to announce.

And there indeed they were, all standing in a row. The two maids I had already seen beside a big, fat, very black, old woman, her head tied up in a turban; next to her a tall, thin female with a much paler complexion and a sickly-looking face, then two men, one very dark, tall and strongly built with greying curls, the other a youth who, except for his negroid features, might have passed as white.

'So, me dears – ' and now Mrs Cradwick's accent and form of speech became truly Jamaican – 'maybe this lady your new Mistress – '

None of them moved, their faces remained totally expressionless.

'Oh Lawd!' she exclaimed, 'must you all stand there like a lot of duppies – come along, Cooky, you're the eldest and the bosswoman here, greet my guest.'

The old woman came forward and awkwardly bobbed the semblance of a curtsy. I stretched out my hand. She wiped hers carefully in her apron then held mine in her big black one. Suddenly her broad face widened into a friendly grin. It was as if something in our physical contact had reassured her.

Then I shook hands all round, Mrs Cradwick introducing one after the other with humorous comments.

'Joycie? Well, you've seen her at table. Best parlourmaid in Jamaica but Lawd what a temper when roused! Kitty? Too pretty by far, yet she's been a good girl up to now. Am I right, me love?' The girl started to laugh, then put her hand over her mouth as if embarrassed.

'Mrs Sutherland lives in the village and only comes to help out occasionally when we have a lot of guests.' This was the thin, rather sour-looking woman. 'Joe, my headman and godson, named after me. The christening was rather late. But better late than never, eh Joe?'

'Mistress right,' he said solemnly.

'Joe sees to the land, the fruit trees, does repairs to the house and is responsible for most things.'

The tall black man stepped back and the young, almost white boy came forward. 'And this is Jackie, supposed to be the gardener. Well, he still has a lot to learn.' He grinned sheepishly.

Two little black faces peered out from behind the woman's wide skirts.

'How often have I told you, Cooky, that I don't want children running all over the place?'

'Only my nephew and niece come visiting.'

'I've never seen these before.'

'Mine is a large family,' Cooky said with dignity.

'Don't I know it,' Mrs Cradwick sighed. 'They eat me out of house and home.' Her bright blue eyes met Cooky's dark ones. Then both women laughed as if they shared a joke.

'Well, back to work, all of you,' Mrs Cradwick ordered.

'They are good people,' she said. 'I hope you didn't believe everything you heard last evening?'

'I never take anything for granted that I've not found out for myself,' I said quite truthfully, thinking of my many follies and mistakes and knowing that nothing would deter me from what was probably one more.

'I am going to write to our friend and ask him to buy Tan-Y-Bryn.'

That evening I did, describing everything as best I could and wrote almost the same to Leopold. After all, they had left it to me to choose. And I knew they would accept my decision.

68

After 'C' had telegraphed permission to buy Tan-Y-Bryn I came to an arrangement with Mrs Cradwick that suited us both. We would remain with her as paying guests until the sale was legally confirmed and completed which would take some weeks; meanwhile she would teach me everything about housekeeping, marketing and the guest-house business that she felt I and Leopold ought to know.

She did her best to do so. Shrewd and capable as she was, I soon learnt that she had made her profits by the most careful budgeting, by doing all her own shopping, buying only what was cheap and in season and stringently controlling how much was used up in the kitchen.

Not that she stinted her guests. The food was adequate, plentiful and rather good. If lunch was only a light meal of salad and fruit, there was always roast or boiled or curried meat for dinner accompanied by vegetables and followed by one of Cooky's rich puddings.

Several times I drove down with Mrs Cradwick to the weekly market in Mandeville. She had a ramshackle old car with which she was on the best of terms, guiding it down the steep hill with evident confidence, though I doubt it had any brakes left since it never slackened speed till it reached level ground. Whatever might have got in the way was warned long before we endangered it by prolonged hooting.

Our return journeys were much slower as constantly changing gears she managed to coax the protesting, rattling old machine to climb up towards Tan-Y-Bryn. I did not enjoy these expeditions. I didn't mind the drive, perilous as it seemed, it was the marketing I couldn't stand. It took place under a large corrugated iron roof, supported on wooden pillars. The heat, the crowds, the noise, the smells and the dirt were too much for me. Fruit and vegetables piled on the ground, tossed and fingered for ripeness or rottenness by so many black hands, carcases of dead beasts from which cuts were hacked off with a cutlass, heads and feet of slaughtered cattle or pigs reeking of blood and covered with flies, the heaps of stinking salt fish and the fowl still alive, lying in helpless twitching bundles, their legs tied, it all nauseated me.

Mrs Cradwick remained quite unperturbed by it all, except for bargaining fiercely with the market women, arguing and protesting, wheedling or pleading, all in the sing-song accent and way of speech of the natives. Little boys carried the vast amount of food she had finally triumphantly acquired for one-half of the price asked, in baskets to the car.

'I will never be able to do it,' I had to confess on one of our drives home. 'Once we have a car, can't I send Cooky or Joycie with Selvyn to do the shopping? I could make lists – '

'Cooky can't read or write. I suppose Joycie would translate the lists for her but letting the servants do the shopping is not very advisable,' Mrs Cradwick warned. 'Market is a great event for them. They get rather carried away when they see so much food. It won't do to tempt them too much. It's not that they are dishonest. You could leave a fortune in money lying around and not one of them would touch it, but they have a funny attitude towards anything edible. They take it where they find it, often from someone else's garden or kitchen if they are hungry and don't consider that stealing. You will have to check your supplies carefully every day too or you will find your larder bare.'

In spite of this warning I was never to go marketing again after Mrs Cradwick had left and neither did Leopold. We took Cooky's word for what was needed and sent one of the maids down to buy it. And if he or I went into the dark kitchen with its old-fashioned wood-burning stove at all, it was rarely to check supplies but to teach a willing Cooky how to boil rice the way we liked it or how to mix and bake a soufflé or some other dish we fancied. If there was enough to eat for everyone after we had taken over, the servants included, it was not at great expense and considering how little they were paid it seemed positively wicked to expect them to buy their own food or have to steal it.

Meanwhile, however, I was still waiting for Leopold to arrive. He had written several times, promising to come soon, saying he was having the furniture, our trunks, the kiln and my ceramic materials shipped, that he had sold the house, finding a buyer who was fond of cats. 'We are very lonely and bored without you here, darling,' he wrote. Whether the 'We' applied to himself and the black cat or Annicka and himself wasn't clear. 'But as always,' he added, 'I can't wait to be with you and now to see Tan-Y-Bryn,' which was as it should be.

Still, I wished he'd hurry, certain little difficulties with Mrs Cradwick having unexpectedly arisen. It had been agreed that the house was to be sold furnished. But seemingly this did not include anything but the barest essentials in every room, the rest she was taking with her to Mandeville. The same applied to china, cutlery and kitchenware and even, when she finally left, to her paying guests. They moved with her to Mandeville where she had meanwhile bought a house.

The first who defected was Mr Peters whom I did not much regret, having felt there was something as phoney about his so very English manners as there were about Mrs Cradwick's. I knew from Mrs Noble that he had a Jamaican wife and children and his arrogant condemnation of everything native was not very appealing under the circumstances. Still, there was no doubt that Mrs Cradwick admired his somewhat over-emphasized masculinity though the servants feared him.

'Him real *busha*,' Kitty, the maid, told me, an expression used in the past for overseers of slave labour.

The young couple from Liverpool were soon also established as paying guests in Mrs Cradwick's little house, eventually to be joined by Baker. Only Les Edmeade remained with us for years. Why, nobody knew, since he rarely spoke to anyone but Kitty with whom he had an interest in common. With our permission he built a hen house, that is a hen palace, so large and elaborate was it with its netted yard and different compartments for sleeping, laying and feeding. Soon it was stocked with three dozen pure white hens and a formidable rooster to defend them from rats or mongooses. When Les came back from his work in the mines in the evenings he and Kitty would collect the eggs together. Half of them he had decided were by rights hers as she fed, tended and cleaned the fowls, the rest ours.

If Mrs Cradwick felt slightly guilty at having deprived us of most of the paying guests, she tried to make up for their loss by giving me addresses of people in England who had been annual visitors of hers, even writing to some herself, recommending the new management of Tan-Y-Bryn.

In spite of her deviousness in some matters, she became and remained throughout our stay in Jamaica a good friend, visiting us frequently, always ready to advise and help.

Meanwhile Diana seemed to be adapting herself quite well to life in Tan-Y-Bryn. No one could have remained oblivious to the beauty of our surroundings or to the comforts we enjoyed, the unaccustomed luxury of not having to cook or clean or wash dishes or do our laundry as we had been obliged to in St Petersburg.

I rose in her estimation, since I was no more the overworked, often bad-tempered, drudge I had been there. At last I had enough leisure to pay attention to my looks and dress, though fully occupied with planning, redecorating the house and arranging my studio, interests in which she could share. Seeing how happy I was in Tan-Y-Bryn and how much Leopold liked it, even his health improving remarkably, I think she realized at last how hard life in Florida had been for both of us.

Of the bauxite engineers with whom we spent our first month she didn't think much, simply accepting their obvious admiration for her good looks as her due. If they tried to flirt with her she remained coolly aloof.

Later she was to attract young men from all over the island. Once the entire English Cricket Team pursued her up to Tan-Y-Bryn and we were rarely without some young English officers, stationed with their regiment above Kingston, coming to call on her. But she remained indifferent to most of them, playing one against the other and favouring none.

Selvyn had taught her to drive the car we had bought. She had passed her test in Mandeville and soon drove to visit friends of hers or ours in Kingston or Montego Bay.

'Miss Diana, she drive real good,' Selvyn said when I asked him if it was safe to let her go alone. 'Danger never to herself, only to others. If car wants to pass, she wave him on – all smiles – brown hair flying. Driver looks at her, not what's coming other side of road towards him. Then, crash! Miss Diana, she drive on – '

She did much the same with her admirers, I thought.

Though at first letters were still exchanged between her and the young man in St Petersburg (he had achieved his ambition to become a jet pilot), the correspondence soon ceased.

Even when a year later we could afford to send her to Washington, where she lived under the kindly protection of friends, took typing lessons and soon got a job, greatly enjoying, according to her letters, the diplomatic dinners, receptions and dances to which she was invited, she, as far as I knew, never tried to meet the jet pilot again. She had outgrown him as she would so much else as time passed. Nevertheless in the six months she remained in Washington she became, as she had always intended, an American citizen.

Meanwhile she seemed quite content in Tan-Y-Bryn, decorating her own room in the cottage according to her taste, playing her gramophone or listening to the radio and making the most elaborate dresses, having borrowed an ancient hand-sewing machine from Mrs Cradwick. She would often talk to Mrs Noble, whom she liked, and sometimes to

Les whose beauty no one could ignore but who was singularly inept at or opposed to speech, limiting his to 'A jolly good morning to you' at breakfast and to 'Nighty night' when he went up to his bedroom.

Then one day, and it proved to be a most important one for all of us, Mrs Cradwick drove me down to Mandeville to meet her friend, Rhoda Jackson, insisting I take my jewel samples with me.

She explained that Rhoda, well-known artist that she was, her pictures selling for big sums on the coast, only remained in Mandeville because of her aged and ailing parents and had started her little boutique as an occasional diversion.

We drove up an overgrown drive through what must once have been a park as there were still groups of fine trees but in between small patches of land roughly cultivated with bananas or vegetables, then stopped before one of those deserted-looking former 'Great-houses' in a sad state of disrepair, of which there were so many around Mandeville. Adjoining it was a long, low modern building with high windows.

'Rhoda's studio,' Mrs Cradwick explained.

Out of its door Miss Jackson stepped to meet us, slight of build, dark hair uncompromisingly drawn back from a high forehead. She had large grey-blue eyes, a small nose and a full-lipped if firm mouth. She wore no make-up at all and as I was soon to discover there was nothing made up or artificial in her nature either.

Standing on easels and littering the floor of her studio were many pictures, all rather alike.

'What great art,' Mrs Cradwick exclaimed.

'As great as a calypso is compared to Beethoven's music,' Rhoda said. 'I know my limitations. All I can do is to capture some of the primitive rhythm of movement, the simple grace of our people, as well as their colourful, absurd costume, gaiety and charm.'

Indeed she had perfectly expressed just that, I thought, and told her so.

She shrugged. 'There are darker, less cheerful aspects of life on the island. If I painted those the tourists would not appreciate it. As it is I've become a most popular artist and earn enough to keep myself and my parents in comfort.'

It was then I told her of my ceramic plans and hopes and showed her the ear-rings and necklaces. She was most enthusiastic, genuinely so I believe, trying on one or the other. 'I'd be grateful to be allowed to sell some in my shop but there's such a limited "clientele" up here, really only old retired colonels and their wives and bauxite people. What you need is for some of the big shops on the coast to become interested. I have a lot of friends down there. Let me have a few of these samples if you can spare them and I'll see what I can do. How soon do you think you can start work?'

'My kiln should be arriving any day now – and Mrs Cradwick thinks she might know of some girls who would help.'

'Well, I think if you can mass-produce these things you'll make a fortune.'

Kind words I had heard so often and which I didn't dare believe in any more.

However I thanked her and gave her my samples to do with whatever she thought best.

'My parents would like to meet you,' she then said, 'they are expecting us for tea.'

To my surprise Mrs Cradwick said, 'Some other time,' looking appealingly at Rhoda as if for understanding.

Rhoda laughed. 'Is it the touch of the tarbrush we have to conceal once more?' she asked.

Mrs Cradwick flushed. Seeing I didn't understand Rhoda said abruptly, 'My mother's English, my father Jamaican. Quite black, you know.'

69

Leopold had still arrived in time to meet Mrs Cradwick and her assembled guests. Again rum punch was served as on our first evening there. Mr Peters played host, Major Reynolds and his wife having left. The punch met with Leopold's approval. It was, once he had taken over the housekeeping, to be served every day before lunch and dinner to ourselves and our guests at no extra charge to them.

His success with Mrs Noble was immediate. Not only because he automatically kissed her hand as he would have that of any old lady in Europe, and later even her cheek, but because there was from the first a sense of relationship between them. She accepted the limping giant with his uninhibited sense of humour as one of her own kind.

Mrs Cradwick, however, did not know what to make of him. Never had she met anyone so lacking in conventional poses. If obviously a foreigner, was he a gentleman? Mrs Noble had to reassure her that he was.

The bauxite engineers cared less as to what class he belonged or what country he came from, but though they had accepted Diana and me as harmless females they had, I think, grave doubts as to what effect a type of man they had never met before would have on their placid lives at Tan-Y-Bryn. They were probably quite right to move to Mandeville. If Leopold was to run a guest-house he would do so in his own highly original way no matter what anyone thought or felt.

After Mrs Cradwick had left Leopold moved into the room that had been hers. It was very small, contained merely a bed, a wash basin, one chair and a desk but it was the only room that overlooked the court-yard, the servants' quarters and the kitchen. From its window she had watched the activities of her staff and controlled them.

So did Leopold if for different reasons.

Fearful at first that they were being spied on, the servants and their visiting relations kept out of his sight. Only gradually did they discover that it was not to reprimand them for idleness or to ascertain how much food was carried out of the kitchen that he watched. It was, in fact, mainly for his own amusement that he leant out of the window to talk and joke with anyone that went by. Soon confidence was established. Black Jamaicans, solemn as they look, love a good laugh as much as he did. He and they were to understand each other to a remarkable degree. Soon they accepted his benevolent rule, willingly called him 'Master', and trusted him.

Occasionally when the servants quarrelled fiercely among each other, swinging their machetes menacingly, he had to call them to order and if this was not immediately effective walked fearlessly between them and took the long knives from their hands, mildly enquiring what it was all about. But it took even him quite a while to discover why these violent quarrels arose. All questioning only brought negative answers. Had one insulted the other? No. Or stolen property or lover? Neither. In any case the last would not have applied. Jealousy was rare among Jamaicans of the labouring classes. They very seldom married and did not remain attached to each other for long, even if they had children together. Nearly always it was the females, more hard-working than the men, who refused marriage.

'Me no work for any man!' as Cooky said. 'Five sons and three daughters and reared them all on my own.'

Many women of her kind thought the same, since there were advantages in remaining unmarried. Whatever they earned was theirs, also, according to law, they were entitled to a quarter of a man's wages if they could prove he had fathered their child.

Finally we had to beg Mrs Cradwick to explain the reason for so many incomprehensible quarrels among our staff.

Very reluctantly she did. 'Nothing but wicked heathen superstitions,' she said, then explained that though *Obeah* (Jamaican witchcraft) was strictly forbidden by law and severely punished if discovered, it was regrettably still practised in secret and that if a misfortune befell one of the natives, or he or she became ill, it was attributed not to normal causes but to someone's having cast an evil spell on them.

'If you see any signs of *Obeah* don't call the servants, remove it yourself.'

'But what are they?' we asked, deeply interested.

Mrs Cradwick looked around as if she feared someone might hear, then lowering her voice said, 'Sticks laid in a certain pattern on a person's path; a knife and fork put cross-wise on a plate; a bunch of cock's feathers tied in a special way, thrown into one's room; a leather pouch suspended from a tree in one's garden; a doll in a drawer, all such-like nonsense. Yet it can kill. Not us whites, of course,' she added hastily, 'but them. Destroy anything that looks suspicious. They'll understand.'

Strangely Leopold didn't laugh but took her advice quite seriously, perhaps because his own religion, which he accepted without doubt or question, was as rich in images and symbols of good and evil as were those in which a people still part-pagan believed.

It was not very often that we came upon anything suspicious-looking either in the house or garden but if so he would quietly remove it.

This was, of course, noticed by the servants. Impressed that he knew of the significance of these things yet did not fear them, they came to believe in his power to avert evil.

'Living among them sometimes makes me feel as if I was God,' he confessed to me laughingly, yet though he joked about it I knew how deeply the black people's confidence and devotion appealed to his primitively paternalistic and feudal nature.

If he did not get on quite as well with some of the guests it was because he soon felt so much at home in Tan-Y-Bryn that he treated those who came to stay as he would have anyone he had invited to Castolovice. He was, in fact, a perfect host, except in that he refused to learn that it was the guests who were bestowing a favour on us by paying for board and lodging and not he on them by allowing them to stay. And if they complained of anything, which was after all their right, he could become most indignant, saying the food was excellent, which by then it was, and the house certainly much more attractively furnished and decorated than in Mrs Cradwick's days. That the bath water always remained rather brown, that rats quite often ran along the verandahs, and that in spite of incessant cleaning and spraying there frequently were cockroaches and ants in the bedrooms, these were things one had to accept in a climate so pleasant that doors and windows could remain open day and night. If he didn't bother about these small disadvantages, how dared his guests?

Neither could he understand that people of different social backgrounds might object to one another when they stayed together in what he considered was his house.

Some of our guests didn't share his tolerance, nor was his lack of racial prejudice approved of by all. Of course we couldn't have foreseen, as Mrs Cradwick who knew everyone on the island would have, that a Mr and Mrs Sutherland who had booked rooms from Kingston would turn out to be black. Still, they seemed nice enough and certainly had better manners and were better educated than the white couple who were staying with us then and who threatened to leave because of our dark-complexioned guests. Oddly even Cooky showed prejudice. 'Them people not good for guest-house business,' she said. But Leopold was having none of this. It was the whites who were asked to leave by him, not the blacks.

Still, only rarely was there any serious trouble. Leopold was by nature slow of anger and only twice can I remember it exploding while we were at Tan-Y-Bryn. The first occasion was when a man, presumably English, of the overseer type which the servants called *busha* arrived in his car in the late evening, dragging a young black girl out of it, clutching her wrist as if he feared she might try to escape.

'We are on our honeymoon,' he said. 'We want a room.'

'Me no want!' the girl exclaimed, trying to free herself. She couldn't have been more than thirteen or fourteen, I thought, if well developed. The man had an unpleasantly brutal face and reeked of rum.

'I'm sorry, we have no rooms available,' I said, firmly.

'Besides,' Leopold added, having sized up the situation, 'even if we had, this is a guest-house, not a brothel.'

The man started to curse and threaten.

'Let go of that girl,' Leopold said calmly. 'Anyone can see that she's under age.'

The child tore herself loose and fled like a frightened animal out into the darkness.

'And now off you go,' Leopold said, raising his heavy stick like a club.

The man retreated. 'Keep her then,' he snarled. 'Nothing but a stupid, useless, ungrateful nigger brat.' He backed towards his car, jumped in and drove off.

We went in search of the girl, to find her sobbing, clasped in Cooky's arms.

'And she no more than a child,' Cooky said indignantly, looking at us over the bowed crimped head. 'Her mother work for that man, she not dare say "no". She sleep with me tonight and better she stay here. That *busha* bad man. She can help in kitchen.'

And so it was decided. She remained with us. Her name was Pearl. She was indeed stupid, useless and ungrateful. Idle and lazy, she soon grew very fat, of use to no one except Mrs Dod Proctor, RA, a painter of much merit who came to stay with us every winter for some months and painted Pearl in all sorts of different poses and costumes while Pearl dozed contentedly.

Only once more can I remember seeing Leopold really angry at Tan-Y-Bryn and this time with the servants.

The mongoose, a small, furry, brown animal rather like a ferret, had been imported from India a century ago to rid the island of snakes. Once there were no snakes left, it survived on frogs, rats and mice but above everything it preferred eggs or young chicks. Though a mongoose is easy to tame it can be very fierce if frightened and the natives hated these little beasts for raiding their poultry yards. If one was caught it was placed in its cage-like trap for all to see, everyone standing around in a circle, prodding it with sticks through the bars to watch the helpless animal's rage and fear with shrieks of laughter. Then kerosene was poured over the cage and set alight, everyone applauding the animal's death agonies with savage delight.

This happened too at Tan-Y-Bryn. Leopold watched from his window, to descend into the courtyard in a towering rage. 'How dare you!' he said. All the round, black eyes rolling with excitement in their white sockets grew still as he looked from one servant to the other and then at the pathetic little heap of ashes in the cage.

'Whom did that mongoose belong to if it was caught on my land?' he roared.

'Why to Master, of course,' Joe said, looking frightened.

'Well, from now on no more burning. You will bring me every mongoose you catch in its cage, alive and unharmed.'

'Certainly, if Master wishes,' Joe said, scratching his head in perplexity. 'Skin not much good though – ' thinking, I suppose, that we wanted the fur.

Several mongooses were caught and brought to Leopold who then ordered Selvyn to drive us into the mountains where we freed them.

Soon there were none left at Tan-Y-Bryn to be trapped, rats and mice rapidly increasing after the mongooses were gone.

As time passed running the guest-house, which in any case had not brought much profit since we never learnt to be as shrewdly economical as Mrs Cradwick, became unimportant compared to my ceramics. My kiln had been installed in the former stables, expertly wired and connected by the efficient engineers of the Mandeville Electricity Company. I would have wondered at their technical ability had not the daily thunderstorms in which all our fuses frequently blew convinced me how much practice they had. Joe, who proved a good carpenter, made work-benches and tables. Soon I had three girls working for me. I installed them together in the cottage where they cooked their own food. I didn't want them to live or mix too much with the servants. I hoped they would feel that as aspiring artists they were in a class of their own.

The first who came was Maria, recommended by Mrs Cradwick. She was a policeman's daughter from Mandeville. Small and very black she was shy and rather timid, except when driving a car. Her father had taught her to do so. This was of great use to us. Behind the wheel she lost all timidity and turned out to be an expert and efficient driver, which saved us hiring Selvyn. If she showed no great gifts at ceramics, she was patient and painstaking, and since there was a lot of purely mechanical work involved I could safely leave most of that to her.

Veronica, was very different. She was a tall, yellow girl, so slim that she looked as if she would break in two. She had grown up in a Catholic orphanage in Kingston and the nuns had taught her to sew and embroider. She had been warmly recommended by them as a girl of superior intelligence and great moral virtue. The trouble was that Veronica knew her worth and believed herself superior to anyone. She was as proud and arrogant as if she had been a princess in disguise. Her surname was Hamilton. Sometimes I wonder if she was descended from some profligate member of that noble Scottish family, at other times if she had Chinese blood. Though she had crinkly black hair, her heart-shaped face was not negroid. No one could have called her pretty, her eyes were too wide apart and slanted, her mouth much too large, in fact she looked very like a cat. Her movements too, graceful and dignified, were feline.

But how talented she was! Not a piece left her fine-fingered hands that wasn't perfectly finished. I never could have produced or achieved as much as I finally did without her help and she knew it. She bossed the other girls mercilessly. Maria didn't mind, knowing herself superior at least in that she could drive a car, which Veronica could not, but Lucie did. She came from a rich family, as she frequently told us. I had met her parents. They owned a small shop in Mandeville and had brought her to Tan-Y-Bryn to see for themselves that their only daughter would be well looked after. It was evident from the start that she needed supervision. She was a pretty, languid, coffee-coloured girl and very fond of boys and they evidently of her, because there was rarely a Saturday or Sunday on which a motor-cycle didn't roar up our hill with a visitor for Lucie. I couldn't really forbid that but I warned the girls that I would allow no overnight guests in the cottage. Veronica and Lucie did not like each other. The latter was not without talent, she painted rather well, but was lazy and had to be constantly prodded by Veronica to work harder, which Veronica did with sarcastic remarks. Though Lucie thought herself better than the other two, she was very stupid, which was taken advantage of by both, mercilessly teasing and often frightening her with gruesome tales.

Thanks to Rhoda Jackson's help I was soon able to sell all I produced. It had started with her little shop in Mandeville, then she had introduced a young American couple to me who lived in Montego Bay. Their name was Claridge. They were both small as to size but they had big ideas and successfully put them into practice. They had started a factory in which Jamaican girls and young women cut, sewed and hand-screened garments designed by them. These clothes were highly original, gay, colourful and inexpensive. Just what the tourists wanted. Soon the Claridges had a large shop in Montego Bay and a smaller one adjoining the Myrtle Bank Hotel in Kingston.

For the printed patterns on their dresses and shirts they used, much as I had in my jewellery in Florida, designs of corals and shells, sea-horses and sea-stars, even crabs and octopuses, as well as all the colourful fruit, flowers and plants of Jamaica.

We decided to collaborate. It became an astonishing success.

If a dress of theirs had a design of fruit or shells or fish or whatever, I made ear-rings, bracelets and necklaces to match. The combination was seemingly irresistible to our customers. They rarely bought a garment without at least a pair of my ear-rings.

The Claridges proved wonderful people to work with, very talented, besides having a keen business sense and a sure instinct as to what would sell best.

Of the greatest advantage to me was that they bought whatever I made outright. I didn't have to bother about anything but my work and designs.

Three or four times a year I would be driven down to Montego Bay with my wares by Maria or by Janet Heron.

This charming, intelligent daughter of a disreputable old Scot and a Jamaican mother, who lived in the neighbourhood, became my secretary and friend.

These expeditions to the coast took us through wild and beautiful mountain country, the open car piled high with baskets of shimmering jewels. Once we arrived in Montego Bay, Janet or Maria would check lists and items with Mr Claridge while I discussed new designs with his wife and then departed with a cheque so large that I couldn't believe it. I was very happy.

At last after so many years of hope and failure I had succeeded. Though I accepted it was to a great extent due to the Claridges' kindness, understanding and scrupulous honesty (they never took any advantage of my lack of business sense) and even more thanks to our friend 'C's' generosity, for without his help we would not have been able to settle in Jamaica, nevertheless I took great pride in my achievement and so did Leopold.

'Pride comes before a fall,' as Mrs Cradwick would have said.

It literally did. Leopold could now afford to travel whenever he wanted to. He flew to New York and from there to Toronto to visit our Czech friends in Beamsville. Walking in the orchards he fell and broke his leg. He was flown on a stretcher to New York and a famous Viennese surgeon who had emigrated to the USA set the shattered kneecap as best he could.

Leopold telephoned from there, telling me the grim facts. That there was not much hope of his ever walking again without a steel brace since because of his old injury and faulty circulation in the other leg there was not a chance that the now damaged one would support his weight.

It was the first time in my life that I had heard fear and despair in his voice.

'I'll fly to New York tomorrow,' I said.

'No, please don't. I'm well taken care of and nothing more can be done. I'll be home in a couple of days. You will have to order a wheelchair at the airport – better get one for Tan-y-Bryn too. I'll telegraph my arrival.' He hung up abruptly.

So that was that, I thought bitterly. What was the good of all that I had at last achieved? It had proved no insurance against disaster.

Janet drove me down to the surgery in Mandeville. I had come to know it well, so had Leopold. Not only had he been frequently in need of medicines for his circulatory troubles but many of our guests suffering from some minor ailment had been taken down by us to consult one or the other of the three doctors. Our favourite was Mr Henriques. Though he was the darkest of complexion he had the brightest of minds and was a skilful surgeon, as I knew since he had once operated on me for a tumour. Thanks to the Bauxite Company and the care they lavished on their employees, Mandeville had a small, well-run, modern hospital with pleasant rooms and a well-equipped operating theatre. Though a gift of the company to the people of Mandeville the hospital was mainly used by whites.

I went to Mr Henriques to ask for a wheelchair. He listened with sympathy and concern when I told him of Leopold's accident. 'Don't worry too much,' he said. 'A man as strong as your husband will probably recover sooner than you think – even if he might have to adapt himself to a different way of life. Overcoming a physical handicap is often a matter of will-power and he certainly has that.'

Henriques proved almost right. When I met Leopold at the airport he waved his crutches cheerfully at me as he was wheeled down the ramp by two pretty air stewardesses who parted from him with evident regret. Though he winced with pain as he was heaved into our car by an airport attendant and looked pale and exhausted, he kept on talking all the way, not about himself, but of friends he had seen in Canada and New York as if nothing had happened, occasionally bolstering his strength with sips from a brandy flask.

Arriving at Tan-Y-Bryn, he allowed himself to be carried upstairs, the entire staff assisting, and to be put to bed.

'It's nice to be home,' he sighed before he fell asleep.

For a few days he rested in bed, pampered by all of us, but soon insisted on lacing his leather brace round his leg and climbing downstairs, supporting himself by the banisters, in considerable pain I could see by his face, but there was no stopping him. He would then be helped into his wheelchair in which he moved himself around, either joining me in the studio, or wheeling himself on to the verandah to contemplate the view, or to be entertained by Mrs Dod Proctor, one of our most permanent guests, of whom he was fond.

'Doddie', as we came to call her, was the only woman I had

actual proof of his having been to bed with. It had happened in the first year of our living in Tan-Y-Bryn, soon after his arrival, Doddie being by then one of our paying guests.

One night I was awakened by a piercing scream, followed by a banging on my door. It was almost dawn and there was enough light for me to recognize her as she leapt into my room. She was dressed in mannish striped pyjamas in which she seemed even smaller and thinner than she was. Her frightened eyes looked enormous, her face a pale blur. She reminded me of a lost Harlequin, which in any case she rather resembled.

'There's a man in my bed,' she gasped.

'Impossible,' I said.

'I felt a body – '

'My dear Mrs Proctor, you must have been dreaming. No one in this house would dare.' Or want to, I thought. Doddie was over sixty.

I switched on the light, took her trembling hand in mine and led her back to her room.

Though the bed was in some disorder, there was, of course, no one in it.

'You've had a nightmare. Now go back to sleep,' I said, severely, indignant of having been woken by this nervous little creature's fantasies.

Crossing the landing between her room and mine, on to which all the other doors led too, I noticed a light in Leopold's room. Probably he had been awakened by the scream, I thought. I found him sitting up in his bed, grinning.

'I got out just in time,' he whispered. 'Thank God she fled.'

'But how could you?'

'It was certainly not intentional. I got up to go to the bathroom, mistook one door for the other and went back to what I thought was my bed. I never noticed there was anyone in it. Just a rather hard, small pillow. I suppose it was her. I only woke when she screamed.'

Doddie, though she eyed our male guests and even Leopold with some suspicion next morning at breakfast, never mentioned the night's events any more, convinced, I hoped, that she had only dreamt them.

We were to grow fond of her, though she was often difficult, excusing her moods as due to her artistic temperament. She sulked at times, especially when no one paid her any attention but when in a good temper and when she had an audience she could be very funny indeed.

Her face revealed no age. It was painted like a clown's, the size of her big, melancholy, black eyes accentuated by kohl and mascara, her mouth bright crimson, the rest covered by a thick layer of white powder. Her hair, probably dyed (Doddie was vain of her appearance), was dark and cut short like a man's.

In her manner and dress she stressed the bohemianism of her youth and after a few glasses of rum could often become very entertaining, reminiscing about artists with whom she had worked in Paris as a student and those she had known in London later. She implied that Augustus John had been more than a friend and 'dear Laura' (Dame Laura Knight) almost as good a painter as she was herself.

Doddie liked dancing. When Diana was staying with us she would persuade her to bring down her gramophone and Doddie would perform solos, either dressed as an Apache, a cigarette dangling from her mouth, a man's cap drawn low over her face, a red scarf round her neck, hand on hip, or waltz all by herself round and round the loggia, waving her thin arms. She was so extraordinarily light that she seemed almost to float, when exhausted fluttering to the ground like a falling leaf. Often Leopold would have to pick her up, she weighed nothing at all, and carry her upstairs to her bed.

As a painter she took herself very seriously and rightly so. When with us, she mainly painted black children. They had to be forced by Cooky to sit for her, which they disliked doing. Doddie was very stingy and wouldn't pay them anything, only occasionally giving them a sweet. Besides she terrified them because she muttered to herself unceasingly when she painted. I often overheard her. She would enthuse about the child's dark complexion. 'Oh, the wonderful deep purple tones of that skin' – 'A touch of indigo there, now some *terre verte*.' Or she would scold herself – 'What a coarse brush stroke, not worthy of Dod Proctor' and out would come the palette knife to scrape it away while the child, believing it was threatened, usually fled. Only Doddie's favourite model whom she called 'Black Pearl' sat placidly for hours chewing sweets, grateful not to have to work in the kitchen.

I am still sorry I couldn't afford to buy any of Doddie's pictures then. She charged high prices and in any case disliked selling them before they had been on show in London. When many years later I visited the Royal Academy I found several portraits by her of Pearl. After wintering in Tan-Y-Bryn for years Doddie decided to go to St Lucie instead, having heard it was even cheaper than staying with us and that the natives there were blacker. We heard from her no more.

The strangest of our guests in all the time we lived at Tan-Y-Bryn were an elderly English couple called Insole who remained with us for over a year. They were quiet, pleasant-mannered, well-behaved people, both rather insignificant-looking. He reminded me of a parson and she of a schoolteacher. They kept very much to themselves, their room always curtained, understandably so because Mrs Insole, who wore a green eyeshade when she came down to lunch, explained that she was allergic to sunlight.

One day I encountered Kitty on the stairs taking down the Insoles' wastepaper baskets to empty them. The verandah door was open and a sudden gust of wind blew the baskets' entire contents all over the place. My glance fell on several pieces of paper covered with drawings. I picked them up. I took them into my room, thinking perhaps they had been thrown away by mistake and that I should return them to the Insoles. But on looking at them more closely I saw I could not possibly do so. I called Leopold, giving him one to look at.

'I can't make head or tail of it,' Leopold said, turning it round and round. 'Looks like a man with horns, or is it a goat? In any case there is no doubt as to its sex.' The rest of the sketches were equally mysterious and indecent.

'It would never do for the servants to see them,' I said, rather shocked. 'Couldn't you talk to Mr Insole, give him back the drawings and warn him to be more careful? It would embarrass me too much.'

However I did ask Mrs Insole if they weren't very bored up there in their rooms. 'Oh, not at all,' she smiled. 'We are very busy. I am writing a novel and Alan, who is a poet as well as an artist, is working on a very beautiful poem.'

Leopold had his talk with Mr Insole too, with astonishing results.

'He was most understanding and, in fact, I think very pleased,' Leopold said, 'to be able to speak about himself and his work. Not that I understood much. Please tell me what is a warlock, which he said he was? Or something called a coven? He seems to have had trouble with his in England, that's why they came here.'

I stared at Leopold aghast. I couldn't believe what I heard. 'But that means he's a male witch!' I exclaimed. 'How can we keep people like that in the house?'

'Oh, I don't know,' Leopold said, 'witches or not they seem perfectly nice, harmless people to me.' Indeed they were.

Taken into their confidence I was shown the Hymn to Lucifer, Mr Insole's life's work, which he was completing. It was all written by hand on vellum like a medieval missal or book of hours, the capital letters with their intricate designs painted in scarlet and blue and covered with gold leaf, the illustrations exquisite, if startlingly explicit, the text, conched in biblical language, reminding me of the ravings of St John of the Apocalypse.

Mrs Insole too gave me her novel to read, coyly saying she hoped it wouldn't shock me too much. It did not, except that the amorous transports of her heroes and heroines left me in no doubt that poor Mrs Insole had no personal knowledge of sex at all.

We remained on the best of terms with them both throughout their long stay. They paid their bills regularly and bothered no one. They left, however, because Mr Insole, his great work finally completed, got bored and begged Leopold's permission to be allowed to instruct young Jackie, the gardener, in certain magical rites.

This Leopold refused, pointing out that the servants were confused enough as it was with *Obeah*. Finally the Insoles moved to Haiti.

Among the many callers who came to sympathize with Leopold and to cheer him up after he had broken his knee was Miss Elsie Walder.

She had proved herself the best of neighbours and had become a good friend through the years, a big, hearty, buxom woman with a high-pinned mass of hair the colour of ripe corn.

I admired her fortitude. I knew how poor she was yet she never complained about her straitened circumstances, doing all the hard work her big house and garden demanded by herself.

Usually she walked over, her land adjoining that of Tan-Y-Bryn, but this time she came with a car, bringing a green parrot in a cage.

We knew the bird well. Its name was 'Pretty', which it repeated incessantly when it was not whistling, dancing or singing. It had belonged to Elsie's aunt, who was so old that she had decided to return to Devon, where some of her relations still lived, before it became too late for her to die in England. 'Pretty' had been her companion for many years and parting from the bird had grieved her deeply. She had implored Elsie to find it a good home, since she knew her niece was not overfond of parrots, so Elsie brought it to Leopold. He had often told her of his liking for them, having had one as a boy.

Soon he and the bird were inseparable. Though he couldn't walk without his kneebrace he had soon managed to do without the wheelchair, supporting himself on his stick as before, and limping around with 'Pretty' on his shoulder he reminded me of Long John Silver in *Treasure Island*.

We could now afford to have guests of our own and many old friends came to stay at Tan-Y-Bryn.

'C' too had come to view his property, and though he rather regretted that I had chosen a place the farthest from the sea as was possible to find on the island, nevertheless he appreciated its beauty and the perfection of its climate and was delighted to see how well his plan had worked out and to find Leopold as content as he would ever be so far from his home and his country.

❦ 70 ❦

Diana had returned from Washington, but only to stay with us briefly. She had enjoyed the social life there and had met many interesting and politically prominent people. So once again as it had been in St Petersburg, though with more tact and understanding than she had shown there, she made us feel that the life we lived, taking in paying guests and working at ceramics, however profitable this had become, was slightly unworthy. Also that the island in spite of its beauty and diversity of people did not compare in interest or importance to the rest of the world.

She now longed to see Europe and we could at last afford to send her there. I wrote to all the relations and friends I could think of, begging them to look after her. She stayed with the Bismarcks in Friedrichsruh, with our old friends from Prague, Adi and Irma Rotter in Bonn, where he was then Austrian Ambassador, and in Vienna with many of our numerous relations. Most of these still had country houses, servants and lived much as we had in Castolovice and everyone spoke of Leopold. She could not help accepting how popular he had been just because of his unconventional behaviour – prince or pauper, everyone remembered him. Intellectuals praised his independence of spirit, people of the sporting world his sportsmanship, politicians his astuteness and courage, barmen, waiters and taxi drivers his generosity, while the young, inspired by the legend of his wild youth, tried to behave just as badly as he had then.

When she finally returned to us after her travels she saw us both, I think, with different eyes. I too had friends left who remembered me with affection. From then on she accepted our faults with much greater tolerance.

After her stay in Austria she had remained in Paris for several months where Eddie had installed her with a highly respectable family to perfect her French. Eddie had old-fashioned ideas about the education of girls. He didn't care how little they had learnt as long as they were attractive and spoke three languages fluently, which Diana did already – English, German and Czech. The latter Eddie discounted as being now useless, whereas 'a lady' had to be fluent in French. Diana learnt quickly, she had a good ear for languages. If she rather resented being, as it were, sent back to school there were compensations.

Mona and Eddie had then a very beautiful apartment in the Palais Lambert in which Voltaire and many other famous people had lived in former centuries and where she met much of French and international society. Mona gave her lovely clothes and she was taken out to dine and dance in all the private houses or restaurants or nightclubs, then considered smart in Paris.

When she came back to Tan-Y-Bryn the finishing off and final polish Eddie had been so anxious for her to acquire had been completed. Not only was she ravishingly pretty and beautifully turned out, her hair and clothes perfect, but so were her manners. And with us at last she was understanding and kind.

Of course I questioned her as to everyone she had met, whom she had liked most and if she had fallen in love.

Though she showed no resentment at being interrogated, she answered rather evasively, mentioning several young Austrians whose parents I knew who had become friends, and boys in Paris, some of them American. One, she laughed, had even sent her twelve dozen red roses, which her small room in the French family's house had not been able to contain, and told me the names of various young Frenchmen and Belgians she had met.

What a success she must have been soon became evident by the amount of letters that arrived for her at Tan-Y-Bryn.

One day she showed us a telegram. It came from Calcutta. It said, 'Will you marry me?' That was all.

'I thought you'd like to know that I probably will,' she said.

'An Indian?' I gasped.

'Well, why not?' Diana laughed.

'A Maharaja, no doubt,' Leopold said, looking pleased.

'Sorry to disappoint you, Papi. He's an American I met in Paris.'

'An American?' Leopold had never fogotten his fear of the jet pilot. 'What does he do?'

'He studies music.'

'Oh, just a student – but why is he in India?'

'To get far enough away to make up his mind, I suppose,' Diana said.

'Seems an awfully long way to go to propose.'

'Not any further than my coming back to Tan-Y-Bryn to ask your permission to marry him,' Diana said calmly.

'But we know nothing of him,' I protested.

'You'll like him,' she said.

'Look, darling, if you're serious about this and really love him we will do the best we can. Perhaps he could help with the ceramics here and I could clear the cottage for you both to live in.'

'I don't think that will really be necessary,' Diana said.

Indeed it was not. I wrote to Eddie and Mona in whose house Diana had met her future husband to enquire about him. 'Don't worry,' Eddie answered. 'She's a lucky girl. Not only is Harry nice, good-looking, intelligent and gifted but he comes from one of the wealthiest families in America. She couldn't do better. Congratulations.'

As to us, certain discreet enquiries had also been made, so we were informed by the Czech Refugee Committee in New York, Harry having merely told his father that he intended to marry a Czech emigrant by the name of Sternberg. I hope Harry's relations were somewhat reassured when they got their answer, if not as to our fortune at least of our respectability.

The wedding was in Kingston. Abe Issa had kindly promised to arrange everything at the Myrtle Bank Hotel. Harry had come to visit us at Tan-Y-Bryn to be approved of and Diana had been taken by him to meet the various members of his large family who lived in Palm Beach or on Long Island. His parents were divorced and had remarried, which had greatly increased the number of his relations.

I hope they approved as much of Diana as I did of Harry.

He was everything Eddie had said but in a way much more.

I came in later years to love him like the son I had never had. Not that I think I would have ever borne a child so close to being a genius or so desperately anxious to achieve perfection. Whether in the simple pastimes of a young man of his kind – games and sports – or in more intellectual pursuits (he was seriously interested in literature, art and music), to excel in so many different fields at once proved impossible even to him. Yet he couldn't tolerate mediocrity, either in himself or in others, and in a deeper sense this applied too to qualities of heart and mind. He simply would not accept human limitations and was to be throughout his short life as if haunted by some vision of perfection beyond mortal capacity to achieve.

Harry's relations, most of whom came to the wedding, were a type of American we had not met before. Quiet in manner and dress, reserved rather than effusive, they were polite and pleasant but extraordinarily shy, we thought.

Perhaps no wonder. None of them were Roman Catholics and the church ceremony must have seemed strange to them. Even more perhaps Mr Issa's kind ideas of nuptial festivities.

On the evening before the wedding a calypso band never stopped playing and singing, which made all conversation between us and Harry's family impossible and at the lunch after church the Royal Jamaican Band in their colourful uniforms (Queen Victoria having been asked how she wished them dressed had said, 'Oh, like those lovely Zouaves') drummed and trumpeted even louder. And though relations of our own had come – Leopold's sister and her husband and 'C' with his pretty wife – to assist us, there was no doubt that many of our Jamaican friends whom we had, of course, invited were of rather dark complexion. My ceramic helpers came too and some of the servants. Joycie in tears over the wedding cake that she had nursed on her lap all the way down to Kingston. The high and splendid sugar-glazed construction that Cooky had insisted on making had melted into an unsightly lump on the drive. It had to be repaired as far as was possible by one of the Myrtle Bank Hotel's chefs.

After the wedding Harry and Diana flew to Cuba for their honeymoon and, except for his mother, the rest of his family returned to America. She stayed with us for a day and night at Tan-Y-Bryn. I liked her very much, even then. I appreciated her good looks and her keen mind but above all the way in which she bridged all differences of nationality, fortune and background by gentle tact and simple warmth of heart. I could not have wished a kinder or more sympathetic mother-in-law for Diana.

Reassured that all was well, though somewhat sad, as I suppose all parents are at having had to part from an only child, life continued at Tan-Y-Bryn much as before.

There were still the cool dawns and resplendent sunrises, high noons of blazing heat, then the gathering clouds exploding in lightning and thunder to bring the welcome rains, the luminous sunsets and calm, clear nights alight with stars.

There was our work and there were friends to keep us amused. We were content with what we had and with each other.

Some months later Leopold died.

I do not like to dwell on his death, only remembering that his gaiety, humour and courage didn't forsake him in the weeks in which I and the entire household nursed him at Tan-Y-Bryn, his temperature rising day after day. He had come back from a brief trip to New York, ill with flu, and though I had called Mr Henriques, who gave him antibiotics, they didn't seem to have any effect. Neither did the potions and herbal baths (God knows what they contained) that Cooky insisted on preparing for him and which he took to please her.

'I will be sorry to leave you, darling,' he smiled on one of the nights when he realized how ill he was. I slept on the couch in his room by then and the parrot at the foot of his bed. 'Please don't worry,' he added, seeing the anxiety in my face. 'I'm not afraid of death. I've been close to it so often. It's not as unpleasant as it looks. Why should it be, since it's as natural as being born?'

Next day he asked me to bring him his black bag in which he kept all his documents and started sorting them: his old passport, his first papers, his Czech National Committee Identity Card that proclaimed him a loyal Czech and all the many letters that vouched for his pro-allied stand in and after the war. 'Of what use?' he asked. 'Nothing but rubbish by now. You had better throw them away.'

There was a bundle of letters tied with string. 'Send them back to Annicka,' he said, 'perhaps she'd like to remember. You'd better keep this paper though.'

I had seen it before. It was a legalized bequest, leaving Castolovice to 'C's' youngest son, provided the boy would add the name of Sternberg to his. If it was a mere gesture under the circumstances, improbable as it was that the property would ever be returned by the Czech state, still at least it proved his gratitude for all 'C' and his family had done for us.

When he started to have hallucinations, believing he was in Czechoslovakia, I sent for Doctor Henriques and we took him down to the hospital in Mandeville. He was given oxygen and various injections and after a week seemed so much better that I thought I could safely leave him for the night. He was sitting up in bed smoking, teasing the indignant nurses and sipping rum.

Next morning a taxi drove up to Tan-Y-Bryn with a note from Doctor Henriques, asking me to come immediately. Leopold had suffered a stroke.

There was no hope after that. I think he still recognized me, then drifted into unconsciousness from which he didn't wake.

Only a few friends attended the funeral service in the church of the Roman Catholic Convent in Mandeville. Mrs Cradwick was there, tears streaming down her face, Rhoda Jackson and Elsie Walder, then we followed the coffin into the churchyard. Our entire staff stood around the open grave, Cooky giving orders to the two men who were still deepening and widening it.

'Master, he too big for small hole like that,' she reproved them indignantly.

She was quite right. They had to continue digging. The sun was hot. We had to wait. Cooky's legs, which were not able to support her great weight for long, finally gave way so she simply sat down on the coffin. 'Master won't mind,' she said. 'Mistress looks tired, sit down too.' I did. I saw the shocked faces of Miss Elsie and Mrs Cradwick but what did I care? They knew less of love and death, I thought, than old Cooky and I.

I also thought of how Leopold would have laughed at it all and that this little cemetery built on a hillside with a view almost as beautiful as that from Tan-Y-Bryn was not a bad place to rest in.

After the coffin had been lowered and covered with earth, Janet drove me to the rectory where I bought space for six more graves so I could surround Leopold's with a garden, then Janet drove me home. She was deeply concerned for my having had to face all this without any members of my family present.

Only then did I remember that I had neither wired nor telephoned Diana nor anyone else. As I wrote out the various telegrams – 'Died peacefully', the standard phrase (well he had) and the date of his death – I wondered why I didn't feel more alone and bereaved. The reason I now know is that one cannot live with someone for almost thirty years as I had with Leopold and acknowledge separation. He was someone I couldn't lose like I had Steinhardt, who, though I had loved him, had always remained a stranger.

As when a great tree dies, the ivy that has been allowed to grow and climb in its sheltering shade, entwined in its roots and branches, remains green and alive even after the tree's death, so would I remain attached to Leopold as long as I lived.

Harry and Diana had flown from Paris as soon as they had received my telegram. They stayed with me for a while, kind and comforting. Diana perhaps sadder than I because to her Leopold was lost for ever.

Some days after the funeral Cooky came to me with a strange request. Would I allow her and the servants to have a wake at the grave?

I asked her to explain what it meant.

'It's so,' Cooky whispered. 'Church don't know or understand but on the ninth night after the burial the spirit goes on its journey. It needs prayers and food and drink to give it strength on its way. So we have a feast round the grave. We would like to do this for Master.'

'I think he would appreciate it very much, Cooky,' I said, trying not to laugh or cry. 'But no one must know, not even me. You see, some people might object.'

'No one see us,' Cooky reassured me. 'We go after dark.'

Perhaps they did. I thought I heard a car late at night leaving Tan-Y-Bryn and returning at dawn.

Next day I drove down to the cemetery. Except for some fresh flowers on the grave and an empty rum bottle near it there were no signs that anyone had been there.

Meanwhile there were hundreds of letters and telegrams, expressing sympathy from all over the world. With Diana's help I tried to answer them all.

Only one amused me. It was from an elderly cousin of Leopold's. She wrote frankly: 'I never liked you because of your free and easy ways but I pity you now that with Leopold dead you will have lost all moral support.'

There was a pathetic scribble from Annicka, thanking me for having sent back her letters and for the gift of Leopold's little gold watch that he always wore, which I had enclosed. 'If I have ever hurt you, please forgive me,' she wrote. Had she? I wondered. Only my pride in that she should ever have become a necessity.

There is not much more to tell. With Leopold's death and Diana's marriage the long journey we had made together ends.

From many sides I was being pressed to leave Tan-Y-Bryn. A close relation of 'C's' came to tell me, quite contrary to his wish I later knew, that I had no right to remain living in a place that had only been lent to Leopold and which had never brought 'C' any profits, which was only too true, and that he was now anxious to sell it.

Diana and Harry urged me to come and live with them, pointing out that Independence would change Jamaica and that it would be dangerous for me to stay on alone. Eddie and Mona wrote much the same. Yet I didn't want to go.

I thought of the first words of the Czech national anthem, 'Kde Domov Muj?' 'Where is my home?' There seemed no answer to that any more.

Eventually it was Phil Nichols and his wife – he had been British Ambassador in Prague and my great liking for them both and their affection for me had never changed through the years – who, when they came to stay with me in Tan-Y-Bryn, persuaded me to move to England.

'Come home,' they said. Home? How often I had heard that word said by Jamaicans who knew almost as little of that country as I did. 'Home to England.'

Well, why not?

I sold my business, my entire stock of ceramic moulds and models, my kilns and tools to the Claridges, teaching some young Jamaicans of their choice how to make my jewels. As far as I know they are still successfully being produced and sold to this day.

Of my girls, Veronica refused to leave me, so I took her with me to England. Joycie who had relations there came too. Maria was already working in a London hospital as a student nurse and Janet Heron had married a young Australian and moved with him to Perth.

Of the servants, Kitty found a good job on the coast, Jackie went to England as a gardener and Cooky, who had grown too old to work but not to rule, went to live with her children and grandchildren and great-grandchildren on a hilltop village in St Catherine's. I took her there myself to see her received like a royal personage, crowds saluting and waving as she rode up the steep hill on a donkey, her descendants walking in procession behind her.

Only Joe remained in Tan-Y-Bryn as caretaker until it was eventually sold.

For the last time I went to Leopold's grave. We had worked hard in the past months, my girls and I, to make it worthy of him.

Inset in the tombstone was the lettering we had formed, fired and glazed in the studio. His name and title, the date and country of his birth and of his death, all in Latin as it had been on the graves of his ancestors at home and in the heraldic colours of the Sternbergs, blue and gold, the coat of arms, the knight's helmet and mantle and the golden star that according to his family motto would never set.

Then I sailed for England.

INDEX